Marion Shoard was bor... spent most of her childh... where she was a pupil at C... ...House Grammar School for Girls. After reading natural science at St Hilda's College, Oxford, and spending a post-graduate year working on pest control for the Agricultural Research Council, she decided to devote her energies to countryside conservation. She took a diploma in town and country planning at Kingston-upon-Thames Polytechnic and then joined the Council for the Protection of Rural England in 1973 as assistant secretary responsible for planning and conservation. She left CPRE in 1977 to go to the Centre for Environmental Studies to carry out research for her first book, *The Theft of The Countryside*, published in 1980 by Maurice Temple Smith. She is now based at the Faculty of the Environment, Polytechnic of Central London, and has been writing articles for a variety of publications on conflicts over the use of rural land.

'No man made the land: it is the original inheritance of the whole species ... The land of every country belongs to the people of that country.'

John Stuart Mill, Principles of Political Economy, 1843

'The first man who, having enclosed a plot of ground, took upon himself to say "This is mine", and found people silly enough to believe him, was the real founder of civil society. How many crimes, how many wars, how many murders, how much misery and horror, would have been spared the human race if someone, tearing up the fence and filling in the ditch, had cried out to his fellows: "Give no heed to this imposter; you are lost if you forget that the produce belongs to all, the land to none." '

Jean Jacques Rousseau, *Discussion on the Origin of Inequality Between Men*, 1753

MARION SHOARD

This Land is Our Land

PALADIN
GRAFTON BOOKS
A Division of the Collins Publishing Group

LONDON GLASGOW
TORONTO SYDNEY AUCKLAND

Paladin
Grafton Books
A Division of the Collins Publishing Group
8 Grafton Street, London W1X 3LA

A Paladin Paperback Original 1987
Reprinted 1989

A CIP catalogue record for
this book is available from
the British Library

ISBN 0-586-08473-8

Printed and bound in Great Britain by
Collins, Glasgow

Set in Baskerville

For Granny, Dace and Stig
and
in loving memory of Harold Shoard

Contents

Acknowledgements   9

Preface   11

Part One: Points of Reference
1. The World   17
2. The Past   29

Part Two: Who Are Britain's Landowners?
3. In Search of Ownership   119

Part Three: What Landowners Want
4. Wealth   165
5. Power   229
6. Private Pleasure   266

Part Four: The Broken Contract
7. Rights of Way   321
8. Freedom to Wander   371
9. Common Land   404
10. Environmental Protection   422

Part Five: At Issue
11. The Heart of the Matter   473

Part Six: Repossession
12. Other Owners   485
13. Sensible Subsidies   493

8   *Contents*

14.   Pleas and Urgings   513
15.   Planning   518

          Part Seven: The Way Forward
16.   A Tax on Land   527
17.   A Right to Roam   537

          Part Eight: Conclusion
18.   This Land is Our Land   549

References   554
Index   582

Acknowledgements

Much of the pleasure in writing this book has come from the exchange of ideas along the way. I treasure many happy memories of profound discussions and generous hospitality in both centres of learning and government and remote corners of rural Britain, from Birse to Botesdale. I am immensely grateful to the many different people, country-dwellers and others, who have given me their thoughts on the rural order over the past five years.

For entertaining my young daughter Catherine on Broadstairs beach and in a variety of other places while I worked on this book, I should like to thank my mother, Gladys Shoard. My brother, John Shoard, the Head of History at Manchester Grammar School, lent a critical eye to the historical section of the book, and I appreciate the helpful comments made on various parts of it by Professor Leonard Cantor, Paul Clayden, Canon C. R. Craston, Dr Roy Douglas, Professor Peter Fowler, Annesley Malley, Dr Derek Ratcliffe, Dr Michael Reed and Alan Vittery.

I am grateful to Professor Margaret Roberts for providing me with facilities at the School of Planning, Faculty of the Environment, Polytechnic of Central London from which to conduct my research, to Sandra Sutton who typed the manuscript, and to Gordon Benningfield for giving me a photograph of his wonderful painting of a barn owl. I should also like to thank Peter Campion and Wendy Siemaszko at Wimbledon Public Library for the enthusiasm with which they met my numerous and often peculiar demands.

My most heartfelt thanks go to David Cox for his help throughout.

Preface

The most fundamental resource of human beings everywhere has always been the land itself. Land is the source not only of the food we eat and the minerals from which we build shelters and shape implements, but of the space we occupy as well. When it has provided for our needs, it accommodates our pleasures. Because it is a finite resource it has always been the subject of struggle between tribes and races, nations and classes, who wish to put it to conflicting uses. Yet in otherwise strife-torn industrial Britain the land itself has been the potential theatre of conflict on which the curtain has so far failed to rise. For the last 200 years, political struggle here has largely revolved round the jobs and incomes and taxes and welfare of a population apparently firmly rooted in the towns and cities of one of the world's most industrialized countries. Eighty per cent of the land surface of Britain is countryside, but rural affairs have been more or less left to the tiny group which happens to own land. Now, however, it looks as though the land question may reassert itself. As in so many other countries today, and in our own past, the fate of the land henceforth seems likely to arouse here the most intense of political passions.

Over the past quarter of a century, city-dwellers have been taking a deeper and deeper interest in their natural environment. This trend has complex origins and exhibits itself in diverse forms. But its effect has been to take more and more people out into the countryside either to set up home or to pursue a variety of leisure interests. Interest in what goes on there has risen sharply, and as a result a real challenge to the existing rural order has emerged.

City-dwellers used to blame themselves for abusing the rural environment through pollution and excessive consumption of the earth's finite resources. Landowners were victims, like the countryside itself, of urban greed. Since 1970, however, this guilt has given way to a new assertiveness. The countryside has come to be seen more and more as playing a vital role in all our lives. As people have come to be aware of what they want from the countryside so they have also become aware that they are often thwarted by the landowners who run it. The loudest complaints have concerned the transformation of the landscape by agricultural change and conifer afforestation, both of which threaten to make the countryside less attractive and less accessible to the ordinary urban visitor.

The discovery that the citizen has little chance of influencing such changes has helped foster a new mood of hostility towards the landowning classes, extending interest in issues of minority concern like factory farming, straw burning and fox hunting.

As such issues multiply and arrive on the mainstream political agenda, it is becoming apparent that two quite different value systems are on course for collision. The tastes and standards, objectives and methods of those who run the countryside are very different from those of the urban population. The landowners see the rural environment as theirs to exploit and enjoy by themselves; the ramblers and weekenders see the countryside and the living things which inhabit it as objects of their own affection and a source of pleasure for themselves. Each side believes the countryside is its birthright, but it does not appear to be big enough for them both. At present the rural landowners are beyond the reach of much of the democratic machinery which has subjected their urban counterparts to the will of their fellow-citizens. Now they are likely to face a determined onslaught aimed at the imposition of similar constraints, but they will not accept these without a fight.

The impending clash could develop into the climax of a struggle for the land of Britain that has remained unresolved for over a thousand years. This book describes the battle-lines and attempts to identify the scope for a resolution of the conflict which would preserve as much as possible of the honour, dignity and interests of the combatants.

Part One outlines the global context of Britain's system of land organization, and sets out the historical backcloth against which present-day relations between landowners and landless in Britain are played out. Part Two describes the present owners of rural land in the United Kingdom, and Part Three analyses the ways in which they exploit their holdings and the impact of their activities on the rest of society. Part Four examines the effectiveness of the present legal framework in protecting the ordinary citizen's interests in the countryside. Part Five lays out the areas of conflict between landowners and the rest of society today, while Part Six discusses ideas currently in play for reconciling these conflicts and notes their limitations. Part Seven puts forward new approaches to the problem. Part Eight provides an assessment of the likelihood of successful reform.

PART ONE
Points of Reference

1. The World

Today, the British system of rural land ownership, in which owners have absolute control of their domains, can be found in many different parts of the world. As far away as you can get from Britain, in New Zealand, sturdy farmers of largely Scottish descent run their holdings on much the same basis as their counterparts in Ayrshire. But we need only contemplate the way things were before Captain Cook landed at Tolaga Bay on the eastern knuckle of North Island in 1769 to appreciate that the traditionally British approach to rural land management is far from being the only one.

The Maoris had no conception of the freehold ownership of land. The idea that one man could possess all rights to one stretch of land to the exclusion of everybody else was outside their understanding when the first British settlers arrived. Maori land was owned not by individuals, but in common by all the members of whatever tribe had laid claim to the area. Even the chieftain had no greater rights in the tribe's land than anybody else.

What was distributed to tribe members was not plots of land but rights of use, or usufruct. Though all land 'belonged' to all, one family might have the right to snare birds in a particular tree and the right to cultivate a particular plot. A different family might enjoy the right to glean the edible roots of the fern growing around the same tree and to catch birds on the same plot that the first family was cultivating. The distribution of these rights was based on the principle that every individual or family was entitled to an equal share in the community's resources. To make sure nobody acquired an excessive share, a right of use was forfeited if not continually exercised; and no man had any right to more produce than he could glean. So nobody was going to build up capital for expansion or become an absentee owner.

Small wonder then that when the Maoris encountered British settlers there was some misunderstanding.[1] The tribe which sold 200 acres of land to Rev. Samuel Marsden for twelve axes in 1815 literally did not know what it was giving away. Nor did the other Maori tribes which were to make similar deals during the next quarter of a century. Under the Treaty of Waitangi of 1840, the Maoris became subjects of Queen Victoria. But by 1980 only 4.5 per cent of New Zealand belonged to Maoris.[2] They had been dispossessed by the new class of landowners from Britain. Today, the descendants of once proud tribesmen are to be found aimlessly hanging round the street corners of Auckland.

Elsewhere in Britain's former dominions, settlers encountered other attitudes to land ownership among indigenous peoples. In Canada, the Ojibwa Indians of Ontario organized their society on a fiercely individual basis.[3] Co-operation and even contact between households was reduced to a minimum. In winter, when the Ojibwa hunted big game and fur animals, their lands were divided into tracts subject to total individual ownership. A trespasser on another man's territory could be shot on sight. Every hunter was absolutely dependent on his own efforts. In summer, when individual households came together in groups as villages, activities like the gathering of berries, fishing and the trapping of rabbits were also carried out on an aggressively individualist basis. Individuals, not households, owned things: a husband needed his wife's permission to use her fishing net or to eat her berries or her rice. Similarly, a wife needed her husband's permission to use his canoe or to use the game and fish he had caught. A man owned land outright and in his own name only. He could transfer it when and to whom he pleased; relatives had no claim upon a man's land.

These two examples show how different are the ways in which mankind's key resource may be apportioned. Among 'primitive' tribes, however, the Maori approach is far more common than that of the Ojibwa. Co-operative arrangements reflect a generally lower level of commitment to personal wealth than we are used to encountering in 'advanced' societies. Many tribes have devised sophisticated mechanisms for ensuring that land is used in the way which best suits most members. Although substantial rights in plots of land may be allocated to individuals or households, mechanisms often exist to prevent the strong from appropriating the lion's share.

The Zuni Indians of New Mexico are one tribe which has taken elaborate measures to keep individual members' land hunger in check. The forefathers of the Zuni once occupied territory in Utah, Colorado, Arizona and New Mexico. By the dawn of the twentieth century, the tribe was faced with a harsh physical environment and a strictly limited amount of cultivatable land on a high, arid plateau in New Mexico. Yet they are not a poor people: famine is virtually unknown, and anthropologists describe them as 'well-to-do'.

Under the Zuni property system,[4] land is owned by individuals or households but it is frequently worked co-operatively, and any surplus from one particular holding is redistributed to the community at large. Uncultivated land is considered to belong to the tribe as a whole with no particular member of the tribe having greater rights to it than anybody else. However, if a man clears part of that land, stakes out fields and is seen to work them, they become 'his' – so long as he continues to work them. If he stops, they may become 'owned' by any other member of the tribe who starts to work them.

The idea that land should go to those who demonstrate their need for it, though unfamiliar to us, is extremely widely encountered around the globe.

Among the Zuni, some individuals are better off than others. But when an excessive concentration of surplus wealth appears in the hands of one individual, it is redistributed among the members of the village. In this harsh physical environment competitive individuals are not the most admired. It is rather the co-operative person, ready to share his food and ready to assist others in agricultural labour, who is most respected.

A similar commitment to make the land serve the common good can be found in tropical Africa, even though the forms of tribal organization are very different from those of American Indians. The practices of the Lozi tribe, which dwells in the flood plain of the Upper Zambezi River, are representative not only of present arrangements in central and east Africa; they are also considered likely to be similar to those that existed across the continent before the advent of Europeans in the sixteenth century.

Ultimately the Lozi consider that all the land, and its products, belong to the nation through the king.[5] The king is thus the owner of Loziland and its cattle and wild products, in the sense that he ultimately claims rights over all land. However, the king's total power is balanced by extremely onerous duties. He is obliged to give every subject land to live on and land to cultivate, and he must allow every subject to fish in public waters, to gather wild fruits and to hunt (for food: hunting for pleasure is unknown in most 'primitive' societies). The king must protect all subjects against trespassers or anyone attempting to prevent them from exercising their rights. Once the king has given land for cultivation, or a fishing site, the subject enjoys rights in it which are protected against all comers, including the king himself. Property in Lozi society thus involves not so much rights of people over things, but obligations owed between people in respect of things.

A surprisingly large number of primitive societies seem to be able to sort out equitable and effective methods of land allocation. Yet as societies grow more complex, they find it harder and harder to maintain arrangements which seem 'fair' even if they are trying to achieve this. Technological advance tends to provide new opportunities for the stronger members of a society to get a grip on more than their fair share of a nation's land.[6] When they do, the weak often find themselves capable of enjoying the fruits of the earth only on terms dictated by their new masters.

The emergence of feudalism in Western Europe is a good example of this process. In this case, it seems to have been an advance in military technology that prompted the breakdown of the more equitable arrangements that had previously existed. The armies of the ancient world – the Macedonian phalanxes or the Roman legions – relied heavily primarily on foot soldiers to wage and win wars. But in the eighth century, the face of European warfare was transformed. The commanders of the Frankish army noticed that Arab invaders crossing into Europe used horsemen who, while fighting, were able to maintain their position with the aid of two iron rings on leather thongs. The bareback warriors the Franks had encountered so far, riding on a loose cloth without a saddle, had been able only to throw a lance and then retire. But this new tool, the stirrup, permitted a man on horseback to deliver a powerful blow without any risk of unseating himself. The Franks decided to switch their own forces into cavalry.[7]

However, the Franks found their new horses expensive engines of war. To provide economic support for their cavalry, they seized Church lands or ordered the Church to provide their soldiers with grants of land. This was the origin of the 'fief' – a piece of land conveyed not absolutely but with the condition of military support attached. The fief was to provide the basis of feudalism in Europe.

Within his fiefdom a feudal lord could use the force at his disposal to command the labour of the common people. In time of war he would lead them into battle on behalf of his own master.

A particularly clear-cut form of warrior aristocracy grew up in Japan from the twelfth century onwards to be overthrown only a century ago. At the top of the feudal pyramid was the Shogun. He gave the land of Japan to around three hundred war-lords, known as the *daimyo*, on condition that they fought in his army and supported his court. The *daimyo* in their turn sub-contracted land to tens of thousands of fighters, the *samurai*. For 500 years Japan was ruled by this class of warriors which, with the exception of a small court nobility, alone enjoyed wealth and power. The cultivators of the soil remained an unarmed, helpless mass of serfs forced to give their lords up to 60 per cent of the rice they produced in return for being allowed to cultivate a little land of their own.[8]

In some form or other, feudalism enveloped countries as different as China, Germany, India, Poland and the Philippines. Imperialism arrived too, as a kind of supra-national feudalism, spreading oppressive land-ownership régimes even more widely. Invaders from Scandinavia imposed feudalism on the Slav clans of what was to become Russia in the first century A.D., and European settlers imposed something similar on the peoples they conquered in Asia and Africa. It was South America, however, which was to bear the clearest imprint of this process.

When Spanish and Portuguese *conquistadores* conquered South

America in the sixteenth century they stumbled upon some extremely sophisticated and socially advanced forms of agriculture. The Incas and Aztecs, for instance, were producing enough of a wide range of crops to support urban areas and considerable armies. Irrigation, fertilization methods and the co-operative organization of food production were highly developed; the Inca *allyu* system was an early example of planned collective agriculture, not unlike the present-day Israeli kibbutz. Armed with more sophisticated weapons than the Indians could muster, the *conquistadores* broke up the Indians' communal villages and took possession of the best land. The Indians paid with their wage labour three, four or even more days a week for the right to retain a little of the land they had previously owned in common. In this way the conquerors and their armies were fed for nothing.

In much of South America, feudalism has survived to the present day.[9] Brazil, Argentina, Ecuador, Colombia, Paraguay and Uruguay have around 80 to 85 per cent of the continent's agrarian population and in all these the traditional land ownership structure is still largely intact. This system of major estates known as *latifundios*, reflects the pattern of rural social organization of Spain and Portugal at the time of the conquest and its superimposition on native cultures through large grants of land and Indians by the Spanish Crown to the *conquistadores*.

The *latifundio* system involves the landowner wielding power over the landless not just as landlord but as employer, shopkeeper and money-lender as well. In return for working the landlord's land for up to four days a week, the serf may cultivate a small plot. Often it is the landowner who decides what the serf may cultivate on this plot of land that forms part of his wages; and tradition or contract may oblige the worker to donate part of his holding's produce to the landowner, or at least sell it to him at such prices as the landowner may determine. Any shop within easy reach is usually owned by the landowner. In some places wages, if paid at all, are paid in the form of promissory notes bearing the landowner's signature, and valid only in his stores. It is almost impossible for the serf to save against unforeseen expenses. Every time a member of his family falls ill, gives birth, marries or is buried, he will need credit – and the landowner is often the only available source of it. The credit system binds the serf to the estate; and often children inherit their parents' debts.

Today, the feudal system which for four to five centuries has monopolized much of South America's agriculture still hampers the whole continent's economic, social and political development. At the same time, it adds massively to unemployment. In a continent where new industry cannot possibly absorb the growing labour force, most jobs in the future are going to have to be found in the countryside. Peasant subsistence agriculture is labour-intensive. But the laws of the market working through the *latifundio* system mean that more and more of the existing workers are being replaced with machines.

If the transition from the 'primitive' state towards a more 'advanced' society tends to bring with it more oppressive systems of land ownership, an eventual reaction against this oppression is however almost as regular. In very different ways, in countries as different as Japan and Tanzania, Egypt and China, Mexico and Russia, Cuba and Denmark, some form of revolutionary change has toppled a feudal type of arrangement. And in each case, land taken away from domestic or imperial overlords has been returned, in some degree at least, to the people.

The French Revolution in 1789 provided the model for many subsequent efforts at land reform. First, serfs' obligations to their lords and the landowners' controls over the lives of the serfs were abolished; then the large estates (of the Royal Family, the Church and the large private landowners) were declared national property and sold or granted to the former serfs and to the middle classes. This land redistribution, coupled with the practice of dividing property equally among heirs rather than giving it all to the eldest son, served to institutionalize the small family farm as the agricultural unit in France. This idea of peasant proprietorship flowing from successful revolution left a deep impression – and not only in France. When, for instance, the Government of the United States transferred the nation's land to private ownership in the nineteenth century, it sought to put into practice what it saw as the democratic ideal of a nation of small family farmers like that of post-Revolution France.[10]

Most major land reforms have followed the French model even if peasant proprietorship has subsequently given way in many cases to co-operative or state ownership. Finland is an entirely typical example. By the Smallholdings Law of 1918 and a land reform in 1922, which allowed the expropriation of estates of more than 495 acres, former tenant farmers and landless labourers were given their own land. In the process, more than 90,000 smallholdings were created.

The land reform that revolutionized land ownership in Japan in 1868 did not simply aim to take land away from the small number of war-lords who had held it for centuries and hand it back to the people. The Meiji Emperor who seized power in 1868 from the military, landowning families who had dominated Japan for centuries also wished to increase total farm production and to create a sound rural tax base in order to build up industry. His reform succeeded on all three counts. An 1868 edict declared all agricultural land the property of the former serfs to use or dispose of as they liked: as a result 80 per cent of all serfs became free owner-occupier farmers. Farm output rose dramatically.

A massive increase in food production and great improvements in rural life have also accompanied land reform in Egypt, the home of the earliest large-scale land reform in the Middle East and one which has influenced other countries in the region.[11]

Before 1952, the Egyptian peasants were suffering from worsening poverty; they were also among the most disease-ridden and socially oppressed people in the world. Fewer than 0.1 per cent of all landowners owned 20 per cent of Egypt's agricultural land (which itself made up a narrow, Nile-based belt of land occupying only 3.5 per cent of the country's total land area). This dominance of the large owners left nearly 3 million peasant proprietors to eke out a living on less than one acre each, while around a million and a half families were landless.

A revolutionary coup staged against the king and his landlord-dominated Parliament in 1952 led to a land reform in which the vast royal estates were appropriated and redistributed to the peasants together with all private land over a 200-acre ceiling. Another law ten years later restricted the amount of land that any one person could own to 100 acres, and this was further reduced in 1969 to 50 acres. Strong co-operatives have become necessary in Egypt to reduce the problems of smallholder farming. Food output in Egypt was soon rising faster than population.

In Latin America, Mexico is the only country to have achieved a real transfer of land back to the people. The *hacienda* system had developed after centuries of appropriation of Indian lands by Spanish settlers. By 1910, 1 per cent of the population owned 97 per cent of the land leaving 92 per cent of the rural population landless.

The land redistribution programme that was launched after the 1910 revolution and still continues has resulted in an eclectic mixture of public and private, individual and collective, ownership. Much of the land has been handed to roughly village-sized groups known as *ejidos*; they have retained untilled land like pasture and woodland in communal ownership while permitting the sub-division into small, individual units of much of the crop land, although a small proportion is farmed collectively.

Alongside this is a private farm sector but without the large units that characterized the *haciendas*; large private holdings are confined to semi-desert and tropical jungle. Economically, land reform in Mexico has been a huge success: Mexico is the sole Latin American country to have achieved agricultural self-sufficiency and become a net food exporter.[12]

Of course, not all attempts at land reform are equally successful. In India, reform has failed to improve the lot of the mass of landless people. After Independence in 1947, the Government unequivocally declared that land must belong to the actual tiller of the soil. Since then it has introduced ceilings on the amount of land any one person may own, measures to abolish the old rent collectors or *zamindars* who had raised rents to astronomical levels in order to increase their cut, and measures to regulate tenants' rents and to give them some security of tenure. However, implementation of these steps has rested with individual states, with the result that implementation has been piecemeal and half-hearted. Firmly entrenched class and caste divisions compound the problem: caste rules forbid field labour by members of the upper castes who are usually the landowners and until recently untouchables were not able to own land. While guarantees of tenant security have enabled some middle and rich peasants to improve their position at the expense of large absentee landlords and the *zamindars*, such land reform as has occurred has tended to leave the hundreds of millions that comprise the lowest classes on the land if anything worse off than they were before.

Russia experienced the most catastrophic of all attempts at land reform. Though feudalism had dominated Russian rural society since the fifteenth century, many serfs never really saw the land as belonging to anybody but themselves. There had been an ancient tradition in Russia that title to land went 'wherever axe and plough went': once somebody had cleared land and was working it, ownership naturally fell to him. Even in the nineteenth century the serfs either regarded the land as being under no human ownership ('The Land is God's') or viewed themselves as its rightful owners.

When the Revolutions of 1917 swept the Tsars away, Lenin's reform plan followed closely the French model of peasant proprietorship. After centuries of struggle many Russian peasants thought they had finally achieved the dream of their forefathers. Demand for food from the urban areas grew, and with their new-found ability to buy and dispose of land, some of the peasants became relatively well-to-do.

The Soviet leaders were, however, unhappy to see the emergence of a class of rich peasants or *kulaks* practising capitalism within a socialist society. At the same time, they desperately wanted to industrialize Russia, and came to see agriculture as providing the only available means of raising the necessary money. To produce more food, larger working units would need to be formed. As enlarging peasant proprietorship would have conflicted with communism, Stalin imposed collectivization. First, he shot many kulaks and deported others to Siberia. Then he cajoled the rest of the peasants into joining the collectives through taxation and the threat of being labelled a kulak. So great was the peasants' resistance to collectivization that many of them slaughtered their animals and destroyed their crops rather than give them to a collective.

In Russia today a new feudalism has been imposed. Just as the Russian serfs once had to work for nothing for their lord in return for the right to cultivate a little land of their own, now those on collective farms have to provide the state with labour instead. Land reform in Russia, rather than liberating the peasants, has imposed a new form of oppression on them.

In Red China, however, land reform has taken a very different course. After the Revolution of 1949, the Communist Party at first did no more than dispossess the non-working landlords and distribute the land to the peasants. This created millions of tiny farms, many of them too small to be viable. However, in some areas mutual aid teams were established in which three to six households combined to work on common tasks on each other's land during the busy seasons. This idea spread rapidly and the teams converted themselves to permanent organizations for the whole year, including more households. Animals, tools and reclaimed land were owned in common.

By 1956, more than 90 per cent of China's rural population were involved in producers' co-operatives. But Mao Tse-tung was impatient for collectivization and for a rapid increase in food production to provide the surplus for investment in industry. Conversion of co-operatives to collective farms involved the peasants forfeiting individual ownership of land, animals and tools and joining with other households to make units of 100 to 300 households.

The peasants themselves provided the impetus to convert the collective farms in turn into people's communes in which all economic and social activities took place in common. A typical commune was about thirty times as large as a collective and, unlike the collective, embraced factories and schools, collected taxes and discharged welfare, military and security responsibilities. To improve their effectiveness the communes' size was reduced in the 1960s to an average of 1,900 households; private plots were restored to a limit of 5 per cent of the commune's farmed area; and organization and responsibility within the commune were de-centralized. Now the communes seem to be working well. All members of the commune have a real say in their administration; all officials do some manual labour. Meanwhile, the encouragement of local self-sufficiency seems to give the Chinese peasants a real link with their land.

Such, then, is the background against which we may contemplate our own arrangements for allocating rural land and its benefits. A number of things emerge. Almost all over the world at almost all times rural land has been highly prized. The ingenuity of mankind allows for a vast range of methods of relating command of land to the needs of the people. Some of these methods are equitable. Some are efficient. Some are both. Some are neither. 'Primitive' societies often enjoy equitable arrangements but in 'advanced' societies the strong tend to gain a stranglehold over the weak. Systems that fly in the face of the needs of the people tend eventually to be overthrown. What replaces them is often better but sometimes worse.

None of this tells us what should be the proper arrangements for Britain. What it does tell us is that an infinite variety of possibilities exists. If the status quo does not meet our needs, we should not imagine there is no alternative. What then has been the experience of the British?

2. The Past

> The objects which men aim at when they become possessed of land in the British Isles may, I think, be enumerated as follows. (1) political influence; (2) social importance, founded on territorial possession, the most visible and unmistakable form of wealth; (3) power exercised over tenantry; the pleasure of managing, directing and improving the estate itself; (4) residential enjoyment, including what is called sport; (5) the money return – the rent.
>
> The 15th Earl of Derby, 1881[1]

In Britain today the idea that the land surface should be regarded as the private property of those who happen to 'own' it comes so naturally that alternative arrangements are hard to conceive. But it need not be so and it was not always. The present disposition of our land is the outcome of a struggle between those who have sought to own and those they have thereby dispossessed. Our present arrangements can only be followed in the light of the twists and turns of this long and eventful story. But this story does not just serve to explain our present difficulties. It also points the way to their resolution.

The Dawn of Man

Early Stone-Age man was a hunter and food-gatherer, a way of life that would have lent itself to a relaxed pattern of land ownership. However, we have no way of knowing what arrangements, if any, actually prevailed, for it is not until the Roman Conquest that the first written records appear in Britain. Pollen records indicate that the British environment was being manipulated to enhance food production 4,000 years before the Romans arrived. But no one knows on what basis this prehistoric agriculture was conducted.[2]

Surviving archaeological features give the faintest of clues.
Neolithic relics, like the spectacular causewayed enclosure on
Dorset's Hambledon Hill, the large burial mounds to be found
on several of England's southern downland hills or the henge
monuments of Avebury and Stonehenge, could not have been
constructed by one family group: they must have been the result
of the collective effort of large numbers of people. It may be that
those entombed under the burial mounds (or 'long barrows') –
whose numbers could have represented only a small proportion of the Neolithic communities of southern England – represent an upper tier of Neolithic society. And it may be that the
henge monuments were centres of political power as well as
shrines for religious events. But we shall probably never know
for sure.

After about 1500 B.C., however, no more of these giant public
monuments seem to have been erected. Instead, there is evidence
of small farming settlements apparently tilled by peasant farmers,
living in small groups or as family units. Yet when we examine
the pattern of their fields, we do not always find a hotch-potch of
individual fields appearing to have been worked by one individual or family operating independently. Instead, sites from Sussex
to the west of Ireland have revealed whole networks of fields
sharing common axial lines that often ignore topographical
features, and cover in some cases thousands of acres – networks
which could only be the product of the careful organization of
large numbers of people in a cohesive society. What we cannot
say about this or about any other period of prehistory is that
this organization was controlled by an individual leader or an
oligarchy or an elected assembly or something else. If chiefs
existed in the early part of the second millennium B.C. it may be
that, five hundred years on, they had been overthrown by the
peasant farmers on whom they depended. Or it may be that their
energies were being channelled into practical land management
instead of the more ostentatious activity of earlier years.

If Stone-Age attitudes to land ownership are a mystery, those
of the late Bronze Age and the Iron Age are a little clearer. In
these periods a new class of large structures appear that had a
clearly defensive function – unlike the earlier causewayed enclosures and henge monuments. These hill-forts, with interiors up to

over fifty acres in area, bespeak not only concentrated communal effort but also territorial attitudes. And excavations at one of the best known Iron-Age sites in England, a four-acre enclosure at Little Woodbury near Salisbury, suggest that the form of social order involved was stratified rather than egalitarian. Within the quarter-of-a-mile perimeter of the site there is ample space for thirty small modern houses and their gardens. What has been found, however, are the remains of a single, large, round house, forty-five feet across, in the middle of its own enclosure. Comparison with other sites elsewhere has led archaeologists to suggest that the large house within the Little Woodbury enclosure belonged to a member of the Iron-Age aristocracy. Other Iron-Age sites contain the remains of much smaller dwellings – a site at Glastonbury, for instance, contains the remains of sixty huts within two acres – while others reveal the remains of dwellings of intermediate size. It may be that this variation in size reflects differences in use – perhaps the Little Woodbury structure housed animals as well as people or served as a meeting place. On the other hand, its relatively large size may reflect social supremacy. If it does, we shall probably never know whether the society involved was equitable or oppressive.

We do, however, know that Gaullish society before the Roman Conquest was split into two main classes: Caesar's account in his *Gallic Wars* contrasts the *equites* or knights with the *plebs* or common people. Iron-Age society at least in southern Britain may well have followed a similar pattern.

After 43 A.D. under the Roman occupation, British society was almost certainly highly stratified.[3] For one thing, slavery was probably a feature of Roman rule in Britain as elsewhere in the Empire. It was almost certainly slaves who provided labour for the villas that the Romans set about introducing into the British landscape as the centrepieces of rural estates that could be inherited or bought and sold. The villas arose not out of the countryside itself but from the growing towns and cities as successful town-based families invested wealth in the acquisition of rural estates. Not that all villa farmland was necessarily in private hands: considerable tracts of *ager publicus* existed in the early Roman Empire and the exploitation of such land was normally entrusted to private tenants of the state.

Saxon Innocence

So by the time written records are at hand to give a clearer picture, the signs are that Britain had already experienced several different forms of land organization, some of them possibly quite sophisticated. The written records surviving from the Roman period relate mostly not to Britain but to Gaul, where conditions might or might not have been very similar. We have to wait until Anglo-Saxon times in the early seventh century A.D. for the first British texts on land organization. When the curtain rises at this time we find an England owned by a community of free, independent peasant proprietors or 'ceorls', each family cultivating its own smallholding and relying largely on its own efforts for the procurement of the food it needed. We do not know how each Saxon peasant family came to own that portion of the globe it claimed as its own. But we do know that although the Saxon peasant undoubtedly engaged in some co-operative farming and communal effort, each family owned a certain amount of land itself. There was just one figure with rights over the ceorls, and thereby indirectly over the land, and that was the king, who was entitled to require of each ceorl a certain amount of military service as well as hospitality for himself and his retinue in the form of the annual 'food-rent'. What this meant in the earliest times was a quantity of provisions sufficient to maintain a king and his retinue for twenty-four hours. This requirement did not stop land ownership in Anglo-Saxon times being a more absolute right than it has ever been since. Another characteristic of the period was that all the owners of the land were also cultivators of the soil. In other words, there was no group of non-farming landowners.[4]

However, even at this early stage, a certain amount of perversion of the system was already taking place. Supporting what seems a relatively innocent form of family-subsistence agriculture was a class of slaves – probably Britons who had been expropriated when the Saxons conquered their country. And in so far as the system can be seen as free peasant landholding, it began to crumble further under the impact of the continual warfare of the seventh, eighth and ninth centuries mainly against the well-equipped invading Danes. One of the most admired virtues of the Saxon kings was the generosity they showed towards their supporters. Money was not much used, and so the most obvious way of rewarding supporters was through provisions. What the kings therefore did was to grant charters to their followers – and they in turn granted charters to *their* followers – which transferred the duty of military service and food-rent due to the king to the favoured supporter – or from the favoured supporter to one of his own supporters. This process snowballed, and by the time of the Norman Conquest in 1066, the right to collect food-rent and to raise fighting men had in many areas passed from the king to territorial lords, known as 'thegns'. The land remained in the ownership of the ceorls, but the rights of a territorial lord replaced those of the king.

The impact of this process on the lives of the ceorls must have varied widely from place to place. Some thegns clearly had no qualms about installing large private armies to live off the backs of the ceorls, greatly increasing the food-rents payable. And of course the thegns' monopoly over the means of coercion enabled them to retain their control.

But there were also external forces working to undermine the independence of the ceorls. Without the benefit of such basic farming techniques as four-course rotation, they were not well placed to support not only their own families but an army and navy as well. A series of poor harvests, theft and destruction caused by war left some ceorls unable to pay the food-rent due to their thegns. When this happened, many ceorls had no option but to hand over some of their own land to their thegns in return for relief from immediate hardship. As the thegns claimed land for themselves they were prepared to accept the ceorls' free labour instead of the whole food-rent. Gradually whole communities of ceorls handed their lands over to the thegns and earned their keep by working on the lands they had once owned.

However, much land even in late Saxon England was not under the exclusive ownership of one person or family. Instead, considerable areas were subject to shared rights, common to people of one district, or even one village – rights that had grown up by custom over centuries, and probably pre-dated the emergence of private land ownership. When a thegn sought to appropriate this 'common' land, his ownership could not be absolute, but was subject to the customary rights of others, whether to gather berries or nuts or mushrooms, pasture animals or cut gorse for fuel. The woods, marshes and little clearings of the Kentish Weald, for instance, were almost certainly available for grazing, wood-collecting and other such activities to all the inhabitants of Kent in Saxon times, just as Sherwood Forest was common to all the people of Nottinghamshire. Extensive common lands existed not only in Saxon woodlands but also in the open moorlands of Wales and the north, west and south-west of England, as well as in the fens and marshes around the coast.[5]

Dispossession

We are accustomed to thinking of the Norman Conquest as the subjection of one people by a foreign tribe. And so it was. But this aspect of the affair was ultimately to prove of vastly less significance than one of its immediate consequences. The new Norman régime took control of the land itself (as the Romans, for example, had never bothered to do) and placed it in the hands of a class created for the purpose of managing it. Feudalism, as the new system came to be known, was not as oppressive as is now often thought. On the contrary, it was at root both sensible and benevolent. But by requiring the dispossession of the common people it paved the way for abuse and ultimately catastrophe.

As we have already seen, the form of social organization known as feudalism emerged in the face of the military threats confronting the Franks in the eighth century and in which a man's status turned on his ability to fight from horseback. The skilled troupe of fighting men William brought with him to England in 1066 expected to be richly rewarded for their military service. They were. William immediately threw England under the heel of a landowning class of knights and barons (the most superior form of knight). He claimed all the land for the Monarchy: from henceforth all land would be owned not in any absolute way (as the Saxon ceorls had done) but by permission of the king. William created the same sort of feudal pyramid in England that he had known in Normandy. At the top of the pyramid was the king, the ultimate owner of all land. The king kept some of his kingdom to himself – 'in demesne' was the term used – and divided the rest between about 180 barons on the understanding that they would provide a specified number of knights ready for battle whenever the need arose. Each baron in turn retained demesne lands of his own, and divided the rest of his territory among knights, each of whom was under a military obligation to his baron, and thus to the king. William also exacted knight service from the ancient English churches which, like the knights, retained demesne lands and sub-let the rest of their holdings.

Those thegns and ceorls who had not been killed in war lost their ownership rights and could gain an interest to land only by leave of the new warrior-landowning aristocracy. The Saxons became 'serfs', providing their labour on the knight's lands in return for the right to till some parts of the knight's holdings for their own benefit.

Each knight owned far more land than the average Saxon thegn had controlled. Henry de Ferrers, for instance, the founder of the family of de Ferrers, and the forebear of the present 13th Earl Ferrers, was given estates scattered in fourteen counties. Although the bulk of his estate lay in Derbyshire, Staffordshire and Leicestershire, he also had outlying parts of his estate in Essex, Berkshire and Hampshire. The spreading of barons' interests into many counties helped William to make his new kingdom cohere since each baron would be as anxious as the king himself to keep all his own private kingdom together through the use of his own private army of horsemen. There was thus a military reason for the award to a baron of scattered estates – as indeed there was for more compact gifts like that of land in Cheshire to Hugh Le Gros Veneur (forebear of the Grosvenor family and the present Duke of Westminster), who was charged with the task of keeping invading Welshmen on the left side of the Dee.

The arrival of feudalism clearly reduced the standing of the mass of the people. First, William had abolished the notion of free, independent peasant ownership of the soil. The Saxon ceorl had enjoyed rights in law, if he had not relinquished them, to own, buy, sell, inherit or bequeath the land itself. If he sought the protection of a lord he could always, if he did not like what

he got, seek his fortune somewhere else. William changed all
this. From the time of his arrival nobody could till the soil unless
he paid for it, whether by providing free labour or military
service. Serfs were subjected to all sorts of restrictions. The serf
was by birth and inheritance bound to the soil; he and his family
were sold with an estate when it changed hands. His daughter
could not marry save with his knight's or baron's consent and
the payment of a heavy fine; when he died his best beast,
sometimes his only cow, was seized as 'heriot' by the lord. He
could not migrate or withdraw his services at will. He could not
strike.

The serf was allowed to till the portion of his knight's land
allocated for his own use on a certain number of days of the year
when the knight had no claim on him. And he could pasture his
beasts on the untilled 'waste land of the manor', in common
with the other serfs. But it was the lord of the manor who owned
all these lands.[6]

Rights of Conquest

The Conquest eliminated the early Saxon notion of land *ownership*
by working farmers. What took its place was a form of ownership
by conquest. Tenure sprang from the part the owner's forebears
had played in helping William defeat the English at the Battle of
Hastings. And of course, in many cases it still does, even when
that title to a particular piece of land has since been bought and
sold many times. Ownership through previous conquest is of
course also found in some 'primitive' societies, where the warrior
may own what he can seize in battle. But, as might be expected,
this model is not noted for the social equity to which it gives rise.

The establishment of this system of land allotment in Britain
was perhaps William's most important legacy. But he also left
other marks on the rural régime which were to remain in place
long after his demise. He did not only ensure that land was held
by the Crown through a small class of intermediaries; he also
ensured that this group of landowners would enjoy a privileged
status. Their superiority was reinforced by two special features
of feudal society: the association of the landowners with the
horse, which enabled them literally to look down on the serfs,

who walked; and the erection of castles from which they dominated the landscape. Belvoir Castle reminds us of what Norman
barons' castles must have symbolized to the people who lived
around them. Belvoir, in Leicestershire, was built by William
the Conqueror's standard-bearer at the Battle of Hastings. His
descendant, the present Duke of Rutland, still owns 15,000 acres
of countryside overhung by the same castle. Belvoir Castle so
dominates the Vale of Belvoir that it is almost impossible to be
anywhere in the Vale without feeling overlooked by it.

By ensuring that knight service passed from father to son,
William also ensured that land remained in the ownership of the
same families. William's band of knights and barons were already
closely related when they set foot in England. This sense of
kinship, and a common attitude to the 'lower' orders, was to
endure. As landowners, the Normans went in for judicious
marriages to consolidate and enlarge their families' estates. And
as a result, control of land was to remain vested in a small and
tightly-knit group, rather than becoming ever more fragmented,
as happened in countries without primogeniture such as Ireland
or post-Revolution France. The creation of an enduring breed of
landowners holding total sway over cultivation was to set in
train attitudes of subservience towards the landowning class
which were to persist over the centuries. Deference on the one
hand, and paternalist arrogance on the other, became built into
the bedrock of rural life.

In other words, William the Conqueror did not only establish
the principles of our system of land ownership. He also helped
shape attitudes and habits on the part of the landowning class
which have survived in part to the present day. The enduring
attachment of landowners to bloodsports is a striking example of
this.

Realm of the Huntsman

William brought with him from Normandy a passion for hunting.
So intense was his enthusiasm that he did not hesitate to set
aside huge tracts of his new kingdom as his private playground
for the pursuit of deer and boar – land which would be sterilized
for food production for the rest of the population. These areas,

defined in law as royal forest, extended far beyond the lands the
king owned personally and included territory he had handed out
to freeholders. Most of Essex, Sussex, Surrey, Hampshire, large
stretches of the north and west and parts of Scotland and Wales
were declared royal forest. It is impossible to establish the
precise extent of the royal forests in William's day, but it is clear
that almost a quarter of England was royal forest during the
reign of Henry II in the mid-twelfth century; and that by the
thirteenth century, after a period of decline, they still covered
about one-fifth of the land surface of England.

'Royal forest' did not imply only wooded land: it embraced
villages and cultivated fields as well as common, rough pasture,
field and wood. The term 'royal forest' meant an area in which a
special kind of law – the forest law – applied. To safeguard and
replenish the stocks of deer (red, fallow and roe) and wild boar
was the sole purpose of forest law. Under this régime, deer were
'the principal beauty and ornament of the forest': their needs
overrode those of mere human beings. And unfortunately for the
non-regal inhabitants of medieval England and Scotland, these
needs were considerable. They included feeding grounds well
provided with grass, the leaves of bushes and the lower branches
of trees. As red deer and fallow deer do not consort together
happily, even greater expanses were required to keep them apart.
Cattle could be tolerated in the vicinity of deer, but sheep and
horses, which, like deer, bite the grass close and might therefore
compete with them for pasture, had to be segregated or banished
completely. In winter, the deer required their feed to be supplemented by hay or 'browse wood' (tender twigs, branches of
holly and so on) unobtrusively strewn in their path by keepers.
In mid-summer they had to be kept free from all disturbance
while they fawned. Certain favourite haunts of the deer were left
as 'preserved grounds' throughout the year.

The laws and regulation of the royal forest, enforced by a host
of forest officials, forbade any activities that might impair the
use of the land for hunting. Nobody, not even the baronial
owner of the land, could plough up pasture used by deer in
order to grow crops, nor could trees be cut down; permission
was required to lop branches. Yet to the serf, rough grassland
and woodland was much more than an extra or even a main

source of pasture. It also provided him with wood – an essential material from which his house, farm implements and household utensils were made and which formed his main source of fuel. Some sheep and cattle grazing was allowed in the royal forests, but only at certain places and seasons. Anybody who broke any of the forest regulations could be fined heavily and might have his property confiscated. The poaching of venison was the most serious offence, and for this a man could be castrated and blinded. Explained a writer of the time:

The organisation of the forests . . . is separate from other judgements of the kingdom and is subject only to the will of the king or of some other officer appointed for this purpose. Indeed it observes its own laws, which, it is said, derive not from the common law of the land but from the will and whim of the king. So that whatever has been done according to it may be said to be not *absolutely* just, but *just according to the law of the forest*.[7]

Outside the royal forests, the landowning classes took their cue from the king, and applied the principles of the royal forest to their own lands. Living as warriors at the expense of the cultivators of the soil, they had time on their hands. Hunting provided something to do which was not only entertaining but useful in that it provided peacetime training for war. As the knights and barons took up the royal habit of hunting so they followed the king in creating private hunting domains of their own. To establish a private hunting forest or 'chase', a landowner needed only the permission of the king. Once he had secured this, he could forbid everybody else to take animal food within it. The vast private chases of medieval England, of which there were at least twenty-six at various times in the Middle Ages, owned by both lay and ecclesiastical lords, included Cannock Chase in Staffordshire, Lancashire's Forest of Bowland, Arundel in Sussex, Enfield Chase in Middlesex and Dorset's Cranborne Chase.

Neither the royal forests nor the private chases were actually fenced: their boundaries were so long that this would have been impracticable. Since many embraced strings of villages, ordinary people were permitted to traverse the royal forests and private chases in order to go about their everyday business. However, in the third category of medieval game preserve – the smaller deer parks – no access of any sort seems to have been permitted.

Deer parks were essentially status symbols in which their owners hunted deer. Securely enclosed with a high earth bank topped by a fence of oak stakes, all maintained by serf labour, the deer park was usually situated close to the lord's house and might well occupy potentially productive agricultural land. There is definite evidence for the existence of 1,900 parks in England at various times during the Middle Ages, and they must have been a common feature of the landscape. Hundreds of deer parks could have seen their owners only very occasionally since many of the great landowners and wealthy bishops had large numbers of parks: the Bishop of Winchester, for instance, owned twenty-three, the Dukes of Cornwall twenty-nine and the Earls of Lancaster forty-five.

Clearly the development of the habit of hunting had a decisive impact on the allocation of land in medieval England. A French observer reported, incredulously, in 1549 that a great part of England consisted not of cornfields but of 'waste, desert and savage ground, not inhabited or tilled, but consisting of forests, chases, parks and enclosures'[8], so that he reckoned there must be as many deer in England as there were people in France. (Better population statistics exist for deer in medieval England than for the human beings.) Many are the instances in which the allocation of a stretch of land for private bloodsports (regal or baronial) in medieval times has survived the intervening centuries. Cornbury and Wychwood in Oxfordshire for example, was a favourite hunting ground of the medieval kings; today, two of the main uses to which its owner, Lord Rotherwick, devotes Cornbury Park and Wychwood Forest are pheasant and deer shooting (see pp. 400ff.) The countryside around Alnwick in Northumberland was also established as royal forest; fox-hunting and pheasant shooting are two of the main uses of the enclosed and essentially private headquarters of the present Duke of Northumberland's northern lands, the 3,000-acre Hulne Park at Alnwick (see pp. 128 and 273ff.)

However, the emphasis on hunting in medieval Britain had even more far-reaching consequences. It helped establish two basic principles of land management that were to persist to this day. The first was that facilitating the private pleasure of the privileged few was a legitimate basis for determining the allocation of Britain's land. The second was that the landowner possessed the right to do whatever he liked with his land – irrespective of the impact of his land-use decisions on other members of the community. While some of the vast deer preserves of the Norman landowners were in areas of relatively poor and infertile soils, like the New Forest and Dartmoor, others occupied land that could have grown crops for the poor. Farming was further impaired by deer that strayed from the coverts and woodland pastures on to growing crops in existing fields. The restrictions on grazing in the royal forest, private chases and deer parks meant that serfs and the few free peasants had to seek pasture for their livestock somewhere else, perhaps some distance away. But this inconvenience and hardship had to be tolerated in the interests of the private pleasures of the rich.

The arrival of feudalism in Britain, then, constituted a graphic case of the seizure of power by the strong over the weak. The manorial system had existed in embryo under the Saxon kings, who were themselves fond of hunting. But it was the Normans who cemented the inequalities emerging under the Saxon régime into a fixed and enduring system.

Recovery

As we have seen, elsewhere in the world seizures of power of this kind have tended to reverse themselves, albeit often over hundreds of years. In Britain, however, our landowning class has proved remarkably resilient. It has retained much of its strength and many of its privileges. This is largely because ever since protest first started to surface, our landowners have been prepared to head it off by granting concessions.

For many serfs in England during the early Middle Ages, feudalism was a simple, harsh and oppressive régime. However, towards the end of the fourteenth century, many of the serfs fortunate enough to survive the Black Death of 1349 came to feel a relaxation of their bonds.

About 1.5 million people were wiped out by the Black Death. The drastic reduction in population caused by the plague meant that landowners suddenly found it difficult to recruit enough people to till their demesne lands. To cope with this problem, many converted their arable land to sheep pasture, which required far less labour while wool was becoming more and more lucrative as a crop for export. Once landowners had made this change, they no longer needed so many of the serfs who actually were available, so they agreed to accede to long-standing demands for the commution of feudal dues into the payment of a cash rent. This trend brought the serfs a degree of freedom but it tended to increase the degree of social unrest in the countryside. The serfs who had not had their feudal dues commuted contrasted their situation with the prosperity of those labourers who had managed to secure and retain their freedom. Other serfs whose lords had commuted their feudal dues for a limited term only bitterly resented having to go back under the feudal yoke when the time came. By 1380 many serfs in various parts of England, but in particular Kent, Essex and East Anglia, were discontented. The improvement in conditions some had experienced only made others less compliant and submissive and heightened the consciousness of all serfs to the servility of their position. The attachment of the lower orders to tradition dwindled and with it their respect for authority.

The match that was to set this tinder alight was the imposition in 1380 of an extra tax to pay for the Hundred Years' War with France. All taxes were ultimately paid by the field labourers, and this was no exception. When the king's official went to Brentwood in Essex to gather the tax in 1381 he was met by an angry band of five thousand men armed with sticks and rusty swords. This riot stimulated others and on 11 June 1381, one hundred thousand people marched on London and took over the city for several days. It was an eruption that took the governing classes entirely by surprise. They were faced for a short spell with what was almost complete anarchy – days in which new names like Wat Tyler, John Ball and Jack Straw were on everyone's lips as leaders of a frightening revolt. The rebels' chief demand was the abolition of feudalism through the commutation of all servile dues throughout the land for a money rent. Many of them also demanded the disendowment of the Church, free use of forests and the abolition of the game laws.

Had the Peasants' Revolt succeeded, it could have changed

the whole future history of Britain. What happened instead was, from the serfs point of view, a cruel trick. The king came out and met the rebels' leaders, promised to accede to their demands and guaranteed them safe conduct. In fact, these concessions were revoked the moment the revolt was at an end, the rebels' leaders were arrested and beheaded, and the king's forces put down the revolt.

However, the suppression of the rising by no means ended the strikes and riots against serfdom. It became more and more difficult to get a good day's work out of resentful serfs. And gradually landowners stopped working their demesnes through the forced service of serfs. Instead of requiring labour from the serfs they charged them rent for cultivating their strips, using these rents to hire free labour. Gradually, feudalism was transformed into something else – agrarian capitalism. And for serfs in the closing decades of the fourteenth century and throughout the fifteenth century, the new system brought with it material improvements. Landowners did not only change the system of tenure. They also took other steps to buy off dissent by adding to what concessions they had already accepted to their absolute ownership of the land. What all these concessions began to imply was the acceptance of responsibility for meeting the needs of the community as well as the needs of the landowners themselves.

By the closing years of the fourteenth century, three main elements of a possible 'social contract' between landowners and the landless could be discerned. First, there was the ancient system of common rights which enabled all citizens to graze their animals and carry out certain other activities on special common lands and also, at certain times of year, on the open fields. Second, a right of passage was generally respected for all citizens over all privately held land (except for deer parks) at least within each citizen's own parish. Third, it came to be understood that the laws banning the taking of game and interference with its habitat would not be too vigorously enforced.

A Social Contract

(i) COMMON RIGHTS

We have already seen that common rights in land, gradually restricted from the inhabitants of a whole region to those of perhaps one or two villages, precede the idea of private property in British land. As population pressure increased over the centuries, not only were rights restricted to people from a smaller and smaller geographical area, user rights came also to be shared out within particular communities – in a system not unlike that of pre-colonization Maori tenure. This sharing of rights in farmland continued under Norman feudalism just as it had formed a vital element of food production by free ceorls or those whose land had been granted to thegns.

In fourteenth- and fifteenth-century England, the commons were far from being patches of waste on which the poor turned out a few geese and goats to scratch a living:[9] they encompassed all the open land of each parish and included not only unploughed rough pasture but also the very best meadow land. In the tilled common fields, common pasture lay on the grassy banks that separated the cultivated strips, on the headlands on which the plough was turned in autumn, on strips of grass lying on the banks of streams bounding the fields; in the fallow fields; early in the sowing season on the corn fields; and on the stubble when the harvesting and gleaning were over. In the common meadow, common rights of pasture existed after the hay harvest. The rest of the common pasture was to be found on the uncultivated 'waste' belonging to the lord of the manor. Common 'waste' however, was an inappropriate description in view of the value and variety of the pasture that was often involved. It frequently included the grass verges of the roads running through the parish; the town green or greens; the rough land near streams and rivers; and the uncultivated common itself, which could cover rough grass, wood or fen.

The status of 'commoner' was enjoyed not by a handful of cottagers but by virtually everyone from the richest tenants and the largest yeomen in a parish down to its poorest inhabitants. In Northamptonshire, for example, landless commoners included squatters in the forests and fens owning nothing but their common rights and craftsmen earning their main income from working as weavers, shoemenders or butchers.[10]

Grazing rights in the common pastures were much the most important of the numerous common rights. They enabled people with tiny holdings or no land at all of their own to keep a cow or two, some sheep or pigs, perhaps a few geese, or a horse that could be employed in the carrying trade. What is more, arable farming could not have been carried out without cattle to plough and manure and carry heavy loads. Next in importance to grazing rights were the rights that enabled commoners to collect wood. Wood had to play the part in the economy now played by coal, gas, steel and concrete combined. It was the most widely used fuel; it was used for the building of houses, and for the making of equipment and tools of every kind. So the right to collect wood was immensely important.

But there were many other rights of common, varying from place to place. These could include a right to fish, a right to take bracken (used for thatch, bedding and fuel), a right to take clay (for building), a right to take rushes, and a right to take berries, nuts, peat and gorse.

Commoners' rights helped enable a co-operative farming system to survive underneath the régime of Norman feudalism. Although William the Conqueror had divided up the country into private kingdoms and established basic principles of private ownership in land, the ordinary field labourers attempted to continue the co-operative system of agriculture they had practised in Saxon times, and probably earlier. The permanent grazing pastures or commons, in which any citizen of a particular locality could graze his animals, were a vital part of this intricate system of collective farming. A sophisticated armoury of local bylaws, enforced by the law-makers – in this case the commoners themselves – existed to keep the common pasture in good heart, to protect the grazing animals against disease and accident, and to keep the right of common open to all occupiers. Local manor courts, in which the villagers had a voice, prepared and enforced rules to regulate use of the commons.

So the continued recognition of common rights after the Norman Conquest amounted to a limitation on the total ownership of land by the king through his barons which otherwise applied. It came about because the Norman kings calculated that any attempt to obliterate commoners' rights would stimulate rebellion as well as wrecking the agrarian economy on which their armies depended. But it was to serve as the main symbol of

what was to be regarded as a form of feudalism that could claim
to bear an acceptable face.

But if the common lands were the concession most valued by
the landless, they were also the concession that cost the landowners most dearly. It was not long before some landowners
were seeking to erode the commoners' rights. So deeply ingrained
in the British system was the notion of common rights that,
although the Norman kings and their favoured few 'owned' the
land, common law had not allowed them to fence off the
commons for their own private use without the consent of
their free tenants. Increasing pressure for the enclosure of the
commons led the medieval Parliament in 1235 to give lords the
right to appropriate waste land of the manor – but only provided
that they left sufficient pasture for their free tenants. The Statute
of Merton, as it was called, had limitations: it was vaguely
worded, and provided no safeguards for the mass of the serfs
who were not freemen. However, it did reflect a genuine determination to maintain the limitations on full-blooded feudalism
which were to make Britain's system of land ownership more
resilient than its counterparts elsewhere.

(ii) RIGHT OF PASSAGE

Over common land it was, of course, only natural that access for
right of passage would exist, since people needed to cross
the commons to exercise their rights as commoners. With the
exception of the deer parks, the public seem also to have been
able to pass freely over uncultivated land on which they did not
enjoy common rights, even when this embraced royal forest or
private chase.

Altogether, the density of tracks and paths in typical parishes
was far higher than it is today. Once a path entered a tract of
uncultivated land, for instance, it tended to fan out in all
directions. People appear to have been able to walk straight
across uncultivated land whether or not a marked-out path or
track was present. This custom also seems to have been followed
in the open fields; people were able to use the grassy banks
between strips or around fields not only for access to the fields
themselves but for movement for any other purpose too.

A right of passage across private land for the public was a widely accepted constraint on the rights of the landowner. Access was seen not as a privilege to be granted but as a basic right. A man might not own any land, but he could traverse anybody else's.[11]

Landowners were not only expected to grant a free right of passage across their lands; they were also expected to see that at least the main tracks connecting settlements were adequately maintained. In the fourteenth and fifteenth centuries there appears to have been a considerable amount of travelling. People seem often to have been on the road, going to market, or to a fair, on pilgrimages or visiting towns. The first statute to deal with roads, the Statute of Winchester in 1285, placed the duty of maintaining all the public highways within each manor, without remuneration or reward, on the inhabitants of that manor. What is more, bushes, woods or dykes that came within two hundred feet of either side of the highway and in which robbers might lurk had to be cleared away. Days spent in highway maintenance were deducted from the quota to be worked on the lord's estate. For the landowners involved, the maintenance of roads and bridges was an obligation they were content to discharge in return for the many privileges land ownership brought with it.

(iii) THE RELAXATION OF THE FOREST LAWS

As we have seen, William the Conqueror seized for himself not only all rights over the land of Britain but also the right to kill its wild animals. He allowed some of his subjects to hunt certain creatures but he retained the best for himself and set aside huge tracts of his new kingdom for the preservation of 'his' wild animals.

Until 1217, lands subject to forest law could not be enclosed, nor could timber be felled on them, cultivation take place or game be killed. Some of the Plantagenet kings were even more anxious to preserve deer for themselves than William. On the accession to the throne of Henry II (1154–89) the forests were extended to cover the greatest area they were ever to attain – almost a quarter of England.

However, Henry II's successors during medieval and Tudor times proved less anxious to preserve the royal forest. The bounds of the forests were extremely difficult to police while an increasing population sought to use the forests' resources; at the same time, disafforestation was a way in which the Crown could raise money. Henry III began to permit the felling of royal forest timber, the killing of game and the enclosure of tracts of forest. By about 1330, the area of the royal forests in England as a whole had shrunk to about two-thirds of what it had been in 1250. At the same time, there was a reduction in the stringency of the law's application, so that more and more areas became 'forest' in name only. The penalties for forest offences were reduced. There were fewer convictions involving imprisonment and castration and more fines. The grazing rights that the Crown had reserved for itself in the forests came to be less vigorously enforced. As a result of all this, the poor began to take by stealth much of what the law confirmed to them. They began to drive their cattle into the deer reserves and to take timber freely from the forest. People began to squat in the forests, make clearings for agriculture and exploit all the resources the forest had to offer.

Quite large squatter communities grew up. Beyond the domination of any lord of the manor, these were essentially communities of masterless men, providing a refuge for itinerant people.[12] In the seventeenth century in particular, these communities of men and women, many of them driven out of their homes by landowners' appropriating common rights to themselves, were to form the seed-bed for ideas about land ownership that challenged the basis of the landowners' hegemony head on.

Feudalism Gives Way to Capitalism

It is easy to underrate the significance of this change, yet it is, in a sense, more fundamental than any other; for it marks the transition from the . . . conception of land as the basis of political functions and obligations, to the modern view of it as an income-yielding investment. Landholding tends, in short, to become commercialized.

R. H. Tawney, *The Agrarian Problem in the 16th Century*, 1912

There is no doubt that the arrival of agrarian capitalism and the relaxation of the ownership régime that came with it brought some benefits for the peasants.[13] Feudalism had allowed little scope for the individual serf to improve his position. One of the advantages of capitalism was that it allowed the hard-working peasant blessed with good luck to produce food for the market as well as for his own family. In so doing he stood a chance of eventually being able to enlarge his own holding by buying out other peasants. But it soon became clear that the benefits the new system had brought were not unalloyed.

Feudalism had at least guaranteed the livelihood of large numbers of people by providing them with employment and enabling them to grow their own food on land which their lord was expected to provide for them. The occupier of the soil was in a condition of legal insecurity, but he enjoyed practical economic security since his services were needed for the cultivation of the lord's home farm. But under capitalism, hired labourers and people working land they had leased for a money rent were at the mercy of the laws of the market. And these worked to the advantage of the landowner rather than that of his poorer tenants. The feudal idea of the lord of the manor as a figure with some responsibility for his local community, albeit responsibility of a paternalistic rather than a legal character, came to to be undermined. Landowners came to view their property less and less as a trust to be exercised on behalf of the sovereign and more and more as a source of wealth. The relationship between land ownership and the interests of the community that had begun to take root in the fourteenth century gradually became obscured as land came to be treated as a form of capital.

This change in landowners' attitude to their land was enhanced by two sudden changes in the composition of the landowning class. At the beginning of Tudor times land remained concentrated in the hands of a small number of noble families. A survey for Rutland in 1522, one year and place for which figures happen to be available, showed 4 per cent of the county's population as owning 43 per cent of its land.[14] In so far as new members joined the landowning class, they tended to ape the attitudes of the established aristocrats and gentry rather than introduce new ideas. However, in the middle of the sixteenth century and then again a century later, the sudden influx of a new group of landowners was to accelerate the move towards ruthless commercialism of the whole landowning class.

In 1536, Henry VIII dissolved the monasteries and seized Church lands occupying about a fifth of the land surface of England and Wales. Henry gave a small amount of his new possessions to his most eager subjects, but because he desperately needed money to wage war against the French, he sold the rest outright or let it on long leases. The people who came to take on these new acres were quite different from the nobility – merchants, civil servants and in particular members of the legal profession, which was at this time the surest way of getting rich quickly. These people had never known the mediaeval idea of the lord of the manor as paternalist – in so far as it existed. For them the land was above all a source of profit. They regarded their tenants and lands as things to be exploited automatically, whereas for the established landlords this attitude required something of a rethink. A hundred years later, 1,677 Royalist estates were confiscated by Oliver Cromwell. And these ended up in the hands of another set of equally ignoble and equally commercially-minded parvenus. Their influence on the older landowners, who were in any case changing their attitudes to their land and tenants, helped ensure that land came to be regarded during the sixteenth and seventeenth centuries less as a basis of political power and obligation and more and more as a source of income.

Both older aristocrats and the less noble newcomers were able to turn their land into a secure investment in several ways. On the land they managed themselves they could grow grain or keep livestock for the market or for wool. They could exploit the timber on their estates or the minerals. Alternatively, or simultaneously, they could evict tenants and buy out small freeholders, letting the large profitable units thus created on lucrative leases. One obstacle stood in the way of both these approaches – the system of shared control of the open fields and the peasants' common rights over the waste and over the open fields themselves. If the countryside was to continue to be shared to some degree with the common people, the landowners would have had to work round this obstacle. More profit was certainly available without any encroachment on the rights of the common people. The open-field system had evolved as new agricultural techniques were discovered, and land reclamation was being carried out successfully on a co-operative basis. But by this time the landowners had little interest in the common good. They wanted to increase their own wealth, and that is what, by and large, they did.

Sheep Eat Men

> There is an other [cause of stealing] ... Your sheep ... eat up and swallow down the very men themselves. They consume, destroy and devour whole fields, houses and cities.
>
> Sir Thomas More, *Utopia*, 1516

In Tudor times the most profitable form of agriculture was sheep farming. Wool and cloth could be sold abroad at extremely good prices, yet livestock required much less labour than arable farming.

There were two main ways in which landowners could increase their sheep-run acreage, and both had grim consequences for the rural population. First, they could convert to sheep-run the demesne lands they had retained and which they worked themselves through a bailiff. This deprived many people of their employment. Second, they could evict tenants on land that had been leased out. The terms of such leases varied widely: they might run for a term of a generation or more, for one year only, or at the will of the lord. All that was required for eviction was non-renewal when the leases expired. If an owner would not wait that long he could drive tenants out with astronomical rent increases. The only class of peasant with any legal security was the small number of freeholders. These people were protected by common law from any encroachment on their land. However, even they could be winkled out through the conversion of the common lands which provided food for the cattle that drew their ploughs. To those people, known as 'cottars', who had no right to any land save that provided through common rights, the enclosure of commons meant destitution. 'The greatest grief', declared the preacher Thomas Lever in 1550, 'that hath been done unto the people of this realm, hath been the enclosing of the commons.'[15] Tens of thousands of people left their villages and sought employment elsewhere or joined the swelling band of vagrants already roaming the Tudor countryside.

As we have seen, common land could not survive without the goodwill of landowners, since the Statute of Merton, though valuable, provided only a slim sanction. As commercialism gathered pace among the landowners, the Statute was overriden more and more frequently. The vast acres of common land offered a perpetual temptation to landowners anxious to extend their sheep-runs. And once respect for them began to be eroded, they quickly fell prey to the greedy. All over England and Wales during the sixteenth century, lords seized commons, fenced them in and turned them into private sheep-runs. In some cases an agreement was drawn up between the lord and the commoners providing for a fair and equitable division of the common. Yet unilateral action and high-handed oppressive proceedings appear to have been more usual.

The pursuit of commercial success through enclosure did not, however, mean that landowners lost the time and inclination for bloodsports. They retained both, and the new kinds of landowner acquired them too. And this meant further enclosure. New deer parks were created through the enclosure of rough wood and pasture so that they became an increasingly common feature of the Tudor and Stuart landscape. For the poor, who were losing their own land to sheep, the deer parks were vast tracts of land wasted on the pleasures of the rich. The creation of these parks added extra fire to the protest movement that sprang up against the whole enclosure campaign.

There were hundreds of riots and revolts against enclosure throughout the sixteenth and seventeenth centuries.[16] May 1607, for instance, saw a month of sustained and widespread rioting in Northamptonshire, a county in which many parishes had experienced such complete enclosure that road verges rep-resented the only remaining common land. The armies of the landowners as lord lieutenants put down the rebels and executed their leaders, but in spite of this defeat, further enclosure riots erupted in neighbouring Midland counties. For the most part, however, protests concerned with the clearance of common land, forest or the draining of common fen and marsh were unco-ordinated local events. There was no national movement; no leader emerged who could make his voice heard beyond his parish. Yet in district after district, for two hundred years, villagers rose up to break down the fences and hedges – the symbols of enclosure – to try to win back their common fields. They almost never succeeded.

In the face of the danger of revolt, the Crown took some steps by legislation and penalties to try to arrest enclosure. Henry VIII in particular, although he had helped precipitate the situation by selling off the Church lands, deplored what was happening and in a statute in 1515 ordered that within one year all land converted to pasture should be restored to tillage. This effort to defend the citizenry against the landowning class was very different from the approach of the Norman kings who buttressed their barons' rule. But it was to become a feature of Tudor rule. Nonetheless, Henry's laws and commissions were powerless to stem the tide, for their implementation depended on the very landed classes who were profiting from enclosure. The pivot of local government in Tudor times were the justices of the peace who were almost always major landowners, and who were most reluctant to punish others for an offence they might well be committing themselves.

After the Civil War, however, Oliver Cromwell's Parliament was dominated by landowners. Half the members returned for the Midlands, for instance, had been fined for depopulation or belonged to families which had recently been fined. And it soon became apparent that the English Revolution was to have the effect of strengthening the grip of the landowner over the landless.

Cromwell's Parliament did not only decline to put a stop to the relatively limited efforts at enclosure under way in its own time. It also, indirectly, paved the way for the much greater rash of enclosures that was to follow in the eighteenth century. It did this by altering the legal status of the large landowners. For in 1646, feudalism effectively came to an end with the abolition of feudal tenures and the Court of Wards.

Responsibility Dies – Power Persists

As we have seen, William the Conqueror granted land to his supporters on the condition that they supplied him with an army

whenever the need arose. From about 1166 this obligation was
commuted into money payments called scutage instead of fixed
quotas of knights, and by the latter part of the thirteenth century,
scutage had more or less disappeared. However, because of the
feudal tenure of land, the Crown was still able to impose
arbitrary taxation or death duties on landowners even if in
practice most of them felt pretty safe with their lands. Another
way in which large landowners could feel the grip of the king
was if a man who held land direct from the king died before his
heirs came of age. In this eventuality, the heirs became wards of
the Crown. The right to manage the estate of a ward during his
or her minority and the right to arrange his or her marriage
might each be worth a considerable sum of money. Thus,
particularly in Tudor times, the Court of Wards became an
instrument of financial exploitation by the Monarchy.

The abolition of feudal tenures and the Court of Wards gave
landowners absolute control over their estates.[17] In the security
provided by this condition, they then set about taking steps to
ensure that their estates would always remain within their own
families. One favoured means of achieving this was a special
legal device called the strict settlement. By this means each
succeeding landowner settled the succession of his estate inalien-
ably upon his descendants, in a specified order of precedence.
This system turned a current owner into a trustee for the
transmission of the property to future generations. Although it
was possible to break an entail, the system paved the way for the
concentration of land in the hands of a few families.

However, if the landowners benefited from the abolition of
feudal tenures, the rest of the rural community did not. Tenures
were abolished upwards only, not downwards. An Act of 1660
insisted that the abolition of feudal tenures should not be
understood to make any alteration to the main form of tenure of
the peasant farmers – copyhold. The tens of thousands of
copyholders, whose claim to title rested only on manorial rolls,
thus remained in abject dependence on their landlords. An Act
in 1667 ensured that the property of small freeholders should be
no more secure than that of copyholders unless supported by
written legal title. Since few title deeds had been drawn up in an
era when society was based on loyalty and custom, many small

freeholders found themselves with no real hold over their land at all. These changes removed potential obstacles to enclosure. And as a result, the agricultural boom of the late seventeenth and eighteenth centuries was to entrench the power of the big landowners and capitalist farmers rather than bringing prosperity to the rural population as a whole.[18]

The return of the Stuarts in 1660 did not hail a reversion to the medieval land régime, with a beneficent Sovereign capable of protecting the poor in some measure from the strong landowners. Under Constitutional Monarchy, from 1688 onward, the grip of the Sovereign Parliament, and the powerful interests which ran it, tightened. Until our own century there was no question of universal suffrage. For most of the time, the men who ran Parliament were those who ran everything else – the people who happened to own large tracts of land. Parliament became a means not only of formalizing the power but also of articulating the ideology of the landowning classes.

Even in mid-seventeenth century England, however, there were other ideologies. And if these were never to legitimize a power structure they were able to give meaning to the voices of dissent. By the end of the seventeenth century, a coherent and impressive critique of the prevailing rural order had been worked out. A blueprint for a very different England had been tabled, which retains much of its relevance even today.

The Voice of Dissent

In the middle years of the seventeenth century, in particular from 1645 to 1653, there was a great reappraisal of established values in England. Old institutions, as well as old beliefs, came into question. Within the Revolution which brought about the execution of Charles I and the establishment of a short-lived republic, another revolt took shape. Its roots lay in the undeniable fact that Parliamentary rule benefited the aristocrats, gentry and merchants, not the poorer half of the population. Various groups of common people therefore sought to mobilize support for alternatives to the programme of the new régime.[19]

The revolt took many forms. None of these involved defined organization of the kind which our own pressure groups and political parties enjoy: people moved freely between one group and another. Some, like the Quakers and Baptists, based their case on religious considerations, such as opposition to the tithes and doubt about the necessity for a priesthood. Groups like the Levellers were based around political proposals; others, like the Diggers, Seekers and Ranters, asked fundamental questions about many of the institutions and beliefs of their society. All of these groups were stimulated partly by the temporary liberalization of publishing law. Before 1640 (and after 1660), strict censorship was in force. But for two decades, cheap, portable printing presses were available and active.

The ideas the activists spread fell on receptive ears. For social change was creating a new class of malcontents. The cement of feudal society had been the bond of dependence and loyalty between lord and man: 'No land and no man without a lord.' But by the sixteenth century, people were becoming mobile. Masterless men, free to think what they chose, grew more and more numerous. There was an itinerant trading population – pedlars, carters and craftsmen. There were the squatters on the commons, wastes and in forests. There was the casual labour of the capital, where prospects existed for earning a dishonest living. Above all, there were the large numbers who had been evicted from their holdings by the enclosure movement.

It was natural enough that among the radical ideas floated before such people, ideas about the ownership of land should loom large. 'The earth is the Lord's and the fullness thereof,' wrote one of the Quaker leaders in 1653. 'He hath given it to the sons of men in general, and not to a few lofty ones who lord it over their brethren.' But it was the Levellers and Diggers who developed the most advanced proposals for land reform.

The Diggers sought to overturn society and establish a state in which the poorest would be as free as the richest. They based this idea of democracy on a system of inalienable natural rights, one of which was a right to property and to the fruits of the earth. Their leader, Gerrard Winstanley, wrote: 'The poorest man hath as true a title and just right to the land as the richest man . . . True freedom lies where a man receives his nourishment and preservation, and that is in the use of the earth.'[20]

To draw attention to their demands, Digger groups up and

down England congregated at commons and began to dig them up. They deplored what they saw as the under-utilization of England's land and the impact this had on the price of food. For while the poor went hungry, vast stretches of good, productive earth lay beneath hunting forests or on commons which lords of the manor would not allow the poor to cultivate. One group, calling themselves the True Levellers or Diggers, arrived one Sunday morning in 1649 at St George's Hill Common outside Walton-on-Thames in Surrey and began to dig it up. Their act was intended to be a call for the common people to be allowed to cultivate all forests and wastes; taking place on a Sunday, it was also a symbolic rejection of traditional pieties. The communal cultivation went on but lords of the manors in Surrey harassed the Diggers with legal actions. They moved to Cobham Heath a few miles away but raids and harassment continued and by April 1650 the colony had been forcibly dispersed and their huts and furniture burnt.

This did not, however, stop other Digger colonies from springing up at Wellingborough in Northamptonshire, Cox Hall in Kent, Iver in Buckinghamshire, Barnet in Hertfordshire, Enfield in Middlesex, Dunstable in Bedfordshire, Bosworth in Leicestershire, and at other places in Nottinghamshire and Gloucestershire. Each group seems to have dug up and planted crops on common land, and several published pamphlets.

Gerrard Winstanley was the Diggers' leading thinker and spent many years in a tireless round of writing and campaigning. One of the True Levellers at Walton-on-Thames, he had been a farm labourer in Lancashire, when he felt called by God to take action to ensure that 'the earth should be made a common treasury of livelihood to whole mankind, without respect of persons.'

In his major work, *The Law of Freedom*, Winstanley not only criticized the way in which the land of England was used; he questioned the very basis of private property. He argued that the landowners had no God-given right to the land; indeed, God had given the earth to everybody equally. The right to land was, in his view, a natural right that could not be taken away. But, long ago, men had seized the land by force and the descendants of these robber-barons now owned the land and dictated its use.

He told lords of the manor: 'The power of enclosing land and owning property was brought into creation by your ancestors by the sword; which first did murder their fellow creatures, men, and after plunder or steal away their land, and left this land successively to you, their children. And therefore, though you did not kill or thieve, yet you hold that cursed thing in your hand by the power of the sword.'

Winstanley considered that from a half to two-thirds of England was not properly cultivated: 'If the waste land of England were manured by her children, it would become in a few years the richest, the strongest and [most] flourishing land in the world, and the price of corn would fall from 6s or 7s a bushel to 1s a bushel or less.' Collective cultivation of the waste by the poor could allow for capital investment in improvements without any sacrifice of the interests of the commoners. Crops would be grown to feed the nation rather than, like wool, to produce a profit for the landowners while the poor went hungry. There was land enough to maintain ten times the existing population and make England 'first of the nations' – if only that land were used in the best interests of the people as a whole.

Winstanley did not envisage a bloody revolution and the seizure of the land. He aimed to work through persuasion. He wanted to see the vote extended to all men. Education naturally seemed to him of the greatest importance, and under his plan – and quite exceptionally for the seventeenth century – it was to be universal (for both sexes) and equal, with no specialized scholars.

If the Diggers were prepared to rely on constitutional action, the régime of the day was not willing to leave them alone to do this. After 1660, there was a clamp-down on the publication of radical views. Radicals were purged from official posts, and local commissions (composed of the local gentry) empowered to remove people from public office if they considered this 'expedient for the public safety'. An Act of Parliament in 1661 made it illegal to collect more than twenty signatures to a petition 'for alteration of matters established by law in church or state' unless the petition had first been approved by three justices of the peace (who would normally be major landowners). In 1662 an Act empowered justices of the peace to check migration, a move which made it hard for new Digger communities to set themselves up. JPs were also empowered to displace squatters from the commons and forests.

In so far as any violent resistance was put up, it was mercilessly crushed. In 1649 a group calling themselves the Constitutional Levellers (as opposed to Winstanley's True Levellers) gained sufficient support in the Army to dare a physical trial of strength. The Constitutional Levellers wanted the establishment of a true democracy in Britain, the cultivation of the commons and forests by the poor and the protection of small landowners against the powerful. They would not have dispossessed the rich completely. (Winstanley's True Levellers, in contrast, and in so far as they were a coherent movement, wanted private property ultimately to be abolished.) The Army in the 1640s was a hothouse of political ideas: some of the rank-and-file were calling for an upper limit to the landed property that anyone might hold. And some officers were attracted by the Constitutional Levellers' programme. When it came to a showdown, however, they were defeated by government troops in an armed clash at Burford. Several of the management's leaders were shot.[21]

In so far as anybody knows, Winstanley eventually retired into private life. But his ideas and those of the other radicals did not die with him. Leaders of the American Revolution like Thomas Paine and Thomas Spence (who rejected private property in land and wanted democratic village communities to become sole owners of the land) appear to have been influenced by him. In Britain, *The Law of Freedom* became part of the ideas of the underground, surfacing in a wide variety of places.

As for actual impact on the body politic, the dissidents of the mid-seventeenth century achieved nothing at all. But if this was the radicals' philosophy, the landowners were to develop an equally impressive one. This philosophy was used to buttress in eighteenth century Britain a more oppressive attitude to the landless than Britain had ever seen.

Ideology and Power for Owners

There is nothing which so generally strikes the imagination, and engages the affections of mankind, as the right of property; or that

sole and despotic dominion which one man claims and exercises
over the external things of the world, in total exclusion of the right
of any other individual in the universe.

Sir William Blackstone, *Institutes of Natural Law*, 1754

In the late seventeenth and early eighteenth centuries, Britain's
landowners acquired an ideological framework of their own to
match that of their critics. They ceased to see their legitimacy as
rooted merely in the might of their forebears. Instead, they
looked to philosophers who were presenting the ownership of
property as intrinsically good. Foremost among these was John
Locke, who argued that the accumulation of wealth should be
free of all political and moral controls as it was sanctioned by
natural law. He asserted that the unfettered acquisition of money,
goods and land was part of Nature and therefore ordained by
God, and that 'Government has no other end but the preservation of property'. Later writers embroidered the doctrine. Sir
William Blackstone, a celebrated eighteenth-century writer on
the law, saw not only the existence of private property but also
the inheritance of land and the institutions of government that
protected it as underwritten by natural law. Like Locke, he
argued that private property is acquired under the law of nature,
before civil states are established. But the other foundation of
the property structure of England – the law of England – was,
he argued, also natural because it was the embodiment of natural
justice and 'dictated by God'.

The translation of the twin themes of the right to property and
the rule of law into eighteenth-century statutes was to deepen
the plight of the non-landowning population. Democracy had
yet to arrive, and the group that made and administered the
laws was dominated by landowners.

The House of Lords was extremely important. Landowners
controlled it because most peers were major landowners: the
influence of the Church had been greatly diminished since the
time of Henry VIII. But landowners dominated the Commons
too. Here, the criterion for joining the electoral register and for
standing as a candidate was the same – the ownership of
property. Nobody could qualify for membership of Parliament
unless he owned an estate worth at least £300 a year; while only

men owning the freehold of property capable of attracting rent of at least forty shillings a year could vote – a tiny fraction of the population. Typical of those who sat in the House of Commons was Sir Robert Walpole, who was Prime Minister for nearly twenty-one consecutive years and oversaw many of the mid-century enclosures. Walpole rode and hunted whenever he could. When he received his morning's post-bag, he delighted in opening letters from his gamekeeper in Norfolk before state papers.

To enhance further the power of landed interests, the distribution of constituencies greatly favoured the rural areas, which the landed aristocracy and gentry dominated, as opposed to the industrial areas.[22] Particularly noticeable were the 'rotten boroughs' – tiny constituencies, the smallest of which had no voters at all, but which carried with them Parliamentary seats in the gift of a landowner. Cornwall, for instance, in which tiny hamlets like Tregony, Fowey and Grampound could send two members apiece to the Commons, had more representation in Parliament than Northumberland, Durham and Yorkshire together.[23] In England and Wales as a whole, about a hundred constituencies, each with fewer than five hundred voters, had the right to elect MPs, whereas cities like Birmingham and Manchester, with populations of 75,000 each, were not entitled to send anybody to the Commons.

The ballot was not secret: voters had to declare their votes to the returning officer at the polling stations. Alongside him there was often a representative of the local landowner who was either standing for election himself or sponsoring somebody else. This system helped ensure that the landowner's preferred candidate won the day. Although there were exceptions, most landlords considered it their right to tell tenants how to cast their votes. Some chose instead to rely on various kinds of bribery. These ranged from postponing a rent increase until after an election to handing out a couple of guineas to each elector who voted the right way.

The choice for the electors did not lie between a party representing the strong and another representing the weak. Instead, family relationships and personal loyalties were the basic elements of politics. It was not extraordinary for a Member to have fifty relatives in the House. The Whigs and Tories dissolved into a confusion of 'interests' influenced by common economic concerns and 'connections' based on patronage and kinship. And through all this, the power of the rural landowner remained unchallenged.

The justices of the peace who were responsible for meting out justice under the law were chosen, except in the corporate towns, from the ranks of the landowners. Thus a man accused, say, of poaching would be summoned to appear in the mansion of his local squire who, acting as JP, would hear his case.

Under a landowner-dominated Executive and Judiciary, the law came to be more and more closely involved with property matters. Eventually, as the historian E. P. Thompson put it, justice came to be 'no more than the outworks and defences of property and its attendant status'.[24] Increasingly, intrusions against property became capital offences.

Ranged against the ideology of property clothed in the rule of law were the traditional rights of the landless. These were extensive, including the right to collect firewood, to graze animals over lands regarded as common, to take small game like rabbits, and to walk freely over other people's land. But such rights were not backed up by law, merely by the unwritten social contract between landowner and landless dating back to medieval times. In an increasingly legalistic age, an unwritten agreement counted for little in the face of the new law of the land based on supposed natural law. In earlier times the Sovereign, mindful of the responsibility that came with the divine right of kings, had intervened on behalf of the underclass. Now, however, the king was no more than a figurehead. Divine right without any accompanying sense of responsibility seemed to be re-emerging through in the shape of the law of property. As Adam Smith, the high priest of laissez-faire, put it in 1776: 'Civil government, so far as it is instituted for the security of property, is in reality instituted for the defence of the rich against the poor, or of those who have some property against those who have none at all.'[25] It was not long before such sentiments were transforming the relationship between landowners and the landless.

(i) DEATH TO POACHERS

It was in a revision of the game laws that the new ruthlessness made itself felt most starkly. If the wild creatures which roamed the land were property, then their owners' rights in them were going to receive the fullest protection the law could devise. By the mid-eighteenth century, deer stealing had become a capital offence; indeed, a man's life could be taken for catching one fish or damaging a young tree. The landowning classes' new passion for justice had done nothing to diminish their old passion for bloodsports. 'The game laws, therefore, united the two great preoccupations of the landed ruling class in one knot of emotion', as historian Douglas Hay has put it.[26]

The screw began to tighten with the Restoration Parliament of Charles II, which enacted our first national game laws in the late seventeenth century.[27] These laws took away from the vast majority of people not only the right to take traditional game animals like deer, pheasants and partridges but also the right to fish and the right to kill some animals (hares and rabbits in particular) which provided the only source of meat for many people. The Game Act of 1671 forbade all people to hunt game except those who (a) held freeholds worth at least £100 a year or (b) held leases of at least ninety-nine years worth at least £150 a year or (c) were heirs to esquires or persons 'of higher degree' or (d) held a royal franchise of a park, chase or warren. Through this high landed property qualification, the game of England was appropriated not by the mass of the people, nor even necessarily by the wealthy, nor by all owners of land, but by one group – the country gentlemen.

The main problem these men faced in protecting all the game they now 'owned' was that it was to be found not only on their own land but also on the commons and the land of smallholders. To meet this difficulty, not only poaching itself but the possession of implements like dogs, nets and snares that could be used to take game was made a punishable offence. A mass of statutes re-enacted and stiffened the penalties for taking game unlawfully. There was to be three months' imprisonment or a £5 fine for killing rabbits in warrens, the same for keeping dogs or snares, a year's imprisonment or a £30 fine for taking deer. Three months in gaol may not seem too bad, but in those days the incarceration of a breadwinner for three months could bring a whole family to the brink of starvation. Gamekeepers were empowered to search houses and confiscate nets, snares and guns: this right to search soon became the keepers' most potent weapon.

The law-makers did not only rely on the sanctity of property to justify measures like these. They also argued that the new laws were of benefit to the poor in that they saved them from idleness. The game laws were 'to prevent persons of inferior rank from squandering that time which their station in life requireth to be more profitably employed'.[28]

The poor, however, were not convinced, and in the early 1720s in places like Windsor Forest, Richmond Park, Enfield Chase, Waltham Chase and Woolmer Forest, gangs of men, their faces blacked to escape detection, made night raids to take deer. The areas most affected were the royal forests, over which control had slackened since the days of the Norman barons. The new game laws were seen as an attempt to reassert control and were bitterly resented. At the same time, deer, which relish young corn and vegetables, had to be allowed to eat growing crops in the fields unmolested. Small wonder, then, that those who staged the 'Blacking' attacks were fired by rage as well as hunger.

Parliament's response to these local disturbances was the introduction in 1723 of the death penalty not just for poaching deer, but for taking rabbits and fish. For the sake of the deer, not only was poaching being outlawed, but so were the collection of firewood (the main and in many cases the only source of fuel for heating and cooking), the cultivation of waste land and the cutting of turf, peat and heather by the poor. At a stroke, what came to be known as the Black Act created fifty new offences punishable by death. 'It is very doubtful whether any country possessed a criminal code with anything like so many capital provisions as there were in this single statute,' the eminent historian of criminal law Professor Leon Radzinowicz wrote in 1945.[29]

Sixteen of the 'Blacks' from Windsor, Hampshire, Enfield and Richmond were hanged in the first two years of the Black Act's operation. The number of deer the accused had killed is not recorded, but two gamekeepers were killed and several injured. An unknown number of Blacks died in gaol; others were transported, while some forty who escaped arrest became outlaws. As the century progressed, the Act was successively renewed, extended and enlarged, through both statute and case-law. It remained on the statute book for a century, until its virtual repeal in 1823. As the years passed, recourse to the Act occurred most frequently in response to the riots which were often sparked by enclosure. As it fell to the justices of the peace to decide whether or not the full rigour of the game laws was to be applied, their importance in their local communities grew even further. From his study of the operation of the game laws in Cannock Chase during the eighteenth century, historian Douglas Hay concluded:

Such discretionary power, exercised directly as a prerogative of class, was an integral part of the justice of the eighteenth century: it was used to legitimize power, to tie men in gratitude, to prove the humanity of the English law. At the highest level, royal pardons mitigated the barbarous criminal code by commuting death sentences to transportation or imprisonment; and at the lowest, in rural parishes, the power to intervene in the execution of the laws gave landed gentlemen and peers the opportunity to exercise the same prerogatives of 'mercy' and 'justice'.[30]

Nonetheless, the introduction of the game laws was not the only or even the main unwelcome consequence for the poor of the ferocious possessiveness now coming to the fore among the landowning classes.

(ii) THE LOSS OF COMMON RIGHTS

It was not long before the landowners of the eighteenth century turned their attention to the most obvious legacy of the spirit of compromise of previous centuries – common rights.

The early method of enclosure – private agreement, sometimes confirmed by court decree – could be awkward to implement. In the eighteenth century, however, the landowning oligarchy was able to overcome this difficulty by getting Parliament to pass private enclosure Acts, which gave the landowners immediate

powers to enclose the areas specified. It was possible for those
adversely affected to resist an Enclosure Bill by petitioning
Parliament. In practice, though, this did not often happen. The
historian Christopher Hill explains why: 'The poorest cottager
was always free to oppose a Parliamentary enclosure bill. All he
had to do was to learn to read, hire an expensive lawyer, spend
a few weeks in London and be prepared to face the wrath of the
powerful men in his village.'[31]

In England as a whole, some 5,400 individual enclosures
during the eighteenth and nineteenth centuries, under 4,200
private Acts and various general enclosure Acts, caused the
enclosure of more than 7 million acres of land. About a third of
these acres had been permanent common pasture and waste.
Seven million acres is more than the total area of the following
ten contemporary English counties: Derbyshire, Nottinghamshire, Northamptonshire, Buckinghamshire, Bedfordshire, Hertfordshire, Cambridgeshire, Essex, Norfolk and Suffolk.

After enclosure, all common rights disappeared except, in
some cases, the right to glean fields after harvest. The poor lost
their right to graze animals, cut turf, gather wood, collect berries
and so on. In countless villages in England and Wales, the effect
of the changes was to destroy the subsistence economy that
supported the poor.[32] But it was by no means only the very poor
with no rights to land other than common rights who suffered
through enclosure. Copyholders with no legal proof of the
tenancy or other rights their families had enjoyed for generations
were rarely compensated. And many smallholders who succeeded
in establishing their claims were left with a parcel of land too
small to provide them with a livelihood and a disproportionate
share of the very high cost of putting in the hedges or fences.
Many of these people, working smaller holdings without common
right elsewhere and without the support of common farming
practice, were soon forced to sell out to their richer neighbours.

The objectives for which Parliamentary enclosure was
employed included not only the production of wool, but also
clearance for quarrying, mining, cattle-rearing and the growing
of grain for market. Through enclosure many landowners
increased the value of their estates enormously. By gaining
absolute control of large tracts of land they were able to produce

commercially for the growing urban market in a way that had not been possible before. The estates of Sir Thomas Coke at Holkham in Norfolk had an annual rental value of £2,200 in 1767; by 1816 this had increased almost ten times, to £20,000.[33]

Many people, rendered landless by enclosure, stayed on in the countryside, relying on the poor rate, which had been introduced by the Tudors. More and more, however, moved to the towns. Once this had begun to happen on a large scale, the rural protest movement that had campaigned almost unabated for three hundred years, indulging in sporadic hedge-levelling, deer-park attacks and rioting, started to die down. Gradually land became a less contentious issue, not just because the enclosers had proved themselves irresistible but because their victims had moved out of the firing line into urban communities where they were less aware of what was being taken from them. In any case, they had little time for anything except their most immediate concerns. Life had been hard in the countryside, but in the cities people were required to work up to sixteen or eighteen hours a day, six days a week, in hot and often unhealthy conditions. When children of five or six were working eighteen hours a day in mills, sometimes falling into machines and losing arms or legs, the urban poor had understandably little time to worry about the erosion of their rights in a countryside which no longer played any part in their lives.

(iii) TRESPASSERS WILL BE PROSECUTED

> All Persons found trespassing in any of the Woods, Plantations, Coppice or Grounds belonging to the Right Honourable Lord Bolton, whether for NUTTING, or any other Purpose, will be prosecuted with the utmost Rigour of the Law.[34]

The third major feature of the fifteenth-century understanding between landowners and landless that came under threat was the free access to the countryside that had been available to all. In the eighteenth century, this gave way to a more rigid system of regulation together with the enforcement of provisions to curb trespass.

After enclosure, the ordinary people of England and Wales

came to find themselves shut out of their countryside not only figuratively but literally too. During the sixteenth and seventeenth centuries, the freedom to travel through the countryside which had existed in late medieval Britain started to be withdrawn.

The enclosure of so many kinds of common land curtailed directly some of the freedom of movement villagers had hitherto enjoyed. The old custom of walking in a line across cultivated land rather than keeping to the uncultivated field edge was soon on the way out – to the impotent regret of villagers, like 'Old Tom Lynes', for instance, of Tysoe in Northamptonshire: 'In the old days' (before enclosure) 'you could walk all through the parish and all round it by the balks and headlands and cut wood on the waste, if there was any. And what can you do now, Jasper?', asked Lynes. 'Make a farmer mad and you be done.'[35]

However, it was not only from the enclosed commons that people came to be excluded. As we have seen, villagers had walked freely through private woods even when these lacked the status of commons. Private woods seem to have been seen as a partial, unofficial extension of the commons: commoners crossed woods frequently, gathering nuts and berries, picking up dead wood and probably taking a few hares and rabbits as well. But in Northamptonshire, as the pace of parliamentary enclosure quickened in the 1760s and 1770s, warning notices to trespassers sprang up in these woods. Landowners seem to have been specially anxious to prevent the gathering of nuts. The Earl Spencer, one landowner among many, threatened anyone caught nutting in his woods with being 'taken before a Magistrate and sent for a Soldier'.[36] Later, in the nineteenth century, Richard Jefferies described the way in which 'in many places, where nutting was once freely permitted, it is now rigidly repressed'.[37]

Gradually, access to the countryside came to be confined more and more to predetermined routes. Even these, however, diminished in number. Many enclosure schemes stopped up old roads. After such a scheme had taken effect, anybody trying to use one of these roads could be deemed guilty of trespass.

At the time, the loss of access, like that of common grazing rights, seemed to matter primarily because of the economic implications. These were real enough: a man who needed to drive his cattle to pasture along a certain track could be ruined if it was blocked by a hedge. But the pattern of recreation in the countryside was also to change for ever.

The recreation pursuits of the landowning classes did not suffer. Indeed, enclosure incidentally enhanced what were fast becoming their most popular sports. The new hedges provided cover for partridges to nest in, and by providing jumps for horses, increased the excitement of fox hunting.[38] But activities from which the rest of the population had sought relaxation for centuries were damaged and sometimes destroyed. 'Owing to the inclosure of open lands and commons, the poor have no place in which they may amuse themselves in summer evenings when the labour of the day is over, or when a holiday occurs', wrote Robert Slaney, a vicar, in 1824.[39] Communal activities from fairs to football, wrestling to quoits, skittles, cudgelling (fighting with sticks), foot races, ball-running and stool-ball (an ancestor of cricket) all depended either on easy movement through the countryside for participants and spectators or the occasional use of an open field which might have an agricultural use for most of the year. As enclosure reallocated old hay meadows and common land to individual farmers, it robbed the poor of the space for their traditional recreation pursuits.

The landowners who were wreaking this destruction on recreation opportunities did not consider they had much to answer for. They applauded the demise of these traditional features of rural life as a sign of national improvement, and as a means of securing a better-disciplined labour force. In the wake of the Puritan revolution, popular recreations were largely seen as self-indulgent diversions involving idleness and the loss of precious time that would have been better spent in work. But in later times, when attitudes changed, the old games and festivals were not to return. They had gone for good, taking with them much of the character of rural life in Britain.

The Highland Clearances

One of the most vivid recollections which I retain of Kilbride is that of the eviction and clearance of the crofts of Suishnish. The corner of Strath . . . had been for ages occupied by a community that cultivated the lower ground where their huts formed a kind of scattered village. The land belonged to the wide domain of Lord Macdonald, whose affairs were in such a state that he had to place himself in the hands of trustees. These men had little local knowledge of the estate, and though they doubtless administered it to the best of their ability, their main object was to make as much money as possible out of the rents, so as on one hand, to satisfy the creditors, and on the other, to hasten the time when the proprietor might be able to resume possession. The interests of the crofters formed a very secondary consideration. With these aims, the trustees determined to clear out the whole population of Suishnish and convert the ground into one large sheep farm, to be placed in the hands of a responsible grazier, if possible, from the south country . . .

I had heard some rumours of these intentions, but I did not realize that they were in process of being carried into effect, until one afternoon, as I was returning from my ramble, a strange wailing sound reached my ears . . . It was a miscellaneous gathering of at least three generations of crofters. There were old men and women, too feeble to walk, who were placed in carts; the younger members of the community on foot were carrying their bundles of clothes and household effects, while the children, with looks of alarm, walked alongside. There was a pause in the notes of woe as the last words were exchanged with the [minister's] family of Kilbride. Everyone was in tears; each wished to clasp the hands that had so often befriended them, and it seemed as if they could not tear themselves away. When they set forth once more, a cry of grief went up to heaven, the long plaintive wail, like a funeral coronach, was resumed, and after the last of the emigrants had disappeared behind the hill, the sound seemed to re-echo through the whole wide valley of Strath in one prolonged note of desolation. The people were on their way to be shipped to Canada. I have often wandered since then over the solitary ground of Suishnish. Not a soul is to be seen there now, but the greener patches of field and the crumbling walls mark where an active and happy community once lived.

Sir Archibald Geikie, the distinguished geologist, in his autobiography *Scottish Reminiscences*, Glasgow, 1906 (recalling a clearance in Skye in 1854)[40]

The Highland Clearances – the enclosures that took place in Highland Scotland between 1780 and 1855 – demonstrated in particularly extreme form the power which the landowner can wield over his fellow-citizens. For north of the border the institutional safeguards that existed in England – such as they were – to protect the poor were completely absent.

Before the twelfth century, Scotland was parcelled out among different tribes or clans. Each clan consisted of a set of men and women bearing the same surname and believing themselves to be related to one another and descended from the same common stock. All members of the clan owed their allegiance to the clan chief and looked upon it as their duty to support him in all his adventures. The chief for his part played the role of father and head of the family to all his kinsmen. He administered justice and a clan 'welfare state', providing for widows and the elderly. And he also acted as trustee of the clan's lands. He did not own the land, since this belonged, in common, to the whole clan. But he collected rent from clan members and required military and labour service from them. In return he protected the clan from outside attack. There was neither recognition of, nor claim to, absolute and unrestricted land ownership; and security of tenure was rooted in the customs of the people, even though it was not enshrined in law.

By the time David I succeeded to the Scottish throne in 1124, he had spent many years at court in England and acquired, through marriage, vast estates in Northamptonshire and Huntingdonshire. Under David I and his immediate successors, something like a peaceful Norman Conquest of Scotland took place. David took land out of the collective hands of clans and appropriated it himself. He then granted parcels of it to a few favoured men. Some were Anglo-Normans brought up from Northamptonshire; others were former clan chiefs who now became owners rather than trustees. Each chief holding land was required to render military and other services to the Crown. The chief retained a small parcel of land and sub-contracted the remainder to 'tacksmen' who paid only a nominal rent for their farms on the understanding that they would provide the chief with skilled soldiers when these were needed. The tacksmen rented out their land to joint-tenants who worked it with the help of cottars (people who held a small amount of land in return for their labour) and landless servants – all of whom also served a vital function in the clan's military machine.

Under the feudal ownership régime, relatively little changed at first. The prime objective of land management remained the support of as large as possible a number of people to provide an army to fight. Before feudalism the fighting had been with other clans. Afterwards it was with the English. The clan chiefs were prepared to accept low rents from their land, for their true wealth lay in the size of their armies. But if agricultural efficiency was of secondary importance, that did not mean that agriculture was inefficient. Its organization, called 'runrig', had many similarities with the pre-enclosure situation south of the border and also with the Irish system of 'rundale'.[41] The whole system was shot through with the notion of shared rights. Cultivation in both infield and outfield was frequently carried out communally; while beyond lay common grazing lands over which members of the 'clachan' (or hamlet) including the cottars held common rights. These lands, known in Scotland as 'commonties', were to all intents and purposes the same as the commons of England and Wales. Scottish agriculture was essentially at subsistence level; by 1700 populations were large and there was considerable underemployment. But then the system's purpose was the support of an efficient military machine – not high rents from agriculture.

This régime persisted until the defeat of the Scots at Culloden in 1746. The British Government had been shaken by successive Jacobite risings and after its final victory it was determined that the Highlands should never again prove a breeding ground for rebellion. The brutal and bloody repression that followed Culloden included the prohibition of the wearing of Highland dress and the abolition of the chiefs' judicial powers over their clans.

But the other main steps taken to undermine the threat posed by the clansmen were more subtle. In particular, efforts were made to co-opt the Highland chiefs on the government side by buttressing and rewarding them. Acts of Parliament in 1746 and 1747 made former chiefs outright owners of their land and placed them in a new landlord/tenant relationship with the rest of their people. Henceforth the land was to become a commodity enabling the clan chiefs to profit directly from the efforts of their people. The class stability and the military loyalty that had gone with it began to diminish. In their new role, Highland land-owners began to take an interest in their counterparts in the rest of Britain. Contact with English landowners gave them a taste for wealth and an aristocratic life-style. And released from their old feudal obligations, they began to devote their land to the single-minded pursuit of profit. Through this process, English attitudes to land ownership began to penetrate the Highlands.

One consequence of the changing social pattern accelerated this process even further. Some of the chiefs seeking to ape the extravagant life-style of their southern counterparts by buying up more and more land on borrowed money over-reached themselves. A trail of bankruptcies in the Highland estates during the early nineteenth century provided splendid pickings for well-to-do Englishmen looking for openings in land. Nouveaux riches from the south, many of them former soldiers or English sheep-ranchers, moved into the Highlands to merge with the successful clan chiefs. Their attitudes reinforced the new commercial approach to land ownership. Many of them did not actually live in the Highlands. While they enjoyed the greater comforts to be found in lowland England or the south of France, they entrusted a new salaried bureaucracy, equivalent to the English and Welsh land agents and known as the 'factors', to manage their estates.

As this revolution became complete, the vast majority of the people who owned no land found themselves at the mercy of whatever form of land-use an owner or his factor considered likely to produce the highest money rents.[42] Unfortunately for the Highlanders, the most lucrative agricultural products during much of the eighteenth and nineteenth centuries were wool and mutton. Scotland soon found itself ravaged by the same kind of enclosure movement as had gripped England a century earlier, but without any of the limited constraints that had operated south of the border in the interests of the poor.

In England, the small owner, tenant or landless labourer at least had rights over the common land, which might or might not survive enclosure. But in Scotland, common land had effectively been abolished by an Act of Parliament in 1695 which had authorized the division of most commonties by the landowner-dominated Court of Sessions. So no separate Parliamentary enclosure bills were required as had been in England. As there were no Parliamentary bills, there were none of the Enclosure Commissioners who in

England had served as the only protection of the weak against the major landowners. With hindsight, it is clear some change needed to come to the organization of Highland society if the growing rural population was to be fed at anything above subsistence level. But the absence of legal safeguards for the great mass of the population left them powerless to ensure that they received some material benefit from land reform.

Once evicted – whether by poverty, starvation or brute force – from their traditional lands, some Highlanders were deposited by their landlords on the very edge of the land mass. Here they could provide cheap labour for the lucrative fishing and kelp (the conversion of seaweed into soap) industries. To keep these workers alive, landlords allowed them to rent small allotments of land known as 'crofts' together with common grazing pasture. But the size of each croft was deliberately kept too small to support a family, thus ensuring the landlords a supply of labour. Tens of thousands of other Highlanders emigrated, the lucky ones with financial assistance from their landlords and the even luckier ones with enough strength to survive smallpox and other diseases that swept through many of the emigrants' ships. Conditions on emigrant ships were worse, it was commonly said at the time, than conditions on the vessels transporting slaves from Africa.

Despite the catastrophic impact of the Clearances on countless Highland communities, there is little evidence of violent resistance to them. It is true that some insurrections took place, both in lowland Scotland (where runrig farming and the clachan communities it sustained were also being replaced with large-scale arable and cattle farming) and in the Highlands. Evictions by landowners in lowland Galloway in the 1720s, for instance, gave rise to the Levellers' Rising in which people dispossessed of their right to graze animals ripped out the enclosers' low turf walls or dykes, maintaining that the landlords had no right to turn them off 'their' land; this rising had to be put down by military force. What however was absent was any campaign of resistance to the Clearances as they occurred. Perhaps the most obvious reason is that in the harsh climatic conditions particularly of the Highlands people were far too preoccupied with day-to-day survival to be able to plan any campaign of resistance. Another

factor was the departure of the clans' natural leaders after the
chiefs, for the tacksmen had been some of the first to leave.
Unable or unwilling to be transformed into businessmen farmers
who would replace their kinsmen with sheep, the tacksmens'
tenancies were often ended and the land offered to the highest
bidder. But perhaps the most important reason for the Highlanders' relative unwillingness to take up arms against their landlords
was their inheritance of a social system of loyalty to one's chief.
In the words of historian John Prebble, 'Unprepared for change,
the Highlanders held to the old ways, of which an acceptance of
the chief's authority was among the strongest. He might dispose
of them as he thought fit, but he was also their only protector,
and when he began to use the power and ignore the obligation
they were helpless. Aware of betrayal, they sometimes walked
into exile with the meekness of the animals that replaced them.'[43]

The Promise of Parliament

At the close of the eighteenth century, the position of the landless
north and south of the border seemed grim indeed. Little
remained of the accommodation with the landowners which in
earlier times had ensured that the landless enjoyed some kind of
stake in the fruits of the earth. There seemed few indications
within the rural economy that the position of the landless was
likely to improve. But in the next century, the balance did start
to tilt once more away from the landowners – not because of
changes in rural conditions, but because of changes in the
political life of the nation as a whole.

By the end of the 1820s, pressure for Parliamentary reform
had become overwhelming. The Industrial Revolution had made
the middle class stronger. Its leading figures had grown extremely
concerned about the extent of working-class despair in both
town and country, and convinced that an uprising could no
longer be averted by mere repression. Instead, they wanted a
meaningful gesture of some kind. They quickly fastened upon
the sacrifice of the rotten boroughs as a suitable step, and in
1832 brought a Reform Bill into Parliament designed to bring
this about. In the eighteenth century, the aristocratic owners of
these boroughs had been regarded with obsequious deference.

Now they had come to be generally abhorred as 'borough-mongers' who had stolen the nation's birthright. The ruling class, fearing that the abolition of the rotten boroughs would be but a first step in a general widening of the franchise, fought the Bill tooth and nail, and political agitation unparalleled in the history of Great Britain accompanied its passage through Parliament.

A general election was fought and won over the Bill, but the Tory peers blocked it in the Lords. As popular anger at the Lords' behaviour threatened the country with chaos, it became clear that the peace of the country depended on the passage of the Bill. The peers eventually surrendered and the Bill was passed.

Fears that this victory would lead to a general widening of the franchise were soon being proved well founded. An Act in 1835 gave ratepayers in the larger towns the right to vote for new municipal corporations; the rural areas, however, stayed under the administrative control of the justices of the peace until elected county councils appeared in 1888. The difference between the methods of government in force in town and country reflected the continued domination of rural England by the landowning ruling class that was losing control of the towns. It was not until 1884 that agricultural labourers got the vote; town workmen were enfranchised nearly twenty years earlier, in 1867.

The rural sphere in which democracy had its first major impact was in the price and availability of food. The food problem can be traced back to the loss of the subsistence farming rights which the poor had enjoyed under feudalism. As enclosure deprived them of land, they became dependent on such wages as they could extract from capitalist farmers. Although they worked on the land, they were forced to buy most of their food retail at market prices. The farmers wanted the highest price they could get for their produce. This might be obtained by exporting it or storing it in anticipation of higher prices to come. And these courses were adopted even if the poor happened to be starving at the time.

The Tudor and early Stuart monarchs passed laws to protect the consumer, but after 1660 things changed. Parliament repealed old regulations controlling the activities of middlemen and gave both middlemen and farmers freedom to buy corn, store it and sell it again at a future date as they saw fit. They were also allowed to export it regardless of demand for corn at home. All customs duties on the export of corn were removed in 1689.

The hungry poor of town and country, lacking any access to land they could cultivate themselves and facing the death penalty for poaching, took to rioting. Food riots were a common feature of eighteenth- and nineteenth-century English life.[44] Most frequently the protests took place in major grain-growing regions and at or around ports from which grain was being shipped, usually at times when shortages were either anticipated or already being felt. The enactment of the death penalty for rioting did little to diminish the activity. Two typical newspaper stories of the second half of the eighteenth century:

My servant informed me this morning that a man, his wife and three children had perished for want in one of the poor houses and that the floor of their wretched hovel was covered with their naked and emaciated carcasses . . . I will only add to this sad relation that several poor of this parish are in almost as wretched a condition. (Extract of a letter from Datchworth, Hertfordshire published in *The Kentish Gazette*, 25 January 1769)

A mob has rose here [at Great Colton, Warwickshire] consisting of upwards of 1,000 men, who divide themselves into Gangs of 3 or 400 each, and continue traversing from one Market Town to another, doing incredible mischief wherever they come; the Reason they alledge for their assembling in the manner is the Farmers sending their new Corn to Bristol for exportation, which has raised its price to Eight Shillings per bushel . . . If some speedy method is not found out to relieve the Distresses of the people, there is no knowing where this will end. (*Adams Weekly Courant*, 14 October 1766)

Things became even worse for the poor in 1815 with the passage of the first Corn Law, which guaranteed farmers a minimum price for their produce by forbidding the importation of any foreign wheat into Britain until the price of home-grown wheat had fallen to a certain point. The object of those who promoted the Corn Laws was to defend the interests of the landowning class; they justified the measure by invoking strategic necessity. The Napoleonic Wars had demonstrated the nation's vulnerability to food shortages in wartime: security depended, it was argued, on a strong and therefore protected agriculture industry. Exactly the same argument was to lead to the installation of our present régime of agricultural support in the aftermath of World War II.

The overthrow of the Corn Laws was eventually achieved by the ever-more-powerful urban interests. The Anti Corn Law League, formed in Manchester in 1839, won its most significant backing from manufacturers who feared that the Corn Laws would inhibit their efforts to spread free trade and objected to being forced to pay higher wages so their workers could buy dear food. They argued that the imposition of the Corn Laws not only kept the price of bread artificially high; it also discouraged foreign corn-producing countries from buying British-manufactured goods – an argument that finds echoes today in discussion of the Common Agricultural Policy. After a quarter of a century of pressure for reform, the prospect of a famine in 1845 converted the Conservative Prime Minister Sir Robert Peel to the idea of free trade in food. Many of the members of his own party denounced him as a traitor. They forced him to resign but in 1846 the Repeal of the Corn Laws went through.

Revolution in the Air

'There is in nature no such thing as a fee simple in land . . . If we are all here by the equal permission of the Creator, we are all here with an equal title to the enjoyment of His bounty . . . This is a right which is natural and inalienable.'

Henry George, *Progress and Poverty*, 1879

With their success in overthrowing the Corn Laws behind them, the MPs of the mid-nineteenth century soon turned their attention to the land on which British corn was grown. Fundamental questions were asked about the landowner's right to appropriate the soil – questions that echoed those posed by Gerrard Winstanley two hundred and fifty years earlier. But for the intervention of World War I, the resulting agitation might have brought about a revolution in our land-holding system.

Those asking these questions had fallen to some degree under the influence of one particularly impressive land radical – an American named Henry George.

George was a journalist and intellectual whose imagination had been fired by the gulf between fabulous riches and extreme poverty he had encountered in New York City. He saw the urban poverty of the New World as the direct consequence of the dispossession from rural land in Europe. His masterwork *Progress and Poverty*, which first appeared in 1879, made him the most discussed man in Britain after Gladstone by the mid-1880s. *Progress and Poverty* sold hundreds of thousands of copies in Britain and George followed up these sales with four extremely successful lecture tours.[45] George's thesis was that the root cause of continuing poverty in the wake of technological progress was the ability of the owners of land – upon which all industrial production ultimately depends – to levy a toll in the form of rent upon the earnings of labour. This toll was levied constantly and continuously by those who, in George's eyes, had robbed the human race of its heritage. He questioned the right of landowners to charge other people payment (rent) simply for the use of the natural opportunities which the land provided. Such rent, he considered, represented not a fair exchange but 'a levy wrung from producers by those who in no wise contributed to production'.

It was not only the industrial life of towns that was sapped: in areas of countryside like Ireland, the levy resulted in famine and death as landless labourers were forced to pay rent to often absentee landowners. To make matters even worse, these land-lords were able to decree that the land produce not nourishment for the starving labourers and their families, but food for export. Merely through being fortunate enough to stake their claims first, landowners were able to make slaves of the rest of the people. 'If it were true that land had always been treated as private property, that would not prove the justice or necessity of continuing so to treat it, any more than the universal existence of slavery, which might once have been safely affirmed, would prove the justice or necessity of making property of human flesh and blood,' Henry George declared.[46]

The message in *Progress and Poverty* was that natural resources like land, air, water and sunshine, having no cost of production, are God-given and belong to everyone. Nobody can truly own these things, and everybody has as much right to their benefits as everybody else. 'Consider what rent is,' wrote George. 'It does not arise spontaneously from the land; it is due to nothing the landowners have done. It represents a value created by the whole community ... Rent, the creation of the whole community, necessarily belongs to the whole community.' He contended that the most efficient and just means of securing government revenue was not a tax on income or on capital but a tax on land values. The major reform George proposed was a 100 per cent tax on the annual rental value of all land and the simultaneous abolition of other forms of taxation, since he believed his tax on site values would generate enough money to cover all government spending. Landowners would thus retain their ownership of the land, but land ownership would be redefined to exclude the right of the private owner to site value rent. Landowners would therefore no longer be entitled to appropriate rent in respect of the land itself. Nor, George believed, should they be entitled to that portion of the rent that could be attributed to society's demands on land: if the rent a landowner could charge was artificially raised because a railway station had been built next to it, this increase in land values should also go to the State. All the landowner was morally entitled to exact in the form of rent payments, considered George, was in respect of any improvements he himself had made to the land – for instance through preparing it for cultivation, growing crops on it or putting up buildings. After that, the landowner or anybody else would be perfectly free to claim all the profits from whatever activity he conducted on the land. In a nutshell, 'We may safely leave them the shell, if we take the kernel.'

George believed that the change in the system of taxation he was proposing would benefit the nation by stopping the one-way flow of resources to a group who contributed nothing to the process of industrial production. At the same time, the shift of the burden of taxation from production and exchange to rent would give new stimulus to the production of wealth. For it would not only leave more money in the hands of the workers: it would also encourage landowners to find a productive use for their land, since site value tax would fall equally on the idle land in town and country as on that in productive, profitable use. This, he hoped, would stop speculative landowners holding land back from use in the hope that they would one day get a high price for it when it was developed for housing or industry.

In late nineteenth-century Britain three groups looked as if they might serve as the vanguards of such a revolution in Britain's land-holding system: tenant farmers, that peculiar class in between landowners and landless; farm labourers; and the urban proletariat through its representatives in Parliament. All these groups were becoming exercised about the land issue to a greater or lesser extent.

IN BETWEEN: THE TENANTS

The thousands of riots that took place in the English countryside from the beginning of the sixteenth century until the end of the nineteenth were carried out in the main by people with no title to land at all. Tenant farmers did not in general join in these protests: for much of the period, tenant farmers in England were doing well enough. They often controlled substantial areas of land and themselves employed workers for wages. As a result, they tended to throw in their lot with their landlords rather than the landless. In Ireland, Wales and Scotland, however, tenants usually held only as much land as their own family could till – if this much. At the same time there was no obviously more disadvantaged group, as most landless labourers had emigrated or, in Ireland at least, been killed by famine.

So in these Celtic areas the gulf between tenant farmer and landlord was almost as great as that between landless and landlord in England. Conflict between tenant and landlord became a regular feature of Irish life, and in the second half of the nineteenth century it spread to Wales and Scotland. In Ireland it was to culminate in the overthrow of the existing land organization pattern.

The Irish Land War

We went down to Mayo and we preached the eternal truth that the land of a country, the air of a country, the water of a country, belong to no man. They were made by no man. They belong to the human race.

Charles Stewart Parnell, the leader of the Irish Land League, talking of his speech to launch the land war in Ireland[47]

Though England has not known foreign conquest since 1066, the Irish experience has been different. In the twelfth century, the Celtic people of Ireland saw the south and east of their country overtaken by Anglo-Norman colonizers intent on making Ireland an integral part of the feudal world of Western Europe. But though the invaders built castles and walled towns and imposed feudalism on the countryside, they never succeeded in bringing the whole country to heel. By the beginning of the fourteenth century, the native Irish were gaining the ascendancy. By the fifteenth century, English authority was confined to a small area around Dublin known as The Pale.

All this did not stop Elizabeth I and the Stuart monarchs attempting to subjugate Ireland by settling or 'planting' large English Protestant communities in the country. The post-Plantation period, up to the first two decades of the nineteenth century, was a time of relative peace and stability with expansion both in farming and industry. However, not everybody nor every part of the country benefited equally, and by the 1870s Ireland was a poor, peasant country with little industry, peopled by small tenant farmers who eked out precarious livelihoods on small plots paying rent to absentee English landlords. They risked eviction at any time, even if they paid their rent – unlike their counterparts in England whose annual tenancies were renewed so long as the rent was paid. Religion deepened the divide between landlord and tenant in Ireland: the tenants were Catholics, while the landlords belonged to the Church of Ireland, which was part of the Anglican community. In remote districts, the peasant tenant farmers even spoke a different language from their landlords.

The match that lit the tinder of the Irish tenants' long-held grievances was a famine in 1879–80 and the widespread eviction of tenants unable to pay their rent (5,000 in 1882 alone).[48] The ensuing distress greatly facilitated the rise of the Irish Land League, a farm tenants' movement, founded in 1879. What the Irish tenants most wanted was to own the land they rented; but the League's demands were for the 'Three Fs': Fair Rent, which should be fixed by some kind of tribunal; Fixity of Tenure, which meant that a tenant should be irremovable so long as he paid his rent; and Free Sale of the tenant's interest, that is, the right to sell the value of improvements to a successor tenant. These demands were forcefully put to the House of Commons by the League's president and principal parliamentary spokesman, Charles Stewart Parnell, then at the start of his career as leader of the Irish party at Westminster. The real strength of the League lay in its mass following in rural Ireland where rent strikes and violence quickly threatened to undermine, and even destroy, the enormous power of Ireland's landlord class. While landlords and their agents went in fear of their lives and Gladstone's Government tried desperately, but unsuccessfully, to crush the League by force, it occurred to the Government that a country whose people had a stake in its land would be less prone to crime and civil disturbance than one peopled by an aggrieved and desperate peasantry. Gladstone's government decided to concede to the League's demands.

The Irish Land Act of 1881 granted the Irish tenants security of tenure and judicially-determined rents and heralded a revolution in land ownership in Ireland. Four years later, the Irish Land Purchase Act of 1885 made it easier for Irish tenants to buy their land through the Government advancing them four-fifths of the purchase cost and giving them forty-nine years in which to repay. Feudalism in Ireland was effectively overthrown. And today, while a few large estates remain, Ireland is essentially a land of peasant proprietors, with an average holding of only sixty acres, compared to an average of 280 acres on the British mainland.

The Highland Land War

Set foot on the Isle of Skye nowadays and you could be forgiven for imagining it the most peaceful place on earth. Less than a century ago, however, it was the scene of a fierce land struggle between landlords and their tenants.

Many of those Highlanders who did not flee the Highlands completely during the Clearances of the eighteenth century settled on newly-created coastal smallholdings or crofts. But they were not safe even here, as profit-hungry landowners continued to extend their sheep-runs and deer forests. Though the Irish tenants complained most bitterly of high rents, it was the shortage of land that irked the Scottish crofters more than anything else. Most crofts had been allocated by landlords on the principle of the allotment: they were deliberately made too small to sustain a whole family, so that crofters would be forced to make themselves available to labour on the landlord's estate or in his sea-related industries like kelp.

The Highlanders refused however to accept their subjection. Old Celtic ideas about land ownership had survived the Clearances and challenged those of the land-holding class. Many crofters questioned the idea that a piece of parchment and a lump of wax gave a man a right to own land. They held to the pre-Culloden view that prolonged occupation of land gave a family permanent rights to it. Nor could they accept the private ownership of game, believing that the landlord had no more right to deer, salmon or grouse than anybody else. Echoing the convictions of Gerrard Winstanley 220 years before, one of the leaders of the Highland Land War, the Rev Donald MacCallum proclaimed, 'The land is our birthright, even as the air, the light of the sun, and the water belong to us as our birthright'.[49] It was the Irish example that was to turn these ideas into action.

In 1881 some Skye fishermen landed in County Cork and picked up the infectious ideas of the Irish Land League. When they returned to their crofts at The Braes in Skye, they persuaded the other crofters to sign a petition demanding that their landlord return to them as of right the land of Ben Lee. This area had been converted to sheep ranch during the Clearances, but the crofters claimed it had once been part of the common pastures of the settlements at the foot of the mountain. The petition was presented to Lord MacDonald's factor only to be at once rejected. Thereupon the crofters announced that they intended to stop paying rent.[50]

Lord MacDonald tried to put down the rebellion by serving eviction notices on a dozen of the crofters. But when a sheriff-officer set out to serve the notices, a crowd of about 150 people assaulted him and burned the notices on the spot.

The Sheriff of Inverness-shire sent fifty policemen to The Braes to apprehend the leaders of the uprising. Local people surrounded the policemen and stoned them in an attempt to rescue the five wanted men, but the policemen were victorious in what became known as The Battle of The Braes.

Support for the Highland Land League grew in the towns of Scotland as well as the countryside. In the North West, crofters illegally occupied sheep ranches and deer forests and refused to pay their rent. In general elections in 1885 and 1886, candidates supporting the Highland Land League were successful in many of the crofting constituencies. And, with the crofters' grievances being put more and more forcefully at Westminster, Gladstone's Government finally, in 1886, passed the first Crofters' Act which set up a rent tribunal called the Crofters' Commission. It also granted the crofters security of tenure as long as they paid their rent. Riots continued, however, because the Act did nothing to provide the extra land that the crofters needed – in particular the land from which they had been dispossessed during the Clearances.

But if attitudes to the justification for owning land died hard among the Highlanders so too did other parts of clan folklore: the loyalty of the chief to his clansmen. Unlike the situation in Ireland, the landless of Scotland were used to inter-clan conflict rather than warfare on class lines and many of them, even when faced with overwhelming evidence to the contrary, found it almost impossible to believe that their own chief could betray them. If the Irish evidence is anything to go by, it seems that what lost the Highlanders the war was their reluctance to engage in the violence of their Irish cousins. The British Government's post-Culloden policy vis-à-vis the Highland clans of divide and rule had been so successful that when the time came for the old clan members to join with others and rise up against their English and Scottish rulers, they were unable to wage the sort of terror campaign necessary.

The Welsh Land Movement

Nineteenth-century Wales was a land of vast estates let out to poor tenant farmers. Even less land in Wales was owned by the people who farmed it than in England or Scotland: only 10.2 per cent of the cultivated area of the country was held by freeholders. (The figure for Scotland in 1887 was 12.7 per cent and for

England 15.5 per cent.) The remaining 90 per cent of Wales was in the hands of a few families. Estates of a thousand acres and above covered 60 per cent of the cultivated land of Wales and 53 per cent of that of England. Just six landlords, with 25,000 acres apiece, owned half the cultivated land of Caernarvonshire, for instance.[51]

In nineteenth-century Wales, religion, politics and nationality sharply divided landlord on the one hand from farm tenant and farm labourer on the other. The landlord was English-speaking, Anglican and Conservative; the farm tenant or labourer was Welsh-speaking, Nonconformist and Liberal. Landowners, often absentees, represented all three groups in Parliament while the lesser gentry acted as magistrates.

Population growth in the countryside and large-scale enclosure fuelled social unrest. Nineteenth-century Wales saw the destruction of landlords' enclosure fences as well as food and corn riots. The most spectacular disturbances were the Rebecca riots.[52] From 1839 till 1844, from Swansea to Aberystwyth and from Haverfordwest to Carmarthen, hundreds of rural protests took place. The people complained of high rents and the payment of tithes; the poor law; the game laws that forbad the poor to take fish from the rivers; and the erection of toll-gates along the roads operated by turnpike trusts. Scores of toll-gates were smashed down, hayricks burned, salmon weirs destroyed and workhouses attacked. One hundred and fifty metropolitan policemen and 1,800 troops were sent in to quell the riots.

In the 1880s, in the aftermath of a severe agricultural depression, new disturbances mushroomed in Wales, involving in the main farm tenants and labourers aggrieved at the high rents their landlords demanded. Local 'land leagues' began to be formed, and a Welsh Land League was proposed. But although the founder of the Irish Land League, Michael Davitt, addressed meetings in Wales, the Welsh disturbances of the early 1880s involved no substantial measure of unlawful activity against the landlords. At this time, according to historian Dr Roy Douglas, the Welsh land movement was 'impeccably "constitutional", operating through political channels, and there was no agitation comparable with the disturbances which had been endemic for years in Ireland, and had recently occurred in the Hebrides.'[53]

Compared with the achievements of their Irish counterparts, the short-term benefits secured by the Welsh tenants were limited. All they managed to achieve in Parliament was an Act in 1890 providing that tithes (compulsory payments to the Anglican Church) should be paid by the owner rather than by the occupier of land. In the long-term, perhaps the most important effect of the Welsh land movement was the impetus it gave to the career of David Lloyd George. As a young man in Wales he had acquired considerable antipathy to the landlords. His radical views on the ownership of land were to play an important role when the battle for the land came to the cities of Britain in the 1890s.

The English Tenants

In the mid-1880s, when illegal and violent activities were widespread in the Celtic areas of the United Kingdom, it appeared that these could easily infect the country as a whole. All that was required was the English tenant farmers to align themselves with their Celtic brothers. Then, the pressure for a fundamental reform of land tenure throughout the country might have been irresistible. But this never happened. The tenant farmers of England did not join the Celtic rebels. For they were different.

Far from being subsistence peasants like the Irish tenants, the English tenant farmers of the nineteenth century often controlled substantial areas of land and themselves employed workers for wages. They were even more passionately committed than their landlords to the protection of agriculture through the Corn Laws. Indeed the only possible cause of a rift between landlord and tenant in nineteenth-century England would have come because of tenant resentment of their landlords' failure to work hard enough at safeguarding agriculture's privileges.

Although English tenants were not summarily evicted in the way that Irish tenants were, they did however often have to put up with extremely onerous tenancy contracts.[54] It was they rather than the landlords who shouldered the financial risks of farming, yet restrictive covenants in their tenancies dictated the system of cropping to be practised and the way produce would

be disposed of. These convenants also prevented them from
killing rabbits, hares, pheasants, partridges and deer which were
devouring their crops. Indeed, if they did kill such animals they
risked prosecution for poaching. Nonetheless, tenants, particularly after the Napoleonic Wars and before the repeal of the
Corn Laws, were prepared to put up with these severe leases
essentially because they knew they could make money out of
agriculture. High rents and stiff conditions in return for security
of tenure was a good deal. 'A good farm offered a short cut to a
fortune' was a saying of the time. Paradoxically, the enclosure
movement boded well for tenant farmers: as small freehold
farmers were squeezed out, their land was bought by the landed
aristocracy who then proceeded to let it out.

It was the agricultural depression of the 1880s that strengthened the tenants' position. As the depression began to bite,
landlords found it harder and harder to attract tenants. To find
takers, landlords had to abandon the stiff terms of traditional
tenancies. At the same time, the news from Ireland was making
landlords wary. More concessions were made as a hedge against
rebellion.

The concessions came in two main areas. The first at last
permitted tenant farmers to kill ground game (hares and rabbits
but not pheasants and partridges) if they were damaging crops.
Then in 1906 one of the first steps of the Liberal Government
when it regained office after a long period of Conservative rule,
was to enable tenants to claim compensation from their landlords
for damage to crops caused by the main game species.

The English tenants accepted these concessions cheerfully and
abandoned any thoughts they may have had of land revolution.

AGRICULTURAL LABOURERS

> Thus far the agricultural labourer has been regarded . . . as a
> mere machine – an instrument to be used for the creation of
> wealth, deposited in the hands of the few; not as a human being
> whose comfort, health, and home are to be considered, and who
> has a claim to such benefits as were conferred by the Factory Acts
> upon the labourers in towns.

Joseph Chamberlain, MP, *The Radical Programme,* 1885

The first feature which attracts the attention of a stranger on entering the village, is the total want of cleanliness which pervades it. . . . The worst malignant fevers have raged here at different times.

Another fruitful source of misery as well as immorality, is the great inadequacy of the number and size of the houses to the number of the population. It is by no means an uncommon thing for the whole family to sleep in the same room.

The rents of these hovels vary, with few exceptions from 1s. a week up to £3 and even £4 per annum . . .

Dishes, plates and other articles of crockery, seem almost unknown; there is, however, the less need for them, as grist bread forms the principal, and I believe the only kind of food which falls to the labourer's lot. In no single instance did I observe meat of any kind during my progress through the parish . . . Want, famine and misery are the features of the village.

The findings of a *Times* special correspondent sent to investigate the condition of the rural poor in Dorset in 1846, writing of Stourpaine parish outside Blandford Forum[55]

If privilege was the reason why England's agricultural tenants chose not to follow their Irish counterparts into a land war, the same brake was not available to restrain any revolutionary inclinations on the part of the English agricultural labourers. These people were undoubtedly subject to deprivation on a considerable scale. Nonetheless, they too failed to take up the cudgels of revolution for reasons of their own.

Lacking any land of their own, agricultural labourers were forced to depend on such wages as they could extract from farmers and landowners (less than half the average industrial wage in the middle of the century), or to fall back on poor relief. The men who sowed the seeds, hoed, weeded, mowed, made hurdles, cut chaff, spread dung, threshed the corn and built and maintained hedges, ditches and farm roads while their landowning masters hunted, shot, went to the races and ran the country formed a kind of underclass – occupying not only the lowest rung of rural society but an even more depressed situation than their urban counterparts. Significantly, they were the last group of men to get the vote, seventeen years after urban workers and fifty-two years after tenant farmers.

Agricultural workers did not share in the booming farm profits of the Napoleonic Wars. Indeed, the agricultural boom was to make their condition even worse, for it induced farmers to adopt machinery, especially threshing machines, for the first time on a wide scale. When the war was over many farmers laid off their workers, but kept their threshing machines. Threshing had provided the traditional mainstay of the already scanty winter employment for labourers and for them the development had dire consequences.

Unemployment – aggravated by the introduction of threshing machines – was one in a list of the labourers' grievances. Others included low wages, high prices, the absence of any land they could call their own, and the requirement by Act of Parliament in 1834 that any able-bodied pauper who wished to receive poor law relief leave his or her home and live in a workhouse in which men were segregated from their wives and children.

To survive, many farm labourers turned to poaching. The game laws had been relaxed since the Black Act of 1723 in that poachers were no longer hanged or transported but fined or imprisoned instead. Nonetheless, the game laws were still bitterly resented, particularly after the introduction of stop-and-search powers for the police in 1862. One in four of all convictions in Suffolk in 1843 was obtained under the game laws, and in neighbouring Norfolk over 2,000 poachers were fined or imprisoned in the years 1863–72.[56]

Destitute and bitter, some labourers moved on from poaching to sheep stealing, horse rustling and rick burning. Labourers were also prepared to come out into the open in overt crowd protests. Enclosure riots, bread riots, poor law riots, the smashing of threshing machines were all common features of life in the eastern counties of England during the first half of the nineteenth century. 'No year in the first half of the nineteenth century was a quiet year in the east. Every year was violent, and the amount of violence that took place was very great indeed.'[57]

The labourers' distress found a tragic outlet in 1830, when there took place what has been called 'The Last Labourers' Revolt'.[58] Through most of southern England, East Anglia and the southern Midlands, labourers burnt hayricks and destroyed the new threshing machines that were taking their jobs. They demanded higher wages and higher rates of poor relief, together with a reduction in rents and tithes. There was little violence and no one was killed. But the Government took brutal measures to punish the labourers. Nineteen men were hanged (including a youth of nineteen who had knocked off the hat of a wealthy landlord) and 457 transported; over 600 more were imprisoned.

This episode left behind bitter memories in the countryside of southern England and East Anglia. It also had the result that the farmworkers' rumblings of discontent never again flared into mass violence. To right what they saw as the wrongs inflicted on them, they did not turn to revolution. Their energies went instead into the formation of unions. Although the first attempt at Tolpuddle in the 1830s ended in tragedy (with the transportation to Botany Bay of the six leaders), a trade union was formed in the Midlands forty years later which was to form the seed from which the national farmworkers' union of England would grow.[59]

The English labourers' protests – whether individual acts of sabotage or organized trade unionism – never converged with the Irish tenant farmers' efforts to regain the land for themselves. The English workers did not make claims on the land itself at all, never awakening in themselves an overt sense of entitlement to title. They accepted their situation but wanted better terms.

This failure to take a really radical view reflects the length of their estrangement from land ownership. The land had been taken from the Saxons through the Norman Conquest more than 800 years before. A landless class had again been created in the countryside through enclosure more than a hundred years before. For nineteenth-century English labourers, dispossession was the natural state. Their collective memory did not accommodate the idea of land ownership by people like themselves. As a defeated class they looked only to improve the terms of their subjection, and in their own time, they failed even in that.

Instead, like the English tenants they proved ripe for being bought off by concessions, even though in their case these were to be of no more than a nominal character. The labourers were not to gain command of the land. But they were to gain custody of little patches of ground of their own – allotments. Even this small gain came only after half-a-century's campaigning. It was not until 1906 that allotments became available to all – rather than to those chosen by a landowner as beneficiaries of an act of private charity.[60] But in comparison with the rights of more privileged peoples, the English labourer's right to his allotment would be seen more as a symbol of his dispossession than of privilege.

THE URBAN MAJORITY

> Who ordained that a few should have the land of Britain as a perquisite, who made 10,000 people owners of the soil and the rest of us trespassers in the land of our birth? Who is it – who is responsible for the scheme of things whereby one man is engaged through life in grinding labour, to win a bare and precarious subsistence for himself . . . while another man who does not toil receives every hour of the day, every hour of the night, whilst he slumbers, more than his poor neighbour receives in a whole year of toil?
>
> David Lloyd George, Chancellor of the Exchequer, speaking in Newcastle, 1909[61]

Those driven off the land to find a new life in the factories of the Industrial Revolution were for many years too preoccupied with the problems confronting them in their new environment to give much thought to the rural world they had lost. Nonetheless, in the late nineteenth century, an upsurge of interest in the land question was evident in Britain's cities.

The ideas in play this time were very different from those of the rebel leaders in the Irish Land War. Peasant proprietorship, unpersuasive as it was as an objective to the landless English farm labourer, was completely meaningless to city-dwellers. Instead, interest centred upon Henry George's idea of a common and universal right to the land, his belief in the right of the community as a whole to land rent and his conviction that the land should be devoted to productive communal use rather than the whims of those who happened to own it.

In the 1880s, land reform societies reflecting Henry George's alternative view of land ownership began to spring up in Britain. Some, like the extremely influential English Land Restoration League, propounded George's views more or less unchanged. Others, like the Land Nationalization Society, took on board George's basic questioning of the rights of landowners but proposed specific remedies of their own.[62] The Land Nationalization Society, for example, was prepared to see land taxation, but only as a step on the way to the total abolition of private land ownership. In its People's Land Charter, the Society called for the state to become supreme owner of all land and the minerals it contained. Thereafter, local authorities would ensure that the land was put to the use that would best serve the community as a whole: this was seen at the time as likely to mean that far less land would be 'wasted' as game preserves; instead it would be devoted to food and timber production and the provision of land for houses where these were most needed.

When Gerrard Winstanley had preached similar ideas in the 1650s, no politician was prepared to march behind his banner. But in the far freer political atmosphere of late nineteenth- and early twentieth-century Britain, the land question was discussed more freely. Eventually the Liberal Party came to espouse the ideas of the land taxers. It wrote George's land tax into its constitution, and in the early years of the twentieth century, distinguished Liberals like Winston Churchill took the message to the hustings with remorseless attacks on land monopoly. The Liberal Party's foremost thinker on land was however Joseph Chamberlain. Chamberlain was the first leading politician to urge a tax on land values; but it was George's theme of the power of landowners to dictate the economic development of the whole community which struck the strongest chord in him. In speeches he made up and down the country on the land question and in his book *The Radical Programme* (1885), Chamberlain blamed the squalid and overcrowded housing conditions of the poor both in large towns and villages on the refusal of landlords to let any land at reasonable rents for houses. He condemned those landowners who held up economic development by refusing to sell land to the community for public purposes such as the building of railway stations. In the countryside, Chamberlain deplored what he saw as the waste of fertile British soil where land was used for game preservation or left uncultivated because landowners, fearful of incurring obligations to tenants, refused to sign leases. Meanwhile, Chamberlain observed, farm labourers were being forced to eke out an existence on meagre wages supplemented by small allotments for which they paid high rents. When land was brought into production, greedy owners would often stop up public footpaths and even fence in roadside land and other odd corners where children had played.

This line of thought attracted considerable support for the Liberal Party. But it also helped to split it. As ideas for land reform surfaced, and as the Liberal Government of the 1880s passed legislation to enable the Irish tenants to buy their own land, the great Whig landowners who had helped to establish the party in the middle of the nineteenth century began to break away and join the Conservatives. This step left the Liberal Party more open to influence from the radicals, among whom were to be numbered many enthusiastic land reformers.

Lloyd George was one of the Liberal Party's most committed land reformers. In 1908, shortly after a Liberal government was returned with a vast programme of social reform, he was made Chancellor of the Exchequer. Lloyd George's first attempts at land reform were thrown out by the Lords. But in his 1909 'People's Budget', he proposed not only a heavy increase in death duties but two new land-based taxes as well which he believed the Lords would accept. His Government had already provided for the valuation of all land throughout Britain, and the Budget imposed a modest tax (1d in the pound) on the capital value of all undeveloped urban and suburban land. Though this initial rate of tax was very low, the proposal clearly opened the way for the hard-hitting land tax which Henry George had called for. Lloyd George also proposed a new tax on the unearned increment of land values – the increase in value that resulted not from landowners' actions but from a public decision or public spending, such as the building of a new main road next to a landowner's acres. From thenceforth, landowners would be taxed at 20 per cent on this unearned increment. Of this tax (which foreshadowed the 1974 Labour Government's Community Land Act), Winston Churchill declared: 'No more fair, considerate or salutary proposal for taxation has ever been made in the House of Commons.'

But the Lords passed a wrecking amendment. Soon the issue of land taxation was superseded by the issue of the power of the Lords to thwart the will of the Commons. The Commons declared the Lords' rejection of the Finance Bill to be unconstitutional, and Parliament was dissolved.

The General Election that followed asserted the Commons' authority over that of the Lords. A Parliament Act in 1911 abolished the Lords' power to block Finance Bills. But the election also gave the Unionists almost as many seats as the Liberals. These Unionists were prepared to see local authorities collecting rates based on site value, but they would not support a national system of land taxation.

While the Government was deciding what to do, a number of by-elections suggested that the electorate supported land taxation. At Hanley in the Potteries in 1912, for instance, the land tax question swept all others aside. At one point in the campaign, three public meetings were being conducted by the land taxers each day, from 11 A.M. until midnight. From innumerable gramophone records and on innumerable occasions was sung The Land Song, culminating in the chorus:

> 'The Land! The Land! 'Twas God who gave the Land!
> The Land! The Land! The ground on which we stand!
> Why should we be beggars, with the Ballot in our hand?
> "God gave the Land to the People!" '[63]

The Liberal candidate at Hanley who championed the land taxers' cause, was triumphantly returned. But the Government needed the support of the Unionist MPs in order to survive, and, rather than introduce immediate legislation, it chose to set up a Land Inquiry Committee.

The Committee's report, published in 1913, recommended improvements in the conditions of farm workers, the setting up of a Land Court to fix rents and measures to prevent damage by game. On land taxation, the Committee supported Lloyd George's proposals for a 1d rate on all capital values but went further, recommending that local authorities should be empowered to levy a higher site value rate if they wished. It also recommended that local authorities should be given powers to develop land nationalization pilot schemes. To this end, they were to be given powers to buy land either to use themselves or to lease to other people. The Government set about implementing the proposals at once.

A few months later, nearly 5,000 men were already at work valuing Britain's land so it could be taxed. A Ministry of Lands was also to be set up primarily to administer the new tax. But then, with dramatic suddenness, came World War I. The land issue, divisive as it obviously appeared, was thrust into the background in the interests of national unity. And when the war was over, everything had changed.

The pre-war support for land taxation had dissipated. Shifting party alignments had left the movement's most influential advocates in Parliament on opposite sides of the House. Lloyd George, though now Prime Minister, was heading a coalition government in which Conservatives outnumbered all the other groups combined. In this position he was no longer able to promote land tax legislation. In 1920, eleven years after he had first broached land taxes and valuation, Lloyd George found himself presiding over the Government that was to abolish both.

Because the Liberals could not advance the cause of land taxation from within the Coalition, several Liberal MPs who had supported it drifted to the infant Labour Party, which had growing electoral support and substantial funds. But though the Labour Party supported land taxation, it had many higher priorities. As the slump of the 1930s grew deeper, unemployment became the Labour Party's foremost concern. The land-taxers within the Party could and did argue that the taxation of land was the long-term cure for unemployment, but other supposed remedies appeared to offer quicker returns. It was on these that the Party concentrated.

When Labour won the election in 1929, the stage again seemed set for a programme of land reform. The new Government opted for a Liberal-style taxation policy rather than the nationalization schemes Labour had advocated in opposition. Legislation almost identical to that contained in Lloyd George's People's Budget of twenty years earlier was approved – after a fight – by both Houses of Parliament. The 1931 Land Valuation Act provided for the valuation of all land with provision for the revision of the valuation rolls every seven years. At the same time, the Budget introduced a tax of 1d in the pound on the value of every acre of British land.

Once again, however, the cup was dashed from the lips of the landless. Less than two months had passed after the passage of the Finance Bill before a mounting financial crisis brought Labour down. A National Government, predominantly Conservative, took office. Like Lloyd George in 1920, some of the Ministers who had sponsored the land taxation legislation now presided over its obsequies. The cause of land taxation had been won and lost again, this time within four months. It was never to be embodied in a statute again.

Landowners Consolidate and Regroup

As prospects of a concerted challenge to the landowners faded, new factors made their position even more impregnable than before. The main change was the absorption into the landowning class of much of the tenant class that in England had proved such an effective bulwark against change.

In the 1870s, though the landowners wielded immense power, they were still small in number – as they found out for themselves. The 15th Earl of Derby, the representative of the 'lords of Lancashire', whose family's land holdings in the North West dated back to the twelfth century and who owned 69,000 acres of land in Lancashire, Cheshire, Kent and Surrey in the late nineteenth century, was one of many landowners angered by what he termed 'the wildest and most reckless exaggerations' about landowners and their power put forward by disciples of Henry George. To dispel charges of a concentration of landed power, Lord Derby managed to procure in 1876 an official return of the landowners of the United Kingdom, the first such survey since the Domesday survey of 1086.

But as a weapon in the controversy over land, the survey boomeranged. Although it revealed that nearly a million people in England and Wales owned some land (even if this was frequently no more than a cabbage patch or a back garden), it also showed that only 7,000 people held title to 75 per cent of the land in England, Wales and Scotland, and that of these a mere 710 individuals owned more than a quarter of England and Wales.[64]

One of the drawbacks of the New Domesday Survey was that it simply listed landowners in alphabetical order, county by

county, without distinguishing major landowners from those
with more modest holdings or indicating holdings in different
places that shared the same owner. Under Bedfordshire, for
instance, the name of the Duke of Bedford, with 33,589 acres at
Woburn Abbey, appears alongside that of Robert Beechener, the
owner of just over one acre.

John Bateman, a Victorian squire, who seems to have been
motivated by no more than a deep interest in the subject, decided
to refine the New Domesday Survey. He solicited corrections
from landowners, and in his work *The Great Landowners of Great
Britain and Ireland*, listed the acreage and annual value of the
land of all individuals shown by the New Domesday Survey to
have at least 3,000 acres worth at least £3,000 a year. The fourth
edition of his work, published in 1883, provides a reasonably
reliable guide to the structure of British land ownership at the
close of the century.[65] Again, any hopes that this survey would
dispel what the landowners saw as the myth of land monopoly
by the great territorial magnates were dashed. Bateman's survey
detailed, for instance, the five different estates of the Duke
of Sutherland, covering well over 1.25 million acres in Ross,
Sutherland, Shropshire, Staffordshire and Yorkshire and worth
£141,500 every year; or the fourteen rural properties of the Duke
of Buccleuch – 95,000 acres in Dumfries, 26,500 in Northamptonshire, 39,000 in Roxburgh, 12,500 in Warwickshire, for example,
totalling an incredible 460,000 acres and with a gross annual
value of £217,000. In the Highlands, Bateman revealed that
fifteen owners with at least 34,580 acres apiece owned 50 per
cent of the land.[66]

In fact, the 1873 Return and Bateman's survey were to provide
a picture of the large private estate at its zenith. The blatant
concentration of power the survey showed was a political liability
for the landowning class, and in the early years of the twentieth
century, it began to be broken down as the biggest change in
land ownership in England and Wales since the dissolution of
the monasteries took place.

The first batch of sales followed the return of the strong
Liberal Government of 1906: its Agricultural Holdings Act of
1906 and land legislation of 1908 strengthened tenants' rights to
compensation from their landlords for unnecessary disturbance

and gave county councils compulsory power to buy land to let as
farm smallholdings. The last straw for many landowners seems
to have been Lloyd George's 1909 budget, with its provision for
the valuation of all the land in Britain in order to introduce a tax
on land. The Duke of Bedford is credited with starting a process
that was to snowball until the outbreak of war in 1914 as the
owners of large landed estates sold off outlying portions: in 1909
the Duke offered his 18,000-acre estate in Cambridgeshire to the
Crown as it had become financially unattractive. When it
declined the purchase, he sold to his sitting tenants. Between
1910 and 1913, about 650,000 acres of English rural land changed
hands, and the tenants were the most frequent purchasers.[67]

Fear of land taxation was not the only reason for selling.
Many owners wanted to liberate capital for more profitable uses,
and as there were many tenants in a position to buy, they sold to
them or to middlemen speculators who then resold to the former
tenants. As the large family estates contracted through the sale
of outlying parts, a new class of owner-occupiers appeared on
the scene – former tenant farmers – who were to inject new
vigour into the landowning class without in any way reducing
the firmness of its grip on rural Britain.

At the same time as the landowning class was strengthening
itself by assimilating the former tenant farmers, it began to forge
closer links with Britain's other élite groups. This came about
partly through the sale of land to wealthy men, among whom
bankers, brewers and lawyers figured prominently. These groups
wanted to own land largely to enhance their social status. So
when they arrived in the countryside, the last thing they wanted
to do was to adopt attitudes which would be at odds with those
of the existing landowning aristocracy. To gain social acceptance
they were more than happy to ape the habits of their betters:
they were even prepared to lay on lavish hunt breakfasts, to
subscribe munificently to the local foxhounds and to cram their
coverts full of pheasants. This process was, of course, but one
aspect of the much vaunted readiness of the British élite to
absorb the cream of lower classes that presented a potential
challenge – the process to which some historians attribute
Britain's avoidance of a French-style revolution. In this case it

left Britain's parvenu landowners often more firmly committed to traditional landowning attitudes than the aristocrats themselves.

The actual numbers of men who amassed fortunes from the Industrial Revolution and then went on to become major British landowners is, however, small. Only about 6 per cent of all the country seats in Northamptonshire, Hertfordshire and Northumberland between 1540 and 1880, for instance, were occupied by people who had bought their way in from business.[68] But many more leading lights of industrial Britain were introduced to the rituals of upper-class landowners than actually became landowners themselves. For you did not have to become a landowner to indulge in the landowner's most glamorous pursuit – bloodsports.

It was shooting – of pheasants, grouse and deer – that enabled many of the rich men of late nineteenth-century urban Britain to absorb and therefore identify with rural landowning culture. Rented shooting rights enabled even those who were not in a position to become landowners to see themselves as country gents in spirit, if only on a spare-time basis.

The landowners did not deliberately set out to consolidate their position by forging stronger links with the rest of the Establishment. This development, useful though it was to be to them, occurred largely as an unforeseen product of their efforts to consolidate their position in purely financial terms.[69]

The idea of letting sporting rights to outsiders surfaced early in the nineteenth century. At first the lets were modest: huge areas of Scottish deer forest could be secured for tiny rents because the sport was uncertain and the forests had no facilities like hunting lodges. But it quickly emerged that immense demand existed. By the 1870s, landowners were finding they could rent out deer forests at considerable profits. They needed the money. For by the 1870s, the repeal of the Corn Laws and the influx of cheaper food from abroad had cut back the profitability of many types of agriculture. Yet landowners had no desire to cut back the lavish standard of living to which many of them had grown accustomed. The Game Act of 1831 had removed an ancient restriction limiting most forms of hunting and shooting to the owners of land or their eldest sons; from henceforth anybody with the necessary certificate could kill game either on his land or on that of any other person with his permission. So landowners were handed an ideal opportunity to make up the income they were losing from agriculture.

Scottish landowners were particularly quick to exploit the sporting potential of their land. Sheep farming, of which landowners had enjoyed such high hopes when clearing crofters out to make way for sheep-runs, suffered badly in the face of new competition from the refrigerated lamb of New Zealand and Australia. Between the 1860s and the 1880s, the rents of Scottish sheep farms were halved. At the same time deer stalking was becoming more and more fashionable. To own stalking was to own the greatest of status symbols – all the more so after Queen Victoria and Prince Albert bought the Balmoral Estate in 1848 and started to retreat there every August and September. By the 1920s, businessmen were paying £44 in rent payments alone for the privilege of killing one stag, quite apart from the cost incurred in travel and equipment. In many places, sheep were cleared from estates to make way for deer and new hunting lodges were built. By the end of the century a quarter of the entire area of Scotland had been turned over to deer forest. Yet over this vast area, deer stalking employed only 800 men full-time and another 1,000 part-time.[70]

If deer stalking was the most exclusive sport, grouse shooting, pheasant shooting and salmon fishing were also attracting larger and larger numbers of rich non-landowning devotees. The number of shooters that could be accommodated in any one area was greatly increased by a change in the way grouse or pheasants were shot: instead of one or two men pursuing birds on foot and shooting any that their dogs might frighten up into the air, the shooters were lined up and hundreds or even thousands of birds were driven over their heads by beaters. The profitability of Scottish salmon fishing was transformed when the sport became a craze among rich Englishmen in the 1850s and '60s. Before these years, rivers like the Tweed in the Border Country south of Edinburgh had been fished only by country folk and a few shoemakers and other artisans. These were all quickly driven out as the annual migration of Englishmen pushed rents higher and higher. By 1868, visitors were paying £1 a day for the privilege of fishing (but not taking away any fish they caught).

Salmon fishing too had become the exclusive preserve of the rich.

In Scotland, the involvement of the nouveaux riches in bloodsports played a particularly strong part in strengthening the landowners' position in the social system. But it sharpened the divide between these privileged classes and the rural poor. Although the deer did not cause clearances on the scale of the sheep evictions, they were bitterly resented by those poor Highlanders who remained. The historian Professor Eric Richards has written:

The deer simply exacerbated the land hunger of the region and symbolized, in the most dramatic way, the existence of the two nations that inhabited the Highlands. There were, on the one hand, the sporting magnates, the 'Nimrods', who massacred animals in the strenuous pursuit of leisure and prestige; and, on the other, the crofters and cottars who eked out their lives on the fringe of the land mass, unable to gain access to the pastoral lands because of the greater profitability of capitalist sheep farming and the new sports industry, neither of which had much use for crofters.[71]

The newcomers who bought sporting estates were no more accommodating to the poor than the traditional owners. In about 1890, an American millionaire, W.L. Winans, bought a 300-square-mile Highland deer forest and installed an army of sentinels to protect his quarry. He even took a crofter to court for allowing his child's pet lamb to stray into the vast deer preserve.

Grazing animals were not the only creatures which the owners of sporting lands wished to exclude: they also wanted to keep out ramblers from towns. As intensive and expensive forms of shooting and stalking grew more and more elaborate, landowners grew ever more anxious to protect game from any conceivable threat. So what had been freely accessible moors and mountains, woods and parks, rivers and lakes were closed off. Around Edinburgh, for instance, 'the public were gradually man-trapped off everything beyond the high road', according to the then Lord Advocate of Scotland, Lord Cockburn. When he was a boy, nearly all the countryside in the vicinity of the city was freely open to the public, but by the middle of the nineteenth century, the seaside, the riverside, and the open moors of the Pentland Hills, Edinburgh's traditional country playground, had been closed.[72]

In Scotland it was the closure to public access of deer stalking lands that caused the greatest resentment. Deer are elusive beasts, easily startled. So, to increase the certainty of sport, paths and even roads were closed and ordinary people were stopped from roaming over open country. 'The aim of the owners of deer forests', explained the mountaineer and campaigner for access to open land E. A. Baker, 'is to create a huge solitude, first by removing such of the human population and their stock as survived the great clearances, and then by closing the mountains and glens to the public.'[73] Walkers could not even land on the island of Rhum, for instance, 97 per cent of the area of which was given over to grouse and deer and whose total human population amounted to less than a hundred. Of 543 Scottish mountain peaks rising higher than 3,000 feet above sea level, more than 450 were situated in the 'forbidden land'; and Baker estimated that landowners had succeeded in closing off to general public access large portions of ten counties. The means deployed ranged from keeping gates across popular roads locked in the shooting season and putting up notices warning tourists of the danger of getting shot, to forbidding tenants to take in lodgers and applying pressure to get inn licences removed in remote areas. The tourist ban enraged not only the walkers. Others complained that by turning the Highlands into a huge game preserve and inhibiting the development of tourism, land-owners were frustrating economic progress in the countryside. They contrasted the Highlands with the Alps, pointing out that what have turned out to be the real sources of the Alps' prosperity would have lain undeveloped had the Swiss allowed their mountains to become a great closed area where private individuals stalked deer or chamois for a month or two of the year.

A New Vision of the Countryside

To many of us city life can only be rendered tolerable on the condition of frequent holidays in the real country. Civilized man now feels the desire and need for the wildness and greatness of untamed, aboriginal nature, which his predecessors did not feel. ... By the side of religion, by the side of science, by the side of poetry and art, stands Natural Beauty, not as a rival to these, but as the common inspirer and nourisher of them all, and with a secret of her own beside.

G. M. Trevelyan, 'The Call and Claims of Natural Beauty', 1931[74]

By the early twentieth century, the idea of struggle to dispossess the landowners and to hand the land back to the people for subsistence farming had receded into unreality. But in many quarters there remained a sense of dissatisfaction at the tightness of the landowners' grip on the rural life of the nation. Pressure for change developed, no longer directed at a reallocation of the economic spoils of rural ownership, but at something else. Efforts began to be made to secure the countryside as a source of recreation, spiritual refreshment and artistic inspiration for the people – in particular for the ever-growing numbers of city-dwellers.

The idea of the countryside as the key to recreation had acquired great force in Victorian Britain. Not that such an attitude was unprecedented. In Tudor London, merchants took weekends off in the country, and on May Day Elizabethan Londoners 'would walk into the sweet meadows and green woods, there to rejoice their spirits with the beauty and savour of sweet flowers, and with the harmony of birds', according to a reporter of the time, John Stow.[75]

During the seventeenth and eighteenth centuries popular enthusiasm for the pastoral pleasures faded. Its phenomenal resurgence in the nineteenth century is understandable enough.

The root cause was a sharp fall in the quality of the urban environment. As late as 1790, four people out of five in England and Wales lived in the country. Forty years later, one in two lived in a town, and there were already five towns with more than a hundred thousand people each. By 1891, the number had risen to twenty-three. The housing conditions in these towns were desperate, with overcrowding and rat-infestation rife. The fumes and waste generated by industries like brick manufacture, brewing and dyeing, which were located in the middle of cities, made urban life extremely unhealthy. Smoke from coal burning filled the air with so much sooty deposit that London's statues of kings came to look more like chimney sweeps. Little wonder then that in this urban hell, people should prove willing to contemplate the idea of a refuge from the dirt, smoke, and noise of the city. The countryside came to play this role, largely because of a change in the way people thought of the natural world.

A new confidence developed about venturing out into the wild outdoors. Medieval man had viewed the countryside with mistrust and suspicion – it was a hostile world to be subjugated and made safe rather than a place in which to relax. If natural things were to be enjoyed at all it was in the secure conditions of, for example, a walled-in garden. Outside, preferred landscapes were cultivated, fertile and Man-dominated. But the Enlightenment, celebrating dispassion and objectivity, stripped the natural world of its menace. And once people were no longer cowed by the woods and mountains, wild plants and animals, they were able to establish a new relationship with them. Before the nineteenth century, the study of natural history and admiration for picturesque scenery were already developing among the middle and upper classes. Some people made vast collections of anything from stuffed birds and butterflies to shells and fossils; others merely observed wildlife, like Gilbert White. Gradually a greater understanding of other living things began to erode the idea of the uniqueness of Man, an idea which had helped justify the ruthless exploitation of the natural world for profit.

Medieval people had interpreted literally the biblical account of Creation: God had given Man dominion over all other living things for his benefit. In Tudor and Stuart England, the interpretation persisted, so in early seventeenth-century poems we find birds and beasts finding their fulfilment in yielding themselves up to be eaten by Man. The spectacle of a man riding a horse proclaimed not only his social superiority over his fellow human beings but also his dominion over animal creation.

Scientific discovery had started to erode this anthropocentric tradition by the late seventeenth century. Biological studies revealed that other living things shared many of the physiological and behavioural characteristics which Man had thought were his exclusively. At the same time, astronomers revealed that the known world was vastly bigger than anybody had previously believed. The study of geology completed the dethronement of Man: fossils showed that other living things had existed for millions of years before Man arrived on the scene. So the earth and the creatures on it had a life and history of their own, independent of humanity.

These developments, coming as the monolith of Christian belief was cracking up, gave rise to a growing feeling that the earth and its creatures should not be exploited for Man's benefit but accorded rights of partnership in the experience of life. From here it was but a small step to begin according the natural world some of the veneration that was no longer the exclusive preserve of the Creator.

The Romanticism of the nineteenth century brought with it a sharp turning away from the utilitarian values that had prevailed hitherto. Useless and spectacular scenery quickly came to be seen as powerfully alluring. And, crucially for future attitudes to the countryside, landscape came to be associated with a new emphasis on the individual and self-development.

In Britain, the poet William Wordsworth did more than anyone else to invest the countryside with the aura of splendour and significance it has retained to this day. His own view was that God was actually present in the hills, woods, dales and streams. This pantheism was not widely shared. Nonetheless, the sanctification of the countryside which his poetry implied struck a resounding chord among large numbers of people seeking a repository for their dreams and yearnings.

One theme that he established was the role of the countryside as wilderness: a place where urban Man could retreat alone or with a few friends, and seek himself. For all Romantics, the delineation of individual identity was of vital importance. Wordsworth established the countryside as the ideal canvas on which the individual could paint himself. The countryside was to offer a context for the human experience which the unnatural environment of the city was incapable of providing.

It is to Wordsworth as much as anyone that we also owe the idea that the proper way of communing with Nature is by walking through the countryside. The idea of walking through the countryside continuously for the sole purpose of enjoying the experience was an entirely new one. De Quincey calculated that by middle age Wordsworth must have walked between 175,000 and 180,000 miles.[76] Going for a country walk became, and has remained ever since, the spiritual as well as the physical exercise of a significant chunk of the population.

By investing the countryside with so much importance in the private life of Man, Wordsworth paved the way for the public role which it was soon to play. Once the countryside had come to be seen as of almost mystical importance in the lives of a wide range of citizens, its fate soon became a matter of widespread concern.

It was one particular kind of countryside that first provoked the zeal of policy-makers and campaigners – the remaining tracts of still unenclosed common land which were dotted up and down the country. Those commons which had escaped enclosure and happened to lie round towns and cities had become extremely important to the growing urban population for fresh air, exercise and recreation. While fewer and fewer people relied for a major part of their economic existence on rights to graze animals, take wood or fish, or collect wood for fuel from their lord's land, they found the open commons fulfilling a vital new role as open-air recreation grounds. The idea that enclosure was the concern of all the local inhabitants not just those who held common rights was developed in the General Inclosure Act of 1845, which ordained that where commons lay within five miles of towns of a population of 10,000 or more, the need for any proposed enclosure had to be proved while allotments had to be provided for recreation and for field gardens.

But such safeguards as the Acts of 1836 and 1845 provided were insufficient to stem the continuing tide of enclosure. Well over half a million acres of common were enclosed between 1845 and 1864, yet only 0.3 per cent of this land was set aside for recreation or for the benefit of the poor. Matters came to a head in the late nineteenth century, which saw a spate of enclosure plans for commons in and around London. Earl Spencer, the lord of the manors of Wimbledon and Battersea, proposed to sell Putney Heath as building land and to use the proceeds to buy out and thereby extinguish common rights over the remainder of Wimbledon and Putney Commons. Then he wanted to fence the area, turn part of it into a public park, build a residence for himself in the centre and make money out of letting pasture and extracting gravel. Wandsworth Common had been reduced to a fraction of its former size by enclosures in the eighteenth and nineteenth centuries. Sir Thomas Maryon-Wilson was using Hampstead Heath, of which he was lord of the manor, for the large-scale extraction of sand and gravel for building in north London; he also wished to build over the Heath and, as evidence of his determination, began to put up houses on the highest, most conspicuous areas. On London's eastern edge, Epping Forest (a former royal chase over which common rights pre-dating the Norman Conquest had gradually been re-established) was also performing an increasingly important role as an open space for Londoners. However, the Forest's nineteen lords of the manor were enclosing large blocks of it. In one incident, a man and his two sons, who had made their living during the winter by lopping wood, were convicted of malicious trespass on property and sent to prison for two months with hard labour. They argued they were exercising an ancient right since the lord had enclosed what was a common without the sanction of a private Act of Parliament. Finally, at Berkhamsted Common, only twenty-five miles from the capital and easily accessible by rail, the Trustees of Lord Brownlow planned a major enclosure. They set to work to purchase the rights of those commoners who objected to their plans so as to reduce the number of people who could legally resist them. Impatient to get the job done, the agent of the estate even went so far as unlawfully to fence in a large section of the Common with two miles of iron railings.

It was against this background that England's first-ever national countryside campaigning organization was born.[77] The man behind it was a radical Liberal MP called George Shaw-Lefèvre. His first interest had been in securing access to the countryside. As Commissioner for Works – one of several government offices he held in the late nineteenth century – he succeeded in opening up Kew Gardens, Hampton Court Park and parts of Regent's Park which had all previously been out of bounds. When the Liberals were out of government, he devoted his

energy instead to trying to save commons. In 1865 he formed
the Commons Preservation Society. The Society formed local
committees to fight all existing plans to enclose or build on
commons, seeking out public-spirited men of substance prepared
to put money into the legal battles. In a series of cases the
Society was successful in saving many commons including the
large London commons. Most of the battles took place in law
courts: at Wimbledon for instance, four years of litigation with
Earl Spencer finally resulted in his handing over the common to
a Board of Conservators charged with defending it from all
encroachments.

The Commons Preservation Society was prepared to resort to
direct action where necessary: at Berkhamsted, the Society hired
a team of navvies, armed with crowbars, to go to the common at
dead of night and tear down Lord Brownlow's Trustees' railings.
They were never put up again and Berkhamsted Common has
remained open and unenclosed ever since.

These successes and the legal precedents they set encouraged
the Society to press Parliament for new legislation to safeguard
the interests of landless city-dwellers in common land. Years of
campaigning eventually bore fruit in the Law of Property Act of
1925. This forbade the erection of any building or fence that
would prevent or impede access to a common unless the consent
of the Minister of Agriculture had first been obtained. And,
because a legal right of access to the public existed over only a
handful of commons, the Act ordained that the public should
have such a right over all urban and metropolitan commons. It
also made provision for landowners to declare by deed that the
public should have access over commons in their domains.

Long before this, however, the commons campaigners had
come to appreciate that they should not be confining their efforts
to commons. Many tracts of countryside of vital importance for
recreation were not commons. What common rights had once
existed over the chalk downs and woods of southern England,
for instance, had long since disappeared. Yet these areas were
favoured retreats for Londoners and also under intense pressure
for development. In any case, some of the campaigners began to
feel that they had to do more than frustrate individual development schemes. They wanted to be able to preserve sites in

perpetuity for the nation, removing them from subjection to the whims of whoever happened to own them.

This feeling led in 1895 to the formation of the National Trust. The three main founding figures were Robert Hunter, who had been working for a number of years as the Commons Society's treasurer; a priest in the Lake District named Canon Rawsley; and Octavia Hill, the campaigner for better housing for the poor. All three were motivated not only by a personal love for the countryside of England and Wales; they were also deeply anxious to provide people shut away in cities with opportunities for rural refreshment. In 1895 the trio formed a company with the object of holding land in the public interest.

The National Trust soon became a force throughout the Kingdom, although its activities in the early years were concentrated in England. Properties that came to the Trust during the first thirty years of the twentieth century either through gift, purchase or, after an Act of Parliament in 1931 in lieu of death duties, included Box Hill, Bodiam Castle, Toys Hill, Dunkery Beacon, the Farne Islands, Wicken Fen and large areas of the Lake District. Their acquisition saved key sites from building development, but valuable though this was, it made little difference to the face of the countryside as a whole. It was clear that the Trust's resources, both financial and human, were never going to be up to the task of protecting the countryside generally.

To meet this need, the Council for the Preservation of Rural England (CPRE) was born in 1926 with the planner Professor Patrick Abercrombie as its first honorary secretary. 'The greatest historical monument that we possess', declared Abercrombie, 'the most essential thing which *is* England, is the Countryside, the Market Town, the Village, the Hedgerow Trees, the Lanes, the Copses, the Streams and the Farmsteads.'[78] A similar Association for the Preservation of Rural Scotland followed in 1927 and the Council for the Preservation of Rural Wales was founded in 1928.

The first target of the new organizations was urban sprawl. Between 1900 and 1939, the built-up area of London quadrupled, and other British cities also expanded dramatically. The Councils' activists saw towns shooting out their arms into the countryside as though they were octopuses and engulfing fresh areas of green within their tentacles of builders' pink.[79] Semis, telegraph poles, factories, pylons, mineral workings, huts, and unsightly advertisement hoardings all threatened to penetrate the mystery of the countryside, laying the dead hand of suburban uniformity on what had been rustic and remote.

Partly in response to the efforts of the Councils, Parliament provided through Acts of 1929 and 1932 for local authorities to enter into agreements with developers to regulate the nature and size of new building in the countryside. However, the Acts required planning authorities to pay compensation to developers whose plans were changed, and they could rarely afford to do this. The only other means of curbing building expansion available to local councils was purchase of the land involved – which was of course a great deal more expensive still. So they ended up for the most part merely accepting and ratifying existing trends.

Throughout the 1930s the CPRE campaigned vigorously for more effective planning legislation to cover the whole country, as well as extra special protection for the wildest areas, which would be known as 'national parks'. Neither the CPRE nor the National Trust sought to overturn the existing landownership régime. Instead they hoped to work alongside it. The Trust would accept any land that landowners wished to dedicate to the nation or buy such important land coming on to the market as it could afford but never seek to force landowners to sell or use compulsion. The CPRE would work shoulder to shoulder with traditional owners some of the time in fighting off pressures for urbanization. Both the Trust and the CPRE had strong links with the landowning classes right from the start: both organizations sought out the Queen as their patron. The Duke of Westminster was the first president of the National Trust and the Duke of Atholl and the Earl of Crawford and Balcarres performed the same role for the National Trust for Scotland and CPRE respectively.

But if the CPRE and National Trust saw themselves as on the same side as the landowners most of the time, the same cannot be said of the groups which began to campaign for greater public access to the countryside. Such indeed was their hostility to the prevailing régime that they proved ready to break the law.

The campaign for public access to the countryside got off the

ground in Scotland during the period when many former sheep
ranges and other kinds of agricultural land were being converted
to deer forest.[80] In 1845, a society 'for protecting the public
against being robbed of its walks by private cunning and
perseverance' was founded in Edinburgh. The Edinburgh Society
soon became embroiled in legal battles over what they claimed
were public rights of way along which landowners were refusing
access. Generally, the argument turned on whether or not a path
had been used by the public from time immemorial. In 1884,
despairing at the number of court cases that would have to be
fought, the society persuaded the then MP for Aberdeen West,
James Bryce, to introduce in Parliament the Access to Mountains
(Scotland) Bill, which proposed that the public should have a
legal right of access to all uncultivated moor and mountain in
Scotland. Bryce tried eight times to get his Bill passed. He did
not succeed, but his efforts and those of the Edinburgh Society,
which became the Scottish Rights of Way Society, began to
attract attention south of the border.

In England, the cult of walking in the countryside came to
enjoy even more of a following than it did in Scotland. During
the nineteenth century, Wordsworth's message filtered down
through the professional and artisan classes to ordinary working
people. Walking became a national pastime. By the time the
twentieth century dawned, thousands of ramblers and cyclists
were pouring into the countryside every weekend, many of them
via the now extensive railway network on which special tickets
were available for walkers. Rural tea-rooms and cheap cafés
were far more numerous than they are today and local newspapers featured recommended walks in their rambling columns.
It has been estimated that in the early 1930s, 15,000 people left
Sheffield and a further 15,000 left Manchester on the average
Sunday to explore the Peak District alone.[81]

However, in England as in Scotland, vast tracts of what was
often the most spectacular countryside were locked up by their
owners – usually to protect sporting rights. Professor Cyril Joad,
writing in 1937, deplored the fact that in the woods of southern
England, 'a pair of lovers may not walk in privacy, a little girl
may not go to pick primroses, without being harried and chivvied
by angry men, whose sole concern is to ensure that the greatest

possible number of pheasants shall be offered every autumn as living targets to the guns of lazy townsmen.'[82] Nonetheless, in those days, a dense network of paths criss-crossed lowland England, providing delightful walking country outside the sporting preserves. It was in the North, where vast tracts of completely inaccessible land lay almost cheek by jowl with conurbations housing hundreds of thousands of people that feelings grew most intense.

In 1935, throughout the moorland area in and adjacent to the Peak District and covering about 215 square miles, there were only twelve footpaths that exceeded two miles in length.[83] The remainder were mainly short paths near the edge of the moors. The best and largest moors, centred on Kinder Scout and Bleaklow Ridge, were without public access of any kind. These wild and magnificent moors, only sixteen miles as the crow flies from both Manchester and Sheffield, had been closed off in the space of a generation for exclusive use as grouse preserves. Other large areas controlled by water boards as water-gathering grounds were barred to the general public on the grounds that they might infect the water with typhoid. This rule was, however, flexible enough to allow the water boards to recoup some of their expenses by leasing shooting and grazing rights.

Many of the early English ramblers were idealists with strong socialist views and an unshakeable belief in the rights of man and the freedom of the hills. Their convictions were strengthened by the impact of World War I: they felt entitled to walk on the land for which they had fought and many of their comrades had died. When the slump of the 1930s started to bite, some came to feel they should fight not only for jobs but also for the right to make the most of their enforced leisure hours. For many of these people, the countryside held the key to recreation, and their battles to gain access to it were soon to prove as fierce as their battles for work.

Ramblers started to give vent to their resentment at annual rallies held in the Winnats Pass in the Peak District: often the crowd exceeded 5,000. The rallies were organized by the local branch of the Ramblers' Association. Sympathetic Members of Parliament would address the crowd on the need for an Access to Mountains Bill, which would give every citizen an unlimited right of access to all Britain's mountain and moorland. Then, in 1932, a new organization arrived on the scene, prepared to take more militant action. The British Workers' Sports Federation, which had campaigned successfully for football pitches in deprived areas of London, began to organize open-air rambles for young people in the North. The Federation soon became outraged at the inaccessibility of large areas of moor in the Peaks. To try to change the situation it organized mass trespasses over the moors. On one spring Sunday in 1932, 400 men and women took part in a mass trespass over Kinder Scout in order to demonstrate, in the words of Benny Rothman one of the leaders, 'for the rights of ordinary people to walk on land stolen from them in earlier times'.[84] The publicity resulting from the trespass itself and from the prison sentences meted out to five of the ring-leaders aroused national interest in their cause. Thousands of ramblers went to view the scene of the mass trespass, and two other mass trespasses followed.

The trespass campaign paid off in the end, but not in the way the campaigners had imagined. The legislation on which their hopes were pinned – the Access to Mountains Bill, 1939 – was emasculated by its opponents, and brought no positive benefit at all. But the campaigners' actions, coupled with the persistent lobbying of groups like the Ramblers' Association, succeeded in implanting firmly in the public consciousness the notion that the status quo in the countryside was unjust and needed amendment.

The Election of the Attlee Government

By the time World War II was underway, there was a widespread feeling that the iron grip of the landowner in rural Britain must now be loosened. Many people believed that the war should be seen as a prelude to the unveiling of a new Britain that would be built not on feudal principles but on principles of equality. Everybody, rich and poor, all who had together survived the dangers of bombing, military and civil defence service would be fairly catered for in a new welfare state. It was widely accepted that among the policies of a post-war administration would be the conservation of the countryside and the provision of public access to it. This being so, the wartime coalition government of

Conservatives, Labour and the now tiny Liberal Party set in motion studies to work out how the countryside should be preserved and access should be provided. In 1941, it appointed a Committee, chaired by Lord Justice Scott, to work out how the right balance could be struck between the needs of industry, agriculture, conservation and the social well-being of the country-side. Meanwhile, the Minister of Works and Buildings, Lord Reith, asked John Dower, an architect and one of the most prominent lobbyists for the establishment of national parks, to prepare a detailed report setting out ways in which national parks in England and Wales should be selected, administered and planned. So while Coventry and Dresden burned, specially appointed teams worked away on the shaping of a new rural order.

When Clement Attlee's Labour Government was swept to power in 1945 it really looked as if fundamental change would sweep the countryside. In the new House of Commons there were far fewer landowners than ever before, and the Government seemed determined to pursue the ideas laid out by Scott[85] and Dower.[86] Within days of taking office, the Minister of Town and Country Planning, Lewis Silkin, had set up a Committee on National Parks in England and Wales, charged with making specific recommendations on the basis of the Dower Report.[87] Another special committee was appointed to put forward pro-posals on footpaths and public access to tracts of countryside;[88] while another was to report on how nature could best be conserved.[89] These committees concerned themselves with England and Wales; but the Scottish Office considered how their ideas could best be applied north of the border.[90] After a thousand years of oppression and exploitation in rural Britain, it looked as if the landless were at last in sight of a real share of the benefits the countryside could bestow.

We shall see shortly (in Part Four) how this promise has been betrayed in our own era. But first we examine the character and attitudes of the landowners of the 1980s.

PART TWO
Who Are Britain's Landowners?

Part Two

Who Are Personality Judges?

3. In Search of Ownership

Shut away as most of us are in built-up areas of one kind or another, we rely for our idea of what happens in the countryside on second-hand impressions. Media cliché tells us that the holdings of the aristocracy have been wiped out by death duties, and that such blue-blooded figures as remain are lucky if they retain the ownership of a garrett within their once stately homes. Faceless state corporations and pension funds are supposed to have taken over from traditional landowners, though we are also expected to believe in a sturdy race of decent farmers held back in an endless struggle to make ends meet by EEC red tape and their own deep sense of social responsibility.

These images owe much to the considerable efforts of those who control the countryside to ensure that they are presented to the urban population in the way they want them to be. The reality is rather different.

The Public Owners

Some people seem to assume that in the era of the welfare state the bulk of the countryside must surely be publicly owned. Perhaps the conspicuous ownership of large individual tracts of land exercised by the Ministry of Defence with its red flags and the Forestry Commission with its familiar signboards has helped give rise to this impression. In 1985 (the most recent year for which figures are available), the Ministry of Defence owned 561,710 acres of Britain including 206 tenanted farms, while in March 1986, the Forestry Commission owned five times this amount: 2,878,785 acres, making it Britain's largest single land-owner. Substantial tracts are also held by local authorities in the UK, water authorities and the Ministry of Transport as well as nationalized industries like the Central Electricity Generating

Board, National Coal Board, British Railways Board, British Waterways Board and the British Steel Corporation.[1] Many of the holdings of these bodies are very noticeable in the countryside. But add together the land owned by all public bodies and together it amounts to 11,740 square miles – 12.6 per cent of the surface of the UK.[2] Put another way, 87 per cent of the land of the United Kingdom lies in private hands – and that means much more than 87 per cent of what we think of as countryside, as opposed to motorways, marshalling yards, sewage works or reservoirs.

The few local studies of land ownership that have been made confirm the overwhelming dominance of the private landowner. In Cheshire, for instance, a study carried out for the Royal Agricultural Society of England in 1963 revealed that public bodies owned just under 7 per cent of the county's land.[3] Of the private individuals and companies that owned the remaining 93 per cent, private individuals not occupying all they own (in other words, letting out some of their holdings) were the category accounting for the single largest proportion of land: 51 per cent of Cheshire. Private owner-occupiers came next (28 per cent of the county), while private companies and the Queen in her capacity as Duke of Lancaster accounted for most of the remainder.

The proportion of land in public ownership in Britain has not been increasing during the 1980s. Quite the reverse. Not only have public bodies from county, district and regional councils to the British Railways Board been selling land to release cash; Britain's largest public owner, the Forestry Commission, succeeded in 'hiving off' 321,100 acres of its estate between 1981 and 1986 mainly to private landowners or forestry companies, in response to pressure from the Thatcher Government. That Government's 1981 Forestry Act made provision for the Commission to sell off its land and forests, and the Commission took advantage of this steadily from 1981. It is planned that by 1989 the Commission will have generated £100 million by selling about 10 per cent of its estate.[4]

The amount of land held by public bodies could drop still more if the emphasis on privatization and public spending curbs continues. By the mid-1980s only a few local authorities had disposed of large areas they rented to tenant farmers as small-holdings, although most had considered doing so. Further financial pressure would force this farmland into the private sector. Scotland's Department of Agriculture and Fisheries sold 105,281 acres or 26 per cent of its estate between 1980 and 1985, including both crofting lands and lowland farms. All the Department's sales of farmland during those years were to sitting tenants as such sales are the only ones permitted by current crofting and agricultural holdings legislation. In 1986, as the number of tenants able and willing to buy was beginning to dry up, the Department told me it was 'actively considering' other ways in which it could increase sales.

As it happens, public bodies that own land often have closer links with private landowners than might be imagined. The Forestry Commission is Britain's largest landowner. Its estate is in theory the forestry estate of the British people. On top of managing this estate, the Commission has the task of adjudicating on behalf of the public between competing uses of rural land in so far as it decides the fate of applications from the private sector for applications to clear woods and copses and for state grants to help finance private afforestation. Yet the membership of the Commission has hardly reflected the make-up of society. Five of the seven men who have chaired the Commission since its birth in 1919 have also been private landowners: Lord Radnor, Lord Robinson, Earl Waldegrave (father of the Minister for the Environment, Countryside and Local Government since 1985, William Waldegrave, MP), Richard (later Lord) Mackie and the chairman since 1979 Sir David Montgomery, Bt. In 1986, Britain's largest state owner of land was led by a titled aristocrat who is reported to own a 6,000-acre landed estate in Kinross. And sitting alongside Sir David on the eleven-man Forestry Commission were two other private landowners.

POPULAR FALLACIES

One of the reasons why so much of the countryside is assumed to be in public hands is misleading terminology. Nine per cent of England and Wales is designated 'national park', a term which in Africa, Australia, North and South America and most of

Europe refers to lands owned by national governments to ensure
their complete protection. But in Britain, a 'national park' is
something altogether different. Our 'national parks' are far from
being nationally owned. True, the ten national parks of England
and Wales (which cover, in order of designation, the Peak
District, the Lake District, Snowdonia, Dartmoor, the Pembrokeshire Coast, the North York Moors, the Yorkshire Dales, Exmoor
and Northumberland's Cheviot Hills) occupy a larger proportion
of our land area than the national parks in many other countries.
But the public bodies (in this case national park authorities)
charged with the responsibility for conserving the parks and
providing for public recreation within them, owned in 1982 only
1 per cent of the parks' land area – 39,115 acres out of a total of
3,359,627 acres.[5] If the land owned by the government agency
for nature conservation, the Nature Conservancy Council, is
added, the area of land within the national parks publicly owned
and managed specifically for the purposes of conservation and
recreation in 1982 rises to a tiny 1.38 per cent.[6] Apart from
stretches owned by the Ministry of Defence, water authorities
and the Forestry Commission, most of the remainder of Britain's
national parks lies in private hands – hands whose owners may
or may not rate the conservation of the parks' beauty above their
own economic objectives. At least in Scotland and Northern
Ireland there is no possibility of the public being misled in this
way. Although government-appointed committees recommended
in 1947 that national parks should be established forthwith in
Scotland and Ulster, (and in Scotland on the international model
of total state ownership of the land), no national parks of any
kind have ever been designated in either country.

The term 'common land' – which is applied to 1.5 million
acres of England and Wales – also suggests public ownership.
But it means nothing of the kind. Common land is land over
which certain individuals other than the owner enjoy certain
carefully circumscribed rights. The designation of land as a
common does not automatically mean that anyone can walk
over the land in question. Apart from any public rights of way
that may pass alongside or through a common, the public enjoys
a legal right to roam at will over only one-fifth of the common
land of England and Wales, much of this in urban areas.[7] Over

around 1.2 million of the 1.5 million acres of common, ordinary
citizens enjoy no legal right to roam and can be treated as
trespassers.

Areas designated by the Nature Conservancy Council as
'national nature reserves' form another kind of land often wrongly
assumed to be owned by the nation. These reserves are tracts of
land of outstanding natural history or geological interest: the
survival of many of Britain's rarest species depends on their
presence. In fact, however, in 1986 of the total area of Great
Britain designated by the Conservancy Council as national
nature reserve, only one quarter was fully owned by the Council
and therefore fully protected.

The Financial Institutions

Another widespread idea about Britain's rural land is that a vast
proportion of it now lies in the hands of faceless financial
institutions like pension funds, insurance companies and property
unit trusts. Through the control exercised by such bodies – it is
sometimes suggested – rural land is effectively under the ultimate
control of the general population as shareholders and pension
contributors even though it is not under direct democratic
control. So what is the part played by the institutions?

Insurance companies and pension funds have to find a safe
haven for the savings of their tens of millions of policy-holders or
pension contributors. Before World War II, they opted mainly
for government securities; during the 1950s, they diversified into
equities. In the early 1970s, they began buying up rural land. At
the same time, another set of new buyers was entering the
property market as well – property unit trusts. These trusts
invest exclusively in property (urban as well as agricultural) on
behalf of corporate investors who wish to invest in property but
do not want to buy and manage it themselves. The vast majority
of property unit trusts are owned by pension funds. All these
institutional investors are looking for steady but secure growth
over the years. And by the 1970s, farmland appeared to be
providing just this.

There was a sharp rise in the price of farmland in England
and Wales during the early 1970s, which continued through the

decade. Reckoning on the substantial capital appreciation this trend implied, the Post Office Pension Fund, to take a typical example, bought the 2,616-acre Saltmarshe estate at Howden, north of Goole, East Yorkshire, in two lots in 1972 and 1973. With their enormous financial resources, financial institutions are in an extremely good position to pour money into land in order to improve its agricultural profitability – through new buildings and equipment, land drainage and so on. And soon after its purchase, the Post Office Pension Fund put in more than £190,000 of its own money at Saltmarshe, as well as taking advantage of capital grants from the Ministry of Agriculture. The resulting increase in the land's productivity set against a national background of steadily rising farm incomes and farmland prices enabled the Fund to increase the rents of its fourteen tenant farmers by almost 200 per cent by 1979 and to see the capital value of the whole estate more than treble within the same period, from £768,000 in 1972/73 to £2.6 million in 1979.[8]

Concern that financial institutions might be taking over much of Britain's land led the Government in 1977 to appoint a committee to look into the acquisition and occupancy of agricultural land in Britain. This committee, under the chairmanship of Lord Northfield, found that insurance companies were the biggest institutional landowners, with 59 per cent of all financial institutional landholding, compared to 22 per cent owned by pension funds and 19 per cent by property unit trusts.[9] But to the surprise of some, the Committee's report published in 1978 revealed that the rural land holdings of all the financial institutions amounted to no more than 529,819 acres – just over 1.2 per cent of all agricultural land in England, Wales and Scotland or 0.9 per cent of these countries' total area. The Committee could find no institutional ownership in Northern Ireland. Of course, the proportion of land owned by the institutions might increase. But the Northfield Committee calculated that even if the sharp upward trend of the 1970s continued, the institutions would still end up with only 11 per cent of the farmland of England, Scotland and Wales by the year 2020, or 8.3 per cent of these countries' total land area. And by 1985 it had come to look as if continued expansion on this scale was not going to materialize. The imposition of milk quotas appeared to mark an end to the fashion for land. Instead of further large-scale purchases, the institutions were doing no more than consolidating their existing holdings by acquiring any land adjacent to farms they owned already, just like owner-occupier farmers.[10] So the idea that the institutions are taking over Britain's countryside seems to be mistaken. Whatever happens to 1 per cent of Britain is not going to be decisive. But in so far as these institutions are imposing their mark on the landscape, how do they behave?

In some cases, land acquisition by a financial institution does bring with it a completely new set of people in charge of the land. This happens when an institution acquires land with vacant possession and asks a farming firm to manage the land on its behalf. In such cases, the institution's land comes to take on the appearance not of other land owned by that institution but of other farms managed by the same firm. Velcourt is the leading firm in this area, managing 20,995 acres of farmland in the United Kingdom in 1985. Velcourt sells itself on its ability to remodel farms into new highly profitable enterprises. On each farm it takes over, whether corn-growing or pastoral, the firm aims to impose what it calls the Velcourt stamp: fields all about fifty acres (three acres less than the area of London's Green Park), with tramlines all following an identical pattern and the same crop grown at the same depth on the same day using identical machinery. Depressing though this may sound, it is not in practice very different from the approach taken now by many family farmers.

To try to find out what happens when an institution buys land, I talked in 1982 to the chief land agent for the financial institution with the largest land portfolio, the Prudential Insurance Company. In 1985, the Prudential owned 82,000 acres of land in England and Scotland, including a 13,000-acre stretch of Herefordshire bought in 1979 from the Trustees of the late Sir Charles Clore in what was probably the largest ever single purchase of land in England by any financial institution. Only 11 per cent of the Prudential's estate was bought with vacant possession. The most common forms of purchase were sale-and-leaseback and purchase of land already let to tenant farmers. Sale-and-leaseback accounts for 49 per cent of the Prudential's land. In these cases, an owner-occupier farmer sells his land or part of it to a financial institution like the Prudential. He often uses the capital from the sale to invest further in this or other farms while leasing back the farm from the institution.

Forty per cent of the Prudential's land was purchased with sitting tenants. (The Clore estate included forty tenanted farms as well as hundreds of rented cottages.) When a landed estate is purchased, the previous landlord may stay on too. When for instance the Prudential bought the 8,500-acre South Esk estate in Angus on the east coast of Scotland from the Earl of South Esk in 1976, the Earl retained Kinnaird Castle at the centre of the estate and 600 acres, together with shooting rights estate-wide until 1992. The tenant farmers who used to pay rent to the Earl have the right to stay on since any land purchase by an institution or anybody else is subject to existing tenancies.

What all this means is that takeover by an institution rarely makes much difference to what happens on the ground. In many cases the previous owners carry on doing as tenants what they would have done anyway as owners. If investors in the institutions wanted to use their position to bring about changes they would face an uphill struggle. Most of the institutions involved do not publish a list of their land holdings to their policy-holders, let alone anybody else. I asked the Prudential's chief land agent Nicholas Woolley the reason for this secrecy. He told me:

You will have read in the papers that we bought the Duke of Norfolk's Kenning Hall Estate in Norfolk the year before last. I've mentioned the Angus estate, the Guy's Hospital estate in Herefordshire and the Watership Down estate. But certainly there are a number of areas where it would be a breach of confidentiality with our existing tenants who, until we purchased, were the owners of the freehold as well. So naturally it would be quite wrong, there's no need to disclose those names.

There is no need either, in the institutions' view, for a different approach to land ownership from that of those from whom they buy. So the arrival of the institutions has made very little difference for better or for worse even in the small part of rural Britain which has fallen under their sway.

In fact, neither financial institutions nor the Government own more than a fraction of Britain's rural land. Around 80 per cent of it is still effectively controlled by individuals, as it has been for a thousand years. This reality is disguised by the fact that for tax and other reasons individual owners today often elect to shroud their ownership in trusts of various kinds. While these preserve their ability to benefit from their holdings and to pass them on intact to their descendants, they often do little to reduce the degree of control which the individuals wield over the land in their power. These people are today's landowners, and they fall into a number of groups which though distinct have a surprising amount in common.

The Landed Aristocracy

First, what of the aristocratic landowner of old. Has he, as is so widely imagined, faded away? The answer comes as a surprise in view of the widespread impression that change has swept through every corner of modern Britain, overturning the old bastions of privilege and creating a new and effectively classless society.

Fundamental to any appreciation of the real power structure in the countryside today is the realization that in fact the vast landowner of aristocratic background and attitudes has *not* faded away, but remains an extremely potent force. This is not only because he still owns much of the land surface; it is also because his attitudes continue to dominate the countryside as a whole, infecting the thinking and behaviour of other, newer kinds of owner.

A hard core of titled families – dukes and marquesses, viscounts, earls, barons, baronets and the Royal Family – own nearly a third of the land of Great Britain. This is the conclusion of Dr Doreen Massey and Alejandrina Catalano who in 1978 calculated from existing published sources – in particular a 50 per cent sample survey of the holdings of Britain's titled families carried out in 1967 by author Roy Perrott – that the titled nobility of Britain (as opposed to her untitled landed gentry or businessmen farmers) owned 31.6 per cent of her land.[11] Two-thirds of these landed aristocrats, or just over two hundred families, each owned at least 5,000 acres (an area more than twice that of Richmond Park), according to Mr Perrott.[12] And there is no reason to suppose the picture has changed much since 1967.

What this means in Scotland is that whole islands, deer forests, ranges of mountains and grouse moors may fall under the ownership of one man – together with the more typical components of the private estates of England and Wales: forests, parks, mineral workings, stretches of river, lakes, villages and occasionally even small towns, but above all agricultural land, much of it peopled by tenants. In economic terms the holdings of this landowning élite constitute a considerable portion of the wealth of the nation. And though these estates have indeed declined in extent since the late nineteenth century, the post-war increase in land values means that many are worth more now in real terms than the larger estate was worth a century ago.

(i) ORIGINS

The tenacity with which Britain's landed aristocrats have clung to their holdings over the centuries belies the popular image of an effete, enfeebled and ineffectual group of human museum-pieces. Some families have managed to hold on to large estates since their forefathers were first given land by William the Conqueror or an Anglo-Norman King of Scotland.

A not untypical specimen of this breed is Hugh Algernon Percy, the 10th Duke of Northumberland. He runs his 105,000 acres (bigger than the Isle of Wight) from a gaunt, austere medieval fortress on the northern edge of the little market town of Alnwick, thirty miles north of Newcastle. To the north and to the west of Alnwick Castle rolls Hulne (meaning home) Park – a magnificent Capability Brown creation, 3,000 acres in all that includes five-and-a-half miles of the River Aln (famous for its trout fishing), vast sweeps of park, field and forest (managed partly for timber and partly as cover for the 2,000 pheasants turned down in the Park every year), the remains of two medieval monasteries and many other historic monuments. The Duke's holdings stretch down to the coast at Alnmouth over land which in the past harboured rich coal seams that provided much of the estate's income in the nineteenth century. Further north lies the remainder of the estate, which, when I visited it in 1982, consisted altogether of 167 separate farms let out to tenants, 7,000 acres of forest, large grouse moors on the Simonside Hills, 620 let houses in thirteen villages and many more miles of the River Aln. This estate had seen no major sales of land for fifty years, although there is more or less continuous buying and selling of bits of land to improve the efficiency of the estate. Increasingly, ownership has been vested in trusts and companies: the Alnwick estate belonged in 1982 to the Percy family through eleven different legal ownerships.

Henry, 1st Lord Percy of Alnwick, who became the first owner of Alnwick Castle in 1309, was the head of a family which was descended from William de Percy, who had accompanied William the Conqueror in 1066, and been granted extensive domains in Yorkshire, Lincolnshire and later in Sussex. When the Percys acquired the barony of Alnwick they became one of the most powerful families in England, a position they were to sustain. During the Wars of the Roses, in the fifteenth century, the Percys, led by the head of their family, the Earl of Northumberland, were in the forefront of the Lancastrian party. During the eighteenth and nineteenth centuries members of the family regularly sat in the House of Commons while other members of the family took their place in the House of Lords – as the present Duke is of course entitled to do.

But the 10th Duke's writ does not stop at Alnwick. He has 3,500 acres of rolling chalk downland and Wealden sandstone and clay country three miles east of Guildford in the Surrey Hills. Here there are farms and forest plantations. There are the famous beauty spots of Newlands Corner, St Martha's Hill and the mysterious and lovely Silent Pool. There is a sawmill and there are estate cottages and buildings. There are pheasant woods and a large, spectacular sand quarry. There is a winding stretch of the little River Tilling Bourne, and there is Albury Park, a magnificent private parkland with avenues of limes and Spanish chestnuts and a redundant Saxon church. Only the main house of Albury Park, now converted to private flats after it was sold in 1965, is no longer owned by the estate.

When in London the Duke resides in Syon House, Brentford – a mansion set in a 200-acre park granted to the 9th Earl of

Northumberland by James I in 1604. Bounded on one side by the river Thames and on the other three by high brick walls, Syon Park is well known for its garden centre, but not for its acres of stately cattle-graced parkland from which the public are excluded.

A far more valuable private estate originating as a gift from a long departed king is the Duchy of Cornwall. To be Duke of Northumberland or Rutland, Beaufort or Devonshire, for instance, is to be rich and powerful; to be Duke of Cornwall is to enjoy enormous tax privileges as well. The Duchy of Cornwall is based on 130,000 acres scattered through nine counties. It includes the whole of the Scilly Isles, 160 miles of foreshore, 11,000 acres of river-bed, five ruined castles, tens of thousands of desirable agricultural acres across the South West, much of Dartmoor and, in London, the Oval cricket ground plus 850 properties in Kennington alone valued in 1981 at almost £100 million. The title was first given, 750 years ago, to Edward, the Black Prince, in order to provide for his upkeep while he was waiting to become king, and this tradition has continued to the present day; the Prince of Wales receives nothing from the Civil List. In 1985, the Duchy made a net profit of £1,462,573. The estates of other private landowners may be larger or even more lucrative, but that of the Prince of Wales alone enjoys the special privilege of exemption from income tax, surtax, capital gains tax, and, when the estate passes to Prince William, inheritance tax. Prince Charles, following a precedent set by Edward VIII, paid half of his Duchy revenues as a gift to the State until his marriage in 1981, when he reduced this to a quarter.

But the Prince of Wales is by no means the largest of our aristocratic landowners. In the mid-1980s, that position fell to the 9th Duke of Buccleuch and Queensbury, who owes much of his good fortune to the parental concern of King Charles II, concern which extended to his fourteen illegitimate children. One of these was the direct ancestor of the present duke. In 1663, this young man was betrothed to a Scottish heiress; Charles II created the dukedom of Buccleuch in celebration of the marriage. By the end of the nineteenth century the family's estates had swelled to half a million acres. In 1970 they stood at a reported 277,000 acres of Scotland[13] (most of this consisting of vast tracts of hill country in the border counties of Dumfries-shire, Roxburghshire, Selkirk and Lanarkshire); and the 11,000-acre Boughton estate in Northamptonshire, which itself includes five villages. 'If Boughton is the most beautiful house in England, then Drumlanrig is the most romantic in Scotland,' wrote Brian Masters in his book *The Dukes* in 1977.[14] Drumlanrig Castle is one of the Duke of Buccleuch's four Scottish mansions, standing on a lofty hill in the wilds of Dumfries-shire while Boughton House shelters a particularly fine private art collection. In 1986, the Duke probably controlled two and a half times as much land north of the border as the National Trust for Scotland. But like a rapidly growing number of Britain's large landowners, the Duke of Buccleuch and Queensbury does not own all this land person-ally. In 1976, ownership of the Duke's estates was vested in a family company, Buccleuch Estates Limited, in which the Duke had the casting vote and which had a controlling interest in twelve subsidiary companies (including three operating in Australia). At Boughton for instance, Buccleuch wealth was split between Boughton Estates Limited (in which Buccleuch Estates Limited owned 100 per cent of the ordinary shares) and the farming company Geddington Farms Limited (in which Buccle-uch Estates Limited owned 99 per cent of the ordinary shares).[15]

Several of our most prominent landowners owe their holdings to the great land windfall that accompanied the Dissolution of the Monasteries in the 1540s. An ancestor of our present Duke of Bedford, for example, was a small-scale Dorset landowner when he came to the notice of King Henry VIII, who was able to reward him for certain services rendered not only with an earldom but also a vast area of what had been monastic land. Other present-day major landowners benefiting from the Dissolution of the Monasteries are the 17th Earl of Pembroke, whose 14,000-acre estate at Wilton near Salisbury is based largely on the lands of the former Abbey of Wilton which his ancestor Sir William Herbert was given at the Dissolution; and the 7th Marquess of Northampton. The Marquess lives on his 3,500-acre estate at Compton Wyngates in Warwickshire, but he also owns a 10,000-acre estate just east of Northampton which includes Castle Ashby, a magnificent Elizabethan house approached by a three-mile avenue, as well as land in Surrey.

His ancestor, Sir William Compton, was able to buy estates in twenty counties, after Henry VIII showered him with offices of state.

It might be assumed that the Industrial Revolution would have produced a new wave of powerful landowners as the fruits of the factory age were ploughed into that most reassuring of all assets, land. In fact, however, this did not happen on a significant scale. Some industrial, commercial and banking families became substantial landowners, but the old, pre-industrial families continued to outnumber them by far. In his book *Men of Property*, 1981, social scientist Dr W. D. Rubinstein lists the men with the greatest landed wealth in Britain in 1883. Of the twenty-nine he credits with gross incomes from land of more than £75,000 a year, only one, Lord Overstone, was a man whose fortune came from the Industrial Revolution. Dr Rubinstein writes:

The riches of all the others were, without exception, pre-Industrial Revolution in origin. They represented the end result of a process of familial acquisition which began, in some cases, with the Norman Conquest, and which was aided and abetted by all of the landmarks of British history through which the aristocracy consolidated its gains, from the spoils of the monasteries, to eighteenth-century 'Old Corruption', to the mineral income and urban rentals of the nineteenth century.[16]

Three main things have enabled Britain's aristocratic families to cling to large holdings of land. The first was the very nature of land ownership as an occupation, which meant that they could rely on the labour of others for generating their income while devoting their own time and energy to the consolidation of political power. The second was the rule of primogeniture, whereby the family estates were always preserved for the first-born male rather than carved up between him and all his sisters and younger brothers as happened elsewhere in Europe. The third factor was the attitude which landowning families took towards marriage. Other than during a short period at the end of the last century and the beginning of this one, few large areas of land ever came on to the market. Estates agglomerated instead through judicious marriages.

The large Scottish estates are no exception to this rule. The Murrays, from whom the dukes of Atholl are descended, were a relatively insignificant family until the seventeenth century when William Murray, 2nd Earl of Tullibardine, won the hand of Lady Dorothea Stewart, the heiress of Atholl. (The Atholl lands had been given by the king to his brother-in-law who became Lady Dorothea's great-grandfather). In the eighteenth century, the 2nd Duke inherited the lordship and lands of the Isle of Man through his maternal great-grandfather; but the 3rd Duke disposed of his sovereignty of the Island to the British Government in 1765 for £70,000, while in 1828 the 4th Duke sold the family's remaining property and privileges in the Isle of Man to the British Crown for £417,144, then a vast sum. Today, the 10th Duke of Atholl has to make do with 130,000 acres of Perthshire.

But perhaps the most successful of all such marital mergers was that in 1677 between Sir Thomas Grosvenor and a twelve-year-old heiress. Gerald Grosvenor, 6th Duke of Westminster, born in 1957, owes the most lucrative part of his inheritance – 100 acres of Mayfair and 200 acres of Belgravia – to this marriage. For Mary Davies' dowry was a collection of marshy meadows covering what is now Belgravia and Mayfair.

The name 'Davies' lives on in the heart of the Duke of Westminster's empire in Davies Street running south from Oxford Street to Berkeley Square – as well it might. But for this marriage, the Grosvenors would probably have carried on as they had since the twelfth century, as landowners restricted to Cheshire. As it is, by the early 1980s, Grosvenor family trusts, valued at £400 million, also owned rural estates in Scotland, Ireland and Lancashire, a massive business empire with investments in Australia, the United States and Hawaii quite apart from the property in central London and Cheshire. For though at the time of her marriage Mary Davies' lands were only swamp and poor pasture, they were spectacularly well-situated. And in 1826 her great-grandson drained the land and built Belgravia. The rich and the fashionable flooded in to be close to the rebuilt Buckingham Palace, and by 1860, three dukes, thirteen peers and thirteen MPs had their town residences in Belgrave Square alone. In the mid-1980s, Britain's reputedly richest citizen was landowner and duke, Gerald Grosvenor. When I interviewed him in 1982, he had recently bought 22,000 acres of Lancashire, mainly grouse moor, only half an hour by helicopter from his 10,800-area estate at Eaton, south of Chester.

(ii) PERSONAL CHARACTERISTICS

High up in their Scottish castles or in their more modest stately homes of England and Wales, Britain's landed aristocrats live at a physical and psychological distance from the rest of the world. But they are not lone individualists, each using his holdings and the power they give him in a different way. After a thousand years of similar experience, they now share a remarkably similar outlook.

Part of the reason for this is the close relationship they enjoy with each other through their tradition of inter-marriage. Take the Duke of Buccleuch. The descendants of Charles II's other children with whom he could be said to be related include the Duke of Grafton, the Duke of Richmond and the Duke of St Albans. But the present Duke is also related through marriage to the Duke of Northumberland, Sir Ian Gilmour Bt, Lord Montagu of Beaulieu, the Earl of Bradford, the Duke of Abercorn, Lord Home, the Duke of Marlborough and the Marquess of Exeter, to name but a few.

A sense of common heritage stares down at Britain's landed aristocrats from the portraits of their ancestors on the walls of their stately homes. Their family histories are documented in works like Debrett's *Peerage* and Burke's *Peerage*. For them, unlike Britain's leading businessmen and professional people, there is no escaping the influence of the collective history of their tribe.

Nor do they seem to want to avoid this influence. The young landed aristocrat tends to enjoy not only a feeling of separateness from society as a whole but also a firm commitment to the traditions of the colourful section of society in which he finds himself. And this natural enthusiasm for the collective heritage is reinforced by social conditioning. 'For "education" one could simply Eton,' says Roy Perrott in *The Aristocrats*.[17] After Britain's young landed aristocrats tend to head either for the Army. Thus upbringing, way of life, family occupation, social outlook and political beliefs all end up conforming to a pattern which the members of what is a loosely-knit club all implicitly endorse. According to Roy Perrott, should the aristocrat need to earn a living, it will not be as a social worker or teacher but as a merchant banker or lawyer. He is most unlikely to be a member of CND, the Labour Party or Friends of the Earth – but he may well be a member of the Conservative Party. He will not be a Quaker, Methodist or an officer in the Salvation Army, but a member of the Church of England or a Catholic. At the same time, the leisure pursuits, in particular fox hunting and other bloodsports, which he shares with other members of his tribe, help him and his peers to see themselves as a race apart.

Among this close-knit tribe, certain attitudes have become endemic, and because the tribe is so homogenous, these tend to be taken for granted by its members. They know no different. Two particular characteristics of the landowning class have implications for the rest of society. The first is their extreme possessiveness. One autumn day in 1982, a hot-air balloon carrying three passengers on a pleasure flight floated over a grouse moor near Ripon in Yorkshire. Viscount Mountgarrett, a major landowner in Yorkshire, who was out with a shooting party, turned his shotgun on the balloon and gave it both barrels. These hit the basket, so he reloaded and fired again.

Not all the owners of Britain's large landed estates would necessarily go as far as Lord Mountgarrett. But most of them are committed to ensuring that all of their land remains in the hands of their own family, for ever. One of them pointed out to me: '*I* am not immortal.' The fact that he felt it necessary to make this clear suggests perhaps that those human beings who have most nearly approached this much-desired state are those of our large landowners who have managed to reproduce themselves and their properties generation after generation for hundreds of years, and look likely to continue to do so for many centuries to come.

The 11th Viscount Downe lives at the picturesque Wykeham Abbey, which incorporates the remains of a twelfth-century nunnery and lies in the depths of the Yorkshire countryside six miles inland from Scarborough. His estate includes 4,000 acres of fine farmland, woodland and parkland. Why would such a man also want 10,000 acres of heather moorland as a separate unit high up in the North York Moors? But he does. The moor is not profitable: the shooting rights just about enable it to break even. But Lord Downe would not think of selling it. 'I keep the moor because it's been in the family for years and because I want to look after it for everybody who cares about it,' he told me in an interview in 1983.

This possessiveness can also extend to estate houses. Many landed aristocrats own houses in the villages on their estates, and they are often extremely reluctant to sell them off. More than half of Northamptonshire's estate villages were still wholly or substantially owned by the local large estate owner in 1983, while in Cheshire at least forty villages were still in single private ownership in that year.[18] This in spite of the high prices attracted by olde-worlde cottages in otherwise unbuilt-up villages.

Another characteristic of the titled aristocrats that has implications for the rest of us is their belief in their right to lead. They may not have experience of many other walks of life, but they take it for granted that they will shape the lives of other people. Conversely, they do not expect to have to respond to the views of the lower orders or a society dominated through the workings of democracy by these same lower orders. This natural superiority is hardly surprising in view of the landed aristocrats' long history of leadership and control. And it is very much to the fore in the field in which they feel most qualified to take the lead – rural land administration. This effortless assumption of authority – though at odds with attitudes elsewhere in British society – has not only proved resilient among the aristocratic landowners. It has spread from them to other kinds of landowners – untitled landowning magnates and owner-occupier farmers, as well as the people who manage large landholdings on behalf of private, state and institutional owners: the land agents.

Major landowners like the Dukes of Westminster and Northumberland or the Marquess of Northampton are far too busy with their other business and public activities to see to the day-to-day administration of their estates, and many have handed this task over to land agents. Some of these men are younger sons of the large landowning families; some of the others are eldest sons who will in time take over their own family's estates. Many play sleeping roles in the private companies or family trusts in which their masters' land is vested. And unlike other land-based employees, the land agents, typically with a public school and Royal Agricultural College background, move within the same social circles as the landowners.

These men do not only look after the large private estates; they also oversee much publicly-owned land too, as well as the estates of pension funds, insurance companies and institutions like the Church, the Crown Estates and the Duchy of Lancaster. Relying on a body of professional knowledge built up on large private estates during the eighteenth and nineteenth centuries, the land agents move from one type of owner to another, unconsciously disseminating the attitudes to land of the large private estate owners, even when their masters are, in theory, the people. In this way they serve as an important buttress of the land ownership régime.

The Untitled Barons

If few people appreciate the extent of the private kingdoms of Britain's titled aristocrats, fewer still have any inkling of the amount of land controlled by an almost equally powerful group: the untitled barons.

In 1967, a shepherd's son and former forestry worker, John McEwen, began the task that was to occupy him for the next decade. By chiselling away at the hard skin of secrecy that conceals the raw data on who owns Britain, he was able to ascertain the ownership of every block of Scottish land over 1,000 acres in extent.

The results, published in his book *Who Owns Scotland?*, reveal that in 1970 87 per cent of Scotland's land was in private hands; and that 63 per cent of the entire country was privately owned in blocks of at least 1,000 acres.[19] Titled aristocrats loom large in Mr McEwen's list of Scotland's top 100 private landowners, but another group of private owners is just as common. These include the Wills tobacco family with 263,000 acres, Captain A. A. C. Farquharson with 119,000 acres and E. H. Vestey with 93,000 acres. These are members of a group of perhaps 1,500 British families[20] without blue blood but with vast land holdings, whom we may call the untitled barons. Like the titled aristocrats, the untitled barons differ from owner-occupier farmers in that while they may well farm sizeable areas directly themselves, usually through a farm manager, their holdings also embrace farmland let to tenants and often other types of country as well such as woodland, deer forest, amenity parkland, grouse moor, villages and other estate buildings and stretches of lake or river.

If the untitled barons lack the breeding of their titled betters, they make sure there are as few other differences as possible. If they are not upper class by blood they certainly are in manner. Apart from the prefix to their name – usually Colonel, Commander, Sir or even Mr instead of His Grace (in the case of a duke) or Lord (in the case of a marquess, earl, viscount or baron) or Sir with a Bt after the surname (indicating a baronet) – these people affect the attitudes and behaviour of the titled class often as completely as the aristocrats themselves, and sometimes more completely. Their estates tend to be slightly smaller than those of the really old aristocratic families, but they fall within the same pattern.

Birse, the southernmost of Aberdeenshire's eighty-five parishes, is one area that is under the sway of untitled barons. It is also a pocket of Britain's land for which detailed information on land ownership is available – the result of research carried out by a resident of the parish, Robin Callander, in 1980.[21]

Drive north from Brechin or Montrose through the misty clouds that so often shroud the high, bare moors of West Kincardineshire, and once you reach the summit, a quite different landscape can be glimpsed below. Through the clouds and rain, the sun shines down on the gentle corn, sheep and cattle fields of the Dee valley. As you begin the descent towards this comforting farmscape, you enter the parish of Birse. Here are 31,500 acres (equivalent to more than thirteen Richmond Parks lying side by side). Much is rich farmland – large, fenced or walled fields around the wide valley of the salmon-heavy Dee; but close at hand are two other types of landscape – huge blocks of conifers covering gently undulating land and, glowering to the south, the great, wild heather moorlands of the Forest of Birse, which is part of the massif from which the Dee springs.

For the eastern Highlands, Birse appears well populated: the roads and lower hill slopes are scattered with small dwellings (usually of one storey with dormer windows in the roof, in the Scottish estate-cottage style). In fact, however, the population of Birse is only about 540. Most of the families own their houses, but since these come with only about a quarter of an acre apiece, these dwelling areas do not account for more than a tiny percentage of Birse's land. In 1980, there was one owner-occupied farm of 470 acres. The other farms were tenanted and together with the forests, the deer lands and grouse moor and the river were the property of four untitled barons. These men were:

i) Charles Pearson, the owner of the 9,000-acre Birse estate, who comes closest to the titled aristocracy of any Birse baron. Born in 1956, as the younger son of the 3rd Viscount Cowdray, Mr Pearson is denied the inheritance of the title and the family's polo-famous Cowdray Park estate in West Sussex. The Cowdrays bought Birse in 1911 from a London-based American. Lord Cowdray sold the Birse estate to his son Charles in 1978, and it remains a small part of the hundreds of square miles the family own in Scotland.

ii) Angus Farquharson, the owner of the 7,900-acre Finzean estate, is the 13th Farquharson laird of Finzean. The Farquharsons already had kinsmen owning extensive tracts of Deeside when they first settled at Birse in 1580.

iii) The third estate of Birse, Ballogie, was also owned by the Farquharsons for many years, but in 1852 the sisters who had succeeded to this estate sold it to James Dyce Nicol. The estate, which now covers 6,000 acres, has remained ever since with the Nicols, who can trace their position as major landowners to James Nicol, who rose from tenant farmer to overseer on the Arbuthnott estate in Kincardineshire in the eighteenth century. His grandson made the family rich by developing tea plantations in India; when he returned to Britain in 1839 it was to become MP for Dover, a JP and Deputy Lord Lieutenant for Kincardineshire. His son, in his turn, was able, after a spell in Bombay, to buy up more land in Scotland.

iv) The final untitled baron of Birse is Hugh Cochran, the fifth generation of the Cochrans to own the 450-acre Balfour estate. Francis Cochran, an Aberdeen lawyer, first bought the estate in 1840 from its previous owner the Earl of Aboyne.

One point illustrated at Birse is that the ownership of the large estates has not been decimated by death duties as it is often imagined to have been. The reverse proves to be the case. In 1700, the land of Birse was divided between fifteen owners. The eighteenth century saw the concentration of this land into four estates, and that situation has continued into the last quarter of the twentieth century. The period since 1801, when the first census of the parish was taken, has, however, seen a marked reduction in the population of the parish – from 1,266 in that year to 541 in 1980.

Just like their titled counterparts, the untitled barons surface in almost every corner of Britain's countryside – and in the most unexpected places. On the southern edge of Luton, that grey industrial conurbation of 200,000 souls, extend the lakes, woods, park and farmland of Luton Hoo crowned by a stately mansion that houses a valuable art collection. This splendid symbol of inherited privilege is the property of Nicholas Phillips. Mr Phillips, who was born in 1947, owes his position as owner of Luton Hoo to his great-grandfather, Sir Julius Wernher. Sir Julius made a fortune from gold- and diamond-mining in South Africa in the latter part of the nineteenth century and used part of this money to buy Luton Hoo in 1903. But perhaps because the Phillipses and Wernhers have not been long established in Bedfordshire they have held relatively few positions of political power in the county – although Nicholas Phillips is a deputy lieutenant of the county.

Drive out of the opposite side of Luton, and nine miles to the north you find yourself amid the woods, well-timbered hedge-rows, private parklands and estate villages belonging to another of Bedfordshire's untitled barons, Samuel Charles Whitbread. In contrast to Nicholas Phillips's family, the Whitbreads have held so many positions of political power in the county that at one time it was known as 'Whitbreadshire'. Three former Samuel Whitbreads of Southill represented the people of Bedford or South Bedfordshire in Parliament and the present owner's father and great-grandfather were leading members of Bedfordshire County Council. The present Samuel Charles Whitbread has also served as a county councillor, with seven years as chairman of the Leisure Committee, which helps set countryside policy for the county. At 10,800 acres, the Southill estate is as big today as it was seven generations ago when Samuel Whitbread I, the founder of the brewing firm, bought it for his son.

It would be wrong, however, to conclude from these two Bedfordshire examples that the untitled barons are all relative newcomers to land ownership compared to their titled cousins. Peter Giffard, who was president of the Country Landowners' Association between 1983 and 1985, is the twenty-eighth member of his family to own the 4,000-acre Chillington estate in Staffordshire. His forebear, Walter Giffard, was William the Conqueror's standard-bearer at the Battle of Hastings.

What distinguishes the history of most of the untitled landowners from that of the landed aristocracy is that their rise to prominence, although the result of similar forces, was normally a little less straightforward. The services for which the present family's ancestors were rewarded may have been a shade less glamorous. Or they may owe their holdings not to the proud line of primogeniture but to the energies of a young son who managed to beat the system. Or they may have acquired land through marriage – like John Greenwood, whose wife Penelope inherited a 4,000-acre estate at Balcombe in Sussex from her grandmother. Mr Greenwood has been High Sheriff of West Sussex since 1971 and sat on the County Council from 1973 until 1985.

Some of the untitled large landowning families, like the forebears of the Whitbreads, the Watneys or the Wills tobacco family, have simply bought into land. In 1855, to take another example, Michael Williams MP invested £170,000 in land, including £50,000 with which he bought Caerhays Castle near Mevagissey and its associated land. Like many of Cornwall's present-day landowning magnates, the Williams fortune was founded in mining. Overlooking Porthlune Cove and the little river that runs into it, the romantic, battlemented and turretted Caerhays Castle is backed by extensive private woods that run northwards up the valley side. The estate's present owner, Julian Williams, is a member of the Council that advises the Prince of Wales on the running of the Duchy of Cornwall. Since 1980, he has also been chairman of Cornwall County Council.

The untitled barons tend to share many of the characteristics of the landed aristocracy – such as a shared delight in blood-sports. For sixteen years until 1982, the chairman of the British Fieldsports Society, which exists to preserve bloodsports in Britain, was Sir Marcus Kimball. The Member of Parliament for Lincolnshire (Gainsborough), Sir Marcus follows in the tradition of Britain's large landowners in maintaining an estate in Scotland (in his case 60,000 acres of Sutherland) to which he and his family repair at the end of each summer to stalk deer.

A mission to keep their land in their family's ownership for ever is characteristic of the untitled barons as well as their ennobled counterparts. Commander Michael Saunders-Watson, whose 4,000-acre Rockingham Castle estate on the outskirts of Corby in Northamptonshire has been owned by members of his family since 1530, is a typical enough member of the breed. His ancestor Edward Watson added greatly to the family's wealth and influence through a judicious marriage, and it was probably through the influence of his father-in-law, Sir Edward Montagu of Boughton, that Edward Watson obtained from Henry VIII a lease on Rockingham Castle and Park. In the nineteenth century, a large part of the estate was sold by its owners to finance Grand Tours. But since he was given the estate by his uncle in 1967, Commander Saunders-Watson has sold very little indeed. Below the castle lies the little village of Rockingham with a population of only 123. In 1982 when I visited Rockingham, Commander Saunders-Watson owned all the housing in the village (seven-teenth- and eighteenth-century cottages and houses along a main road) except for a small council estate behind it and one house that his uncle had sold – forty-three houses in all. Commander Saunders-Watson told me he had never agreed to sell a village dwelling.

Part of the reason for the convergence of the attitudes and behaviour of the titled and the untitled is that the mechanisms that hold the aristocracy together apply equally to the next grade down. Intermarriage and the influence of a particular group of schools bind members of both groups to other members of their own group and to the other group. They do not try to preserve any wall around the aristocracy. For example, Nicholas Phillips's sister Natalia is the Duchess of Westminster; while Commander Saunders-Watson, is distantly related by marriage to the Duke of Buccleuch, the Duke of Rutland, Countess Fitzwilliam, Barons Monson, Feversham and Nugent, Earl Sondes and the Earl of Sandwich.

Owner-Occupier Farmers

Most of the 87 per cent of Britain's land that is in private hands and which is not owned by the titled or untitled barons is controlled by owner-occupier farmers. These people differ from the titled aristocrats and untitled barons in that their relationship with their land is more direct and less complicated: they need it to farm it, rather than farming it because this happens to be a way of realizing wealth from an asset they own.

This does not, however, make the owner-occupier farmer the blameless hero of our story. In his case, as in those of his betters, there are one or two myths which need to be dispelled.

It is the owner-occupier farmer who is the most widely celebrated in popular mythology of all the owners of Britain's countryside. Epitomized by the late Dan Archer, he is seen as working long hours for little financial reward. He is, however, compensated for a lack of material comforts by the close contact he enjoys with the sights and sounds of nature and country life, which to him, bluff and manly figure though he is, are dear indeed. He is trustworthy and reliable, and, were the countryside to reside in his hands, we need have no fears for its future. Even in 'The Archers' a more threateningly aggressive and self-seeking figure like Phil Archer sometimes hoves into view. However, the good sense and decency of his peers ensures that he is kept firmly in his place and prevented from disturbing the order of the rustic scene. Sometimes the jolly farmer can turn into a bit of a moaner who runs a Merc and a Jag while complaining that the weather is bankrupting him. Yet even here the underlying good humour of the farmer normally bursts through in the end.

It is this image of the friendly and reliable family farmer that the landowners themselves work hardest to promote. Their pressure group, the Country Landowners' Association (CLA), whose objective is to preserve private land ownership in Britain in the form in which it exists at present, makes a point of concentrating attention on the small landowner. Whether it is putting forward people to appear on television programmes, issuing press releases or giving evidence to government commissions and committees, it is the image of the small businessman which it tends to project. 'The closer the owner of land, whether owner-occupier or resident landlord, is identified with the small working farmer, the less the likelihood that he will have to bear the brunt of political attack arising from envy,' explained the CLA in 1976, in a document entitled *The Future of Landownership*.[22] Typically, then, when the CLA submitted evidence to a Select Committee of the House of Commons inquiring in 1975 into the feasibility of introducing a tax on wealth, the Association pointed out:

There are no comprehensive statistics on the size of unit of ownership. From the available evidence it is a reasonable conclusion however that few large estates in private hands have survived and of those that have, the majority are but a fraction of their former size. Conversely the numbers of owner-occupiers have increased . . . Land ownership has already become more widely distributed and the process is continuing . . .

Small privately owned businesses, and landowning and food production are businesses, are an integral and essential part of life in this country. Indeed small firms are the most vigorous part of the economy and when successful not only they but the community at large benefits . . . If the Government decides that no individual has a right to own more than a certain amount of productive assets, it will be a fundamental attack on the freedom of the individual and will be doing the nation a disservice.

It is easy to see why the yeoman farmer stereotype persists and even easier to see why the landowners foster this image of themselves. But it is less representative than is usually imagined.

If the typical UK farm were indeed a small business, we should expect the average size of farm to be small. But when we calculate the average size of farm holding – a figure that includes the very many tiny units, part-time holdings and tenant farms, the average turns out to be high. In 1983, the average size of farm holdings in the United Kingdom was 170 acres – far higher than the figure in any of the other member countries of the European Community. Farms in West Germany, for instance, with an average size of thirty-eight acres, were only one-fifth the average size of those in the UK, while the average farm holding in Italy was only one-tenth. France had the second largest average size of farm holding. But this (at sixty-three acres) was only just over one-third of the size of the UK average.[24]

As it is, the British figure would be even higher if holdings in Northern Ireland or tenanted farms were excluded. In Northern Ireland, the land revolution at the end of the nineteenth century left what had been large landed estates in the hands of former tenants who became freeholders in holding units that are on average only about 38 per cent of the average size of those in the UK as a whole. In mainland Britain, about 40 per cent of farmland is let out to tenant farmers on long leases. A figure for the average size of a freehold land ownership unit in Great Britain would be even more out of line with that in the rest of Western Europe (where the proportion of leased land is very much less).

Overall, Great Britain's farmland does include many small units. In 1983, 39.6 per cent of Britain's farm holdings (85,948 out of 216,929) were smaller than fifty acres. Yet all these holdings together amount to only 4 per cent of the farmland of Britain. So in 1983, 96 per cent of our farmland was held in units of more than fifty acres apiece. Farms of between fifty and 494 acres took up 48 per cent of the farmland of Britain; while the 6.6 per cent of farm holdings of more than 494 acres occupied 47 per cent of our farmland. This is not to say that there are no small family farmers in Britain akin to the stereotype so carefully fostered by landowners. There are many of them. The key point to remember is, however, that they control only a tiny fraction of our land.

Of course, some of the farms in the larger size groups in particular will be in the hands of the two groups of private owner we have considered already. What do we know of those men and women who farm the land direct as owner-occupier farmers and whose holdings do not consist of much else?

Many of the present generation of owner-occupiers moved into farming either as tenants or freehold owners during the 1940s or '50s. At this time, farmland was relatively cheap to buy; and tenants could often buy the land they farmed if it came up for sale at far below the market rate. Other owner-occupier farming families today are the descendants of the former tenant

farmers who acquired the freehold of the land they had hitherto
rented during the great land sales at the beginning of the
twentieth century.

Now, however, easy transition from tenant to freeholder is a
thing of the past. Agriculture has become a gold-mine since the
1950s, so land prices have risen. Those best placed to pay the
higher prices are those who have been in on the gold-rush.
Increasingly, Britain's owner-occupier farmers are becoming a
class closed to all but a fortunate few.

What this means is that ownership of Britain's farmland is not
becoming more widely distributed through the population than
it has been in the past. Owner-occupier farms remain in fewer
and fewer hands. Where small owner-occupier farmers sell up,
their place is often taken not by a new small man, but by
existing farmers sufficiently enriched by the agricultural gold-
rush to be able to expand their holdings. At the same time, the
openings for those who want to rent farmland are diminishing.
The ratio of rented to owner-occupied farmland in Great Britain
has changed from 62:38 in 1950 to 40:60 in 1983. In many cases,
where a tenant farmer gives up farming or his tenancy falls
vacant for some other reason, the landlord either merges that
unit with another tenanted farm or he takes it in hand and farms
the land direct himself or through a farm manager along with
any other land he is already farming himself.

One man who has witnessed the relentless increase in farm
size at first-hand is Suffolk farmer Anthony Stocker. Anthony
Stocker, a doctor's son, discovered an interest in growing things
during the war, and decided when peace came to Britain, to put
this interest into practice through becoming a farmer. In 1951,
he and his wife Sheila bought a twenty-five acre farm at Cowlinge
in north Essex for £3,500 and tried their hand at raising pigs,
then cows, sugar beet, strawberries, wheat and barley. In 1958,
they sold the farm at Cowlinge and bought a sixty-acre farm at
Stradbrooke in Suffolk. This second farm appreciated in value
from £5,000 to £8,000 during the three years Mr and Mrs
Stocker used it to rear dairy cattle and grow cereals. Their third
farm, 183 acres in size west of Long Melford in Suffolk, cost
£20,000 when they bought it in 1961 and £300,000 when they
sold it in 1980. With their children grown up, the Stockers

moved in 1980 to a smallholding (twenty-eight acres outside Framlingham including fourteen acres of deciduous woodland) where they grow vines, Christmas trees and flowers for seed.

Each of the three farms which the Stockers occupied during their farming career had been included in much larger units by 1986. Their first farm of twenty-five acres is now part of a 200-acre unit; their second farm is now part of a 300-acre unit and their third part of a 1,200-acre farm. In each case, the old farmhouse has been sold off separately from the farm as a private residence. This feature of the process would make it difficult to reverse the trend towards amalgamation: if now large farms were to redivide, reverting to their former boundaries, there would be no farmhouse for the would-be small farmers.

The Stocker case also shows clearly how the rise in land prices has changed the prospects for would-be entrants to farming. It is now much harder for doctors' sons with a feel for growing things to become farmers, as Mr Stocker did – unless they already happen to be able to lay hands on several hundred thousand pounds.

The impression created by the Stocker snapshot is borne out by the findings of Howard (now Professor) Newby and a team of researchers from Essex University who conducted a detailed sample survey in the mid-1970s. The team talked to farmers from forty-four parishes around Framlingham in mid-Suffolk and conducted another sample survey of all holdings in Norfolk, Suffolk, Cambridgeshire and Essex over 1,000 acres in size. Some of these farmers, particularly those operating on a large-scale, included titled and untitled barons. However, many of the Newby respondents were owner-occupier farmers, and his is the only research available which gives an indication of the personal characteristics, the origins and the position in rural society of owner-occupier farmers.

The Newby team discovered that existing farmers tend to come from farming families; almost 80 per cent of those in the 1,000+ acres sample and nearly three-quarters of those in the forty-four parishes had fathers who were farmers themselves. And it was the family connection more than any other single thing that had enabled the people interviewed to become farmers. Professor Newby and his team write:

When we examine the source of capital which enabled our respondents to become farmers in their own right, the family looms large whether in terms of the inheritance of land or cash to buy land, or in the form of interest-free family loans or straight cash gifts to set up a farm. It is very much a minority who either first made money outside farming and used this as their source of capital or genuinely climbed the farming ladder by thrift, business acumen and the aid of bank loans or loans from the Agricultural Mortgage Corporation.[26]

Seventy per cent of the farmers in the 1,000 acres and above sample and 60 per cent of those in the forty-four parishes sample had inherited the land they farmed.

But Professor Newby and his team did not look only at the origins of their interviewees; they also looked at the personal characteristics of the farmers as a group. The picture they paint is of a relatively closed world, with farmers not only being farmers' sons but often marrying farmers' daughters. They tended to go to local public schools, have a spell at agricultural college and then go straight back to the family farm to work, often in partnership with their fathers, never entering a world in which they would have to sell their labour. Even for rural folk, Professor Newby's interviewees were a clannish crowd: intermarriage with the families of agricultural workers, for instance, was almost unknown.

Professor Newby's research helps build up a picture of a section of the landowning class with a clear identity of its own. But although distinct, this identity is not greatly at variance with that of the bigger and more powerful landowners. In their smaller way, the owner-occupiers share the attitudes of the aristocrats, and because the agriculture industry has become so lucrative they have been able to pursue similar aspirations, for example the desire to take up public positions in rural society.

Take these two entirely typical examples. Peter Blaxell comes from a long-standing farming family in Hickling on the northern edge of Norfolk's Broadland. Like many farmers in the Broads, Mr Blaxell's freehold land, which in 1978 covered between 250 and 300 acres, is part 'upland' or arable land and part lower-lying marshland, much of which he has drained. And, like many farmers, Mr Blaxell is active in local politics. A parish councillor, he has been a member of North Norfolk District Council since 1976 and the chairman of its development committee since

1984. Although farmers comprised only 2 per cent of the adult population of North Norfolk District, they made up 26 per cent of the membership of the District Council in November 1985.

Peter Blaxell also wields considerable influence over rural land through his position as vice-chairman of the Smallburgh Internal Drainage Board, which plans and oversees land drainage over 11,000 acres of the Norfolk Broads. He is also a member of the Broads Authority, the joint committee of local authorities set up in 1978 to try to salvage the attractions of the Broads after decades of environmental neglect. In 1986 35 per cent of the members of the Broads Authority were farmers or landowners like Peter Blaxell.

Across the Irish Sea, farmer Robert Hanna has shown similar civic energy. An active member of the Ulster Farmers' Union (he is a past president of the Union and in 1986, for instance, sat on two of the Union's national committees), Mr Hanna owned 170 acres of dairy land in County Londonderry when I talked to him in 1982 – a land-holding which would be considered on the small side in Great Britain but which is large by Northern Ireland standards. Two influential organizations in rural affairs of which Mr Hanna has been a long-standing member are, first, the Planning Appeals Commission – an independent body set up to determine planning appeals and to hold inquiries and hearings. Members are appointed by the Secretary of State for Northern Ireland, and Mr Hanna has been one of these ever since the Commission was first established in 1973. Eight years earlier, in 1965, the second organization, the Ulster Countryside Committee, was set up. Mr Hanna came on to the Committee when it was first established and has remained a member ever since; since 1975 he has been its chairman. The Ulster Countryside Committee is the only statutory body advising the Department of the Environment in Belfast on all matters relating to countryside conservation and outdoor recreation provision in the Province, including the designation of areas of outstanding natural beauty and the development of country parks.

Northern Ireland – A Special Case

If the portrait of typical ownership by the small-scale owner-occupier farmer is not true of the United Kingdom as a whole, there is however one area where it is typical – Northern Ireland. Ulster provides a complete contrast to the pattern of land ownership on the British mainland, a contrast which demonstrates how different things might be.

The tenant-led revolution of the 1880s which led to the 'break-up' of the large British-owned estates effectively purged the large landowner from the Province. Holdings in Northern Ireland average sixty acres in size – compared with 280 acres in Great Britain. They are also mainly owner-occupied, since the graziers or capitalist tenant farmers were overthrown in the nineteenth century as well as the large landlords.

Even in Ulster, however, the descendants of the owners of the large landed estates have by no means been completely wiped out. Although the purpose of the land reforms – to replace the landlords of the old plantation estates with their former tenants – has indeed been largely effected, the descendants of the former landlords have shown a remarkable ability to hold on to at least some land. Some of them have kept a foothold in the Province through retaining ownership of the home farm, demesne lands and woodland round the great house – land which was not tenanted and so not subject to the nineteenth-century land reforms. The Earl of Abercorn holds on to Baronscourt, the Earl of Erne still owns Crom Castle, the Duke of Westminster still owns Ely Lodge in Fermanagh, the Earl of Antrim still owns Glenarm Castle and Lord O'Neill still owns Shane's Castle. And some of the old landlord families have also retained certain rights over parts of their families' former estates even though they no longer enjoy ownership of them.

Throughout the United Kingdom, alongside freehold rights to land, are other rights which may or may not lie with the same owner – such as the right to work minerals, to shoot game and take fish. What happened to these rights in Northern Ireland while the former tenants were acquiring the freehold of the land they had rented? The right to cut turf for fuel (turbary rights) usually passed automatically to the former tenant; these rights had always gone with farm tenancies since if a family could not cut turf for their own use as fuel they could not survive. In addition, former tenants round the coast kept the right to take seaweed and the right to take sand for their own use. But the landlords retained mineral, timber, fishing and shooting rights, and many of these rights are still in the hands of the old landowning families.[27]

Lough Neagh, which covers 100,000 acres and is from fourteen to sixteen miles long and from six to eight miles broad, is the largest inland lake in the United Kingdom and one of the largest in Europe. Fishing rights in the Lough were originally acquired by Sir Arthur Chichester, Lord Deputy of Ireland at the time of Charles II, and they have passed down through his family so that today they are the property of the 10th Earl of Shaftesbury, who lives in Dorset.

Perhaps more typical is the case of Dick Blakiston-Houston. Mr Blakiston-Houston, who comes from a former landlord family in the Province, owns shooting rights over about 15,000 acres of land he does not own but which adjoin his 240-acre farm and 150-acre woodland in County Down just east of Belfast. In addition, through land purchase by his father of certain rights held by another former landlord family, the Cole-Hamiltons, he also owns the shooting rights over 22,000 acres of County Tyrone.

Oddballs

There are of course some types of landowner who do not fit into any of the categories mentioned so far. Some of these own enough land to command considerable influence, locally.

THE NATIONAL TRUST

From its formation in 1895, the National Trust has been intended to bring to land ownership an approach quite different in character from that of other British landowners. Its object is not profit, but the preservation of land (and buildings) for the nation. In 1986, the National Trust owned 532,657 acres in England, Wales and Northern Ireland. (The separate National Trust for Scotland owned 100,000 acres.) A further 76,742 acres of England, Wales and Northern Ireland were covenanted to the National Trust.

Although hundreds of properties have come into the hands of

the two Trusts since they were formed, the proportion of land in the UK in their hands is still small – exactly 1 per cent of the total. The Trust's acres do tend to embrace much of the United Kingdom's most beautiful and spectacular scenery. And they receive a high level of protection: almost all Trust land is inalienable, which means that no government department, local authority or any other agency may compulsorily acquire it without first winning Parliament's approval – a higher safeguard then applies to any other land in the UK.

Nowadays, National Trust properties fall into three main categories: the open spaces (like commons and including more than 100,000 acres along the coast); country houses and their contents with adjoining parks; and larger stretches of countryside often combining farmed countryside with woodland. Properties come from three main sources. They may be given or bequeathed by a landowner – like the late Ralph Bankes whose bequest to the Trust in 1982 of Kingston Lacy House and 16,000 acres of superb countryside in Dorset was the single largest gift of land the Trust has ever received. Nowadays all gifts and bequests to the Trust of money, land or chattels are exempted from capital gains tax and inheritance tax. Other properties are bought by the Trust with money it is given – like the one thousand £1 notes from a retired Lancashire mill-worker which helped buy the Aberglaslyn Pass in Caernarvonshire in 1944. Yet other properties come to the Trust in lieu of inheritance tax (formerly capital transfer tax and before that death duties), since the Treasury is empowered to accept and then hand over to the National Trust land, buildings or chattels (like works of art) instead of cash as payment of this tax. Hardwick Hall in Derbyshire, for instance, built in 1507 by Bess Hardwick, a forebear of the Dukes of Devonshire, came with adjoining land to the Trust as part settlement of death duties in 1944.

The Trust has no powers of compulsory purchase, so land of outstanding national importance which cannot be acquired by one of these three routes is not acquired at all. For example, the Trust had long had its eye on Land's End and the adjoining coastal heathland, but when the land eventually came on to the market in 1982, it was outbid by property millionaire David Goldstone. In some other places, the Trust has to satisfy itself with ownership of only part of what it would like. Although the Trust would dearly like to own Clandon Park in Surrey, for example, it can do no more than hope that the 7th Earl of Onslow will some day part with it. At Clandon, the Trust owns only fourteen acres comprising the house, garden and a car-park. The house overlooks a beautiful stretch of parkland with a lake but when I visited in 1982 it was all fenced off with a prohibitive warning. The family was prepared to give the Trust the house, which the Trust completely restored and furnished (it had been unoccupied for some time); over the park in front of the house and the lake the Trust has to accept no more than restrictive covenants preventing any major landscape change, but a denial of public access.

The National Trust stands apart from other landowners not only in terms of its objectives but also in its mode of operation. For instance, it employs its own breed of agents to run its estates and does not rely on the established land agents to whom private and many institutional and public landowners turn. Yet the Trust does not operate in a vacuum. Its half-a-million acres are dotted through a countryside dominated by private landowners. And not surprisingly it has strong links with the landowning class.

There are not many landowners on the National Trust Council which ultimately controls the Trust. Half the members are elected from the Trust's 1.32 million members while the other half (almost all of whom are worthies from fields other than landowning) are nominated by relevant organizations like the Society for the Protection of Ancient Buildings and the British Ecological Society. Landowners do, however, figure prominently on the fourteen regional committees which do the Trust's work on the ground. In 1986, seven of the chairmen of these commit-tees were major landowners. In addition, the chairman of the important national properties committee was large-scale York-shire landowner Sir Marcus Worsley (Sir Marcus is also a leading Church Estate Commissioner); while other landowners chaired the Trust's conservation, estates, gardens and architec-tural national panels, which advise the properties committee on the purchase and care of land and buildings.

The Trust does, of course, need links with the landowning

class to enhance its prospects of acquiring the properties it wants and discovering what properties are coming on to the market. But these links do give it an air of appearing to share some of the attitudes of the landowning class.

Take bloodsports. Where a donor of land to the Trust expresses no view on hunting, shooting or fishing, if any of these activities is customarily pursued in the area and has been pursued on the particular stretch of land involved regularly in the past, so long as the Trust does not consider the activity is doing any damage to wildlife, then it is Trust policy to allow the hunting, shooting or fishing to continue to take place over its land. The Trust sees this as part of its 'good neighbour' policy in the countryside – even though a large proportion of its members might, if polled on the subject, be expected to oppose hunting and shooting on Trust land. As a result of this policy, hunting occurs over about a third of the farm and estate land the Trust owns in its southern region (Surrey, West Sussex, the Isle of Wight and Hampshire), for instance.[28]

Perhaps the most striking way in which established landowners maintain their influence in Trust property lies in the practice of allowing the previous owner to remain in residence after he has passed his land (together with the responsibility for upkeep) to the Trust.

Petworth in West Sussex is a good example of the way in which give-and-take between an established landowner and the National Trust works out in practice. Petworth was owned by the 3rd Lord Leconfield, whose family had acquired the estate by marriage in 1750 along with land at Cockermouth in Cumbria and other estates as well as the Earldom of Egremont. When the Trust took over Petworth in 1947, the deal was that in return for a one-off endowment of £0.25 million to help maintain the house, Lord Leconfield and his heirs could go on living in the south wing of this vast mansion in perpetuity. The Trust now owns the house itself and the surrounding 700-acre deer park. When Lord Leconfield died in 1963 no death duty was payable on this land since it was owned by the Trust; his heir, Lord Egremont, has been entitled to live at Petworth since then under the original agreement. Although Lord Leconfield's endowment helps to maintain the property, the Trust, as owners, are responsible for maintaining the house, the park and the house's contents and carrying out major repairs like re-roofing. However, Lord Leconfield did not give all his Petworth estate to the Trust: he retained a 12,000-acre area of land which Lord Egremont is free to use as he wishes.

At West Wycombe in Buckinghamshire too, the family has retained ownership of the 4,000-acre estate outside the house and park together with the right to go on living in the house. The present owner, Sir Francis Dashwood, regrets the fact that his father handed the house and park over to the Trust. According to *Sunday Telegraph* reporter Graham Turner who interviewed him in 1983, he dislikes the presence of the public, and has therefore tried to develop attractions other than the house itself – a garden centre and a series of caves filled with talking waxwork figures from the family's history. He has placed these together with a car-park across a main road from the house, his avowed aim being 'sucking people off from the house and keeping them happy'.[29] The money Sir Francis has made in the City and through land speculation in Australia now enables him to live in the style which his ancestors expected of him without the additional expense of maintaining his house.

When the Trust takes over land, it frequently takes on board any existing tenants working the land. At Mottisfont alongside the River Test in Hampshire, although the donor no longer lives there, the Trust has inherited several of the agricultural, fishing and shooting tenancies, with all the implications these have for land management and public access. Again, at the Trust's 2,500-acre Drovers estate outside Chichester in neighbouring West Sussex, Lord Benson, a former adviser to the Bank of England, has shooting rights.

The rules under which sporting rights and tenancies operate limit the Trust's opportunities to change the régime of the properties it comes to own. Most agricultural tenancies run a lifetime. During their term, all the Trust can do to alter agricultural practices is try to negotiate better clauses. It does not necessarily succeed.

The influence of past owners and existing tenants does not however prevent the National Trust from creating a very different model of land ownership from the norm in rural Britain: it gives a hint of what the countryside might be like if priority were to be accorded to conservation and public access rather than the very different concerns of most other landowners.

THE CHURCH OF ENGLAND

In 1529 Henry VIII snatched the lands and wealth of what was then the single largest landowner in his kingdom – the Church. By 1972, the Church of England had recovered its lost ground sufficiently to be rated in a BBC survey as the tenth largest landowner in Britain.[30] Thirteen years later, in 1985, the Church of England's farm and forest land covered 170,000 acres and attracted a market value of £173 million.

Anybody expecting a particularly Christian approach to the management of these lands would however be disappointed. The Church does not deploy its lands for the furtherance of the public good. It uses them to alleviate its considerable financial problems. Every year the Church of England has to find over £100 million to pay its ministers and to provide them with housing and pensions on retirement. Church property – not just agricultural land but also commercial and residential property in cities – is seen as one of the means of raising the necessary cash. In 1985 the Church Commissioners, who are responsible for the redistribution of wealth within the Church, supported their clergy through a net profit of £45.1 million from their land and other property. The rest came from profits from shares (38.8 million), contributions from Church members (£47.2 million) and interest on loans (£9.6 million).[31]

The most valuable part of the Church's property portfolio in terms of net income are its offices, which generated £20.1 million in 1985. Property in the United States as well as shops, housing and industrial land and buildings each also generated several millions of pounds in 1985. Farm rents and the exploitation of minerals produced a net profit of £7.5 million.

The Church's farms are highly profitable, and their profitability is being further enhanced. History left the Church with a distinctly scattered estate – stretches of land lying wherever a private owner happened to have bequeathed it some property. The Church Commissioners are working to consolidate this estate, selling off unprofitable outlying lands (the Church now owns no hill farms in Wales, for instance) and buying up more lucrative ones closer to its existing holdings. The Church spent £1 million in 1983, for example, on selective purchases of good quality land adjoining its existing estates, while selling isolated and less potentially lucrative properties. In 1982, Sir Ronald Harris, who had been First Church Estate Commissioner in the late 1970s, explained the Church's attitude to farmland to author Richard Norton-Taylor: 'Agricultural land has undoubtedly proved one of the best forms of investment from the point of view of both preserving and enhancing capital value and securing a reliable and growing income, and this must surely be the main incentive for an institution to own farmland.'[32]

Farm rents on Church property are on a par with the rents charged by other landlords, and between 1972 and 1982 the Church increased the rents to its farm tenants by 208 per cent (dividends from shares rose by only 71 per cent over the same period).[33] All in all, then, the pursuit of profit pushes the Church into behaviour none too different from that of other larger landowners.

THE CROWN ESTATE

Who owns the sea-bed round the 2,500-mile-long coast of the United Kingdom out to the limit of territorial waters? Who is therefore in a position as landowner to charge others for the privilege of laying pipelines over this land, extracting minerals from it, dredging sand, building marinas and jetties and establishing fish farms? Who is also the owner of the bed and banks of all Britain's tidal rivers, such as the Severn, the Clyde, the Tyne and the Thames? Not the British people, either as individuals or collectively through local or central government. This land – together with a great deal more above the high-water mark – is the property of the Queen. As Sovereign she has inherited an estate that dates back to the time of the Saxon King Edward the Confessor, known as the Crown Estate. When she came to the throne, she could have kept the estate as her own and held it as a private citizen. If she had, she and her family would have had to forego the Civil List, the money Parliament allocates to the

Royal Family each year for the staff salaries and other expenses of the Royal Household. Instead, the Queen chose to continue the practice started by George III two hundred years ago of passing to Parliament the net receipts derived from rents, mineral royalties and so on from the Crown Estate and receiving in return fixed annual sums in the shape of the Civil List for herself and all other members of the Royal Family (except the Prince and Princess of Wales, who have income from the Duchy of Cornwall).

It is open to the Queen's successor to terminate this arrangement when he or she attains the throne and to appropriate the income from the Crown Estates. In view of the fuss over the Queen's regular 'pay rises' which the Civil List system seems to provoke, such a step might have its attractions. In the year ending 31 March 1986, the revenue to the Exchequer from the Crown Estate was £26.5 million (an increase of 9 per cent over the previous year), while only £5 million was paid out through the Civil List during 1985. Not that the Civil List covers all the costs associated with the Royal Family, however. Buckingham Palace and Windsor Castle are maintained separately by the taxpayer through annual payments from the Department of the Environment, while revenue from the Duchy of Lancaster, which is the other main estate owned by the Queen because she is sovereign but which is not surrendered to the Treasury, goes to feed and clothe Her Majesty.

In the main, the Crown Estate is an accumulation of land that has come to the Crown by a variety of routes since about the tenth century.[34] At the time of his death, William the Conqueror owned an estimated one-quarter to one-third of the landed wealth of England. The Conqueror's successors sold or gave away much of this land, but other kings and queens bought other areas or came by land by other routes, for instance through the dissolution of the monasteries, or through escheat, by which the property of an owner who dies intestate or without heirs passes to the Crown. By 1986, the Crown Estate included 335,402 acres of farmland in England, Wales and Scotland and 38,285 acres of commercial forest.[35] The Crown Estate's urban lands, which provide about 60 per cent of its annual rental income, are widely spread. They include some of Britain's most lucrative sites – in Regent Street, Oxford Street, Kensington, St James's and Victoria – as well as profitable stretches of land in Richmond (Surrey), Edinburgh, Eltham, Egham, Ascot, Bagshot, Oxshott, Devizes, Taunton, Bingham (Nottinghamshire) and Swinley (Berkshire). Two hundred and sixty-six acres of chiefly residential land in Windsor town is also owned by the Crown Estate; the Windsor Estate alone, which also includes the Great Park, Home Park, two farms and much woodland, covers 12,378 acres.

Apart from the tidal rivers and continental shelf, the Queen as owner of the Crown Estate also owns about half of the foreshore of the United Kingdom. (Over the years, the Crown Estate has made grants of part of the foreshore to other owners, while the foreshore around the coasts of Lancashire and Cornwall is the property respectively of the Queen in her capacity as Duke of Lancaster and of the Prince of Wales as Duke of Cornwall.)

The land the Queen owns is by no means confined to the Crown Estate. As a private citizen, she is the owner of 50,000 acres at Balmoral in the eastern Highlands, forty-eight acres at Buckingham Palace and 20,000 acres at Sandringham in north Norfolk. The Duchy of Lancaster covers 50,000 acres of land together with the foreshore of Lancashire.

The Queen does not, of course, have time to see to the day-to-day running of her vast domains; to run the Crown Estate she has appointed eight Crown Estate Commissioners. These men are given a wide measure of freedom under the Crown Estate Act, 1961 to buy, sell and lease land (leases to be for no longer than 150 years) and generally to manage the estate with the overall objective of maintaining and enhancing its value and the return from it, but with due regard to the requirements of good management. The only exception relates to Windsor Forest and Park where the Commissioners are charged with maintaining its character as a royal forest and park, and where they may not sell any land unless it is needed for development by a public authority.

Who are the men the Queen appoints to manage this vast estate of land, river, shore and sea-bed? Are they drawn from backgrounds likely to produce a view of land management different from that of the private landowners among whom they operate? The answer is no. The Crown Estate Commissioners

are drawn from backgrounds likely to reproduce on the Crown
Estate exactly the sort of approach to the use of land and the
relationship between landowner and the rest of society as that
evolved over thousands of years on Britain's large private landed
estates. They are landowners themselves, or comparable figures
like the agents that administer large privately-owned landed
estates. In 1986, the First Commissioner and Chairman of the
Board was Scottish landowner the 8th Earl of Mansfield. The
Earl was reported to own 33,800 acres of Perthshire in 1970,[36]
though he told me in 1986 that this report was inaccurate. (He
would not give a figure of his own.) Three of the other eight
commissioners were also the owners of large private landed estates,
one of them a former president of the Country Landowners' Association. The other commissioners were two chartered surveyors (one
of whom has been a trustee of the Duke of Westminster's Grosvenor
Estate since 1971), a chartered accountant and a former high-
ranking official in the Ministry of Agriculture.

    Though the rental income from the Crown Estate goes into
the Exchequer, the people of Britain have less say in the decisions
of the Crown Estate Commissioners than they do in those of
most other landowners. For the Commissioners are accountable
only to the Queen, who appoints them and to whom they
present their annual report. This freedom from public scrutiny is
confirmed in law since the Crown Estate Act, 1961 lays down in
Section 1(5) that:

The validity of transactions entered into by the Commissioners shall
not be called into question on any suggestion of their not having acted
in accordance with the provisions of this Act regulating the exercise of
their powers, or of their having otherwise acted in excess of their
authority, nor shall any person dealing with the Commissioners be
concerned to inquire as to the extent of their authority or the observance
of any restrictions on the exercise of their powers.

    Since the Crown Estate Commissioners are answerable only
to the Queen, they are immune from the public accountability
through Parliament which applies at least in theory to landowners like the Ministry of Defence or the Ministry of Agriculture, though they share some of the special privileges enjoyed by
government departments in respect of land-use change. Thus

the Crown Estate – like government departments – is exempt from the planning controls that affect building, quarrying and the change of use of urban buildings. This is because it is a general rule of English law that the Crown is not bound by any statute unless that statute specifically says so. 'Crown land' includes land that belongs to a government department or which is held in trust for Her Majesty for the purposes of a government department. But it also includes land in which an interest belongs to the Queen because she is the monarch, and this includes not only the Crown Estate but also the Duchy of Lancaster and the Duchy of Cornwall. All three of these land-owners make it their practice to consult local planning authorities over proposals for which they would otherwise have to apply for planning consent, but they do not require the authorities' approval to proceed.

Two Nations: Landowners and Landless

Britain remains sharply divided between those citizens who own land and those who do not. Two examples.

In May 1981, unemployed, thirty-two-year-old Dave Batty walked from Hull to the Houses of Parliament to deliver a note to the Prime Minister drawing attention to the plight of the unemployed. Mr Batty, an ex-farmworker and ex-lorry driver had called at every Jobcentre along the way, but none had been able to offer work. As he waited in the Commons Central Lobby, he said: 'My idea of heaven would be ten acres of land. If I had that, I'd happily go away and not bother anyone about work ever again.'[37] The chances of Mr Batty getting his hands on ten acres of Britain are virtually nil. In 1981 that amount of land would have cost him about £17,000. No bank would have advanced him that sort of money because, although he could probably grow enough on ten acres to feed himself, his wife and his two children, he would not have had sufficient land to grow food for market and so would not have been able to repay a mortgage. Even if he were in work, on a farmworker's wages (£5,000 a year for a forty-six-hour-week in 1981), he would have had little hope of saving the sum he would need.

In August 1984 Simon George Strangways Morrison was

born. Baby Simon is the heir through his mother to a 3,000-acre Nottinghamshire estate with two mansions, 15,000 acres of Dorset centred on an imposing seventeenth-century mansion called Melbury House, as well as a valuable parcel of London bounded by Holland Park and Kensington High Street. Without any exertion on his part, Simon can look forward to joining a small élite whose grip upon the broad acres of rural Britain is as absolute as that of the Norman barons. Simon's good fortune is bad news for Dave Batty. But what does it mean for the people of Britain as a whole that the land is in the grip of a privileged few?

The answer to that question turns on the use to which Britain's landowners put their property. They turn out to be motivated by whims and aspirations reflecting the peculiar national experience of their breed. Three things obsess them above all: wealth, power and privacy.

PART THREE
What Landowners Want

4. Wealth

THESE DAYS MONEY DOES GROW ON TREES.

Headline for newspaper advertisement for the forestry company Fountain
Forestry in 1984.

It's a business like any other business and we've got our assets
and we've got to make the maximum profit from those assets.
Whatever that involves.

James Townsend, farm manager for the farming company Velcourt,
speaking on television, 1983[1]

Nowadays, rural land does not naturally come to mind as a
major source of wealth. We think of entertainers and businessmen
as our wealthiest citizens, while the stereotypical landowner is
an impoverished aristocrat scrimping to maintain his ancestral
home. In fact, however, two centuries after the Industrial Revolution, few assets can match rural land as a means of enrichment
and of providing the means for further enrichment. And Britain's
landowners are still the country's wealthiest group.

Less information is published on the financial circumstances
of our wealthiest citizens than on those of our poorest. In the
1970s, the Royal Commission on the Distribution of Income and
Wealth in Britain had begun to piece together an overall picture
of its subject when it was abolished in 1979, less than three
months after the Thatcher Government first came to power. An
interim report of the Commission in 1976, however, revealed
that the richest 1 per cent of Britain's population owned more
than half (52 per cent) of all personally owned land. A further 22
per cent of personally owned land was held by the next most
wealthy group, who made up between 2 and 5 per cent of the
population.[2]

Another glimpse of the real standing of landowners can be
obtained from an analysis of wealth in the post-war world by the

social scientist Dr W. D. Rubinstein.[3] He listed the ten people who left most money when they died in the period 1970–79. All left at least £5 million, and five of the ten were landowners: Thomas, 10th Earl Fitzwilliam, Archibald, 6th Earl of Rosebery, Thomas, 5th Earl of Leicester, Sir Richard Boughey, 10th Baronet and William, 7th Earl of Sefton (who owned property in Liverpool as well as land). The remaining five were two property developers, a ship-owner, Lord Rank the entertainment mogul and an Austrian count.

Of course some landowners are poor. But the figures reflect the overwhelming fact that landowning tends to make you rich.

The value of land springs first from its God-given assets, be they soil, water, trees or minerals. But another factor is at work as well: society's demands on the land in question. Clearly, a piece of land next to the M25 is likely to be of far greater value than a piece of land of the same size and similar natural resources in the Outer Hebrides.

The benefits bestowed by both God's gifts and man's needs can be sudden and dramatic. In 1984, the Brecon Beacons National Park Authority paid the Eagle Star Insurance Company £30,000 for a 23,000-acre stretch of common land in the heart of the Brecon Beacons. The same year, another 22,000-acre stretch of common not far away and similar to the first except in one respect – the presence beneath it of anthracite reserves – attracted a selling price of £430,000. In the early 1980s, permission was granted for the building of 380 houses on two adjacent plots of land amounting to 42.5 acres on the edge of the little town of Bisley in north Surrey. The increase in land value prompted simply by the planning permission was £263,235 per acre. For the total area of 42.5 acres, the increase in the value of the land alone was over £11 million.[3] Since development land tax was abolished in the 1985 Budget, a landowner in this sort of situation would be liable only to capital gains tax at 30 per cent, leaving him with a capital gain net of tax of £181,176 per acre or £7.7 million on the increase in the value of the land alone.

In fact, however, mineral extraction and new building affect a relatively small proportion of Britain's rural land. The predominant form of land-use is farming, but here too increases in land value can be sharp and sudden. In 1977 farmer Hughie Batchelor

bought an 800-acre farm in the Alkham valley behind Dover for
£500,000. When he sold it three years later the land fetched
£850,000 – a price rise of 70 per cent, generated partly by the
general increase in the value of farmland and partly by the
clearance of downland turf, bushes and trees. Mr Batchelor went
on to buy a 940-acre farm on the North Downs near Maidstone
in 1983 for £1 million. By 1986, this land was worth around £1.4
million.

Behind such individual windfalls lie certain comforting realities
for landowners. Together with labour and capital, land is one of
the three essential factors of industrial production. But the
possessor of land, as opposed to labour or capital, is in the most
advantageous position for a number of reasons. First, whereas
men and machines depreciate and require maintenance, land
renews itself even if left untended. To profit from his holding,
the landowner need do no more than bide his time. Secondly,
and even more important, the supply of land is finite. Capital
can be created through the deployment of labour. As many
ploughs can be made as farmers have money to buy them, but
the supply of land cannot expand in response to demand. This
gives the owner of land a great advantage over other agents in
the economy. It is this stranglehold that ensures that the greatest
disparities of wealth and poverty are to be found in those
societies where individuals exercise unlimited ownership rights
in land. The exercise of these rights ensures that extreme poverty
can be found not only in lands which lack natural resources (like
the countries of the Sahel) but in some of the richest lands of the
world (like the countries of Latin America).

On top of the wealth which land represents in itself comes the
wealth created by the fruits it produces. Industrial activities like
farming, mineral extraction, forestry and building themselves
provide revenue either directly or through rents from those to
whom the rights to pursue such activities may be leased.

There is a whole host of ways in which somebody who owns
land can charge others for the use of it without himself necessarily
contributing much to the productive process. He may be able to
charge others a toll to use the only road to a particular site. In
1986, it cost £1 (or £2 from April until the end of September) to
drive a car along the only means of access to the beautiful long

sandy beach of Sandwich Bay in east Kent. As thousands of cars
pass through the toll every summer weekend, income to the
owners of the Sandwich Bay Estate must be considerable. The
owner of land may be able to charge others to park cars on his
land or to carry out any number of activities on it – from using it
as a golf course to using it for a film location. Sometimes this
involves allowing people to occupy a stretch of land and use it in
almost any way they please. Thus in 1984, the Prince of Wales
(in his capacity as Duke of Cornwall) offered a lease to the tiny
island of Gugh in the Scillies. In return for £150,000 he would
allow a tenant to possess two houses on two acres for thirty-
seven years and to have the run of the rest of the ninety-four-
acre island.[5]

In other cases, payments are rather more modest. For instance,
in 1983, the wrath of councillors in St Albans came down upon
the 8th Earl Spencer for upping his rent demand on the popular
ninety-two-acre Nomansland Common at Sandridge, Hertfordshire, from £212 to £850. Local councillors claimed the Earl had
not earned his rise because the common is maintained by
ratepayers. (In the end, they paid the rent at the new level.)
Another land-based rent steeped in history is the ability of some
landowners to levy market dues. Lord Romsey, for example, the
owner of the 5,500-acre Broadlands estate in Hampshire, is
entitled through a charter granted to the lord of the manor by
Henry VIII, to market rights at Romsey. When I visited Romsey
in 1984, Lord Romsey was able to decide to whom to grant the
right to hold a market and to levy a percentage payment on
stall-holders' rents.

Some of these forms of revenue involve very little money,
others a lot. Of all the means of generating wealth from land, four
principal means stand out today: mineral extraction, building,
farming and forestry. These activities not only happen to be
extremely profitable; two of them in particular also enjoy protection from the forces which have undermined so many of Britain's
other economic activities. Small wonder then that our landowners
are doing so nicely. But unfortunately the rest of us cannot
afford simply to wish them well. For among the unique qualities
that make land such a profitable asset for landowners is one that
makes it something in which everyone of us has an interest.

Because land is part of the earth on which we all live, we are all affected by the way in which it is deployed. And what landowners are doing with it, as they energetically enrich themselves from it, is far from being always consistent with the public interest.

Mineral Extraction

Minerals can yield the most spectacular bounty land can bestow upon its human 'owners'. It may be that minerals are created by God or Nature and imbued with value by the needs of human society as a whole. But it is the owner of the land under which they happen to lie who, under British laws, gains the full benefit of their presence.

Sometimes the owner of the mineral rights is also the owner of the surface of the land; sometimes he is not. In view of the potential for extreme wealth embodied in mineral deposits landowners tend to hang on to mineral rights even when they sell freeholds. When journalist Jill Tweedie bought in 1984 six acres of rural Essex, she discovered that she was in fact only the partial owner. She explains: 'It appears that a local baron is holding on to everything that lies beneath the surface: the small print allows him to invade and quarry for whatever he thinks he might find, provided he leaves it all, one day, as tidy as he found it. They do not give up easily, those feudal landowners. They yield the topsoil only, they bide their time.'[6]

In Great Britain, there are four exceptions to the rule that the owner of land or some other owner of mineral rights owns the bowels of the earth. Ownership of coal, oil, gold and silver has been transferred to the state through nationalization.

Not that nationalization is always disastrous for a landowner's family fortunes. When coal was nationalized in 1947, astute lawyers of landowning families helped draft the legislation; later they worked hard to get as high a compensation payment for their clients as possible. Not surprisingly, many coal-owning families did well out of nationalization – particularly in view of the run-down state of the mines and the investment needed for modernization. Altogether, £243 million (equivalent to £2,875 million at 1985 prices) was paid to the former royalty owners and coal-owners by the British government in compensation for the unworked coal and assets (plants, building, stock and so on) which were taken over by the National Coal Board (NCB). The annual interest charges were likely, according to the NCB's 1947 annual report, to be between £10 and £12 million. This interest will not finally be paid off by the NCB until 1997.[7]

Even when a mineral has been nationalized, landowners may still benefit from its extraction since they can charge for the privilege of drilling or digging through their land to reach what lies underneath. Prospecting, surveying and drilling for nationalised minerals require the consent of the landowner. During the early 1980s, oil companies were prospecting at many different sites throughout southern England. In 1984, landowners were receiving £500 per acre per year for allowing oil companies to carry out test drilling on their land, with the oil company also paying further sums for disturbance and reinstatement. Should a well prove productive, a much higher rent per acre is payable.[8] By the end of 1985, the going rate for simply allowing test drilling had increased fivefold – to £2,500 an acre.[9] As most oil installations cover several acres – Wytch Farm in Dorset for instance occupied 13.6 acres in 1985 – it is clear that even nationalized minerals bring considerable wealth in their wake.

It is, however, the minerals the landowner actually owns which provide the real pickings. Limestone, sandstone, sand and gravel, slate, iron ore, tin ore, tungsten ore, lead ore, zinc ore, copper ore, silver ore, china clay, fireclay, ball clay, fuller's earth, common clay and shale, gysum, fluorspar, potash, barytes silica and chert and flint are among the non-nationalized minerals from which Britain's landowners today can take whatever return they can secure.

Many of our foremost present-day landowners owe a substantial part of their wealth to past mining income. The families owning the largest amounts of land in general benefited most, simply because the laws of probability dictated that the larger the amount of land somebody owned the greater the likelihood that some profitable mineral would be found beneath it.

The 5th Duke of Buccleuch, the second largest private landowner in Britain in the 1870s and whose descendant the 9th Duke is the largest today, drew £216,473 a year from coal and iron ore in fourteen counties during the 1870s – an amount equivalent to about £5.8 million today.[10] Much of the money with which the Dukes of Devonshire built up their position came from mining: in the nineteenth century the 7th Duke owned more than 31,000 acres rich in lead-mines. The Duke of Rutland's nineteenth-century lead mines were even more widespread than Devonshire's; while Lord Scarsdale, the Duke of Buccleuch, and the Marquess of Bute (who owned Luton Hoo during the nineteenth century) were among the magnates who also derived substantial sums from lead mining. Further north, the minerals of Northumberland, Durham and Scotland made fortunes for many landowners: 'a list of North-Eastern coalowners is almost a roll-call of local landed families,'[11] according to the economic historian Professor J. T. Ward, who notes that the Duke of Northumberland, for instance, had a gross income from minerals of £82,450 in 1918 alone (equivalent to £1.2 million at 1985 prices); while in Scotland the Duke of Hamilton was reputed to be making £113,800 a year at the end of the nineteenth century (equivalent to £3.6 million in 1985). Not only did minerals buttress the fortunes of ancestral landed families: they also aided the rise of new gentry, like the Ridleys, Joiceys and Strakers of the North East (see pages 239–41). Even tiny pockets of land could produce windfalls for their lucky owners. The one acre of Lancashire which John Shaw owned brought him an income through mining of £2,263 a year in the nineteenth century – while his 9,000 acres of rural land elsewhere generated only twice that amount.[12]

What sort of sums of money does the ownership of the minerals bring to individual landowners today? Since no comprehensive information is published on this, and since mineral operators are reluctant to disclose the rates they pay in what is a highly competitive business, it is very difficult to be precise. Just occasionally, however, figures come to light. In particular, since the Duchy of Cornwall and the Crown Estate both publish accounts, we know that in 1985 the Prince of Wales's Duchy of Cornwall, which is relatively badly endowed with minerals, received a mere £150,772, while in the year ending 31 March 1986 the Crown Estate received nearly £3.5 million in mineral royalties.[13]

Apart from published figures such as these, we can only make informed guesses of what mineral royalties mean to landowners in the present day. Take royalties on limestone quarries in Derbyshire. Tarmac Roadstone is the principal operator in Derbyshire (and much of the rest of England) for limestone. In 1985 the company told me that in Derbyshire it much prefers to pay royalties rather than to buy mineral rights in order to avoid having to find large capital sums, and that the average royalty payment to the owners of mineral rights in Derbyshire was 15p per tonne of rock. In 1984 (the most recent year for which figures are available), the total amount of limestone quarried in the whole of Derbyshire was 14,559,000 tonnes.[14] If a similar amount of rock was quarried in 1985, and if other mineral operators in the county like Roadstone were also paying 15p per tonne in royalties rather than acquiring mineral rights outright, Derbyshire's landowners would have picked up just over £2 million in limestone royalties. One half of mineral royalties is subject to income tax, or in the case of a company to corporation tax; the other half is subject to capital gains tax, which is levied at 30 per cent. Mineral valuers in the Inland Revenue to whom I spoke told me these levies usually result in landowners paying 15p in the £1 tax on mineral royalties. So the post-tax takings to the owners of the rights to work Derbyshire's minerals – foremost among whom is the Duke of Devonshire – is probably in the region of £1.8 million every year.

Royalty payments to the owners of mineral rights vary widely for different types of mineral. What is more, royalties vary for the same mineral – according to quality of the reserve, ease of extracting it, nearness to markets and so on. Some minerals have little or no value. The chalk of the South Downs, for example, has been worked only occasionally. There is so much of it and so little demand for it that it has aquired little value. On the other hand, a landowner may have high-value mineral beneath his soil of which only a small quantity exists and which is much in demand. If he also has planning consent to work it, that mineral can acquire an exceptionally high value.

The example of sand and gravel working in south-east England shows that a landowner's income from minerals does not necessarily end with the royalty payments on minerals he permits others to extract from his land. Sand and gravel are among our

most widely worked minerals. In 1984, 106 million tonnes of
sand and gravel worth £388 million were produced in the United
Kingdom. The royalty paid on sand and gravel varies widely.
But in 1984, landowners receiving royalty payments on sand
and gravel in south-east England were getting on average £1 per
tonne of gravel extracted, and paying around 15p in taxes on
each £1 received. In return they were putting up with any
inconvenience caused and foregoing income that might have
accrued from any other activity they might have been able to
carry out on the particular site involved. But once the site is
exhausted, the landowner may then be able to make more money
from it by allowing the holes created by extraction to be used for
the disposal of waste. The rates in mid-1984 were as follows: for
innocuous but non-putrescible industrial waste, 40p per cubic
yard; for household refuse, £1 per cubic yard. As both types of
waste can usually be compressed with a steel-wheeled compactor
down to a quarter of their original volume, it is clear that the
amount of money a landowner can get from allowing holes to be
filled is often more than he got for allowing them to be created in
the first place. So if we take the old GLC area alone, the 2
million tonnes of sand and gravel extracted every year would not
only have generated income, which, calculated on a royalty basis
would have been £2 million a year: this would also have created
1,494,800 cubic yards of space (since the density of sand and
gravel is 1.75 tonnes per cubic metre). If half of this space were
filled with industrial waste and half with domestic waste which
in each case had been compressed to a third of its original
volume, income from permitting infilling would have been over
£3 million per year.

If the landowner works 'his' minerals himself he can, of course,
add in the profits which the extractor would otherwise make.

Building

Building can also provide fabulous riches. The most dramatic
form of benefit comes through the increase in the value of land
that accompanies the granting of planning permission. In 1984,
the average gain in value of one acre of land in the metropolitan
green belt caused by the granting of planning consent for

building was £257,620,[15] leaving a net gain after capital gains
tax of £180,334 per acre. Those fortunate landowners who can
secure planning consents can then sell the land to somebody else
or act as a property developer themselves. In either case they
can pocket the wealth created.

Established rural landowners derive rental income from commercial and residential properties in many towns up and down
the land of Britain. These towns range in size from Balcombe in
West Sussex (where many houses and shops are owned by Mr
and Mrs John Greenwood, the owners of the adjoining 4,000-
acre Balcombe estate) to Barrow-in-Furness (an unlikely but
nonetheless real outpost of the Duke of Devonshire's domains).
Frequently they own not buildings but the land beneath and, as
ground landlords, secure a reliable rent. Thus the Cecil family's
Stamford Estates still own much of the centre of Stamford,
Lincolnshire, while the Trustees of the Chatsworth Settlement,
in which much land formerly under the legal ownership of the
Duke of Devonshire is vested, still own large areas of Eastbourne
and Sheffield (the Duke of Norfolk and the Fitzwilliams, a long-
established landowning family, also own several large sites in
Sheffield). At Eastbourne, for instance, a local council official
estimated to me in 1986 that the Trustees of the Chatsworth
Settlement owned at least 50 per cent of Eastbourne's central
area and far more land there than Eastbourne District Council.

Nobody knows precisely how much landowners based in the
countryside control in Britain's towns and cities – whether
directly or through property or insurance companies in which
they play a prominent position. What we do know is that many
old-established rural landowners made fortunes out of building
development, and the period for which the most information on
this exists is the nineteenth century.[16] There are, of course, very
well-known examples of landowner involvement in urban growth:
such as the building of the northern and eastern parts of Sheffield
including the industrial district of Brightside covering over
12,000 acres of Duke of Norfolk land; or the development on
part of 12,000 acres of the Duke of Devonshire's land in Sussex
in the premier south-coast resort of Eastbourne. But, apart from
these, virtually every county seems to have had a handful of
ancestral families whose fortunes were considerably enhanced by

nineteenth-century building or industrialization. Dr G. Rogers of the University of Lancaster has made a special study of economic and social change on landed estates in nineteenth-century Lancashire.[17] He found that the Cliftons, with 16,000 acres of farmland, benefited mainly from the development of Lytham, while in 1860 the Scarisbricks owned more than 30,000 acres embracing not only parts of Wigan, Eccleston and Scarisbrick but, financially most important of all, the land that formed the heart of the development of Southport. Ground rents on land that became Southport's most fashionable suburbs generated considerable wealth for the Weld-Blundells of Ince-Blundell Hall near Liverpool, whose estates were worth £60,000 a year by 1876 (equivalent to £1.6 million at 1985 prices); while land ownership in what became central Southport also swiftly brought the Hesketh family large urban rents.

If these were the handful of new-rich barons who received windfalls from nineteenth-century building in Lancashire, what of the also long-established estates of the aristocracy? Dr Rogers' research suggests that some of these may have made even larger profits from nineteenth-century urbanization. The Earls of Wilson became one of the wealthiest families in the county through the development of north Manchester; while in the far north, the urban expansion of Barrow-in-Furness (together with dividend payments from Barrow's ship-building yards, steel company and railway) was filling the Duke of Devonshire's estate coffers – at the same time as land he owned in Eastbourne was being lucratively developed. The Earls of Sefton and the Earls of Lilton also made fortunes from the nineteenth-century industrialization of Lancashire, but topping them all must come the Earls of Derby. This 70,000-acre estate included land and property in Bolton, Bury, Salford, Manchester and Liverpool, rents from which (added to income from the agricultural estate), gave the 17th Earl a gross income at the turn of the century of £300,000 a year (equivalent to £9.6 million in 1985).[18]

It was central London, however, which saw the making of some of the biggest fortunes from the development of land during the nineteenth century.[19] And today, it is of course in central London that land commands the highest rents, much of them going to some of Britain's largest and richest rural landowners.

Though local authorities, pension funds and property development companies have been acquiring sites in London, old-
established owners have held their ground in the prime central
area. The six most prominent are the Duke of Westminster,
Viscount Chelsea of the Cadogan Estate, Viscount Portman,
Lord Howard de Walden, the Crown Estate and the Church of
England. All these owners or their families have held on to
substantial tracts of central London for at least two hundred
years. The arrival of the twenty-first century seems unlikely to
shake their grip. 'The idea that these ancient estates have been
broken up and scattered by taxation is largely a myth,' wrote
Oliver Marriott, former financial editor of *The Times* and author
of *The Property Boom* (1967). 'Some, caught on the wrong foot by
death duty, have been weakened. But many have remained
static, or, managed by astute delegates of the beneficiaries, have
adjusted to the changes in the property market and emerged
richer than ever.'[20]

Strolling across central London you might never guess how
small is the band of people who own the land beneath your feet.
If you walk north-eastwards from Marble Arch across Portman
Square with its vast Cumberland Hotel and across Baker Street,
Gloucester Place and Manchester Square, you will pass through
the heart of the smallest of the Big Six estates – the fifty-five-acre
Portman estate, which can trace its beginnings back to the
thirteenth century.[21] Cross Marylebone High Street and you
step into Lord Howard de Walden's country: 110 acres of land
north of Oxford Street with 1,200 properties under its control,
including shops, embassies, hotels, offices and housing. One of
the most profitable parcels of the de Walden estate must however
be Harley Street and Wimpole Street: here, the plaques may
bear the names of some of Britain's most prestigious and expensive doctors and dentists, but the bricks and mortar and the land
beneath belong to the Howard de Walden estate. Slip down
Great Portland Street. As you walk across Oxford Circus, down
Regent Street, across Piccadilly Circus and into St James's and
Pall Mall you are passing through wedges and slivers of land
owned by the Crown Estate. Its properties in St James' alone
brought in £2.5 million in the year ending 31 March 1984, while
total rents from Crown properties in Central London amounted

to £27.6 million in the year ending 31 March 1986 – a net figure of £23 million after payments for repairs and general maintenance.

Now cross Green Park and walk south-westwards from Grosvenor Place right through Belgravia to Pimlico. You are passing through the 200-acre southern block of the Duke of Westminster's Grosvenor estate, a piece of land once swampy marsh but now including some of the smartest addresses in town (like Belgrave, Eaton and Chester Squares) as well as such landmarks as the Inn on the Park and St George's Hospital. Just before you reach Sloane Square, you enter the ninety-acre Cadogan Estate owned by the Earl of Chelsea. Clues to land ownership abound: there are thirty-three street names bearing the name Cadogan, Cheyne or Chelsea. If you retrace your steps through Chelsea, Pimlico and Belgravia and start walking up Park Lane to complete your circular tour at Marble Arch, make a detour off Park Lane in a north-easterly direction and wonder at another great block of Duke of Westminster country: 100 acres of Mayfair bordered by Oxford Street and Park Lane. The only major member of the Big Six whose holdings you have not encountered in your circular tour is the Church Commissioners: to find their land cross Marble Arch and start walking north-westwards. Once you have completed a tour through the Church Commissioners' triangle of land on the northern side of Hyde Park covering around ninety acres you can find their other main stretch covering a further 120 acres further up the Edgware Road in Maida Vale.

Rents from leases on properties built on such land provide the estates that own it with extremely reliable income. To increase yields, old properties may be demolished – subject to the local authority-administered controls of planning and historic building preservation – to be replaced with modern blocks of flats or offices. And existing properties may be converted to more lucrative uses on the expiry of leases. In this category comes the conversion of properties on the Grosvenor estate to embassies and luxury apartments – by 1966 there were twenty-eight embassies on this estate alone, including the gigantic American Embassy in Grosvenor Square, the only American embassy in the world whose freehold is not owned by the United States

Government. The key to all these approaches is of course to ensure that the freehold of the land is never relinquished.

Building development – and quarrying too – provide, then, dramatic examples of the way in which Britain's landowners succeed in charging others for the use of Nature in exactly the way Henry George deplored. It is not obvious why the man whose land includes 20,000 tons of gravel should be entitled to so much of the proceeds from its exploitation while his fellow-citizens should get so little. Nor is it clear why the benefits accruing from the Americans' wish to site their embassy in Grosvenor Square should all go where they do. But what does it mean for the rest of us that Britain's landowners are able to collar the proceeds from building and mineral extraction?

Henry George argued that the ability of landowners to charge others rent for land to use for homes, offices, factories and offices inflicts enormous economic damage on society as a whole. One of George's disciples is author and journalist Fred Harrison, who edits the magazine started by George's followers in Britain a century ago *Land and Liberty*. In his 1981 book *The Power in The Land: An Inquiry into Unemployment, the Profits Crisis and Land Speculation*, Mr Harrison presents evidence from Japan, the United States, Australia and Britain that the ability of those who own land to charge others rent to use it is the fundamental flaw of capitalism that has given rise to the cycles of depression that have dogged it for 150 years. A supporter of capitalism himself, Mr Harrison argues that the free market cannot function effectively if at its base lies a group of people who are not subjected to the rules of competition:

The private appropriation of the *value* of land (as opposed to secure individual possession and use of specific sites) is not a necessary condition for the capitalist mode of production. Capitalism entails the accumulation of wealth based on the provision of goods and services to consumers. It is a two-way exchange: consumers produce wealth in order to exchange it with others – to consume. Land monopoly undermines this creative process because it is a one-way relationship. The monopolist secures legal title to the resources of *nature*, and then claims a portion of the wealth created by others in return for nothing more than the permission to use land. This is the economics of the bandit sanctified by law. The monopolist *per se* does not contribute to production; he is, therefore, an anomalous feature within an otherwise efficient system.[22]

The major reform Mr Harrison advocates is the same as that propounded by Henry George – a 100 per cent tax on the annual rental value of all land and a simultaneous reduction in other forms of taxation, particularly income tax.

Whatever view one takes of the economic justification for urban rent, at least building, like quarrying, affects only a small proportion of the land surface, in spite of the fuss that often surrounds individual development proposals. The activities which dominate the countryside are far more damaging to the interests of non-landowners as a whole and far less subject to control by the community as a whole.

Agriculture

Eighty per cent of Britain is still countryside, and farming continues to be the dominant use of much of that land, as it has been for thousands of years. Indeed, post-war planning controls on building have accentuated the hegemony of agriculture. Farming in Britain today would however take a very different form were it not for the comprehensive system of public subsidy which ensures that what has become a capital-intensive industry brings in high and guaranteed levels of profit. Now, more than at any time since the Enclosures of the eighteenth century, the agriculture industry is increasingly finding itself coming into conflict with the interests of the community as a whole.

The treatment of agriculture in the post-war era has always been hard to justify. Landowners remain free to use 'their' land for maximum wealth creation – regardless of the interest of the rest of society in landscape, wildlife and recreation. Their disenfranchised fellow-citizens have then been paying them subsidies even more extensive than those enshrined in the Corn Laws.

It was the peculiar circumstances of World War II which enabled landowners to secure this remarkable deal. When Hitler's U-boats were threatening to sever food supplies from overseas, Britain seemed ill-equipped to feed her people. Much of Britain's farmland at that time was devoted not to crops like potatoes and cereals that could be fed directly to people, but to grass or barley for animal feed. Britain survived, but the fear of being starved into submission left its mark on post-war policy-makers. They decided to encourage agricultural production by making it lucrative. The import of low-cost food from countries where it could be produced more cheaply would be controlled, and prices in the home market supported through state subsidy.

Under the deficiency payments system set up after the war, the taxpayer guaranteed Britain's farmers a set price for their products – a price that was to be reviewed every year by the Government in consultation with the National Farmers' Union of England and Wales. If farmers found themselves unable to secure the agreed price on the open market, whether through foreign competition or overproduction, the Government would step in to make up the difference with a cash payment, however rich the farmer was.

The system worked. Once the fear of producing unsaleable produce at a loss disappeared, farmers stepped up production. But the system had other effects which were not so clearly foreseen.

One of these was the rise of what some consider the most influential pressure group currently operating in Britain. The National Farmers' Union built on the base provided by its statutory role in price support to work hand-in-glove with the Ministry of Agriculture over the whole range of agricultural matters. One consequence of this relationship was the steady growth of new financial benefits and privileges for farmers on top of the guaranteed prices. During the 1950s, statutory pro-vision was made for a wide range of capital grants to support schemes to improve food output – schemes that ranged from ploughing up uncultivated land to drainage and the deployment of artificial fertilizers. These new forms of support accelerated the growth in agricultural profitability. And as profitability increased, old privileges dating back before the war, like reliefs for farming from death duties and rates, became more valuable. As a result, Britain's farmers invested energetically and became both efficient and prosperous.

It was entry into the Common Market in 1973 that topped up

the farmer's cup with public inducements to prosper. The Common Agricultural Policy (CAP), which now applies in Britain, had not been designed to handle an efficient modern industry like that which existed in Britain. Continental farmers tend to have far smaller holdings than their British counterparts, and they often run amateurish, family-based operations on time-honoured peasant principles. The Common Agricultural Policy had been designed to protect them, like the British system, by guaranteeing their incomes. But to the sophisticated large-scale producers it held out the prospect of even greater profit than the deficiency payments system.

Before examining the conflict that has developed between agriculture and society, it is worth itemizing the separate sources of subsidy, both British and European, which have together turned this most basic of industries into a ravening monster.

A FOOD TAX

The CAP's system of guaranteed prices differs from the deficiency payment system in two main respects. First, the cost of guaranteeing European farmers a set price for their main foodstuffs is borne by the consumer, through higher food prices, rather than by the taxpayer: there is no compensation to farmers from the State for low prices as the prices are always high. But as well as the tax on food produced in the EEC which this system effectively imposes, consumers have to pay a tax on food imported from outside the EEC. Farmers on other continents can produce wheat, barley and other cereals, sheep, beef, sugar and butter at prices far lower than those at which EEC farmers produce them. So in order to ensure that food imported from Africa, Australasia and the Americas in particular does not undercut the prices guaranteed to EEC farmers, an import levy is imposed on these products as they enter the EEC.

These payments are made by European consumers through food prices higher than they would otherwise be. For sugar, cheese, beef and barley, for instance, consumers in Britain are forced by the CAP to pay about twice the price at which these foods are available on the world market. The Common Agricultural Policy was adding in 1986 on average £8.25 a week to the food bill of a British family of four and a further £3.25 to their tax bill – an annual total of £600, according to the University of Newcastle's Agricultural Economics Department.[23]

DIRECT SUBSIDY

Alongside the effective taxes paid by the consumer, the ordinary taxpayer has an additional contribution to make. His money is required to finance the acquisition of food that is not cleared on the open market and then its disposal. The more European farmers produce – spurred on by guaranteed prices – the more taxpayers have to pay to dispose of surpluses. Much of the British wheat that ends up in surplus stores is unfit for human consumption and cannot be sold as animal feed. In 1986, surplus wheat that could be sold was going to the Middle East to be sold there at £57 per tonne, or half what the EEC's taxpayers in the form of the UK Intervention Board had paid for it in the first place. In 1985 alone, the British Exchequer spent £900 million on the storage and disposal of surplus food produced in the UK.[24]

The milk quotas introduced in 1984 have slightly reduced the EEC's mountains of skimmed milk and butter, and the future build-up of these surpluses should also be slowed down by the temporary reduction in dairy quotas agreed by EEC farm ministers in December 1986. However, such savings to the taxpayer as may arise from reductions in the dairy surpluses are likely to be offset by increases in the surplus stores of sheepmeat and cereals. While the December 1986 agreement provides for a reduction in milk production between 1987 and 1988, it leaves the problem of the mounting cereal and sheepmeat surpluses untouched. In 1985 alone, the UK Intervention Board spent £213 million getting rid of surplus sheepmeat, while in 1986 the EEC's cereal mountain stood at 18 million tonnes. Many dairy farmers have switched to sheep rearing or cereal growing, some through the dairy herd conversion scheme, which provides grants for those who undertake to change from dairying to keeping sheep or beef cattle. By the time the sheepmeat surplus gets out of control and the cereals surplus even more so, the milk surplus may have come down to a low enough level for farmers to secure a reverse scheme – getting taxpayers to finance a switch back to dairying.

The only action ever taken to curb the growth of the cereals surplus is a 3 per cent producer tax or 'co-responsibility levy' introduced in April 1986. But the return would have to be cut by up to a half rather than 3 per cent before output would be noticeably reduced according to the House of Lords Select Committee on the European Communities, which considers the levy simply a device for raising extra revenue to finance the disposal of the cereal surpluses, not a means of deterring further accumulation.[26] Certainly the EEC is funding research into ever more exotic means of disposing of surplus cereals, including prospects for converting wheat into ethanol for use in fuel oil.

On top of the benefits flowing from the CAP, British farmers continue to enjoy a wide range of specifically British privileges – capital grants, exemption from rates and so on. Three hundred and sixty million pounds would have been raised in the financial year 1984–5 in England and Wales alone if agricultural land and buildings had been rated, according to Patrick Jenkin, then Secretary of State for the Environment, replying to a parliamentary question in 1984.[27] In the same year, Mrs Thatcher announced that the question of re-rating farmland and buildings would not be investigated in her Government's consideration of the future of local government finance and the alternatives that could be developed to current rating practice.[28] Yet the anomalous character of this concession, granted in 1929 at a time when the profitability of agriculture was at a low ebb, has become peculiarly striking in the 1980s, as hard-pressed manufacturing firms providing vital jobs in depressed areas have been driven to the wall partly by the rates they have had to pay. In 1984, for example, the North British Steel Group had to find £179,000 to pay rates to Lothian Regional Council for its foundries at Bathgate and Armadale west of Edinburgh – although the Group had made a loss of nearly £900,000 for the half year to March 1984. The 180 workers who lost their jobs with North British Steel during the summer of 1984 are among many others who would have been entitled to wonder why pigs and chickens working away in food factories should be so much more privileged than themselves.

Farming's £360 million-worth of exemption from local taxation is only the beginning of the story. Farmers are exempt from payment of VAT (a concession whose value is put at £300 million).[29] They are entitled to exemption from the excise duty on fuel oil (£300 million).[30] They can write off the cost of purchase of new machinery and buildings against tax (£700 million).[31] One of the farmers' most envied privileges is the ability to average out their profits over five years for tax purposes.

The delights of the tax concessions are matched only by the joys of the grants and the special payments known as 'compensatory allowances'. More than half the agricultural area of the United Kingdom has been designated by the EEC as 'less favoured areas' (LFAs). All farmers within these 24 million acres, which cover most of Northern Ireland, Scotland, Wales, the Pennines and Cheviots, the Lake District, Exmoor, Dartmoor, as well as mid-Devon and parts of Cornwall, receive special 'hill livestock compensatory allowances' in respect of every breeding sheep and cow on their holdings. These headage payments amounted to £131 million in 1984–5. The figure looks set to rise since in 1984 a campaign by the National Farmers' Union (NFU) bore fruit in a 3-million-acre extension of the area of the UK covered by the less favoured area designation bringing it up to its present 53 per cent coverage of the UK's farmland area. Farmers in the LFAs also benefit from enhanced rates of grant for activities to improve the profitability of their holdings; these grants are available, but at a lower rate, in the remaining 47 per cent of the UK's farmland. Throughout the UK there are grants to form co-operatives and grants for agricultural training. There are cash payments to people who agree to give up uncommercial holdings and there are grants to plant trees. Since the end of 1984 there have been grants to put in hedgerows and walls in traditional materials. But 90 per cent of the £145 million given to farmers as grants in 1985–6 was used to improve land and buildings in order to increase production. Under the Agriculture Improvement Scheme, grant is available at a basic rate of 30 per cent in the less favoured areas and 15 per cent elsewhere for activities like field drainage, flood protection works, the 'improvement' of grassland, the control of bracken, various

forms of horticultural investment and the provision of farm
buildings, roads, fences and waste disposal systems.

Today, the subsidies Britain's farmers enjoy both from
Europe's consumers and direct from the British taxpayer run
not into millions of pounds a year, or tens of millions of pounds,
or hundreds of millions of pounds: they amount to thousands of
millions of pounds every year. Various estimates have been
made of the total extent of this cash flow. In 1980, I calculated
that Britain's farmers receive around £5,000 million a year from
taxpayers and consumers;[32] in 1984, *Sunday Times* foreign editor
Stephen Milligan put it at £5,860 million – an annual subsidy of
£20,000 per farmer.[33]

These reliefs and grants give farmers a much higher level of
state financial support than any other industry receives; and of
course they are in addition to the protection the industry receives
from overseas competition. Victor Keegan, Economics Editor of
The Guardian, brought this point home when he wrote in 1984, 'If
British Leyland had a "protective" tariff of 100 per cent to keep
out imports of key models; if it paid no rates, no VAT, virtually
no mainstream taxes and the Government agreed to buy all the
cars the company could not sell abroad (at the price well above
the market rate) even you or I could make BL profitable.'[34]

In view of the degree of state support which Britain's farmers
enjoy, it is not surprising that so many rural landowners are rich
men. As agricultural economist Paul Cheshire put it in 1983,
'When you buy agricultural land now, you're essentially buying
a licence to receive very large sums of public money.'[35]

FARM RENTS

For some landowners, the riches that are to be had from farming
come through the simple process of letting out their land for rent
to others who farm it. In 1985, the average rent on tenanted
farms in England and Wales was £35 per acre.[36] In 1984 (the
most recent year for which figures are available), the area of
rented farmland in England and Wales was 10.5 million acres.
On this basis, landowners received over £368 million by way of
farm rents in England and Wales in 1985. Since the abolition of
investment income surcharge in 1984, these rents have been

taxed like any other income, earned or unearned, at a maximum rate of 60 per cent.

Between 1945 and 1985, farm rents in Great Britain doubled in real terms. Yet, increasingly, landowners are proving impatient even with this level of return. Many of them want to get their hands directly on the agricultural profits now to be made, and to do this they are farming more and more of their land themselves. Now, when a tenancy falls vacant, the owner will often decide not to relet it or to sell it as tenanted farmland. Instead he will take the land in hand and farm it directly, usually through a hired farm manager. A hundred years ago the British landowner was no more a farmer than a shipowner was a sailor. But it is not only the prospect of picking up the profit the tenant has enjoyed which leads the owner to step in. He also gains the flexibility to exploit the land value directly by selling up at the best possible price whenever he wants to. Land with vacant possession is worth 40 per cent more than land without. And even if an owner has no intention of selling, if he gets rid of his tenants he can start benefiting from the special tax reliefs available to working farmers on both income and capital.

FARM INCOME

Just how much more a landowner may make from farming his own land rather than renting it out is difficult for the outsider to estimate. The average individual farmer's income from agriculture is not much illuminated by official statistics. The main figures are those published each year by the Ministry of Agriculture, Fisheries and Food in the *Annual Review of Agriculture*,[37] and there is a limit to what can be deduced from them. Yet these particular statistics are the basis for the annual discussions on what changes the British Government should demand in the CAP's guaranteed prices to maintain farmers' incomes at a reasonable level.

The 1986 *Annual Review* tells us that average net incomes for farms in the UK for the year ending February 1985 ranged from £2,672 for a small English arable farm to £20,507 for a large Welsh dairy farm and £63,747 for a large English pig and poultry farm. Net income on an average, medium-sized English arable farm was, according to these figures, £11,683. However, there are several ways in which these official figures give a rather misleading impression.

Ninety-two thousand of Britain's farmers are part-time: yet figures on their income are merged with those of the 199,000 full-time farmers to give the average net farm income figures. Although a part-time farmer may have a relatively low income from farming, he may have a relatively high total income. A survey in 1969 revealed that on nearly a third of English farms, at least one of the business principals had an extra source of earned income outside farming, mainly as the proprietor of other businesses.[38] Fifty-five per cent of these part-time farmers (who might be involved with small, medium or large farms) had full-time occupations outside farming.

Another substantial difference in individual incomes is between those farmers who pay rent to farm and those who do not. Anthony Murray, who farms just east of Wooler in north Northumberland, is a perfectly typical Northumberland tenant farmer. He told me in 1985 that he was paying his pension fund landlord £28,000 a year as rent for 620 acres. These rent payments, together with bank interest charges of £8,000 a year on a further 200 acres he is buying, were reducing Mr Murray's annual income from farming by well over half, from around £50,000 to around £20,000.

What the *Annual Review* figures do is to assume that all farmers pay rent, and to deduct an imputed figure for rent when working out the average figures. Yet in fact 60 per cent of Britain's farmers do not pay rent.

In view of all these difficulties, impressionistic evidence has to play a considerable part in building up an overall picture. This often tends to sound very different from what the farmers themselves would have you believe. *Sunday Times* reporters Ian Jack and Graham Rose had a familiar experience in 1983 talking to a Yorkshire pig, poultry and cereal farmer in an effort to discover the true financial situation of Britain's farmers. The man they talked to told them he thought he might make £5,000 that year (1983) from rearing tens of thousands of pigs and chickens and growing barley and rape on 820 acres of prime farmland. Yet, commented the reporters, 'The family has four cars and lives in an elegant Victorian farmhouse. A home help polished the table as we spoke. It was hard to believe that all this was supported by £5,000 a year or less.'[39]

Not that all farmers believe it is worth trying to convince the public they are poor. Hughie Batchelor, the owner of a 940-acre cereal farm in Kent and one of the very few farmers to talk about their own incomes to the media, confirmed to a 'World in Action' reporter that his farming income in 1983 ran into hundreds of thousands of pounds on which he said he paid 'a little tax'.[40] But according to the *Annual Review* of that year, the income from a large English cereal farm like Mr Batchelor's was a mere £35,424.

Perhaps even more attractive than the high level of agricultural incomes is their security, guaranteed as they are by the taxpayers of twelve of the richest nations on earth.

It was the security of farmers' incomes that came into sharpest relief when the post-war economic order started to falter in the 1980s. As recession turned large areas of urban Britain into industrial desert, the great food factory in the countryside was expanding its grip by swallowing up more and more marginal land, under the CAP, immune from the laws of economics under which such harsh penalties were being meted out elsewhere. Time and again during the 1980s, the Government has refused to prop up ailing industries, like ship-building. But any suggestion that farmers' livelihoods be threatened in any way so that resources could be shifted to other sectors of the economy has been dismissed as unthinkable.

FARMLAND VALUE

Enhanced appreciation of the desirability of this security of income has further compounded the financial well-being of those who own farmland. For it has served to drive up the value of the land itself. The increases in farm incomes and farm rents since the war have been far outstripped by the soaring price of farmland. Between 1945 and 1985, the real value of land in Great Britain increased fivefold.[41] Between 1969 and 1979 alone, the capital gain was about £1,190 per acre – or £270,000 on the average 226-acre farm. The rise in the value of farmland, coupled with the absence of any national tax on land itself, or any local tax on farmland in the form of rates, has made many men very rich for very little effort.

Nineteen eighty-six saw the biggest fall in farmland prices in England since 1974 – a fall attributed to uncertainty over the future of cereal farming in the light of the possibility of grain quotas being introduced by the EEC. This embarrassed some who had borrowed to buy farmland but did little to undermine the wealth and power of the rural landowning class.

With vacant possession farmland in England fetching £1,612 per acre in May 1986, 620 acres were enough to make their owner a paper millionaire. In 1984 (the latest year for which figures are available) there were 4,500 farm holdings of at least that size and so possibly 4,500 English farmer millionaires.[42] A substantial proportion of those owning 2,000 acres of farmland or more are members of the titled aristocracy or untitled but long-standing large landowners; many families which have owned land for centuries now find themselves much richer today than they were a hundred years ago, even if they now own less land.

Financial institutions – property unit trusts, pension funds and insurance companies – have helped increase pressure on prices by entering the market in pursuit of the same guaranteed returns that attract individual buyers. But it is not the financial institutions that mop up most of the farmland that comes on to the market in Britain today, despite a widespread belief that this is so. The people who are most active in the land market are those with the best experience of what it can offer: the farmers themselves. One advantage of their excellent financial standing is that it puts them in a good position to make themselves even richer by increasing the size of their holdings.

Each of the steady improvements in the position of farmers that come along – such as a devaluation by Britain of the green pound, an increase in the EEC's guaranteed prices or the introduction of additional tax advantages for farmers – works through into higher land prices. One measure that was to give land prices a particular boost in recent years was the introduction in 1979 of special 'roll-over relief' for farmers on capital gains tax.

Although capital gains tax is levied only at a flat rate of 30 per cent on what is essentially unearned income, farmers had been complaining, through the National Farmers' Union, about the amounts of capital gains tax they had had to pay when they sold a plot of farmland. The Government replied by introducing a special scheme for owner-occupier farmers whereby the tax could be deferred where a farmer was using the capital gain from the sale of the plot of land to invest in another item of capital – say a new piece of machinery, a new building, or another piece of land. The tax on the first sale would not be payable until a capital gain had been made on the second sale. There is no limit to the number of transfers that can take place, and the liabilities to tax built up over a number of capital gains are cancelled on death, so capital gains tax can often now be avoided completely.

For those who do not own farmland but who would like to do so, its high value is not such good news. High land prices make it extremely difficult for newcomers to break in. As farmland coming on to the market tends to pass into the hands of those who are already landowners, the gulf between the landowning class and the rest of the community is deepened. Redundant industrial workers are not able to benefit easily from the milk and honey flowing through the EEC by setting up as farmers because the cost of doing so is more than their redundancy payments. Because of the level of land prices, Britain is now moving further away from citizen landowning that is much prized in so many other parts of the world.

FARM SUPPORT: WHY?

The original justification for the heavy state subsidies which farmers have enjoyed since the war was to ensure that Britain would be better placed to feed herself from her own resources if she ever needed to do so. This contingency may seem less pressing now that the fear of nuclear annihilation has replaced anxiety about submarine attacks on merchantment as a national preoccupation, but it seemed real enough in the aftermath of World War II.

In fact, howeyer, all the money poured into agriculture by the citizenry has not actually made the country all that secure in the face of interruption of supply from overseas, whether or not such an eventuality is still a fit cause for concern. As we have seen, one of the main problems at the outbreak of World War II was that most of Britain's farmland was producing food for animals, not crops that human beings could eat. Today, after the injection of thousands of millions of pounds of public money, the picture is much the same. The subsidies farmers used to drain the wetlands and plough up the downs were not conditional on food being produced which human beings could consume directly. So farmers used the subsidies to produce what was most profitable at the time, namely barley, most of which went into the manufacture of animal feed, and dairy cattle. At present, only 8 per cent of UK farmland is given over to crops that provide for people direct. So we could not hope to maintain our present diet under siege. In these conditions, we should have to dismantle the vast meat and dairy food production machine which our countryside has become and plough the land afresh to grow cereals. This is, of course, just what was done from scratch during World War II – perfectly successfully but without a vastly subsidized agriculture industry having first existed in peace-time.

Not that subsidy has had no effect. The area of land under intensive cultivation has certainly increased and in the process our countryside has been transformed. But as Professor Kenneth Mellanby demonstrated in his book *Can Britain Feed Herself?*[43] we should still be able to support our entire population on home-produced food under seige conditions only if we replaced the barley and grass grown to feed animals with crops grown for human consumption. Dr Colin Tudge, the author of *The Famine Business*,[44] has estimated that if Britain's farming activity was aimed exclusively at supporting our population, we would need only a fifth of the land area at present under cultivation to achieve this end.

Indeed, so far off providing for strategic needs is our present agricultural activity that our prospects of feeding ourselves in time of siege are in fact worse now than they were in 1939. Then, British soil was inherently fertile. Once ploughed it was available for national service. Post-war gold-rush farming has, however, involved the application of vast quantities of artificial fertilizer. The soil has got used to this, and were the additional input withdrawn, it would be far less productive than it is now. It would be several years before the soil could regain the fertility it used to enjoy from its own resources. Yet these artificial fertilizers on which our soil has become so dependent, together with pesticides and oil, which are equally essential to present farming practice, pretty well all come from overseas. If we are ever cut off from overseas food supplies we shall be equally cut off from the minerals and chemicals on which present agricultural practice is based. The implication is inescapable if ludicrous. The effect of pouring vast sums of public money into agriculture to improve Britain's strategic security has been to reduce that security.

Strategic security is not the same as maximum output, although this is what government policy has effectively assumed. What security requires is an agricultural industry either geared to subsistence or, more realistically, flexible enough to switch easily into subsistence operations from whatever else it is doing should the need arise. A genuinely strategic agricultural policy might provide grants to ensure that farm horses, for example, are maintained in operational condition and that the skills required for operating them continue to be taught. The last thing it should do is turn agriculture into an industry committed irrevocably to producing the wrong things on a massive scale on the basis of technology which would collapse very soon after a crisis struck.

The fact that the strategic arguments on which agricultural support is based do not in fact make sense is fairly apparent to those who have much to do with the industry. It is perhaps for this reason that those who are obliged to defend the status quo in agricultural policy hesitate to stand four-square between them and cast around for other things to call in aid. Their quest is not an easy one. State support is granted to other industries normally on the grounds that they are of strategic importance (as agriculture is meant to be), that they are infant industries which need to be nursed, that they need to be protected from going under during temporarily adverse conditions, or that they provide jobs in large numbers or in areas of high unemployment. Agriculture is not an infant industry nor has it been going through a difficult period. And it contributes remarkably little in the way of employment. Farmers and farmworkers together make up only 2.6 per cent of the civilian workforce. Manufacturing industry employs more than ten times as many people, or 28.3 per cent of the workforce. Construction and tourism, for example, each employ about two and a half times as many people as agriculture. From any employment viewpoint, subsidy would be much better directed to, say, tourism, which remains obstinately labour intensive,[45] whereas the more money goes into agriculture the more automated it becomes.

Rather than employing people, the mechanization that has come with state support has driven people off the land. The number of regular, full-time agricultural workers in Great Britain fell by more than 50 per cent between 1946 and 1966 (from 739,000 to 342,000) – a steady decline of about 20,000 jobs a year. By 1984, the number had fallen still further – to 117,000 throughout the UK. Yet this is one group that certainly was not pricing itself out of jobs with excessive pay rises. What has destroyed many of the farmworkers' jobs is 'unfair' competition from machines subsidized through capital grants and tax concessions. This may have helped make agriculture more efficient but it has made it harder for it to justify the subsidies it receives on the grounds of the employment it provides, though attempts to do this are still sometimes made.

But it is not only the number of farmworkers that has shrunk. The number of farmers, owner-occupier and tenant, has dropped too. Douglas Beba, who rents thirty-three acres at Spalding in Lincolnshire producing a rotation of wheat, potatoes, sugarbeet and tulips and daffodils, explained why in a television programme in 1983: 'The system is all in favour of bigger units, because bigger units can survive on a much smaller profit per acre. For an example, if you have a 1,000-acre farmer and he makes £50 an acre, he's got £50,000. If I make £50 an acre, I've got about £1,600.'[46] In Lincolnshire as a whole, nearly 2,000 farms disappeared between 1974 and 1984, a fall of 25 per cent. The majority lost were less than 100 acres while the number of large farms over 500 acres in size in the county increased.[47] And so the post-war increase in agriculture's profitability and the revolution in farming practices that has accompanied it has resulted – just like the eighteenth-century enclosures – in a sharp drop in the number of Britain's small farmers.

Another attempt to justify agricultural subsidy is an appeal to the 'balance of payments' argument. Jerry Wiggin, MP, the then Parliamentary Secretary at the Ministry of Agriculture and himself a farmer, wrote in 1981: 'We grow only 60 per cent of our own needs and the rest has to be imported. Importing more – or exporting less – costs us foreign exchange, and it is in the national interest to produce more of our own food and improve our self-sufficiency. That is why it is vital for us to have an efficient agricultural industry.'[48]

In fact, in an era of floating exchange rates and oil exports, an even agricultural balance is not necessarily a desirable objective. The country's employment prospects are actually enhanced by the lower exchange rates that trade deficits bring. If, however, we wanted to weight the trade balance by subsidizing producers, it would make much more sense to give the subsidies to industries that employed large numbers of people rather than agriculture. As it happens, our present agricultural policies are doing a certain amount of damage to our trading relations with the rest of the world. A third of the new cars sold in New Zealand are made in Britain. But the New Zealand High Commission has told the Commons Select Committee on Agriculture that Britain's continued access to the New Zealand motor market will depend on New Zealand's ability to export food products to Britain.[49] New Zealand farmers manage to produce butter and lamb, for example, much more cheaply than our own farmers do at present, even with the large subsidies they receive. It will profit the balance of payments nothing if subsidized import substitution of dairy products reduces the prospects of British Leyland.

It is sometimes argued that the massive level of support for agriculture is justified by the improvement in the material condition of our people which it engenders. Vice-president of the National Farmers' Union Christopher Righton explained to readers of *The Times* in 1980 that the product of present agricultural support is 'a vital and dynamic industry which grows at home an ever-increasing proportion of national food supply at ever-decreasing cost to the consumer.'[50]

However, an ever-increasing proportion of national food supplies which is produced at home actually worsens the consumer's position. It is not the case that the more food is produced in Britain the more British consumers benefit, because in the sheltered world of the CAP, more production does not bring lower prices. It brings higher taxation as more has to be spent on disposing of surpluses. Under the CAP, cheap flour, cheap milk, cheap beef, cheap lamb, cheap pork, cheap vegetable oil and cheap sugar are illegal, while foodstuffs produced from these basic commodities like bread, biscuits, yoghurt, cream, butter and breakfast cereals are more expensive than they would otherwise be.

As Mr Righton says, agriculture has become 'a vital and dynamic industry' as the result of billions of pounds of public investment. This is good for farmers but not necessarily for the rest of us. Sometimes though, agricultural apologists hint that whether or not a booming British agricultural industry is good for us, it must be good for the hungry poor of the Third World. This claim too, natural though it sounds, is entirely bogus.

In 1985 the United Kingdom gave away as food aid 105,691 tonnes of cereals, 9,442 tonnes of skimmed milk powder and a substantial quantity of butter-oil. As long as we have food surpluses and the costs of selling them outside Europe require such large export restitution payments from our own taxpayers, it clearly makes sense simply to give the food away. And where people have been hit by disasters like earthquakes or famine and need short-term supplies to tide them over the disaster period, food aid is obviously beneficial. Yet continual dumping of surplus food on Third World countries as 'aid' presents no more of a long-term solution to the problems of the hungry Third World than it does a solution to the inherent defects of the CAP that give rise to the surpluses in the first place. Ghana has good soils, a rich variety of lands, adequate water and a climate that encourages growth. Yet in 1980, only 11 per cent of its arable land was producing crops. Poverty has prevented it developing any more. As a result, the country is forced to spend desperately-needed foreign exchange on importing a commodity it could easily produce itself – food. Senegal has hundreds of thousands of acres of rich alluvial siltlands, which in the UK would be classified as Grade I farmland. Yet the land goes untilled and the people hungry. What Third World countries like these want is the basic wherewithal to develop the very considerable food-producing potential that lies on their doorsteps – not an indefinite reliance on charity from the West on the unpredictable occasions when it is forthcoming. If a little of the money at present channelled into agricultural support to the British agricultural machine that results in the surpluses could be spent instead helping poor countries overcome some of the most basic problems they face, that money would be far better spent. A simple campaign to eradicate the tsetse fly in Africa, for instance, could release nearly 3 million square miles in thirty-five African countries.[51]

Indeed, the dumping of food surpluses can actually damage the countries involved. A well-documented report in 1984 by the Frères des Hommes in France and Belgium contends that food aid (except that given in times of disaster) has made the Third World hungrier and rich 'donors' richer.[52] As aid from America and Europe in the form of wheat has introduced a taste for bread in countries that traditionally produced rice, millet, sorghum or maize, so imports of wheat and flour in Africa have multiplied ten-fold, completely cancelling out earnings from food exports. Not only do the skimmed milk powder and wheat that make up the bulk of food-aid disorganize local production and distort local tastes, they also induce a dependence mentality and drive economies still further into debt.

DESTRUCTION OF THE COUNTRYSIDE

Surely the point about the countryside is that it is used for so many different purposes. Farming is one; looking at it from cars or trains is another. It is also used for exercise, for rambling, for camping, for riding, for adventure-training, and it provides source material for artists, poets, biologists, ornithologists, entomologists, zoologists, archaeologists, architects, historians and many other people.

It also supports other life forms for which, it could be argued, we humans with our unlimited powers of destruction, have special responsibilities beyond the fact that we may find them interesting or beautiful. All these interests, with the possible exception of farming, would seem to be better served by the green field system than by prairies.

Is not this the context in which modern agricultural processes need to be judged?

Professor Sir Colin Buchanan, letter to *The Times*, 18 November 1980

If the present system of agricultural support is damaging to the British economy, it is far more damaging to our environment. The subsidies funded a revolution in agricultural practices which have combined to drain Britain's countryside of beauty and interest.

This agricultural revolution really got under way in the 1950s. Subsidies like the ability to write off the cost of new machinery against tax stimulated the development of more and more sophisticated equipment and encouraged farmers to invest in it. Chemical companies meanwhile scrambled over each other to invent new and more effective pesticides to spray from the bigger and bigger new machines. What rapidly came to amount to state guarantees of income created a climate in which almost any investment began to look profitable. Hedges, ponds, woods and wetlands were cleared aside to make way for the new machines and methods and to create more ploughland or highly productive pasture on which more profit could be made. Farming as Britain had known it for generations gave way to a relentless process of industrialization.

Four aspects of the post-war agricultural revolution have had particular impact on the rural environment. The first is an expansion of the amount of land under cultivation at the expense of hitherto marginal but attractive landscape features like hedges, woods, marshes, heaths and downland turf. The second is the enlargement and standardization of agricultural working units, which pose a further threat to landscape features like woods, hedges, copses, banks, ponds and streams. These features have been swept aside to accommodate the massive new farm machines and to create extra acres on which more crops can be grown or farm animals ranched. The third is new practices in stock-rearing. No longer permitted to munch their way lazily through flowery meadows, many cattle (and pigs and chickens) have been put indoors. Their former pastures are often turned

over to crops like barley, most of which is manufactured into
concentrated animal feed. Where stock is left outdoors, the old
pasture is often subjected to intensive chemical treatment to
improve its productivity. Nitrogenous fertilizers are rained down
upon it often with the accompaniment of herbicides and grass
seed. The old mixture of wild grasses and plants is replaced with
a specially bred strain (evocatively labelled S24, S32 or similar)
of one grass species – perennial ryegrass. This is grown as a
virtual monoculture and efficiently converted to beef, sheepmeat
or milk by grazing beasts. The fourth aspect is the application of
large doses of artificial fertilizer and pesticide to land already
under crops. This has devastated the wildlife of the cornfields –
the poppies and the cornflowers, the hares and the partridges –
as well as disrupting the balance of nature in nearby streams,
dykes and rivers.

For a fuller picture of the impact of the post-war agricultural
revolution on Britain's rural environment the reader may like to
turn to my earlier book, *The Theft of The Countryside*. Now, my
purpose is to set that revolution in the wider context of the abuse
of rural Britain by its owners. For subsidies and technology do
not apply themselves. They are developed within a framework
of assumptions shaped by the long-standing attitudes of our
landowners. Now as in the past they feel entitled to do whatever
suits them with 'their' land. In the past this attitude has had
grim consequences for the rural poor. Today, it is having grim
consequences for everyone who values the countryside but does
not happen to own any of it.

Who does own Britain's wildlife? Who owns Britain's landscape? Who owns Britain's archaeological relics? When Shakespeare wrote in *A Midsummer Night's Dream*, 'I know a bank
whereon the wild thyme blows, where ox-lips and the nodding
violet grows', he did not have to worry about who owned the
thyme, the oxlips or the violets. The existence of these flowers
and a reasonable degree of access to them could be taken for
granted by all citizens. But today the ownership of our rural
heritage is a real issue. Many of those who consider themselves
the absolute 'owners' of rural land are bent on destroying the
charms it holds for others. If our countryside is to be saved, the

rest of us will have to assert our own claim to ownership rights against the absolute rights claimed by landowners.

By 1987, the ravaging of Britain's landscape by agriculture was showing no signs of abating, in spite of farmers' claims to the contrary. For the forces behind the process were still at work, in spite of efforts by the farming lobby to persuade the public that dark days lay ahead for farmers. Cereal production in particular remained so profitable that incentives remained for the further reclamation of marginal land. The suggestion that the Common Market might impose production quotas on cereals was if anything intensifying moves in this direction as farmers sought to ensure that if quotas came their own output would be frozen at as high a level as possible. The expansion of cereal growing during the six years up to 1984 alone was accompanied by the removal of 17,500 miles of hedgerow throughout Britain, the construction of 105,500 new farm buildings (one for every other farm holding) and the clearance of ninety-three square miles of deciduous woodland, according to a survey by scientists at the Institute of Terrestrial Ecology.[54] Although landowners planted a considerable amount of broad-leafed woodland during the same period, the scientists pointed out that these new plantations would have nothing like the ecological value of the deciduous woods that had been uprooted.

Among the treasures of which we are being robbed is irreplaceable evidence of our past. By world standards Britain has an impressive array of such relics, from neolithic standing stones and burial mounds to Iron-Age hill forts and Roman villas. They are of real importance in understanding the past, yet they are being wiped off the landscape at a startling rate.

A survey of plough damage to archaeological sites in Sussex in 1976 provides a snapshot of a process that has continued across Britain through the 1980s. This survey, conducted by Dr Peter Drewett of London University's Institute of Archaeology, found two out of five causewayed enclosures, five out of fifteen long barrows, eleven out of twenty-seven Iron-Age hill forts, three out of five Roman forts and posting stations and nine out of fourteen Bronze-Age settlements were being destroyed by ploughing.[55] A tiny proportion of Britain's archaeological sites (less than 2 per cent) have been scheduled by the Department of the Environment on account of their outstanding archaeological significance; the same survey found nearly one-fifth of these being damaged by ploughing.

The relics that are disappearing form part of the only raw data that exist about the 50,000 years of human life in Britain before the Romans introduced the first limited written records. Only a fraction have ever been excavated.

Alongside the loss of our history, the loss of other treasures of our national life to modern agriculture have become increasingly well documented – like the loss of the once common plants and animals of our countryside. Ninety-five per cent of our hay meadows, with their characteristic constellations of yellow flags and buttercups, fritillaries and cowslips, early purple and green-winged orchids, ragged robin and meadowsweet have been subjected to agricultural 'improvement' since the war. Most of them now consist simply of cereals or perennial ryegrass sown as a monoculture. Shakespeare's oxlip, to take an entirely typical example, has declined dramatically both in range and population numbers as its habitat, the often centuries-old damp oak and ash woods of Suffolk and Essex, has been cleared away.[56] Woods that are probably the present-day remains of Britain's post-Ice-Age forest cover and have never been converted to any other use are known by naturalists as 'ancient woods'. Between 1933 and 1983 Suffolk, which is a reasonably representative case, saw 38 per cent of her ancient woods turned over to farmland or restocked with conifers, either of which processes as we shall see eliminates most of the existing wildlife.[57] Suffolk naturalist Francis Simpson writes in a 1982 book of the heady scent emitted by the tiny, cream heads of the oxlip in these Suffolk woods: 'The flowers presented a sight of unparalleled beauty and filled the whole atmosphere with a scent like apricots. Very few woods and copses exist today where such a profusion of flowers can be seen.' He goes on:

It may be difficult for younger readers to visualize the beauty of the Suffolk countryside and its many wild flowers that still existed in the period between the two World Wars. Changes were taking place, but not on such a large scale as we have seen in recent times . . . It was no

problem finding many of the wild flowers which are rare or local today
... In springtime a magic existed in the woods with their carpets of
flowers. They seemed lit up, beautiful and enchanting and there was a
chorus of birdsong such as is never heard today. There were carpets of
Archangel, Anemones, Violets, Primroses, Oxlips and Water Avens,
followed by Bluebells, Foxgloves, Herb Paris and Orchids. Many of the
old woods have now changed beyond recognition or gone forever.[58]

The fen violet and fen orchid, the frog orchid and dwarf
orchid, purple crocus and corn bedstraw are six of the twenty-
nine species of flowering plant which became extinct in Suffolk
between 1950 and 1982. During the present century, a further
189 species have become so reduced in numbers that they are
now rare or local to Suffolk: these include the wild tulip and the
yellow star of Bethlehem, the lizard orchid, lady's tresses, juniper
mezereon and deadly nightshade. The picture in Suffolk is not
unusual. The national populations of the vast majority of our
native flora have been drastically reduced since the war. Twelve
of our native flowering plants and ferns died out completely
between 1930 and 1984. Agricultural intensification was responsible for two-thirds of these extinctions.[59]

Animals have fared little better than plants. Great Britain has
three species of native newt (only one of which also extends to
Ireland). Over the centuries, these primitive-looking creatures,
like tiny dinosaurs (with which beasts they share a common
ancestor), have given rise to a wealth of folklore. Much of this
springs from their interesting habits: their shed skin is frequently
swallowed whole by its former wearer; the female places each of
her annual lay of 200–300 eggs singly on water plants, bending
a small leaf round each egg as a form of protection. The largest
and most distinctive of the three species is the Great Crested
Newt, named on account of the beautiful crimson-tipped, jagged
crest that extends along the back and tail of the male during the
breeding season and waves constantly when he is in water.
Members of this bizarre species can live to be twenty-seven
years of age and were believed by many country people in the
nineteenth century to be poisonous: if a cow died after drinking
from a trough in which crested newts were subsequently found,
the death would often be attributed to the newts.
Although the great crested newt lives on land once it is

mature, breathing by means of lungs and through its skin, it needs ponds or dykewater in which to breed. Each newt returns to the pond of its own metamorphosis to find a mate, relying on a curious homing instinct which can take it distances of several miles if moved. Unfortunately for these newts, however, the number of great crested newt breeding sites has declined sharply. The eight years between 1966 and 1974 alone saw a 50 per cent drop in the number of breeding sites, according to a survey by Dr Trevor Beebee on behalf of the British Herpetological Society. The decline is also unfortunate for the children who might have come across one of these strange beasts in the mud at the bottom of their tadpole nets. Dr Beebee writes, 'Most areas have suffered declines in their crested newt populations which have accelerated to alarming proportions. Lowland areas of England, where the species is most abundant, have suffered more than the remote highland districts ... Extinction on a local scale is already occurring.'[60] Dr Beebee goes on to express a hope that the crested newt may not come to share the fate of the natterjack toad. A less common species than the crested newt but nonetheless once widely distributed on coastal dunes and marshes and inland heaths, the natterjack toad is now classed as an 'endangered' species. Between 1930 and 1974 the creature disappeared from fifty-seven of its seventy-seven known breeding sites in the British Isles, many of which were changed (often but not always by agricultural intensification) out of all recognition.[61]

When Gilbert White was writing *The Natural History of Selborne* in the eighteenth century, that remarkable bird the nightjar was so common in the Hampshire parish that local people used to gather and eat nightjar eggs. This nocturnal bird depends on open woodland and wood borders, heaths and other open roughlands with a cover of bracken, heather, gorse or bushes. It migrates from equatorial East Africa, rearing its young in Britain in a mere four-month sojourn between May and August. For White, 'There is no bird, I believe, whose manners I have studied more than that of the goatsucker, as it is a wonderful and curious creature'[62] – an opinion no doubt shared by those people lucky enough to have heard its weird churring call on a June night, to have seen its moth-like form fly and wheel silently in pursuit of insects, or even to have stumbled across it on the ground with its curious frog-like face, open-mouthed, waiting for moths to fly in.

Until the end of the nineteenth century, the nightjar remained a common bird. Its decline in our own time, particularly since 1950, has however been dramatic. In Essex, for instance, numbers dropped from eighteen to twenty pairs in 1952 to not more than three pairs in 1972.[63] Nobody knows the whole story of the decline. One factor may be that average temperatures in April and May since the 1950s have been lower than they used to be while summers have tended to become wetter. But according to the ornithologist F. C. Gribble, who has made a special study of the decline of the nightjar, 'another factor is undoubtedly the destruction and fragmentation of former Nightjar breeding sites throughout the English regions by the ploughing up of heathland, downland and marginal land or its conversion to forestry'.[64] The fate of the nightjar perhaps demonstrates that if a species' population is already under pressure, habitat loss can vastly accelerate its decline.

It is not only through the loss of wildlife, landscape and archaeological relics that new approaches to agriculture have disadvantaged the community as a whole. The clearance of a woodland, or the fencing, draining and reseeding of a stretch of moor, down, marsh or rough meadow does not only alter the content of the stretch of countryside involved; it often also results in a reduction in the degree of access to it. The sort of countryside which has seen most change has often been those remnants to which de facto access has survived – the areas where anybody has been allowed to walk freely in practice whether or not a legal right to do so exists. When these patches of wood or roughland disappear, so too do our ancient playgrounds. Thirty years ago, large tracts of chalk downland turf in Sussex, Hampshire, Berkshire, Dorset, Wiltshire and East Yorkshire provided freely accessible land over which the walker could roam at will alongside the sheep, the butterflies and the kestrels on a carpet of orchid, cowslip and harebell-studded turf. Indeed, rough chalk downland turf was one of Britain's main landscape types. The proximity of these downs to the towns and cities of the southeast made them especially valuable. Now, the experience of walking over a great wilderness of springy downland turf amid thyme-scented air survives mainly in the writings of Kipling, Belloc, Hardy and W. H. Hudson.

The area of chalk downland turf in England has declined by around 80 per cent since World War II, according to calculations by the Nature Conservancy Council.[65] Two large stretches of uninterrupted downland – the East Sussex Downs and the Berkshire and Marlborough Downs – were put forward for national park designation by the architects of Britain's national parks system just after the war.[66] These hills' wide open spaces, freely accessible and strewn with a multitude of wildflowers and archaeological relics, seemed just the sort of countryside for which the national park designators were looking. But both areas were subsequently rejected because they had ceased to possess the necessary qualities. Vast stretches of their downland turf had been ploughed up to grow grain. Today, the rolling curves of what might have been the people's playgrounds of southern England have been cut into a giant's chequerboard of barley prairies punctuated only by miles of wire fence. As a result, not only the stone curlews and the chalkhill blue butterflies but the people too have disappeared. So too has the strong presence of the past that used to haunt these open downs. When, for instance, archaeologists surveyed upstanding remains of prehistoric monuments on the Marlborough Downs in 1971 they discovered that 64 per cent by area of the ancient remains which had been identified before World War II had since been flattened.[67] Unless something is done, there is no reason to suppose that the remaining prehistoric monuments will not all in their turn be flattened by the plough, revealing themselves in years to come only as 'crop-marks'. Yet, according to the eminent archaeologist Professor Peter Fowler: 'Archaeology is the only approach for 99 per cent of human history.'[68]

Just as the eighteenth-century enclosures banished the landless from Britain's countryside as a place to make a living so the post-war agricultural revolution has turned them out of large areas of the countryside as a place to play. Not that the economic role of the countryside in the life of ordinary people has not continued to decline as well: today machines rather than sheep have proved 'eaters of men', in Sir Thomas More's phrase. But the loss of further agricultural jobs has affected only a small section of the population. The numbers who seek inspiration from the countryside to refresh their daily lives run into many millions. Now they find the arcadia celebrated by our poets turning into a grim and featureless food factory which can offer them less and less. And at present, their feelings are scarcely any more heeded than were those of the commoners driven by wealthy landowners from their lands to starve two, three, four and five hundred years ago.

During 1986, it became fashionable to talk of the impending derailment of the agricultural gravy train. However, this development owed more to the public relations efforts of the redoubtable agricultural lobby than any real change in the position which agriculture enjoys. The introduction of quotas for the production of dairy products does not appear to herald the collapse of the CAP. However, if agriculture does at some stage in the future prove less profitable than it is now, landowners can be expected to switch their effort deftly into another sphere which will allow them to secure their age-old goals. One such sphere already suggests itself. This is forestry. Minister of Agriculture Michael Jopling prophesised in 1986, 'If surplus agricultural production throughout the European Community is to be reduced – as it must – then I see forestry as offering perhaps the most promising alternative use for land which may no longer be required for agricultural production.'[69] The NFU proposed in 1986 that one and a quarter million acres of farmland in England and Wales – 4.6 per cent of the total – should be turned over to forestry during a twenty-five year period through annual income supplements from the taxpayer of £50 million.[70] At the same time, the organisations that lobby on behalf of forestry have been energetically considering the various forms which lowland forestry might take and calling for an array of new government grants to support it. For instance, farmers might sell some of their land to forestry companies. Or, they might retain ownership and shift production from crops to trees concentrated in plantations. Or, they could combine forestry with cash-cropping of cereals and livestock on the same establishment. If forestry does come to play a bigger role in the lowlands it will bring with it an array of implications for the rest of the community which upland Britain already knows all too well.

Forestry

Glen Ample is a wild glen in the hills of west Perthshire which between 1983 and 1986 underwent a subtle, yet far-reaching change.

This glen is among the first you come across if you drive north into the Highlands from Edinburgh or Stirling. It lies in the shadow of Scotland's first two 'Munros' (mountains over 3,000 feet high), Ben Vorlich and Stuc a' Chroin. Beneath their majestic forms, the Glen is smaller and more delicately shaped than many of its better known Highland counterparts. Before 1983, for seven miles its folds embraced the walker in a delicate, constantly changing U-shaped paradise offering seclusion but on what seemed a human scale. Above the little burn that runs the length of the Glen rose gentle slopes clad in a mosaic of heather, bracken and rough mountain grass. At the top of the glensides these gave way to rocky crags. From these crags, countless little streams fed into the main burn – streams which in summer were crowded with bog pimpernel, bog asphodel and clumps of yellow stonecrop which seemed to tumble with them down the mountainsides.

Walkers were attracted to Glen Ample not only by its seclusion but also by its location relatively close to Scotland's main population centres, which made it the ideal target for a day's outing, winter or summer. Along the glen bottom runs one of Scotland's few agreed and signposted public footpaths which together with the red deer's habit of assembling here for the autumn rut has led Stirling District Council to make Glen Ample the subject of one of its autumn guided walks. Parties of thirty to forty walkers have regularly been able to marvel at the roaring that has marked the autumn rut of the monarchs of this glen set against the autumn russets of the fading bracken.

The changes that came to Glen Ample in the mid-1980s did not transform it overnight. In 1983 and 1984, the 762-acre north-west flank of the Glen was fenced off and the heathery turf cut into countless parallel ridges. Two roads were cut along the hillside and the whole area was covered with tens of thousands of what looked in 1985 like small dark green pimples. Within five years 80 per cent of these pimples will reveal themselves as sprouting Sitka spruces. The remaining 20 per cent will turn out to be Douglas fir (9 per cent), Japanese larch (5 per cent), Scots pine (3 per cent), Lodgepole pine (2 per cent) and mixed hardwoods (1 per cent). In fifteen years this stretch of wild, open, freely accessible moor will have become a dark and forbidding timber factory. Then, any walkers who still wend their way along this part of the foot of the Glen will find their views to one side cut off by a dense screen of conifers, punctuated only by the existing alder and rowan trees that climb the glenside by the tributary streams.

The rest of the Glen was not, however, left untouched. In 1986, a 615-acre stretch of open moor on Glen Ample's north-eastern and south-western flanks was enclosed and planted, together with a further 1,040 acres running due south for three miles from the southern end of Glen Ample over the hillside known as Ardchullarie. Sitka spruce will make up 82 per cent of the 1986 planting at Glen Ample and 89 per cent of that at Ardchullarie. Some of Glen Ample is being left as bare land. But the overall aspect of this unique little valley is changing dramatically. The graceful contours of the Glen will be broken up by vast rectangular blocks of gloomy conifers. In a few years the eagles, which are often spotted hunting over the Glen's open spaces, may be seen no more. The red deer too will have gone – 200 were shot in 1984 to make way for the trees. Afforestation will have plunged yet another of Scotland's scenic gems into drabness and desolation.

By the dawn of the twenty-first century, Glen Ample will be far from unique. Views of large stretches of dazzling heather moorland are growing scarcer in the Highlands. In the southern part of Glen Ample in the summer of 1985 it was still possible to imagine that the open heather rolled on for miles. But in fact, substantial conifer plantations were already only a stone's throw away. Climb over Glen Ample's western ridge and you find yourself in the Forestry Commission's 23,000-acre Strathyre Forest plantation. Drive north past Strathyre Forest and you will see many more blocks of conifers, some mature, others in 1985 no more than the familiar, sinister grid of regular green pimples.

Altogether, 90 square miles of the land of Great Britain, much of it bare moor and glen like Glen Ample, were afforested in the year ending 31 March 1986.[71] Four per cent of this new planting consisted of broad-leafed trees; the remaining 96 per cent conifers. While the government agency for forestry, the Forestry Commission, carried out one fifth of the new planting, the private sector was responsible for the remaining eighty-one square miles of new planting. During the sixty years up to 1986, the planting of new forests in Britain proceeded at the average rate of about 41,000 acres a year; the result is new planting of around 2.7 million acres, the vast amount of it coniferous.[72] And there is much, much more to come.

Imagine an area the size of Kent, Lancashire, Nottinghamshire, Northamptonshire and Warwickshire combined: 3 million acres in all. This is the area that will be covered in new plantations by the middle of the next century if the plans of the Government and the Forestry Commission are fulfilled. In 1980, the Government gave an essentially open-ended commitment to the expansion of forestry. The then Secretary of State for Scotland and Forestry Minister, George Younger MP, told the House of Commons that new planting (as opposed to the restocking of existing forests) should continue at broadly the rate of the past quarter century, but with the private sector playing a greater part than hitherto.[73] On this basis an extra 3 million acres of Britain's land will be under forest by the year 2031. As no absolute limit has been set on the ultimate target area for planting, and as applications for grants from the private sector for new planting have essentially been given on demand, the figure could rise higher still. If past trends are anything to go by, the vast forest that will blanket most of Britain's uplands by the middle of the next century will not have room for many broad-leafed trees. Britain's foresters prefer to plant conifers because they grow quicker and provide faster returns than the traditional broad-leafed species of Britain like oak, beech, birch, hornbeam, ash, maple and lime. The species most often planted over the past half-century have been Norway and Sitka spruce, larch, Scots, Corsican and Lodgepole pine. Eighty-five per cent of the Commission's own forests are conifer; and in 1986, more than 95 per cent of the area of private planting in Great Britain consisted of conifers. An appealing prospect for our grandchildren? Certainly an appealing financial prospect for the men, women and companies engaged in a mad scramble to afforest what remains of Britain's wild country outside the food factories.

Who are the private landowners who are afforesting places like Glen Ample and who look set to be even more active in the future? Where do they come from and what are their motives?

Scottish landowner and the then chairman of the Forestry Commission, Sir David Montgomery Bt, told a conference in 1980, 'Foresters are by nature countrymen with an instinctive feel for the countryside in which they live and work.'[74] It is true that many traditional landowners are active foresters but forestry is also an activity that attracts new entrants to the ranks of the landowners.

It is by no means only countrymen who are responsible for the transformation of Glen Ample. The open moors that were afforested in the mid-1980s belong partly to the Rolls Royce Pension Fund and partly to the British International Cable Corporation which are together entitled to around £225,000 of Forestry Commission grant for their pains. A specialist company, Tilhill Forestry, is managing the forestry schemes on behalf of both landowners.

Tilhill Forestry is one of the four main private forestry companies operating in Britain which are energetically buying land to cover it with conifers. Forestry companies like Tilhill, the Scottish Woodland Owners' Association (Commercial) and the Economic Forestry Group manage land for existing landowners, whether they be large, old-established estates or pension funds. The company will apply for the forestry grants and do all the necessary paperwork as well as installing and managing the plantation. Other forestry companies, like Fountain Forestry, operate slightly differently: they acquire plantable land or forests themselves and then sell much of it in relatively small parcels to large numbers of investors; the company then manages the whole block on behalf of its clients. By 1985, Fountain Forestry either owned or managed more than 250,000 acres of forest land in the UK (mainly in Scotland) and more than 100,000 acres in the United States. Fountain Forestry's clients are not in general country folk. Far from it. People who invest in forestry companies are largely businessmen who have made large sums and are looking for a way of investing their gains in a way which makes them liable to as little tax as possible.[75] For forestry happens to provide unique opportunities for the conversion of income into capital which the Inland Revenue cannot touch.

The financial arrangements are as follows. At the beginning of the forestry cycle, start-up costs are offset under Schedule D against income from other sources. Thus the considerable capital cost of establishing a new forest is money the Exchequer might otherwise have claimed. Instead, the Exchequer through the Forestry Commission provides individuals and companies with the extra bonus of planting grants. Anybody, however rich, can avail himself of these grants, which can go towards not only the cost of planting but also of fencing, drainage and building any roads that will be needed.

Most people investing in forestry are paying 60 per cent income tax. On hill land planting costs about £344 per acre. After the grant of £93 has been subtracted, an investor will claim 60 per cent tax relief on the remaining £251. While the young trees are growing, the private forester can continue to write off the costs of managing his woodland against pre-tax profits from other businesses. The trick when the wood starts generating profits that exceed expenses is to sell it or pass it on to a family trust. The trees are now worth a lot more money, but capital gains tax is payable only on the bare land value, not the trees. What is more, the change of ownership automatically brings the woodlands into Schedule B, which means that the timber can be cut and sold free of income tax. Once this has been done, the new owner can opt for Schedule D and the cycle can begin again. An additional advantage is that developing land for forestry (like developing land for intensive farming) has never attracted development land tax, while, as in the case of farmland, the burden of inheritance tax (or capital transfer tax as it was before 1986) bears relatively lightly on forests.

Conifer plantations also provide the ideal means of storing up money to meet such inheritance tax bills as may arise. It also happens to be an attractive way of transferring wealth, for inheritance tax is not charged on standing timber until that timber is sold, given away or otherwise disposed of.

The forestry tax privilege of Schedule B now being exploited so energetically in Great Britain dates back to 1915. Combined with the option for a woodland owner to switch to Schedule D, it provides the tax-avoider's dream: tax-deductible costs and tax-free revenue.

The reason for granting what was to be the first of many financial privileges to the private forester was strategic. As the strategic argument has become outmoded forestry has become a system of enrichment for the privileged at the expense of the rest – a pattern strikingly similar to that followed by agriculture.

FORESTRY SUPPORT: WHY?

(i) *The Strategic Argument*

From the 1860s until the outbreak of World War I, British forestry was declining in the face of imports of timber from countries abroad where it can be produced at a fraction of the cost of production in Britain. During the war, however, it became apparent that even if ships were no longer made of oak, large amounts of timber were needed suddenly for pit-props and hutments, in munitions and engineering. Yet the U-boats made supplies from abroad uncertain. Britain was forced to look to a far greater extent than hitherto within her own shores for her timber needs.

In 1919 the Government, anxious to equip the country with adequate timber supplies in the event of another war, set up a new agency, the Forestry Commission, and charged it with the tasks of replacing the timber felled during the war and creating a strategic stock of standing timber that could be called on in the event of another war. It was to do this mainly by acquiring and planting land itself but also by encouraging, through the provision of grants, investment by private landowners. The 1920s and '30s saw a programme of frantic (mainly Forestry Commission) afforestation in the hills of Britain. However, by the time war broke out again in 1939, the trees were not big enough to meet the need for which they had been planted. But another U-boat campaign appeared to underline the importance of domestic production.

By the late 1950s, however, the strategic argument was losing ground. It had become clear that a strategic stockpile of felled timber would serve the country in time of war far better than standing timber in remote corners of the country. And as the threat of nuclear war began to rear its head, the strategic role of timber began to seem increasingly quaint as a subject for concern. In 1958, meeting the needs of a future war was officially abandoned as an aim of government support to the forestry industry.

In fact, however, the policy of building a strategic reserve has had its intended result. Today Britain possesses a large stock of standing timber that could be felled in an emergency. However, even if this were still considered important, there would be no further need to add to it. But as in the case of agriculture, new arguments have emerged to justify a practice conceived for purposes which are no longer valid. In his policy statement on forestry in 1980, Secretary of State for Scotland George Younger told the House of Commons: 'A continuing expansion of forestry is in the national interest, both to reduce our dependence on imported wood in the long-term and to provide continued employment in forestry and associated industries.'[76]

(ii) The Trade Argument

The phrase 'reducing our dependence on imported wood' is designed to carry some of the resonance of the strategic argument without laying itself open to having to be required to support the strategic argument in circumstances when it is no longer supportable. What this is now supposed to mean is to reap the benefit of the national asset which our hill country represents by turning it into a form of wealth which will reduce our need to import timber products. This argument has more force than does the comparable argument for agriculture because timber, unlike most of the agricultural goods that are produced, is not in surplus. Britain at present imports over 90 per cent of her timber requirements at an annual cost of £4.5 million. Therefore, the argument runs, if we do grow more timber, we shall use it rather than stockpiling it in the way that we stockpile and eventually destroy so many agricultural products.

But does this argument stand up? In a letter published in *Farmers' Weekly* in 1986, timber merchant B. P. Moor warned farmers to think carefully before taking land out of food production and turning it over to forestry.[77] He pointed out that timber grown in Britain can substitute for only a fraction of our present imports of timber from overseas. More than 40 per cent of Britain's timber imports consist of sheet materials like plywoods and chipboards which are already being considerably overproduced in Third World countries where wage rates are highly competitive. A further 12 per cent of Britain's timber imports consist of tropical hardwoods which will not grow here, like mahogany and teak. This leaves about 47 per cent of conifer imports which may appear to be available for British producers to attack as a potential market. However, Mr Moor points out that conifers reared in the UK grow too rapidly to produce a stable enough timber for joinery and house construction and builders are not willing to risk encountering the problems of warping and twisting of construction timbers which could follow from buying British. All this leaves only the packing case market, pit props and fencing as promising users of UK conifers. However, since countries like Russian, Scandinavia and Canada want to offload their low-grade timber on to the UK, this part of the trade will always be highly competitive. Success in this sector would only offer farmers who entered it 'a standard of living about equal to that of a Russian peasant timber worker', according to Mr Moor.

So it is not as obvious as is claimed that good economic arguments underpin the continuing expansion of forestry. Timber planted *now* will be of use only in thirty-five years time. By then, world demand for timber products is likely to have been reduced dramatically as electronic forms of communication take over from those based on paper, and tropical producers have geared up to capitalize on the advantage of being able to grow wood five times as fast as is possible in the temperate climate. Any assessment of the claims of the conifer to take over our countryside ought to weigh these considerations as well as recreation and wildlife interests so that a proper balance can be struck. Instead, our hill country and increasingly the lowlands too are being stripped bare of their potential for wildlife and recreation in pursuit of a doubtful economic gain sometime in the next millennium. The eventual prospect of mountains of unwanted conifer timber comparable to the mountains of unuseable surplus butter and grain of the 1970s and 1980s is far from fanciful.

(iii) The Employment Argument

Though employment is now the second most often advanced reason for public support for forestry, it in fact employs very, very few people indeed. Nature has always done most of the work in bringing trees to maturity. Plantations like that at Glen Ample require people to prepare the ground (perhaps involving draining, ditching, fencing, weeding and bulldozing roads) and to plant the trees. Long past are the days when weeding involved groups of workers with sickles: any weed control of a young plantation now usually involves spraying herbicides from a tractor or from an aeroplane; while any thinning of the trees up till the time they are about twelve years old is likely to be carried out by one man perched high up in a harvester machine rather than gangs of men on the ground. The trees may then be left for another twenty-three years until, thirty-five years after they were first planted, workers armed with chainsaws chop them down, clear the ground and start again.

If one firm has a large number of forests at different stages of growth in any one area, there may be enough work for a permanent force of men. But the work of planting virgin territory in the hills of Scotland and Wales is carried out in the main by contract labour moved round the country as work demands. Their temporary presence in a rural area does little for its long-term economic stability.

Indeed, forestry serves to reduce many of the employment opportunities in remote rural areas of Britain. Once forestry comes, farming and deer stalking go. And as the wildest parts of Britain come to take on the dull, impenetrable uniformity which conifer plantations impart, tourism can be expected to suffer.

It is by no means only the private sector that has shed labour in order to operate more efficiently and increase profits. The Forestry Commission itself shed half its workforce between 1950 and 1984 – although the size of the Commission's estate almost doubled during the same period. In 1978, James Lamond MP, a member of the Public Accounts Committee of the House of Commons, elicited the admission from George Holmes, then Director General of the Forestry Commission, that, in the years before 1977, the Commission had been laying off workers when one of its chief justifications was the reduction of rural unemployment.[78]

If the overt reasons for state support of forestry are so slender, why then does it persist? By far the most important reason is the power of a vested interest in maintaining the status quo – through the Forestry Commission itself and through the forestry pressure groups like the Timber Growers' Association and the Scottish Woodland Owners' Association. Like the NFU, these bodies rely heavily on their ability to pull strings in high places. Also like the NFU, they put considerable effort into propaganda. They rely not on the appeal of a jolly lumberjack equivalent of the cheery yeoman farmer but on the appeal to the collective subconscious of trees themselves.

Most people are in favour of trees in principle and the word 'forest' does not necessarily conjure up the dark and forbidding image of the Sitka spruce and Douglas fir to which it nowadays tends to relate in practice. Also, the fact that decisions on forestry concern the distant future mean there is always some reason or other why more forests might turn out eventually to be a good thing. We get the benefit (if any) from a new forest at a point so far in the future that anything might have happened by then. If oil grows scarce, may we not have to substitute other raw materials, like timber, for purposes at present supplied by petroleum? Who knows? But the idea of tall silent trees watching over our future in massed ranks has a certain something.

THE DAMAGE

The weakness of the case for the afforestation of Britain's hill country makes even more deplorable the damage the policy is wreaking on our countryside.

In cases where conifers are planted simply as an alternative to arable crops on land that has been under intensive cultivation (as happens, for instance, in lowland Scotland and Wales) this probably does not matter too much. But afforestation is destroying those parts of the United Kingdom's reserve of untouched, natural or semi-natural environment which have managed to escape the ravages of the post-war agricultural revolution and urban or industrial development. Afforestation threatens two main types of uncultivated land. The first is the deciduous woodland of lowland Britain, which is being bulldozed away or

replaced with conifer plantations. The second is the heathery
carpet over our moors and mountains. Both type of country are
vital for wildlife and recreation.

(i) The Loss of The Woods

Apart from sharing a common reliance on photosynthesis,
modern forestry has little to do with the ancient practice of
harvesting naturally growing trees as they reach maturity. Like
modern agriculture, modern forestry takes little more account of
the natural environment than does an engineering factory on an
industrial estate.

In the past, woodland was not cleared and replanted wholesale
every few decades. Nature's bounty was literally plucked from
the forest. Foresters took advantage of the ability of trees to
live for ever. Normally, they coppiced or pollarded trees, only
occasionally felling them whole. This meant that the ground
vegetation of the woods was never radically disturbed. The
coppicing and pollarding actually increased the diversity of the
wild plants and minibeasts of the woodland floor by letting in
more light. What is more, since traditional woodland management relied on nature, it revolved around naturally-occurring
tree species. In one area maple would dominate, in another lime,
in others elm, hazel, oak, beech or ash, or, in the highest
mountains of Scotland and Wales, Scots pine.

Modern forestry, by contrast, imposes its own environment.
First, the trees of any existing deciduous wood are felled and the
stumps bulldozed out or poisoned to prevent regeneration. The
ground is then usually ploughed to a depth of eighteen to twenty-
nine inches and the new crop, which is almost always a conifer
species, planted. Herbicides suppress any plants that might
compete with the saplings while fertilizers force the speed of tree
growth to the maximum possible rate. The impact of all this on
the ecosystem not only of what was once an upland hillside but
also of what was once a deciduous wood is almost as devastating
as if the land had been cleared to make way for a barley field or
a motorway. Many of the woods that have been the subject of
post-war coniferization have been not simply old-established
deciduous woods but woods whose origins go back thousands of
years to the time before Man himself appeared in Britain. They

are the remnants of the post-Ice-Age forest cover – the ancient woodlands. One result of the gradual evolution of these woods over thousands of years is that the mixture of tree species varies even from one part of the wood to another. An expert on ancient woodlands Dr Oliver Rackham of Cambridge University explained the unique value of ancient woodlands to a Commons Committee in 1980:

Ancient woods are of value not only for their tree assemblages but also for their communities of herbaceous plants ... In Eastern England more than fifty such species have been listed, including *Primula elatior* (the oxlip), *Anemone nemorosa* (the wood anemone), *Euphorbia amygdaloides* (wood spurge) and *Carex pallescens* (pale sedge), besides trees and shrubs such as *Tilia cordata* (small-leaved lime) and *Crataegus laevigata* (two-styled hawthorn). These are a characteristic and irreplaceable part of ancient woodland. Woods are part of our cultural history as well as of our native vegetation. A medieval wood, with its boundary bank and other earthworks, ancient coppice stools, and soil profiles and land-forms undisturbed by cultivation, is a record of our environment and civilization as complex and as irreplaceable as a medieval church.[79]

Leicestershire and Pembrokeshire, Lincolnshire and Gwynedd, Somerset, Clwyd and Cornwall – all these counties share the tragic distinction of having lost around half their ancient woodland over the last fifty years according to Nature Conservancy Council figures.[80] Cropland or conifer plantation has been the most common fate of the land involved. While Surrey, north Cumbria, Bedfordshire and Hertfordshire have lost slightly less of their ancient woodland – around 40 per cent each – in several counties, notably Gwent, Shropshire and Northamptonshire, landowners have seen fit to clear away well over 60 per cent of the county's ancient woodland during the last fifty years.

Though conifers may yield financial dividends, they spell wholesale losses for wildlife. Fir is the food plant for only sixteen different insect species – compared to the 284 that live on the bountiful oak. The range of creatures that prey on insects – and of the creatures that prey on them – is similarly denuded. It is not only the conifers themselves which are less attractive to wildlife. They shelter far fewer secondary plants, like hazel, holly, rowan, elder, willow, spindle, dogwood or guelder rose.

There are usually few climbers such as ivy, clematis and honey-suckle, and the trunks and branches are home to few mosses and lichens.

Though it is the destruction of ancient woodland that causes the most striking loss, the disappearance or coniferization of the much greater areas of ordinary, deciduous woodland have probably done more damage to our countryside. In 1811, 95 per cent of the woodland of Dorset consisted of deciduous trees; only 3 per cent was coniferous. By 1972, the area of pure deciduous woodland had fallen to only 23 per cent. Fifty per cent was pure conifer, and in much of the remainder conifers were mixed with broad-leafed trees.[81] In place of the rounded, bushy-topped trees that have for so long complemented the rounded curves and gentle hills of Britain march more and more ranks of regular, spiky-topped conifers. They strike a chill into lowland land-scapes, stripping them of the seasonal variety provided not only by the ever-changing colour and shape of foliage of deciduous trees but also by the galaxy of flowers and bushes that thrive in Britain's traditional deciduous woodlands but not among coni-fers. In place of the bosky delights recorded in our woods by our poets, there is increasingly to be found a gloomy emptiness.

The forestry situation in Northern Ireland provides an illumi-nating contrast with that on the British mainland. Fly over the Province and one of the most striking features of the lowland landscape is the almost complete absence of woodland. This was not always so. There was a saying in the seventeenth century that you could walk all the way from Belfast to Loughinsh-olin[82] (40 miles away) on the tops of the trees. But trees were cut down to provide barrel staves and to remove hiding places for rebels. During the land reforms at the end of the last century, many landowners chopped down woodland for which they considered they were not being adequately compensated by the Government; while during the second half of the twentieth century, agricultural change has been the main force behind the removal of many of the few tracts of woodland that survived – including ecologically valuable stretches like the alder carr on the eastern edge of Lough Neagh. Such natural woodland as survives today tends to be confined to deep glens.

So far, the Province's private landowners have not followed

their counterparts on the British mainland in planting conifer
forests on the sites of felled deciduous woodland. One reason is
that the size of the holdings makes afforestation less attractive
than it is in Britain. Apart from the core remnants of some of the
old plantation estates, which may extend to 2,000 or 3,000 acres,
land holdings in the Province are so small – sixty acres on
average – that commercial forestry is not a viable economic
proposition. At the same time, the smaller size of holdings means
fewer people have large fortunes tied up in land on which they
are seeking to avoid paying tax. Two further factors have been a
shortage of capital for investment in forestry and the political
situation, which has militated against tying up funds in such a
long-term (and inflammable) asset as trees.

(ii) The Loss of the Moors

I was born in Plymouth, so one did see in those days fields outside
Plymouth, and a little village where we were sometimes taken to
church. But none of that meant anything. It was the moors . . . As
a child the very air was magic because it was so different, so clean
and so pure and absolutely heady. And that was part of one's
childhood remembrances of the moor and part of its magic.

I suppose it's really inspiration and freedom. I think even as a
child I used to feel it, and so much now. One feels in a way that
with so much happiness deriving from Dartmoor that one owes it
a debt.

When Dartmoor is dressed in her lovely purple heather it is
breathtaking, both the sight and the smell of it . . . Colours come
into it tremendously, but it's everything, it's the monuments. I can
recognize an ancient monument although it's never been mapped
and nobody else has seen it, and there are many such of course,
undiscovered. The ancient monuments have this great fascination:
there were your forerunners and they lived on the moor and they
could wring some sort of a living out of its soil. There are some
landscapes I could take you to on Dartmoor that literally cannot
change. That gives one an extraordinary security, as though one
knew where one's roots were.

When the heather is finished I love the lovely space, the long
views, the long distances. When you find yourself robbed of those,
as in a forestry plantation, you feel at once absolutely cheated.

I agree with Frank Fraser-Darling who says that even though
people may not go to the wild areas, there is something in human
nature which benefits from their just being there and knowing that
they are there and that you can escape to them if you are really
hard pushed.

Lady Sylvia Sayer, who has energetically campaigned for more than half a
century to conserve the beauties of Dartmoor, talking to the author in
1977

The heaths and rough grasslands of the moors that are disappearing under blankets of conifers are not noted for ecological variety
like deciduous woods. However, they are of great ecological
importance in that they support combinations of plants not
found anywhere else in the world. The sheer abundance of plants
like ling, three species of gorse, the cross-leaved heath and
the common bell heather and the peculiar combinations and
constellations in which these species exist in Britain endow our
moorlands with global significance in plant conservation. At the
same time, the boggy stretches of moorland that survive in the
north and west of Britain with their mixtures of sphagnum
mosses and heath rush, studded with the little yellow stars of
bog asphodel, represent a type of peatland vegetation which is
also of extremely restricted global distribution.

Most of Britain's moors have been gradually evolving towards
their present state over the past 4,000 years. Created after the
felling of the Wildwood by people seeking timber, charcoal or
sheep-runs, and maintained as moorland through grazing and
burning, most of the moors are a great deal older than many of
the historic medieval and even Saxon buildings meticulously
preserved in our towns and cities.

Much of the moorland now being afforested or ploughed and
reseeded for intensive grazing has either never been ploughed or
has not been broken by a mould-board plough (one that turns
over the ground as well as cutting it) in the past 1,000 years.
Because it has lain undisturbed for so long, much of this
moorland is of enormous archaeological value.

One region of moorland hills in which this archaeological
value is coming to light only as ancient monuments are sliced
through with deep forestry ploughs is Galloway. Here, groups of
stone monuments from the Bronze Age of unknown function
known as cairnfields and the ramparts of ancient hill forts are
particularly at risk.[83] But it is not only the archaeological relics
of Galloway that are disappearing through afforestation – the
whole character of the region has been transformed.

One addict to the wild moorland hills of south-west Scotland (Galloway and southern Ayrshire) was Derek Ratcliffe who, as a schoolboy just after World War II, explored them during his holidays, in search of birds of prey.

Each spring saw me roaming the Lakeland fells, but I was drawn even more strongly to the quieter hills of the Southern Uplands, where there was the additional satisfaction of prospecting unknown ground, and working out the distribution of Peregrines and Ravens for myself . . . Galloway, especially, was a magic country to which I returned every year with renewed enthusiasm . . . I well remember the sudden feeling of solitude when the train set me down with my bicycle at the lonely station on the moors, and I headed along the rough road across the wild and windswept uplands towards the abrupt granite crags that were always my first call.

These explorations were the beginning of a lifetime devoted to the study of natural history (the extract is taken from Dr Ratcliffe's book *The Peregrine Falcon*, published in 1980)[84] and to pioneering work in the field of nature conservation (Dr Ratcliffe has been the Chief Scientist at the Nature Conservancy Council since 1974).

Since the war about 50 per cent of the moorland area of Galloway has been transformed – mainly to conifer plantation; much of the rest to reseeded grassland for intensive livestock production. Vast blankets of conifers now wall in any solitary cyclists blotting out not only the rough vegetation, the streams and the archaeological relics but also reducing the prospects for the region's kings of the air. Ravens and buzzards in particular have declined markedly over the hills of Galloway and southern Ayrshire. A survey in 1981 showed only thirteen raven territories still occupied by breeding pairs, compared with thirty-one pairs in the 1940s and '50s. The Nature Conservancy Council believes that 83 per cent of the decline is the result of afforestation having removed these magnificent acrobats' food supply of sheep and lamb carrion. Similarly, all but two of the twenty-five regularly breeding pairs of buzzards in these hills disappeared during the same period.[85]

More worrying still, the Forestry Commission revealed in 1980 that it regards southern Scotland as a region suitable for substantial further expansion of forestry, and went on to identify 864,500 acres of Dumfries, Galloway and the Borders as suitable for new planting[86] – a figure which must amount to virtually all the unplanted moorland below 1,500 feet left within the whole of the Southern Uplands.

Britain's total moorland area is not threatened with virtual extinction by conifers in the way that the chalk downlands have been almost eliminated by agriculture. Nonetheless, it has shrunk and the character of remaining areas has been changed by the brooding presence of conifer forests on the horizon or over the next hill. A study commissioned by the Royal Society for the Protection of Birds published in 1984 revealed that parts of England and Wales have lost more than half their rough moorland since 1946; what is more, the national rate of loss in the late 1970s was found to be four times what it had been in the period 1946–51 and to be increasing.[87] The whole process of upland afforestation involves losses to the community of several different kinds. I will single out four.

First, the hills and moors play host to a distinctive wildlife which cannot survive among mature conifer plantations or down in the lowlands. Species include many of Britain's most striking birds of prey, such as the golden eagle, the hen harrier, the short-eared owl, the buzzard and Britain's smallest raptor, the merlin. All these are highly adapted to hunting over open spaces and are all therefore threatened by their disappearance. The merlin, a bird which plays a key role in our folklore, is now threatened with extinction in many parts of Britain because of loss or moorland habitat. Other birds of the moors which also stand to lose include greenshank, curlew, wheatear, raven, dunlin, skylark, golden plover, red grouse and meadow pipit. Although one or two species benefit from afforestation, such as the capercaillie and goldcrest, the conifer forests on the whole support very little wildlife.[88] On the wild moors and bogs of Caithness and Sutherland, to take one area under threat, almost 70 per cent of the UK's population of greenshanks, 30 per cent of our dunlin, as well as red-throated divers, golden eagles and merlin find a home. Forestry interests already own one third of this land, and the Royal Society for the Protection of Birds considers the blanket afforestation that is proceeding apace there to be 'the single biggest threat to birds in the UK this century.'[89]

The second reason for conserving the wildness of Britain's uplands is that they play some role in supporting employment. Afforestation may make investors richer than they would otherwise be, but it brings few jobs.

Where it does bring jobs, these tend to come at great expense to the public purse. Fountain Forestry's operations over 103,000 acres of Caithness and Sutherland with Exchequer help of £9.5 million have resulted in forty permanent jobs. The Royal Society for the Protection of Birds commented in 1986, 'Assuming that all of these jobs result from the above investment, the cost per job is over £238,000. Compared with this, the average cost per job created or retained by the Highlands and Islands Development Board in the financial year 1983–4 was £4,400.[90]

In contrast to forestry, tourism is an efficient job creator in hill lands. But to sustain tourism the hills will need to retain their wild, open character. In the 9,800 square miles of Scotland making up the Highland Region, forestry employs only about 1,200 people directly with a further 800 working in downstream activities such as saw-milling and processing. Tourism, in contrast, provides over 6,000 jobs directly, while agriculture also employs 6,000 people directly throughout the region.[91] Visitors to the Highlands and Islands – as well as to Exmoor, Dartmoor, the Cheviots, North Yorkshire and the hills of Wales expect to see rising up above little hedged fields in the valleys, a purple blaze of heather – and to know that here are great open spaces over which they may walk freely. They will not be attracted by an unending sea of perennial ryegrass or conifer plantation from which most of the birds and butterflies of the moors have been banished and from which they themselves may be effectively denied access by fencing.

Third, the moors and dales are of value for education. Here, it is possible to see the basic phenomena of geology and geography at first hand – the imprint of the glaciers, the formation of streams and rivers, the weathering process – stark and unconcealed. Children tend to have a greater awareness than adults of the immediate environment and less concern for the more abstract qualities of landscape. Since heather moorland consists of only one storey of vegetation, wildflowers are easy to find. Similarly, caterpillars, beetles and other minibeasts are often quickly spotted. The moors also provide opportunities for education in survival. Here people can learn to pit themselves against the elements, for example in one of the Duke of Edinburgh's Award expeditions which depend on the moors.[92]

Fourth, many people find spiritual refreshment on the open moors of Britain's hill country which they can find nowhere else. Moors and mountains, probably more than any other type of landscape in Britain, are sought out by those who are attracted by high, wild Romantic landscapes in which they can walk long distances and commune with God or their own inner beings.

Moorland clearly offers these people something which they cannot find in apparently similar landscape types, like lowland heaths or ancient woods. What is it? To try to find out, I talked at length with five leading countryside conservationists who are also moorland enthusiasts. Wildness – the antithesis of domestication – turned out to be the key quality of moorland in their eyes. Openness too is central to its appeal. As conservationist Gerald McGuire explained to me: 'The appeal of moorland in contrast particularly to mountains is this openness: this great vista and you're in the middle of it and you're preferably very much alone in it.' Both wildness and openness, I concluded, are central ingredients of the appeal of the moors. Five other characteristics also rated a mention: height (distinguishing moorland from lowland heath); the absence of human handiwork; asymmetry and homogeneity: the landscape must be essentially simple and devoid of any obvious imposed pattern; and finally the freedom to wander at will. Devotees of moorland exult in the liberation they feel on the moors – liberation not only from imprisonment in the towns where they must spend most of their lives, but also from the confinement of lowland countryside, where public access is largely restricted to predetermined routes. And although the moorland as wilderness must appear natural and untouched by Man, free of the accoutrements of modern civilisation like electricity pylons and nuclear power stations, relics of ancient Man and traces of past civilisations in the form of hut circles, rings of standing stones, cairns or prehistoric burial mounds heighten the appeal of moors by setting modern

Man in the context of his own past. The imposition of a forestry plantation, destroying most of the favoured characteristics of moorland, robs the moors of their capacity to play the role sought of them by wilderness lovers.

For many of these people, other natural environments are no substitute. Yet impenetrable blocks of conifers continue to march over Britain's hills and moors, obliterating their wild, open character, eliminating freedom to wander and blotting out views of lochs and lakes, rivers and streams, meadows and crags – all in all destroying the whole point of hill walking.

A report by Parliament's main financial watchdog, the National Audit Office, published in December 1986, questioned the economic usefulness of this destruction.[93] In particular, like the only other independent economic review of British forestry (that of a Treasury team whose report was published in 1972), the Audit Office pointed out that the vociferous claims on the part of the Forestry Commission and Britain's landowner-foresters that forestry is a valuable means of job-creation are ill-founded. The Audit Office also confirmed the Treasury's earlier conclusion that new forestry investment provides an extremely low rate of return. While most public sector investment is meant to achieve a 5 per cent rate of return, the Audit Office calculates that the return on the Commission's planting in north-east Scotland, for instance, which, alongside that of private foresters, threatens to devastate wild bird populations, will be only 1.25 per cent.

Such observations suggest that the time has come when the Government should allocate forestry a role consistent with the economic and environmental needs of Britain. Before we can work out what this role should be we need to ask ourselves what is the role of Britain's hill country in the modern world? Should it become a matchstick factory and if so why? Or do we need at least some of it for other purposes? And when we have answered these questions for the uplands, we need to go on to consider what the role of afforestation ought to be in the lowlands which are beginning to fall under the same dark shadow of the conifer.

The Plea of Poverty

There are, then, many ways in which landowners can make money simply through their ownership of the unique resource

that land represents. However, landowners are anxious to avoid
giving the impression that they are wealthy men and women.
The image they cultivate is that of Boot-Magna-style charm
encompassing genteel poverty.

In support of their claim to be poor, an argument put forward
frequently is that the hefty capital taxes they say they have to
pay reduce the real value of their holdings, and indeed force
them to maximize output from the land while it is in their hands.
In a letter to *The Times* published on 15 November 1980,
for instance, Commander George Marten, a prominent Dorset
landowner, deplored the way in which 'capital taxation regularly
and persistently drains the land of the resources essential to its
proper care'.

However, inheritance tax strikes only when land is actually
transferred and its impact needs to be set against the various
substantial fiscal benefits which landowners enjoy. Farmers, for
instance, are exempt not only from rates on their land and
farm buildings but also from VAT, while their incomes are
safeguarded by the taxpayers of twelve of the richest nations on
earth.

Capital transfer tax was an attempt by the Government in
1975 to claw back some of the hundreds of millions of pounds
lost to the Exchequer every year through the avoidance of
payment of death duties. We do not know the views of those
who had to submit to what was probably the earliest and most
onerous kind of death duty on the transfer of property rights
Britain has known – the 'heriot', a death duty common in
medieval England, in which the son of a deceased serf could not
take over his father's holding until he paid the duty – usually his
father's best animal – to the lord of the manor. Certainly
landowners in modern times always complained bitterly of death
duties after the measure was first extended to them in 1894.
However, as landowners could avoid the tax completely and
quite legally by the simple expedient of giving their property
away at least seven years before their death, very little money
was paid in death duties. The 8th Duke of Buccleuch, for
instance, neatly avoid an estimated £10 million in death duties
simply by settling the major part of his personal shareholding in
Buccleuch Estates Limited on his son the Earl of Dalkeith who

became the 9th Duke of Buccleuch in 1973.[94] Only when several
unforeseen deaths occurred in close succession did death duties
normally cause serious problems.

After capital transfer tax replaced estate duty in 1974, property
was no longer taxed only when handed over at death: to prevent
tax avoidance, duty was also levied – albeit at a lower rate – on
any gifts made during a person's lifetime.

The burden this imposed was, however, much reduced after
1981 through a succession of beneficial CTT concessions to
landowners and farmers introduced in successive budgets by the
Thatcher Government.[95] Finally in 1986, CTT was abolished
altogether on lifetime transfers. Its replacement, inheritance tax,
now resembles the old estate duty abolished by the Labour
government twelve years before because it enabled wealth to be
protected by its transfer through gifts during the lifetime of the
donor instead of bequests.

Taxation has but nibbled at landowners' ability to claim for
themselves increases in the value of land arising from society's
demands on it or society's actions in granting planning permission to develop it. The only tax payable in these situations is
capital gains tax, levied at a standard rate of 30 per cent. In
1983, capital gains tax raised £838 million. Most of the gains
involved came from land, so a great deal of money was being
made. Small wonder then in view of the range of concessions
available to landowners that the leading estate agents firm of
Savills advised in 1984: 'There has never been a better time to
use land to transfer wealth from one generation to the next.'[96]

Development land tax, which was introduced by the Callaghan
Government in 1976, was bringing in only about £70 million a
year when it was abolished by the Thatcher Government in
1985. The reason was the large number of exceptions and
possibilities for deferral of the tax. For example, although charged
at 60 per cent, the first £75,000 capital gain in any one year was
exempt, while relief from double taxation was provided when
development land tax would otherwise have been additional to
the liability for income tax, corporation tax or capital gains tax.

If there were any genuine doubt about the real value of land
today the workings of the market should remove it. There is no
shortage of people wanting to own land. When it is up for sale,

there is nearly always a taker to be found. The reason of course is that, for a great many people, to have dominion over the land and what goes on in it is wealth enough. That power is a benefit, a form of wealth, and one that is universally sought by mankind. It may be nice to have some treasure as well, but that is nowhere near as satisfying a form of wealth as having control over the Earth's surface and those who depend on it.

5. Power

Through the ages it is the power wielded by landowners over the lives of others that has marked them out most clearly from other groups. Today, how much of this control do they retain at local, regional and national levels?

Local

High on an isolated spur of the Lincolnshire Wolds where Nottinghamshire, Leicestershire and Lincolnshire meet rises an imposing and many-towered castle. Its mellow gold stone walls, towers and ramparts crown the lush, tree-clad hill rising out of the flat Vale of Belvoir below from which it takes its name. This castle is the fairy-tale Leicestershire home of Charles John Robert Manners, CBE, 10th Duke of Rutland, and the headquarters of a 15,000-acre landed estate. The estate includes one sizeable reservoir, two large lakes and several small ones, 300 cottages mainly in five villages, a mausoleum, kennels for hounds and various other buildings, 10,000 acres of tenanted farmland and 3,000 acres of land farmed direct by the Duke and his agents together with woodlands which include the largest heronry in Leicestershire.

Forty-two miles away to the north-west lies the Duke of Rutland's Derbyshire residence, Haddon Hall, a romantic medieval castle-cum-manor house in gracious parkland above the Derbyshire Wye. This 3,000-acre estate, which abuts the Duke of Devonshire's vast Chatsworth kingdom to the north, also bears the conspicuous imprint of the Manners family: Manners Wood, for instance, runs for two miles along the valley top ending just east of Bakewell. Altogether, the Duke of Rutland owns 18,000 acres of Britain's land — an area fifty times that of Hyde Park. He is also the possessor of mineral deposits in the

Midlands sometimes, but not always, lying beneath the land he owns.

Like most landowners, the Duke is most powerful on his own property. Naturally enough, it is he who determines the use to which his land should be put and who should use it. It is up to him to decide whether the minerals he owns should be worked or not. He has it in his power to choose his ninety mainly land-based employees. And he can choose who may live in his 300 houses from the converted dairy in a commanding position high up amid Belvoir's woods to the more modest cottages of Knipton and Woolsthorpe.

The people of Belvoir and the area around may or may not approve of the control which the Duke of Rutland exercises over the lives of others and of the land itself; they may or may not agree with the way he wields his power. But they live with the knowledge that his control will continue more or less unchanged for the foreseeable future.

Visit the vast landed estates of Scotland, however, and a rather different picture emerges. The control wielded by these private owners over the lives of others is just as great. But many of Scotland's landless citizens have to cope with change as well as subjection. When ownership changes, the landless may find their lives turned upside down as they find themselves subject to the new whims of a new laird. Unlike the great English and Welsh landed estates, those of the Highlands of Scotland change hands frequently. This is because many of them are considered by their owners less as the seat of a family's power than as a financial investment or a place of resort in August and September to enjoy what bloodsports the estate can offer. This approach enables and indeed encourages owners to buy and sell if they calculate they will gain a financial advantage by selling or if they tire of a particular location.

Knoydart is one of many Scottish estates whose resident families have lived under a cloud of uncertainty about the future of their homes and their livelihoods. This estate – an eighty-five-square-mile peninsula of spectacular mountains, rivers and coastline jutting out into the sea opposite the Isle of Skye – has changed hands seven times this century. In only one case was the transfer from father to son; the other owners came in from outside. As ownership of the estate also includes ownership not only of nearly all the houses but also of all the land that could be developed for tourism, coastal smallholdings, fish farming and so on, the personality of the owner is of vital importance to local people. A combination of the uncertainty engendered by changes of ownership and the preference given to bloodsports over other uses of land has led many people to leave Knoydart. Archie MacDougall, for instance, left Knoydart in 1948 after taking place in a 'land raid' – an attempt to get the then owner, the 2nd Baron Brocket, to release land for cultivation. Despite the mountainous terrain that dominates Knoydart, there are many stretches of land, particularly around the coast and in the valleys, that could be cultivated. Mr MacDougall believes the majority of Knoydart's owners this century have imposed a stranglehold on the economic development of its land. He told me in 1985: 'It's just a closed book. What goes on on these estates is nobody's business but their own. Yet everybody on the estate is completely dependent on them for employment.'

(i) EMPLOYERS AND LANDLORDS

One way in which landowners exert direct power over other human beings is as employers – of farm and forestry workers, huntservants, kennel-maids, gardeners, gamekeepers, grooms, farm managers and land agents. But while anybody who sells his labour to an employer necessarily subjects himself to the power and influence of that employer, the extent of the subjection for most land-based workers is often far greater since they may well depend on their employers not only for their weekly wage, but for their accommodation as well.

The double hold over home and job puts a landowner in a strong position. A dispute with the boss can put a labourer's home at risk as well as his job. According to a survey for Shelter, 70 per cent of agricultural workers live in tied cottages.[1] They do not all have bad relations with their employer-landlords, but they all share a special sense of insecurity unknown to the council tenant or owner-occupier. They cannot be sure they will be able to live in their home in retirement and have to bear this in mind when contemplating improvements.

The position of the farmworker in a tied cottage has been strengthened in recent years. Before 1976, an employer who wanted his tied house back could simply go to the county court and get a possession order; the only protection the farmworker had in such situations was the possibility of having the possession order delayed by up to six months. After that, it was automatic eviction – whether or not the employee had managed to find another home. The 1976 Rent Act requires employers to establish agricultural need before they can repossess a cottage. Even if he does not succeed the first time, an employer can ask for a re-hearing at any time, so there is never absolute security for a former farmworker whose tenancy is secured by this legislation.

The 1976 Act does not extend to Scotland or Northern Ireland nor does it embrace landworkers in any part of the UK who are not strictly farmworkers. Instead these workers – like Britain's 5,000 huntservants or 6,000 gamekeepers – are normally on service tenancies. If their job ends, their employer can take them to the county court and evict them through a possession order within twenty-eight days. A former Yorkshire huntservant explained to me in 1982 the conditions under which he had worked:

Huntservants are usually bred into the job – your father's a huntservant. The attraction of the job is that you're always in the countryside. Jobs in agriculture are going, so it's one of the only jobs if you want to stay in the countryside and you don't have your own land. A huntservant would earn the basic agricultural wage: £60–£65 a week, whether you work fifty hours or seventy hours. I've worked 90 hours some weeks. To a huntservant, a day's hunting is relaxation – he's not working physically, just mentally ... When you take the job on whether it's gamekeeper or huntservant you take it on as a paid servant, on a set wage, without overtime payments, with a tied cottage and no pension fund. If you've stayed in the job a lifetime, you get no pension. And you have to leave the house. They say 'Thank you very much; you're on your own, mate'.

In view of working conditions such as these, it is hardly surprising that Britain's land-based workers tend to be deferential and subservient to their landed masters. Looming in the background all the time is the fear of redundancy. In East Anglia and the South East, to take one example, the full-time agricultural labour force was cut by 55 per cent in the sixteen years between 1969 and 1985.[2]

In Britain, the ownership of, say, the Duke of Rutland's 18,000 acres or the owner since 1984 of Knoydart Philip Rhodes' 52,000 acres can be seen not simply as physical ownership of the land itself insofar as that can be said to be owned, but ownership of a position in a whole nexus of rights relating to land and property. Some of these rights, such as the right to appoint tenants or bar people from walking where they want to flow naturally from the fact of ownership. But in Britain land ownership may also bring with it other rights that bear no obvious relationship with the land at all but which are inherited from history. One of several examples of this type of power is the control many private landowners possess over appointments to livings in the Church of England.

(ii) CHURCH OF ENGLAND LIVINGS

In medieval times and before, it was either the monasteries or the people in charge of virtually every aspect of life – the local secular lords – who ordered the construction of churches and put in the priest. For the lay lords, a church on the estate was a status symbol, an opportunity for influence and a source of profit. Over the years, the Church itself has taken over much of the exercise of patronage, or the right of presentation of a priest to a church living. However, patronage exercised by individual people, usually landowners, is still by no means uncommon. In 1964, the most recent year for which comprehensive figures are available, 2,570 church livings were in private hands.[3] These amounted to 22 per cent of all paid clergy livings in the Church of England. This proportion was considerably less than the proportion more than a century ago: figures that happen to be available for 1836 reveal that private owners controlled at that time 47 per cent of all Church of England livings.[4] Nonetheless, in 1964, private individuals made up the second most important category of patron after bishops and archbishops. And because the 2,570 livings involve far fewer than this number of patrons, one man can, over the years, control a large number of appointments. Yorkshire landowner the 11th Baron Middleton, for

example, who died in 1970, had presented fifty-two vicars in
forty years.[5] Of course, some of the bishops themselves are
landowners as well. The 1964 survey revealed that more than
half of England's bishops owned land either by birth or through
marriage.[6]

Until the twentieth century, the most obvious benefit for the
Church of landowner involvement was financial. The landowner
would give the parish lands from whose income it could draw or
he would make direct payments. For instance, there was a time
in the nineteenth century when the income of the parish of Bury
in Lancashire was £2,000 a year greater than the stipend of the
Archbishop of Canterbury. In return for his bounty the landowner secured the effective right to appoint anyone, who might
be a relative, to a living. That parish of Bury was and still is in
the gift of the Earls of Derby, and in the nineteenth century
members of the family were regularly appointed to the living.
During our own century, however, endowments to particular
parishes have been divided between all parishes by Act of
Parliament and while patrons are free to make financial
donations to the parish, for instance for the upkeep of the
parsonage, they do not support the priest financially.

Some private patrons are newcomers to land ownership who
have come to own land and with it any livings that happen to
have been attached to it recently – like Leicester Racecourse
Holdings Limited, for instance, which came to own the Church
living of Oadby when it bought land there in 1883 to build a
new racecourse. The company controlled the living for a century
until it transferred it to the bishop in 1984.

More frequently, however, private patrons are old-established
landowners. The Duke of Rutland, for example, possessed six
Church livings in 1986. In three of these the Duke was the sole
patron; in one other patronage was controlled jointly by the
Duke, the Bishop and the Diocesan Board of Patronage; while
the Duke shared the remaining two livings either with Major-
General Sir Humphry Tollemache Bt on his own or also with
Baron Gretton. Private patrons in the Winchester diocese in
1986 (to take another typical example) included the Earl of
Portsmouth, Lord Ashburton, the Earl of Caernarvon and Lord
Northbrook, each with two livings apiece; Lord Montagu of

Beaulieu, the Earl of Normanton, Viscount Camrose, Sir Westrow Hulse, Sir James Scott and the Earl of Selborne with one living each; and the Duke of Wellington with three livings in his gift. In towns, the bishop tends to be the patron of a benefice – although private landowners do survive as patrons in towns and cities. The 6th Duke of Westminster, for instance, has three benefices in Belgravia. However, the vast majority of a landowner's livings do tend to be in the country: the 6th Marquess of Exeter, who died in 1981, was the patron of one church living in London and fourteen in and around his 19,700-acre estate based at Stamford, Lincolnshire. Once the terms of his will have been put into effect, these livings will pass to members of his family; the 7th Marquess lives in Canada.

The power of private patrons lies in being able to appoint priests – whether the local bishop, the local parishioners or anybody else agrees with their choice or not. It is certainly true that some patrons consult the bishop and perhaps churchwardens about an appointment; but they are under no obligation to do so, let alone to take their wishes into account.

The power to appoint priests was once considered so valuable that this power used to be bought and sold on its own. Parish records contain numerous reports of these transactions – in 1679, for instance, Lawrence Alcock of Midhurst paid £60 to Anthony Kemp of Goodwood for the right of patronage of the parish church of Binsted in Sussex and a further £60 for the right of patronage at South Stoke. An Act of Parliament in 1923 made such transactions illegal, and since that time, private patronage has existed almost invariably as a right alongside other rights belonging to the owners of a particular tract of land, not transferable on its own.

It is the treatment of the right to appoint priests as real property, or in other words a right attaching to land, that is at the heart of the debate over private patronage that has exercised Church of England synods and assemblies for decades. Canon C. R. Craston, who chaired one stage in the process of devising a new Benefices Measure in the late 1970s, told me in 1985:

Patronage is an anachronism. It is indefensible on New Testament principles. If the choosing of parish priests is in the hands of anybody, it should be in the hands of the diocese plus the parish. Other churches [which are] the subject of possible union moves with the Church of England could not have accepted patronage. The Church of England is the only church in Christendom across the world with this system.

Since the early 1960s, there have been calls for the radical reform of a number of aspects of the organization of the Church of England such as the compulsory retirement of clergy. Patronage is one element that has resisted wholesale change. However, after decades of committees and proposals and debates and resignations a new Benefices Measure has been approved by the General Synod. Published in 1985 as the Patronage (Benefices) Measure, it was approved by Parliament in 1986, and makes a number of changes to the present system of private patronage. First, the new Measure requires that from October 1987 every patron must declare that he is a member of the Church of England before he appoints an incumbent. (Hitherto, only Roman Catholics were disqualified: athiests could appoint.) If the patron is not a Church of England member, he will have to nominate another person who is an Anglican to make the appointment in his place. The other part of the Measure, which comes into effect in 1989, alters the procedure by which priests are appointed. It provides that the parochial church council may by resolution request a meeting with the patron to discuss an appointment, and if such a meeting is requested, the bishop must also be present. Once a patron has decided on the priest to whom he proposes to offer the living, he will have under the new Measure to obtain the approval of the bishop and that of representatives of the parish concerned. Finally, a patron will no longer be able to sell a benefice as a right attached to a piece of land, although it will still be perfectly possible for a right of patronage to be inherited or given away along with a piece of property.

The patronage system is therefore not being abolished but modified. Critics of the system do not believe these changes are all that radical. On what appears at first sight the most significant change – the power of veto over appointments given to bishops and parishes – Canon Craston observed: 'A veto looks like a black mark against somebody. You have got to have strong grounds for applying it. The fact that a bishop or the church-wardens think somebody is not quite the right person will hardly be grounds for their vetoing an appointment.'

So even after the 1986 Benefices Measure comes into effect, landowners look like continuing to wield considerable power in this area for the foreseeable future.

Regional

(i) LOCAL GOVERNMENT

Just as Britain's landowners have helped shape the institutions of the Church of England so they have left their imprint on local government. Our landowners' enduring power today still draws sustenance through its historic roots. Industry, trade unions and conservation groups are relatively new phenomena while landowners were in at the shaping of many of the institutions through which power now flows – both Houses of Parliament, the Crown, the Church of England and local authorities.

Today they still play a crucial role in local government. There is no reason to suppose that landowners abuse the positions of public trust they hold to advance their personal interests. The significance of the role they play in public authorities is that their efforts to promote the public good necessarily reflect the special view of what is right which is held by the group to which they belong.

For thirty-nine years, from 1946 until his retirement in 1985, the 10th Duke of Rutland was a member of Leicestershire County Council. After local government reorganization, he was the first chairman of the new Leicestershire County Council, from 1973 until 1977. His term on both county councils has included membership of most committees although his main interest has been in the policy and resources committee and the police committee (of which he was chairman from 1979 until 1985). There are plenty more like him. Throughout our own century, landowners have continued to play an active part in local politics, and today their representation on rural county and district councils is out of all proportion to their minuscule numbers in the population as a whole.

In April 1985, for example, landowners or farmers (including retired farmers and farmers' wives) made up the following proportions of the membership of the following county councils (the 1981 census figure for the proportion of farmers in the adult population of the counties concerned is given in brackets afterwards): North Yorkshire: 16 per cent (2 per cent); Suffolk: 18 per cent (1 per cent); Oxfordshire: 9 per cent (0.6 per cent); Lincolnshire: 22 per cent (2 per cent); Buckinghamshire 17 per cent (0.5 per cent); Cornwall: 28 per cent (2.3 per cent). A look at some district councils yields the following equivalent figures: South Lakeland: 8 per cent (2.7 per cent of the total adult population); West Dorset: 25 per cent (2.8 per cent); Taunton Deane: 10 per cent (1.9 per cent). On five of the six county councils (North Yorkshire, Suffolk, Lincolnshire, Buckinghamshire and Cornwall) and one of the three district councils (Taunton Deane), a farmer or landowner held the position of either chairman or leader of the council in April 1985.

Why should farmers and landowners be so numerically strong in local government compared to their numbers in the population as a whole? There seem to be two main reasons. First, it is far easier for any self-employed person to take part in local government than an employed person because he does not have to ask his boss for time off to attend meetings; if he is also rich he does not have to worry about losing working time as a taxi driver might. Secondly, the Conservative Party in particular tends to prefer to choose farmers or landowners as candidates in elections.

(ii) REGIONAL INSTITUTIONS

Other regional institutions which are not strictly local authorities also tend to have more than their fair share of landowners or farmers. Take the nine regional water authorities of England and Wales. As far as impact on the attractions of the countryside are concerned, the most influential aspect of the water authorities' work is the drainage of land. Water authorities carry out large-scale drainage schemes both to alleviate floods in built-up areas and to enable farmers to grow crops more profitably by artificially lowering water tables. In 1983–4, the water authorities spent £22.7 million of public money on drainage, about half for town flooding and about half for agriculture. Drainage for agricultural improvement has attracted much concern in recent years because of the devastating effect it can have on wildlife. Yet in 1983–4, the chairmen of all nine water authorities' agriculture and land drainage committees responsible for administering this money and for deciding how conflicts between drainage and conservation should be reconciled were farmers.

To a lesser but real extent, the imprint of the landowner is also to be found on private regional institutions such as building societies, television companies and commercial and industrial companies.

Landowners also exert considerable influence regionally through their positions in a variety of state or state-financed agencies, from the National Coal Board to new town development agencies, industrial development boards to higher education institutions. Research by the Benwell Community Development Project of West Newcastle illustrates the way in which rural landowners have continued to exert great economic and social power in what is primarily an industrial region – the North East – throughout the twentieth century.

The Benwell team examined the changing fortunes of seventeen dynastic families all heavily involved in the industries of West Newcastle during the nineteenth century. By the turn of the century, most of these families were major rural landowners as they have continued to be. Some had always been landowners and had also become industrialists; others came from merchant backgrounds but involvement in industries like coal, heavy engineering and shipbuilding enabled them to buy rural estates. During the nineteenth century, these families wielded enormous economic power. By the end of the century, many of the mines in the region were run down and needed massive investment and the mine-owning families declined to invest heavily in either the mines or the other industries. Instead, they chose to diversify their portfolios, channelling funds into finance, property and land. Investment in rural land in particular had an advantage over and above its financial return: it enabled the industrial families to enhance their status still further by joining their aristocratic landowning allies within the county élite.

Today, the Benwell landowning families also wield considerable economic power through holding key positions in the state apparatus. Sir Michael Straker, for instance, a present-day member of one of the seventeen families, has held various positions in the state machinery within the region; since 1982 he has been chairman of the Northumbria Water Authority and since 1980 of the Peterlee and Aycliffe Development Corporations. The 4th Viscount Ridley, a member of another of the Benwell team's families, is a director of the Northern Rock Building Society, Tyne Tees Television, Barclays Bank (North-East) and Municipal Mutual Insurance, and chairman of the Newcastle University Development Trust, which develops academic projects to benefit the region.

But the present-day influence of the Benwell landowning families does not end with economic power. Although excluded from the elected local authorities of staunch Labour strongholds like Tyneside, they continue to exert considerable social and political power not only in the shire counties around but also through membership of both Houses of Parliament. While Sir Michael Straker is a former Northumberland County Councillor, Lord Ridley was chairman of the old Northumberland County Council between 1967 and 1974, and then chaired the new County Council between 1974 and 1979. He is Lord Lieutenant and Custos Rotulorum of Northumberland and like many major landowners holds several high-ranking positions in the Territorial Army. His brother, Nicholas Ridley, has been Member of Parliament since 1959 for the Cirencester and Tewkesbury division of Gloucestershire. After holding various lesser position in government, he became Secretary of State for Transport in 1983 and, in 1986, Secretary of State for the Environment.

Dr Bill Williamson of Durham University, who supervised the Benwell research, explained in 1985 of the Benwell families, 'Their money once invested in coal, ships and railways remains secure in the modern financial world. They have moved their investments out – into finance, into property and into land. But we shouldn't underestimate the role that they still play. They do play a role in property, they do play a major role in the financial institutions of the region, and of course some of them play a major role in the multinational companies which are so much part now of the economic life of this region and which in effect control that economic life.'[8]

The Benwell work also illustrates an important buttress of landowners' power: the social prestige attached to the ownership of land. Many of those of the West Newcastle families who were not originally landowners bought into land at least partly because of the social status attached to it. And once they had done so, they did not develop a view of their own of the role of the landowner but were content to adopt the ways of the existing landowning class. Today, people who achieve status in government, industry, banking or entertainment often turn out to be aspirant landowners. As such they are naturally slow to move against the class they seek to join. So he who would tangle with the landowners in Britain finds he attracts less support than he might hope in the corridors of power of the nation. For power, however it originates, tends to turn into landowning power.

(iii) NATIONAL PARK AUTHORITIES

Within the structure of rural local government, one area where one might expect the dominance of farmers and landowners to be challenged is in the special committees and boards set up to administer and plan Britain's ten national parks. Right from the point in 1949 when the idea of national parks was introduced to the statute book, it was recognized that if the national parks were to be adequately conserved and their recreation potential exploited, then the local landowners' interest would need to be countered by representation of the national interest. To this end, Attlee's 1949 National Parks and Access to the Countryside Act laid down that the task of planning and administering the parks should be given to special national park authorities, two-thirds of whose members should be drawn from the local councils in whose areas the parks lie and one-third of whom should be appointed by the Minister of Town and Country Planning (a responsibility which has now passed to the Secretary of State for the Environment). The task of this latter group is to uphold the national role of the parks in conserving the nation's best scenery and providing for outdoor recreation for the British people as a whole whenever this conflicts with local concerns. But have the authorities now become responsive to the general will?

Three of Britain's national parks lie in Wales – the Snowdonia National Park, the Brecon Beacons National Park and the Pembrokeshire Coast National Park. I asked each of the authorities for these parks to let me have details of the profile of their membership as at April 1985. What emerged was the opposite of what might be expected. For farmers and landowners were proportionately even better represented on these authorities than on many local planning authorities outside national parks. Landowners and farmers made up an average of exactly one-third of the membership of the Welsh park authorities in April 1985 (the actual figures are 35 per cent, 26 per cent and 39 per cent respectively).

These figures cannot be seen simply as providing evidence that local economic interests are well represented. If this were so, then tourism, which employs about the same number of people as agriculture in all the parks, should be well represented on the park authorities. In fact, however, in only two of the three Welsh national parks was there any member connected with the tourist trade. (The Brecon Beacons and the Pembrokeshire Coast park authorities included one hotelier apiece.) In all the Welsh parks, landowners and farmers were numerous both among the local authority representatives and among the nominated members of the park authorities. Even the Ministerial nominees rarely included people living outside the park area let alone in the urban areas whose populations might be expected to look to the parks concerned for recreation. The Pembrokeshire Park authority for instance included just one member with an address outside Pembrokeshire – and he lived not in Birmingham, Bristol or Cardiff but in Carmarthen.

The situation in the English national parks is hardly different from that in Wales. A recent survey of the membership characteristics of the appointed members of all ten national parks shows the same domination of local and in particular landowning interests. Dr Ian Brotherton of Sheffield University who carried out the survey found that 40 per cent of the appointed members of the national parks in 1983–4 had as their main occupation farming or forestry.[9] Although the figure was smaller during periods of Labour administration, it was not much smaller: the proportions of nominated members with their main occupations in farming and forestry was 30 per cent in 1974–5, 26 per cent in 1979–80, and 39 per cent in 1982–3. No one would suggest that park authorities should not include people who are acquainted with agriculture and forestry, but there is no way that the present composition of the park authorities can be squared with their supposed purpose. Once again the mysterious power of the landowners has aborted a potential challenge to their position.

(iv) LORD LIEUTENANTS

Knowledge is power and in any county, alongside the elected councillors and their officials, there is a select circle of people who exercise influence by being 'in the know'.

A key member of this group is the lord lieutenant. Former Bedfordshire county planning officer Geoffrey Cowley explained to me in 1984: 'The Lord Lieutenant is very well placed to know just what is afoot, and has an automatic entry to any place of relative privilege. It is difficult to say "no" to the Lord Lieutenant.'

Henry VIII appointed lord lieutenants to discharge responsibility for the maintenance of law and order and for all military measures needed to be taken for local defence. Their military function led sovereigns to look to those citizens on whom they had traditionally relied to raise an army – the landowners. And an automatic assumption that lord lieutenants should be found among the ranks of a county's main landowners still seems to obtain.

In 1985, twenty-six of the lord lieutenants of the thirty-one counties of Scotland, for example, were landowners. The people involved were the owners of large, landed estates, not small-time farmers. Large landowners who are not themselves lord lieutenants will often be among each county's several deputy lieutenants and as such privy to the information circulating within the élite.

Insofar as most people have any idea of the duties which the office of lord lieutenant confers, they know that he acts as the representative of the Sovereign in his county. He is the first to receive a royal visitor into his area and, on the Sovereign's behalf, he presents awards and medals.

Few people realize, however, that the lord lieutenant retains one very real power from the days when he was the sole upholder of the king's peace. Each lord lieutenant is automatically Custos Rotulorum, or the chief magistrate within his county. As a result, he is normally chairman of the Lord Chancellor's County Advisory Committee. This committee, whose proceedings and membership (apart from the name and address of the secretary) are secret, advise the Lord Chancellor on the appointment and conduct of magistrates in the county concerned.

National

PARLIAMENT

One hundred years ago, in 1885, Lord John Manners, Member of Parliament and later 7th Duke of Rutland (and great-grand-father of the 10th Duke), took on the job of Postmaster-General in Gladstone's Government for the second time. The following year he was to become Chancellor of the Duchy of Lancaster, and he had already been MP for Newark, Colchester and the Melton division of Leicestershire in turn in a parliamentary career that was to span forty-four years. The present 10th Duke of Rutland has been confined in his membership of Parliament, however, to the House of Lords. An incumbent Duke of Rutland has not sat in the House of Commons since 1895.

In the House of Commons as a whole, farmers and landowners are far less numerous than they were a century ago. Nonetheless, they form a sizeable bunch of people. After the 1983 General Election, for example, fifty-nine members of the Lower House, or 9 per cent, described themselves either as landowners, farmers, the directors of agricultural firms or members of the National Farmers' Union, according to a count by Richard Howarth of the University College of North Wales at Bangor.[10]

In politics as elsewhere in public life, landowners and farmers are often to be found holding the most important jobs. Take the European Parliament. Landowners are not particularly well represented among the UK's Euro-MPs. Nonetheless, Warwick-shire farmer Sir Henry Plumb, whose long career in the National

Farmers' Union included nine years as its president, was chairman of the European Parliament's highly influential Agriculture Committee between 1979 and 1982, and rejoined that committee in 1984. The same tendency for landowners and farmers to rise to the top applies in the Cabinet. In April 1985, nearly one-third of Mrs Thatcher's Cabinet were farmers or landowners – and this *after* the departure of Lord Carrington (whose family owns a reported 25,000 acres spread over three counties), Francis Pym (the owner of a landed estate and stately home in Bedfordshire), Cornwall landowner Sir John Nott and Suffolk farmer and former Minister of Agriculture James Prior.

Since there is no register of interests of members of the Upper House comparable to the register of MPs' interests, it is hard to say precisely how many peers are landowners or farmers. However, in 1985, of the 1,176 Members of the House 762 (65 per cent) were hereditary peers by succession, many of them from old-established landowning families.

In some matters, the over-representation of major landowners in the House of Lords may not matter much. But where there is a conflict of interest between these people and other groups, the unrepresentative nature of the Lords is a matter of deep concern. Few members of the Upper Chamber can, for instance, speak with authority and first-hand experience about the needs of farmworkers or Hebridean fishermen, let alone city-dwellers seeking access to the countryside. Yet a large number of peers are extremely conversant with the problems faced by the agricultural landlord or forest owner.

Lobbies

The parliamentary strength of Britain's landowners and farmers is far from being their only political asset. Like other interest groups, they organize to lobby Parliament, Government and the media. Yet they have influence way beyond that of most other pressure groups by virtue of their wealth, history and close ties with Establishment institutions.

THE LAND OWNERSHIP LOBBY

The Country Landowners' Association (CLA) and its counterpart north of the border, the Scottish Landowners' Federation, exist to preserve private land ownership in its present form and to protect landowners' interests. These organizations not only advise their members on issues related to land ownership – anything from tied cottage matters to the formation of family trusts to hold land – they also lobby persistently and successfully on their members' behalf.

We have already seen that history lends support to the present-day power of Britain's landowners. One implication of this – which is illustrated well by the activities of the Country Landowners' Association – is that, in asserting their own interests, unlike most interest groups in the political marketplace, landowners do not have to secure changes. Whether it is a matter of law or custom or tax regulation or whatever, all they usually have to do is to prevent other interests from securing changes to the status quo. They do not have to explain why they should be given power. The burden of argument is on those who would strip it from them and these have first to organize and articulate a case before they need even be resisted.

Three typical CLA achievements on the national political stage in 1984. First, the Association could claim at least part of the credit for the removal of investment income surcharge. Before 1984, unearned income from rents was taxed at a higher rate than earned income. Investment income would be taxed at a person's marginal rate of income tax and an extra 15 per cent added on for unearned income. Since 1984, however, earned and unearned income have been lumped together and taxed at the marginal rate. In 1984, the Country Landowners' Association also played a part in securing a substantial cut in the top rate of capital transfer tax, and in the 'toppling' (the CLA's own word)[11] of the 1976 Agriculture (Miscellaneous Provisions) Act. This Act had granted security of tenure for three generations of farm tenants: the 1984 Agricultural Holdings Act, which replaces the relevant provision, provides that new farm tenancies made after the Act comes into force will exclude this right to succession. These three changes were the result of constant pressure over several years, but the CLA also keeps watch for any new legislation that might erode their members' privileges and interests. For instance, a private Bill promoted by Oxfordshire County Council in 1982 would have given the Council a veto over the disposal of land covered by an agreement with the Council dealing with the provision of public facilities like roads, parking, open space, rights of way and drains in private developments. The CLA reported: 'After friendly discussion, the council dropped the offending provision and the CLA chalked up another score in its defence of private ownership.'[12]

The success of the CLA in such matters does not depend on its ability to secure the attention of news editors or to worry governments by activating back-bench revolts. Unlike other pressure groups it can rely on long-established personal contacts between its activists and key figures in the national élite. The constant contact that occurs between CLA staff and top civil servants, ministers or peers is usually enough to secure the organization's objectives. And one of the objectives most success- fully achieved is the maintenance of a low profile. Enhancing the position of the privileged at a time of national decline is much easier if it can be done behind closed doors. The fact that so few know of the CLA's achievements is itself one of the more valuable of those achievements.

THE FARMING LOBBY

Though it does not enjoy the same cachet in the upper reaches of the British Establishment, the farmers' lobby is even more effective than the landowners'.

The National Farmers' Union of England and Wales (it has counterparts in Scotland and Ulster), works less through élite contacts than through thorough-going detailed collaboration with civil servants coupled with a formidable publicity machine. The NFU's power is based not in the old-boy network but in the wealth that enables it to employ hundreds of professional lobby- ists and specialist advisers. In 1985, the NFU's expenditure was £8.8 million. The organization used this money to support campaigning on behalf of its members at three main levels – local, national and European.

Taking Europe first, we find that in 1984 alone the NFU spent £300,000 on its Brussels office. This office not only main- tains close contact with members of the European Parliament, the European Commission, farmers' groups in other Common

Market countries, but also key individuals – like, for instance, Sir Henry Plumb.

If we turn to the local level, we find the NFU organized in county branches each of which has its own structure of committees and officers. In 1984, the East Sussex County Branch alone, for example, had separate county committees, each meeting every month and answerable to the monthly meeting of the executive committee on each of the following topics: publicity, finance, employment and education, cereals, seeds, milk, pigs, potatoes and vegetables as well as a working party on countryside and environment. The NFU's county branches provide the basis of the Union's financial support and play a very active part in the lobbying process, applying pressure on their own constituency MPs, local councils, local television stations and local newspapers as well as providing advice to national office and a corps of active members ready to join deputations to London or Brussels. Should a new MP take his seat, for instance, the county branch staff will be at the House of Commons meeting him and arranging for him to spend days on farms in his constituency. In this way the number of MPs sympathetic to farmers' interests are kept up, ready for recourse from the county branch or headquarters whenever this should prove necessary.

Such feelers to MPs carry with them the taste of invitation into a club – and one into which the new MP can throw himself without appearing to alienate any obvious rival interest group.

At national level, the same kind of approach is followed. John Silkin tells what happened when he became Minister of Agriculture, Fisheries and Food in 1976: 'On Day One, a few hours after I had become Minister, I received a letter addressing me by my Christian name from the President of the NFU. I didn't even know who he was at that time I regret to say, but it was "Dear John", signed "Yours sincerely, Henry", and that was what gave us what the relationship was.'[13]

Not that the NFU's contact with the Ministry of Agriculture is confined to a chummy relationship with the Minister: it operates at all levels. The NFU has far closer and more comprehensive contact with a Whitehall department than any other pressure group. NFU Parliamentary Secretary Barney Holbeche told a 'World in Action' reporter in 1983: 'At official level as

between NFU staff officials and civil servants there is regular
contact often almost on a day-to-day basis. Most of us know our
opposite numbers by Christian names.'[14]

It was World War II which opened the doors of the Ministry
of Agriculture to the National Farmers' Union. In 1939, the
Ministry of Agriculture depended on the Union's help to put
agriculture on a war footing. The authors of a study of the
relationship of farmers to government in Britain, Peter Self and
Herbert Storing, write of this crucial period in the NFU's history:

Regular consultations between the Minister of Agriculture and representatives of the Union were begun in 1939 and continued throughout the
war . . . The Union shouldered widening responsibility for agricultural
policy in exchange for an increasing measure of influence over it . . . In
hundreds of matters of detail, from the supply of binder twine to the
acquisition of land for military purposes, and on dozens of official
advisory committees, Whitehall and the Union's old headquarters at
Bedford Square were drawn together.[15]

After the war, when agriculture policy-making acquired such
a high priority as a peace-time task for Government, officials
looked to a continuation of their war-time relationship with the
NFU to put their policy into practice.

The 1947 Agriculture Act consolidated the Union's consulta-
tive position with the Ministry still further. It guaranteed British
farmers high prices for their main products and made it a duty
of the Ministry to consult the National Farmers' Union each
year before setting these prices. This annual, statutory consultation was to enhance and perpetuate the close relationship
between the Union and the Ministry that had been forged in the
war.

Constant contact with a government department not only
enables a pressure group to imbue the ministry officials with its
own philosophy; it also enables it to keep abreast of all developments that might conceivably affect its interests. Crucially, it
can then apply pressure while ideas are still being crystallized in
Whitehall and before a Minister commits himself even at the
level of a green paper or a consultation paper to affected
organizations. This is a happy situation for the NFU: the
pressure group that enjoys access to an official when some new

scheme is but a gleam in his eye can influence the limits within which any public debate will subsequently be conducted.

The NFU's success in maintaining its grip on Whitehall is not allowed to become an exercise for slackness on other fronts – like Parliament. NFU Parliamentary Secretary Barney Holbeche: 'We have a lot of contact I would say with something of the order of a hundred MPs out of the 635 but we also have perhaps rather less contact with 350, 400, something of that nature.'[16]

Close contact with the Ministry of Agriculture and with both Houses of Parliament are two of the three main elements that combine to produce what former Minister of Agriculture John Silkin has described as 'the most effective, well-organized lobby in Britain, possibly in Europe'.[17]

The third element is a truly formidable publicity machine, of which the central cog is the large and experienced headquarters press and information office. Way back in 1950, the report of the Union's publicity section makes impressive reading: sixty-nine press releases issued and thirteen press conferences organized. Thirty-three years on, in 1983, the Union was still putting a massive effort into publicity with 161 press notices and eleven press conferences, as well as hosting informal lunches for top people in television and newspapers. All this helped to ensure that the NFU message would be widely broadcast: during 1983 alone, broadcasts by NFU office-holders, chairmen and vice-chairmen of headquarters committees and headquarters staff totalled 240 – an average of 4.6 every week. Those who appear on radio or television on behalf of the Union are well prepared. One section of Agriculture House runs courses to teach Union representatives down to the level of county branch members the techniques of radio and television, while another section issues them with briefing and speech notes.

There is also plenty of effort outside Agriculture House. A key element in the dissemination of the NFU's view of the world is its network of regional information officers. These people maintain close contact with local radio, television and newspapers. So successful are they, and so peculiar are the standards of objectivity in the broadcasting institutions in this area, that in some cases they actually present regional and local programmes themselves.

Alongside the Union's steady stream of reactive comment on issues affecting farmers are specific campaigns aimed at improving the public image of the farmer and the farming industry. Since the early 1980s, an annual public opinion survey conducted for the Union by the market research firm MORI has sought to identify any changes in the public perception of farmers that might call for a change of emphasis in the Union's publicity effort. The 1984 campaign *He Cares* for instance was specifically designed to fight the growing impression that farmers are damaging the landscape: 'The farmers made the countryside what it is. And it is, essentially, a masterpiece,' declares *He Cares*, a glossy, colour brochure showing farmers going about their apparently customary occupations of thatching, laying hedges and building traditional dry stone walls – alongside ramblers who trample down their fields of corn.

The idea of the farmer as custodian of the countryside was just one theme in a campaign launched by the Union in 1982 under the banner 'Farming – the Backbone of Britain'. In this case, the accent was placed mainly on the contribution farming is supposed to make to the British economy. This campaign, launched by the NFU President at a press conference, and with the full support of the Minister of Agriculture, was followed by a conference of county branch chairmen, travelling displays and a full-colour book written by the Union. Such material gradually comes to form part of the Union's library of books, films and videos it has produced itself and which can be used in the classroom, conference room or village hall.

Whether fielding people to appear on local radio phone-ins or top-level conferences and farming programmes, or encouraging them to write letters to the newspapers, the Union is able, by virtue of the wide range of its membership, to call on many different kinds of people to put forward its views. Naturally enough it does not choose rich barley barons if it can help it. Most of the farm support policies in Britain since the war have proved of most benefit to large-scale, high-production farmers. However, the Union is in the fortunate position of being able to draw on three other groups for the figures to put forward as typical farmers.

First, there are the tenant farmers. These people are especially attractive to the NFU as symbols for the public of farmers since they are not in general the product of inherited privilege but epitomize instead honest toil for well-earned rewards. The NFU has burgeoned from a small organization originally formed in Lincolnshire in 1904 which deliberately restricted its membership to farmers – owner-occupiers and tenants. Landlords and their middlemen like factors and agents were not permitted to join the fledgling organization. This state of affairs has, however, long since changed, and now, within the NFU, the tenants and the landlords, the Ted Burgesses and the Lord Triminghams, exist side by side. A few of the tenants have gone on to become as powerful as some of the NFU's owner members. Tenant Ralph Baker, for example to take a particularly outstanding example, pioneered the post-war drainage of the Somerset Levels. He was one of the first farmers in the Levels to take advantage of generous Ministry of Agriculture grants to install electrically-powered pumps in order to lower the water table and thereby increase the quality of his grassland and thus milk yields. As a result of land drainage, Mr Baker was able to increase his herd of cattle (from forty to 350) and the amount of land he rented (from 100 acres to 450 acres) between 1963 and 1977 alone. A long-serving member of the NFU's national council, Mr Baker has been chairman of the Agriculture and Land Drainage Committee of the Wessex Water Authority since 1983. In this capacity he influences millions of pounds worth of major schemes covering Somerset, Dorset and Avon that reduce the risk of flooding in towns and increase farmers' potential for greater profits.

Another group of farmers almost as valuable in image terms as the tenant farmers are the horticulturalists, growing flowers, mushrooms, tomatoes, orchard and soft fruit and posing few environmental problems in the process. The fact that their holdings cover only 1 per cent of Britain's total area under crops does not prevent them from being pressed into service to put the Union's case. Finally, there are the small farmers, the men and women most comparable to the peasant farmers on the Continent. Their activities also tend to be far more benign than those of their large, richer brethren, though, as we have seen, their holdings amount to only a tiny fraction of Great Britain's land.

Of this group it is the small farmers in the hills, working under difficult conditions in some cases for little financial reward whose condition can be most effectively highlighted when the NFU needs an example of what it may wish to present as the sterling qualities of its under-appreciated and ill-rewarded membership.

Why are the small farmers prepared to be used as the acceptable face of modern agriculture? The answer is that in return for their co-operation in this matter the large producers maintain a fiction that benefits their smaller brethren. This is the myth that the small farmers play a necessary role in food production. In fact, Britain's small farmers produce only an insignificant proportion of our food. Within the warm embrace of the NFU their need for financial support is both supported and used as a means of buttressing the financial support of their bigger counterparts who do not need it.

There is, of course, nothing wrong with a pressure group advancing its own particular case and grinding its own particular axe in whatever way it thinks will prove most effective. However, democracy breaks down if one pressure group far outweighs in influence all others that might put forward an alternative point of view. This is the case with the farming lobby. Its power and influence is so overwhelming that it is almost as if it were part of the Government. And the NFU can engage in all this activity only because its members are rich enough to finance it. They are rich enough largely because the rest of the population as tax-payers and consumers pay them large sums of money. Compare the Union's expenditure with that of other pressure groups putting forward opposing points of view. In 1985, the Ramblers' Association, for example, found £350,000 for its battles to keep open public footpaths and to campaign in other fields of rural public access and conservation. The Union spent £8.8 million on its activities in 1985 – twenty-five times as much.

THE FORESTRY LOBBY

The timber growers' organizations, co-ordinated under the umbrella of Timber Growers United Kingdom, are based along-side the National Farmers' Union at Agriculture House in Knightsbridge. They conduct political activity in Parliament and Whitehall, negotiating in particular on grants and tax allowances for forestry and generally defending the industry's privileges, such as its exemption along with agriculture, but unlike any other industry, from town and country planning controls. And as it happens, landowners as foresters are even better placed to influence the relevant arms of government than landowners as farmers.

Much of the influence of Britain's formidable agricultural lobby is exercised through the extremely close relationship established by the National Farmers' Union between itself and the relevant department of government. To promote their interests as the owners of forest, Britain's landowners have not had to pull off any such feat of manipulation: the relevant state agency has effectively been run by the landowners themselves from the time the Forestry Commission was set up in 1919.

In 1986 three out of the eleven members of the Forestry Commission, including the chairman Sir David Montgomery, were landowners. Advising the Forestry Commissioners are three national committees, and in 1986 the chairmen of two of these committees were also landowners. On the third and bottom tier of the system that supports the Commission advising it on a wide range of matters, including possible conflicts between forestry and other land-uses, is a network of seven regional advisory committees. In 1986, five of these were chaired by landowners, while many other landowners sat as members. Five of the nine members of the South Scotland Regional Advisory Committee were also landowners or land agents as were five of the nine members of the East England Committee, to take two perfectly typical examples.

Alongside the landowners, the other major group on the Forestry Commission has always consisted of civil servants. Indeed, career civil servant Leslie Jenkins chaired the Commission from 1965 until 1970; and in 1986 three of the Forestry Commissioners were civil servants. But the civil servants on the Commission have not seen it as their place to assert forcefully the interests of the rest of society against that of the landowner/forester.

Nor have the remaining members of the Forestry Commission, whose identity has been influenced by a number of unpublished rules governing their selection. Two interest groups which might have been expected to challenge the status quo on afforestation methods – the forestry trade-union interest and the countryside conservation and recreation interest – have always been muffled within the Commission. And yet it was employment, amenity and recreation which were specifically mentioned in a government statement on the purpose of state finance for forestry in 1972. A team of Treasury economists concluded in a report that there was no sound economic reason for Britain to continue providing large-scale state subsidies to state or private forestry.[18] The team had applied a cost-benefit analysis to forestry and found it unable to meet the rate of return required for other nationalized industries. An innocent observer might have expected the immediate withdrawal of all state aid to forestry. Instead, Mr Heath's Government responded by altering the objectives which Forestry Commission planting was to pursue. A new government policy paper on forestry declared:

The Government have concluded that the main justification for Forestry Commission planting is to be found in the part which it can play in sustaining the rural economy, especially in areas which might otherwise be threatened with depopulation. The Government consider that, in the management of the Commission's commercial forests, there should be a marked increase of emphasis both on visual amenity and on realizing their potential for recreation.[19]

It might be imagined that this clear statement of new aims would have resulted in a rash of new appointments to the Commission itself of officials from the forestry workers' union primed to resist the industry's relentless de-manning together with activists from the ranks of Britain's most knowledgeable and committed countryside conservation and recreation campaigners. Nothing could be further from what happened. Forestry worker John Hose, the chairman of the Agricultural Workers' Trade Group Committee of the Transport and General Workers' Union, told me in 1985 he believes it is an unwritten rule that the odd trade unionist who gets appointed to the Commission should never come from the forestry workers' own union; the union representative on the Commission since 1978, for example, John Pollock, is General Secretary of the Scottish Teachers' Union.

Similarly, the 1973 statement did not result in a conservationist being appointed to the Commission, despite the continuing criticism of modern forestry methods from bodies like the Council for the Protection of Rural England. Instead, the landowner members of the Commission are assumed to take account of conservation. As Commission Press Officer Mrs Hazel Clowes explained to me in 1985 when I asked her who the amenity representatives on the Commission have been: 'One would hope that the landowning interest would take that on board.'

The Committee Committed

The Forestry Commission is only one of a handful of agencies of government holding such limited power as exists to influence the outcome of conflicts arising between our two major rural industries – farming and forestry – and the needs and interests of the non-landowning public. And in the other agencies too we find many members firmly committed to landowners' values.

The Countryside Commission for England and Wales and the Countryside Commission for Scotland are the government agencies charged with conserving the landscape beauty of Great Britain and of enhancing opportunities for open-air informal recreation. The Commissions also designate long-distance paths, national parks (although there are none in Scotland) and approve grant-aid for local recreation facilities like country parks. The Nature Conservancy Council is the government agency charged with conserving the wildlife of Great Britain.

Scrutiny of the membership of such organizations as the Countryside Commission, the Countryside Commission for Scotland and the Nature Conservancy Council reveals a constant landowner presence – albeit proportionately less marked than on the Forestry Commission. In May 1985, for instance, landowners, land agents or farmers made up about a quarter of the membership of each of these three bodies. But when examining the influence of the landowning community within government agencies such as these, it is instructive to examine the identity of the remaining members of the organizations in question. Think of, say, five of Britain's foremost countryside conservation and access campaigners, and names that come to mind might include

Lady Sylvia Sayer (with a lifetime's work on behalf of the Dartmoor Preservation Association and several national voluntary campaigning bodies including the Council for National Parks and the Open Spaces Society); Chris Rose (author and wildlife campaigner principally on behalf of Friends of the Earth and the World Wildlife Fund); Christopher Hall (vice-chairman since 1984 of the Ramblers' Association, former vice-chairman of the Southern Regional Council for Sport and Recreation, former director of the Council for the Protection of Rural England and former president of the Holiday Fellowship); Mrs Alison Kemp (a vice-chairman since 1978 of the Council for the Protection of Rural England and a member of the Common Land Forum as well as a former chairman of CPRE Oxfordshire and of the Oxfordshire Fieldpaths Society); and Drennan Watson (teacher of applied biology in agriculture, mountaineer and chairman of Scotland's North East Mountain Trust). However, you would look in vain for such names in the ranks of the Countryside Commissions or the Nature Conservancy Council. It is almost as if an unspoken rule lays down that no radical conservationist should ever be appointed to the government agencies they are perhaps better equipped than anybody else to serve. The only person from the top ranks of the voluntary conservation and access movement to have been appointed to either of these three agencies is the slightly less radical but firmly committed conservation and access campaigner Gerald McGuire. Before his appointment to the Countryside Commission, Mr McGuire had served as deputy secretary of the Youth Hostels' Association and as a member of a national park committee. But Mr McGuire was to survive on the Commission for just three years: the incoming Conservative Government of 1979 declined to reappoint him.

So what sort of people have swollen the ranks of the Countryside Commission since it was founded in 1968? Apart from the landowners and farmers, they have tended to be people drawn from diverse backgrounds – leading figures in local government and the trade unions or retired county planning officers. Many of these people are highly regarded public servants. But they are not committed to conservation and access: their interests are diverse. Like the civil servants on the Forestry Commission they are therefore incapable of forming a counterweight to the organized and determined landowners with whom they sit.

One example will illustrate the way in which the system operates in practice. In 1984, the Countryside Commission published a policy document on the uplands which called for the introduction of limited constraints on landowners' freedom to plant conifer forests on the moors and mountains of England and Wales.[20] The endorsement of this policy by the Nature Conservancy Council would have done much to strengthen the hand of the Commission in seeking controls over forestry. But the Conservancy held back precisely because of what the Commission said about controlling forestry. Editor of *The Countryman* Christopher Hall reports that when the Commission's proposals came to a meeting of the Conservancy Council, two members refused to endorse the Commission's line and their colleagues lacked the resolution to override them. The two who opposed a radical line on forestry were two former conveners of the Scottish Landowners' Federation, Sir Hector Munro and Viscount Arbuthnott.[21]

The landowner members of bodies like the Forestry Commission, the Countryside Commissions and the Nature Conservancy Council do not simply share a common culture: they are very often the same people. After serving an apprenticeship in local government, they often find that once elevated to these national land-use quangos they serve on several of them – sometimes at the same time.

In 1979 Sir David Montgomery Bt, the reported owner of a 6,000-acre estate in Kinross, took on the chair of the Forestry Commission after twenty years in local government including five as a member of Tayside Regional Council and spells both as vice-convener of the Regional Council and vice-president of the Convention of Scottish Local Authorities. On taking on the chair of the Forestry Commission, Sir David resigned from his positions in local government, and from the Nature Conservancy Council, where his six-year term of office had included a four-year tenure of the most important position in nature conservation affairs in Scotland: the chair of the Nature Conservancy Council's Advisory Committee for Scotland.

In a country like Scotland where so many major landowners

are absentees, preferring the warmth of the South for most of the
year, those relatively few large landowners who live in Scotland
all year round and are willing to take on public appointments
tend, like Sir David Montgomery, to have a finger in several
important pies. Dr Jean Balfour is the owner with her husband
of 18,000 acres of Sutherland. She also owns 1,000 acres of forest
in south-west Scotland, while a Balfour family trust own the
4,500-acre farm which she and her husband run. Like Sir
David, Dr Balfour also served in local government (as a county
councillor in Fife for twelve years) before accepting a host of
national appointments in land-use from the Heath Government
in the early 1970s. For nearly eleven years, between 1972 and
1982, Dr Balfour was chairman of the Countryside Commission
for Scotland. Between 1973 and 1980 she was also a member
of the Nature Conservancy Council, the Scottish Agricultural
Development Council (1972–7), and the Oil Development Council (1973–8). Between 1976 and 1985, she was chairman of the
Forestry Commission's Regional Advisory Committee for East
Scotland.

Even more striking is the record of John, 16th Viscount of
Arbuthnott of Arbuthnott House, Arbuthnott, Kincardineshire.
Lord Arbuthnott's ancestor, Hugh of Swinton in Berwickshire,
received the Arbuthnott estate in about 1195 from Osbert Olifard
who in his turn had been granted the land as a knight's fee from
William the Lion, King of Scots. Hugh's son, Duncan, adopted
the surname 'of Arbuthnott' which has been used by all his
successors. Between 1980 and his retirement in 1985, Lord
Arbuthnott was chairman of the highly influential Advisory
Committee for Scotland of the Nature Conservancy Council.
Over the same period, he also held the position of vice-chairman
of the Nature Conservancy Council covering the whole of Great
Britain. This former convener of the Scottish Landowners' Federation also served as a member of the Countryside Commission
for Scotland for four years and as chairman for six years of the
government-funded agency charged with managing Scotland's
deer populations, the Red Deer Commission. Since 1977, he has
also been lord lieutenant of Kincardineshire.

This is not to say that some landowning members of the
official agencies do not have considerable knowledge of the

area within which the agency works. Viscount Arbuthnott, for instance, worked as a land agent for the (then) Nature Conservancy before inheriting the viscountcy, while Dr Balfour has a degree in botany.

South of the border one man who has held most of the available appointments on government quangos concerned with conservation and recreation provision is Sir Ralph Verney Bt. Buckinghamshire landowner Sir Ralph, who lists shooting as his only recreation in *Who's Who*, was chairman of the Nature Conservancy Council between 1980 and 1983. For thirteen years up till 1980 he was chairman of the Forestry Commission's Committee for England and a member of the Forestry Commission itself for twelve years. For part of this time he also sat as an ordinary member on the Nature Conservancy Council. During the early 1960s, Sir Ralph was the president of the Country Landowners' Association. His public appointments in Buckinghamshire have included chairman of the County Council's Planning Committee and Finance Committee as well as high sheriff of Buckinghamshire and deputy lord lieutenant.

One slightly different type of landowner who looks set to take some of the key positions in the countryside during the next decade is John Dunning. Mr Dunning's membership of the executive committee of the Country Landowners' Association derives not from the ownership of a large landed estate but from the freehold ownership of a 700-acre Lake District farm. Mr Dunning is exactly the sort of person the CLA likes to put forward as a typical landowner: non-aristocratic, a farmer from the hills, relatively youthful, charming and a persuasive public speaker. In 1971, the Heath Government appointed Mr Dunning to the Lake District Special Planning Board to represent the national conservation and recreation interest in the planning of the Lake District national park. After sitting on the Lakes Board for seven years, Mr Dunning was appointed to the Countryside Commission in 1978 where he remained until 1983. In 1985, Mr Dunning became the chairman of Rural Voice – an alliance of nine national organizations concerned with the social and economic life of rural areas – after chairing the Cumbria Countryside Conference, the Rural Voice branch in that county. Mr Dunning, representing the national Rural Voice organization, told a fringe meeting at the 1985 Conservative Party conference that rural renewal could help to sustain the Conservative Government, even swinging seats presently held by other parties towards the Conservatives. A former vice-chairman of the Northern Council for Sport and Recreation, Mr Dunning is a member of a Forestry Commission working group examining the integration of forestry and farming in the lowlands and serves as specialist adviser to the House of Lords Select Committee on European Communities Rural Policies. Mr Dunning is well placed to secure the chair of the Countryside Commission when farmer Sir Derek Barber retires in 1989 after nine years at the helm.

The Secret Club

Britain's landowners are helped in the preservation of their privileges by the secrecy that surrounds matters affecting the ownership of land. It is far easier to cling to privileges if few are privy to their extent.

Look up the 9th Duke of Buccleuch and Queensbury in *Who's Who*. You will find no mention whatsoever of his role as a landowner. Yet, with a reported 277,000 acres in Scotland and 11,000 acres in Northamptonshire, the Duke is probably Britain's largest private landowner. Among the endless details of public appointments, company directorships and war service, there is very rarely any mention in directories like *Who's Who* of the holdings of Britain's landowners.

Contrast this situation with the position on the ownership of companies. At Companies House in London, anybody may discover the names of all the shareholders of every limited company in Great Britain as well as details of the company's profits and losses; a company that fails to give details of its shareholders can be fined or struck off the companies register.

In the 1870s, the Government was able to accede easily to the Earl of Derby's request for a register of landowners because at that time local valuation rolls prepared for the levying of rates on farmland gave all the necessary information. But in 1929, at the instigation of the National Farmers' Union, the Government granted agriculture the special privilege of exemption from payment of rates. As a result, for well over a half a century there have been no valuation rolls that could indicate who owns a vast amount of Britain's agricultural land.

The most easily comprehensible land register publicly available deals only with Northern Ireland. A little less than half of Ulster's rural land has been registered, which means that ownership details are available to the general public at the Province's land registry in Belfast. (Northern Ireland also has a publicly available register of deeds, but this records only information about all land transactions in the Province since 1923 and does not provide comprehensive data on land ownership.) In Scotland, the Register of Sasines, lodged in Edinburgh, provides publicly-available information on land ownership, though it is less easy to interpret than its counterpart across the Irish Sea. It does not include all titles to Scottish land, does not always provide a complete description of the land involved and does not reveal the identity of the individuals who make up the private trusts and companies which now hold much of Scotland's land. The Register is, however, open to public inspection. For the rest of the United Kingdom, no publicly available land register of any kind exists. Data held in the Land Registry in London would however provide a useful basis for a public land register, were one ever to be introduced. Index maps at the Registry give the number of the relevant certificate of registration of a piece of land in England or Wales. Such a certificate records the names of the legal owners of the property together with beneficial easements, restrictions upon the land and encumbrances such as mortgages. These certificates are at the moment private and are available for inspection only with the permission of the land's owner. There would however be problems with using the Land Registry as a basis for a public land register south of the border. First the question of registering land arises only when land is bought and sold. Details of land which passes to members of a family by will, for example, never come to the Land Registry. Secondly, the Registry records only the legal owner of land, not the beneficial owner: it does not seek to penetrate the nominal ownership vested in trusts and companies to identify the individuals in whose hands control really lies. Thirdly, at the beginning of 1987, compulsory land registration applied to only about 55 per cent of the land area of England and Wales.

Despite these deficiencies, the Law Commission (among several other organizations, including the National Consumer Council) has urged that the Register of Title at the Land Registry should be opened to the public. The Law Commission (which is a branch of the Lord Chancellor's office and draws up proposals for law reform in a variety of fields) pointed out in a report in 1985 that information on apparently private matters, such as wills, births, marriages and deaths, is available to anybody – in line with the absence of any general right of privacy recognized by English law. Curiously, however, information on the ownership of land – 'a finite resource, which carries social responsibilities and is a matter of legitimate public interest' – is secret. The lawyers could see no sound reason for retaining this secrecy rule.[22]

It is not as easy as might be thought to discover who owns Britain simply by asking. A writer for *The Spectator* ran up against an elegant smokescreen when he was compiling a 1977 version of the Domesday book for his journal. The only way to win the necessary information, the reporter Stephen Glover concluded, was to ask the owners in person:

This was usually attempted on the telephone and naturally entailed difficulties. Often, the landowner was out shooting; once he unfortunately turned out to be dead; and once he was drunk. One landowner could not decide whether he owned 10,000 acres or 100,000 acres: 'I do find it so difficult to remember what an acre looks like when I drive across the estate.' The younger ones tended to be fairly candid, the older ones suspicious . . . There were those, too, who sheltered behind half-truths: they would say that they did not own any land at all when in fact their estates were owned by trusts of which they, or their families, were the sole beneficiaries.[23]

The hesitancy shown by some of Mr Glover's respondents is at odds with the public importance of the information he was seeking. As things stand, it may well be impossible even to make a request to a landowner relating to his land as it may not be possible to discover whom to approach. Many individuals and organizations would dearly like to know who or what have bought the tens of thousands of acres of woodland that the Forestry Commission has sold mainly to the private sector during the 1980s. The Ramblers' Association would like to be able to write to these new owners asking them to continue the public access policies of the Commission. For while the Forestry Commission adopted a policy of allowing the public to visit all its forests, it did so almost always on a permissive basis and was very reluctant to allow permissive paths to be converted to public rights of way; any future owner is therefore perfectly free to terminate permissive access. Yet the Forestry Commission has consistently refused to publish the names of the new owners of these forests and woods. It has also consistently refused to publish the price at which its land and forests have been sold, on the grounds that if it did so it might not get the best possible price for future land and forest. Nor has the Commission changed this policy since an all-party House of Commons committee condemned it for its secrecy in this area. The Public Accounts Committee reported in 1984:

The Commission maintained that, for reasons of commercial confidentiality they were unable to disclose publicly the selling price of any land or the name of the purchaser. The Committee is not satisfied with the reasons given by the Commission for refusing to publish the selling price of publicly-owned land. Furthermore, we do not consider that the information provided has shown sufficient reason for the Commission's present policy, and consider that it is necessary for the purpose of ensuring proper accountability that this information should be made public.[24]

There are wider, national reasons why a public register of the ownership of Britain's land is essential. How can public policy on the use of land be formulated without this basic information? How can government commissions and committees do anything but lay themselves open to misleading impressions on this score if they are denied this basic information? In 1974, a House of Commons Select Committee looking into the feasibility of introducing a wealth tax in Britain was seriously handicapped in its investigations by the lack of information on the ownership of land. Another Committee set up by the Minister of Agriculture John Silkin to examine the impact on Britain's agricultural industry of recent trends in land acquisition pointed out in its 1979 report that the absence of ownership information made it extremely difficult to work out the impact of agricultural subsidies on the industry. More knowledge was needed, said this Committee, 'on almost every aspect of land ownership, acquisition and occupancy if Government policy is to be formulated on an adequately informed basis'.[25]

Another, perhaps even more important inquiry which soon found itself floundering in the absence of data on land ownership was the Royal Commission on the Distribution of Income and Wealth. Established by Royal Warrant in 1974 to carry out 'a thorough and comprehensive inquiry into the existing distribution of income and wealth' so as 'to help secure a fairer distribution of income and wealth in the community', the Commission published five major reports before the Thatcher Government abolished it in 1979. While the Commission devoted whole volumes to such matters as higher incomes from employment (240 pages), lower incomes (394 pages) and income from companies (176 pages), it found it could carry out only the most crude analysis of the distribution of wealth through the ownership of land. Its consideration of wealth in land, limited to just four pages, ended abruptly with the conclusion: 'The paucity of comprehensive up-to-date information on land ownership is remarkable. In the absence of a survey yielding data on the lines of the 1873 survey it is difficult to carry our analysis any further.'[26]

For the landowners, however, perhaps the main advantage of anonymity is that it protects them from the impact of public opinion. If people are upset at the stance taken by a trade union they know that they can direct their anger at the union's clearly identifiable officials. But people cannot organize demonstrations outside the offices of landowners if they do not know who they are.

6. Private Pleasure

> I have just become the legal owner of six of the thirty-two million
> thirty-four thousand acres of England . . . So what is to be done
> with this inheritance of which I am the guardian for a while? . . .
> The village . . . show me how I should react. Put up gates they
> say, and Keep Out notices and padlocks . . . No urban ghetto has
> a fraction of the territorial imperative of the countryside.

Jill Tweedie, *The Guardian*, 31 January 1984

> The Duke of Roxburgh, 28, will be up at the crack of dawn today,
> potting the defenceless birds that become fair game on the Glorious
> Twelfth. Those shot on his 60,000-acre grouse moor at Lammer-
> muirs will be available for breakfast at his hotel near Floors Castle.

Daily Mail, 12 August 1983

Britain's landowners are often conscious of their land less as a
source of wealth or power than as their personal playground.
Outsiders may be struck by the degree of wealth and power
which the ownership of land may bestow. But, traditionally the
British landowner has not cared to be seen to be concerned
about such things. For him, the habit of thought persists that the
serious business of life is play.

A particularly British feature of the pleasure a landowner
takes in his holdings is that it is a *private* pleasure. In Britain,
more completely than in some other countries, the law allows
landowners to keep their land very much to themselves. Their
own inclinations lead them to take full advantage of this privilege.
In an essay about a Surrey wood he had just bought, E. M.
Forster put his finger on this attitude:

Does my wood belong to me or doesn't it? And, if it does, should I not
own it best by allowing no one else to walk there? There is a wood near
Lyme Regis, also cursed by a public footpath, where the owner has not
hesitated on this point. He has built high stone walls each side of the

path, and has spanned it by bridges, so the public circulate like termites while he gorges on the blackberries unseen. He really does own his wood, this able chap. Dives in Hell did pretty well, but the gulf dividing him from Lazarus could be traversed by vision, and nothing traverses it here. And perhaps I shall come to this in time. I shall wall in and fence out until I really taste the sweets of property.[1]

In fact, however, gorging blackberries is not the most usual occupation in which Britain's landowners indulge behind the barricades enclosing their secret domains. Nor is it picnicking or botanizing. The private pursuit of game has been the primary leisure activity which the land of Britain has sustained since the time of William the Conqueror. Today, most of the land in Britain dedicated to pleasure rather than profit is primarily devoted to bloodsports.

Hunting, Shooting and Fishing

'I remember the first pheasant I shot. I remember the first woodcock I shot. I remember the first every game bird I've shot, I think. There are moments in one's childhood which one never forgets, because I was eight when I shot most of my first game birds,' reminisced Gerald Grosvenor, the then thirty-two-year-old 6th Duke of Westminster in Robert Lacey's television series *The Aristocrats*, first broadcast in 1983.[2] Explained Mr Lacey, 'Gerald Grosvenor's favourite pastimes are fishing and shooting, as befits his family name.' (Le Gros Veneur was the nickname given to a Norman huntsman of generous bulk who was one of William the Conqueror's closest companions when he took possession of England in 1066. Le Gros Veneur was rewarded with estates in Cheshire and the earldom of Chester; the Grosvenors and the Dukes of Westminster are descended from him.) Of Gerald Grosvenor Mr Lacey went on, 'In July, he catches salmon. In August, he shoots grouse. And in the autumn, he walks up the hedges and thickets of Eaton in pursuit of pheasant.'

The ritual of bloodsports not only links Britain's landowners with their past but also enables them and their hangers-on to maintain the exclusivity of their club today. For those who seek to join the landowning élite, hunting, shooting, stalking and game fishing are initiation rites. Nouveaux riches newcomers to landownership are not usually to be found transforming the rural scene by putting the land to unusual uses. Instead, like their eighteenth- and nineteenth-century counterparts, their first concern is normally to ape the ways of their betters by getting accepted by the local hunt or stocking their coverts with pheasants to provide good sport for their neighbours.

Game for Conservation

The extent to which the land serves as its owner's plaything is not obvious to the casual observer. From the train window, evidence of the pursuit of wealth through mining, forestry and above all agriculture appears to monopolize the landscape. In fact, however, the shape our countryside takes is intimately bound up with the peculiar leisure tastes of the landowning élite.

We are fortunate in one sense at least that our landowners' pleasure has taken the form that it does. For it has served to mitigate the destructive effects which their other appetites have come to unleash on the landscape. It used to be the case that all the landowners' main activities, including the two most widespread – agriculture and forestry – served to enhance rather than damage the beauty of the landscape. Until World War II, the requirements of farming, forestry and bloodsports combined to require the conservation of the features that made the landscape attractive. The hedgerows that enclosed stock, sheltered crops and provided timber for a huge variety of purposes also served as cover for pheasants and partridge and provided jumps to add to the thrill of fox hunting. The small woods and spinneys that also provided timber lent shelter and nesting sites for pheasants as well as tall trees under which the guns could stand. And in the uplands, the young shoots of heather nourished grouse chicks while their parents nested in the deep, woody stands of the older heather plants which also provided shelter for sheep.

In our own time, this picture has been transformed. Modern agriculture has no use for traditional features like hedgerows, deciduous woods, ponds and streams, flower-rich downland and moor. Modern forestry has no time for small woods and spinneys of native deciduous trees but deals only in vast expanses of

gloomy conifers. Only the requirements of sport now sustain
most of the features that make our landscape attractive and
without sport our countryside would have been far more savagely
devastated than it has been. Grouse love to feed on and nest in
rough heather moorland – not perennial ryegrass or conifer
plantations. They have thereby ensured the survival of moorland
which incidentally continues to provide a habitat for golden
plover, dunlin, curlew, peregrine falcons and golden eagles.
Despite strong commercial pressures for afforestation, between 2
and 3 million acres of the relatively dry east of Scotland are still
occupied by grouse moor; while grouse moor covers perhaps as
much land again in south and west Scotland, Yorkshire, Lancashire and Northumberland.[3] Trout and salmon savour the little
pools and shallows of winding streams and watercourses that
have evolved over centuries – not uniform drainage channels. It
is no coincidence that many of Britain's most magically beautiful
rivers, like the Test and Itchen in Hampshire, the Wye, the Usk,
the Tamar, the Teifi, Devon's Taw, Tavy and Teign, the Pang
in Berkshire, and Scotland's Tweed, Tay and Dee run through
those areas most prized for salmon and trout fishing. The joys of
fox hunting have encouraged otherwise profit-hungry farmers to
maintain hedges as jumps and rough copses where foxes may
make their earths. Three million acres of the Scottish Highlands,
mainly in the wetter west, are given over to deer stalking.
Stalking is considered most satisfying when it involves the stalker
in scrambling long distances over different varieties of wild
terrain. So it serves to preserve the delights of vast areas of this
kind of country, even though less than 4,500 people a year go
stalking in Britain.[4]

Perhaps the most successful of all the unwitting furred and
feathered conservationists is the pheasant, which has done more
to safeguard what remains of the traditional British landscape
than all of the voluntary conservation groups put together. This
exotic, unEnglish-looking creature, introduced by the Romans,
is both widely distributed (though less common in Wales,
Scotland and Northern Ireland than in England) and the most
popular victim of the country sportsman. Every year, landowners, their friends and the syndicates of businessmen to whom
they rent out shooting claim hundreds of thousands of pheasants

in woods, spinneys, private parks and grassy rides, many of which would not exist were it not for this sporting activity. Like the British public, the pheasant likes deciduous woodland interspersed with small fields separated by thick hedgerows with marshy areas and ponds: features which furnish a good supply of spots the birds consider suitable for nesting, feeding, hiding, sleeping and raising their young. They do not like draughts, so the woods must contain plenty of undergrowth. Almost equally attractive to pheasants (and to partridges, which exist in lesser numbers alongside the pheasants in many areas) is rolling, wooded hill country with open valleys. Wherever possible, the guns stand in a line on the low ground at the bottom of a high hedge or narrow belt of tall trees over which the victims are driven. It is considered better sport if the pheasants, by nature reluctant to take wing, are high in the air rather than only a few feet off the ground; while a line of tall trees also prevents the birds from seeing the guns until they are almost on top of them.

But if bloodsports have ensured the conservation of many of our landscape treasures, they have also served as the reason, or at least the pretext, for denying their enjoyment to the people.

Private: Keep Out

For most of the last thousand years, the landless have been complaining that the landowners' penchant for bloodsports was denying them their rights in the countryside. For most of that time, what was being denied was the opportunity to find or grow food. While the poor went hungry, land that could have fed them was reserved as private playgrounds for the pursuit of game. Sometimes resentment was dormant; at other times it was active, and on at least two occasions – the Peasants' Revolt of 1381 and the challenge to land ownership in the 1880s – it threatened the very basis of the rural land ownership régime. Nowadays, when food is being overproduced, no one starves in Britain because of bloodsports. But in modern times a new hunger has arisen – hunger for the joys the countryside can bring to the oppressed urban spirit. And hungry souls seeking open-air recreation are disbarred from the hunting grounds just as their more literally hungry forefathers were before them.

It is not inevitable that hunting grounds should be closed to the public. But accompanying the passion for bloodsports that has survived among Britain's landowners down the ages has come the notion firmly established in medieval times that hunting grounds should be private. The principle established 900 years ago in Britain that land ownership carries with it an almost complete right to exclude others has become entangled with the idea that a proper use for the British countryside is to provide a private playground for the privileged few. The poor, who used to be deprived of the land to grow food and collect firewood are deprived of it as a place for enjoyment today for the same reasons supported by the same laws.

According to British law no right of access exists in the countryside unless there is some clear indication to the contrary. This presumption against access is the complete reverse of the situation across the Channel. In France, access is presumed to exist unless a landowner has put up notices at sixteen-yard intervals indicating that he wants his fellow citizens to keep out of what he regards as *Propriété Privée*. In Sweden, the ancient customary right of *Allemansrätten* authorizes any citizen to walk over another person's land provided no damage or disturbance is caused, apart from limited exceptions. In practice this permits access everywhere except in the curtilage of private houses, across growing crops or young trees and in certain defence and nature conservation areas. It even enables a person to camp.

In Britain, by contrast, anybody setting foot on land where no public right of way exists without the consent of the land's owner is a trespasser. Except in certain carefully-defined circumstances, trespass is not a criminal offence, and despite the many notices to the contrary, trespassers cannot normally be prosecuted. It is a civil wrong or tort. The law says that a landowner can use reasonable force to evict a trespasser and that he can sue him for any damage he causes while trespassing. These sanctions are not in themselves grave, but they underline the fact that trespassing is illegal, and that owners are therefore perfectly at liberty to put up fences to keep people out. And the 'Trespassers will be Prosecuted' signs, although no more than a 'wooden falsehood', in the words of the lawyer J. A. Jolowicz,[5] effectively deter people from venturing on to private land.

In Britain's countryside, a walker is *not* trespassing only when he is using a legal right of way or where he is on land by express permission of its owner. Even on a public right of way he is a trespasser if he is doing something other than travelling from one place to another – for instance if he is picnicking or sitting down to rest.

In Scotland, though as in England and Wales trespass is a tort not a criminal offence, certain associated activities are criminal, including lighting fires and pitching tents without permission. So the position north of the border is if anything more restrictive than it is to the south. A widespread impression to the contrary doubtless arises from the particular difficulty faced by Scotland's lairds in making their writ run on their often vast and remote estates.

In parts of France and Sweden the sheer size of the land seems to lessen the possibility of conflict between public access and other land-based activities. But the difference in the legal position on access and the way in which landowners approach it also reflects a fundamentally different approach to the ownership of land. Partly because both France and Scandinavia underwent land revolutions in which the barons were dispossessed and the land was handed to peasant farmers, land is not identified with social status in quite the way it is in Britain. The tradition of the French peasant, for instance, is that the land is a means of growing crops and of subsisting; he uses his land and does not seek to possess it totally as a British landowner does and may indeed be quite happy for other people to use his land freely for purposes which do not conflict with his own.

In Britain, the casual observer may not readily appreciate how private the countryside is. At first glance it may appear to be part of 'the national property' of which Wordsworth spoke a century ago when talking of the Lake District. Public footpath signs crop up along the roads; notices proclaim the opening hours of large country houses or safari parks. Yet those non-landowners who seek their own pleasure in Britain's countryside, whether they be ramblers, bird-watchers, painters, photographers or mere picnickers, are gravely handicapped in their pursuits.

The 200,000 people who live in the Luton–Dunstable conurbation of south Bedfordshire face circumstances mirrored all over the country. On the edge of their town lies spacious parkland with enticing lakes. But this is private. They may not spread their tired limbs on its inviting grass, walk in its graceful woods or along its peaceful lakeside. They may motor round the largely hedgeless sea of ploughed earth or monochrome crops that is the typical landscape of South Bedfordshire. They will even find some public footpaths there. But after decades of agricultural intensification they will not find many delights to match the forbidden charms of the park on their doorstep.

The Luton Hoo estate lies behind a wall on the south side of Luton. Here are woods, farms, lakes, a Capability-Brown-modelled park, cottages, outhouses and, in the centre, a Robert-Adam-designed mansion. In 1986 no rights of access existed within this little kingdom, though paying visitors could go round the mansion with its valuable art collection and the gardens next to it. Lutonians visited Luton Hoo only when its owner, Nicholas Phillips, decreed that they might and then only on his terms.

Grace and Favour

The total control which the landowner wields is in a sense rendered all the more apparent when he chooses in his munificence to toss a crumb to the masses from the table of landed pleasure. When it suits them, some landowners do allow the public to visit what are usually carefully selected parts of their estates under what are usually carefully controlled conditions. Access arrangements over the three extensive parks and associated woods owned by the Duke of Northumberland in different parts of England illustrates some of the forms this permissive access for the general public can take.

Look at the 3,000-acre Hulne Park, Alnwick on the Ordnance Survey map and your appetite may well be whetted by the glories the map reveals – many woodlands, a lazily meandering river, much parkland and names redolent of the past like Friar's Well, Alnwick Abbey, Standing Stone, Brizlee Hill Tower and Hulne Priory. However, closer examination of the map will reveal virtually no means of access for the likes of you and you will probably look elsewhere for a trip to the country. Only two short stretches of public footpath seem to provide any means for the general public to explore Hulne Park and both of these lie outside the main area of the park which with its associated woods covers about 2,500 acres.

If, however, you went down one road leading to the park – a fairly unlikely event since it does not really lead anywhere – you would find, as I did when I was shown round the estate by the Duke's agent W. F. P. Hugonin in 1982, an unobtrusive sign informing you that between one in the afternoon and sunset on Saturdays and Sundays you are allowed to walk on all the main drives and paths in Hulne Park. The Duke had also granted special access privileges in 1982 to about 200 local people who, armed with special permits, could visit Hulne Park during the week as well.

Albury Park in Surrey is much smaller than Hulne (around 70 acres) and here the access situation is very different. Two public footpaths penetrate Albury Park, there is a criss-cross of bridleways just inside one of the woods and in addition there is a notice informing people that they may go along a road into the park to view a redundant Saxon church. However, the public are kept firmly to these rights of way and to the permissive path to the church. When I visited the Park in 1982 I found that people using the two public footpaths across the Park for instance are instructed that their rights are firmly restricted – 'Footpath Only', 'No Picnicking Allowed' and 'Private Parkland' notices confronted the walker where these paths left the road on the northern edge of the estate. And on the fence round the enticing beechwoods a little further along the road, the potential rambler was warned: 'Private Woodlands. Trespassers will be Prosecuted. By Order.' Nor were the villagers of Albury and Shere or the people of nearby Guildford paddling in the enticing waters of the little River Tilling Bourne. Public access alongside this river is forbidden for most of its length through Albury Park with warning notices carrying messages like 'Private Fishing: Keep Out'.

Permissive access to the park at the Duke's London seat is on yet a different basis. Syon Park in Brentford covers about 200 acres – twice the area of St James's Park. Visiting the Park in 1985, I found it surrounded by a high brick wall, bounded by the River Thames on its south-eastern side and bisected by its main drive, which was also a public footpath. Down this drive, just near Syon House itself, the Duke had provided a cluster of facilities open to the public. There was an art shop, a large garden centre, a gift shop, a cafeteria, lavatories and a car park. For a payment in each case, visitors could look round Syon House itself, a stretch of formal gardens with a lake and a conservatory, a motor museum and a butterfly collection. There were odd stretches of ground on which anybody might sit or lie – like the wide verge on one side of the main drive. However, these facilities formed but an island in what was otherwise private, inaccessible and extremely beautiful parkland. If you walked down the main drive from the western end of the Park towards the house you could easily imagine yourself in the depths of the country. Far from the noise and dirt of Brentford's London Road, which runs along the northern boundary of the Park, only the top of the occasional tall chimney or tower away behind the parkland, trees and a lake revealed the proximity of London. Stately limes, chestnuts and little hawthorn trees adorned this lovely grassland, lightly grazed by cattle, and in the distance swans could be glimpsed on the lake. However, you could not set foot on this land. These eighty acres of outer park land plus a further sixty acres of land on the other side of the estate where Syon House fronts on to the River Thames, were barred to the general public. They had to content themselves with the fifty-five acres of the estate that contained the more formal attractions. A good few of the 16,500 people of Brentford who lived beyond Syon Park's northern wall and of the 24,500 citizens of Isleworth behind the west wall must sometimes have longed to feel these broad, inviting acres of soft grass under their feet.

Where landowners do allow permissive access without charge (as opposed to access based on legal rights for the public) it is usually confined to special groups of people (like the scouts, guides, disabled or naturalists), or, where it exists for a wider group, few people usually know about it. In particular, when landowners make a practice of granting named individuals special permits to visit their land the practice is normally very little known. People who live near big but inaccessible country estates are often unaware of the opportunity that might be available to walk in attractive countryside near them – admittedly on terms which would bring home forcefully the fact that they did so on sufferance.

Of course where permissive access does exist, it may be withdrawn or reduced at any time, to the distress of those who have come to rely on it. This happened in 1964 at the 800-acre Southill Park, which forms the centrepiece of the Whitbread family's 10,800-acre estate in north Bedfordshire. From the terrace of Southill House stretches an expanse of park with a large lake in the distance, the farther banks of which are heavily wooded and almost conceal a charming, white-brick fishing temple. Famous for its shoals of rudd and a favourite haunt of wintering wildfowl, the lake was freely accessible at weekends to people from Luton, Dunstable, Hertford, north London and elsewhere for some years. But when the estate's present owner, Samuel Whitbread, came to Southill in 1961, he decided that the general public should be barred. Giving bad behaviour by visitors as the reason, Mr Whitbread introduced a formal permit system whereby only residents of Southill and bona fide naturalists might be given access to the lake. Local sea scouts and boy scouts were allowed to camp in the park, but ordinary people from Luton, Bedford and further afield were denied access to this magnificent landscape.

It may be that landowners see access by permit as a means of heading off protest. Certainly it sometimes serves to enlist the support of local villagers for a régime that disadvantages outsiders. The Fitzwilliam family have an estate at Wentworth-Woodhouse near Rotherham in Yorkshire as well as the 9,000-acre Milton estate in the East Midlands. Michael Thompson, the Fitzwilliam's chief land agent, reminded a conference in 1982 that the opening up of the 400-acre Milton Park on Peterborough's western edge twice a year for annual shows provides 'an opportunity for the locals to view their home countryside and this is naturally of interest to them. It also prevents a build up of ill-will that can easily arise where members of the public are permanently excluded from a local country estate'.[6]

Dodges such as these are not the only things serving to disguise the limitations on access to Britain's countryside. Perhaps the most obviously misleading indication of all is the practice of stately home owners of permitting the public to view (for a consideration) the very part of their property that might be thought to be most private – the interior of their houses and, usually, adjoining gardens.

The 13th Duke of Bedford began the practice in 1955 for financial reasons and, as it happens, opened up a far larger slice of his domain than most of the landowners who have followed his example. Before 1955, Woburn had been a very private place indeed. A former duke was so anxious to avoid contact with the villagers at his gate that he insisted that the estate cottages in the villages that surround Woburn Park (Eversholt, Ridgmont, Milton Bryan and Husborne Crawley) should have no front doors: he did not wish to see women chattering at their front doorsteps as he went down the drive in his carriage and pair.

However, the 13th Duke was faced with heavy death duty bills after the demise in close succession of two of his predecessors. The refusal of successive dukes to talk to each other had prevented the usual avoidance of death duties by transferring property before death. To pay his tax bills the 13th Duke opened Woburn Abbey and part of the grounds to the public, on payment of a fee. Today, Woburn is thought to be Britain's most popular privately owned stately home, with a reported 1.6 million visitors a year. Most of the landowners who have followed the Duke of Bedford's example have also done so for financial reasons. Heating, repairing, maintaining and running a country mansion is extremely expensive. Receipts from visitors can help cover these costs. What is more, if a landowner can convince the Inland Revenue that the showing of his house and its contents has become a trade or business within the terms of Schedule D, Class XI, then all these expenses can be written off against tax, less some agreed proportion deemed to relate to the portion of the house kept completely private. And although an invasion by crowds of wondering visitors might be thought enough to disturb any home-owner's sense of privacy, many landowners seem to reside happily enough in some smaller dwelling in their grounds or an out-of-the-way wing of their mansion. And one of the most interesting features of the whole business is that the landowners involved actually seem readier to allow the public into their homes than on to their lands.

Most of the landowners who open their property to the public impose strict limits not on how close to the family hearth the visitor may go but on how far he may stray away from it. Broadlands, in Hampshire, provides a typical example of these limits. Broadlands House is a Palladian mansion overlooking the River Test half a mile south of the little town of Romsey in Hampshire. The former country seat of Earl Mountbatten of Burma, it was in the news in 1981 as the place where the Prince and Princess of Wales spent the first part of their honeymoon. The house stands near the centre of the 5,500-acre Broadlands estate, which contains estate-run farms amounting to 2,500 acres with five dairies and 1,000 acres of cereals; over 1,100 acres of commercial and amenity woodland; 1,250 acres of farms which have been let out, parkland, gravel workings, a fishing lake, a golf course, several miles of river and stream and over 150 houses and cottages. When Lord Mountbatten was assassinated by the IRA in 1979 while on his annual August visit to his Irish mansion, Classiebawn Castle, Broadlands passed to his grandson, Norton Knatchbull, now Lord Romsey, who will succeed to the title Earl Mountbatten on the death of his mother and who plans to hand on the estate in time to his son. Born in 1947, Lord Romsey accompanies the running of Broadlands with film-making and with business interests in radio and television companies.

Broadlands estate, which is fifteen times the size of Hyde Park, overshadows the little town of Romsey. The gate at the end of Broadlands' main drive is but a stone's throw from the centre of this town of fewer than 14,000 people. Before 1977, few of these people had ever set foot behind Broadlands' enclosing wall. But in that year, the four-member family group who ran the estate decided in the face of the rising costs of maintaining and running the house that they would open the house to the public. When I visited the estate and talked with Lord Romsey in 1984, the public were permitted to make their way along the private drive to the house near which they could park, and to stroll and picnic in the parking area and in a small piece of land between the house and the river – about six acres altogether. The house and these parts of the grounds were open to the public six days a week from April to September. In addition, anybody could walk along the public footpaths that penetrated the estate all year round. These rights of way skirted and occasionally crossed some of the estate's woods, crossed slices of farmland, and followed little streams. But they avoided whole features of the estate landscape such as a 120-acre stretch of woodland criss-crossed by streams and private tracks known as Burnt Grove and a 22-acre square of park and grazing land with the house at its south-western corner and Romsey town along its nothern edge. Another 225-acre belt of woodland with two lakes, streams and private tracks was skirted along part of one edge by a public path but nowhere penetrated by one; while public paths barely touched upon the three miles of the lovely River Test that run through the estate.

What all this means is that ordinary people could visit only a tiny part of the estate. The 22-acre stretch of parkland and grazing lands on the southern edge of the town alone, with its oaks and beeches, pines, planes and sweet and horse chestnuts, willows, hawthorns and stately ash trees, poplars and willows, here standing singly, there in groups, copses or lines of trees, offered countless shady spots to sit matched only by the river-bank's many opportunities for staring at the clear, cool waters on a summer's afternoon. But they were all out of bounds.

Lord Romsey has excepted from the general bar on access to his estate about twelve individuals and groups to whom he has granted special access permits. These are people with a special interest in the estate, say, in an aspect of its wildlife. Permits are not issued to people who simply want to enjoy the beauties of the place. 'Definitely not' was Lord Romsey's reply when I asked him whether he would issue a permit to a resident of Romsey who wrote in saying he would simply like to walk in the grounds. However, Lord Romsey has provided a piece of land on the edge of town for the exclusive use of local voluntary groups like the guides and scouts and radio amateurs. Lord Romsey told me: 'I sacrifice that piece of land totally to public use. It isn't farmed; I get not a penny of rent or whatever from it and if you like it is the concession that we wanted to make to the

area to provide space where any organization can come and
hold these events – something very few other landowners in this
area are prepared to do.' However, this area of grassland next to
the Romsey Sports Centre and bounded on two sides by main
roads is not intended as an area for informal walking. It is in
any case only three acres in extent.

At Broadlands, however, as at most country mansions open to
the public, the visitor feels he is being taken to the heart of the
family. The guidebook begins with a welcome to visitors signed
by Lord Romsey himself. Turn the pages, and pictures of the
interior of the house are interspersed with recent family photos:
Lord and Lady Romsey and their eldest son as a baby with two
dogs, their son's christening party, Lord and Lady Romsey's
wedding party, Lord Romsey with his mother and grandfather,
as well as innumerable photographs of Lord Mountbatten. Lord
Romsey is far from being alone in being readier to show strangers
his family snaps than the broad acres under his control. He is
actually less restrictive than some other stately home owners,
most of whom seem to be more concerned to preserve the privacy
of their land than that of their furniture and paintings.

The holdings of lesser landowners are just as effectively barred
to the public. A typical picture was painted by Dr Charles
Watkins, who studied a 15 per cent sample of Nottinghamshire
woodlands spanning estates of all shapes and sizes in 1982.
Thirty per cent of the woods that Dr Watkins surveyed were
owned by the Forestry Commission, Nottinghamshire County
Council and the National Trust, and in these he found the
public could wander freely. The other 70 per cent were privately
owned and inaccessible, except for any linear access provided
where a public footpath happened to skirt or pass through them
– which happened in only a small proportion of cases. In most of
these private woods pheasants were reared or encouraged to nest
in the wild. Only one private owner that Dr Watkins interviewed
was prepared to allow access to his woods. This man commented:
'I see public access to the countryside as a major problem. It is a
pity that so little land is open to the public. I am pleased that
they should enjoy the woods, and the tenant farmers don't seem
to mind.'[7]

Oxfordshire is another county for which figures are available.

In an area like Oxfordshire in which so much of the countryside is intensively farmed, rural parklands which have escaped the plough seem particularly well suited to rural recreation. And, indeed, the Oxfordshire countryside is dotted with enticing parklands, usually sited close to country mansions. However, a study in 1977 revealed that of the county's thirty-nine stretches of rural parkland, only a handful were open to the public at all times. The same survey revealed that of the county's 27,000 acres of woodland, only 111 acres, or 0.4 per cent, were open to the public at all times.[8] The remainder, like most of the county's rural parks, are reserved for private use, which usually means pheasant shooting.

The notion that the private recreation of a few should take priority over rural enjoyment is so widespread among landowners of all types in Britain's countryside that it has penetrated the attitudes even of owners like financial institutions and government agencies.

In 1984 a farmer, Tom Meakin, who lives near the hamlet of Capel Coch on Anglesey wrote to me expressing concern at what he considered was the over-shooting of a national nature reserve owned by the Nature Conservancy Council. The land in question is a twenty-acre stretch of wet pastureland and lake south-east of Capel Coch which was acquired by the Council earlier in 1984 when the previous owner died. There is a tradition of pheasant shooting on this part of Anglesey and although the site is a grade one site in the Council's Nature Conservation Review on account of its rare wild plants (including columbine and the marsh and fly orchids), the Council decided to continue the practice of the previous owner and allow shooting over the land. In return for £15 a year, the local man to whom the Council has granted a licence together with up to three of his guests may shoot pheasant, partridge, Canada geese, mallard, teal, widgeon, snipe, woodcock, magpie, carrion crow, wood pigeon, rabbit and other wild animals on not more than one day every three weeks during the open season. The Council is not convinced that shooting is causing damage to the natural history interest of the site. Be that as it may, the site is not accessible to the general public and what the Council has done is to take on board the orthodoxy on recreation of the private landowning class – deference to bloodsports but no access for ordinary people for informal outdoor recreation. The Council has good reason for keeping the local landowning fraternity on this part of Anglesey happy: it is trying to acquire as much land as possible around the edge of its national nature reserve so that it can maintain a high water level within it without affecting water levels of neighbouring landowners. As Brian Ducker, the Regional Officer for North Wales of the Nature Conservancy Council, explained to me in 1984:

We are anxious to maintain relations with our neighbours in a way which is going to invoke a positive and neighbourly response, but at the same time I can assure you that we wouldn't allow any level of shooting to take place that was deleterious from a conservation point of view . . . There isn't open access here as there is on some of the properties that we acquire. But of course we are always anxious to assist any member of the public who writes to us and is anxious to visit the land we hold whether or not it's been declared a national nature reserve and we will invariably issue a permit if we are satisfied that the person concerned is interested and will benefit from access to the land.

Those landowners who exclude their fellow citizens from their domains even more rigorously than the Nature Conservancy Council have their own explanations for their practice. Some speak of regrettable necessity, some even of high-minded altruism. But these 'reasons' do not stand up well to close scrutiny.

'Game Would Be Frightened'

Landowners frequently argue that bloodsports, and in particular the rearing of game, cannot be carried on successfully if people are allowed to blunder freely on to the game preserves. They say it is not that they prefer to engage in their sport in private, but that the sport itself would actually be impaired if people could frighten away their pheasants, deer, salmon, grouse or whatever. As many landowners could not possibly kill all the game on their land themselves, they rent out shooting or fishing to others, often syndicates of businessmen, and thus argue that they are excluding the public to protect their business as well as their pleasure. But are bloodsports really incompatible with recreation?

ACCESS AND PHEASANTS: THE FACTS

Every year 10 million young pheasants are turned down (i.e. released) into the British countryside to supplement the numbers that are born in the wild. On their account, the public are excluded from a high proportion of Britain's woods, parks and farmland – including in many cases, the only really attractive stretches of country close to centres of population. The argument put forward in support of this is very much that the pheasants require it.

The 9,000-acre Milton estate on the edge of Peterborough provides a typical example of the measures thought necessary. Between 3,000 and 4,000 pheasants are turned down on the estate every year, according to the Chief Agent to the Fitzwilliam Estates, Michael Thompson, (with whom I talked in 1982) in order to provide sport for the Fitzwilliam family and a small amount of commercial shooting. The needs of pheasants for cover is one of the main reasons why Milton estate lands are so well endowed with woodland, while the jewel in the Milton crown, Milton Park, in which 1,000 were being turned down in 1982, contains many fine woods alongside its parkland, string of lakes, heronry and eighteenth-century mansion occupying 400 acres in all. The estate is situated in a region denuded of much of its former cover by the requirements of modern farming and the Park itself lies on the very edge of Peterborough New Town, in which 133,000 people live. So the whole estate and in particular the Park could provide superb opportunities for open-air recreation. Yet the overall approach is to keep the people out rather than to share the glories of Milton with them. The situation in 1982 was that the Park itself was closed to the public except on one day a year, and visitors were not encouraged to stray from the two public footpaths that penetrate it but do not provide access to the string of lakes or the heronry or most of the woods in and on the edge of the Park. Michael Thompson told me that pheasant rearing was the main reason why the public had to be kept out of the estate's woods (though in the Park the requirements of stock-rearing were the main reasons for restricting public access). In any case, he considered Peterborough people were well provided with open-air recreation opportunities at the Nene Park (a country park established around disused gravel pits) on the edge of the new town. Mr Thompson told me, 'Wildlife, like game pheasants, cannot really accept a lot of interference and disturbance. It is the one thing that they like, to be left in peace. So a high degree of public presence will just drive every pheasant out of the wood or off the Park or wherever it may be because they just like to be left alone and not disturbed. That is the problem.'

Let us look in detail at the argument that pheasant rearing and shooting are incompatible with public recreation. It is certainly possible that human beings venturing into pheasant woods in April might frighten a hen bird off eggs she was incubating and that these eggs might as a result be lost. Few estates however rely primarily on birds being hatched in the wild. On most pheasant estates, the majority of young birds are reared indoors from eggs incubated in special cabinets in which the temperature, humidity and the rate at which eggs are turned over mimic conditions under the female pheasant.

At Highclere in north Hampshire for instance, the seat of the 6th Earl of Caernarvon, about 6,000 pheasants were being reared artificially indoors each year when I visited the estate in 1978, while about 3,000 pheasant chicks were hatching naturally among Highclere's 6,500 acres of fields, thick hedgerows, rough downland turf and beech woods. The agent to the estate told me that of the 3,000 that hatched outside, two-thirds each year were killed by the rain, the cold or foxes. So the eventual number of birds likely to be affected by the activities of noisy picnickers when the eggs are being incubated or the young chicks hatching would not be that great.

Once Britain's artificially reared pheasant chicks hatch, they are carefully reared by hand and then transferred to brooder houses out of doors, rather like broiler houses, where they live together (some are debeaked to stop them pecking each other's feathers out) till they are nearly two months old. From the brooder houses, they go to release pens in the wood in which they will probably spend the rest of their relatively short lives. In these pheasant coverts, gamekeepers feed the birds twice a day on grain (about forty tonnes per 7,000 birds each year). In the coverts they are joined by any pheasants that have been reared naturally in the wild.

Were the public to intrude upon these complex arrangements, it is argued, especially if they were accompanied by children or dogs, not only might those hen birds sitting on eggs in the wild be frightened off them, but young or full-grown birds reared indoors might also be frightened out of the wood in which they had been released, never to return. Some pheasants might be frightened away from the woods in which they were reared on to land outside their home estate. This would be serious for the landowner if shooting was in progress on an adjoining estate because then the birds would legally become his neighbour's property.

However, if access were also allowed on adjoining or nearby estates, all this would mean would be that the pheasant populations would get a little more mixed up than they do anyway. In any case the whole idea that pheasants would flee their home woods the minute a rambler arrived is somewhat doubtful. Because of the problem of getting pheasants to take to the air, some landowners deliberately startle the birds by running packs of foxhounds through pheasant coverts a day or two before a shoot. Certainly plenty of landowners are quite happy to welcome the hunt in their pheasant preserves – spectacular though the disturbance caused by fox hunting necessarily has to be.

Controlled experiments by the British Field Sports Society itself have shown that pheasants are not easily rattled even by foxhounds and mounted huntsmen tearing through their coverts. The experiments were conducted in the early 1970s, in the face of conflict within the ranks of the British Field Sports Society. Shooting folk claimed that hunting posed a threat to their sport by frightening birds away. The Society ran packs of hounds through pheasant woods to determine just how flighty pheasants are. At the first such experiment, at Batsford Park in Gloucestershire, the Heythrop Hunt crashed through the Park coverts. Yet three days later, when the same coverts were shot, they were found to contain the usual number of pheasants.[9] When a similar experiment was carried out in different kind of country at Thurlow in Suffolk, and the whole of a wood was given 'a thorough shaking up' with the hounds, fewer than 5 per cent of birds flew for cover to adjoining coverts. The pheasant bag four days later showed no significant difference from that of the preceding year.[10] At Cirencester Park in Gloucestershire, twenty-three hounds ran through a wood where, six weeks earlier, seven-week-old poults had been released. The vast majority returned to the usual feeding ground in the wood that same evening.[11]

If it is indeed true that a pack of hounds tearing helter-skelter through a pheasant covert does not harm the shoot, it seems unlikely that walkers and picnickers would do much damage.

It is also sometimes suggested that walkers might accidentally get shot. But this is a danger that could easily be avoided. Shooting occurs for only half the year (October to April) and may well involve only about twenty days. The area over which shooting takes place on any one day – the beat involved – usually covers only a tiny area of the whole estate, and it would not be too difficult to post notices warning ramblers of the locations of shoots.

Poaching does not seem to be something landowners are seeking to prevent as a reason for inhibiting public access – perhaps because such poaching as occurs is carried out in the main by organized, professional gangs who would not be affected one way or the other by greater legal access.

There are already some private estates where public access and pheasant shooting do co-exist without apparent damage to the shoot. Thirty-seven miles from Hyde Park corner, in some of the most beautiful scenery in south-east England, for example, lies the 4,000-acre estate of Mr and Mrs John Greenwood at Balcombe in Sussex. When Mrs Greenwood inherited the estate from her grandmother in 1955, she found the area criss-crossed by public footpaths, bridleways and roads. Yet despite this high level of public access, the Greenwoods turn down as many as 16,000 pheasants every year in order to let out ten days shooting a year commercially and to have another ten days to themselves. Pheasants at Balcombe therefore have to put up with a high level of human contact. Yet this does not seem to harm the shoot. When I visited the estate in 1982, Mrs Greenwood showed me two release pens within yards of public footpaths. At one, as many as twenty people come and watch the keeper feeding the pheasants. Mrs Greenwood told me that not one pheasant had ever been stolen from the estate.

Twenty-five miles to the south-west, at Arundel in West Sussex, lies another privately-owned estate in which pheasant shooting and public access co-exist happily. The 11th Duke of Norfolk, who created Arundel Park in 1789, was 'a Foxite Whig of advanced views' in the words of historian of the Dukes of Norfolk, J. Martin Robinson. He allowed anybody to walk in the Park and this tradition of free public access has been maintained at Arundel by the successive members of the Fitzalan family who have owned the estate ever since (apart from a ten-year period in the 1840s when the 12th Duke closed the park). During most of the nineteenth century Arundel Park was a favourite spot for bank holiday picnics not only for local Sussex people but also for visitors from further afield who made their way by train. Arundel Park is now owned by the son and heir of the 17th Duke of Norfolk, the Earl of Arundel and Surrey, who was born in 1956. Public access through the Park is guaranteed by the existence of a two and a half mile public footpath running through the middle of the Park. But people can also wander off it where they like throughout 1,000 acres of woodland, lakeside and grazing pasture. They may also make their way along any of the tracks in the Park which are not public footpaths. This freedom to wander anywhere is withheld on one day every year to ensure that access rights cannot be registered over the whole Park – something which can happen if it is possible to demonstrate at least twenty years' uninterrupted passage as of right.

Arundel Park is a well-known beauty spot not only in Arundel but also in the populous South Coast towns of Portsmouth, Southampton, Chichester, Bognor Regis and Worthing. Yet when I talked to the assistant agent for the estate, Ralph Percy, in 1985, he reported no serious conflicts between public access and other uses. No restrictions are imposed even on the fifteen days a year when the pheasants are actually being shot. However, dogs are not allowed in Arundel Park. On shooting versus access Mr Percy told me: 'People are fairly sensible and keep out of the way. Shooting is usually in the middle of winter when there aren't many people walking through anyway.'

If public access and pheasant shooting can co-exist in places like the Greenwood Estate and Arundel Park, why should they not do so elsewhere? Clearly, public access need not damage shooting. And landowners who continue to deny the truth of this proposition still have to face a question put by Professor Cyril Joad in 1946. He asked:

Is it socially more important, ethically more desirable, that rich men should slaughter game-birds, than that those who make them rich should wander freely in the waste and woodland places where wild birds make their home; more important that birds should be killed, than that work-worn men and women should regain spiritual health? Is it, or is it not? The answer is, one would have thought, obvious enough. And so I would take down the 'Trespassers will be Prosecuted' notices, and give people access to the English woodlands.[12]

There are other game targets whose welfare is cited by landowners as the justification for excluding the public from vast tracts of Britain's countryside. The most important are the red deer, salmon and trout and the red grouse.

THE RED DEER

Visitors to Richmond Park know well what damage deer can impose on ecosystems. The island of Isabella's Plantation, enclosed by high, deer-proof fencing, abounds with wildflowers: in May sheets of bluebells dazzle visitors. Outside the Plantation, the park is also dotted with mature oak trees. But the undergrowth is like a desert in comparison. For outside the Plantation, herds of browsing deer are allowed to roam freely and they nibble off the shoots of any flowering plants that attempt to settle leaving only the grass and bracken plants that are able to withstand frequent decapitation.

Around 260,000 red deer range over 7.75 million acres of Scotland. Of this area, red deer co-exist with sheep over about 4 million acres leaving over 3 million acres as pure deer forest. 'Forest', however, is a misleading term for a deer forest has few trees: the term refers simply to open hill ground which has traditionally been deer country. And just as the fallow and red deer of Richmond Park reduce its ecological diversity, so the red, roe and Sika deer of the Highlands reduce substantially the ecological diversity of Scotland's hills. Without the constant decapitation of tree saplings and wild flowers, Scotland's mountain flora would be far more diverse. At present, the woolly willow and the downy willow, the juniper tree and plants like the globe flower, melancholy thistle, woody cranesbill and milk thistle are almost absent except on rock faces.

Deer damage can be prodigious in scale. Fifty per cent of the silver birch trees in belts and scattered clumps on the Scottish Wildlife Trust's nature reserve at Glen Muick on the Balmoral estate and another 50 per cent of birches on the Morrone National Nature Reserve near Braemar disappeared in less than thirty years (between 1947 and 1976) because grazing deer prevented seedlings regenerating. The situation at Glen Muick and Morrone is typical of what is happening throughout the eastern Highlands, according to Sandy Payne of the Scottish Wildlife Trust who carried out these surveys using large-scale aerial photographs to count individual trees.

Not that the red deer really thrives in the present-day Highlands. Although the population is substantial, each specimen is but a pale imitation of the deer that roamed these hills and mountains 7,000 years ago. In those days, Scotland's red deer were literally twice the weight of their present-day descendants: they were woodland animals, and the ancient Caledonian Forest of birch and pine that then clothed most of the Highlands provided them with more shelter and better feed than today's open moors and sparser woods.

The great red deer fell prey to packs of wolves and another ferocious carnivore, the European lynx. Today, however, Scotland's red deer have no natural predator, and if they were not so enthusiastically culled their population would increase further and individuals would become smaller and smaller and scraggier and scraggier.

In this context, deer stalking can reasonably be presented as pest control, except that, fortunately for the landowners, the activity has acquired rather more social cachet than rat catching. Landowners can command high prices for allowing others to shoot deer on their property, as well as enjoying the aristocratic pursuit of deer stalking themselves.

Sir Marcus Kimball is one landowner who retains the pleasure of stalking deer on his Highland estate purely for himself, his family and friends. The Member of Parliament for Gainsborough in Lincolnshire and former President of the British Field Sports Society, Sir Marcus told me in an interview in 1982 that he and his entourage take themselves to Altnaharra each August to shoot the stags that roam over the 40,000-acre deer forest that occupies two-thirds of his estate in Sutherland.

The 10th Duke of Atholl's 130,000-acre domain based at Blair Castle, Blair Atholl, Perthshire, includes 100,000 acres of deer forest. In an interview with me in 1983, the Duke explained that he needs to kill 380 stags and 380 hinds every year to keep the numbers under control. Each day throughout the stag-stalking season (from 1 July to 20 October) he told me he let between seven and nine stalkers loose over his forest, charging each of them over £1,000 a week for the privilege of stalking and the services of a ghillie, two ponies and any vehicles that might be needed. In 1983, the deer-stalking enterprise at Atholl employed fifteen people all year round with an extra three or four in the stag season.

In 1986, the going rate for shooting one stag in Scotland was £150. However, the stalker is normally allowed to take away only the head while the estate retains the venison, which is worth about another £100. In other words one stag is worth not less than £250 to an estate.

As with other bloodsports, the requirements of deer stalking can be used as a reason for the exclusion of unwanted walkers. Sir Marcus Kimball attempts to keep visitors off his deer forest all year round through notices and advice to visitors from his employees and local people. He told me that he is however perfectly happy for walkers to use the 20,000 acres that make up the remainder of his estate, and indeed public use of that part of the estate provides revenue to Sir Marcus through the sale of day-fishing tickets and charges from a caravan site.

The Duke of Atholl tries to persuade people not to go on to his deer lands during the second half of August, the whole of September and preferably the first half of October: at that time, he told me, they can go to National Trust properties instead. It is the policy of the National Trust for Scotland not to permit commercial stalking on its estates. When the mountaineer Percy

Unna donated his Glencoe property to the Trust in the 1930s, he did so only on condition that commercial deer stalking should not be allowed since he feared it would conflict with public access. This lead was followed on the Trust's other properties, many of them managed with the help of a bequest from Percy Unna on his death where trust employees simply carry out essential culling. However, the Trust's total holdings in Scotland are not all that great – 100,000 acres or just 0.5 per cent of the country's land – 30,000 acres less than the Duke of Atholl's estate on its own. So visitors who find their way restricted at private stalking estates might not find it all that easy to seek out Trust properties instead, particularly if they have no car. In Perthshire, for example, the Trust's main property is Ben Lawers, twenty miles as the crow flies from the headquarters of the Atholl estate at Blair Atholl.

Why should owners go to the trouble of trying to keep people away when deer stalking is in progress?

The most obvious reason is safety. Many of the notices which landowners erect through the Highlands to discourage people from straying on to deer country emphasize the safety aspect. A typical form of words is: 'Deer culling with high-velocity rifles is in progress. For your own safety keep to the path.' In fact, however, the likelihood of a stalker shooting a rambler is not very great. There are no recorded instances of this having ever occurred in the Highlands: stalkers do not take lots of pot shots at their quarry but carefully aim before pulling the trigger. In the absence of trees to block their view (the cause of many American hunting accidents), they are unlikely to kill people.

Another concern that seems to weigh heavily with landowners is that human beings may frighten deer away. The accepted wisdom is that the mere scent of a human being can send the quarry running away for miles and miles, perhaps never to return. Norman McCulloch, then Secretary to the Red Deer Commission (the government-funded agency that advises land-owners on the control of deer), told me in 1985: 'One walker going along a ridge can clear that hillside of deer for twenty-four hours.'

But just what disturbance is likely to spoil a day's stalking? No stalking occurs in Scotland on the Sabbath, so it might be thought all right for the public to wander over the deer ranges at least on this day during the stalking season. The Duke of Atholl is one of many landowners who will not even allow this because he believes if his deer get the scent of human beings they could rush off miles away from the stalking area.

This notion has much greater implications for walkers than does the similar idea that walkers may frighten pheasants. In pheasant shooting, the area over which slaughter takes place is normally limited. But if deer are to be kept secure from human contact vast areas must be declared out of bounds to ramblers. Yet the evidence that walkers do frighten away deer is little more than anecdotal.

The only scientific study of the impact of human disturbance on red deer pointed to the opposite conclusion from that assumed by Scotland's landowners. In 1973, scientists from the Brathay Hall Trust based in Cumbria observed the movements of deer and people on the mountainside of Meall a' Ghiubhais in the Beinn Eighe National Nature Reserve in Wester Ross. Hidden in four stone hides carefully positioned over the mountain, they plotted deer and human movements on map overlays using binoculars, two-way radios and compasses; they also took regular measurements of wind speed, wind direction and humidity. This is what they discovered:

The deer movements were generally of a slow progressional nature with the beasts stopping to gaze and then moving on. In some cases though deer were seen to be moving at speed for some distance, sometimes this movement could be accounted for by disturbance from people and on other occasions it seemed unrelated to such factors. When deer were disturbed by people, and it was clear that it was people off recognized tracks that would be more likely to disturb beasts, they generally only moved short distances (up to half a mile), enough to get out of view (and scent one supposes). It was noticeable that deer often watched people walking along paths without being particularly concerned.[13]

These observations square with what might be expected in view of the red deer's natural history. Like all wild animals, deer are creatures of habit. Furthermore, deer grow very much accustomed to staying in a small area. What this means is that though they may panic if badly disturbed, they will come back later. One herd at least that seems to be able to live alongside human visitors is that of the Martindale deer of the Lake District. This herd of 150 beasts lives in an area popular with hikers in winter as well as summer. But the herd stays – and thrives.

In spite of these considerations, Scotland's landowners continue to labour to keep walkers off their deer lands. As the areas involved are so vast, they can achieve complete success only by employing great numbers of keepers. In the nineteenth century, many estates could afford to do just this and the result was considerable conflict between those wishing to walk and climb and those wishing to stalk deer. It was because of this conflict that the first attempts to legalize public access to open countryside came from Scotland. Today, however, the overall situation is less difficult for walkers. Although during the stalking season from mid-August to mid-October many regions of the Highlands sport warnings to walkers to keep out of deer lands, the constraints are not nearly as great as they were in the nineteenth century since there are fewer keepers on the ground to turn people away. Three facts, however, remain. Where restrictions remain they are imposed entirely at the will of the landowners themselves usually without any say whatsoever for the public. Secondly, most of the restrictions are applied at the time when many people have to take their holidays. Thirdly, the last ten years in particular have seen an increase rather than a reduction in the incidence of 'Keep Off' notices in the Highlands.

The problem for ordinary people visiting the Highlands in August and September is not simply that access to odd estates like Altnaharra or Atholl is restricted: it is that these estates lie among other estates that will also be trying to exclude the public from at least part of their deer forest during the stalking season. The Atholl Estate for example occupies the south-western flank of the Cairngorms. Its neighbour to the north-east, the Mar Lodge Estate, owned by a company called Harlow and Jones Investments, also tries to restrict access. It operates a 'restricted period' from 1 August until 20 October in which walkers are asked to confine their incursions into this 65,000-acre estate to public footpaths to and from Cairngorm Nature Reserve, Glen Tilt, Larig Ghru and Glen Feshie while walking over Bein Bhrotein, Carn Ealar and Scarsoch only on Saturdays and

Sundays. Walkers who decide to try their luck elsewhere in the region will find that the Glenfeshie estate, which also borders the Duke of Atholl's estate, is also out of bounds. Glenfeshie is owned by the 2nd Baron Dulverton and is part of the quarter of a million acres of Scotland owned by members of the Wills tobacco family. It operates an even longer restricted period (mid-August until mid-October, and also 4 November until 31 January), with one 'preferred route' right of way through this 48,000-acre domain. The 19,800-acre Rothiemurchus Estate adjoining Glen Feshie has a 1 September until 20 October restricted period, although it does permit access to the summit of Brae Riach even during the cull.

The 'restricted periods' operated by many of Scotland's largest estates are listed in a widely available booklet entitled *Access for Mountaineers and Hill-Walkers*, prepared by the Scottish Land-owners' Federation and the Mountaineering Council of Scotland and published by the Royal Bank of Scotland. In fact 'restricted' does not always mean that all walking is banned, but the booklet and the various signs undoubtedly give that impression at first glance. The booklet explains, however, that a particular activity like deer stalking is likely to be taking place on the estate during the restricted period, that conflicts can arise between stalking and access, and adds, 'It is therefore important that contact should be made to check on this possibility'. For each estate a phone number is given.

Dr Robert Aitken, the chairman of the Scottish Countryside Activities Council which embraces all the country's main conservation and access organizations, has had considerable experience of telephoning estates to check about access. He told me in an interview in 1985:

Unless you phone very early in the morning, in which case you might get somebody out of bed angrily, you will very often not get the stalker but you will get the stalker's wife. The stalker's wife may not know where the party have gone shooting that day anyway, or she will have been fed the local policy that you shouldn't be on the ground at all, in other words she can't recommend to you it's safe to go up. Quite often even if you get the stalker he says, 'Well if it was up to me I wouldn't mind you going, but the boss says "no", and that's the end of the story.'

The result in the Cairngorms is that some places are very
heavily used – like Cairngorm itself with its ski-lift, and other
mountain peaks particularly in the Rothiemurchus Estate like
Ben Macdui, Einich Cairn and Braeriach. But many visitors,
particularly those with children, are deterred from wandering
freely into the heart of the Cairngorms except along the predetermined 'restricted routes'.

The problems for would-be walkers over Scotland's deer
country do not end with the restrictions imposed during the
stalking season. They go far wider than this. Some owners try to
restrict access during the hind-culling season as well as when the
stags are being stalked. It is not considered sport to shoot the
hinds (for one thing, as they are pregnant for ten months of the
year, culling necessarily occurs when many are in fawn), but an
equal number of hinds to stags have to be killed for the deer
population to be maintained at the desired level, so estate keepers
round up the hinds and shoot them. Walkers are just as likely
(or as unlikely) to disturb hinds as stags; certainly keepers
consider that walkers cause extra inconvenience. The females
may be legally shot in Scotland at any time from 20 October
(one day after the stag season begins), until 16 February,
although most hind-culling occurs from mid-November until
mid-February.

It might seem paradoxical that some landowners also try to
keep the public away when the hinds are giving birth in May
and June. They argue that human disturbance could lead a hind
to abandon her calf. In other cases notices intended to keep the
public at bay during the stag stalking season are left up all year
round. While notices like 'Danger: Stray Bullets: Walk here at
your own risk' might be laughed at out of season by the hiker
well-versed in the esoteric details of Scotland's game regulations,
visitors from towns in Scotland or further south, particularly if
accompanied by children or old people, tend to be more easily
intimidated.

As if all that was not enough, the restrictions on public access
in the interests of deer stalking are paralleled by other restrictions
at other times in the interests of other bloodsports.

Take almost any other tract of Scotland that embraces both
hill and lowland country. No sooner have the restrictions imposed

by the stag cull been lifted on the higher ground in mid-October than pheasant and partridge shooting begins on the lower fields, if it has not begun already. One family in the parish of Birse in Aberdeenshire told me that pheasant shooters stand in a line around their garden for three weekends every autumn bagging birds. They dare not venture into the garden to gather up the lead shot until the sportsmen have left.

The colder months of the year are the easiest as far as access is concerned, but only between mid-February when hind-culling stops and April when the grouse and pheasants start nesting is the pressure off completely. Thereafter if it is not the nesting grouse, pheasants or partridges which are providing the excuse for barring walkers, it will be anything from the hill sheep lambing in April and May, the grouse chicks hatching in June and July, the adult grouse being shot from Mid-August until the end of October, the roe deer being shot in the woods from April until October – on top of the supposed needs of the red deer when they are calving in May and June and when they are being shot in summer and autumn. In other words, the most relaxed attitude to walkers is during the second half of February and the whole of March – except, that is, along Scotland's rivers, for the salmon and trout fishing season begins in March and extends through the summer until September.

In fixing their restricted periods and the detailed public access arrangements on their estates, landowners usually pay some attention to established access patterns and public pressure. For instance, they tend to leave the most popular mountain peaks, especially the Munros, free for walkers. Nonetheless, large areas remain in which landowners seek to restrict walkers and the walkers themselves have no formal say in the matter.

Starting in 1984 landowners in the eastern Grampians sought to co-ordinate restrictions on public access. These landowners control 300,000 acres (469 square miles) of magnificent scenery bounded to the north by the River Dee, to the west by the A93 Braemar to Blairgowrie road and to the south by the Angus glens. This land forms the territory of one of Scotland's forty 'deer management groups'. These are areas isolated from one another by the sea, sea-lochs, roads or railways which contain more or less isolated populations of red deer. In implementing

an annual cull of one-sixth of the adult population of males and
females, the Red Deer Commission has found it convenient to
use these units as a base. The deer management groups seek to
attain not only the target cull for their area but also a balanced
cull: ownership boundaries tend to be unfenced and one landowner will be upset if all the stags that have been grazing his
land go on to his neighbour's land, perhaps lured by a herd of
hinds, at the very time he is letting out stag stalking. According
to the Red Deer Commission, half of these groups also try to
develop a concerted policy on public access within the group's
area.

The East Grampian group implemented its access policy first
through putting up fifty notices at all the main access points in
its territory. This notice suggested to would-be walkers that if
they strayed off the hill tracks at certain times they might be
endangering people's jobs; what is more, it mentioned a stalking
season that embraced both the killing of stags and of hinds. The
notice read:

Hill walkers and visitors are welcome in the East Grampians but are
asked to bear in mind that deer management, farm and estate activities
continue throughout the year and that undue disturbance in sensitive
areas may be a threat to the well-being of the deer and to the livelihood
of farm and estate workers. The stalking seasons, involving the use of
firearms, take place between 1 July and 16 February but the most
important period is from 12 August to 20 October. During this shorter
period please remain on the recognized hill tracks indicated by a red
line, and where possible notify estate personnel of your proposed route.'

In other words, the East Grampian owners are not simply
asking the public to check before walking in the hills during a
restricted period; they ask them to walk only on hill tracks
throughout an important holiday period. The map to which the
notice refers marked these tracks and existing roads. Together
they make up a sparse network which leaves vast areas out of
bounds to walkers.

The other main way in which the East Grampian Group
sought to put their message across was through leaflets which
were made available at hotels, youth hostels, tourist offices, and
estate offices. These leaflets took a similar line to the notices but
also called in aid the well-being of the deer:

The stalking season for Red Deer Stags runs from 1 July to 20 October
and for Hinds from 21 October to 16 February. The period of most
significant stalking activity is from mid-August to 20 October. In
addition Red Deer calve in the early Summer and it is highly desirable
that disturbance in the hill should be kept to a minimum at this time.
In deep snow conditions during the Winter it is also important to
minimize disturbance, as Red Deer are subjected to prolonged harsh
conditions and the increased stress of disturbance by walkers and cross-
country skiers can be the cause of high levels of mortality.

Present-day restrictions on walkers in Highland deer forests
are not as blindly selfish as those of the nineteenth century.
Today's landowners may enjoy the feeling of power they get
from excluding their fellow-citizens but many are rather more
concerned about their finances. For many Highland estates, deer
stalking now provides the main income. Highland landowners
playing host to people paying £150 and more for the pleasure of
shooting one stag consider it understandably important that the
stalker should be disturbed as little as possible. Nonetheless, it
should be perfectly possible to give the public a far greater say in
determining when, where and how any restrictions on access
genuinely required for the benefit of stalking should be imposed.

GAME FISHING

The rivers, streams, lakes and lochs of Britain bring out their
owners' instinct for privacy in a peculiarly virulent form. And as
ownership of dry land is seen as revolving round game, so our
landowners' passion for their waters is bound up with fish.

At the time of the Norman invasion, the right to take any kind
of fish from all the rivers and lakes of the British Isles seems to
have been as freely availed of by ordinary people as the right to
fish from the open sea. Gradually, however, ordinary people
came to be legally excluded.

Long before Britain became one nation, kings north and south
of the border had decreed that salmon and trout were to be
aristocrats among fish and that salmon and trout fishing was to
belong to the monarch. Having appropriated this right, they
gave back the privilege to a favoured few. In many cases, the
descendants of those favoured have hung on to this privilege.

The 10th Duke of Atholl, for instance, owns the right to take salmon and sea-trout from the whole of Strathardle even though he does not own all the land alongside the river. His ancestors were given this right and it has always accompanied the earldom of Atholl.

Like many other rights in land, the right to fish can be bought and sold quite separately from the land in question. When salmon and trout fishing became popular with the rich during the nineteenth century, fishing rights became extremely valuable. Waters came to be managed more and more in the interests of fish and fishermen and 'poachers' to be dealt with more and more severely.

The absence of any legal right of public access alongside the rivers and lakes of Britain ensured landowners a free hand. Whole stretches of river were bought and stocked and turned into commercial fishing enterprises. And as part of this process the public was often firmly excluded from the banks.

Only occasionally do public footpaths or roads run along river-banks. In general, rights of way alongside rivers are scarce, particularly as one moves southwards through England. Paths along the Cheshire Dee are patchy, but they exist. Move into Shropshire, and rivers like the Teme and Lugg are very badly served by public paths. Few rights of way exist alongside Dorset's Stour and Yeo; or Dyfed's River Teifi. The people of Hampshire may not walk far alongside the Test, while Cornish people are barred from the Rivers Tamar and Tavy. In Scotland, very few paths or roads provide access to the banks of such beautiful rivers as the Dee, the Tweed and the Tay.

Along our coasts, de facto access exists in much of England and Wales, though to a lesser degree in Scotland. Long-distance paths like the one running right round the coast of Somerset, Devon, Cornwall and Dorset have enshrined in legal form the general belief that you can walk along the coast. But along the edges of Britain's rivers, streams and lakes, no comparable form of customary access exists. Where these contain salmon or trout, they are likely to be jealously guarded.

Fortunately for Britain's landowners and salmon and trout fishermen, but unfortunately for the rest of us, both salmon and trout will live in virtually all the rivers of Scotland, Northern

Ireland, Cumbria, Lancashire, most of Wales, Devon, Cornwall, Dorset, Hampshire and parts of West Sussex. Salmon disdain the lesser waters of Kent, East Anglia, and the East Midlands, although trout will co-exist along with the lower orders of the fish world – 'coarse fish' – in parts of East Kent, Berkshire, Oxfordshire, the Cotswolds and the West Midlands.

As with rivers, so with many lakes. Hammer ponds, remnants of industry but now bordered by hanging woods, are one of the most characteristic landscape features of the High Weald. Yet the public may gaze on many of them only from afar. Hawkins and Hammer Pond, both about three miles outside Horsham in St Leonard's Forest, are typical examples. In both cases the fishing rights have been let to an angling club and, as so often happens where this occurs, the general public are denied access.

In some places where walkers and indeed canoeists are allowed alongside salmon and trout fishermen, however, they seem to co-exist perfectly well. Rutland Water in Leicestershire, for instance, attracts around 12,000 visitors every fine summer Sunday – strolling, riding, cycling, picnicking or observing wildlife around the twenty-four mile perimeter. But such a fine summer Sunday also brings up to 400 fishermen to Rutland Water, pursuing some of the upper-crust of the fishing world – the brown and rainbow trout. Indeed, Rutland Water is the main still-water trout fishery in Britain. On top of the visitors round the water's edge the fishermen have also to contend on the water itself with wind-surfers and underwater divers, canoeists and yachtsmen, not to mention a pleasure cruiser. The only zoning that is imposed over the whole 3,200-acre reservoir restricts sailing craft (not fishermen's motor boats) from entering the shallow lagoons within a nature reserve area since the flapping of sails can frighten waterbirds. The whole of Rutland Water is a designated Site of Special Scientific Interest. I asked Frank Knights, the Reservoirs Manager for the Oundle Division of the Anglian Water Authority, in an interview in 1985 how the supposed conflicts that can arise between anglers and others are tackled at Rutland Water. He told me:

Most of the public come from twelve o'clock until half past four when they go home. That's when the pressure is on, and at that time anglers are doing one of three things: (a) they are asleep on the bank, because having travelled a vast distance to get here, they fished early morning and then they are tired; (b) they are at the pub; (c) they are out in deeper water, wading to try and get out to the fish which traditionally feed further out in the daytime in deeper, cooler water and then come in to the margins at night . . . We rely basically on the good relationship between the various people. We have a thing called a reservoir users' panel on which every interest is represented and which meets twice a year to discuss problems that might be arising and new ways of dealing with them. I think it's the sense of balance that we get at that meeting: there are so many different things taking place there's a realization that the water is not just there for them. I think that's the main thing.

There seems no reason to suppose that the problems of combining public access with trout fishing would be any different on a lake or, say, a Wealden hammer pond, than they are on Rutland Water – or indeed on other waters where these uses have been successfully combined like Tayside Regional Council's Monikie and Clatto country parks just outside Dundee or the National Trust's Waggoners' Wells near Hindhead. The problems on a narrow stretch of river can be different, however. On a lake there is enough wave action to spoil the vision of a trout so that it is not frightened away (or 'spooked' in the angler's jargon) by somebody walking along the bank. But on a river, from which trout can see clearly and through a wide angle, a trout can be spooked by a silhouette from the bank. However, there are several ways in which possible conflict could be minimized. For one thing, salmon and trout tend to hold up at certain traditional spots along rivers. An angler does not fish the whole length of a river but will go to a spot or salmon pool where, perhaps because of the presence of deep holes where the fish can lie in cooler water, or bushes, or the presence of food, he knows from past experience he is likely to make a catch. Subtle zoning could keep walkers away from those particular spots when fishing is in progress. Some landowners even encourage the public to walk along angling rivers because they believe any disturbance to the fish is outweighed by the role the public play in discouraging poaching. The Duke of Atholl told me he does this at Glen Tilt.

Of course surveys show that among the things many anglers value in their sport is the peace and quiet they enjoy by the river or lakeside. It is this more than the sport itself that is threatened by the suggestion that the rest of us should walk along the watersides. This and the landowner's feeling that in letting out fishing rights he has not entirely relinquished his grip on his land in the way that he would if it were opened up to all. But should these considerations be allowed to continue to bar the people from their rivers, streams and lakes? W. H. Hudson said in 1909: 'The stream invites us to follow. The impulse is so common that it might be set down as an instinct; and certainly there is no more fascinating pastime than to keep company with a river from its source to the sea. Unfortunately this is not easy in a country where running waters have been enclosed, which should be as free as the rain and the sunshine to all, and were once free, when England was England still, before landowners annexed them, even as they annexed or stole the commons, and shut up the footpaths and made it an offence for a man to go aside from the road to feel God's grass under his feet.' (*Afoot in England*)

RED GROUSE

The landowners' argument that visitors would frighten game is undermined by the experience of one area where game and ramblers have come to co-exist very well in spite of earlier claims that this would be impossible. During the 1920s and 1930s, the vast grouse moors between Sheffield and Manchester were one of the places in which the idea of public access was most fiercely resisted. Few game preserves can ever have been more jealously guarded. And the arguments put forward for the exclusion of the public seemed convincing enough to many at the time. The red grouse is, after all, a choosy bird. Indigenous to Britain (attempts to get it to breed outside our shores have always failed), it will nest only on the relatively dry heather moors of upland Britain. It was also thought to be an extremely nervous bird: landowners argued that the sight of ramblers, especially in the breeding season, would be bound to ruin the sport completely. Were this to have happened, real economic loss would have occurred, for grouse shooting commands high rents.

However, nearly one-third of the human inhabitants of the British Isles live within fifty miles of the Peak moors, in such cities as Leeds, Sheffield, Nottingham and Manchester. And it was the position of these very moors on which mass trespasses had occurred that led to the enactment in 1949 of radical legislation on access. This enabled planning authorities to open up hitherto inaccessible areas of uncultivated land through access agreements with landowners. In the face of immense public pressure for access, the new Peak Park Special Planning Board secured access agreements with landowners over seventy-six square miles of moorland, including the very areas where conflict over access in the 1930s had been most intense.

Access agreement land in the Peak does not only cover land devoted to grouse rearing: there are also sheep grazing lands and some land devoted to both uses over which legal public access has also now been introduced. Under the agreements, the public have a right to wander at will over the land concerned without being treated as trespassers. This freedom continues throughout lambing time and the grouse breeding season; it is only when the grouse are actually being shot that access is suspended: the landowners who have entered into these agreements are allowed to nominate up to twelve days a year for shooting. The Planning Board makes provision for this multiple use of the land by publicizing days on which shooting is to take place in local newspapers and through circular letters to 500 affected organizations. In addition, its team of rangers post up warning signs on the moors on shooting days. And so far no walker has been shot or injured since the agreements have been in force. (Such accidents as have occurred have involved the shooters shooting each other.) In addition to operating the moor closures on shooting days, the Peak Board rangers enforce by-laws to prevent damage – for instance the lighting of fires. Landowners receive modest compensation for access designed to compensate for inconvenience: the annual rates in 1986 were 13.4p an acre, 32.5p per ewe grazed where appropriate, and £87.36 and £43.68 a mile respectively for external and internal wall or fence.[14]

The Peak Board estimates that the access agreement moors receive up to 700,000 visits every year. Kinder Scout, where some of the most violent skirmishes between walkers and game-keepers took place during the mass trespasses of the 1930s, now welcomes nearly 66,000 people each year. Yet this intense public pressure has had no detrimental impact on grouse bags. When Nicholas Picozzi of the Nature Conservancy Council was asked in 1967 to investigate complaints from moor-owners that access was reducing their grouse bags, he discovered that grouse bred no less successfully on moors over which people and their dogs had unrestricted access. If anything, the birds on these moors had done rather better than their counterparts elsewhere. At the same time, grouse bags showed no evidence of a decline in the wake of the access agreements.[15] Most moors in the Peak District have shown a decrease in game bag figures since the war, but such decreases, which have also characterized grouse moors elsewhere, do not seem to be related to disturbance. They may have been partly due to poor heather management: to reach maximum numbers, grouse need a large amount of young heather shoots, and this requires the burning of plots of heather about every fifteen years.

As yet, public access does not exist on all grouse moors even in the Peak. Although 44 per cent of the Peak Park moors are covered by access agreements, and a further 11 per cent is moorland owned by bodies like the National Trust or Sheffield City Council which is freely open to the public, 45 per cent is still legally closed, including areas that are fenced off with 'Private' notices. Elsewhere, there are still many grouse moors that sport 'Keep Out' notices. Yet, as a former huntservant from Yorkshire put it to me in 1982:

How can two or three people walking across several thousand acres of moorland disturb the grouse? I can't see how they can, and I've been in the country all my life. You're not likely to stumble over a grouse nest – if you do it's a chance in a million. Most game birds – pheasant, partridge, grouse, if you come to them when they're nesting, they lie ever so low and only when you're on top of them will they move. Mostly they won't, they'll remain stationary. Unless you actually stand on the nest you haven't disturbed them and if you do disturb them they'll perhaps fly away twenty yards, they'll settle down and then they'll run back through the undergrowth to their nest. So why close a whole moor down for fear of disturbing a bird for a few seconds?

'Wildlife would be Disturbed'

Landowners often view themselves genuinely enough as custodians to whom fate has allocated the task of safeguarding their

For thousands of years the people of Britain have freely enjoyed a common heritage of wonderful countryside full of charms like those of these flowers in a Suffolk meadow. But though we all have a stake in our environment, control of it lies in the half a per cent of the community who hold legal title to land, who may treat it as they will. These flowers were destroyed when the meadow's owner ploughed it up in the early 1980s. Should owners have a totally free hand to do what they like with our countryside? *Photo by Peter Stocker*

Attitudes to the ownership of land in Britain dating back to the Norman Conquest have been transmitted down generations of aristocratic landowning families. Today these traditional landowners are far from extinct. The 10th Duke of Northumberland *(above)* owns 105,000 acres in Northumberland and more in the South of England. The 10th Duke of Rutland *(right, above)* owns 18,000 acres of The Midlands including Belvoir Castle *(right, below).* Aristocratic landowners still own one third of Britain's land.

Photos by Northumberland and Morpeth Gazette, Leicester Mercury

Attitudes of landowners and landless continue to diverge. Conflicting views on bloodsports are but one facet of a deepening conflict. To the ladies of the hunt, foxes exist for Man to do with as he wishes. But for young London Wildlife Trust volunteers *(left and below),* foxes are fellow citizens of our environment entitled to protection and affection. *Photos by Suresh Karadia,* The Times, *Garry Weaser,* The Guardian, The Times

Landowners see the land as theirs to exploit for profit. That often means intensive agriculture and that often means the destruction of attractive and interesting landscape features as here at Newdigate Wood in Surrey in 1983 *(left)*. But the rest of us prefer our countryside to retain its variety as seen at Newdigate Wood before the bulldozers came *(below)*. *Photos by Marion Shoard*

Among the silent victims of the post-war agricultural revolution are Britain's wild creatures. Once widespread, the barn owl has become an uncommon bird in modern Britain, as its traditional nest sites in old trees and barns have been torn down and the rough cover that used to harbour its prey has been ploughed up. Yet according to the painter of this picture, Gordon Beningfield, 'The countryside is the most important source of inspiration for Britain's painters, sculptors, composers, poets and novelists'. *Photo by Gordon Beningfield*

Henge monuments like the one at Avebury *(above)* have imparted character and magic to the landscape for four thousand years, as well as embodying irreplaceable data about past human life in Britain. Once levelled, they show up only as cropmarks in the growing corn, like this one at Marton-le-Moor near Ripon in Yorkshire.

Photos from the Cambridge University Collection of Air Photographs: copyright reserved

Landscape change is
totally in the hands of
landowners, so there is no
redress for people like
Florence MacDonald
(above), whose home at
Botesdale in Suffolk now
looks out on a modern
agricultural 'prairie'
where once there was a
patchwork of flowery
meadows and hedges.
Emergency powers under
the Wildlife and
Countryside Act 1981 did
enable steps to be taken to
stop the complete
destruction in 1984 of this
site at Udden's Heath in
Dorset *(right),* but the
Act's provisions have
safeguarded only a tiny
fraction of Britain's land.
Photos by Marion Shoard,
The Guardian

Modern farming need not eliminate beauty and wildlife. Peter and Sheila Stocker 'made a good living' and reared four children between 1961 and 1980 on their 83-acre Suffolk farm *(left).* However, when they sold up, the farm became part of the much larger unit of a neighbouring farmer, who has made radical changes to increase output *(above).*
Photos by Peter Stocker, Marion Shoard

Glen Ample *(above)* is a tiny but unique glen in Scotland's southern Highlands scoured in the classic U-shape by glaciation. The lines of much of the valley are however soon to be obscured by conifer afforestation. Afforestation obliterates contours and cuts out views, as over Loch Lubnaig in Stirling District *(left)*. It destroys wildlife habitats and makes hill walking tedious. *Photos by Marion Shoard*

Since the Middle Ages, landowners' rights to exploit their land to the full commercially have been limited in the interests of the rest of the community on the widely scattered patches of land known as commons. Today, tobogganing, butterfly spotting and orienteering are just a few of the hundreds of different activities that take place on Britain's 1½ million acres of commons, including Ashtead Common in Surrey *(above)*. The commons are however fast disappearing and Hampshire's Hazeley Heath *(right)* could soon join the many commons which have been enclosed by their owners for farming, forestry or building in the course of this century.
Photos by Marion Shoard

Britain's countryside is far less accessible than many people imagine. Away from rights of way walkers find themselves barred from much of Britain – including this stretch of peaceful parkland in the Duke of Northumberland's Syon Park in Brentford *(above)*, or this part of Lord Romsey's Broadlands estate *(left)*, photographed on one of the three days in July 1984 when it was open to the general public as the venue for the Game Fair. A new right of access to our countryside, turning the existing law of trespass on its head, would enable all to share the delights of the countryside. *Photos by Marion Shoard*

The supposed needs of the
pheasant, red grouse,
salmon, trout and red deer
for peace and quiet are
used as reasons for
excluding most of the
British people from much
of Britain's finest countryside, as at Highclere in
north Hampshire (above)
and in the south-east
Cairngorms (right). Yet in
the few game preserves
where walking is allowed,
it does little obvious harm
to the game. *Photos by
Marion Shoard,
Dr Robert Aitken*

DANGER
PLEASE DO NOT CLIMB
THE HILLS DURING THE
STALKING SEASON —
AUG. 1ST TO OCT. 20TH

In the absence of any right of access to most of the countryside, the British people have to rely largely on such permissive access as landowners are prepared to tolerate. On one day each year, Lord Rotherwick permits the general public to enter part of Wychwood Forest, north Oxfordshire's most impressive woodland. Thousands take advantage of the offer, including these people leaving the Forest on Palm Sunday in 1982. At other times, the Forest's 1,550 acres, and the adjoining 600 acres of Cornbury Park, are closed to the public, save for a short section of public footpath crossing one corner of the park. It was from here that the bottom photo was taken in 1984. *Photos by Marion Shoard*

Along with the evils we have inherited from our rural past, we have also inherited the germ of a policy for people in the countryside. Our public footpaths system (though threatened) is an enormous asset, and our country buses (though decimated) show how opportunities can be provided for all the people to enjoy their countryside. The top photo is in the West Sussex Downs near Arundel; the bottom at Branscombe in South Devon. *Photos by Marion Shoard*

Overseas the grip of the landowner can sometimes be even tighter than it is in Britain. British settlers in New Zealand took with them the possessiveness of the mother country without British concessions to the landless like the public footpaths system. Today, in attractive areas of New Zealand, like this hillside near Sanson in the North Island *(above)*, walking in the countryside is often virtually impossible. In countries with a non-British heritage, things can however be very different. In these woods near Abisko in Sweden *(left)*, as everywhere else in the country, walkers have a legal right to go where they please. *Photos by David Cox*

heritage for future generations. When in this frame of mind they often defend the exclusion of the public from their land as a regrettable necessity imposed upon them by their duty to protect the nation's wildlife from damaging disturbance.

Lord Romsey, the owner of the 5,500-acre Broadlands estate in south Hampshire, had this to say to me on the subject of public access:

Letting people in is akin to cutting down a rain forest in South America: you are actually destroying animals' habitat . . . Anywhere that I've been where there's been this attempt by a local authority or by an extremely altruistic landowner to open up an estate, there's a great deal of destruction, destruction not necessarily visible to the eyes of the average person living in Romsey or wherever, they probably wouldn't understand. It can be as simple as constant feet destroying the sward . . .

People will say 'We walk along and keep quiet, we don't have dogs, we won't cause any distress.' The very fact that there are humans there at all will drive the hares, the rabbits and the duck and everything away . . . What you would do is scare away all the species that were there long before us: classes of animals that are dying out every year because they require total privacy.

But are people really such a threat to wildlife? A good place to look for evidence not far from Lord Romsey's estate is the much-visited New Forest. Lord Romsey believes that visitors have done much damage here: 'You've only got to go and look at the New Forest to see an environment which has been virtually totally destroyed,' he told me. He believes allowing the public access in the New Forest must have resulted in loss of species. But has it? Colin Tubbs is the Nature Conservancy Council assistant regional officer responsible for Hampshire; he is also the author of a book on the ecological history of the New Forest. When in 1984 I asked him for his view of the impact of visitors on the wildlife content of the New Forest, he told me:

It is perfectly true that around parking and camping sites the land has become very trampled and worn; there is also the secondary impact of safety tree fellings around car-parks. Locally this is having an effect and if you multiply it up it is significant. However, no species changes in the forest can be attributed to recreation. The wildlife population changes that have taken place have been due to quite different factors, like over-grazing. From an ecological point of view, the problem of over-grazing is far greater than recreation.

What has been happening in the New Forest is that ponies and cattle in particular have seriously reduced the diversity of grasses and plants, eliminating the most palatable species. Comparisons by Mr Tubbs show that woodland on similar soils nearby but fenced to keep out grazing animals has a hazel understorey; in the New Forest, in contrast, hazel as well as elm and lime have been eliminated. The other woods contain abundant bramble while the herb layer of grasses and flowering plants is more prolific and rich in species than that in the Forest. Mr Tubbs also considers the relative scarcity of butterflies in the New Forest is almost certainly the result of cattle, ponies and deer eating the food plants of the butterfly larvae; while these grazing animals have severely reduced the food available for rabbits, voles and other herbivores that are the traditional prey of kestrels and buzzards all of which are relatively scarce in the New Forest. Finally, although the New Forest as the largest area of unsown vegetation in lowland England supports most of the British population of the rare Dartford Warbler, surveys by Mr Tubbs have demonstrated that burning (to produce better grazing pasture) and heavy grazing have significantly reduced this bird's habitat.[16]

So the effect of visitor pressure in the New Forest is not really to eliminate wildlife. There is wearing away of grass in some areas and there is a litter problem – but these phenomena are not to be compared in significance with the felling of the Amazonian rain forest.

The Duke of Rutland is another landowner who defends the exclusion of the public from his estate on the grounds of nature conservation. His Belvoir estate covers 11,000 acres (more than thirty times the size of Hyde Park) on the borders of Lincolnshire, Leicestershire and Northamptonshire. When I visited Belvoir in 1982 the Duke allowed a certain amount of permissive access: the guides, scouts and mentally handicapped were allowed to camp on one fifty-acre site on the estate, while the disabled were permitted to fish on the lower lake on Sundays for free. In addition, people from two local villages could walk along the estate's tarmacced private roads, and bona fide organizations might get permission to hold sponsored walks or other special events on the estate. The general public could visit the Castle on payment of a fee and walk in gardens close to it. A Leicestershire County Council-designated footpath, the Jubilee Way, runs through part of the estate; overall, however, there are very few public footpaths. What this meant was that there was no access whatsoever for the general public over many of Belvoir's most spectacular woods, grasslands, parkland and lakes. I asked Andrew Thompson, the Duke's land agent, why the public were not allowed to walk on the paths through the estate's woodlands and uncultivated land and around the lakes. He conceded that the public would not cause 'terrible damage', but went on to say: 'I think you have got to have islands of peace and non-disturbance to try and preserve forms of wildlife . . . One is not being selfish for an individual; one is being selfish for the environment.'

Locally of course, the problems caused when very large numbers of visitors converge on one spot can be real enough, as a few small, heavily-used areas like Kynance Cove, Tarn Hows or Loch Lomond bear witness. Ecological studies carried out in the 1970s have demonstrated that different forms of countryside recreation can indeed change ecosystems.[17] Indeed, it would be surprising if they did not. Walking and picnicking on grass, for example, can cause species changes as those grasses and flowers most resistant to nutrient enrichment or trampling replace those less resistant. In very heavily used spots, even resistant species are unable to survive the trampling they receive and the bare ground that is exposed may be eroded by wind and rain. But this is a small problem. Very, very little countryside is actually trampled away. The threat to landscape or wildlife caused by public recreation is just not a sufficient reason for keeping people out.

Landowners sometimes present the danger posed by public visits in terms of wilful destruction rather than mere pressure of numbers. Belvoir agent Andrew Thompson, who opposes extra access to Belvoir on the grounds that the public would disturb wildlife, distinguished a small minority as much more trouble-some than most. He told me:

The vast majority of people you meet on the footpaths, the Jubilee Way or what have you wish you a cheery 'Good Morning'. They are jolly pleased to be out in the countryside, they appreciate the fact that one is trying to keep the countryside looking more or less as it has always done, that one's trying to preserve the countryside as best one can. They appreciate it, they have a discerning eye. Yet get the 5 per cent idiot who will go out and wilfully do damage. He is probably the same idiot who beats up a telephone box in an urban environment. He will therefore beat up hang-gates and scratch his name on trees and so on.

There is obviously something in the idea that the countryside provides opportunities for vandalism. Indeed, a fair amount of deliberate destruction occurs already. One of the nastiest incidents reported to me came from Michael Thompson, the agent for the Fitzwilliams' Milton estate. He wrote in a letter:

In the last estate I managed a group of ten-year-old children came upon some eight-week-old ducklings just released by a riverbank. Over twenty of them were clubbed to death with sticks by the three children concerned. These actions are the work of a small minority but they are sufficient to convince me that a lot more trouble would arise if uncontrolled access were allowed over private farmland.

However, vandals are a group one could expect to be less affected by access restrictions than others. I put it to Andrew Thompson (of Belvoir) that such people as might want to wreak damage in the countryside would probably do so whether they enjoyed legal access or not. He agreed that that was so.

Townspeople confronted by landowners' fears that they might vandalize the countryside might well retort that much deliberate damage is done in the countryside anyway. This, however, is tolerated in the name of 'traditional country sports'. Michael Thompson at Milton, for example, told me he takes steps to maintain the numbers of foxes on his estate, so that the hunting fraternity can enjoy themselves – despite the damage foxes do to pheasants, poultry and lambs. In spring 1981, for instance, foxes killed between fifteen and twenty lambs at Milton within a month.

But it is the actual killing of creatures like foxes by Man – what landowners call 'country sports', what many others terms 'bloodsports' – that bring the double standards into sharpest focus. Some landowners deliberately try to maintain deer by feeding them in winter or encourage foxes on their property. Of course it can be asserted that even if there were no artificial maintenance of deer and fox stocks, hunting would still be necessary as a means of culling wild populations that now lack any natural predators. The same cannot be said for pheasant shooting.

Although some pheasants exist in the wild, a great many more are deliberately reared for the purposes of shooting them. And while traditional deer stalking by men on foot (if not stag hunting with hounds) is relatively humane in that many stags are killed by the first shot and very few escape wounded, a pheasant shoot can involve the wounding of hundreds of birds. The theory is that the agony of these wounded birds is soon put to an end by dogs or foxes 'mopping up' after a shoot. But those that flee into tangled undergrowth may never be retrieved and their agony may last for hours. Or, if a pheasant's wings have been shot in but its legs are still in working order, the wounded pheasant, known as 'a runner', runs frantically from the dog which is trying to catch it. If it succeeds in catching its prey, the dog may not have the bite to kill the bird, so it has to take it to the shooter for its neck to be broken. If a shoot involves inexperienced guns, as many as half the pheasants shot may be wounded rather than killed outright.

What some people regard as the greatest cruelty of all is the deception wrought on game birds by human beings. Most pheasants that are shot start life as hand-reared day-old chicks, brought up to look upon Man as their friend. When they are put out in the coverts they know their own keeper and come to him when he calls them to be fed. Some country people say that one of the real reasons why landowners are so anxious to keep the public out of pheasant woods is that the arrival of strangers might upset the birds' illusion that human beings are their friends – an illusion to be kept up at all costs until the birds are cruelly jolted into reality by their own deaths.

As well as the lingering deaths of pheasants in the woods and spinneys of our countryside there are the deaths of the creatures which are snared or poisoned by gamekeepers for preying on pheasants' eggs or young. Every year hundreds of thousands of wild animals, mainly jays and magpies, crows and rooks, stoats and weasels and hedgehogs are killed by gamekeepers on the grounds that they might eat wild pheasants' eggs or the newly-hatched chicks. Naturally enough, abundant eggs and young pheasants attract potential predators from the countryside all around. The elimination of these predators can affect the balance of nature over a wide area. Relatively common wild creatures that prey on pheasant and partridge chicks direct are by no means the only victims of keepering practices. Poisons like strychnine laid for vermin also kill indiscriminately many non-target species. These victims then kill other species which feed on them. Eighty-nine buzzards, nine golden eagles, four gos-hawks, six red kites, a marsh harrier, three hen harriers and four peregrine falcons were known to be killed in this way between 1966 and 1978 – along with forty-two cats and 119 dogs and thirteen badgers – according to the report *Silent Death* published by the Royal Society for the Protection of Birds in 1980.[18]

So although game preservation helps protect valuable land-scape features it is not blameless. Double standards have to be employed to present the potential urban vandal as introducing something new into the countryside. Nowhere is this more obviously true than in the case of fox-hunting. Landowners are prepared to tolerate the hunt crashing willy-nilly over their land and the large amount of damage and inconvenience this causes. Yet the threat of townspeople wandering quietly over the same land is presented as a grave threat to agriculture, wildlife or shooting. If a townsman cuts his initials into the bark of a tree this is 'vandalism'; if the hunt pounds over a field of daffodils killing half the blooms, this is 'traditional country life'.

'Farming would be disrupted'

'Farming is a business, and one can't afford to have people running loose over the farm – same as British Leyland wouldn't like people wandering over their factories. It's the same thing – farming is big business.'[19] This view, put by a Suffolk farmer with 1,000 acres at his command to sociologist Howard Newby of the University of Essex in 1976 reflects what is perhaps the favourite argument of the landowner challenged on the issue of public access.

In fact, the notion that greater countryside access means

enabling people to wander willy-nilly through farmers' crops is one dreamt up by farmers to confuse the argument. Not even the most radical access campaigners have proposed that walkers should fan out across fields of young corn. The system that is sometimes held up as the model of what should be sought in Britain – the Swedish *Allemansrätten* or right to walk – specifically forbids people from wandering over growing crops or young trees. And in Britain there is certainly no demand for the opportunity to stumble over ploughed earth or through crops which may have been sprayed with dangerous chemicals. However, there are people who do not see why they should not be allowed to walk along field edges and along private roads and tracks in the countryside. There is little reason to suppose that if they were free to do these things they would cause much harm.

Horses and hounds do damage agriculture. Here again, though, there is one rule for society at large and another for the landowners themselves.

There are 206 hunts in England, Scotland and Wales, meeting on average three times a week from September to April. Their route is not confined to fortified tracks: they go wherever the fox leads. And a fox will go anywhere to save his life – into people's gardens, up village streets, into buildings, across plantations of young trees, through streams and across growing crops. Sometimes the master keeps the hounds off specially vulnerable areas, and he also tries to keep them off the land of farmers and others who have told him the hunt is not welcome on their land. But sometimes the hounds simply get out of control, and the whole spectacle is simply imposed on whatever and whoever happen to be around.

'A terrified fox which tried to take refuge in Gainsborough Lea Road railway station was followed by a pack of hounds and savaged to death in front of a horrified passenger,' reported the *Lincolnshire Echo* of 20 February 1981. The *Western Gazette* of 16 February 1981 reported that a Yeovil businessman alleged that between thirty and forty hounds ran over land he had developed as a wildlife sanctuary. 'They churned up the ground over the whole area, smashed down a lot of nesting undergrowth used by wild birds, and wrecked several hundred beech trees he had planted to aid wildlife', according to the paper. Perhaps the deepest impact of 'traditional country sports' is made on elderly people and children, like the youngsters from Bridgwater in Somerset enjoying a Sunday school outing in the Quantocks in 1980 who suddenly found themselves witnessing the killing of a stag by the Quantock Staghounds. The *Daily Express* for 9 April 1980 reported:

Children on a church ramble screamed and wept as a hunt reached its horrific climax before them. First there was fear as shouting huntsmen approached at full gallop with a pack of bloodthirsty hounds. Then came the kill. An exhausted stag was cornered in a stream only yards away, shot and dragged past where children had been playing.'

And eighty-two-year-old Alfred Holt is one elderly person who is unlikely to forget the harm foxhounds can do. A pack of hounds savaged his ten-year-old pet collie as he took it for a walk in his Sussex village. 'The lead was wrenched from my hand and before I knew what was happening fifty hounds were tearing poor Simon to pieces. It was horrible. I will never forget it and I wake up at night crying.' (*Daily Mirror*, 26 August 1986)

Many hunts operate a system of going round the day after they have been out, repairing fences and, where necessary, paying farmers compensation for damage. However, it is often very difficult to estimate damage. As a former huntservant explained to me one February:

You've got corn growing now till the hard frost comes and stunts the growth, and if the hunt went through with 100 or 150 horses, you can't really say how much damage has been caused. You won't know until the harvest, and then again it depends on the harvest itself: it could be a poor quality harvest anyway. A lot of tenant farmers daren't ask for too much compensation because their landlord probably hunts and he could turn nasty about the tenancy agreement, for instance increasing their rent. So when they are compensated, it's usually a minimal figure. There is resentment about hunt damage by farmers anyway but they daren't voice it too much because there's other people who can influence their livelihood. A farmer who owns his own land, the hunt cause damage to his land, he's offered a certain amount of money to reimburse him. If he doesn't agree with that and makes a stink or whatever he might find the next time he goes to market with some cattle nobody will buy his cattle because he's upset the master of the hunt.

Landowners opposing public access are particularly fond of arguing that visitors would upset farm animals. Pregnant ewes, which might miscarry after being startled, or young lambs which might be abandoned if their mothers were frightened, are examples cited. The dogs visitors might bring are often presented as more dangerous than the visitors themselves.

It is undoubtedly true that sheep have died or aborted foetuses after being frightened by walkers' dogs. However, it is also true that sheep and lambs have been killed by foxhounds – sometimes in horrific incidents.

If dogs turn out to be a threat to sheep or other animals on farmland, farmers are well placed to defend their stock. The Animals Act of 1971 permits them to shoot on sight any dog – other than a guide dog, police dog, sheep dog, gun dog or hunting hound – seen worrying a farm animal if there is no other reasonable means of stopping the worrying. Any person whose pet dog was worrying livestock could also, under legislation dating back to 1953, be prosecuted. The Wildlife and Country-side Act 1981 further strengthens the farmer's hand. Now it is an offence simply for a pet dog (but not of course a fox hound) to be 'at large' in any field containing sheep. 'At large' is defined as not on a lead or under close control.

Less obvious fears than sheep-worrying are sometimes voiced as arguments against public access. The land agent for the Belvoir estate, Andrew Thompson, told me that the possible presence of the public on a network of footpaths through his woods would mean that 'you could hardly dare fell a tree without thinking that somebody might be standing in its way'. When he agreed that tree felling does not usually involve a very large area at any one time, Mr Thompson went on to say that forestry workers would have to lock up valuable machines if there was a possibility of the public being nearby, and that people might hurt themselves if saws and other tools were left lying about. These risks the public might however be expected to bear. The experience of the National Trust estates and lands owned by public bodies like the Peak Park Planning Board as well as private estates in which forestry co-exists with public access suggests that they are not too terrible in practice. Ralph Percy of Arundel Park, for instance, told me in 1985: 'Public access doesn't really affect us. People are quite sensible and keep out of the woods on the whole. There are just one or two chaps with chainsaws and a tractor with a grab on it.' And when I asked him if there was a conflict between access and farming, Mr Percy said: 'Not really. There's only ever any conflict when people leave gates open.' The general situation: 'The only problem we do have sometimes with people is with fences, when groups of small boys climb all over the fences and in places they come down. There is very little in the way of conflicts. You obviously get the odd one – a teddy-boy gang going into the wood and setting light to the bushes or something. But it's very rare.'

'Nobody Wants to Come'

We have already seen that landowners or their agents on the edge of towns (like Michael Thompson at Milton on the edge of Peterborough or Lord Romsey at Broadlands) justify the exclusion of the general public from most of their estate land by arguing that the public would cause damage. So what about landowners whose estates lie further out in the country?

The core of Samuel Whitbread's 10,800-acre estate in north Bedfordshire includes parkland, woodland and two lakes. There is very little public access. When I asked Mr Whitbread in 1982 why he did not permit greater public access to this magnificent landscape he told me:

I don't believe that the demand is there. It is being whipped up, if you like perhaps by your book [*The Theft of the Countryside*] amongst other things, but people are not actually clamouring to do this . . . If we were in a tourist area, where there was a lot of tourist traffic, I think there would be a strong case . . . But I don't think that the demand that you are supposing is there is really there. It is very easy to say 'Yes, let's open everything up and let everybody walk everywhere they like' and really find that it is a bit of a non-event because people basically don't want it.

Mr Whitbread is firmly of the view that wider public access is unnecessary. At first sight his argument has force. No one is demonstrating for access with banners outside his gate. Nonetheless there are people who would travel to the Whitbread estate if they thought they could get in. If owners in Mr Whitbread's position could be persuaded of this they might well become as convinced as Lord Romsey that they ought to be excluded for fear of the damage they might do. In theory, of course, Mr Whitbread's argument defeats itself. If landowners really believe nobody would come, they should have nothing to fear from allowing them to. ·

It is impossible to measure precisely the demand for facilities that have not existed before. At present, our main leisure activity is watching television, but before television was provided, nobody was demanding that it should be. What we do know is that visiting the countryside is an extremely popular activity – second only to gardening as the most popular outdoor recreation pursuit among British people, according to a survey conducted by the Countryside Commission in 1977.[20]

Future Prospects

In 1983, the Country Landowners' Association mounted a survey in an attempt to counter the argument that demand for access to the countryside was not being met. It sent a questionnaire to its members asking them about present and likely future access to their lands. The Association selected 800 of the replies it received from its members and then drew up a policy document entitled *Agreeing on Access*.

The Country Landowners' Association's conclusion from this survey was that there is not under-provision of access to the countryside of England and Wales but over-provision. And when it asked its members 'If suitable controls were agreed, either by formal or informal agreement, and supervised, would you be willing to allow more access on to all or part of your land?' a resounding 74 per cent said 'No'. The figure was even higher in the case of a Countryside Commission survey published in 1986. Eighty-seven per cent of the 257 farmers (tenants as well as landowners) interviewed in this sample survey across England and Wales were against further public access to their land. Seventy-nine per cent were against further access even if payments were available to

them from the public purse in respect of the access and 74 per cent
if a ranger service were also provided.[21]

But if agricultural intensification and expansion and the march
of the conifers continue to claim more and more of the de facto
access lands and to wipe away the attractions of ordinary
countryside penetrated by public roads and paths, is there not
an even greater case than there was in the past for opening up
the great private playgrounds? The evidence of these two surveys
is that so far Britain's landowners have not been persuaded that
there is. Perhaps more worrying still are signs that restrictions
on access may grow even greater in future. In 1982 Scottish
landowner and past president of the British Field Sports Society
Sir Marcus Kimball MP told me:

As the area which is beautiful and people want to go to gets smaller
and smaller, you must be very careful that those people don't destroy
the very thing they want to preserve . . . I think you have got to limit
access as the pressure mounts, and as more Bedfordshires are created
then you will have to limit access to the Yorkshire Dales . . . We may
well be forced to restrict access, and the only fair way to restrict it is by
the purse.

One new threat with some potential consequences for the landless of Britain reared its head in 1986: a change in the law of trespass. In Britain, trespassing on private land was not a criminal
offence before November 1986. But in 1985 the Country Landowners' Association sought to get trespass criminalised in certain
circumstances. It proposed that if a small group of people trespassed on any privately-owned land in defiance of the objections
of the landowners, knowing they had no right to be on the land,
the police could be called and the trespassers prosecuted. The
CLA's original proposals related to groups of three or more people,
but it raised the number to six in the face of opposition from
ramblers and other organizations. The occasions when the CLA
clearly believed such a provision could be useful appeared to
include trespass by demonstrators such as hunt saboteurs, a peace
convoy encampment and trespass in order to damage shooting
butts.

The intrusion into the Queen's bedroom by Michael Fagan in
1984 had provided the impetus for the CLA's 1985 proposals.
Then, in June 1986, the encampment by the hippie convoy in

Somerset farmer Les Attwell's field provided an extra spur to
the campaign. Leading landowners tabled amendments to the
Thatcher Government's Public Order Bill then on its way
through Parliament urging a change in the law to make trespass
a criminal offence if somebody trespassed on private land with at
least one other person and with the intention of depriving the
owner or occupier of the land of the use and enjoyment of it, or if
somebody trespassed on land in a manner likely to cause
harassment, alarm or distress to people present at the scene –
both vaguely and widely drawn circumstances. Such circumstances could clearly have embraced the activities of two ramblers
or a family party who had strayed off rights of way. The
Government did not, however, go quite this far. Its Public
Order Act, which received the Royal Assent in November 1986,
empowers a senior police officer to direct two or more people to
leave land if he believes they are trespassers and that they plan
to reside on the land concerned 'for any period', that the occupier
of the land has asked them to leave and that any of the alleged
trespassers have caused damage to property on the land or have
used threatening or insulting words towards the occupier or an
agent of his. If the trespasser thereupon fails to leave the land or
having left returns within three months, he is committing a
criminal offence and can be sent to prison or fined up to £1,000.

The new law lays a considerable burden on the police officer
concerned to judge whether, for instance, a backpacker plans to
'reside' (camp?) on land on which he is trespassing. Though the
requirement that the trespassers should plan to 'reside' before
they fall foul of this law appears to protect the ordinary rambler
accidently trespassing, the terms of the clause could easily be
widened in future now the law is on the statute book. Perhaps
the most serious immediate consequence will be that the vague
knowledge that the law on trespass has been tightened up may
inhibit nervous townspeople disconcerted by the now slightly
less bogus 'Trespassers will be Prosecuted' signs that already
deter potential visitors to the countryside.

Conclusion: Tyranny Unmitigated

Today, then, the landowners bend the countryside to their
private purposes as surely as any of their predecessors have ever

done, justifying their behaviour on the rare occasions when they are called upon to do so with arguments that do not hold water. So what became of the historic compromise between landowners and the rest which was forged amidst such clamour in the aftermath of World War II – a compromise growing out of a tradition of such civilizing deals which goes back to the fifteenth century? What has happened to the post-war dream of a country-side shared by all? It is to the character and practical effects of the post-war social contract for the countryside that we turn next.

PART FOUR

The Broken Contract

7. Rights of Way

Within the countryside, the single most important recreational 'facility' is the rights of way network.

Adrian Phillips, then Director of the Countryside Commission, speaking at a conference in 1985[1]

Look at an Ordnance Survey map of any part of England and Wales and you will see a straggly network of red broken lines marking the footpaths and bridleways which enjoy the status of public rights of way. Altogether there are about 120,000 miles of these public paths.[2] They give the public the legal right to walk (in the case of footpaths) or walk, ride or cycle (in the case of bridleways) along predetermined routes whether the owner of the land traversed likes it or not. In Northern Ireland and Scotland public footpaths and bridleways are relatively uncommon. Overseas they are largely unknown. But in England and Wales, they are the linchpin of rural recreation facilities.

On any winter Sunday, around 12.5 million trips will be made to the countryside of England and Wales – a figure which rises to 17 million in spring and over 18 million on a typical summer Sunday, according to a Countryside Commission survey conducted in 1984.[3] In the same survey, a random sample of 1,000 people interviewed in their homes were asked which of twenty recreation activities they had undertaken during the previous four weeks. Visiting the countryside (whether to go for long walks, outings or picnics, visiting friends living in the country, walking along the coast or taking part in informal sport in the countryside) was far more popular than simply going to a seaside resort, watching or taking part in organized sport, visiting an historic building or country park, or going riding or fishing. So the sample saw the whole countryside, not just specific sites in it, as their favourite place of recreation. And it is in opening up the countryside as a whole that the network of public footpaths and bridleways plays its most crucial role.

Recognized public rights of way have always existed in Britain. They have evolved over the centuries along with roads and stretches of completely open land as vital elements in the national transport system: landowners had to tolerate the passage of their fellow-citizens across their land because the economic life of the countryside depended upon the ability of all to get to and from their places of work. The paths crossed all kinds of country and penetrated all sorts of unlikely places. And when, in the nineteenth and twentieth centuries, city-dwellers were looking for a means of exploring the countryside at weekends and holidays, they found the footpaths of unique value as avenues for rustic exploration. It was to the protection and extension of what had by then become a unique recreation resource that Attlee and his team of legislators addressed themselves in 1949.

They faced two main problems. No institution shouldered the responsibility of keeping rights of way open. And there was no means by which the public could tell what was a public right of way and what was not. In the absence of such simple but necessary devices, walkers trying to get about by public footpath found themselves continually obstructed. In the Lake District, for example, which had become one of the most popular resorts for city-dwellers, landowners closed twenty-two supposed public rights of way during the 1880s. They erected huge barriers of iron and wood, saturated with coal tar, to stop an organized protest walk over one path. Frequently the reason for path closure was the conversion of land to deer forest, salmon stream, pheasant covert or grouse moor. Doctor's Gate in the Peak District was the site of another protest walk in 1912 after its owner, Lord Howard, closed it to preserve the privacy of his grouse moor.[4]

All would-be walkers could do when public paths were blocked was to try and persuade the landowner to re-open them, smash the padlocks or take him to court. The 1835 Highways Act had made the wilful obstruction of public rights of way an offence, but in any such case walkers had to prove in court that the path involved was a public right of way – by arguing, for example, that the path's public status was indicated on an enclosure award or that passage had been enjoyed by the public as of right and without interruption for several decades – before they could go on to seek to prosecute for obstruction. The expense of lengthy court actions against wealthy landowners meant that few such cases were fought. Even when they were, and victory ensued, this was often far from being the end of the story. The Edinburgh Society fought a protracted legal battle against the 6th Duke of Atholl, who in 1847 had tried to prevent a party of botanists from going down Glen Tilt, on an old public right of way that had been used from time immemorial and had been maintained at public expense. The Society won the case, but this did not stop the Duke forcibly intercepting two other undergraduates as they descended Glen Tilt in 1850 when the His Grace was pursuing deer.

Pressure for legislation that would guarantee for all time public access along predetermined rights of way built up steadily. No fewer than eleven Rights of Way bills were introduced into the Houses of Parliament between 1906 and 1932, but it was not until 1932 that one of these became law. This Rights of Way Act was much weaker than the original Bill and in view of its defects, the war-time Government appointed a committee under Sir Arthur Hobhouse to draw up a blueprint for post-war footpath and access legislation. It was this Committee's recommendations on *Footpaths and Access to the Countryside*,[5] published in 1947, which formed the basis of the rights of way provisions in Attlee's 1949 National Parks and Access to the Countryside Act.

The 1949 Act required every county council in England and Wales to map all the rights of way in its area. Provision was made for objection, but once paths had finally been entered on the county maps of definitive rights of way, this status could be upheld in the courts and ran with the land in perpetuity. At the same time, the Act laid a duty on the county councils to assert and protect the right of passage of the public along these designated paths – a task made easier by the fact that councils no longer had to prove in court that a path was a right of way before they could get an obstruction removed: the existence of a path on the definitive map was enough.

The public path provisions of the 1949 Act, which are still in force,[6] reflect a clear understanding between landowners and landless: what the American radical Elihu Burritt has called 'the inheritance of the landless millions'. The rights of the walking and riding public are clearly limited to the right to pass and repass along a particular route with any deviation constituting trespass. Yet landowners have a real obligation to respect these rights. The law has imposed severe limits on a landowner's room for manoeuvre as far as public rights of way are concerned. Though permissive paths can be closed or changed at the whim of the owner, specified legal procedures have to be implemented before a public right of way may be diverted or destroyed. Because the fate of public paths is now a public issue, the procedures to divert or extinguish them involve not just the landowner himself, but his county council together with the Secretary of State for the Environment. It is county (or district) councils who make extinguishment orders for public paths. The only admissible grounds are that the path in question 'is not needed for public use'. The council is obliged by law to give publicity to the order in local newspapers, on site and to the parish and district or county councils over whose land the path passes. Any member of the public can object and unless any such objections are withdrawn, the Secretary of State for the Environment is obliged to hold a public inquiry. After this it is the Secretary of State who either confirms the order, rejects it or confirms it subject to modification. The same procedure applies for diversion orders.

What happens in practice is illustrated by the following example. In 1976, landowner J. E. Heathcote Ball asked Charnwood District Council in Leicestershire to make orders to divert paths on his land in Charnwood Forest. Mr Heathcote Ball said vandalism had occurred; path realignments would stop walkers passing through his farmyard by putting the path 150 yards away. However, the Leicestershire Footpaths Association, the local branch of the Ramblers' Association and the local branch of the Countrywide Holidays Association told the Council that the paths Mr Heathcote Ball wished to re-route formed an interesting and ancient crossroads within the Forest. They said his proposal would result in a net loss of paths of 800 yards and force people to walk longer distances along roads in what is Leicestershire's foremost recreation region. They also argued that Mr Heathcote Ball's proposals would not in fact improve the agricultural value of the land. Charnwood District Council responded by turning down the landowner's application for the changes, and the paths have remained in their old location ever since.

However, the rights of way network is by no means a fossilized, unchanging set of routes. Around 1,500 formal proposals to alter the network of England and Wales are made every year, the majority of which are upheld. Seventy per cent of the diversion, extinguishment and creation orders made in 1983, for example, were confirmed and only 9 per cent rejected, according to the Ramblers' Association. The outcome of the remaining 21 per cent of orders was still unknown at the time of writing.[7]

To appreciate what a remarkable amenity our rights of way represent we have only to consider the situation in less favoured lands. In many respects, New Zealand is more like England than any other country in the world. But not in this. There, the absence of a tradition of rights of way makes it virtually impossible for many New Zealanders to walk in the ordinary countryside near their homes. They can approach a landowner to ask permission to walk on his land but this may well be refused. If they are found on private land without permission they can be prosecuted (under the 1980 Trespass Act). They can even be prosecuted for failing to give their names and addresses to a landowner to enable him to launch proceedings against them. If they want to walk in the countryside, they must look to their nearest (state-owned) national park, which may be hundreds of miles away, or to the limited number of 'walkways' recently created by statute. In the face of these difficulties, many New Zealanders forget about their countryside altogether and head for the beach instead. The reason for this state of affairs is that the English settlers who emigrated to New Zealand took with them the traditional attitudes of English landowners without encountering the moderating influence of the long years of struggle between landowners and landless which in England resulted in, among other things, the public footpath network.

New Zealand country-lovers are not alone in the outside world in envying the English and Welsh public footpaths and bridleways which have traditionally given every citizen, regardless of status or means, access of some kind to countryside near his home wherever he lives.

But how complete is the access to the countryside provided by the rights of way network of England and Wales? Is the network shown on Ordnance Survey maps adequate for recreation needs? And how many of the paths marked on the maps actually exist on the ground in passable shape?

Where the Network Runs

Compare an Ordnance Survey map of Norfolk with one covering Suffolk and you will notice that public footpaths and bridleways in Suffolk are more than three times as numerous as they are in Norfolk: on average there are three miles of path per square mile of countryside in Suffolk compared with only 0.9 miles in Norfolk. In Devon, the density of public paths is only one-eighth of what it is in Worcestershire; in Pembrokeshire it is half that of Anglesey; while in Lincolnshire, public paths are only a third as dense on the ground as in Somerset. (All these figures were worked out in 1969 by Michael Holroyd of the Ramblers' Association and related to pre-1974 county boundaries.)[8] So if one could argue that the rights of way that exist in, say, Buckinghamshire (with 3.2 miles of path per square mile of countryside) represent a fair share for the landless, could this also be argued for neighbouring Bedfordshire (with 2.1 miles)?

Of course the areas where there are most footpaths are not necessarily those most suitable for recreation, even though the 1949 legislators hoped that footpaths would contribute a great deal to popular enjoyment of the countryside. If you try to pick out on a map what are likely to be the most attractive stretches of landscape – river valleys perhaps and, after thirty years of hedgerow removal, the non-farmed landscape of woodland and country parkland, it will often be apparent that such areas tend to be the worst served by public rights of way. Rights of way may be fairly common on farmland but in Dorset, for example, landscape gems more or less by-passed by the path network include Sherborne Park and Lake on the edge of the little town of Sherborne, Milton Abbas lake and the areas of deciduous woodland that stretch northwards from the village, Charborough Park with its associated woods and farmland (over two square miles in all) and the western half of Melbury Park and Great High Wood in north-west Dorset. Of Melbury Park a reporter on *Country Life* lucky enough to be allowed in wrote in 1899, 'Dorsetshire has no more beautiful place.'[9] We have already seen that there are many other inner citadels of large rural estates as well as more widespread woods, lakes, parks, riversides and moors which are almost completely cut off from general view and which the public path system rarely penetrates.

So why do our public paths leave out so much of the best countryside? Why have they failed to penetrate so many of the forbidden woods and parks, lakes and river-banks of England and Wales?

To answer these questions we need to look carefully at the process by which the definitive maps were drawn up.

DEFINING EXISTING RIGHTS OF WAY

The keystone of the 1949 Act was the requirement that county councils should draw up maps of all paths in every county that were commonly agreed to be public rights of way as opposed to merely private tracks. But the idea of what constituted a right of way was by no means an invention of the post-war Labour Government: this was a fundamental concept that reached far back into British history. When the county councils which prepared the definitive maps established what were rights of way they made use of the age-old maxim of footpath law, 'once a highway, always a highway'. For a path to become a public right of way the test was whether it had already been used by the public without interference from the landowner for the preceding twenty years.

Six hundred years earlier, the test had been the same. In 1320, during the reign of Edward II, the authority responsible for maintaining a track running from the tiny settlement of Stodmarsh to Canterbury in Kent tried to close it to save the cost of maintenance. In protest, the riders and pedestrians who used the path (mainly monks at a local monastery) took the case to court. The result was that the sheriff ordered his men to re-open the path since it was clearly an 'ancient and allowed highway'. The route exists to this day, now as a ridge-top road through Trenley Park Wood, providing fine views of the marshes that still lie below.

Since the paths that formed the old communications network of the countryside were to form the basis of the definitive maps, it was important that the maps drawn up in the 1950s should be as comprehensive as possible. Unfortunately, however, the maps prepared in many areas almost certainly understated the extent of the rights of passage won from the landowners by the landless over the centuries. The main reason is that the landless population was not adequately represented during the establish-ment of the definitive network.

On the whole, local authorities dealing with the countryside are different from those covering the major towns and cities in which most people live: Londoners for instance have no say in the decisions made by the councils of the Home Counties, and Mancunians have no say in the affairs of Cheshire or Lancashire. In 1949 this was even more true than it is now, for not only metropolitan areas but every sizeable town as well was cut off from the surrounding county in an autonomous county borough. County boroughs had the option of preparing definitive maps for their own areas. But the substantial proportion of the population living in them were denied any formal say in the drawing up of footpath maps for the countryside around their home towns. Instead, decisions on the definitive maps were in the hands of representatives of the rural, landowner-dominated population of the shire counties rather than those of the British people as a whole.

What this meant was that in Devon, for example, 37 per cent of the county's population were denied a say in the establishment of the county's rights of way network simply because in the 1950s Exeter and Plymouth, where they lived, happened to be county boroughs. Other counties in which census figures for 1951 reveal that the exclusion of townspeople from the process was particularly complete because of the county borough system include Oxfordshire, where more than a third of the county's population lived in the county borough of Oxford when the definitive map for the county was drawn up in the 1950s, and Nottinghamshire, where 36 per cent of the population lived in the county town. In Leicestershire, East Sussex and Northumberland 45 per cent of the county's population in each case lived in county boroughs. In Gloucestershire and the East Riding, to take two other examples, over half of the county population were disenfranchised.

Meanwhile, the county councils which were to draw up the maps were dominated by landowners. And to make matters even worse, they turned for help in the mapping task to a set of administrative units in which the power of the landowners was even more strongly felt than on county councils – the parishes.

As a first step in the preparation of the definitive map of rights of way for its area, each county council in England and Wales had to draw up a draft map indicating whether routes were footpath or bridleway, their starting and ending points, the number and location of bridges and stiles and so on, after consulting all parish and rural district councils within its boundaries. What many county councils seem to have done in practice is to send a blank map to all of the parish councils asking them to mark on it the paths which they understood to be public rights of way. On receiving the maps back from parishes, most county councils seem to have done little more than check that the paths claimed by adjoining parishes fitted together. If a footpath changed into a bridleway at a parish boundary in such a way that riders would be unable to get to or off the stretch of bridleway, county councils would go back to the parishes concerned and try to sort things out. Sometimes they checked with parish enclosure awards to make sure that paths had not been omitted. But on the whole they used the parish maps as the basis of their drafts. The general public had the right to object to these draft maps when published, and the Minister of Housing and Local Government was empowered to hold an inquiry into the objections. This opportunity was however little used by urban recreation interests at a time when footpath societies were barely beginning to get off the ground. Even when it was, the objectors did not get far, for as Northamptonshire County Council's rights of way officer, Dennis Nightingale pointed out to me in an interview in 1982, the views of somebody from a parish carried far more weight with an inspector than those of townspeople, as it was taken for granted that local people were in the best position to know what were the rights of way. After any inquiries county councils then had to publish the provisional map of rights of way taking on board the Minister's recommendations. After this, the owners and occupiers of land involved – but not the general public – had a second opportunity to make representations. Once these had been resolved, the final definitive map of public rights of way was published. In this whole process, it was therefore the approach taken by the parish councils which really determined the outcome. Yet these parish councils were even more unsuited to carrying out the will of the Attlee Government than were the county councils.

The parish councils of the time did not have much professional expertise to help them carry out what has since proved to be a crucially important task in determining public access to the countryside. Many parishes – an estimated 20 per cent in Northamptonshire for example according to Dennis Nightingale – had no parish council at all, but simply a parish meeting at which only the chairman was elected. So uneven were the parishes that some energetically claimed a high density of public rights of way while others did not. One measure of what parishes missed out is the number of paths now being claimed which it is asserted were mistakenly omitted in the 1950s. Take the Macclesfield district of Cheshire. The definitive map for this area shows 986 rights of way running for a total distance of 386 miles. But since the definitive map was published, claims have been submitted for a further 260 paths supposedly left off the original map. If three-quarters of these claims turn out to be well founded, the definitive map will have underestimated the number of paths in Macclesfield District by one-fifth. In the old East Riding of Yorkshire, to take another example, the definitive map published in 1968 failed to include nearly 1,200 footpaths and bridleways that ramblers and others claimed as rights of way – potentially a large proportion of the total number of rights of way in the county.[10]

How did parishes determine what was a public right of way and what simply a permissive route? Parish council clerks to whom I spoke were unable to offer a coherent account of any guidelines used. Some parishes operated in the (mistaken) belief that, if a coffin had been carried to a road, the route the coffin had taken automatically became a public right of way. Dennis Nightingale told me he thinks that few public rights of way were claimed in the Northamptonshire parish of Naseby not because few existed there but because the parishioners were superstitious about walking over land where a battle had been fought and many people had been killed. More seriously, there was a presumption in many areas that paths which simply led to a beauty spot but did not serve a utilitarian purpose in rural life would not be admissible as rights of way. This does not, however, explain the omission from Cornwall's definitive map of the important path from the end of the A30 to the point of Land's End. Cornwall County Council's footpaths officer, J. W. Hill, told me in 1986 that he believes there was a tendency for many Cornish parish councils to leave off the maps tracks over which they considered the existence of a right of way was not in dispute, marking instead rights of way which were more likely to go out of existence. The omission of this particular track has caused the County Council not a little time and trouble during the 1980s. The headland changed hands and its new owner, Surrey property developer David Goldstone, started charging people to walk along the track. However the Council could not simply require the removal of this obstruction: they would have had to take Mr Goldstone to the High Court to establish first that the route was a public path. In the event, a compromise arrangement was reached. Mr Goldstone agreed to allow the public to walk freely along the route in question for a trial period and to charge them only to park their cars or to go into the various attractions he has developed at Land's End. The path is still omitted from the definitive map of rights of way.

Parishes, then, seem to have decided which paths to claim on the basis of intuition rather than any real criteria. In the absence of clear criteria, the attitudes of those who ran the parish councils played an important part in deciding what rights were to be claimed. And these attitudes were very different from those of the Attlee Government. The thinking of most parish councils

was on the whole dominated by the ideas of the landowning
rural ruling class. In many of the parishes of England and Wales
in the early 1950s, the parish and the estate were one and the
same thing, and the chairman of the parish council or parish
meeting was the local landowner or his land agent or somebody
else in some way beholden to him. This was the period when
many of the old land workers had left the countryside for the
towns and cities but the exodus from the cities of middle-class
commuters, retired people and second-home owners had yet to
take place. Taking a few examples from Northamptonshire, at
Rockingham, the then owner of the castle and 4,000-acre estate,
Commander Michael Culme-Seymour, was chairman of the
parish meeting as well as representing Rockingham on the
county council and at Courteenhall the then chairman of the
parish meeting as well as its landowner was Sir Hereward Wake.
At Althorp, the large estate on Northampton's north-western
edge, the 7th Earl Spencer, the owner of the estate, was chairman
of the parish council for forty years, including 1950; J. R. Tong,
the clerk to the parish council in 1950, worked as land agent for
the estate at that time. Diagonally opposite Althorp, on the
south-eastern side of Northampton, the land agent for the 6th
Marquess of Northampton's 10,000 acre estate, H. V. Phelps,
was also chairman of the Castle Ashby parish council. (The
Marquess was himself chairman of the county council at the
time, while Earl Spencer was chairman of the county council's
planning committee.) Not surprisingly, parish councils run by
such figures did not go out of their way to propose paths whose
status was in doubt.

CREATING NEW PATHS

(i) New Byways

Our present field paths are a brief though lovely suggestion of
what is required. But they are unrelated, ill-defined, insecure.
They should be co-ordinated and extended into a complete system
– a network of footpaths running through field and copse and
wood, along streamside and riverside, along the margin of the
coast, through parkland, past farmyard ponds, low in the valleys,
high on the hilltops, wandering across the plains – a systematized
network of paths, tracks, and bridleways, that will enable a man

to walk ten or twenty miles a day if he wishes without ever having
to pass along a busy road.

Thomas Sharp, 'Planning the Countryside', *Out of Doors*, winter 1945–6

It was clear to those who formulated the 1949 Act that the
existing network of rights of way in the countryside would be
insufficient to enable everyone to explore all of the countryside
on foot or horseback. So the Act empowered county councils as
highway authorities to create entirely new paths for the purpose
of adding to people's convenience or enjoyment. They could do
this either by entering into footpath creation agreements with
landowners or, failing agreement, making orders, which would
be subject to confirmation by the Minister of Housing and Local
Government. There was to be no limit on the number of new
paths which could be created. And it was believed at the time
that the new powers would enable the gaps in the existing
network to be filled, opening up hitherto inaccessible features
and landscapes.

However, this has not happened. Hampshire is one county
where the new powers could have proved particularly beneficial.
Some of the finest countryside in the county borders the Rivers
Test and Rother. Countless private tracks thread through the
woods and marshes by these rivers, yet almost none of these
were claimed as public rights of way when the definitive map
was drawn up. Here, the creation of new public paths along the
riverside could have transformed recreation opportunities in one
of the finest areas of rural Britain. By 1985, however, only four
public paths provided any means of access on foot to the ten-
mile stretch of the river Test between Stockbridge and Romsey
together with the very many miles of waterways that run
alongside it. In each case, the public path provided a way across
the river but not alongside it, apart from one quarter of a mile
stretch. This section of the Test is typical of many of the rivers of
southern England in this respect.

In England and Wales as a whole, few new paths have
been created and of these hardly any have penetrated hitherto
inaccessible areas. Instead, new paths have usually been created
to provide access to new housing estates, to fill in missing links

in Countryside Commission long-distance paths or to replace other paths lost in diversion and rationalization schemes.

The replacement of one public path by another in a process of give-and-take under a rationalization scheme does occasionally mean that walkers benefit. Unfortunately, reliance on this approach means that in areas where there are no rights of way at present no new ones can be created because there is nothing to exchange them for.

There appear to be three main reasons why highway authorities have failed to make much use of the opportunities provided for the creation of entirely new paths.

First, the enthusiasm of the 1949 legislators for footpaths as a recreation resource does not seem to have been shared by the highway authorities as they began to put the Act into practice in the 1950s. Northamptonshire County Council's rights of way officer Dennis Nightingale told me: 'I don't think the word "recreation" was in use then, certainly not in this context.' In those days, recreation provision was thought to consist of swimming pools, golf courses and the like, not country walkways. In council offices public paths were usually seen in their old role as facilitating communication rather than promoting recreation. Dennis Nightingale again: 'The normal purpose of a right of way is to get from A to B. It is possible to have one to a vantage or viewpoint, but it is not normal.'

In view of this attitude, and the decline of the transport function of the footpath, it is not too surprising that when councils drew up the definitive maps in the early 1950s they did not really consider radically extending the network. Kent County Council's then principal assistant, amenities and recreation, C. J. Ashdown, told me in 1984: 'We were recognizing the network as it existed. There was no fuss and bother about creating new paths.'

A complicating factor has been highway authorities' liability to pay compensation to landowners if public paths are created by order. A highway authority is not required to pay compensation to a landowner for a new public path if it is created by agreement, but if there is a creation order, it is liable to compensate him to the extent to which his land depreciates in value as a result of the order or in respect of any damage he suffers. The actual amounts are not usually high, but it is the fact that highway authorities are laying themselves open to compensation claims that often seems to tilt the argument against attempts to create new rights of way.

In recent times, when rural recreation has loomed larger in planners' thinking, there has been another obstacle to footpath creation, even when money is available for compensation. This is the resistance of landowners. Footpath creation agreements have not been made largely because landowners have made it clear that they would refuse to enter into them. That leaves orders as the only available weapon, and even apart from the compensation problem, it is unrealistic to expect highway authorities to deploy these on a meaningful scale, given the rural power structure in Britain. Use of compulsory powers would be 'a political hot-cake' Bedfordshire County Council's rights of way officer Clive Beckett told me in 1984. And in fact few highway authorities are well placed to take on their landowners in the way that would be required. The landowners' position in their communities is too strong.

A landowner does not actually have to be a member of the county council for the council to feel his influence. It is enough that he should be perceived as a powerful local figure who can cause difficulties if antagonized. In Cornwall a swathe of glorious land to which there is hardly any legal right of access is owned by the 9th Viscount Falmouth, whose family made much of their money through exploiting Cornwall's mineral wealth. Lord Falmouth is not a member of the county council, but as lord lieutenant he is a prominent figure in the county. His vast Tregothnan estate lies on the eastern edge of the county town, Truro, and is bounded to the south and west by the snake-like estuaries of the Rivers Fal and Tresillian. When I visited the area in 1982, a few minor roads crossed the estate, and there was a certain amount of permissive access. But hardly any public paths penetrated this secret kingdom.

Although they live in a region popular with tourists, the 16,000 inhabitants of Truro have very little open space available to them. The town, situated as it is at the top of an estuary, is many miles from a beach, and the woods scattered in the countryside around Truro tend to be badly served by public paths. Tregothnan might, perhaps through the provision of rights of way along the private tracks skirting the estuaries, therefore seem to be a suitable target for footpath creation. Cornwall County Council's surveyor, B. W. Mansell, who is responsible for footpaths as well as for other highways, told me of Tregothnan in an interview in 1982: 'I doubt if you would find another area in England as thinly served with public footpaths as this area. Twenty square miles of countryside is virtually inaccessible.' But he went on:

Under no circumstances would I approach Lord Falmouth [for greater access] at Tregothnan: it's clearly been created to keep people at arm's length . . . I can't visualize a situation where I would phone Lord Falmouth and ask him. He is a very influential figure. If I do something silly in that direction, I lose credibility with a very influential group of people and there's trouble. It's all about a common-sense political approach. Clearly you don't talk to a major landowner in the same way as you talk to a tenant of a smallholding. I am sure the committee wouldn't say this [i.e. access to Tregothnan] is important enough for me to press ahead.

(ii) Long-Distance Paths

Much of the most enchanting countryside in Cornwall – from the tidal woods and deer park of Tregothnan on the Fal estuary to the tree-clad slopes of the Helford estuary, the woods around Looe Pool, the woods, river and lake of Caerhays Castle, the Pencarrow woods north of Bodmin, the extensive woods and parkland of Boconnoc in the Lerryn valley east of Lostwithiel and the (often wooded) valleys of the Rivers Tamar, Torridge, Ottery, Inny, Lynher, Tiddy, Camel and Fowey – is pretty much inaccessible by public right of way. But what Cornwall does have – along with many other similarly impenetrable parts of Britain – is a so-called 'long-distance path'.

In the post-war era the vast majority of the new rights of way that have been created form links in these increasingly fashionable long-distance routes. The 1949 National Parks and Access to the Countryside Act empowered the National Parks Commission (since 1968 the Countryside Commission) to designate as long-distance paths rural routes in England and Wales along which it considers the public should be enabled to make extensive journeys on foot or horseback. In practice, long-distance paths are usually at least seventy miles in length and they avoid for the most part metalled roads. Once the Secretary of State for the Environment (or the Secretary of State for Wales) has approved the designated route, the Countryside Commission can implement its proposal by co-ordinating the assertion of the relevant rights of way on the ground by county councils as highway authorities. A similar system, based on the 1967 Countryside (Scotland) Act, empowers the Countryside Commission for Scotland to designate long-distance paths and regional councils to put them into effect; while in Northern Ireland, in the absence of any government agency for conservation and rural recreation on a par with the Countryside Commissions, district councils may together designate a long-distance path, and put it into effect once approval for the scheme has been received from the Secretary of State for Northern Ireland.

Altogether, Great Britain has 1,941 miles of long-distance path, made up, in order of the date in which designation was confirmed, of the Pennine Way, the Cleveland Way, the Pembrokeshire Coast Path, Offa's Dyke Path, the South Downs Way, the North Downs Way, the Ridgeway Path, the South-West Peninsula Coast Path, the West Highland Way, the Speyside Way, the Southern Uplands Way and the Wolds Way. Northern Ireland's only long-distance path, the Ulster Way, a 500-mile uneven circle, is slightly different from the long-distance paths on the British mainland. District councils' formal long-distance path creation powers have existed in Northern Ireland only since 1983. The Ulster Way was devised long before this date largely by the honorary secretary to the Ulster Society for the Preservation of the Countryside, Wilfrid Capper. It was put into effect during the 1970s and early '80s by a steering group financed by the Sports Council of Northern Ireland, which means that in 1987 there were still several stretches of the Ulster Way along which access on the ground was not yet guaranteed by rights of way. However, the Ulster Way has many positive features. In traversing each of the Province's main types of landscape, from the hills and forests of north Londonderry to the Mourne mountains and the Antrim coast, it embraces a wider variety of scenery than any other long-distance path in the

British Isles. Another special feature of the Ulster Way is that it
runs along the edge of Belfast and has paths connecting it to the
heart of the Province's other urban areas.

The UK's longest long-distance path, the South-West Peninsula Coast Path, which strides 514 miles from Minehead around
Land's End to Studland, is more typical of the nine long-distance
paths of England and Wales in that it follows one particular
feature of the landscape rather than crossing a variety of different
kinds. Similar in character is the Pembrokeshire Coast Path.
Most of the remainder of the paths in England and Wales follow
ridges or high-up linear features like Offa's Dyke Path, based
upon an earthwork constructed along the Welsh border to
overlook Wales, or Britain's most famous long-distance path and
the first to be created – the Pennine Way – snaking along the
very backbone of England and, for a short distance, into the hills
of southern Scotland. Scotland itself has three long-distance
paths – the ninety-five-mile West Highland Way from the
outskirts of Glasgow to Fort William and the 212-mile west-to-
east-coast Southern Upland Way. Thirty-three miles of what
was originally proposed as a sixty-one-mile long-distance path,
the Speyside Way, were opened in 1980. They run along a
stretch of the River Spey to its estuary on the north coast of
Scotland's east-thrusting knuckle. In the whole of the United
Kingdom, the South Downs Way is the only long-distance
bridleway.

Although many of the new public footpaths and bridleways
that have been created in the UK since 1949 lie along long-
distance paths, these tend to be links joining established rights of
way rather than pioneering their way through virgin territory.
The long-distance paths have not been devised like motorways,
imposing a completely new route pattern across the land of
Britain. Instead they step from one established right of way to
another, broadly following a particular direction. The West
Highland Way, for instance, makes extensive use of military
roads built in the eighteenth century to control clans rebelling
against British rule, old coaching roads and, to a lesser extent,
disused railway lines. Eighty-five per cent of the South-West
Peninsula Coast Path (one route for which figures happen to be
available) follows existing public paths, which originated as

smugglers' and coastguards' routes.[11] Three-quarters of the
North Downs Way, more than 90 per cent of the Ridgeway and
much of the South Downs Way and Wolds Way too lie on
established rights of way: they follow ancient routes along the
tops of the chalk downs – routes that thousands of years ago
were developed because the chalk hills were far easier to clear of
vegetation than the wetter clay vales below and which in the
1950s were given legal status as rights of way. Part of the interest
in walking these paths lies in this link with the past. The Ulster
Way also follows mainly established rights of way, like the North
Antrim Coastal Path, or it runs through state forests or National
Trust lands. Here and there new rights of way have indeed been
established, in particular across the mountains of Mourne.

Although the long-distance paths are undoubtedly the jewel in
the crown of Britain's public paths régime (they are usually
better signposted, better maintained and less often obstructed
than ordinary field paths), there are plenty of cases in which the
Countryside Commissions have sacrificed some of their recreation potential in the face of landowner pressure. This may
mean a path goes along many sections of road rather than
countryside or makes detours to avoid the estate of a particularly
influential owner. One of the victims of landowner pressure
was the Cambrian Way, a proposal which the Countryside
Commission dropped in 1982, after ten years of controversy.
Had it gone ahead it would have been the only long-distance
path to march across the mountains of central and north Wales.
In the face of overwhelming opposition from landowners, farmers
and farmer- and landowner-dominated local authorities, the
proposed route was first changed: originally intended to scale
the highest, roughest and most wildly beautiful stretches of
Wales from Cardiff to Conway, the route was altered to one that
would have involved 'crawling ignominiously' in the foothills,
according to rambler Tony Drake, who designed the original
route. When even this plan was finally dropped, Mr Drake
commented: 'In some ways, I'm relieved it's off. It had been
emasculated. I did not want the compromise that the Countryside Commission envisaged. It was an act of appeasement to
Welsh farmers.'[12]

The same year in which the Cambrian Way was dropped,

another long-distance path, the Wolds Way, stretching seventy-nine miles over the chalk wolds of East Yorkshire, was opened, marking, in the opinion of the Countryside Commission chairman Sir Derek Barber, 'a triumph of common sense and cooperation between the farmers and landowners along it and those who planned the route'.[13] The Ramblers' Association however, was not so impressed. It boycotted the Countryside Commission's opening ceremony and held a rally of its own. The reason was the Commission's choice of person to cut the tape and declare the Way open: the 12th Baron Middleton and the then president of the Country Landowners' Association. Earlier, Lord Middleton had successfully objected to the Wolds Way going through Wharram Percy in a beautiful downland valley. Wharram Percy, with its ruined medieval church, the remains of a twelfth-century manor house and, according to Yorkshire historian Keith Allison 'one of the finest deserted village sites in the country', was considered by the Ramblers' Association to be the highlight in the original route of the Wolds Way proposed by the Countryside Commission. However, Lord Middleton, who owns a reported 12,000 acres of land in this part of Yorkshire including the area around Wharram Percy, convinced the Countryside Commission that extra numbers of visitors might damage the medieval village. Though in 1985 Lord Middleton agreed to the dedication as a right of way of a path linking Wharram Percy to the Wolds Way, the Way itself now avoids the deserted village.

The controversy over Wharram Percy was one of the reasons for the six-year delay in the opening of the Wolds Way. There are several other places along the Way where objections from landowners have been followed by a change of route to a course which the Ramblers' Association considers much inferior to the original.

Long-distance paths have undoubtedly been a benefit, and, particularly in the case of those paths like the West Highland Way which begin close to conurbations, they have helped draw people into the countryside who might otherwise never have gone there. But long-distance paths are no more than a small part of the answer to the question of countryside access. They do not provide freedom to roam, to explore and to be alone with nature. For these things we shall continue to need by-ways penetrating the nooks and crannies of our countryside – as well as other open spaces over which we can wander at will.

Britain's network of public paths is then far from being an ideal pattern of recreation routes. It is the result of historical accident modified by the muscle of landowners. Nonetheless, these paths are the main means of access to our countryside. In view of their importance, then, what is their condition?

On the Ground

I've ploughed up two footpaths. I don't stop people walking them. Trouble is, now nobody knows where they go. When they stray off them, I threaten them with prosecution for trespass.

A Suffolk farmer interviewed by Howard Newby of Essex University, 1977[14]

It is of real public moment that no genuine public footpath should be lost, without statutory action to close it.

Lord Justice Scott, 1938[15]

In 1971, *Observer* reporter Jeremy Bugler took a walk along the public paths in a fifteen-square-mile corner of north Dorset he had randomly picked from the map. Dorset enjoys a relatively high density of public paths – 2.3 miles of path per square mile of land, compared to the average for England and Wales of 2 miles. But when Mr Bugler tried to use what should have been a good network, he found things were not quite what they seemed.[16] He found his way blocked on no fewer than twenty-two occasions. In several cases the obstruction took the form of a barbed wire fence; in others, paths had been ploughed up and crops planted over them with no indication of where the path lay. In two cases the path was heavily overgrown with natural vegetation, and in one case a barn had been erected straight across the path. It did not take Mr Bugler long to conclude that to walk Britain's public paths you need enough climbing skill to scale barbed wire fences, the tracking ability of a Sioux, the map-reading qualifications of a master mariner and enough courage to disregard threatening notices. Mr Bugler found only four signposts; under the terms of the Countryside Act 1968, which requires highways authorities to signpost public paths where they leave a metalled road, there should have been at least twenty-seven.

Since Jeremy Bugler's expedition, the kind of obstructions with which walkers have to grapple have grown even more forbidding. Some of the new crops to which our farmers are turning, such as maize, sweet corn and above all oil-seed rape, are completely impenetrable. While it may be possible to stumble across deep plough ridges and furrows or through a field of waist-high wheat, you need at least a machete to penetrate rape which, when fully grown, presents an eight-foot-high jungle to the walker. And in the summer of 1983, the Ramblers' Association found rape alone obstructing no fewer than ten public paths within a ten-mile radius of Maidstone in Kent, for example.[17]

To try to get a comprehensive picture of the state of the public paths throughout their counties, the local branches of the Ramblers' Association for East Sussex and south Cambridgeshire carried out sample surveys in 1983 and 1982/3 respectively.

In East Sussex, the ramblers took every twenty-fifth path on the list of definitive rights of way and then walked its length, making a detailed description of its state. The resulting picture indicates that passage was not just difficult but actually impossible along many public paths. Thirteen per cent of the paths were blocked with physical obstructions, while a further 16 per cent had been illegally ploughed up. Thirty-seven per cent of the sample paths needed stiles to enable walkers to scale fences while 18 per cent needed at least one bridge. In all, 84 per cent of the paths needed attention of some kind.[18]

In south Cambridgeshire, only 726 of the 1,276 paths inspected met a minimum standard of effectiveness. The remaining 43 per cent were either ploughed up, overgrown, in need of bridges or deliberately blocked.[19]

The extent to which public paths are restored after ploughing was the subject of a study in 1984 by researchers from Reading University and the Royal Agricultural College at Cirencester for the Countryside Commission.[20] Farmers are required by law to restore public paths after ploughing, and as they need do no more than run a roller or smooth wheel over the line of the path to make good the surface, it might be expected that most public rights of way in arable areas would be restored after ploughing. In fact, however, the team found that 59 per cent of public paths in its six study areas (comprising nine parishes of England and Wales) lay unrestored after ploughing. Those paths in arable areas that did survive the plough were almost always those running around field edges, often as concrete tracks. More than 90 per cent of the paths that crossed arable fields were not restored.

What these surveys confirm is the emergence of a vast yet growing mileage of unusable paths. A 120,000-mile network may exist on the map, but on the ground large chunks of it are effectively closed, even though they have not been subjected to extinguishment orders.

Many of the public paths of England and Wales are obstructed with impunity. Yet they are supposed to be as much a part of the Queen's highway as the M1. Those landowners who wilfully obstruct public paths, who grow crops over them or who fail to reinstate surfaces after ploughing are committing a criminal offence for which they can be brought before magistrates and fined. They are required by law to maintain any stiles along paths on their land (and can claim 25 per cent of the cost of so doing from their county council). For their part, county councils have a statutory duty to secure the removal of any obstructions and also to carry out any other maintenance of the paths that may be necessary to ensure the free passage of those using them. So what has gone wrong?

(i) SOCIAL CHANGE

The first reason for the deterioration of the public paths network in England and Wales is a change in the size and composition of our rural population. What kept footpaths open until the beginning of the twentieth century was the feet of a substantial rural population going about its business and pleasure. Then, footpaths were still a vital element in the transport system, as they had been for the previous thousand years. By the 1930s, however, the rural population had declined dramatically as former agricultural labourers and other poorer members of the rural community left the countryside in search of better wages and living conditions in towns.

The heroine of Flora Thompson's novel *Still Glides the Stream*, first published in 1948, observes at first-hand the impact of population change on footpaths in a village in Oxfordshire. In 1945, Charity Finch returns after a long absence to the Oxford-shire village where she grew up in the 1880s. She finds herself drawn to the stile leading out of the churchyard into a grassy meadow and, leaning on the stile, she visualizes the scene as it would have been half a century before:

In the days of her childhood the footpath over the meadow had been a hard, well-defined track, much used by men going to their fieldwork, by children going blackberrying, nutting, or in search of violets or mush-rooms, and, on Sunday evenings, by pairs of sweethearts who preferred the seclusion of the fields and copses beyond to the more public pathways.[21]

In 1945, however, Miss Finch is confronted by a different picture. The footpath that had once played such an important part in village life had become faint from disuse: not entirely obliterated, it could still just be discerned winding up and down the gently undulating meadow.

It is not only frequency of use that used to keep the footpath system in good condition. Countryfolk often used to be descended from families who had lived in the same small locality for generations, and thus knew very well where they could and could not walk. If a farmer planted crops over the line of a path, everyone would know that they could be trampled out with impunity. More deliberate attempts to encroach on rights of way were quickly dealt with by rural dwellers well aware of their rights. 'In the old days, we would have gone through the gateposts with a hacksaw,' declared an eighty-year-old former horse-and-cart-driver when commenting upon the erection of four gates across an ancient bridleway at Liphook in Hampshire in 1981.[22]

In England, the size of the rural population peaked in about 1850. At that time, a village of 500 or so people in a remote part of the country would have been largely self-sufficient, housing

not only people who worked on the land but a wide range of
craftsmen as well – perhaps a thatcher, a carpenter, two tailors,
a boot- and shoe-maker, a baker, a blacksmith, a wheelwright,
two masons and two dairymen. In addition, there would have
been several shopkeepers and a teacher and a parson.[23]

It was the agricultural depression following the repeal of the
protectionist Corn Laws, and then the beginnings of mechanization, that led the farmworkers to leave. Village craftsmen
followed as they were priced out of the market once cheap
and rapid transport was bringing factory-made consumer goods
within the reach of all.

In our own time, the drift away from the countryside has been
to some extent reversed – but not in a way that does much for
the footpath system. Today, the population of Britain's rural
areas is rising fast, even in remote areas. The population of rural
Wales and the Scottish Islands, for example, rose by more than
7 per cent between 1961 and 1981. But the people who have
moved into the countryside to work – hoteliers for instance or
people working in defence establishments – do not depend on
footpaths to get about. Like the commuters to nearby towns and
the retired people they are often car-owners. Some people do still
use the paths regularly to get from place to place: the elderly
and mothers with young children in one-car households, for
example, frequently prefer the safety of the paths to the danger
of narrow country roads. But neither these people nor those of
their fellow rural dwellers who use the paths for pleasure in the
evenings, at weekends and during holidays are as well informed
as their rural predecessors were about either the routes the paths
have traditionally taken or the rights of those who walk them.

A large proportion of Britain's footpath users do not live in
the countryside at all nowadays but in towns and cities. And of
course these people – seeking recreation – are even more intermit-
tent in their use of the paths. City-dwelling families may spend a
lot of their leisure time walking in the countryside; but if they do
they will almost certainly visit a wide variety of areas without
getting to know any of them intimately. So under-used paths
quickly become overgrown and thus hard to follow even by
those who believed a right of way existed. Landowners, who
often maintained a network of estate or private roads and paths

for their own use and that of their employees and tenants, were usually happy enough to see public paths degenerate in this way. As a result public access to whole swathes of countryside disappeared.

(ii) AGRICULTURAL CHANGE

After World War II, the increase in the profitability of agriculture accelerated this process. As more land came under the plough, farmers found public paths more and more of a nuisance. If a public path crosses an arable field, the farmer is supposed to refrain from running his tractor over the path or, if he does, to roll the path out afterwards. Many have preferred to plough up not only paths running diagonally across fields, but paths round field edges as well.

As a result, thousands of miles of path have been effectively lost as uncultivated rough land or pasture has been converted to cereal fields. A Leicestershire villager explained to me in 1982 his view of the ploughing of public paths:

The biggest loss of public footpaths is through the ploughing of grass fields and turning them over to arable. You can't walk across a field if somebody's got corn in it: any public path across it is then closed. If you complain you're told you have the right to walk across it. But how can you cross the farmer's land, because if you do he's going to sue you for damage? Or, a farmer might say walk round the edge of the field rather than straight across. But if you're trying to get from point A to point B after ten years one mile could increase to five or ten miles with the increase in arable area and field size. Unless someone stands up for their rights all these footpaths and bridleways are going to be closed and there's going to be no access at all to the countryside.

The case of Graffham Down in Sussex illustrates well how agricultural intensification can produce a threat to public access.

Before 1979, Graffham Down was a delightful spot. Two wide ribbons of rough chalk downland turf snaked their way along the Down, covered throughout the spring and summer with myriad wildflowers. Many people enjoyed access to Graffham Down both by virtue of the public footpaths that penetrated it and the de facto ability to wander all over the whole site – 120 acres of downland, scrub and woodland. In 1979, however, a new owner acquired the farm of which Graffham Down was a part. Between August 1979 and July 1980 he cleared away most of the downland turf and woodland and ploughed the land in order to grow arable crops. The wood, scrub and down where nightingales had sung and badgers scuttled became an expanse of barley prairie, like so much of the rest of the South Downs.[24] Inevitably the freedom to roam and picnic, to gather blackberries and to play among the butterflies and cowslips, disappeared.

By 1980, yet another owner had taken over Graffham Down. He decided that three of the public paths that had survived the ploughing interfered with his farming operations. He asked West Sussex County Council to make diversion orders taking these paths off the Down itself and re-routeing them round the edge and through Forestry Commission woodland further down the scarp.

In 1984, West Sussex County Council agreed to make the diversion orders. Strong objections came from Chichester District Council, local amenity bodies and Graffham Parish Council. At the time of writing, the possibility of a public inquiry into the diversion orders was awaited. After such an inquiry, it would be open to the Department of the Environment to overturn the orders. But hopes were not high.

Even if the paths survive the diversion orders, their future will depend partly on the willingness of the owner to reinstate them after ploughing. Even if they are reinstated, they will be less and less used as they are no longer so attractive to walk along. Because of this, a future application for diversion might well succeed.

(iii) WATCHDOGS THAT DO NOT BITE

In devising the means for safeguarding the paths, Sir Arthur Hobhouse and his committee on footpaths and access to the countryside in 1947 looked very much to long-established traditions affecting public rights of way. The main tradition on which they fastened was the idea that the maintenance of footpaths should be the responsibility of localities. In the Middle Ages, all the inhabitants of any area had to keep the area's paths to a high standard regardless of how much use was made of

them or how inconvenient it might be to take time to repair
them. The maintenance of the King's Highway, including footpaths, was one of the duties imposed upon each manor. The lord
of the manor then threw this duty upon his tenants, their various
obligations being adjusted and enforced by the court leet.

Mary Tudor considered the maintenance of roads and paths
so important that she established new arrangements for dealing
with the matter which applied throughout her kingdom. A
statute of 1555, setting up the new system, was to form the basis
of highway maintenance organization for the next 300 years.
Like its predecessor, this system was based on an obligation
imposed on every inhabitant of each parish to keep the paths of
that parish open and in good order. A Surveyor of Highways
was appointed in each parish whose task it was to ensure that
the parish's rights of way were being maintained. If he discovered
an obstruction, he stood up in church after the sermon the very
next Sunday and denounced the offender, giving notice that if
the matter were not put right within thirty days he would deal
with it himself and charge his expenses to the parishioner
responsible.[25]

In keeping with this tradition of local responsibility, Attlee's
1949 Act laid the duty of highway maintenance in each county
on the county council, which thus became the highway authority.
Each of these councils was required to protect and assert the
rights of the public to the use and enjoyment of the highways for
which it was the highway authority and to prevent the obstruction of these rights of way. Today, under this Act, (as slightly
amended by the Highways Act, 1980 and the Wildlife and
Countryside Act, 1981), powers very similar to those of the
old Surveyor of Highways entitle any highway authority that
discovers an obstruction on one of its public footpaths or bridleways to serve a notice requiring the removal of the obstruction
within a specified time by the person responsible for the obstruction. If the obstruction is not then removed, the authority may
remove it itself and recover the expenses incurred in so doing
from the person concerned. Each highway authority also has the
power to prosecute for wilful obstruction. It is an offence wilfully
to obstruct free passage along a highway and offenders can be
fined up to £200.

This array of weaponry is actually quite formidable, and on occasion it has been used quite effectively. Take almost any of the thirty-six public paths in the little parish of Steep outside Petersfield, Hampshire, and you will find it well-trodden and well-signposted with bridges in good repair and aids for the walker. Steps have been hewn into the hillside and a wooden handrail has been erected on one specially popular path leading up what would otherwise be a slippery chalk slope through a beech hanger. Paths, once frequented by the poet Edward Thomas, are now kept open partly through regular use – both for leisure purposes and for people going about their daily business. Any problems are reported to the footpaths representative on the parish council and, as Rollo Wickstead, the parish council chairman, told me in 1985: 'If there is one item that is bound to be on a parish council agenda meeting it is footpaths; and if you look back at the minutes you will see it has been a regular item at parish council meetings for the last one hundred years.' To ensure that all the paths are in good condition, the parish council aims to survey all of them systematically every five years. East Hampshire District Council's footpaths officer carries out any prosecutions that are necessary but local villagers carry out much minor maintenance work themselves on a voluntary basis.

Outside the national parks, the largest area of well-maintained public paths is probably to be found in South Yorkshire – the 602 square miles of land administered between 1974 and April 1986 by South Yorkshire Metropolitan County Council.

The rolling countryside between Sheffield, Rotherham and Doncaster – a contrasting mix of cereal prairies cheek by jowl with pockets of traditional thickly wooded and hedged farmland and patches of derelict industrial wasteland – contain some rights of way still regularly used on a workaday basis by local people travelling between home and coal-pit or industrial estate. Use keeps these paths open just as it used to keep all paths open. Nonetheless, the metropolitan local authority in this area took steps to ensure that less regularly used paths would remain equally operational. Most of the paths in the county are used mainly by its million or so urban inhabitants as they seek rural refreshment at weekends. In 1980, South Yorkshire Metropolitan

County Council introduced a scheme unique in Britain: 'Adopt-A-Path.' The Council felt at that time that many people wished to walk in the countryside but were afraid they might be trespassing because they did not know where the public paths were. At the same time, they felt that the more the paths were used, the less they would be obstructed. 'Adopt-A-Path' worked like this: through an introductory leaflet distributed at public libraries and the like, the Council invited people to adopt one path in the county and to walk it whenever they could – perhaps once every six weeks – and to report any problems they encountered to the County Council. Each volunteer was issued with a copy of the definitive map for the county and a round route of three or four miles which became his or her path. By 1984, over 500 people or groups were participating in the scheme and three-quarters of the county's paths had been adopted.

As well as mobilizing the citizens in this way ('the volunteers are our eyes' one official told me), the County Council proved prepared to take a tough line with landowners who disregarded the law. Prosecution was only a last resort: the Council preferred to serve a notice on an offending landowner to the effect that an offence had been committed and that the Council would remove the obstruction and send the landowner the bill. However, where this did not have the desired effect, the Council was prepared to prosecute for wilful obstruction, and did so on six occasions between 1979 and 1984, for example.

All four of the district councils which took over South Yorkshire's footpath responsibilities on the abolition of the metropolitan county councils in April 1986 had said they would like to continue the Adopt-A-Path scheme. However, only two (Sheffield and Barnsley District Councils) had made firm plans to do this. In the other two districts (Rotherham and Doncaster) the scheme was threatened by budgetary pressures: in 1986 Doncaster District Council, for example, was expecting to have to bear a shortfall in funds in 1986–7 of £9 million.

Lancashire County Council is another authority which takes a relatively tough line with landowners who obstruct public footpaths. The Council, which is responsible for about 4,000 miles of path and bridleway, took out twenty-one prosecutions for footpath obstruction between 1980 and 1984 of which eighteen were successful. It has found that removing an obstruction and then recovering the cost from the landowner can have its drawbacks. Once removed, an obstruction may be replaced soon afterwards. And it may take a legal action to recover costs. Because of this, Lancashire County Council sometimes moves straight to prosecution.

Hampshire County Council, on the other hand, has made much use of its power to issue 'day notices' under Section 143 of the Highways Act, 1980. Once the council receives a complaint about a blocked path, an official verifies the obstruction and finds out who owns the land concerned. He asks the landowner to remove the obstruction, and this visit is confirmed by a letter enclosing an official notice that if the obstruction is not removed within fifty-six days, the council will do the work itself and charge the costs to the landowner. Hampshire County Council issued about 400 such notices a year between 1980 and 1985.

Finally, Humberside County Council offers another example of a highway authority prepared to use its powers to tackle head-on those landowners who block public paths. In 1983 this council started warning landowners who allow crops to block rights of way that it will itself cut down any offending crops if they decline to do so. By 1985, around fifty paths a year in Humberside were being cleared in this way.

The uncompromising attitude taken by Humberside, Hampshire, South Yorkshire and Lancashire County Councils is, however, very much the exception rather than the rule. The extent and frequency of path obstruction shows that, in the majority of cases, highway authorities decline to tell landowners to keep this part of the Queen's Highway open free for passage.

Prosecution for footpath obstruction is rare in many counties. Between 1 January 1980 and 1 January 1985, Leicestershire County Council, for example, prosecuted just two landowners in respect of three obstructions, while nearby Nottinghamshire took only one landowner to court during this same period. Hertfordshire County Council prosecuted twice during this period, Somerset County Council told me it has never prosecuted a landowner for obstructing a right of way. Complaining in 1984 about the extent of path obstruction in north Buckinghamshire, local footpath secretary Joseph Lowrey declared: 'Winslow is in

country where the civil war raged in the seventeenth century –
but parliamentary rule is still not universally acknowledged as
applying beyond tarred roads.'[26]

One indication of the extent to which landowners expect their
highway authorities to enforce the law on rights of way is the
response of most landowners to the statutory requirement under
the National Parks and Access to the Countryside Act, 1949,
that highway authorities should be given seven days' notice of
an intention to plough a path (coupled with a requirement for
reinstatement soon afterwards). In Cheshire, to take one entirely
typical example, only one of the county's several thousand
farmers used regularly to write to the council each year to give
such advance warning. Now, farmers do not have to: this
requirement was repealed in 1981.

Why are the public's interest in rights of way so badly
defended? The answer lies ultimately in the Hobhouse Committee's decision to follow tradition and make footpath maintenance
subject to local control. For appropriate as this approach may
have been in Elizabethan England and Wales, it was not the
way to secure rights of way once the majority of the population
had moved to towns and cities.

In the absence of effective representation for millions of people
who use the countryside for recreation but who do not live in it,
many county councils are dominated by the landowning class.
Even allowing for the non-representation of city-dwellers in the
affairs of shire counties, the influence of landowners over their
affairs is disproportionate.

The power wielded by landowning interests in rural local
authorities goes some way to explaining the lack of zeal these
authorities display in curbing the excesses of landowners. In the
countryside, local control tends to turn out to be not all that
different from landowner control, as it has done for hundreds of
years. This situation is not likely to change as long as local
authorities continue to be controlled by those with the time,
money, inclination and influence to win power.

But if county councils fail to uphold the recreation interest in
footpath policy themselves, they often make matters even worse
by passing on their responsibility to parish councils, on which
landed interests are often represented even more powerfully. The

present policy of some county councils is to refer any public path obstruction to the parish councils to sort out in the first instance. One such is Lincolnshire County Council. Major Brett Collier, the secretary of the Lincolnshire Fieldpaths Committee for the Preservation of Rights of Way in Lincolnshire and South Humberside, told me what this meant: 'The chief culprit is often the chairman of the parish council, and therefore little gets done about the complaint. Alternatively, members of the parish council have to live with their neighbours and meet them socially in a small community hence, "in the interest of good relations" a fieldpath problem is not pursued.'

It is perhaps significant that those authorities whose rights of way are in the best condition are often also those on which city-dwellers are best represented. The Peak District National Park is run by a planning board many of whose members are drawn from towns and cities and one-third of whom are nominated by the Secretary of State for the Environment to represent the national conservation and recreation interest. The Peak has a path network in a far better condition than those in many other parts of Britain. At Steep the presence of Bedales School has provided the parish with a group of people not reliant on the established landowning régime and with high-level expectations of being able to enjoy the local countryside. In 1985 the chairman of Steep Parish Council was a lecturer at a technical college; the other members comprised only one farmer, together with a retired journalist, two housewives, a local businessman and a retired education inspector.

Of course, the membership of South Yorkshire Metropolitan County Council was very different from that of a typical shire county council. Instead of a landowner or farmer, the chairman of the South Yorkshire committee with overall responsibility for footpaths, recreation, culture and health, was in 1984 an educational social worker. This committee had set up a special sub-committee to look after footpaths and on this body, which in 1984 was chaired by a teacher, representatives of working-class areas and user groups like the Ramblers' Association predominated. Neighbouring Nottinghamshire, in contrast, presents a far more typical picture. This council has never set up a special sub-committee to look after footpaths: they have always

been looked after by the environment committee, alongside roads
and town and country planning.

Lack of use ought not then in theory to have posed as much of
a threat to our rights of way as it has done. For the post-war
legislators provided machinery to safeguard public footpaths
whether they were used or not. Unfortunately, however, the
machinery was set up in a way that failed to take into account
key political realities in modern Britain.

But the problems of Britain's public footpaths and bridleways
do not end with the fact that many are blocked and that there
are many areas without any. A combination of other factors is
cutting back the size of the network on the ground.

A DISINTEGRATING NETWORK

One result of widespread footpath obstruction is that the paths
are far less used for recreation than they otherwise might be.
The obstruction of one path affects the degree of use of others
with which it connects. The loss of access to a path that includes
a bridge over a stream can effectively cut off a whole swathe of
countryside from would-be walkers on the other side.

Path obstruction has another unwelcome consequence: it can
make it easier for a path to be legally extinguished. The only
grounds on which a right of way can be extinguished is that the
path is not needed for public use. If a path has been obstructed
for some time, use will have suffered. And if a path is not
being used the landowner will often find it easy to obtain an
extinguishment order from his local authority. If there are
protests against this order, there may be an inquiry and the
inspector at such an inquiry is supposed to disregard any
temporary circumstances that might have affected the degree of
use. But his position is difficult: how can he assess what the
degree of use would be if a path were in perfect condition when
it has long been obstructed? Only if he is confronted by large
numbers of people saying they would like to use the path or if he
is presented with evidence of large numbers of complaints about
the obstruction is he likely to refuse the application. But once a
path has become impenetrable complaints and protests may ebb
away as people adjust their lives to the new reality.

Obstruction, then, can lead to under-use which can lead to extinction. Obstruction can also make easier the legal diversion of paths, which can equally lead to the exclusion of the public from large tracts of land. Take the case of a path going around the edge of a field, perhaps alongside a hedge. The farmer clears away the hedge, and amalgamates his two fields. Our first path round the edge of a field now goes through the middle. Cross-field paths are even more irksome to farmers than paths that go round field edges. Suppose the farmer ploughs up the path and fails to reinstate it afterwards. Walkers continually confronted by growing crops or a churned-up mass of earth may start walking around the edge of the new enlarged field. The farmer may choose to encourage this by leaving a margin around the edge for them to walk on even though there is no official right of way. After a few years, he may formally apply to his council for a path diversion order, diverting the cross-field path on to the track the public now use. Once the order is granted, the whole cycle may begin all over again with yet another field enlargement, until the perimeter route becomes a diversion of many miles from the line of the original path.

A combination of other factors is serving to reduce the effective path network.

The 1949 legislators did not only make path obstruction a criminal offence and highway authorities responsible for removing obstructions, whether or not these were deliberately placed. They also required the authorities to 'maintain' public rights of way in their areas, that is, to keep them reasonably passable by the ordinary traffic of the neighbourhood at all seasons of the year. This means that as well as prosecuting those who wilfully obstruct paths, highway authorities are required to clear any natural vegetation that encroaches upon paths and to repair stiles, gates and bridges, fill in potholes and so on. Unfortunately, however, the highway authorities are no more vigorous in resisting natural than human pressure on the paths. When paths become overgrown or stiles collapse, it is relatively unusual for the local council to step in to restore the position.

Many highway authorities decline to fulfil their statutory duty to maintain paths in reasonable repair because of the pressure of other tasks. But some leave paths to run to seed with the deliberate intention of securing their destruction. Cornwall

County Council's surveyor explained to me in an interview in 1982 that as about 50 per cent of Cornwall's paths were in his view not used, the County Council declined to maintain them. He was anxious to get rid of paths which no longer fulfilled their original function, in his words, 'to clear out the dross'. He agreed that he was not creating large numbers of new paths to make up for the loss and that there would inevitably be a reduction in Cornwall's overall rights of way mileage.

A former chief executive officer of Preseli District Council in south-west Wales was equally frank. Much of the Pembrokeshire Coast National Park lies within Preseli District, and because of the particular importance of this park (Britain's loveliest, some believe) the paths there are especially valuable. Yet Eric Jenkins, Preseli's chief executive officer between 1974 and 1981, consistently argued for a large reduction in the district's path network. In a paper in 1978, for instance, he recommended a reduction of 840 miles in Preseli's network of rights of way.[27] The Pembrokeshire Coastal Path, 107 miles of which runs through the district, would be retained. So would 100 miles out of the then remaining 940 extra miles of right of way. The remainder would go, and to facilitate this process, Mr Jenkins proposed a simplification of the procedure for creating, closing or diverting paths. Mr Jenkins based his approach on the importance of agriculture in the economy and the need for as little interference as possible with agricultural operations; and on the belief that the country cannot afford the expenditure required to maintain the entire path network.

In 1987, Mr Jenkins' proposals were not being put forward as council policy. However, the council's decision to refrain from maintaining many paths is leading to an effective reduction of the usable mileage of paths in the district – if not the 80 per cent reduction advocated by Mr Jenkins. A survey in 1981 found that within Britain's only coastal national park – the Pembrokeshire Coast Park – 27 per cent of the public footpaths and bridleways for which Preseli and South Pembrokeshire District Councils are responsible were completely impassable.[28]

SIGNPOSTING

Public paths will only be used to any extent if they are clear and clearly marked, whereas routes which are obstructed or not marked in any way are most unlikely to be used.[29]

Footpath inspector Vice-Admiral Sir Stephen Berthon after a public inquiry into a proposal to re-route public paths in part of Lincolnshire, 1982

In view of the real and imagined dangers which the countryside holds for townspeople and the lack of adequate maintenance of public paths, footpath signposts have a vital role to play. They both alert urban visitors to the whereabouts of rights of way and help inspire in them the confidence to exercise these rights. Path signposts can prove a very reassuring sight to townspeople in a world that may appear alien and does indeed include unfriendly figures in the shape of territorially aggressive farmers and their dogs, bulls and stallions. A mere line on a map, even if the would-be walker is armed with one, does not instil anything like the same aplomb, especially if, as often happens, its message appears to be countermanded on the ground by forbidding 'Private' and 'Keep Out' notices.

To encourage public paths to be used to the full, the law requires highway authorities to erect and maintain a signpost at every point where a public path leaves a metalled road. And yet when the Gloucestershire branch of the Ramblers' Association carried out a sample survey of the public paths in Gloucestershire in 1981, it found that 90 per cent of the paths surveyed lacked signposts at the points at which they left metalled roads. Of the 105 potential sights for signs where paths left roads, only eleven had signposts. (Two of these signposts pointed in the wrong direction.)[30] A similar survey by the East Sussex branch of the Ramblers' Association in 1983 revealed that to fulfil its statutory duty to signpost all public paths where they leave the road, East Sussex County Council would need to erect 3,000 signs on 2,025 paths.[31]

The reason why so few signs go up seems to be a combination of opposition from landowners who do not want rights of way across their land advertised in any way, and reluctance on the part of many councils to allocate money out of highway budgets which county surveyors consider better spent on road signs. The absence of signs in particular localities sometimes reflects a particular landowner's dislike of them. And some landowners will even go so far as to pull down signs which the highway authority has put up.

In 1984, Lancashire's rights of way officer G. A. Alker reported
to me an increase in vandalism of public footpath signs. The
Council suspect farmers and landowners may be to blame for
much of the damage, since some of the signs have been sawn off
or pulled out of their cement bases – an operation that would
require the use of a tractor and front-loader – equipment not
usually available to the schoolboy prankster. He considers the
disappearance of signs a big problem, but until he can catch
somebody red-handed, there is little he can do except replace the
signs. In 1982, South Yorkshire Council *did* catch somebody
pulling a footpath sign out of its cement base. When police
searched the culprit's farm, they found another eight signposts
stacked in the barn. South Yorkshire Police prosecuted the man,
charging him with criminal damage. He was given a conditional
discharge for one year and ordered to pay costs and to compensate the County Council for the costs incurred in replacing the
damaged signposts.

Highway authorities are not the only organizations that put
up footpath signs. A few exceptional landowners erect them
voluntarily. And the Ramblers' Association has put up large
numbers of waymarks away from metalled roads where landowners are prepared to give them permission. These signs can
prove just as vulnerable to attack as those erected by highway
authorities. As Scottish landowner and former president of the
British Field Sports Society Sir Marcus Kimball MP explained
to members of the Standing Committee considering the details of
the Wildlife and Countryside Bill in 1981, 'The Pony Club in
my constituency has a most enjoyable battle with one especially
active member of the Ramblers' Association who spends all his
time putting up footpath signs. The members of the Pony Club
find happy occupation in the summer going round taking them
down again.'[32]

Sir Marcus went on to give a reason for the Pony Club's
'happy occupation': 'That is purely because that man has got
the atmosphere wrong.' The man to whom he was referring is
Major Brett Collier, and I asked him for his comment on what
Sir Marcus had said. Major Collier, then area secretary of the
Ramblers' Association in Lincolnshire, told me: 'At the time we
were acting, quite legitimately and without charge, as "agents of

the County Council" to assist them in their statutory duties and to save ratepayers expense. After all, the County Council supplied the signposts.'

One Step Forward . . .

If Major Collier has got the 'atmosphere' wrong, what is the atmosphere that Sir Marcus Kimball, a particularly influential landowner, would like to see? In 1982, he gave me his views. Sir Marcus believes – and many other landowners seem to feel much the same way – that there should be a shift from the notion of public footpaths and bridleways as rights to their being seen as privileges whose continued existence must depend on what Sir Marcus calls the 'goodwill' of landowners and farmers. He would like to see the Ramblers' Association taking responsibility for protecting, asserting and maintaining public rights of way instead of the highway authorities. Each county footpaths officer of the Ramblers' Association would seek to deal with footpath obstructions by persuading landowners to remove them. If persuasion failed, the Ramblers' Association man would, of course, have no sanctions to fall back on. Yet he would be expected to respond to complaints from landowners about damage to their land caused by walking or riding by paying out compensation (presumably paid out of members' subscriptions). Sir Marcus proposes that to enable the RA to be well equipped to perform this central conciliatory role in the countryside the president of each county branch of the RA should be that county's leading landowner.

For proposals such as these to be implemented, there would need to be a radical change in the law. And although no Bill embodying these proposals has been brought before Parliament, there is more or less continuous pressure for changes in the direction Sir Marcus would like to see. In 1984, for example, Tony Baldry, MP for Banbury, made an unsuccessful attempt through a private member's bill to remove the need for a public inquiry into proposals to divert public footpaths. Instead, the county council would both promote diversion as at present and take over what is now the Secretary of State's job of deciding whether a public inquiry should take place and of adjudicating on its proceedings. In 1986, as we have seen, (p 317) landowners secured the criminalisation of trespass in certain circumstances through the Public Order Act. And as we shall see in the next chapter, there is an alarming tendency among at least some local authorities to think in terms of permissive paths subject to a landowner's ultimate power of withdrawal as opposed to guaranteed public rights of way when considering how to extend access.

Had it not been for the continuous and consistent work of the Ramblers' Association over the past quarter century, the concept of public paths in Britain's countryside would be far less secure than it is now. But even with the Association's vigilance, it might take less than we think for the basic notion of rights of access throughout our land to degenerate fast. We could easily see the extension of criminal trespass, a much reduced network on the map and an even more reduced one on the ground together with greater and greater pressure for those who wish to explore the countryside on foot to be confined outside open areas in national parks to a skeletal network of long-distance paths much like New Zealand's segregated 'walkways'.

But if the access situation provided by public paths in England and Wales is deteriorating, the situation in the rest of the United Kingdom calls out for even more concern. For in Northern Ireland and Scotland, the law does not even provide the basic guarantees on rights of way provided by the framework of the 1949 Act.

Rights of Way in Scotland

Look at the Ordnance Survey maps of Scotland and you will not find any public footpaths or bridleways marked at all apart from the country's three long-distance paths. The National Parks and Access to the Countryside Act of 1949 passed Scotland by, and, when some of its provisions were extended north of the border in the Countryside (Scotland) Act of 1967, these did not include Attlee's more rigorous measures on footpaths and access.

Such powers as Scotland's highway authorities hold on public paths are essentially permissive. The Scottish legislation empowers local planning authorities (in this case Scotland's fifty-three district councils) to create new public paths, to divert existing ones and to close paths not needed for public use. They are also required 'to assert, protect and keep open and free from obstruction or encroachment' any public rights of way falling wholly or partly within their areas. And the Countryside Commission for Scotland, which was set up by the 1967 Act, is empowered to designate long distance routes; regional councils establish and maintain long-distance paths on the ground.

What the Scottish Act most conspicuously failed to do was to require the preparation of definitive maps of rights of way like those required in England and Wales. The point of such a requirement would not only have been to ensure that information about rights of way could have been provided for walkers; even more importantly it would have endowed such routes as got on to the definitive map with enduring legal status. The absence of such maps has meant that anyone engaging in a legal dispute with a landowner over a footpath (in the case of obstruction, say) has first had to prove that a public footpath exists. Often this task is far more difficult than making the substantive complaint. On top of being left free of the duty of mapping public footpaths, Scottish local authorities were left free of the responsibility of signposting them where they leave a metalled road. These concessions to Scottish landowners have helped maintain a less favourable climate for rights of way than that which exists in the South.

Nonetheless, by 1987, Scotland had at least three different types of paths that approximated in some respect to the rights of way of England and Wales.

By far the most common of these types is the path claimed to be a right of way on the grounds that it has been in continuous use by the public. The claim may be made either by local people or by a voluntary society like the Scottish Rights of Way Society or the North East Mountain Trust. Sometimes societies put up signs besides paths they are claiming denoting the claim, and landowners, without necessarily acknowledging the claim, may allow the signs to remain. Details of these claimed paths are not published, but most district councils hold maps that show their routes. To try to get some idea of the density of the network, I obtained copies of these maps for the whole of Scotland from the Countryside Commission for Scotland and then measured the

total length of such paths for four districts that seemed to me to
reflect the variety of the Scottish countryside. These districts
were intensively-farmed Berwick in the Borders, Stirling District
in the southern Highlands, Angus in the eastern Highlands and
Skye and Lochalsh in the north-west. Berwick had the highest
density of paths: 0.4 miles of path per square mile of countryside.
In Stirling, the density was half as great. In Angus and in Skye
and Lochalsh, the density was half again: 0.1 mile of path per
square mile of countryside. All these densities are far lower than
those of England and Wales where the average path density in
1969 was 2 miles of right of way per square mile of land. Even in
the worst served English counties the density of paths is far
higher than in my Scottish examples – Norfolk, for example,
which is notorious for a shortage of footpaths, has 0.9 miles of
path per square mile of land.

Of course, Scotland's claimed paths do not guarantee a right
of way on the ground like the public rights of way of England
and Wales. People using Scotland's claimed routes may consider
themselves entitled to do so, but landowners may consider such
use permissive and feel able to veto it at will. Dr Robert Aitken,
the Chairman of the Scottish Council for Countryside Activities
(the coordinating body for voluntary conservation and recreation
groups in Scotland) and the author of several reports on footpaths
in Scotland, told me in 1985 that in his view landowners would
be likely, if asked, to deny the existence of a right of passage
along two-thirds of these claimed rights of way.

The second group of 'public' paths in Scotland is the handful
of the first category of paths over which a claim for a right of
way has gone to the courts and been upheld. The bridleway
running through Glen Tilt, the scene of a confrontation between
the 6th Duke of Atholl and botanists in the nineteenth century
and the subject of a subsequent court case, is one of Scotland's
few 'vindicated' rights of way. Paths like this are formally
registered as a right over land in Scotland's land registry, the
Register of Sasines, lodged in Edinburgh. However, even when
such a right has been registered, a walker may find no evidence
of this to reassure him on the ground.

The third category consists of those paths which have been
formally asserted by local authorities under a requirement of the

Scottish Countryside Act requiring them to do this (but not to draw up definitive maps). Yet of those authorities that assert paths, very few do any more than mark claimed paths (category one) on their own unpublished maps. One of the few authorities to do more than this is Perth and Kinross District Council, which has followed a procedure for path assertion similar to that of path registration south of the border. The district council has asked the fifty-one community councils in its area to mark on maps paths they consider to be public rights of way. From the 65 per cent response to this request and from maps supplied by the Scottish Rights of Way Society, the district council has built up a picture of over 500 claimed public rights of way in its 2,022 square-mile area. Of these, the council had by 1985 formally asserted 167. In each case of formal assertion, the council has first established evidence of usage of the route as a right of way, evidence involving at least six signatures. It has then gone to the landowner concerned with this evidence and asked him for his views. The landowner concerned may object to the actual route proposed and want a diversion; or he may object altogether in which case the council can proceed only through a legal battle, or he may agree to the route on a permissive basis only, or he may agree to the original proposal. And even Perth and Kinross will assert a path only if it appears to be challenged; because it ignores paths where access is tolerated, it is not assembling anything like the definitive maps of England and Wales.

The vast majority of Scotland's 'public' paths fall into the first category: in other words, they are at best only de facto rights of way. They have never been formally tested, and so their statutory existence is always open to question. Dr Robert Aitken said in an interview with me in 1985:

The fact that these routes exist on the map doesn't necessarily mean that they are either used, signposted, or even that they are not obstructed. In some cases they will be completely derelict. If they are not posted with signs saying 'No Entry', then the gates will have no stiles or the paths will have barbed wire fences across them, things of that sort.

The absence of more than a handful of vindicated public rights of way in the whole of Scotland has a number of unfortunate consequences. First, if a walker meets an obstruction while walking along what he understands to be a public right of way, he cannot simply report the matter to his local authority and expect them to get the obstruction removed, as he can in England and Wales. For unless the path involved happens to be one of the very few vindicated or formally asserted paths, a local authority faced with such a request would have to establish in a court of law that the path in question was a public right of way before it could take any legal action to get the obstruction removed. In England and Wales this was the situation that existed before the 1949 Act made provision for the systematic mapping of all rights of way and the granting of legal status as rights of way to those routes not successfully challenged when mapped.

The difficulties to which the Scottish situation gives rise are illustrated by the three-year battle over a claimed right of way in the western Highlands near Glencoe. In 1978, the proprietor of land to the north of Loch Leven, Gordon Paine, began challenging parties of walkers based at a nearby Holiday Fellowship hostel when they were using the route from Callert on the shores of Loch Leven to Larigmor, three miles to the north. This path through high, bare hills, wooded on their lower slopes, affords good views across Loch Leven up Glencoe and of the magnificent range of the Mamores to the north as well as providing one of the very few ways across these hills. Indeed, it was because of the strategic importance of the Callert route that walkers concluded it had been a long standing right of way providing a link from an old ferry crossing over Loch Leven to Larigmor which stands on a former military road to Fort William.

The Holiday Fellowship asked its local authority, Highland Regional Council, to take action on behalf of the walkers, but the Council refused. However, one of Scotland's oldest voluntary footpath societies, the Scottish Rights of Way Society, agreed to take up the case (had Highland Council taken it up the procedure it would have had to follow would have been the same). The Society collected as much evidence as it could from people who had used the route as well as employees of the estate in an attempt to demonstrate that use of the route had traditionally been viewed as a right rather than a privilege. The Society traced the route as a right of way back to 1755 and assembled witnesses who declared that in the early 1980s the public had never given up its right of passage along the Callert route. When it presented this evidence to Mr Paine, he proposed an alternative route which the Society found unacceptable. Unable to reach agreement, the Society in 1979 issued a summons to take Mr Paine to court to establish the right of way. A further meeting between the two sides took place and again an alternative route was rejected by the Society. Finally, just before the date of the hearing in 1981, Mr Paine agreed to recognize the route as a right of way.

The whole procedure had cost the Rights of Way Society £1,230. Had Mr Paine not backed down at the door of the court, the case could easily have cost the Society ten times this figure. The right of way will now be registered as a burden on the estate in the Register of Sasines. If a future owner prevents walkers using the route, a local authority will not have to spend several years proving the existence of the right of way before going on to try to deal with the obstruction.

In view of the essentially de facto nature of most of Scotland's rights of way, action in the majority of cases to deal with footpath obstruction is informal. Angus District, which covers 785 square miles of mainly rural land including the popular Glens of Angus and the settlements of Forfar, Brechin, Montrose and Glamis, has no rights of way whatsoever which are any more than claimed rights. In a typical case in 1983, walkers reported to Donald Baxter, the District Council's chief technical officer, that a farmer was preventing them from using what they understood to be a right of way. Mr Baxter told me: 'When I had a word with Angus he said "Och aye, you can pass this way: I was only being difficult."' Fine when a landowner co-operates, but not such a sound approach in cases where landowners continue to be obstructive.

The absence of definitive maps means that local councils seeking to get rights of way put in a fit condition for use face the same difficulties as those trying to get obstructions removed. In 1984, for instance, Perth and Kinross District Council became concerned that a lade bridge alongside the River Tay at Thistlebridge a few miles north of Perth had got broken. Perth is a long way from the sea, and local people had traditionally crossed the bridge to bathe from a pleasant sandy spot on the Tay riverside. The land concerned is part of Scone Estates owned by the family of the 8th Earl of Mansfield, based at Scone Palace, and the District Council wrote to the estate offering to repair the bridge itself. In a letter in May 1984, the factor to Scone Estates, J. B. Farquar, refused the offer. He said that the question of public access to the Thistlebridge area had always been of concern to the estate, primarily because of fire risk and to a lesser extent because of the risk of interference to salmon fishings. He said he did not think it had ever been suggested that the public should have a legal right of access to the area and so he was unable to agree that the bridge should be rebuilt.

The absence of a definitive map of rights of way in Scotland has another unfortunate consequence. It means that such rights of way as do exist in Scotland are completely unco-ordinated. Look, say, at Dundee District Council's map of rights of way in its area and you will see a concentration of routes running a short distance from the district's main towns and villages, separated by large tracts of countryside penetrated by no rights of way whatsoever. Even those running out from the towns do not provide for circular walks. Because they do not preside over comprehensive footpath maps, like their English counterparts, Scottish local authorities are not in the habit of seeking to extend rights of way in response to recreation needs. This means, for example, that there are extremely few rights of way around Scotland's coastline. And within the hills and mountains where most tolerated access exists, bloodsports cut down the extent of this access during particular months of the year. In lowland Scotland, the fences and dykes around many fields preclude de facto access altogether, cutting off not only walks along field edges but also across the stretches of rough wood and heathland beyond.

To make things worse, the existence of the few public rights of way that do occur in Scotland is known only to a small circle of people. In the words of the deputy director of the Countryside Commission for Scotland, Tom Huxley: 'There is no way for the world at large to know what is a right of way in Scotland beyond peradventure.'[33]

Because there is no statutory requirement for local authorities to signpost such public paths as exist where they leave the road, you can drive for miles and miles and miles in Scotland without spotting any indication of any right of way. This may not be too much of a problem in those hill and mountain regions where there is much de facto access to unfenced forests and moors. But in the large area of lowland Scotland, where the vast majority of the country's people live, it can be very hard indeed to find somewhere to walk. Since local authorities are under no obligation to prepare definitive maps of rights of way even for their own use it is no surprise to learn that they do not prepare any footpath maps for publication. Local country people may know where they can walk in the countryside without being stopped. But the inhabitants of nearby cities or those visiting Scotland from the south cannot hope to get hold of this information readily. There are well over 183,000 people living in Dundee, just outside Angus District. Peter Marshall, Dundee District Council's footpaths officer told me in 1984: 'There are traditional areas where Dundee people go, but a vast amount of people don't know where they can walk.'

Perhaps the most worrying long-term implication of the absence of any formal requirement for the registration of public paths north of the Border is that many paths are likely to be lost altogether. Much knowledge about rural rights of way survives only in people's memories, which can fade and disappear like the paths themselves. To be legally upheld as a right of way, a path must have been used for twenty years or more and must still have been in use less than twenty years ago. Changes in the size and lifestyle of the rural population could mean great loss of rights of way. The North East Mountain Trust, an association of hillwalkers and mountaineers based in Aberdeen and founded to safeguard the environment of the Scottish uplands for the benefit of people taking recreation there, estimated in 1982 that 1,000 miles of public rural rights of way could be lost in this way in north-east Scotland alone.[34]

It is sometimes argued that the existence of widespread de facto access to Scotland's upland countryside makes public rights of way redundant. In fact, however, the moors are much less open than they seem, and such public paths as do exist in

Scotland are often of crucial importance. Though there is certainly much tolerated access over Scotland's hills and mountains,
there are also vast sporting estates embracing some of the most
dazzling heather moorlands and the most wild, conifer-free
scenery which are quite effectively barred to walkers: all fenced
next to roads, they sport notices advising walkers to keep to any
public footpaths from August to February. Were it not for the
public paths, these areas might very well be completely private.
And because individual Highland estates are so often very large,
one owner who wished to keep the general public out could bar
literally tens of thousands of acres to ordinary holiday-makers or
hill-walkers. What this means is not only are such public paths
as exist in Scotland of great importance; there is also a great
need for more guaranteed rights of access in Scotland's countryside. The Dee Valley, for instance, running westwards from
Aberdeen to Braemar and then south to the mountains between
Cairn Toul and Ben Macdui, is one of Scotland's landscape
jewels. The nineteen-mile stretch between Ballater and Braemar
is particularly outstanding. Here are some of Scotland's few
remaining fields of wildflowers in an extraordinarily varied
riverscape. Yet the road is everywhere fenced and there are no
public footpaths. A handful of picnic places, most of them little
more than lay-bys, mock the walker: they are fenced in and
mostly situated in conifer plantation rather than the emerald
riverside. It must be possible to marry the needs of the salmon
industry of the Dee with a better deal for tourists and walkers –
a long-distance path from source to the sea would be a good
start.

In lowland Scotland networks of rights of way would provide
an invaluable means for people, particularly city-dwellers, to
walk in countryside close to their homes. In the Highlands,
however, there are fears that definitive maps on the English
model could have an unwelcome side-effect. If a proper network
of genuine rights of way existed, would landowners feel they
could toughen up on de facto access? Alongside stretches of
Scotland's first long-distance footpath, the West Highland Way,
there have been signs of more restrictive attitudes. The fear that
this pattern might spread has led some footpath societies in

Scotland to oppose definitive maps. What might be more appropriate for large open areas like the Highlands is the enactment of a general right to wander at will over untilled land. There would then still be scope for the protection and creation of particular routes which would have to be properly maintained. What should not be allowed to persist is the absence from Scotland of a central feature of Britain's rural heritage – the genuinely public footpath.

Rights of Way in Northern Ireland

A combination of guaranteed rural rights of way and a right to walk over any untilled rural land might also work well in Ulster. In the Province, perhaps more than in any other part of the United Kingdom, there has traditionally been a relaxed attitude to public access: in most rural areas, people have long been permitted to walk where they like. The picture one Belfast woman gave me in 1982 of the position in the 1950s is that of a countryside still largely unchanged:

I grew up in the countryside near Clandy in the Sperrin Mountains. As children, we could walk anywhere along the valley bottoms and through the fields, moving the whin bushes to get in and out of a field. People who lived in the area just wandered around as they wished. There were cart tracks up to the open hill land where you could also walk at will and which was used for turf cutting and for common grazing.

In many parts of the Province, this situation seems little different today.

Legislation consolidating this agreeable picture might be accepted by landowners as little more than tidying up. But this is not what the Province got when the matter was considered in 1983. Instead the Government provided a pale imitation of the access provisions of Attlee's post-war contract for the countryside of England and Wales. In view of the special nature of public access in the Province, this measure could even prove counter-productive in the long-term.

The Access to the Countryside (Northern Ireland) Order, 1983, follows the Scottish approach far more closely than the more comprehensive rights of way legislation of England and

Wales. The order lays a duty on Northern Ireland's district councils to 'assert, protect, and keep open and free from obstruction or encroachment any public right of way'. They may maintain public rights of way in their areas and are required to compile and keep maps of public rights of way in their areas. They may also, after consultation with the owner or occupier of the land concerned, put up and maintain signposts. The problem is that, as in Scotland, although Northern Ireland's district councils will be able and be required to protect public rights of way where they exist, there will be little incentive for them to create any to protect in the first place. There is no requirement for a statutory survey of rights or the preparation of definitive maps on the English and Welsh model. So the sort of maps that are likely to emerge, district by district, are likely to consist of lines that are no more than claimed rights of way, forming no co-ordinated network within a district, let alone over the Province as a whole. If the emergence of a few unco-ordinated route lines is treated by the Province's landowners as an excuse to abandon their hitherto relaxed attitude to public access, walkers will have little cause to welcome the new legislation.

8. Freedom to Wander

> Now at last we shall be able to see that the mountains of Snowdonia, the Lakes, and the waters of the Broads, the moors and dales of the Peak, the South Downs and the tors of the West Country belong to the people as a right and not as a concession. This is not just a Bill. It is a people's charter – a people's charter for the open-air, for the hikers and the ramblers, for everyone who loves to get out into the open air and enjoy the countryside. Without it they are fettered, deprived of their powers of access and facilities needed to make holidays enjoyable. With it the country-side is theirs to preserve, to cherish, to enjoy and to make their own.
>
> Minister of Town and Country Planning Lewis Silkin MP, during the second-reading debate on the National Parks and Access to the Countryside Bill in 1949[1]

The present law on access to open countryside emerged after half a century of protest against the exclusion of city-dwellers from large stretches of rural Britain. This protest, which had its origins in the nineteenth-century struggle over the vast and energetically guarded deer stalking grounds of Scotland, reached its climax in the 1930s as the working people of Sheffield and Manchester fought to gain access to the wild, open grouse moors of the Peak District, some of them going to prison for the cause.

The protesters won the argument. When the war-time coalition government set about planning the better Britain that peace would herald, it felt obliged to set up a special committee including representatives of the Ramblers' Association to con-sider the issues of footpaths and access to open countryside. This Committee, chaired by Sir Arthur Hobhouse, proposed a fundamental change in the access law when it reported in 1947.[2] The public footpath network was no longer to be regarded as providing sufficient access to the countryside. Footpaths might enable people to penetrate the countryside and glimpse its secret ponds and manor houses, bluebell woods and follies; but to experience true rural freedom they would need to be able to wander at will, especially over wild, open land. So the public, argued the Committee, had to be given a legal right to roam without impediment over what might have been termed 'rough-land' – untilled mountain, moor, heath, down, cliff, shore and lakeside throughout England and Wales. Landowners would no longer be able to treat those who walked on any such land without their consent as trespassers; instead the onus would be on the landowner to apply for special exemption from the new right to roam if he could show sufficient cause. Such exemption might be granted temporarily if, say, a landowner wished to reseed his land to improve grazing, or permanently if the Minister of Housing and Local Government decided that the land needed to be used for some special purpose which was incompatible with general public access, like the training of soldiers.

Lewis Silkin, the Minister of Town and Country Planning in Clement Attlee's post-war government, was determined to implement the bulk of the Hobhouse Committee's recommendations. He devoted one whole Section of his 1949 National Parks and Access to the Countryside Bill to the issue of public access to open countryside, accepting the Hobhouse view that public access should not be confined to rights of way across private land. He believed that as well as maintaining a network of public footpaths he had to open up whole tracts of countryside for recreation.

But although Silkin adopted the Hobhouse Committee's recommendations on footpaths virtually unchanged, he stopped short of providing a new legal right to wander at will over all designated access land of the kind the Committee had urged. Silkin feared that such a measure would trigger too much resistance from landowners, so he opted instead for a more limited measure, though he believed his scheme would still amount to a real breakthrough – 'a people's charter for the open-air'.

However, the access measures embodied in Part V of the 1949 Act, which are still in force, are not by any means as imposing as Mr Silkin's words quoted at the head of this chapter might

suggest. Effectively they turn the Hobhouse Committee's recommendation for automatic, universal access on its head by
conferring the right to wander only in areas over which local
planning authorities have made special arrangements. In these
lands the public are no longer to be treated as trespassers, but
have a legal right to wander at will, provided they observe
certain restrictions designed to prevent damage. But elsewhere,
the public have to continue to rely on such de facto access as
landowners are prepared to allow to get on to wild open spaces.

Three and a half decades later, what impact are these arrangements having on access to our countryside?

Drive north out of Bradford or Leeds towards the Yorkshire
Dales. Six miles from Skipton ('The Gateway to the Dales'), in
the deep gulf of the Wharfe Valley, two high, dome-shaped hills
rise up on either side of the road. Fourteen thousand acres of
moorland cover their upper slopes. The hills are called Barden
Moor and Barden Fell. Geographically, Barden Moor and
Barden Fell form part of the Yorkshire Dales. Yet they could not
be more different from the archetypal Dales-scape of green
pastures, dotted with ash trees and criss-crossed by a multitude
of enclosing white limestone walls. Unfenced and wild, clad in
an unending variety of heather and bracken, ling, cowberry,
bilberry and rough grass, these great gritstone moors are
imposingly unique. Grazed by sheep and favoured by red grouse,
they also provide a home for (among others) the cloudberry and
the sundew, the slow worm, adder and common lizard, the
emperor moth and the green hairstreak butterfly. Short-eared
owls, sparrowhawks, meadow pipits, whinchats, ring ouzels and
black-headed gulls are some of the birds to look out for on
Barden Moor and Barden Fell.

Cheek by jowl beneath their rough, open spaces, nestle the
smooth, grassy, stone-walled fields of this part of Wharfedale.
But the moors and the lower fields do not just complement each
other in landscape terms. This stretch of swiftly-flowing river,
the meadowlands with the ruins of Bolton Priory, Bolton Hall,
the fir plantations, deciduous woodland and the two great moors
all form part of the Bolton Abbey estate of the 11th Duke of
Devonshire (headquarters: sixty miles to the south at
Chatsworth).

Thirty years ago, the scene was different in one crucial respect. While the lower ground was accessible by path and road, the moors that tower over it were out of bounds – jealously guarded as a grouse preserve. No roads penetrated far into Barden Moor and Barden Fell, and as few public paths crossed them, only those walkers prepared to run the gauntlet of the then Duke of Devonshire's gamekeepers could savour their wild beauty. For both moors were guarded all year round in order that, for four weeks of the year, the then Duke and his friends could enjoy shooting as many as 6,000 red grouse in a season.

Now, however, anybody may freely tread these moors without being treated as a trespasser. You need not keep to the paths and car-parks but may experience fully the freedom and splendour of Barden Moor and Barden Fell by wandering where you will. Tens of thousands of people do so every year. For in 1960 the Duke of Devonshire's private family trust in which this land is now vested signed an access agreement with the then West Yorkshire County Council. The agreement, now between the Trustees of the Chatsworth Settlement and the Yorkshire Dales National Park Authority, superimposes public access on the established uses, which included in 1987, along with the rearing of grouse, the grazing of sheep by thirty tenant farmers. Only two reservoirs and a small area around them on Barden Moor are fenced off permanently from the public. In addition, the general public is excluded for thirty days a year when the grouse are being shot. The days on which the moors are to be closed are publicized in advance each year in local newspapers and, along with a list of by-laws, are posted on boards at the access points on to the moors. These by-laws enable sheep farming, grouse rearing and public access to co-exist for the remaining 335 days of the year mainly by banning picnic fires or stoves (since fire is a considerable hazard), dogs (since they can unsettle grouse and ewes), and kites (grouse can mistake kites for birds of prey and abandon their nests).

The Barden arrangement is a good example of what an access agreement under the 1949 Act is meant to achieve. Under the terms of one of these agreements between a landowner and a planning authority, the landowner agrees to grant the public the right to roam freely over a tract of land. The planning authority usually agrees to manage the recreation uses of the land and to pay the landowner compensation in respect of any damage caused by public access. Agreements can be made only over land defined in the 1949 Act as 'open country': mountain, moor, heath, down, cliff or foreshore, a definition which was widened through the Countryside Act 1968 to include woodland, lakeside, canalside and riverbank. Land exempted from the access provisions is termed 'excepted land' and includes agricultural land except rough grazing, nature reserves, land covered by buildings or the curtilage of buildings, parks, gardens, pleasure grounds, quarries, golf courses, land which is being developed and land covered by the works of a statutory undertaker like a gas, electricity or water board. If it cannot secure an access agreement, a local planning authority may, with the permission of the Secretary of State for the Environment, make an access order. Authorities can also buy land for the purpose of securing public access to it.

But if Barden Moor and Barden Fell show how an access agreement can succeed, the history of the agreement shows how difficult it can be to bring one into being. Access to Barden Moor and Barden Fell was not achieved overnight, but required over a decade of continuous pressure from ramblers. Yet the area was among the first in Britain to be selected as the possible target for an access agreement.

Preparation of access agreements was not intended to be a random business but to be based on strategic planning. Every county council in England and Wales was required to prepare a 'review map' for its area within two years of the 1949 Act becoming law. This had to show all land coming within the 1949 definition of 'open country' and indicate where action to secure access was proposed. It was left to the councils to decide what action was needed, but they were obliged to bear in mind the amount of access which would exist without action being taken and the degree of need for greater access in their area both for residents and for people from outside. Any member of the public could make representations about the review map and its accompanying statement. Where an objector and the county council involved could not resolve their differences, the Minister of Housing and Local Government had to hold a public inquiry.

Finally, the Minister could direct a council to take action to secure access or make an access order himself if a council failed to do what he thought was necessary.

Despite pressure from Yorkshire rambling interests for far greater access to the county's moors, particularly those which lie between the thickly populated industrial towns, the West Riding County Council's initial reaction to the requirement for a review map was to tell the Minister that, in its view, no action was needed to secure access agreements anywhere in the county. Landowners that had been approached by the Council about access to four main areas of moorland – one of them Barden Moor and Barden Fell – had said they would not enter into access agreements but would accept new footpaths. Though the Council considered this a satisfactory compromise, the ramblers continued to protest. A public inquiry into access needs in the county was held in 1955. The inquiry inspector concluded that access agreements should be sought over five areas, one of them being Barden Moor and Barden Fell. His recommendation was upheld by the Minister in 1957.

However, the Minister's decision had little impact on the ground: the Council stuck to its policy of footpath access only. It took an election in the West Riding which changed the political complexion of the Council together with the appointment of a new county planning officer to bring about progress. And in 1960, the first access agreement in the West Riding opened up 2,700 acres of Barden Moor and Barden Fell. A second agreement, eight years later, extended the area in three stages to give public access to nearly 14,000 acres in all by 1974.

Despite the existence of agreements at Barden Moor and Barden Fell and several other locations, there were in 1984 still at least 300,000 acres of moorland fell within the old West Riding county area where walkers could be ordered off unless on a right of way.[3] And, unlike rights of way, access agreements do not guarantee a right to walk in perpetuity. They can be freely terminated by either party whenever they come up for renegotiation.

One hundred and eighty miles south of the moors of Yorkshire, amid the wide, flat cornfields of south Oxfordshire rise two hills that are also the subject of an access agreement. One hundred and thirty acres of the little-known Sinodun Hills, which stand about three miles from both Didcot and Wallingford and nine miles south of Oxford, are now available for the public to wander over at all times. Like Barden Moor and Barden Fell, these southern hills are not devoted exclusively to recreation. Over the more extensive twin hump, Wittenham Clumps, cows graze the fertilized pasture that covers the whole area apart from a small clump of trees at the summit. On the more compact Castle Hill, the public can roam over the rough grassland that covers the ramparts and in the beech wood on the summit of this prehistoric hill-fort. The previous owner, the Hedges family, had allowed de facto access to the Hills, and was willing to enter into more formal access arrangements with the old Berkshire County Council. The access agreement, signed in 1970, allowed the public access at all times for open-air recreation to the two hills while providing for the County Council to lease land at a small charge for the provision of parking and lavatories. On local government reorganization in 1974, the area moved into Oxfordshire whose county council took over the agreement. Ten years later, the Northmoor Trust, a private charity devoted to conservation and environmental education, bought the land and it reaffirmed the agreement in 1985.

Stand on the summit of Wittenham Clumps and look northwards across the lush wide valley of the River Thames to the woods and fields of central and northern Oxfordshire beyond. You could be forgiven for assuming that your feet could take you not only down this gentle grassy slope but also over the whole of the Oxfordshire countryside laid out before you. You would however be wrong. Like Barden Moor and Barden Fell in Yorkshire, the Sinodun Hills are exceptional in Oxfordshire: they comprise the only access agreement site in the whole of the county (total area 1,006 square miles). In fact, in Oxfordshire there are only a handful of other sites at which the public have any right to be in the countryside at all, other than on public footpaths. In 1985, these consisted of the Giant's Cave Picnic Site near Banbury (area: seven acres), Adderbury Picnic Site near Banbury (two acres), Mapledurham Country Park (twenty-five acres of meadow on the banks of the Thames), and the 309-acre Shotover Country Park, a mosaic of woodland and acid grassland to the east of Oxford. Public access exists to a few other sites, notably the 300-acre Port Meadow on the western edge of Oxford which is also common land, the Forestry Commission's Cowleaze Wood and several other woods and commons in the Chilterns in the far south of the county and, by invitation, to 1,500 acres of the Duke of Marlborough's Blenheim Park. Outside these sites lie tens of thousands of acres of attractive landscape that fit the definition of 'open country' yet which may not be looked upon, let alone walked over. As we have seen (page 281), only 0.4 per cent of Oxfordshire's woodland was freely open to the public in 1974, and there has been no significant change since then. The woods and parklands of rural Oxfordshire have taken on a new importance as this is one of the many counties in which the post-war agricultural revolution has made farmland less and less attractive to the walker. Yet it is through the agricultural, intensively cultivated land that most of Oxfordshire's public footpaths run. There is therefore an urgent need for the land that is not cultivated to be opened up.

Yorkshire and Oxfordshire are not untypical. The fact is that the access agreement as laid out in 1949 has not opened up rural Britain because it has been applied only rarely. It has to be judged a practical failure – the victim of landowners' desire for privacy and local councils' failure to use the powers available to them.

By April 1973, access had been secured through the 1949 Act over only 136 square miles of England and Wales, or 0.2 per cent of the land surface, according to a survey by researchers at Newcastle University.[4] The situation has not changed significantly since then. Why have the local authorities which have had the access powers been so reluctant to use them?

A number of factors seem to have played a part. One is the vulnerability to local pressures of the planning authorities charged with the task of prising the countryside from the grip of its owners. Recreation is a need that spans local council boundaries: above all it embraces cities as well as the countryside. However, the rural authorities charged with implementing the access provisions were frequently reluctant to take note of the needs of the millions outside their areas as well as their own constituents. And, especially before local government reorganization in 1974, they were often dominated by the very landowning class that the access provisions required them to confront.

It is significant that by far the most active user of the Part V powers has been the one rural planning authority with more independence from local interests than any other – the Peak Park Special Planning Board.

In 1951, the Peak District became the first area of Britain to receive the accolade of national park designation. The creation of national parks was a product of the same 1949 Act that introduced the access agreements. The prime objectives which the 1949 legislators had laid down for national parks were the preservation and enhancement of natural beauty and the promotion of their enjoyment by the public. To further these objectives they had proposed the establishment of special planning boards to run the parks, boards which would exist outside the normal machinery of local government. The Peak Park Special Planning Board was the first such board to be set up and embodies the procedure envisaged by the 1949 Parliament more directly than any other body handling any other park. One third of the members of the Peak Park Special Planning Board were drawn not from local councils in the area but were nominated by the Government to ensure that the national conservation and access interests were properly brought to the fore. To establish its independence from local government, the Peak Board was given its own power to impose a precept upon the rates of surrounding local councils; it is also the only park authority to have its own staff separate from that of local authorities. When it came to access, the Peak Board's officers were not shy about approaching even those landowners who had most vehemently opposed the idea in the past. By 1954, the Peak Board had completed its survey of open country (one of several tasks it took over from the local authorities), and drawn up access agreements over more than 9,000 acres. A survey in 1973 revealed that, twenty years later, access had been secured mainly through agreement but also through land acquisition to seventy-six square miles of open country in the Peak Park, and that this accounted for 56 per cent of the 136 square miles of England and Wales covered by the Part V provisions by 1973.[5]

A few other planning authorities have made some use of the Part V powers, notably the Lake District Special Planning Board, the Exmoor National Park Authority, and Surrey, Lancashire, Hampshire, and Staffordshire County Councils. Elsewhere, planning authorities have, in the main, chosen to avoid confronting landowners in their areas, often the most influential local citizens, over public access.

The inertia of the local authorities was compounded by the difference in most cases between their political colours and those of the often noisily socialist campaigners for access. Dr Judith Rossiter of Cambridge University, who has carried out a study of the operation of the access legislation in England and Wales between 1949 and 1968, put it like this:

It must be regretted that much of the responsibility for seeking public access to private land was passed to an amenity group with a distinct political image, as this inevitably reduced the support their proposals might receive both from the traditionally Conservative landowners and county councils which were, immediately after the passing of the Act of 1949, predominantly Conservative.[6]

There is no doubt that conservatism with a small 'c' also played a part in inhibiting moves to provide access. To the planning authorities of the 1950s and '60s, the access agreement and access order were entirely novel concepts. At that time, their main function – development control – was essentially negative. They had not been required to go out and impose their own view of the shape the environment should take. The proposals to open up the countryside by access agreements and access orders, based as they were on an implicitly prescriptive approach, were a far more radical innovation than urban development control or the mapping of public rights of way. More advice from central government on how the access provisions could be made to work might have helped. The provision of model clauses for access agreements or advice on the financial implications of securing access might have resulted in more agreements. It was not until 1970, twenty-one years after the passing of the 1949 Act, that the Countryside Commission came up with such model clauses. Indeed, central government probably bears at least as much responsibility as the local planning authorities for the lack of use of the Part V powers.

Because the 1949 legislators knew that some councils might drag their feet, they did provide for central government intervention at more than one point. The first and most important point was provided by a compulsory central government assessment of councils' review maps of open country and their proposals for securing access to it. On receipt of a local council's review map and access proposals, the Minister could direct that further action should be taken. Yet Ministers declined to take this opportunity in almost every case. Thirty-eight councils in England and all those in Wales responded to their access obligations by informing the Minister in the early 1950s that they considered no action necessary (thirty-one cases) or that they considered they had no open country (seven cases). In only one case did the Minister direct that further action should be taken – that of the West Riding County Council.

The most significant event in determining central government's attitude to the access legislation and in particular to the review maps seems to have been the change of government in 1951. Attlee's team which had forged the social contract for the countryside was replaced by the government of Winston Churchill, heralding thirteen years of unbroken Conservative rule. Many members of Churchill's Cabinet were landowners, and if the other members did not actually own land themselves, many had close links with the landowning class – like Harold Macmillan. As Minister of Housing and Local Government between 1951 and 1954, Macmillan was responsible for vetting the vast majority of review maps and access proposals that came in. He had married into the family of the Duke of Devonshire and was a frequent visitor as a sportsman to the then inaccessible grouse moors of Barden Moor and Barden Fell. Macmillan was known to have strong feelings about the demands for access over Barden Moor and Barden Fell, and Dr Rossiter observes that he described them as 'outrageous' in a ministerial minute dated 1957.[7] There is no need to suppose that Macmillan abused his position to promote the interests of his family and friends: it is simply that his associations would inevitably have influenced his attitude to what was right and proper.

When county councils began sending in their review maps and access proposals during 1952 and 1953, the Government simply declined to pull up those which were falling short of the mark which the 1949 legislators had in mind. In demonstrating the government's expectations of local authorities, the case of Devon County Council was specially significant. Here, the County Council had notified the Minister that, in its view, no action whatsoever was necessary to secure access agreements to open country in the county. After a public inquiry in 1957, the Minister supported the County Council's decision, despite the incontrovertible fact that areas of moorland, designated without dispute as open country, were enclosed by barbed wire and padlocked gates. If Ministers were not going to insist on action in Devon – a county then with a large amount of open country and containing the whole or part of two national parks – they could hardly be expected to concern themselves with the lack of action in more ordinary counties. Not surprisingly therefore, according to Dr Rossiter: 'For many authorities, the consideration of access agreements ceased after publication of their notice that no action was necessary.'[8]

In 1969, however, it did seem as if the Part V powers might at last come into their own. One year after the passing of their Countryside Act, the 1966–70 Labour Government announced a new review of potential access land. They pointed out that their 1968 Act had greatly widened the definition of open country (to woodland and waterside), and that the demand for access had greatly increased since the reviews of the early 1950s. Unfortunately, however, the Conservative Government that came to power in 1970 quickly countermanded this review. No new review has been announced since 1969 and county councils are currently under no obligation to discover what areas are suitable for access agreements or to draw up proposals for action.

The consequences of the failure of the 1949 rural access arrangements go beyond the continuing inadequacy of the provision of access for recreation. The lack of guaranteed public access has helped to ensure that much of rural Britain has taken on a character which would make free wandering impracticable even if it were permitted. The 'open country' which the legislators identified in 1949 is now fast disappearing in a way that would have been much less complete if it had been formally-agreed 'access land'.

Thirty-one thousand acres or two-thirds of the heathland of Dorset, immortalized by Hardy as Egdon Heath and offering freedom to wander were converted by their owners to more profitable uses in the fifty years up to 1983.[9] Exmoor and Dartmoor have seen substantial losses of open country but outside these two national parks 69,000 acres of Devonshire's rough grass, heath and gorse lands have been turned over to intensive agriculture in this century.[10] The recreation opportunities for the people of the Cotswolds have been drastically reduced by the ploughing of rough grassland: only 4 per cent of the county's flower-spangled natural turf remains – the rest has been destroyed mainly to make way for barley prairies and ryegrass lots.[11] To all these areas and many more some access had been available on a de facto basis. But once they have been enclosed, fenced and converted to intensive agricultural land or to conifer plantation the point of wandering across them disappears with the opportunity. Had these areas been established as recreation lands by right they could not have been sacrificed so readily.

The Use of the Access Powers in Scotland and Northern Ireland

When the Part V access legislation was extended to Scotland in 1967, the requirement on local planning authorities to draw up review maps of open country and to assess access needs strategically was left out – just as the requirement for the preparation of definitive rights of way had been. Scottish local planning authorities were merely empowered to secure access agreements or orders or to buy land for access if they so wished.

The result is that very few area-wide access agreements of the Barden-Moor type have ever been signed in Scotland. In the early 1970s, when the legislation was just becoming known, two landowners were in serious discussion with Inverness County Council over possible agreements (Lord Burton of Dochfour, for an agreement at Glen Quoich, and Lt-Col. J. P. Grant for an agreement over 6,500 acres at Rothiemurchus in the northern

Cairngorms). However, ramblers' groups opposed these proposed agreements on the grounds that certain clauses in the
agreements, in particular those barring access during the stalking
season and restricting access to limited routes, would have
increased legal restraint on walkers in areas in which they had
traditionally enjoyed a large measure of de facto free access, and
the agreements were never signed. Since then, access agreements
have been made only very occasionally. By 1985, the single
largest area covered by access agreements in Scotland was almost
certainly the 2,105 acres of Glen Nevis which was subject to two
agreements secured by Highland Regional Council. But Stirling
District Council is probably the planning authority in Scotland
with the largest number of access agreements; as in the case of
Highland Region, action has depended on the enthusiasm of a
small number of planning officials. By 1985, Stirling District
Council was party to fifteen access agreements, many covering
less than twenty acres, with a total extent of 546 acres. Some
involve land to which de facto access already existed; others
land where walkers were not welcomed. Stirling District has
maintained a strong countryside ranger service which, among
other things, leads guided walks, and chief planning officer
Maurice Dobson explained to me in 1985: 'It does help if you're
running, say, a ranger service if there are areas where the ranger
knows he can go and he's there by right, with the knowledge of
the owner, and that he's not going to be challenged – which is
perhaps embarrassing if he's got a group of twenty people in tow
explaining to them the beauties of the countryside.' Why had
access agreements been chosen as a means of legalizing access?
'It did strike us as a fairly reasonable way in which the District
Council could get public access to the land without having to
commit themselves to large capital expenditures on acquiring
land. And it was also an area that was attractive to the
landowners because they in turn didn't lose control of their
own land, but were eased of the problems of dealing with the
public.'[12] In Scotland as a whole, very, very few other access
agreements have been made apart from those in Highland
Region and Stirling District.

The model of Scotland's access powers was extended to
Northern Ireland in the Access to the Countryside (Northern

Ireland) Order, 1983. As this involves no legal requirement to assess access needs or map 'open country' over which access agreements might be made, use of the powers in the Province looks likely to be just as haphazard, infrequent and opportunistic as it has been in Scotland. As the benefits provided by the Common Agricultural Policy continue to encourage farmers to bring land into cultivation thereby eroding 'open country' from the Mournes to the Sperrins, the failure to deploy access powers in Northern Ireland could well be seen, thirty years hence, as a missed opportunity in the same way as it is now seen to have been over the downs, heaths and moors of England and Wales.

Country Parks and Picnic Sites

The first Wilson Government wanted access to be extended over beautiful, inaccessible areas. To this end, it widened the definition of 'open country' to embrace woodland, lakeside, canalside and riverbank and extended the powers to make access agreements and orders to Scotland. But it also introduced two entirely new tools to the recreation planner's kit. As it turned out, these two new schemes were to be taken up by many more local planning authorities than the access agreement powers. The Countryside Act of 1968, which included the new provisions, reflected a revolution in the thinking of recreation planners. Whereas the policy-makers of 1949 had sought to give every man, woman and child relatively general access to all the countryside, the planners of the late 1960s were actively opposed to indiscriminate public access. They were preoccupied less with helping people enjoy the countryside than with protecting it from dangers – one of which was seen as the trampling feet of city-dwellers.

The idea that urban visitors posed a threat to the countryside had surfaced in the mid-1960s. Anxiety about the environment quickly became intense as a few catastrophes brought it home to everyone that the Earth's resources were finite. Too many people appeared to be trying to exploit too few resources. There was much talk of population control; and it seemed natural enough in such a climate to class 'recreation pressure' as one more ill from which the countryside needed to be safeguarded.

An influential report of the period by architect and planner Michael Dower advised planners to 'see people like ants, scurrying from coast to coast, on holiday, swarming out of cities in July and August by car, coach, train and aeroplane to a multitude of resorts and hidden places throughout the isles of Britain.'[13] To handle this sinister menace, Dower proposed a new approach to rural recreation planning. In his own words, instead of spreading 'a thin layer of gambolling humanity across the whole island', people were to be herded into small areas of little scenic or wildlife value where they could not do much harm. Maintaining the view of the citizenry as insects, albeit with a change of species, the planners came to term these places 'honeypots'. A similar view of visitors to the countryside as a plague of noxious, greedy insects which needed to be carefully contained lay behind the other new rural recreation concept of the 1968 Act – picnic sites.

By the mid-1970s it was clear that the simple equation of numbers of visitors with pressure on the countryside was mistaken. Experience in other fields of environmental concern, such as whale protection, had shown that it was not the size of the potential demand for a resource that mattered but the way in which that resource was actually exploited. In any case, the projections of demand for rural recreation which caused so much alarm in the mid-1960s soon turned out to be fallacious. The population scare gave way to anxiety about a baby famine as births per head fell in the late 1960s. And car ownership projections based on the assumption of endless growth looked much less convincing once the recession of 1973 had begun to bite. However, these new realities did not bring about a change in the planning attitudes embodied in the 1968 Act. Country parks and picnic sites sprang up all over Britain, particularly near towns and on main routes while the 1949 access powers remained virtually unused.

'Country parks' are, as the term implies, essentially parks in the countryside. Unlike access agreements, which secure the co-existence of recreation and other established uses, recreation provision in a country park usually dominates and often excludes other uses. The 1968 Act empowered the Countryside Commission to give 75 per cent grant to local authorities to help finance the establishment of country parks. To be recognized by the Commission, a country park must have parking facilities, lavatories and a wardening service. The Act specified that the grant could cover the acquisition of land as well as the erection of buildings, the collection of litter and the provision of wardens. As a result, country parks are usually owned by a local authority – another difference from the concept of the access agreement. Country parks can, however, remain in private ownership: in this case the owner receives the same entitlement to 75 per cent grant-aid to help him provide visitor facilities. At the attractive 230-acre Fritton Lake Country Park outside Great Yarmouth, on part of the estate of the 3rd Baron Somerleyton, visitors can take advantage of woodland and garden walks, go boating, and let their children run loose in the adventure play area as well as using the shop, tea-room, information centre, lavatories and car-parking provided. Some of the best-known local-authority-owned country parks include Lyme Park near Stockport, Frensham Common in Surrey and Dunstable Downs in Bedfordshire.

The parks do not however normally enshrine stretches of the most attractive countryside, nor were they intended to. Instead, as the then Ministry of Housing and Local Government advised in 1968: 'The parks should be in country surroundings, not necessarily beauty spots, where people can go to relax and enjoy themselves. They are primarily intended to meet the demand resulting from the increased leisure and mobility of large numbers of the population living in cities and urban areas and looking for a change of environment within easy reach.'[14]

The other new tool introduced in 1968, the picnic site, is essentially a miniature version of the country park. Some of them run to about twenty-five acres in size, while others are essentially glorified lay-bys, used as a stopping point for motorists and holiday-makers on a long journey and often combined with other services for which the motorist breaks his journey like lavatories, filling stations and cafés. It was the Government's intention that picnic sites should be located on similar principles to those proposed for country parks.

By March 1986, local authorities in England and Wales had established 177 country parks and 217 picnic sites. Private individuals and organizations had created an additional twenty-nine country parks and twenty-three picnic sites.

In locating country parks and picnic sites, councils have followed the advice of the Government, normally coming through the Countryside Commission, fairly closely. Today, rings of country parks all but encircle London, Birmingham, Leeds, Manchester and Liverpool, and Newcastle and Sunderland, while Scotland's thirty-four country parks are concentrated in the central industrial belt, with a scatter of parks behind Dundee and Aberdeen. In remote rural areas, on the other hand, country parks are very scarce. Take the South West Peninsula, for example. By 1986, there were only six local-council country parks in the whole of the South West (one each in Devon and Somerset; two each in Cornwall and Dorset). Of the twenty-three country parks in Wales, to take another example of an area where the importance of tourism might be expected to spur councils to action, the vast majority are clustered behind Newport, Swansea and Cardiff or on the south-western fringes of Merseyside. Dyfed, whose 2,225 square miles make it Wales's largest county, had only four country parks by March 1986 and Powys, which runs the length of mid-Wales, only one. Anglesey had no country parks whatsoever.

The motorist heading out of population centres will nowadays encounter signs pointing to country parks and picnic sites rather frequently. But the extent to which these parks and sites increase the availability of the countryside to the population as a whole is very limited. The majority of country parks are on land to which the public already had access. Of the seven country parks that had been established in the West Midlands by 1972, for example, five are on land that was already open to the public.[15]

Where the land was not previously open to the public this is often because it was a mineral working. Mineral operators have taken advantage of the generous grants to provide visitor facilities on disused workings. It is doubtless desirable that land which might otherwise have lain derelict should be put to some use. But few would claim that disused quarries and pits constitute Britain's most prepossessing landscape.

Country parks and picnic sites do, of course, fulfil a valuable function in reducing the risk to remote and solitary places by easing visitor pressure upon them and in providing recreation facilities close to towns. But if we are to begin to use our countryside to its best advantage, country parks and picnic sites need to be complemented by a host of other measures. Local authorities must open up countryside of the highest quality as well as providing playgrounds in drabber, if more convenient, places.

The country parks of Scotland and Northern Ireland are slightly different from those in the rest of the United Kingdom in that a larger proportion of them embrace really attractive land. Culzean, the grounds of a stately home on the Ayrshire coast, was the first country park to be established in Scotland, and it has set a pattern followed by many others north of the border. In this case, the country park designation enabled the owner, the National Trust for Scotland, to attract government money to help pay for the upkeep and management of the estate. Although relatively remote from population centres (Culzean is twenty miles down the coast from Ayr, the nearest town of any size), the country park's 560 acres of woodland and park, together with a visitors' centre, adventure playground, forestry exhibition and swan pond are heavily used. In the same way as at Culzean, country park designation has been used elsewhere in Scotland on several occasions by the National Trust for Scotland or local authorities as a mechanism for attracting finance from the Countryside Commission for Scotland to conserve an old estate core that is a major heritage resource. However, for a country the size of Scotland with so few access agreements, the number of country parks is not that high: by November 1986 there were thirty-four. Though Northern Ireland's country parks often consist of land as attractive as that in the Scottish parks, they too are few in number. By January 1987 there were only seven in the Province, all managed not by local authorities as in the rest of the UK but by the Department of the Environment based at Stormont.

Why did the 1968 provisions catch on when the 1949 provisions – which could have done so much more to open the land to the people – did not? There are several reasons. As we have seen in England and Wales, the membership of many rural councils is dominated by landowners. These people saw in the

1968 Act a means of appearing to satisfy the public need for rural recreation in a way that did not threaten their own interests anything like as much as the 1949 proposals. And the professional staff of the authorities had their own reasons for willingly putting their political masters' wishes into effect. Providing country parks and picnic sites fitted much more easily into local authority activity than would have the negotiation of access agreements with private landlords. Council recreation departments which had been busily providing swimming pools as a publicly-owned and maintained recreation resource in the 1950s and 1960s, switched happily into providing country parks and picnic sites in the 1970s on a similar basis. The whole operation could be comfortably controlled by bureaucrats who had no desire to forge a new deal between landowners and landless by negotiating endless access agreements. The fact that they were able to get away with the approach they adopted reflects the thoroughness with which the grip of the landowning classes on the countryside had come to be accepted in the post-war era. The brief environmental panic of the 1960s was all that it took to blow away what remained of the spirit of Kinder Scout and the ideas it had spawned in the 1949 Act. Indeed, the setting up of country parks and picnic sites in the countryside as miniature Red-Indian reservations for the urban underclass marked a moment when the hegemony of the landowner was as complete as it had ever been. Certainly, the landowners themselves had few complaints about the direction which public policy was taking.

The idea of invading townspeople being decoyed into country parks and picnic sites before they got as far as the real countryside suited landowners very well. After half a century of full democracy, they found themselves still able to enjoy their often vast territories safe in the knowledge that people who might otherwise have sought to disturb them were safely controlled miles away in some reclaimed gravel pit. Some of them even felt they could strengthen their claim to a right to exclude their fellow-citizens from their land by setting up a country park or a picnic site on a small part of it. In *Humberts Commentary* (published by a firm of chartered surveyors), the Earl of March and Kinrara, who, with his father the 9th Duke of Richmond owns the 12,000-acre

Goodwood Estate in West Sussex, had a tip for fellow landowners:

We deliberately created a Country Park under the Countryside Act on 60 acres of poor-quality land on the top of the Downs. It is an open area where people can park their cars, play games with their children, eat a picnic and exercise their dogs. There is no charge for admission, but it gives us the opportunity to say: 'You can't go there, but you can go to the Country Park.'[16]

For the mass of the people, however, the rural planning attitudes which took root in the late 1960s have constituted a betrayal of the ideals of 1949. Indeed, the idea that the country-side should be opened up has been stood on its head as planners have sought to cage visitors in carefully confined locations.

While all this was going on, there was one institution that might have been expected to push for the public interest. This is the Countryside Commission, which Parliament created in 1968 by enlarging and widening the powers of the National Parks Commission set up in 1949. The Countryside Commission was required to keep under review three things: the conservation and enhancement of the natural beauty of the countryside of England and Wales; the provision and improvement of facilities for the enjoyment of the countryside; and 'the need to secure public access to the countryside for the purposes of open-air recreation'. Yet as far as this last was concerned, the Commission turned out to be a watchdog which did not bark. It is certainly true that in 1970 the Commission published a set of model clauses for access agreements it had taken several years to prepare. But by 1973, when the statement *Countryside Commission: Guidelines for Priorities in Work* was published, it contained no reference whatsoever to the need to secure access to open country.

The Countryside Commission is prepared on occasion to call for greater access to the countryside but not to do anything to secure it that might upset landowners too much. 'There should be – and could be – more public access to the countryside,' the Commission declared in a press notice in January 1984, while in 1986 the Commission launched a public debate on the future of countryside recreation provision. Sir Derek Barber, chairman of the Commission since 1981, certainly accepts that there is much

inaccessible land in lowland England, for example. But he is not
prepared to take radical action to open it up. His reasons are
political. In an interview in 1982 he told me: 'What we need is
better maintenance of and better signposting of the existing
footpath system. I wouldn't want to go much beyond that as a
first step. The existing internal footpath system is adequate.' He
told me that he believed there was a distinct problem of over-use
of some parts of the country and I asked him what solution he
would propose for the over-use and subsequent erosion of parts
of the Cornish coast like Land's End. He told me he would like
to encourage people to go to the parts of Bodmin Moor and
Dartmoor which are little used. 'What about opening up all
those woodlands and river-banks in Cornwall itself which are
inaccessible?' I suggested. He told me; 'I don't at this stage of
the game think this should be done for practical political reasons.
This is something farmers and landowners are fairly nervous
about. Now these people are more interested in conservation
than they have been for fifty years, and to raise access problems
in the same way as conservation problems are being raised
might lose us the good will of landowners . . . Efforts to this end
now would be counter-productive in conservation terms.'

In sacrificing the opening up of the countryside in the interests
of conservation, Derek Barber was very much in step with the
conventional wisdom of 1968.

Decline into Opportunism

Though country parks and picnic sites mushroomed in the 1970s,
their growth did not last into the 1980s. After 1980, there was far
less money around for marginal local authority endeavour of any
kind. And the need to acquire land made country parks and
picnic sites a particularly expensive proposition – certainly they
cost far more than access agreements would have done. So
have hard-up councils now switched to the pursuit of access
agreements over ready-made recreation areas – the glorious
countryside that remains in private hands?

They have not. Far from a switch towards the ideals of 1949,
there has instead been a decline into opportunism. Time and
again in the early 1980s planning officials told me they were now

'responding to opportunities'. If a landowner approached them with suggestions for new facilities, they would respond, but they were not taking the initiative. When, for instance, I asked Cheshire County Council planners in an interview in 1982 whether they were seeking greater public access over two of the county's loveliest yet most inaccessible stretches of rural land – the Combermere estate in the south-west of the county (which includes Cheshire's largest lake) and the Cholmondeley Castle estate near Malpas – they told me they thought if they did so they would receive 'a dusty answer'. They explained it was part of the Council's philosophy to secure facilities by agreement: they did not want to push too hard and create animosity and bad feeling on the part of landowners.

As the push for country parks and picnic sites has run out of steam, many councils are left with no strategic plan for rural recreation provision. One Cheshire County Council official told me: 'There are no official policy documents: the department responds to opportunities'.

This approach leads to very few major advances on public access. The opportunities to be responded to are opportunities to enter a negotiation in which give-and-take is expected. This approach cannot solve the biggest access problem – opening up large inaccessible estates. Where there are no existing footpaths to trade, councils have nothing to offer landowners keen to preserve their seclusion. So much of the best countryside remains a closed book. As one family from Nantwich told me:

The main problem with living in Cheshire is the lack of open space. The countryside is out of bounds. It's beautiful countryside, but you can't get into it. There just isn't countryside that's open to the public. You can go in Delamere Forest in the north [owned by the Forestry Commission] or the National Trust's Beeston Castle. But there's nowhere else. And as you go along the roads you see very few public footpath signs.

Just occasionally the prospect of a major gain for public access looms enticingly into view. In Northamptonshire, to take a not untypical example, there has been just one occasion since 1949 when the county council has come somewhere near breaking the landowners' stranglehold over that county's prize countryside. This is what happened.

Early in 1975, the 7th Earl Spencer, grandfather of the Princess of Wales and the then owner of the large Althorp Estate, asked Northamptonshire County Council if it would be interested in some kind of partnership arrangement whereby provision for recreation would be made over 300 acres of heath and conifer woodland on the edge of the estate known as Harlestone Firs and Dallington Heath. Although this site is essentially a conifer plantation, it is fairly attractive: several different conifer species grow here; there is a wide variety of birds including three species of woodpecker; and heath bedstraw, wavy hair-grass and other little heathland plants still flourish in the rides. Earl Spencer had traditionally permitted de facto access to the Firs, which are also well served by public rights of way including bridleways, a relatively scarce phenomenon in the county as a whole. By 1975, the Firs was a popular weekend haunt of Northamptonshire people, but the lack of regulation of this use worried Earl Spencer's land agent, particularly as far as parking was concerned.

The plan was variously described as an access agreement and a country park. What it involved was Earl Spencer agreeing to allow the public to wander at will over the entire 300 acres. At the same time the existing forestry operations would continue. The County Council would manage the visitors, providing separate trails for riders and walkers, lavatories, and most important of all a car-park, since such parking as occurred was haphazard and along the main Northampton to Rugby highway. The County Council would also provide a warden to iron out any difficulties over the use of the site and to explain to people the wildlife of the site and its management as a working wood.

In Northamptonshire as in Cheshire the public is effectively barred from most of the countryside by the character of agriculture. Yet where there are large tracts of untilled park and woodland they almost always lie outside the reach of the public.

Northamptonshire County Council was delighted by the Earl's offer. In the past the Council had found difficulty in acquiring sites for public open-air recreation and they had high hopes that Earl Spencer's example would encourage other landowners to move in the same direction. In addition, Harlestone Firs would become the county's largest country park, and, in view of its location, would at last provide a valuable resource for the non-motoring public. The Council heralded the arrangement in a press statement as 'a major breakthrough'. The landowner too seemed pleased: 'I am most grateful to the County Council for backing me over this project which I am determined to see through to a successful and rewarding conclusion', he told the *Northampton Chronicle and Echo*.[17]

But only a few months later, the 7th Earl was dead. His heir, the 8th Earl Spencer, decided not to proceed with the scheme. By the end of 1976, it had been abandoned.

Today, the people of Northampton are still allowed to wander over the Heaths on a de facto access basis. But they do so at their own risk. The absence of any special provision for visitors means that parking still takes place as it did in 1975: along the verge of the busy Northampton to Rugby main road. Parking, as well as crossing the road with children and dogs, can be a dangerous business. As Alan Teulon, the County Council leisure and libraries officer told me in 1984, the parking situation at the site was and still is complete chaos: 'There is no parking at the Heaths, no lavatories and no facilities at all in the general sense of visitor provision.'

I asked the Northamptonshire County Council official responsible for rural recreation provision, Howard Rose, why he did not seek to open up the county's attractive but inaccessible lands by trying to secure access agreements. He replied, 'To be honest, I suppose what you are suggesting has never really been seriously considered, maybe because at the back of our mind we know that there is a strong sort of land ownership lobby in the county.' Yet he and his colleagues are very worried about the lack of facilities: 'All we know is that our country parks get an awful lot of visitors, they're bursting and we could do with some more.' In the absence of what it considered in 1982 any prospect of access agreements over extensive, spectacular private countryside like that of Castle Ashby, Rockingham Outer Park, Althorp Park or Boughton Park and woods to name but a few places, Northamptonshire County Council, like other local authorities relying on responding to opportunities finds itself resorting to the

costly business of buying worked-out quarries and adapting them
for recreation. The only two country parks so far established by
Northamptonshire County Council are both on the sites of
disused mineral workings. Mr Rose's major project at the time
he talked to me in 1982 was seeking some recreational after-use
from the areas of the Nene Valley then being worked for sand
and gravel.

If major new access areas are not being created, this does not
mean that things are standing still. De facto access lands continue
to be lost. And there is nothing to stop a landowner withdrawing
from one of the small number of access agreements that have
been made if he so desires.

The Newlands Corner, Silent Pool and St Martha's Hill
access agreements, for instance, provide some of Surrey's most
important open spaces. In each case, access is guaranteed
through an access agreement between the trustees of the 10th
Duke of Northumberland (the sites lie on his Albury estate) and
Surrey County Council. When I spoke to him in 1986, the
agent for the estate, John Evans-Freke, was actively considering
withdrawing the estate from the agreements over Newlands
Corner and St Martha's Hill. The reasons Mr Evans-Freke gave
me were not that the public was inflicting damage on these sites
but that the County Council was not maintaining them properly.
He complained that bushes were being allowed to encroach on
the downland turf at Newlands Corner and that unsuitable
fencing had been put up and saplings had been badly sited on St
Martha's Hill. At the same time, the erection of standard 'Surrey
County Council Open Space' signs was giving the public the
wrong idea of by whose grace they could enjoy this countryside.
The future of the agreements was in question in 1986.

Access by Permission Only

At present, the only circumstance in which full access will occur
is in the event of a benevolent landowner volunteering to open
up his prized domain. Given the characteristic attitudes of the
landowning class, there are not many such benevolent people.
But there are one or two. And what they have done gives us a
tantalizing hint of what real rural access might mean.

In 1982, the 4th Baron Melchett voluntarily dedicated as new public rights of way a network of routes which he considers offers the best views and most interesting walks on his land. These new public footpaths, which are well-signposted, run for a total of five miles through the woods and along the field edges of Lord Melchett's 750-acre arable and beef farm in north Norfolk. He explained to me the reasons for opting for rights of way rather than permissive paths:

We did it as rights of way because I think it's important that people should have a right to be somewhere in the countryside and that they should feel they have a right to be there and that they should feel that that bit of countryside is as much theirs as anybody else's. I wanted to emphasize the fact that anybody has the right to use these paths whenever they want to. That was the main reason. The secondary one was I wanted the paths to be permanent: permissive paths come and go. The third reason was it's not just the right to walk down a public right of way: there is the right to take a dog, a bicycle for the kids and those sorts of things, and I see our walks as things that different people will enjoy for lots of different reasons.

In 1986 I asked the Ramblers' Association head office for details of other cases in which landowners have voluntarily granted a network of new rights of way over their land during the preceding six years. Lord Melchett's Courtyard Farm was the only case of which they were aware. So the goodwill of landowners is not something by which we may set much store in the absence of sufficiently vigorous legislation and adequate effort on the part of local authorities.

Coupled with the trend of local councils simply responding to opportunities from landowners rather than actively seeking access over the best stretches of Britain's countryside is another alarming trend. This is that increasingly there are signs that local authorities are coming to see access as something to be taken up when a landowner appears willing to give it and on his terms rather than something to be secured with a firm legal basis where people's needs require it.

Two cases from the early 1980s indicative of this new attitude are that of the Arans in the mountains of north Wales and that of Wychwood Forest in north Oxfordshire.

Approach the Snowdonia National Park from the south-east

and, as you drive along the road from Welshpool, the first mountain range to greet you is the great north-south backbone of the Arans. It embraces two main peaks, Aran Benllyn and Aran Fawddwy, each marked by a prehistoric cairn and sheltering a lake-filled corrie, while from the upper slopes of the ridge twenty rivers radiate out in every direction. This four-and-a-half-mile wild, rocky spine (the highest massif in Britain south of Snowdon) provides one of the most exhilarating and challenging walks in Snowdonia with magnificent views over Bala, Coed-y-Brenin and the Dovey Forest as well as the rest of the southern part of the national park.

But there are no public footpaths or bridleways to the two Aran peaks or along the ridge itself. The definitive rights of way map covering Snowdonia, drawn up in the 1950s, recorded the old-established footpath and bridleway routes which were mainly those used by the local population to go about their daily business. These routes made great use of the low passes over the mountains but avoided the heights. As a result it is the routes across the passes, together with some old quarry routes that make up the majority of public footpaths in the mountains of Snowdonia today: there are very few rights of way up the mountains. The exceptions are Snowdon itself and Cader Idris: these have always been the most famous summits and had for years before the definitive map was drawn up been visited by visitors on ponies (hence the bridleway status of several of these rights of way). There are no rights of way to the summits of either the Carnedd mountains or the Glyders, for instance, and people wishing to climb these are guaranteed access only along the paths across the passes connecting the valleys. Fortunately for walkers, in the absence of grouse shooting and the presence of a large amount of untilled land of open character, landowners have tolerated de facto access over large areas on which the public have no legal right to walk.

The absence of any legal right of access to the Arans did, however, mean that its owners were perfectly entitled to turn people off their land if they so wished. In April 1978, they prevented a party of Merseyside ramblers from climbing the ridge and thenceforth made it clear in the local press and at meetings with staff from local outdoor pursuits centres that walkers were not welcome on the Arans. For four years there was an effective ban on access to the Arans until in 1982 the Snowdonia National Park Authority (charged as it is with a legal duty to promote recreational uses of the national park) finally secured a compromise arrangement with the Arans farmers. During the negotiations, the landowners refused to countenance an access agreement or a public path creation agreement; while the national park authority ruled out an access order or public path creation order because, as a park official told me: 'Our committee is very much in the business of working with the farming community.' The arrangement that was finally secured in 1982 is a 'courtesy footpath'. In return for an annual payment in recognition of the agreement and a wardening service provided by the national park authority, the Arans owners permit the public to walk along and round the ridge on the courtesy path. The public are not permitted to wander off the path nor to bring dogs with them; the renewal of the courtesy path agreement every year depends on the public's 'reasonable use' and adherence to the conditions.

The arrangement since 1982 has at least provided something. However, the courtesy path could be withdrawn in any future year. Even more disturbingly, its existence may encourage other farmers on the Arans and elsewhere to seek to turn access into revenue at the expense of the public. In the late 1960s, the Nantlle Valley, twenty miles to the north of the Arans, became known as Shotgun Valley because of a dispute over public access. If farmers in those other parts of Snowdonia where an uneasy tension between landowners and visitors exists follow the example of the Arans landowners, and if the park authority declines to use compulsion, walkers could find the substitution of freedom to roam with a predetermined permissive route becoming more general. If the costs of compensation mount, even the permissive routes may disappear. This process, together with activities like conifer planting and agricultural intensification which are cutting down the amount of land over which free wandering is possible, could lead to the further concentration of walkers on a few peaks like Snowdon which are already subject to erosion.

One hundred and fifty miles from the Arans, amid the

intensively cultivated fields of north Oxfordshire, is Wychwood
Forest. It is a remnant of a huge medieval hunting domain and,
at 1,550 acres, the largest remaining ancient woodland between
the Cotswolds and the Chilterns. Wychwood Forest is no dreary
conifer plantation. It is mixed, broad-leaved woodland of ash
and oak supported by a rich shrub layer of blackthorn, hawthorn,
hazel, elder and field maple and flowers that include early purple
orchid, pyramidal orchid, columbine and deadly nightshade.
Through the heart of Wychwood Forest and the adjoining 600-
acre Cornbury Park run two tributary streams of the River
Evenlode. A previous owner of the estate dammed these to form
a string of six lakes and ponds which contain anything from
trout to crayfish and ten-spined sticklebacks. Lying only eight
miles from Oxford on the edge of the little town of Charlbury,
which enjoys a fast train service to London, the Forest is easy to
get to. But not to get into.

Legal rights of way through Wychwood Forest and Cornbury
Park – 2,150 acres in all or nearly six times the size of Hyde
Park – are confined to one public footpath that crosses a far
corner of Cornbury Park. A private enclosure act in 1857
promoted by the Spencer-Churchill family who owned Wychwood and surrounding land at that time failed to indicate any
public paths while setting out new roads and closing others.
This enclosure award has been described by local rambler and
conservationist Alison Kemp, who has made a special study of
the history of Wychwood, as 'legalized robbery'.[18] When, a
century later in the 1950s, various people sought to assert public
footpaths over Wychwood, this proved very difficult. The parish
concerned, Cornbury and Wychwood, marked only two paths
on the draft definitive map, both outside the estate walls; the
chairman of the parish meeting at the time (Cornbury and
Wychwood had no parish council) was the owner of the estate,
Oliver Watney, and the clerk was his farm secretary. Although
Mr Watney was prepared to permit some de facto access to the
Forest, he was not prepared to convert this into legal rights of
way. After the submission of the draft parish map, a succession
of attempts was made by ramblers' groups to assert public paths
across Wychwood. But since the parish has no church and very
few houses, it proved impossible to prove uninterrupted use by

the public for a twenty-year period throughout the length of any one path.

Opportunities for public enjoyment of all of the Forest and most of the Park are therefore limited to what access the owner chooses to permit by grace and favour. Oliver Watney, a member of the brewing family, allowed a certain amount of de facto access to Wychwood as his father, Vernon Watney, who bought the estate in 1900, had done. But when the 2nd Baron Rotherwick took over Wychwood in 1967 he decided to tighten up. He restricted permissive access for the general public to the use of one path into the Forest on one day a year. 'On that day the Forest is alive with visitors,' wrote Alison Kemp in 1978. 'Scores pour in, rejoicing at this one meagre opportunity to wander in this glorious historic woodland.'[19] Such other permissive access as Lord Rotherwick allows is for particular groups of people only. On specified weekday mornings, residents of the local parishes of Finstock and Leafield are allowed to gather fallen wood in the Forest for kindling. And in 1984, for example, the estate issued twenty-seven individuals and groups with permits to enter the Forest on specified dates for particular purposes such as the study of wildlife. The only people with permits that allow them free access at any time are certain officials of the Nature Conservancy Council (NCC): the central part of Wychwood is a designated national nature reserve. It was an official of the NCC who turned me off when I tried to enter the forest in July 1984 – a rather sinister example of the permit-holder enforcing the system on those less fortunate than himself.

In 1982, local ramblers redoubled their efforts to get access to Wychwood. *The Secret Forest*, a report published by the Oxfordshire branch of the Council for the Protection of Rural England with considerable local publicity, urged the creation of a network of new rights of way which would 'enable the public to walk with reasonable freedom and variety in the Forest, but by no means on every existing path or track, and without infringing the privacy of Cornbury Park'.[20] Fifteen months later, West Oxfordshire District Council made a formal approach to Lord Rotherwick to allow public access to Wychwood. However, the Council declined to urge either an access agreement or the creation of new public rights of way. Instead, it sought a permissive path across the middle of the estate in a north-west to south-east direction, along a route that had been claimed as a right of way by local people in the 1960s and placed on the draft definitive map during the first review of Oxfordshire's definitive map, but later removed after objections from Lord Rotherwick. However, the permissive path sought by West Oxfordshire District Council could never have become a right of way. Section 30 of the Highways Act 1980, under which the path would have been made, provides that even twenty years of uninterrupted use of the path could not have resulted in it becoming a public path without the agreement of Lord Rotherwick, who would in any case have been free to terminate the arrangement at any time.

By October 1985, West Oxfordshire District Council had not managed to secure even this permissive path from Lord Rotherwick. However, a change in the political complexion of Oxfordshire County Council in May 1985, replacing a Conservative majority with a hung council, began to make that council more assertive. The County Council persuaded Cornbury Estates to allow between six and eight guided and chaperoned theme walks into Wychwood each year as part of a proposed council programme of guided walls. But it then concluded that more was required than mere persuasion would deliver. In June 1986 it decided to make a public path creation order following the route of West Oxfordshire's proposed permissive path. The cost of the legal fees and compensation for disrupting commercial deer and pheasant shooting was expected in 1986 to be about £31,000. But the price of the order might also include the loss of the guided walks and even the Palm Sunday permissive walk, if Lord Rotherwick chooses to retaliate. And even if the path order survives the public inquiry it may face, the most it will achieve will probably be to create a tunnel through the Forest bounded on each side by deer fencing. Glimpses of some of the glories of Wychwood through a seven-foot-high net of wire would still not really meet the needs of the walkers, picnickers and birdwatchers of Oxfordshire.

Access: No Way

To break the stranglehold which Britain's landowners exert over access to their countryside was always going to be a formidable undertaking. And Silkin's 1949 Act with its access agreements and access orders has just not been up to the job. Blame for its failure does not all lie with county councils who have been too deferential to their local landowners. Tougher legislation was needed, particularly as regards access to whole stretches of land rather than merely along footpaths. In the case of public paths, frequent passage of people along the same route over many years is enough to confer automatically a public right of access along that route that can be upheld in the courts. But the frequent use of an area of land, even from time immemorial, confers no similar legal right to wander.

A more robust scheme was available to Mr Silkin in the Hobhouse Committee's recommendation for a general right of access to all uncultivated land. This would not have required any heart-searching on the part of local authorities. Now, alongside the failure of the 1949 provisions we have seen an enormous loss of lands which before 1949 were, de facto, people's playgrounds. For our generation, with cause to be sadder and wiser than Attlee's where the countryside is concerned, a clear obligation presents itself. For our sake, our children's sake and our grandchildren's sake we have to do properly the job that was botched in 1949.

9. Common Land

I would just remind you that any enthusiasm for wholesale changes of land-use on common land should be tempered with the thought that while we can journey to the moon, or rebuild Westminster Abbey, the likelihood of re-creating the national glories of common land is extremely small.

Dr Derek Wells of the Nature Conservancy Council, 1983[1]

Imagine a typical autumn scene on Wimbledon Common in 1805. The appearance of the Common is not unlike its appearance in 1987: swathes of rough turf interspersed with oak and holly woods, stands of silver birch and stretches of gorse and heather. Though the railway has not yet brought London's commuters and their Edwardian villas to Wimbledon (the population of the parish in 1801 was 1,591), the Common is at least as alive with people as it would be today. Some are crossing the Common to and from all directions, some are enjoying a stroll while others are collecting water from the wells. In the woods, local people are gathering firewood, while others are cutting furze or gorse for fuel. If the day we have visited the Common is in the early autumn, these wood-gatherers will be especially heavily laden since wood-gathering has been forbidden all summer, until on Michaelmas, the Parish Beadle went round with his bell to 'cry the Common open'. All winter the poor are allowed to gather as much wood and furze as they need for their own use until on Lady-Day the Beadle cries the Common shut.

While the custom of the manor stipulates that nobody may take more wood than he needs for his own household, certain people are allowed special privileges, in particular local bakers, brewers and innkeepers. Bakers are allowed more faggots than other people with which to fire their ovens; just as in Elizabethan days bakers and brewers, unlike other cottagers, were allowed to keep a great hog on the Common after the Christmas feast. In

1867, there were two old men alive (one living in Kingston Workhouse) who had made a living cutting furze for bakers and others until the Common's owner, the 5th Earl Spencer, made an order forbidding the activity.

Some of the wood-gatherers on our 1805 morning may be Lord Spencer's tenants; his home estate is Althorp in Northamptonshire but he includes Wimbledon among his many other land holdings. The rights of Earl Spencer's Wimbledon copyhold tenants, like those of the other inhabitants of the neighbourhood, have become established by custom over the centuries and are set down in the court rolls of the Manor of Wimbledon. The copyhold tenants enjoy extra rights over and above the right to gather wood and furze enjoyed by all local inhabitants. They enjoy the right to take gravel and to cut turves for fuel. And they can pasture their animals upon the Common at all times of the year. But just as there are rules to prevent the over-exploitation of the firewood of the Common, so there is a long-established mechanism for preventing over-grazing. Each tenant is permitted to pasture only a stipulated number of his own animals according to the extent of his tenure. The court rolls tell us that for every cottager who was also a copyhold tenant, this meant an entitlement to graze twenty-five sheep, two cows, one mare and a colt. To check that no tenant had exceeded his allotted number of stock, common-keepers periodically 'drove' the Common. They gathered together all the Common's cattle, and impounded any trespassing animals while requiring their owners to pay fines to the Earl.

Some of the people on the Common are the direct employees of Earl Spencer himself. Certain of these are looking after animals; others may well be digging out gravel and cutting turf, loam and bog-earth for sale. For the Earl has a presumptive right to the mines and minerals of the Common, and the records tell us that by the middle of the nineteenth century, the Earl was making about £1,000 a year from the sale of gravel and probably the same sum for the sale of turf, loam and bog-earth.

If this was the picture 180 years ago, how does it compare with what happens on Britain's most famous common today? Nearly 200 years on, the wildlife survives relatively unchanged even though the Common is now surrounded by the urban sprawl of Greater London. Woodpeckers (green, lesser spotted and great spotted), kestrels, blackcaps, coal tits and willow warblers are among a total of forty-odd bird species breeding on Wimbledon Common and neighbouring Putney Common, while a further forty-odd species visit each year. By night, these Commons remain a hunting ground for badgers and tawny owls, foxes and hedgehogs, frogs and toads. On spring and summer nights more than twenty different moth species can be encountered, while by day, over the endlessly varying woodlands, grassy rides, and stretches of heather, gorse and bog, flutter an equally large number of species of butterfly.

Like the wild creatures, human beings remain very active on the Common although the nature of their activities has changed. In 1987, no common rights existed over any part of the Common (the last remaining rights were extinguished in 1871). Yet for most of the year the Common is thronged with people. It plays host to two fairs and numerous horse shows. Two thousand people a week run over it, including members of the Thames Hare and Hounds and the Belgrave Harriers. Army cadets use it to practise orienteering, while for local schoolchildren it is the focus of many educational visits. At dawn on May Day, Morris Dancers dance on it. Even more important in the lives of the people of the surrounding suburbs are the less formal uses to which the Common is put. These vary from ice-skating and tobogganing in winter, to kite-flying, blackberrying, sunbathing, tadpoling, birdwatching, playing hide-and-seek, fungus foraying, tree-climbing, picnicking, sketching, painting and taking photographs, to walking the dog. Ten thousand people use Wimbledon and Putney Commons on an average summer weekend, according to estimates by the chief ranger for the Wimbledon and Putney Commons Conservators who now run both commons on behalf of the nation.

In providing for a wide range of the open-air needs of local people, commons like Wimbledon now play as vital a role in the recreation life of the nation as they once played in its economic life. Their importance in both roles goes back a very long way, for common land has its origins in practices dating back before the emergence of private land ownership in Britain.

Essentially, common land provided a means for large numbers

of people to a share in the natural benefits flowing from land which they did not own. We have already seen that the idea of common rights was so strongly established in Britain that it re-emerged after the Norman kings had imposed their own land ownership régime. In our own time, access to the benefits of common land has been widened to embrace the nation as a whole rather than just local people.

But what precisely is a common? The term does not mean that the land concerned is owned collectively by all the British people. Common land may be publicly or privately owned, by groups or individuals, just like any other tract of land. The term 'common' simply implies that one of three special considerations apply. The first is that people other than the landowner, known as commoners, have the legal right to carry out specified activities on the land in question. These rights of common come in a bewildering if rather charming variety. They may include rights of pasture; pannage (the right of a commoner to let his pigs eat beech mast or acorns); estovers (the right to take underwood and small branches for fuel or building repairs, or bracken to feed to animals); turbary (the right to dig turf or peat for use as a fuel in the commoner's house); piscary (the right to take fish from lakes, ponds or streams to consume in the commoner's household); and soil (the right to take sand, gravel, stone or minerals for use on the commoner's land).

Some commons, however, have no commoners. A second group of commons constitutes what is known as 'waste land of the manor not subject to rights of common'. In this case, the land has to be open, uncultivated and unoccupied and form part of a manor without being demesne lands.

Both these two kinds of common are defined as such in the Commons Act, 1965. The third kind of common is not however recognized as such in law, though it includes some of our best-known commons. These are the areas no longer falling within the legal definition because they have ceased to be commons by Act of Parliament but have become instead estates, often publicly owned, which are managed for the good of the community. Wimbledon Common falls into this category. Earl Spencer had bought out many common rights in the late nineteenth century; after a bitter struggle over the future of the Common (see pages 108–9) the remaining rights disappeared altogether in 1876 when an Act of Parliament provided for the Earl to hand the Common over to a Board of Conservators. In return, he received an annuity of £1,200 which was finally paid off as a lump sum of £22,500 in 1958.

Where the Commons Lie

Within these definitions come about 1.5 million acres of the land of England and Wales, all of it owned by somebody and most of it either comprising waste land of the manor or land subject to rights of common, or both. There are no commons as such in Scotland or Northern Ireland, though there is some land that enjoys similar status.

Dictated as it is by historical accident, the distribution of common land within England and Wales is distinctly uneven. The great sweep of the chalk downlands of Sussex, Hampshire, Dorset and Wiltshire which has in the past included large expanses of rough open space in fact contains hardly any common land. In East Sussex, for example, at least half of the chalk downland over which lords of the manor and their tenants once pastured their sheep had been enclosed by the lords for their own exclusive use as early as the fifteenth century – 350 years in advance of England's main period of parliamentary enclosure.[4] Similarly, widespread enclosure in the past has left Wiltshire with only 1,913 acres of common – 0.2 per cent of the surface area of the county.[5] On the other hand, 41 per cent of Dartmoor is still common land, with the Prince of Wales as Duke of Cornwall the single largest owner. Common land covers 5.4 per cent of Devon as a whole, while in North Yorkshire the proportion rises to 7 per cent. In Wales, energetic enclosure in the past has left Anglesey with common land covering less than 1 per cent of the island – yet central Wales is well endowed. Commons cover 8 per cent of the total land area of Powys, Gwynedd and Clywd: the average common here is 262 acres in size and has ten holders of common rights.

In lowland England, commons tend to consist of widely scattered scraps of common land, each less than 25 acres, punctuated here and there by larger stretches that include some of our most popular beauty spots. Epping Forest and the Malvern Hills, the Forest of Dean and Wenlock Edge, the New Forest and Harting Down in Sussex, Cambridge's Midsummer Meadow and Oxford's Port Meadow, the Strays of York and Newcastle's Town Moor, Hampstead Heath and Blackheath all owe their survival in their present form at least in part to their status as common land.

The Effect of Common Land Status

The importance of our commons nowadays springs from the fact that common land status helps protect attractive stretches of countryside from destructive change. It can also help ensure that these areas remain open to people who like visiting such places. As agricultural change and conifer planting have eaten into Britain's stock of unenclosed land, commons have often survived intact, providing reservoirs of refreshment in an otherwise increasingly dismal landscape.

Commons are also particularly valuable in securing habitats for wildlife which might otherwise disappear. Over the commons of mid-Wales like Plynlimon Common fifteen miles behind Aberystwyth, some of our most spectacular and rare birds of prey find food and often a nest place as well – birds like the red kite and the peregrine falcon, the merlin, the hen harrier and the short-eared owl. The commons also provide a refuge for once familiar plants and animals that are losing their habitat to landscape change. Harebells, cowslips and campions, night-ingales, dragonflies and toads are some of the plants and animals which are now most easily found by many people on their nearest commons.

The ecological value of our commons arises from several causes. They embrace unploughed land, a characteristic which has become more important as post-war agricultural change has destroyed more and more natural or semi-natural communities of plants and animals. Though patchily distributed, common land is widely scattered and thus helps keep reservoir populations of species surviving over large areas of the country. It also includes a wide range of soil types and climatic conditions, providing a good cross-section of traditional British habitats.

And it sometimes plays host to old methods of agricultural management of great benefit to wildlife which have more or less died out elsewhere. Over Huntingdon's Port Holme Meadow, for instance, legal clauses forbid grazing from mid-February until mid-August so that the meadow's luxuriant grasses can be allowed to grow for hay. One beneficial side-effect of this management régime, which has operated for centuries, is that the plants which agricultural intensification has banished from most of the other meadows alongside the River Ouse are here permitted to flower and multiply.

As the legal status of commons often prevents their owners from excluding the public, the wildlife which they help to survive is available for the enjoyment of people who might not otherwise have an opportunity to see it. The accessibility of commons also enables them to provide opportunities for walking and climbing in many different kinds of country. At the latest count, the public actually enjoyed a legal right to wander freely over one-fifth of the commons, around 300,000 acres.[6] This does mean that walkers can be treated as trespassers on the remaining four-fifths, and indeed, there is nothing to stop the erection of 'Trespassers will be Prosecuted' signs on these lands. But a custom of de facto access allowing people to wander at will rather than to stick to particular routes, is enjoyed over Britain's commons more than over any other category of private land. Because of this tradition, roads across many upland commons, like Dartmoor, are unfenced.

So although commons cover only 4 per cent of the land of England and Wales, they are far more important than this figure suggests. Most of the regions relatively well-endowed with open, walking country almost always turn out to be well-endowed with common land. Thus, Surrey is known to its own inhabitants as well as those of South London as a county far richer in public open space than neighbouring Kent; Surrey's area of common land is more than seven times that of Kent. Drive south from Birmingham looking for a place to stretch your legs and you will be unlucky in the tightly enclosed countryside of Warwickshire. Better to bear west instead and follow the tide of country-loving West Midlanders seeking a climb on Worcestershire's Clent

Hills or, farther away, the Clee Hills, Stiperstones or Long Mynd of Shropshire, all of which are commons.

The Commons' Defences

A number of different legal considerations help the commons keep plough and conifer at bay while providing the public with access.

The chief constraint on the enclosure of common land has always been the owner's need to get the consent of the commoners. If an owner does anything that interferes with the rights of commoners without their consent – say, clearing away woodland over which they have a right to collect dead wood – they can take legal action to force him to restore the common to its original state. One problem with this used to be that there was plenty of scope for dispute about who possessed what rights. But in 1955, a Royal Commission was set up to look into the future of commons following the uncertainty exposed when many commons were ploughed up under emergency powers during World War II. The Commission proposed the creation of a nation-wide, comprehensive register of commons, indicating who their owners were, and who owned what common rights. This recommendation was translated into legislation in the Commons Registration Act 1965, which provided the machinery for a modern Domesday Book of common land. All county councils were required to draw up registers of all tracts of common land in their areas. Two eighteen-month periods were set for the registration of common rights, beginning in 1967 and ending in 1970, each followed by a two-year period for the receipt of objections. Commons Commissioners, appointed by the Secretary of State for the Environment, resolve, often by public inquiry, contested registrations, with aggrieved objectors having the right of appeal to the High Court. And since about 1970 all common rights throughout England and Wales have been recorded on special county-by-county commons registers.

The registration process was intended to preserve commons against enclosure in circumstances where this would be undesirable: in the words of the Royal Commission, 'Land which is common at the passing of the Act should remain common. There should be no enclosure except in cases of compulsory acquisition by public authorities in accordance with Special Parliamentary Procedure and of unimportant pieces of roadside strip.'[7] The Royal Commission also recommended that the public should be granted a legal right of access to all common land, but this has not been implemented. So commoners' rights, though now clearly recorded, do not provide an absolutely watertight guarantee of public access. Nonetheless, in practice they provide pretty effective de facto arrangements.

On top of commoners' rights, three different legislative provisions help safeguard the public interest in common land.

First, the compulsory purchase by government or local authorities of a stretch of common land for use, say, as a new road, a roundabout, an old people's home or a school, must be approved by Parliament unless suitable land is given in exchange (under the Acquisition of Land [Authorization Procedure] Act, 1946). When, for instance, the Department of the Environment sought to acquire a fifty-five-acre slice across the middle of Esher Common for a by-pass, the Secretary of State for the Environment, as consenting authority to the appropriation of common land, actually ruled against himself in his decision in 1972. As transport authority, the Department had offered sixty-six acres in exchange, accepting the argument of the local council and the Commons, Open Spaces and Footpaths Preservation Society that, as the land to be taken was in the middle of the common and therefore especially valuable, a larger area should be given by way of compensation. But the Department of the Environment as protector of the nation's common land ruled that the exchange land should be larger still and amount to eighty-nine acres, part of which now links up what were two separate commons to make one large one.

Both the remaining legal provisions that help safeguard the public interest in common land stem from the Law of Property Act of 1925, and both were the result of prolonged and intense pressure from the Commons, Open Spaces and Footpaths Preservation Society from the 1880s onward. Section 193, which is still in force, granted the public a legal right of access for air and exercise to all commons lying wholly or partly within urban and metropolitan areas, save for those held by the Armed Services.

Section 194, which is also still in force, prohibits building, fencing or other works to commons which prevent or impede public access except with the Secretary of State's consent. At the same time, by reference to the Commons Act 1876, it ensures that the Secretary of State must take into account 'the benefit of the neighbourhood' when deciding whether to give permission for the work in question.[8] The law does not only therefore provide a means for the community as a whole to fight off threats to build on commons; because fencing is usually a necessary prerequisite for the conversion of rough grassland to arable cropland, intensive pasture or conifer plantation, it also provides a means for preventing the loss of stretches of open access land to intensive agriculture and forestry.

The case of Plynlimon Common in mid-Wales provides a good example of the way in which the fencing requirement can enable community needs to be taken into account when an owner is proposing land-use change. In 1982, the Crown Estate Commissioners proudly announced a project to commemorate the marriage of the Prince and Princess of Wales. They planned to change land-uses to increase revenue over four square miles of the western slopes of Plynlimon Common, a wild, treeless, heather and grass moor that rises 2,459 feet in the hills behind Aberystwyth – the highest point in Dyfed and the source of the River Severn. When the Commissioners went ahead and started implementing their plan with the erection of 1.6 miles of wire fence across the Common, dividing its slopes in two, without the consent they should first have obtained from the Secretary of State for Wales, the Open Spaces Society (formerly the Commons, Open Spaces and Footpaths Preservation Society)[9] protested. The Commissioners thereupon applied for permission for this fencing, incorporating two gates, and the Secretary of State for Wales replied that he would permit it only if the fence was punctuated with five stiles to ensure that access would be impeded as little as possible. Later the same year the Commissioners sought consent for the erection of a further 5.5 miles of fencing so as to mark off areas in which they wished to plant trees (mainly conifers) and re-seed grassland. Since no common rights exist over this part of Plynlimon Common (the Crown Estate having acquired the last remaining common right in

1981), it was only the interest of the Crown as owner and the
benefit of the neighbourhood that were relevant considerations.
The Secretary of State defined 'the benefit of the neighbourhood'
as 'the effect of the proposals on the wild, open landscape of the
western slopes of Plynlimon ... Unless the proposals are in
keeping with the general landscape qualities of the area they
could be detrimental to public enjoyment of the common as
understood in its wider context.'[10]

After weighing up these matters and visiting the site himself,
the Secretary of State for Wales turned down half the Commissioners' proposal, disallowing fencing over the higher slopes
and imposing a number of limitations on fencing lower down, for
which he gave permission. He considered the proposed fencing
of the upper slopes would impair the landscape beauty and
wildness of the Common and hence its value for public access.

However, the Plynlimon case was special in one main respect.
Consent for fencing in this case was clearly required because a
legal right of access covers the land concerned: Plynlimon
Common forms part of the 75,000 acres of waste-of-the-manor
commons owned by the Crown Estate and over which the Estate
granted a right of access by deed of covenant in 1932. This fact
is important not just because it ensures the public may roam
freely over this land without fear of being thrown off as trespassers; it is also crucial because Section 194 prohibits fencing
without the Secretary of State's prior consent only where this
fencing might impede access. Now, the Law of Property Act
never defined 'access'. So if the owner of a common has always
kept people off it, there is clearly no access to it that might be
impeded by fencing and he would seem not to be covered.
Owners who allow de facto access over commons may or may
not consider themselves required to seek consent for fencing
under Section 194. In the case of commons where legal access is
confined to any public rights of way that happen to cross them,
owners tend to consider that Section 194 applies only if their
plans would affect these rights of way: if changes are confined to
areas from which the rights of way are fenced off they consider
themselves under no legal requirement to seek the Secretary of
State's permission to fence.

The result is that commons covered by a legal right of access enjoy far better protection than commons without. And as it was the urban commons to which legal access was granted in 1925, it is these which enjoy the best protection against fencing and enclosure through the Law of Property Act.

In fact, the Law of Property Bill as first published would have given the public such a right of free access to all the commons of England and Wales. But after pressure from landowners, the 1925 Act granted this right only in respect of commons lying in urban or metropolitan areas; for rural commons the Act simply made provision for landowners to enter voluntarily into deeds of covenant granting the public access.

At first, several public-spirited landowners did enter into such deeds of covenant, and by 1930, more than 13,000 acres of common were subject to voluntary covenants.[11] Then two years later, to the great delight of the Commons Society, came a remarkable breakthrough. The Crown Estate Commissioners had sought to make several enclosures on its extensive waste-of-the-manor Welsh commons. The Commons Society raised the matter with the Government with the result that the Ministry of Agriculture indicated that, in the absence of exceptional circumstances, it would try to discourage further enclosure of Crown commons. Thereupon, the Crown Estate Commissioners voluntarily entered into the access deed of covenant over the whole of its Welsh commons which has never been revoked and which provided the ultimate safeguard for Plynlimon.

However, the rush to grant deeds of access stopped in the mid-1930s. It has never been resumed – not surprisingly, in view of the possibilities that emerged during and after the war for the conversion of commons to forestry plantations and intensive agricultural land. There are other categories of common to which the public enjoys a legal right of access besides those in urban and metropolitan areas: those owned by organizations like the National Trust and county councils as providers of recreation lands, and those subject to particular covenants and agreements sometimes going back a long time. However, when all these areas of common to which a right of public access applies are added up, they amount to only about one-fifth of Britain's common land, according to calculations by the Department of the Environment in 1978.

Disappearing Commons

Forty per cent of the area of common land existing in 1858 had been enclosed by 1958 – one million acres in all – according to the Royal Commission on Common Land. The losses are continuing. And the pressures for enclosure are not diminishing. Today, the greatest threat to our upland commons comes from forestry. Many of those stretches of our hills, moors and dales that have escaped the march of the conifers are commons. However, there is no doubt that Britain's foresters would like to get their hands on them, and the Government has been considering making it easier to enclose commons for forestry. Nicholas Edwards MP, then Secretary of State for Wales, told a conference of landowners and foresters in 1982:

If we are to develop fully the opportunities that exist for further forest planting, and particularly this is true of Wales, we will have to find a better way of making use of the vast areas of common land in Wales, or land subject to common grazing rights. There are no easy solutions, but we recognize the need for new legislation to make it easier to obtain better management of common land.[12]

There are three main ways in which commons are being enclosed and turned over to intensive uses without the involvement of the Secretary of State for the Environment.

First, some are going because their owners do not consider their commons covered by Section 194. In theory at least, nearly four-fifths of our common land is at risk on this account.

Second, some commons are being enclosed simply because commoners are agreeing to enclosure. Particularly if the common rights involved – say to graze one goat – are of little economic value, a commoner may readily agree to surrender his common rights to the landowner for cash. However, what he is also surrendering is the public safeguards in the common concerned. For once a common has no commoners (unless it is a 'waste land of the manor' common) its owner can successfully apply for its excision from the Commons Register. Once off the Register, the owner is then free to treat the former common like any other stretch of rural land – in other words, to do what he likes with it. In other cases, rough, common grazing is fenced off and apportioned into individual lots, in some of which commoners may be granted freehold. New techniques for reclaiming steep hills and dales together with subsidies like the EEC's sheepmeat régime make the offer of ownership of a parcel of land which can be fenced in, drained and re-seeded with ryegrass extremely attractive to commoners.

The other main reason for the continuing enclosure of commons is the emergence of all sorts of legal loopholes in the complicated system of commons safeguards. A relatively new threat – with alarming implications – now faces waste-land-of-the-manor commons.

Hazeley Heath, a common in north Hampshire, 337 acres in extent, covers what could be profitable agricultural land. It extends for well over a mile either side of the road leading northwards out of the little town of Hartney Wintney, and several tracks wind their way across it from the roadside. The heath gives the impression of having attained its present form through years of evolution: at ground level little red cups of lichen are sprinkled on the sandy soil, with, here and there, thick beds of sphagnum moss, tufts of moor grass and three different types of heather. Above this layer, rise bracken, brambles, head-high gorse and, towering above these, a third dimension of scattered trees – mainly silver birch and scots pine. The effect is of a tiny but complex wilderness in which the walker can lose his way along grassy tracks offering for orientation only the occasional glimpse of Bramshill (an attractive, brick Jacobean mansion standing three-quarters of a mile away on a slope).

In 1977, the owner of the Heath applied for consent under Section 194 to fence the central 170 acres of it. He said his reasons were to deter unauthorized camping, to prevent the possible tipping of waste scrap, to minimize the risk of heath fires and to make sheep- and cattle-rearing possible.

No common rights over Hazeley Heath were ever registered, but objections to the application poured in from three local parish councils, the district council, the county council, private individuals, the local branch of the Ramblers' Association and the Commons, Open Spaces and Footpaths Preservation Society.

The Secretary of State for the Environment decided to reject the application. In doing so he said he considered any benefit

that might accrue to the neighbourhood as a result of the release
of land for agriculture as well as through reductions in fire risk,
dumping and unauthorized camping would be insufficient to
justify the granting of the application. 'The loss of 170 acres of
open land from the centre of the heath represents a large
proportion of the common and there would be considerable
impact on the landscape and the visual amenity. A great deal of
wildlife habitat would also be lost . . . The application is accordingly refused.'

In reply, the Common's owner emphasized that the public
had no legal right of access to the land, except by way of the
public footpaths, along which access would not be impaired
since these would be fenced off as corridors. However, the
Secretary of State considered that public access to the Common
had become established firmly enough for him to make it the
overriding consideration. He said:

Whatever the legal position, it is clear that the heath has been open to
the public for many years, and that substantial use is still made of it by
the local inhabitants. No action appears to have been taken in the past
to prevent the local inhabitants from wandering at will over the land
and indeed this was encouraged during the years 1962–71 by the
existence of a Deed of Declaration made by the owner under Section
194 of the Law of Property Act 1925, which legalized public access to
the land during those years.[13]

So far so good. But in 1983 events took a different turn.
Hazeley Heath is a common only by virtue of falling within the
definition 'waste land of the manor not subject to rights of
common'. In that year, the owner of Hazeley Heath sold his
lordship of the manor while retaining his ownership of the
Heath. The following year he applied to Hampshire County
Council to have the Heath removed from the register of commons. Nowadays, a lordship of the manor may be worth little
money: it may simply consist of the title together with certain
usually nominal rights – worth in some cases as little as £1,000.
And by selling the title the lordship of the manor and thereby
severing the common from the manor a landowner may be able
to destroy the common land status of land he owns.

At the time of going to press, the Hazeley Heath case is before the courts. If the application for de-registration is ultimately granted, there is every reason to suppose that owners of other waste of the manor commons will follow suit.

The Future of the Commons

An obvious means of protecting Britain's commons would be an extension of the legal right of access applying to urban commons to embrace rural ones as well, as recommended by the Royal Commission on Common Land in 1958. The Commission considered that the public needed to know that there would be a legal right to roam over all common land in town or country. 'In a sense,' it observed, 'the interest of the vanished commoners in keeping the land open would be bequeathed to the public by virtue of the latter's possession of a right of access.'

As might be expected, this is a move The Open Spaces Society has been urging for many years. In both 1980 and 1982, for instance, the Society's chairman, Dr David Clark, MP for South Shields, sought to introduce a bill in the House of Commons that would have extended legal access in this way. But both attempts, like others before, have failed because the step did not have government support.

In 1986, a Common Land Forum that included representatives of the local authority associations, landowners, farmers and recreation and amenity bodies, did agree to recommend reforms including a legal right of access, albeit somewhat hedged around, and moves to curb de-registrations.[14] It remains to be seen whether the Government will treat the Forum's proposals as a cue for action. If it does not, the outlook for Britain's surviving commons is bleak. Unless some real protection is afforded them, the rate of enclosure is likely to be maintained. The result seems likely to be that most privately owned rural commons will have disappeared by the middle of the next century, with only those owned by conservation bodies having a good chance of survival.

Scotland and Northern Ireland

If the registration of a stretch of land as a common provides at least a slim sanction against its enclosure in England and Wales,

the same is not true in the rest of the United Kingdom. For in
Scotland and Northern Ireland there is no 'common land' as
legally defined.

The nineteenth-century land reforms in Northern Ireland
usually resulted in grazing, turbary and other rights being
divided up on an individual basis. Here and there, in areas
where the land reforms have not reached, common rights survive.
One type of area where this happens is in the relatively infertile
hill areas, like parts of the Sperrins and Mournes. Another is
lakes and rivers, which were largely untouched by the land
reforms. Here, although the bed, soil and banks of a river or lake
may be owned by one individual, the general public may have a
right of piscary, though this often excludes the taking of salmon
and trout.

The completeness with which enclosure occurred in Scotland
where, as we have seen, the landless did not even enjoy the
protection of England's Enclosure Commissioners, has left that
country too without any land whatsoever bearing the legal
definition of 'common land'. The only category of Scottish land
that has some similarities with the common land south of the
border is the common grazing land used by groups of crofters.
The importance of the Scottish shielings – the hill pasture to
which cattle were taken in the summer months – led those
landowners who allocated crofts on their land to include along
with each individual croft's land, a stretch of grazing land to be
used by all the crofters' animals in common. To this day, no
landowner or crofter may change the nature of croft land in a
way that might impair the legal rights of other crofters or the
landowner without the agreement of all parties. But there is no
provision for any national say in the fate of these lands of the
kind provided by Section 194 in England. Nor do the crofters
enjoy any rights other than grazing and, in some cases, peat
cutting.

The crofting common grazing lands consist of a strip of land a
few miles wide around the north and north-west coasts of
Scotland. But the stronghold of these common grazing lands is
Shetland (where it is known as the 'scattald') and the Hebrides
(where it includes the 'machair' – the long strip of sandy
calcareous grassland behind the beach).[15] When the machair

remains undrained and free of artificial fertilizers and herbicides, its summer flowering is on a par with an Alpine meadow. But the machair is coming under pressure as crofters seek to enclose and 'improve' it for agriculture, with the help of EEC grants. If the Scottish common grazing lands had an equivalent legal status to the common lands of England and Wales, sub-division through fencing would not be possible without the Secretary of State's say-so.

10. Environmental Protection

The fourth and final strand of the twentieth-century social contract for the countryside involves the protection of the environment from landowners' attempts to exploit it for commercial gain. The primary means of such protection is the town and country planning system.

Planning Controls

The comprehensive and radical array of town planning measures embodied in the Town and Country Planning Act, 1947, and the similar measures that have extended planning to Scotland and Northern Ireland, grew out of a century's steady refinement of the mechanism whereby public authorities sought to safeguard the environmental needs of the community in the face of land-use change.

The earliest planning measures had sprung originally from concern about the physical well-being of the poor in the crowded cities of Victorian Britain. Appalled at rat-infested, overcrowded tenements and disease-ridden, dingy streets, social reformers urged Parliament to regulate the density and layout of new building. Concern soon widened to embrace the need for open spaces in towns to satisfy spiritual as well as physical needs. The housing reformer Octavia Hill, for instance, told a meeting of the National Health Society in 1877: 'There are two great wants in the life of the poor of our large towns, which ought to be realized more than they are – the want of space and the want of beauty.' Octavia Hill's enthusiasm was to lead her to co-found the National Trust in the hope that it would help factory workers to join the middle classes in experiencing the freedom of the countryside. And from the early 1900s onwards, the efforts of Octavia Hill and others like her bore fruit in a succession of planning acts empowering local authorities to intervene against the forces of commercial gain to maintain the beauty and recreation potential of the countryside.

The 1932 Town and Country Planning Act empowered local authorities to prepare the first planning schemes. These were essentially maps indicating in which areas the authority considered that the public interest dictated that building and other major changes to the land should or should not take place. In putting their ideas into effect, however, the authorities found themselves severely hampered by the requirement that landowners disadvantaged by their decisions should be entitled to compensation for any increase in land value that they would forego. Because building was extremely profitable in the 1930s, compensation could often be very high. So regulation in fact had little influence on what took place. The sprawl of new houses over the countryside, which many people feared would swallow up, octopus-like, its peace and beauty, continued virtually unabated.

The 1947 Town and Country Planning Act removed at a stroke the requirement for large compensation payments by transferring the right to make certain changes in land-use from the landowner to the State. The nationalization of development rights altered the terms under which landowners could operate, considerably reducing their ancient freedom to do exactly what they liked with their land. The authority to make certain kinds of change in land-use, termed 'development', was vested in the State. A landowner could recover this authority only by applying to the community's representatives for 'planning permission'. If this was refused, landowners would no longer be compensated as they no longer enjoyed a right to make the change in use and to profit from it.

In the aftermath of World War II it might have been supposed that there would have been little stomach to impede the activities needed to put the country back on its feet, such as new building and the extraction of minerals. Not so.

Parliament insisted on looking beyond the immediate needs of post-war reconstruction towards a new Britain of the future in which the people would be able to enjoy a pleasing environment. This is why arrangements were sanctioned which ensured there would be no building even of desperately needed housing, roads and factories or extraction of the sand, gravel or iron ore from new sites without the consent of the people's representatives.

When it came to the selection of the activities to be designated 'development' and subjected to control, the criterion was the extent to which recent experience had shown that the activity in question could mar the living and working environment of the British people. The list was long. Included were not only building of almost every kind and the extraction of minerals, but also the erection of advertisement hoardings (which had peppered areas like the South Downs before the war), and certain changes in the use of buildings – from a house to two flats or a shop, a shop to a garage, a pet shop to a hot food shop, any building to a factory or office, and a light industrial factory to a factory for heavy industry.

There was no attempt to confine the arrangements to a few exceptional prized areas or to begin with geographically limited pilot schemes. From the start, planning applied to the whole of England and Wales: even the most unprepossessing area was to enjoy the environmental safety-net of planning control.

The Act did, however, embody safety-valves in keeping with long-standing principles of British justice. The most important was the right of any individual to appeal to the Secretary of State for the Environment against local authority refusal of planning permission or imposition of conditions on the granting of it. In addition, if a landowner considered that a refusal of planning consent or conditions attached to approval made the land involved incapable of beneficial use, he could serve on the authority a purchase notice requiring the authority to buy the land from him. The planning authority in turn could appeal against the notice.

The planning arrangements introduced in 1947 remain in force today. But there have been additions to the system. Subsequent legislation provided that particularly firm restraint should be exercised on development on land around and between particular conurbations which was designated 'green belt'. Also, land of special natural beauty, designated 'national park' or 'area of outstanding natural beauty', received similar privileged treatment. As in the rest of the country, no compensation was offered to the owners of such land if they were stopped from carrying out development, even though they were that much more likely to fall foul of the system in these special areas.

So throughout the UK, for some years now, planning consent has been required before development can go ahead. The range of activities controlled in this way has stayed remarkably constant since 1947, although the planning tools involved have been considerably refined during the four decades since then.

One feature of the system which has grown more and more sophisticated is the development plan. Clearly, planning decisions cannot meaningfully be taken in isolation from one another. So the 1947 Act obliged planning authorities in England and Wales to prepare 'development plans', showing how they proposed that the land in their area should be used. The plans also had to show the stages by which any development should be carried out, and to indicate the sites of proposed parks, public buildings, roads, nature reserves and airfields.

In 1968 the system of 'development plans' of England and Wales was replaced with one of 'structure plans'. A similar change came to Scotland in 1969, while legislation in 1972 introduced to Northern Ireland 'area plans' prepared by the Department of the Environment after consultation with district councils. These developments marked a shift in the planner's role from simply reacting to the proposals of the developer to the more positive function of setting goals for environmental conservation and improvement. County council structure plans for rural areas cover anything from policies to improve country bus services, to encourage certain types of rural industry, to safeguard the position of local people in the private housing market or to improve the look of village centres, as well as indicating the terms under which building, mineral working and so on will be allowed.

In 1968 there began a new era of public involvement both in the drawing up of plans and in the handling of applications to develop. Development plans had been subjected to public inquiries, but the Town and Country Planning Act of 1968 required each planning authority in England and Wales to carry out a substantial public participation exercise as soon as it had completed a survey of its area and before it set about drawing up plans and proposals. Once the structure plan was published, this too was to be open to an examination-in-public and to require the consent of the Secretary of State for the Environment before it could come into effect.

In addition to these developments, planners have also acquired greater expertise in the particular fields in which they are empowered to act. The mining and quarrying sector provides a good illustration. By the late 1950s, it had become clear that mineral extraction presented unique problems for planners. Most forms of 'development' were a once-and-for-all change to the land that was accomplished in the space of months. But mineral working was a continuous process lasting years, even decades, varying over time in its impact on the environment, and requiring guarantees before it even began that all sorts of restoration work would be carried out when landowners or mineral operators had ceased to enjoy any financial return. To try to work out how best planners could ensure adequate restoration, the Government appointed a Committee on Planning Control over Mineral Working whose recommendations bore fruit in the 1981 Town and Country Planning (Minerals) Act. This empowered planning authorities to impose a time limit on every planning permission for the winning and working of minerals. Where a planning authority chooses not to impose a time limit, an automatic sixty-year limit now comes into force. The Act also makes the person last using the land for mineral extraction financially responsible for after-care of that land, and it empowers planning authorities to impose 'after-care' conditions on planning permissions for mineral working in addition to restoration conditions. As a result, mineral operators now have to agree with a planning authority not only a scheme of working including details on hours of activity, noise levels and the methods by which the mineral will be extracted and topsoil and subsoil stored for restoration; but an after-care scheme setting out how they propose to look after the site for five years after restoration. After-care schemes set out precisely how a mineral operator applying for planning consent proposes to look after a site once extraction has been completed and, where the land is to be restored for farming, for instance, include such details as the type and frequency of soil sampling, when and how the land will be drained, fertilized and ploughed.

County council planning officers normally make spot checks on sites being worked and follow up any complaints, in order to enforce conditions imposed on planning consents. The new Act also requires all county planning authorities to review every mineral site in their areas at least every five years. If they consider in the light of new information that extra after-care conditions need to be imposed on top of any restoration conditions, they may impose them. And if they find extraction on a site has stopped for two years or more without restoration, they may issue a prohibition order stopping any more work on that site until a new planning application has been approved. These developments since 1981 have certainly affected what happens on the ground. In 1984, for example, the Greater London Council successfully resisted on appeal a plan to extract gravel over fifty-six acres in the borough of Havering – a plan which, the Secretary of State's inspector judged, did not make adequate provision of restoration of the arable farmland involved to its existing quality.

This continuing development of our planning system has been made possible by the support given to planning by both Labour and Conservative governments. Underlying Britain's town and country planning system are certain assumptions which have never been seriously questioned since Attlee's post-war Labour Government embodied them in law. One of these is that land ownership in Britain is less than absolute: citizens may do what they will with a chattel such as a table, but the rights attached to the 'ownership' of land are circumscribed by a degree of consideration for the interest of the community. The condition of the environment is deemed sufficiently important for the State to appropriate a share of the available rights over it. A secondary assumption is that the rights which the owner forfeits and the state acquires are universal. They are transferred across the whole land surface and not just in respect of special sites. Governments of different political colours have differed in their view of the rights of landowners to benefit financially from developing their land, but both Tory and Labour governments have upheld the system of environmental regulation embodied in the planning system. It has been regarded as an essential element of modern civilization – even at the expense of economic growth. Nothing has brought this out more clearly than the guarantees which the Thatcher Government has given that the green belt of south-east England will be protected, even though individual ministers have pointed out that the economic development of Britain could be severely handicapped by this policy.

The effect of planning on landowners has been to deprive them of immense financial benefits that would otherwise have accrued to them from building development. From the beginning of the twentieth century, many landowners had amassed fortunes from selling land to developers or builders or developing it themselves. After 1947, however, they were forced to concentrate on activities that were not restricted by the new legislation.

Such activities existed. The Act had exempted from the definition of 'development' changes made in pursuit of both agriculture and forestry. It was to these pursuits that landowners therefore looked to replace the profits they might otherwise have earned from building development. Landowners were totally free to change summer pasture to intensive cereal land, rough scrub to conifer plantation or vacant land to intensive pig or poultry unit. In the process, they could eliminate any landscape features they liked. And they could pocket the considerable increases in the value of their land that resulted from such changes without even notifying any public body of their intentions, let alone seeking permission.

Had the planning system arrived ten or fifteen years later, agricultural and forestry operations might well have been classed as 'development'. They were omitted in 1947 because they appeared then to be not only harmless but positively beneficial to the landscape. Agriculture had not yet begun to transform the face of Britain and was not expected to do so. 'It is scarcely probable that the extension of agriculture will go much further, for the limits of profitable agricultural land must have been reached in most places,' wrote leading nature conservationist A. G. Tansley in 1945,[1] as he and other like-minded individuals set about devising the post-war apparatus for conserving Britain's wildlife. At this time, agriculture and forestry were still in many parts of Britain more of a way of life than an industrial process.

And many of the city-based, Wordsworth- and Morris-inspired conservationists of the 1920s and '30s regarded these activities as the embodiment of the simple life untainted by materialism and modern technology for which they yearned. These people were understandably slow to envisage the disfigurement of the countryside by agriculture, which leading conservationist Vaughan Cornish, for example, described as 'the least changing of industrial rural pursuits'.[2] Such people saw the threat to what they valued as posed by the trappings of modern technology: gas-works, telegraph and telephone wires, power stations, radar and radio establishments, electricity pylons, as well as signs of modern living – bungalows along the coast, shacks, ribbon development, mineral workings and quarries. It was the speculative builder who was seen as the main threat to the beauty of the countryside; the farmer was the willing but ailing guardian of the landscape who should be given whatever support he needed. Some areas, like the Wiltshire and Sussex Downs, had been radically changed during the war as their rough downland turf was ploughed to feed a people threatened with starvation by German U-boats. But the impact of these changes had been localized. Had any challenge to agriculture been made it would then have been possible to present the industry as a vital part of the country's defences, as well as a major employer.

There was some appreciation of the threat posed by conifer afforestation. During the 1930s hostility had developed among those seeking the freedom of the open hills for rambling both to the enclosure of open grass and heather moorland and to the replacement of oak and beech woods with dark, impenetrable stands of conifers. In this case, the supposed strategic importance of the industry was called in its aid. In any case, conservationists fell victim to a number of misapprehensions which blunted their attack.

One of the most influential of these conservationists was John Dower, who had been appointed by the war-time Government to consider what form Britain's national parks should take. Writing in 1945, Dower in his report *National Parks in England and Wales*, deplored 'the solidly-massed plantations of spruces and firs, typically in "single-age, single-species" blocks and with sharp, straight edges and "ride" divisions . . . in the mountain

and moorland areas of the North and West (including the
Cheviots, the Lake District, the North York Moors, the Peak
District, Dartmoor and many parts of the uplands of Wales).'[3]
But Dower saw this conifer afforestation as the result of the
Forestry Commission's frantic efforts to meet the brief given to it
by government in 1919: to provide a three-year reserve of timber
for time of war. Dower could not have been expected to foresee
the post-war expansion of private forestry. How was he to know
that private landowners and new forestry companies would seek
to exploit the tax haven forestry was to come to provide?
Virtually all the new afforestation between the wars had been
carried out by a government agency which could be expected to
pose fewer problems in peace-time. In 1945 it did not seem
unreasonable for Dower to hope that the Commission's policy of
upland afforestation

with its emphasis on the production of softwood timber and its disregard
of secondary consequences, will be replaced, at the close of the present
war, by a much more comprehensive policy which gives hardwoods a
larger share in the planting programme, which treats the amenity values
of trees as of no less national importance than their strategic and
economic values, and which makes positive provision for the integration
of silvicultural, agricultural and recreational development.[4]

This hope that the Commission would mellow was reinforced
by apparent evidence that it was susceptible to reason. The
Forestry Commission had entered into an agreement with the
Council for the Preservation of Rural England in 1936 in which
it had agreed to refrain from planting conifers in the central
Lake District – at the time the focus of conservationists' anxieties
about the impact of forestry. Altogether, there appeared to be
cause for optimism.

As it was to turn out, the exemption of agriculture and forestry
was to prove a flaw in the planning process so serious that it was
ultimately to nullify the claim of its architects to be providing a
satisfactory settlement of the long struggle between owners and
people. As landowners turned to farming and forestry to make
money, and as the profitability of the two activities increased,
the rural environment began to be transformed. The appeal and
recreation potential of rural land came to be destroyed over a far

larger area than would ever have been affected by unrestricted building. Wondrous as the Act seemed in 1947, within a couple of decades it was proving hopelessly inadequate as a means of protecting the public interest in land.

Nonetheless, no government has since seen fit to widen the scope of 'development' to include those land clearance, drainage, afforestation and other farming and forestry operations that have been transforming the British landscape. The overriding reason for this is the strengthened power of the lobbies which these industries have managed to set up.

The Shadow of the Conifer

In the post-war era forestry was the first of these major rural activities to attract attention. During the 1960s, private planting by established landowners as well as the new private forestry companies began to gather pace. Conservation bodies found their activities no easier to influence than the block planting still being carried on by the Forestry Commission. In 1961 arrangements were introduced for voluntary consultation between the national park authorities, the Forestry Commission and the Timber Growers' Association, which represented the private planters. However, these arrangements soon proved inadequate, and valued landscapes continued to disappear under conifers both inside and outside the national parks. In the course of public discussion of the issue during the early 1970s, the Council for the Preservation of Rural England, the Ramblers' Association, the Forestry Action Group and the Council for National Parks all urged the Government to extend planning controls to the afforestation of bare land.

But the Heath Government, in which landowners were prominently represented, was not willing to go this far. Instead, in 1973 it introduced a consultation process which remains in force, with minor changes.

Under this system (which applies to Great Britain excluding Northern Ireland), the Forestry Commission has to implement specific procedures whenever it receives certain kinds of application from private owners for grant to plant trees. Where conflict between agricultural and forestry interests are concerned, these arrangements come into force for all applications over certain limits. A landowner or occupier may receive a grant to afforest an area of land as small as 0.6 acres, but if the area of planting includes forty-nine acres or more of rough grazing (or ninety-nine acres or more in Scotland) or if it includes twenty-five acres or more of existing farmland in England and Wales (twelve and a half acres in Scotland), then the Forestry Commission has to seek the views of the relevant agriculture department (in England, the Ministry of Agriculture, Fisheries and Food; in Wales, the Welsh Office Agriculture Department; in Scotland, the Department of Agriculture and Fisheries for Scotland). Consultation with local planning authorities takes place only in the entirely different circumstances which occur where a planting proposal falls within a national park (in England and Wales), a national scenic area (in Scotland), or 'in other areas or circumstances of particular sensitivity where it has been agreed by the Commission and the local authority concerned that consultation should take place'.[5] For proposed afforestation within a site of special scientific interest or national nature reserve, the Commission consults the Nature Conservancy Council; while it consults the Red Deer Commission on new planting of 123.5 acres or more in specified parts of the Highlands.

All these authorities have twenty-eight days to formulate their views, and it is open to them to consult other bodies, like amenity societies, if they consider this necessary. If, on receiving the views of these various bodies the Forestry Commission cannot get them and the landowner to agree, if necessary to a modified proposal, the case is referred to one of the Forestry Commission's seven Regional Advisory Committees. Each committee consists of seven to nine members, of whom at least four must be representatives of woodland owners, timber merchants or organizations concerned with the study and promotion of forestry. Representatives of farmers, amenity interests, planning authorities and trade unions make up the remainder. The regional advisory committees try to reconcile the opposing interests. If they are unable to do so, they make a recommendation on whether or not the scheme in question should go ahead. If either the applicant or the objectors are still dissatisfied, the case goes to the Minister of Agriculture or the Secretary of State for Wales or the Secretary of State for Scotland. The Minister, after consulting the Secretary of State for the Environment, issues his decision. However, this decision has only the status of advice, as it is the Forestry Commission, not the Minister, which is empowered to give grants for afforestation. So at the end of what certainly seems on paper to be an impressively ponderous process, the Commission gives its ruling.

As far as the Forestry Commission's own planting and felling operations are concerned, it is up to local authorities to tell the Commission if they wish to be consulted. If there is failure to agree, the case goes to the same Regional Advisory Committees that consider contested applications for grants from the private sector. The only difference in the procedure is that at the end of the day the Minister of Agriculture (or the Secretary of State for Wales or Scotland) is empowered to tell the Forestry Commission what it should do rather than simply issuing a recommendation.

(Applications to the Forestry Commission from the private sector for felling licences go through a procedure similar to that which precedes grants for planting. Felling licences are required by anyone seeking to chop down more than 176 cubic feet of timber in any one calendar quarter, unless the proposed felling forms part of a planting scheme which has already been approved for grant-aid.)

Elaborate though these arrangements sound, they do not amount to a satisfactory means of ensuring that forestry operations are prevented from interfering with other activities of greater social value. There is more about them of appearance than of substance. The regional advisory committees that play such an important role in the procedures are not democratically elected: effectively, they are creatures of the Forestry Commission. These committees have retained their original function of advising the Forestry Commissioners on forestry matters after taking on the new job of trying to resolve conflicts between forestry and conservation in 1973. They were not designed for the arbitration job, and their membership, loaded as it is in favour of forestry interests, does not leave them well suited to the task.

As we have already seen (page 254), the chairmen of five of

the seven regional advisory committees covering the whole of Britain in 1986 were landowners. And although there is a requirement on the Forestry Commission to appoint to these committees people representing trade union, amenity, farming and planning interests, the people they choose are often also landowners. Take the East of England Committee, for instance, which covers nineteen counties from Kent and the Isle of Wight to Derbyshire and Lincolnshire. The regional advisory committees are required to include a representative of planning authorities and a representative of the amenity interest. Both of these on the East of England Committee in 1986 happen to also have been landowners. J. P. M. H. Evelyn, a former planning committee chairman of the Mole Valley District Council and a leading landowner near Dorking, was the planning authority representative, and H. W. Mackworth-Praed the amenity representative. Mr Mackworth-Praed is chairman of the Surrey Naturalists' Trust and has worked as a conservation officer for the National Trust; he owns a small estate at Headley. This is not to say that either Mr Evelyn or Mr Mackworth-Praed are not perfectly capable and sound people, but they are taking places which could have gone to people more completely identified with recreation and conservation. On the East of England Committee, apart from the chairman, an employee of a private forestry company and a timber merchant (both representing the forestry interest) and a trade union representative the remaining five members of the committee were all landowners.

In practice, the regional advisory system leaves the forester as judge and jury in his own case. It is as if planning control in towns were administered by planning committees half of whose members were developers and the other half chosen by developers, with an organization devoted to development empowered to overrule the committee should it come up with the wrong decision.

Those who wish to object to an afforestation proposal or suggest modifications find that the bias in the make-up of the adjudicating bodies is compounded by excessive secrecy throughout the decision-making process.

Take the case of Glen Ample, for instance, the valley in Stirling District that was the subject of large-scale planting between 1983 and 1986, (see p. 206). If somebody wished to build a hotel or even a single house in the Glen or on any other spot of land in the United Kingdom, his local planning authority (or in the case of Northern Ireland the Department of the Environment) would publicize the proposal and invite objections. Anybody in any part of the country could get details of the proposal from the planning authority and expect to be heard at any public inquiry that might be held. If an inquiry was indeed held such an objector would automatically receive a copy of the inspector's decision letter. But when I telephoned Stirling District Council in 1985 to ask for details of the 1985 afforestation proposals, the group development officer of the District Council, Graham Law, told me: 'The difficulty is that this is reputedly confidential between us and the Forestry Commission. Although the information has been publicized in the press, we can't give details. The Forestry Commission only consult us on the basis that the information is treated as confidential.' Mr Law gave me the name of the local official of the Forestry Commission who, he said, might be able to supply me with information. When I wrote to this official to ask for these details and for those of the large block of planting carried out in 1983, he passed my letter on to the Conservator for Mid-Scotland who told me:

Applications for entry into the Forestry Grant Scheme are confidential between the applicant and the Forestry Commission other than for the necessary land use consultations which are made prior to acceptance. It follows therefore that I am not at liberty to provide you with the details you request for the recent planting on the western side of Glen Ample. However the agents who act for the owners are Tilhill Forestry Ltd, Old Sauchie, Sauchieburn, Stirling, and you might like to approach them to see if they will supply the information you wish.

The press reports to which Mr Law referred were references in the *Stirling Observer*, which receives copies of the development schedule: a list of development applications and consultations that is circulated to members of the district council planning committee and to the press. I therefore went back to Mr Law and asked him if I could see the relevant sections of the development schedule since if these had been released to the press surely the information was in the public domain. He agreed.

However, Stirling District Council is not informed by the Forestry Commission of the outcome of applications for forestry grant, so I still needed to find out whether the applications for grant had been rejected or accepted, and if the latter, with or without conditions. As it happened, Tilhill Forestry was prepared to give me the details I needed. But if the company had refused there would have been nothing I could have done about it.

Why, many people might ask, should afforestation proposals be treated as confidential while a proposal to build, say a hypermarket, which may involve divulging all manner of commercial information about a company's plans, is public? The Forestry Commission's answer is that afforestation proposals involve somebody applying for a grant, and it is for this reason that applications should be treated confidentially. An alternative view might be that the involvement of substantial sums of taxpayers' money in grant handouts provides even more of a reason why other interests should be fully and properly consulted. As it is, the 90 square miles of Great Britain converted in the twelve months ending 31 March 1986 to forest plantation as a result of secret decisions was three times the total area of farmland converted to urban and industrial uses in Britain during the same period after proper democratic scrutiny.[6]

The planning register is not the only element in the planning process that finds no equivalent in the forestry machinery. If an aggrieved applicant appeals to the Secretary of State for the Environment against the refusal of planning consent, the inspector he appoints will hold a public inquiry and later fully and publicly report all the arguments. Similarly, the Secretary of State, when he makes a decision, will make his reasons public. But when a regional advisory committee considers a disputed afforestation proposal, all information to be placed before it must be channelled through the Forestry Commission and the reasons behind its decisions are not made public. The Forestry Commission does not explain its attitude to its advisory committee's recommendation, nor are explanations to be had from the Minister of Agriculture or the Secretaries of State for Scotland or Wales. Only in finally issuing its decision on the application is the Forestry Commission required to explain its reasons to the parties concerned. But the letters containing these decisions are not easily understood by those who have not been privy to the formal consultations.

Two views of non-foresters involved in this bizarre process:

The present procedure is not satisfactory and never will be satisfactory because the regional advisory committees regard their job as mediation between an objecting local planning authority and the people who want to carry out the proposal. Unlike the planning applications system, the regional advisory committees seek not to arrive at a satisfactory result in the public interest but at a satisfactory agreement between two parties. Therefore, there is pressure on both parties to compromise, when what is in the interest of the wider community might be an all-or-nothing solution. (J. H. Bradley, National Park Officer for the Brecon Beacons National Park, talking to me in 1985)

The Regional Advisory Committee procedure . . . is a travesty of justice. (Graham Watson, a former member of the Lake District National Park Special Planning Board, speaking at a conference in 1980)[7]

In any case, the whole laborious and perhaps ridiculous procedure of forestry grant disbursement can be circumvented by any private sector company or individual who is dead set on afforesting an area. For the controls, such as they are, apply only to the issuing of a grant. Anyone who is refused grant can of course go ahead without it if he chooses to – and still get his tax relief.

So, in spite of the 1973 measures, any individual or company is still perfectly free to afforest thousands of acres of bare land, build forest roads and replant over the stumps of a deciduous wood without any need to ensure that the proposals will not damage unduly the interests of other members of the community. The body responsible for such control as exists over private forestry, though accountable to a minister of Parliament through the Minister of Agriculture, is in practice remote from public influence. The proportion of cases in which grants for afforestation are withheld or felling licence applications turned down gives an indication of the impact of the slim sanctions that exist. Between 1974 and 1985, the Forestry Commission turned down only twenty-five of the 26,000 applications it received for planting grants and felling licences[8] – a refusal rate of 0.09 per cent. In other words, forestry remains completely outside planning control, and such controls as have existed over afforestation and deforestation have provided no more than a fig-leaf for the otherwise naked pursuit by landowners of their own ends without regard to the concerns of the wider community. Minor changes to the system mooted in 1986 would very slightly improve public participation in the decision-making process while slightly relaxing constraints on afforestation.[9]

The Wildlife and Countryside Act and the Development of a Conservation Protection Racket

In the early 1980s concern about the march of the conifers over Britain's wild upland country was overtaken by public disquiet at the impact on landscape, wildlife, employment and access of forestry's sister-industry, agriculture. Post-war agricultural change was continuing to sweep aside Britain's characteristic small-scale, intimate lowland landscape of hedged fields, spinneys, woods, downs and streams, leaving in its wake a featureless prairie reminiscent of the American Mid-West. Ironically, Britain boasted a planning system which had succeeded in keeping the countryside free from urban intrusions and in conserving the best of the built environment. But this system did not cover agricultural operations and concern over the havoc which the post-war agricultural revolution was wreaking on the rural landscape had never been greater. The Thatcher Government's response was a piece of legislation entitled the Wildlife and Countryside Bill, 1980.

The Conservatives brought about the destruction of the Callaghan Government's Countryside Bill which had fallen when Mrs Thatcher came to power in 1979. But the new Tory Government could not avoid an obligation to effect five international conservation agreements, which dealt mainly with safeguarding locations important for bird migration.[10] As the problem these commitments posed was considered, the Department of the Environment made it known that it had a number of rural tidying-up measures to dispose of, ranging from the legal status of the Countryside Commission to the question of bulls on public footpaths. A Bill was constructed out of these bits and pieces and the international conservation matters. It was expected to pass without comment, but these expectations were to prove extremely misplaced.

The Wildlife and Countryside Bill happened to emerge at a time of particular concern about the landscape. Newspaper columns and television programmes were full of the growing conflict between modern agriculture and conservation. In such a climate, a Bill called the Wildlife and Countryside Bill was taken as being the Government's solution to the central problem, though it had been designed as no more than a tidying-up measure. Amid the ensuing controversy the Bill took eleven months to reach the statute book – far longer than most bills. It attracted a huge number of amendments, many of them seeking far wider and tougher controls on agriculturally-motivated landscape change. The Bill's critics did not only demand that controls on landowners' freedom to make substantial changes in land-use should apply throughout the countryside of Great Britain; they also condemned the measures the Government had put forward for the fragments of land to which the Bill restricted itself (notified Sites of Special Scientific Interest and National Parks) as hopelessly inadequate even as protection for these areas.

Sites of Special Scientific Interest (SSSIs) are areas of land embracing anything from one ditch to a whole estuary, which are supposed to include the best remaining examples of particular wildlife habitats, provide a home for rare plants and animals, or contain interesting geological or physiographical features. Their origins lie in the National Parks and Access to the Countryside Act of 1949 which laid a duty on the Nature Conservancy (which became the Nature Conservancy Council in 1973) to notify local planning authorities of 'areas of special scientific interest'. A succession of statutory instruments of the town and country planning acts subsequently required planning authorities to consult the Nature Conservancy Council over planning applications affecting SSSIs and to take their scientific interest into account when adjudicating such applications. The first SSSIs were selected in 1951, and by 31 March 1986 4,842 sites covering a total of 5,521 square miles (6 per cent of Great Britain) had been carefully selected to embody the highest quality wildlife habitats and geological features and to provide a minimum skeleton environment such as would render the main indigenous wildlife species of Britain free from the risk of extinction whatever happened elsewhere.

Already by 1981, SSSIs had experienced a well-documented history of damage and destruction, caused mainly by agricultural and forestry change. In Wiltshire in 1977, for example, 35 per cent of the SSSIs had been partially destroyed and 5 per cent completely wiped out, according to a study by Mrs Jennifer Tubbs.[11] In almost all cases agricultural reclamation or forestry operations were to blame. Attempts by the Conservancy Council in Wiltshire to influence landowners' plans for SSSIs on their land were not proving successful, the survey found. For example, a letter sent to all SSSI owners and tenants in 1975 asking their intentions about future management resulted in replies from only 2 per cent. However, Mrs Tubbs found that the planning machinery was proving effective in protecting SSSIs from development as defined in the planning Acts. Of thirteen public inquiries into development proposals in neighbouring Hampshire, for instance, the conservation case had prevailed in all but two.

The widespread erosion of SSSIs throughout Great Britain was confirmed by a Nature Conservancy Council study in 1981, just as the Wildlife and Countryside Bill was beginning its passage through Parliament. The previous year, the Conservancy Council had carried out two surveys to discover to what extent all the SSSIs of Great Britain had altered during that year alone. In the first survey, local Conservancy Council officials made lists of known cases of damage to or loss of SSSIs; in the second, site visits were made to a 15 per cent random sample of SSSIs to ascertain whether any changes had been made to them. The first survey revealed that 8 per cent of the SSSIs of Great Britain were known to have been significantly damaged or completely wiped out during 1980. But the sample survey uncovered a far worse situation: 15 per cent of the SSSIs sampled were significantly damaged, or completely destroyed in 1980 alone.[12]

The problem was that the Conservancy Council lacked any power – comparable, say, to the refusal of planning consent – to prevent the destruction of an SSSI by agricultural or forestry change. It had to rely instead on persuading the landowner to exercise self-restraint, or on enticing him to be bought off with a special agreement under Section 15 of the Countryside Act 1968, whereby he would agree to refrain from the operation he planned in return for compensation paid by the Conservancy Council. Lack of funds meant that the Conservancy Council almost always had to rely on the first option. But by 1981 it was abundantly clear that most landowners were not going to agree voluntarily to leave features intact when they could make a lot of money by ploughing them up or covering them with conifers.

So it might have been expected that when the Government drew up its new Act it would introduce some statutory power to prevent the destruction of these environmentally valuable fragments of land – perhaps by an extension of the town and country planning system which might place the owners of SSSIs under obligations similar to those affecting the owners of Britain's 355,000 listed historic buildings. (These controls restrict the buildings' owners' freedom of action: if they are refused consent to make minor changes to the listed buildings they own, they are not entitled to compensation.)

But it did not. During the two-year period before the Bill was published, the National Farmers' Union was consulted by government officials drafting the bill. It suggested, and the officials agreed, that voluntary conservation should be a central plank of the Wildlife and Countryside Act: landowners were to be expected to exercise restraint rather than being forced to do so. Another principle agreed was that any landowner denied the opportunity of maximizing his income from agriculture or forestry through the need to conserve an SSSI should be entitled to be given the extra profit he would forego in the form of a compensation payment from the taxpayer. As Jerry Wiggin MP, then Parliamentary Secretary at the Ministry of Agriculture, explained when the Bill was on its passage through Parliament:

With one or two important exceptions, the Government's philosophy has been firmly that such controls as are to be exercised in the countryside shall be exercised with the agreement and the co-operation of the farmer and landowner . . . I welcome therefore the emphasis that has been given to a code of practice and to the use of management agreements so that farmers or landowners who have to curtail their agricultural operations shall at least receive some monetary benefit in lieu.[13]

The Wildlife and Countryside Act, 1981, which is still in force, requires landowners to notify the Nature Conservancy Council or their national park planning authority respectively should they plan to make a damaging change to two categories of land: all SSSIs; and those areas of moor and heath in national parks or any other special areas that are the subject of special ministerial order. These orders, made under Section 42 of the Act, differ from those made under a similar provision of the 1968 Countryside Act only in that the period of advance notice required by landowners proposing radical change to land covered by an order is extended from the three months in the 1968 statute to nine months, and in that afforestation is covered as well as agricultural change. However, ministers said during debates on the Wildlife and Countryside Bill that they did not envisage any Section 42 orders ever being made, and by 1986 none had been made. (Two orders were made under the Countryside Act 1968, both on Exmoor, covering a total of 344 acres, but they have since been cancelled.) There is thus no statutory requirement on landowners to tell their national park authority when they plan to plough up or 'improve' in some other way for agriculture stretches of moor or heath in national parks.

In practice however, the provisions of the 1981 Act are not limited to SSSIs. This is because a second factor can bring the mechanisms of the Act into play – an application by a farmer or landowner in a national park to the Ministry of Agriculture for a farm capital grant. Such grants have been available for a wide range of activities like the clearance of bushes and natural moorland vegetation, the drainage of wetlands and the spraying of herbicides and fertilizers. All of these things can wipe out much of the natural wildlife of the land concerned or, particularly in the case of the enclosure and ploughing of open moorland, destroy its value for walking. In the past, the Ministry of Agriculture had been reluctant to withhold grant for even the most environmentally damaging schemes. By 1981, out of the thousands of millions of pounds-worth of capital grants it had been responsible for issuing, the Ministry had turned down a grant application on environmental grounds on only a handful of occasions. The Wildlife and Countryside Act is intended to make the withholding of capital grants affecting land in SSSIs or national parks a less rare occurrence. For when a farmer in a national park or SSSI puts in his claim to the Ministry of Agriculture for a grant, that claim now has to be accompanied by a statement from the park authority or Conservancy Council saying they approve the application. In order to get this statement, the farmer has to notify the Conservancy Council or park authority before he undertakes the work for which he plans to claim a grant.

The Wildlife and Countryside Act requires the Nature Conservancy Council or a national park authority which objects to a proposal of which it has been notified under the Act and from which it fails to persuade a landowner or occupier to refrain, to offer him a management agreement whereby he agrees to leave the landscape feature intact and the Conservancy Council or park authority agree to pay him compensation for so doing. If no management agreement is concluded within the three-month period provided for negotiation in SSSIs, the Secretary of State may be asked to make a nature conservation order that extends the period during which the landowner may not alter the SSSI for a further eight months. If an agreement is still not reached, the only option open to the Conservancy Council – apart from allowing the work to proceed – is compulsory purchase. This option is not available to national park authorities (which have only two months in which to try to thwart damaging landscape changes through management agreements). For they are empowered to seek a compulsory purchase order only to secure access to land, and in practice no such order has been made since the enabling legislation was passed in 1949. The Government twice defeated by narrow majorities amendments moved during the passage of the Wildlife and Countryside Bill to enable national park authorities to impose moorland conservation orders in cases where they could not reach agreement with landowners. As a concession, the Government introduced into the Bill a requirement that park authorities should publish annual maps showing those areas of moor and heath the authorities consider it particularly important to conserve. The 1981 Act also provided for Ministers to publish a code of guidance advising landowners on the management of their SSSIs; this code has no statutory force. And in 1985, the Wildlife and Countryside (Amendment)

Act plugged a loophole preventing landowners who have received notice that the Conservancy Council is planning to notify land in their ownership as an SSSI from ploughing it up or otherwise altering it by extending the protection of the Act to the consultation period before the SSSI designation becomes official.

But despite its small number of positive features, the 1981 Act amounts to a puny shield for the countryside. It embraces the principles of voluntarism and compensation, even though this is not required for consistency's sake. There is no more reason why the nation should rely on voluntary self-restraint to conserve the nation's rural heritage than it should rely on such altruism to stop building developers despoiling the urban skyline. And why should farmers, foresters and landowners be compensated for refraining from damaging the environment when other industrialists, often labouring under much tighter financial constraints, are expected to bear any losses occasioned through environmental restrictions?

No Minister sought to justify these principles during the passage of the Wildlife and Countryside Act, despite their enormous implications both for public spending and for the future shape of the British countryside. So where did they come from? By what process was the conclusion established that the conservation of the countryside against agricultural and forestry change should depend on persuasion and compensation?

The first occasion on which these two principles attracted public notice seems to have been the *Countryside in 1970* conferences. These conferences consisted of discussions between landowning and conservation bodies and government agencies about the future shape of the British countryside. To consider how conflicts between modern farming and forestry on the one hand and conservation on the other should be resolved, a special committee on agriculture, forestry and land management was set up and asked to report to the final 1970 conference. This group not only set out the principles of voluntarism and compensation that were to bear fruit in the 1981 Wildlife and Countryside Act; it also assumed that agriculture must always take priority: 'It is unwise to pursue any policy which discourages the proper agricultural use of land,' declared the group. If wildlife was to be conserved, it should be done in such a way that agriculture was not impaired: 'Every effort should be made to retain as much wildlife habitat as is consistent with efficient land management.' On compensation, the group asserted: 'Where a farmer is required to keep at least some land in a condition that is acceptable to amenity interests but thereby inflicts loss on himself, he must be clearly entitled to proper compensation.' Its final unequivocal conclusion: 'The public must be prepared to pay for amenity and conservation.'[14]

Who were the people who came to this conclusion and in what sort of environment did they work? The group consisted of eleven men. Four of these were representatives of the National Farmers' Union. Two more represented the Country Land-owners' Association. One represented the Forestry Commission. In addition, there was one academic (an expert on agricultural economics) and two independent members. Both of the independent members owned land and were also interested in conservation. The chairman of the group was Walter Lane, who at the time was clerk to Lindsey County Council and the person designated by the County Councils' Association from its membership to take a special interest in conservation. Robert Boote, the then deputy director of the Nature Conservancy, acted as secretary to the organizing standing committee of the *Countryside in 1970* conferences and attended several meetings of this and the various other study groups.

In spite of the presence of these last two, the membership profile of the group reflected the deference to the landowning and farming community that has characterized the making of public policy on the countryside for so long. There was nobody on the group with a special knowledge of outdoor recreation provision and access, landscape conservation or archaeology, for example. And the group went on to deliberate in an atmosphere when 'conservation enjoyed neither the backing in the country nor the recognition in official circles that it enjoys today' (Walter Lane in an interview in 1985).

The group also deliberated before the present disquiet at the scale of public subsidy to farmers had taken shape. Yet this unrepresentative group's view that conservation should depend on persuasion and compensation continued to dominate country-side policy-making during the 1970s. Conservationists who

despaired of achieving an effective means of defending the
countryside started to throw in their lot with persuasion-and-
compensation in the absence of any prospect of anything better.
And although the *Countryside in 1970* group had not dealt with
forestry, its assertion of the principle of compensation came to be
applied in respect not only of farmers but also of foresters
deprived of potential profit in the interests of conservation.

What the Wildlife and Countryside Act has done is to set
the seal of legislative approval on the system of 'voluntary'
conservation and compensation. The Act contains few improvements on the slim sanctions against landscape destruction that
have existed since 1968. But by enshrining the principle of
compensation in law where SSSIs and national parks are concerned, it creates a precedent. What has happened is that
society's demand for conservation fired by criticism of landowners' actions has led to the provision of a financial haven for
farmers even more cosy than agricultural price support.

Once the Wildlife and Countryside Act had been passed,
the Nature Conservancy Council committed itself to offering
landowners management agreements with compensation in cases
where it succeeded in persuading the Forestry Commission to
withhold a planting grant for the afforestation of open country or
the replacement of broad-leafed woodland with conifers. As in
the case of agriculture, the compensation includes payment in
respect of the loss of many of the subsidies the landowner would
have received. So cosy is the compensation system that the
Conservancy Council or the national park authority are expected
to pay the legal and other professional fees run up by the
landowner in negotiating or objecting to a management agreement.[15] The fact that the landowner may be a millionaire or a
forestry company seeking tax avoidance opportunities for rich
clients is irrelevant.

In line with the 'voluntary' principle underlying the Wildlife
and Countryside Act, a landowner is perfectly free to decline the
offer of a management agreement. And in this case there is little
to stop him going ahead with his original plans since, as we have
seen, the only sanction available to the Conservancy Council is
compulsory acquisition of the land involved, a course open to a
park authority only if it is seeking to secure public access over a

tract of land. Should a landowner plan works in a national park
without seeking a capital grant, he is naturally unaffected by the
efforts of the 1981 legislators to stiffen the procedures whereby
such grants are made. He is still perfectly free to pipe streams
underground, clear away hedges and bushes, straighten river-
banks, apply herbicide to whole hillsides and so on without
telling anyone what he plans, so long as he does this at his own
expense and the land involved does not lie within an SSSI. Nor
is a farmer who wishes to claim grant but has failed to notify a
park authority of what he has in mind breaking the law: he is
merely breaking a condition of the grant scheme and thereby
jeopardizing his grant application.

The existence of the Wildlife and Countryside Act undoubtedly
means that some stretches of land have remained unploughed
that would otherwise now be supporting profitable crops or
conifer trees. But the number involved is tiny.

Let us consider the impact of the Act on national parks by
looking at the Act's consequences for the North York Moors
National Park, whose experience has been typical. This park,
serving in particular the people of Middlesbrough, Hartlepool,
Scarborough and York has seen a considerable loss of open
moorland to agricultural intensification and conifer planting –
sixty-three square miles or 25 per cent of the park's moorland
between 1950 and 1985. But the park committee's efforts to
conserve land that is the subject of potentially damaging farm
grant applications have been largely frustrated by landowners'
lack of interest in management agreements. During the first
three years of the operation of the Act, the park authority
responded to eighteen of the farm grant applications it received
with the offer of a management agreement and compensation. In
six of these cases, the landowner ignored the management
agreement offer and went ahead with the operation he had
planned. In only three cases have terms been agreed. In the
other cases, negotiations may drag on for years, since there is no
time limit imposed by the Act on the landowner (though the
park authority has to comply with a very tight timetable for
consultation). As the park authority has to pay the landowners'
legal and professional fees in negotiating a management agreement as well as its own, the landowner has little incentive to

bring negotiations to a quick conclusion in order to keep down
his solicitor's fees. On occasion landowners have been ready to
go and destroy ecologically rich woodland and hay meadows
without advance notification even though they have thereby
been putting at risk their farm grant award. To stop such things
happening, 'The National Park Committee sees no alternative in
cases of basic land-use change, such as the ploughing of moorland
and the drainage of wetlands, to a system of control analogous to
planning control,' it told the House of Commons Environment
Committee for its examination in 1984 of the operation and
effectiveness of the Wildlife and Countryside Act.[16]

Nonetheless, the North York Moors National Park Committee
may come to look back on the period up to 1985 as a relatively
successful time for moorland conservation. For in the autumn of
1985, in response to calls that it should pay greater heed to
conservation, the Ministry of Agriculture withdrew the capital
grant that had been available for the replacement of moor and
heath with ryegrass. Helpful as this move may seem for the
countryside as a whole, in the national parks an incidental effect
of the change is to remove the mechanism by which national
park authorities have been alerted to landowners' plans to
replace open moorland with ryegrass lots. In 1985, the Ministry
also cut the rates of capital grant available for a wide range of
activities – a step which is likely to mean that landowners in
national parks will more often go ahead with operations like
fencing, drainage or making farm roads without bothering to
apply for capital grant and therefore without notifying the park
authorities of their plans.

The Act has been little more successful in rescuing threatened
SSSIs. For an idea of the trouble and expense involved in
conserving any SSSI using the legislation, consider the case of
one site which has been saved.

Baddesley Common, a thirty-seven-acre SSSI in Hampshire,
is an area of wet heathland and developing woodland. It is
unique in southern England in that its communities of plants
and (especially invertebrate) animals have been able to develop
in the absence of the heavy grazing that has impoverished other
otherwise similar habitats like the woods and heaths of the New
Forest.

In June 1982, a local builder and his wife, Mr and Mrs John Burns, bought 155 acres of land including the SSSI: they planned to clear the land for grazing as a 'second string to their bow', although they knew that part of the land was an SSSI and that this would mean the Nature Conservancy Council would seek to restrain their activities on it. In July 1982, the Conservancy Council formally renotified this part of Baddesley Common as an SSSI and sent to Mr and Mrs Burns a list of the activities it considered would damage the scientific value of the site and for which it required advance notification. A month later the Council received notice from the new owners that they intended to drain the land, clear away bushes, plough it and convert it to pasture.

The Council offered Mr and Mrs Burns a management agreement with compensation payments, but the Council and the owners were unable to reach any agreement and towards the end of the consultation period, Mr and Mrs Burns reiterated their intention to clear, drain and plough, as they were perfectly entitled to do once the three-month period was up. To save the site, the Conservancy Council's local official, Colin Tubbs, asked the Secretary of State for the Environment to make an order under Section 29 of the Act. This order, made in October 1982, extended the three-month period during which Mr and Mrs Burns could not plough up the site for a further eight months. Mr and Mrs Burns appealed against this order, and in February 1984, a public hearing was held by an inspector appointed by the Secretary of State for the Environment. In his report the inspector wrote: 'I am satisfied from the unchallenged evidence of the Nature Conservancy Council that the SSSI in question constitutes an area of immense value as a reservoir of species and habitats and that its importance is enhanced by the fact that there are few, if any, comparable sites in Britain.' In July 1983, the Secretary of State upheld the view of his inspector that the section 29 order be neither revoked nor amended.

This still however left the Council with the task of negotiating with Mr and Mrs Burns, a task it found no easier in the six weeks left before the Section 29 order ran out than it had been before. Finally it told Mr and Mrs Burns that unless terms of purchase were agreed before the consultation period was up, it would serve a compulsory purchase order. Had such an order

been made, Mr and Mrs Burns could have appealed against it;
they were also legally entitled to appeal to the High Court
against the Secretary of State's decision on the Section 29 order.
Instead, they agreed to sell, but only on condition that the
Conservancy Council also bought some land outside that covered
by the order.

This case – which has to be regarded as one of the Act's
success stories – illustrates two of its defects. First, the procedures
which the Act provides are cumbersome. If the activities which
Mr and Mrs Burns had proposed for Baddesley had involved
building, the precision instrument of planning control would
have enabled the Nature Conservancy Council to secure the
area completely by recommending that planning permission be
turned down. Since agricultural activity was what was proposed,
no such measure was available; all the Conservancy could do at
the end of the day was to take on ownership of the site itself.
Second, rescuing Baddesley Common has been a very expensive
operation indeed for the taxpayer. Not only has he had to find
the £82,500 to buy the site, he has had to pay Mr and Mrs
Burns' legal costs. Mr and Mrs Burns certainly do not seem to
have lost out on the deal. They paid £99,000 for 154.6 acres in
1982; the Conservancy Council paid £82,500 for sixty-eight acres
(44 per cent of the total) in 1984. So the average price of an acre
of Baddesley Common almost doubled during the two years –
from £640 per acre to £1,213 per acre, or a net capital gain on
the sixty-eight acres the Burns sold to the Conservancy Council
of £38,964.

So high are the levels of compensation landowners can claim
under management agreements that this is forcing up the price
of land over which agreements might be made, thereby making
conservation by land purchase far less likely than it was in the
past. The Sampher SSSI at Sandwich Bay in Kent is a good
case in point.

Together, Pegwell Bay and Sandwich Bay on the Kent coast
south of Ramsgate make up one of the most magnificently wild
areas of south-east England. Separated by the estuary of the
river Stour, the gentle curve of Pegwell Bay embraces salt marsh
and mudflats (a favourite haunt for wading birds) while the
straight sand and shingle shore of Sandwich Bay is backed by

miles of sand dunes, much of both shingle and dune covered in a dazzling variety of wild flowers. The Sampher lies in the middle of this complex, a 268-acre area which is part salt-marsh, bank and river, and part (about two-thirds) marshy rough grazing with hawthorn bushes.

Adjacent to The Sampher is productive arable land – testimony both to modern technology and to the large subsidies available for land reclamation. Anxious to prevent The Sampher coming similarly under the plough, the Kent Trust for Nature Conservation, a voluntary conservation organization relying on members' contributions, began negotiations in 1983 to buy The Sampher from the farmer who had just bought it. The Trust was anxious to preserve The Sampher's rare plants like the sharp rush and the rest harrow, and the rest harrow moth, which naturalists say occurs only here and at one other site near Folkestone. At first, the Trust understood that the owner, Tim Hulme of Merton Farm, Canterbury, was willing to sell them The Sampher, and the price discussed was £160,000. But when the Trust's land agent went to see the owner in 1984 to agree the terms of purchase, Mr Hulme told him that he would not part with the land for £160,000. The reason was that Mr Hulme had discovered that he could get more for The Sampher through a management agreement with the Nature Conservancy Council under the Wildlife and Countryside Act without parting with the freehold of his land. Under such an agreement, the Council would pay him compensation of £110 per acre every year for leaving The Sampher as it is. Calculated over twenty years, this makes the land worth £410,000. The Trust, unable to find this sort of money, found itself gazumped by the Wildlife and Countryside Act. The most the Trust can hope for is that it will be included in the management agreement the Nature Conservancy Council may eventually sign with Mr Hulme and which the Conservancy will pay for. In August 1985, however, terms had not been agreed and Mr Hulme told me that he would not have parted with the land for £410,000: indeed, so valuable was the land in his opinion that under conditions of free negotiation, no figure would ever be enough.

If the compensation provisions of the Wildlife and Countryside Act provide a protection racket rather than protection in the sphere of agricultural intensification, the same thing happens with large-scale afforestation schemes. Here again, the guarantee of juicy state subsidies means that land developers find themselves in the happy position of heads we win, tails we win.

Creag Meagaidh, an important SSSI in Inverness-shire, was eventually sold to the Nature Conservancy Council in 1985 after much controversy over an application by its owner, Fountain Forestry Limited, for a Forestry Commission grant to afforest much of the open valley and hillside. The Conservancy Council paid the private forestry company £430,000, or £130,000 more than Fountain Forestry had paid for the land two years earlier.

Nonetheless, for the Conservancy Council, land acquisition is cheaper than a management agreement in the long run; it also ensures total control of a site and obviates the need for the monitoring of a management agreement. However, the Conservancy Council is not allowed to buy land unless either the landowner is willing to sell or he has been offered a management agreement and has rejected this, in which latter case compulsory purchase is possible.

At Boulsbury Wood on the Hampshire/Dorset border, the Nature Conservancy Council secured in 1984 a management agreement involving curbs on forestry which requires annual compensation payments amounting to more than three times what the Council paid to buy the far larger site at Creag Meagaidh.

Boulsbury Wood, a stretch of ancient woodland carpeted with autumn crocus and lily-of-the-valley, became a candidate for conservation only by chance after a local woodman who happened to be a knowledgeable amateur botanist was awakened one morning by the roar of bulldozers on a piece of scrub next to the Wood. He knew this patch of scrub to be home to one of Britain's rarest plants, the wood vetch, and told local amateur naturalists what was afoot. Eventually, the Nature Conservancy Council became involved. It decided that Boulsbury Wood was the most species-rich stretch of woodland in the whole of southern England. Under a management agreement secured in 1984, the Council is committed to compensating the Wood's owners (Viscount Cranborne, the MP for South Dorset, and others) to the tune of £21,150 every year. The agreement runs for sixty-five years, and the payments are index-linked. At 1983 prices, this means that the benefit to the owners will be £1.3 million. The nation will benefit from the conservation of the essential features of Boulsbury Wood. However, the agreement confers no extra public access to the Wood, so apart from what can be glimpsed from the public path and road the bulk of what is conserved must be left to the imagination of those citizens who will be contributing the money.

In 1986, further scope for compensation for farmers who volunteer to conserve landscape against damaging agricultural change emerged in the proposals for 'environmentally sensitive areas' of the Conservative Government. In response to undiminished concern at the destruction of landscapes and wildlife habitats by agricultural expansion, the Government provided in its Agriculture Act 1986 for the Minister of Agriculture, Fisheries and Food to designate environmentally sensitive areas in which farmers would be entitled to receive payments for refraining from damaging landscape change. An eventual target of £6 million was set for spending, though initial reactions from farmers were not enthusiastic.

Despite the publicity given to the environmentally sensitive area, the tool does not look like proving the salvation of the countryside. Add together the acreage of land that will be eligible for payment in each of the six areas named for England and Wales, and it amounts to no more than 0.6 per cent of the land surface of these two countries.

The Inheritance Tax Cop-out

Alongside the procedure for compensating landowners through management agreements under the Wildlife and Countryside Act is another procedure designed to bring about improvements in landowner behaviour at a cost to the public purse. This works through the tax system. But though the transfers involved are less painful to the authorities – since nobody regards tax foregone in exactly the same way as direct subsidy – the procedure is unsatisfactory not just because it is less surgical in its effect but also because it is enshrined in secrecy which does much to undermine its usefulness and helps turn the system into more of a device for propping up the financial position of landowning families than a real help to the community at large.

The system works through reliefs from inheritance tax (see p 227). Anybody who transfers on death capital worth at least £71,000 to somebody else is liable to pay inheritance tax to the Treasury. The rate of the tax ranged in 1986 from 30 per cent for capital worth £71,000 to 60 per cent for capital of over £317,000. Landowners can however reduce their liability to inheritance tax by 50 per cent through claiming business relief or agricultural relief – as they could for capital transfer tax which was introduced in 1975 as a replacement for death duty and was in its turn replaced by inheritance tax in the 1986 Budget. The main difference between capital transfer tax (CTT) and inheritance tax is that under CTT tax, albeit at a slightly lower rate than on death, was also payable on transfers made during the life of the donor. However, the replacement in the 1981 Budget of the principle of the cumulation over an individual's lifetime for the assessment of CTT to that of cumulation over ten years made possible considerable reduction of the CTT payable.

There were however certain circumstances in which a landowner could receive complete exemption from capital transfer tax and these circumstances also apply to inheritance tax. These circumstances arise from the efforts of a Labour government to secure for the public some stake in its heritage of outstanding landscapes and buildings without actually nationalizing them. The Finance Act, 1976 provides that a landowner may attract complete exemption from CTT in respect of a building which, in the opinion of the Treasury, is of outstanding interest or in respect of land of outstanding scenic, scientific or historic interest, provided that in each case he agrees to conserve it and to grant reasonable public access to it.[17] (Similar exemptions are available for works of art.) The Treasury looks to the relevant government agency (such as one of the Countryside Commissions or the Nature Conservancy Council) to advise it on whether the property in question is of outstanding interest and what sort of undertakings on conservation and access should be required of the owner in return for his tax exemption. The typical stretch of rural land for which exemption is granted consists of a country house that is a grade I or grade II listed historic building, together with the land around needed to 'protect' it – say the acreage that can be seen from the window of the principal bedroom. Or, the land around an historic house may be granted exemption in its own right, as may other stretches of rural land without buildings on them. The exemption is granted only when a taxable event takes place – which may be not only transfers on death but also the transfer of money into a trust fund whose object is to maintain property deemed to be of outstanding interest. There is nothing to stop owners generating income from the property covered by an inheritance tax or a CTT exemption – whether it be from letting out grouse shooting or charging entrance fees to their houses.

In 1984, the Capital Taxes Office told me that on average fifty claims for exemption for CTT for outstanding buildings and land are granted every year in the United Kingdom. The figure in the late 1970s was smaller because fewer people knew of the scheme's existence. This information on the total number of claims is the only information about this system that officially exists in the public domain. The rest is secret, on the grounds that what is involved is confidential information about an individual's tax affairs. What this means is that the public cannot know what are the sites involved, the areas concerned or the undertakings given. It therefore cannot judge whether the benefits conferred are worth the loss of revenue.

During negotiations over management agreements, organizations like the Nature Conservancy Council administer a budget from which they make payments of compensation according to clear priorities. The CTT exemptions occur on a very different basis. Here, the budget is open-ended: there is no limit to the total value of exemptions that can be granted. But the government agency officials negotiating the undertakings do not have enough information. As one former official who had been involved in these negotiations explained to me:

We were fighting in the dark. They were seeking exemptions and we were asking for undertakings. They were squealing and saying 'Oh, no, we couldn't possibly afford to do that.' Yet we never knew the value of the exemption that was being offered. So they might have been offered

£1 million-worth of exemption while we were asking for £2,000-worth of undertakings. Unless you knew the value of the exemption, you couldn't judge the level of undertakings.

The secrecy surrounding the system also brings its enforcement into question. In open hill and moorland areas of Scotland, 'reasonable public access' is usually interpreted to mean that the owner will allow the public to wander at will, although he can close the area for certain periods, for instance when stalking is in progress, so long as he provides agreed excepted routes. This information (without any mention of the tax exemption) will usually be posted on a landowner's territory, like similar access notices on other Scottish estates. Suppose that, in contravention of the undertaking, a landowner or his factor turns people off the land in question. Unless they are turned off a right of way, most people, ignorant of the fact of the CTT exemption and access undertaking, would not even think of complaining to anybody. Even if they did, they would have no way of knowing that the Countryside Commission for Scotland was the relevant body. The Commission itself is in no position to undertake spot checks.

South of the border, county planning authorities or national park authorities often act as the Countryside Commission's local agents in putting the undertakings of a CTT exemption into effect, whether this means steps like the creation of new rights of way or monitoring developments on the ground. It is this process which has yielded most of such information as exists about the working of CTT exemption schemes. Not that much gets out. When planning authorities are asked to act as the Countryside Commission's agents over CTT exemption undertakings, they are cautioned by the Commission not to disclose the fact that a CTT exemption is involved. This can mean that officials know that a CTT exemption exists, but even their own elected masters are ignorant of the fact, learning only that, for instance, a particular owner has agreed to dedicate a new right of way.

Detailed information has come into the public domain in respect of just two exemptions granted to land. The first concerns an exemption granted in 1978 to the Trustees of the Nawton Tower Estate (who include the Countess of Feversham and her daughter Lady Clarissa Collins) in respect of a 14,500-acre stretch of moorland consisting of Bransdale Moor and parts of other moors, in the heart of the North York Moors National Park. Once the exemption had been granted over these moors, the Countryside Commission asked the national park authority to act as its agent in ensuring that the Trustees conserved the landscape and allowed public access. The management plan drawn up and – unusually – published by the North York Moors National Park Committee (which, as a matter of policy, makes public as much information about its activities as possible) sets out the undertakings required of the landowner;[18] and there is no reason to suppose these are in any way untypical of other CTT exemption undertakings.

What the Trustees are required to do is to consult with the national park authority on any proposal that might affect ancient monuments on the land or its scenic or scientific interest. This applies not only to developments requiring planning permission, but also to the construction of estate roads, farm or forestry buildings, the felling of woodland, tree planting, the ploughing and reclamation of moorland and the installation of new drainage facilities. The Trustees are allowed to continue to burn the moor to stimulate the new growth of heather to maintain grouse shooting, but under the exemption they do so only under a plan agreed with the national park authority. Finally, the undertaking stipulates that they will allow reasonable public access to the area. What access means on the ground is that the estate must grant public access along existing rights of way, but it is allowed to ask members of the public not to leave these rights of way during April and May (in case they trample grouse nests), during August and September (in case they interfere with grouse shooting) and at other times when moor burning is taking place or when rehabilitation measures are in progress to restore eroded tracks.

Essentially, these undertakings amount to little more than a continuation of previous practice. Nor do they actually forbid the Trustees from ploughing up stretches of the moor, since they are required only to consult with the park authority if they wish to plough. In practice they would probably be unlikely to go ahead with ploughing to which the park authority had objected because they might well then lose their tax exemption over that stretch of moor. In those circumstances, the Trustees would, however, be entitled to a management agreement under the Wildlife and Countryside Act. The undertakings on access do not significantly change the situation before the exemption was granted. So the exemption appears to be a good deal for the Trustees and a bad deal for the public.

Where new public access facilities are granted, these sometimes take the form of new public rights of way. In 1981, land in the Yorkshire Pennines on Penyghent forming part of the Langliffe estate, passed from Michael Dawson to his nephew, Robert Bell. There was a CTT exemption, and as in the Nawton Towers case, the terms of this required the landowner to consult with the planning authority, in this case the Yorkshire Dales National Park Authority, over any proposal that might affect the scenic or nature conservation value of the 8.8 square miles involved. On public access, the estate undertook to continue its agreements with the Council of Northern Caving Clubs (this is prime pot-holing country) and to create four new rights of way. By 1986, three of these had been agreed, but the fourth was subject to dispute. In addition, the public were to be allowed to wander freely on the summit of Penyghent. Up till now, however, the public have enjoyed de facto freedom to wander over a much larger area than the Penyghent summit alone: some of the many parts of the area covered by the exemption that are covered by no public rights of way but where people have walked freely include Penyghent's gritstone crags (one of the best sites in the Pennines to practise rock- and ice-climbing), while others have looked for nesting ravens over Plover Hill or searched widely for the area's botanical speciality, the purple mountain saxifrage. The exemption undertaking states that, except on the summit of Penyghent where de facto access will be maintained, access in future will be on public rights of way. So there is a distinct possibility that although the public will have more guaranteed rights of way in the area than before the agreement was signed, their freedom to wander on the ground will in practice be reduced.

The advantage of the CTT exemption arrangements is that they may well secure the protection of outstanding pieces of

Britain's landscape heritage which would otherwise be irrevocably changed. As the whole thing is a secret, no one can know for sure. Does the cost of the tax foregone exceed the sums paid as compensation under the Wildlife and Countryside Act management agreements? Again, no one knows. Is this a wise use of public money? Unlike those sites covered by management agreements, the landscapes covered by CTT exemption agreements are not necessarily threatened by destruction. Indeed, they seem to be the very stretches of land most unlikely to be radically altered. This is not only the case with the amenity land around a country house. The Bransdale moors covered by the CTT exemption lie in the very heart of the North York Moors, in an area which, more than any other, has been free from ploughing because this is less practicable in such places than it is elsewhere. If several million pounds are to be spent on the conservation of the moorland of the North York Moors and this is to be handed over to landowners, the money might well be better spent on some of the border moorland areas far more likely than Bransdale to be ploughed up or planted with conifers. Nor do the access undertakings given under CTT exemption agreements seem to be worth such a lot of money. Six of the proposed new rights of way which the Countryside Commission proposed to the Trustees of the Chatsworth Settlement when discussing a possible exemption agreement for the Bolton Abbey estate (including Barden Moor and Barden Fell) were routes that were claimed when the draft definitive map of public rights of way for the old West Riding was being drawn up in the 1950s. These, along with many other paths, were dropped by the County Council when landowners' objections had to be considered at quarter sessions – a lengthy and expensive procedure. In other words, some of the access benefits being granted are no more than the buying back of what some people at least considered to be their rights.

But should landowners receive such large rewards anyway? And if they should, should they not come from profits from the exploitation of land that is not in the public interest, whether this be by other landowners or by the same landowners as are receiving the CTT exemptions on other parts of their property? Like the compensation payments made under the Wildlife and

Countryside Act, the CTT exemption scheme emerges as another
misguided, half-baked non-solution. On its own it cannot provide
a means of conserving the whole of the British countryside. On
the other hand, the secrecy that envelops the system, coupled
with the open-ended nature of the total exemptions provided,
turns the system into a means of further enhancing the financial
position of the landowning class at the expense of the rest of the
community.

Shamefully Naked

Most of Britain's land enjoys the protection neither of such
safeguards as the Wildlife and Countryside Act provides, nor of
the benefits of the inheritance tax exemption system, let alone of
planning machinery comparable to that operating in the built
environment. Instead the whims and wishes of the men and
women who own land take effect without any real scope for
intervention on the part of the community.

In lowland Britain, the contrast between the safeguards that
planning provides for our urban environment and their absence
in the countryside is stark indeed. Thousands of meticulously
preserved historic towns and villages from Rye, Framlingham
and Avebury to Berwick-on-Tweed, once framed by luxuriant,
and colourful countryside, now stand isolated in their dignity
and elegance amid crude, featureless expanses of barley or
ryegrass; while the view from many of the small ancient towns of
our hill country – like Doune near Stirling, for example, with its
ruined medieval castle – is limited to rank upon rank of dark
and forbidding conifers.

The reason why the towns retain their charms while the
countryside does not is of course that forestry is totally exempt
from planning control and agricultural operations are almost
completely so. Massive landscape change can occur without the
elected representatives of the people having any real say in the
matter. Apart from the tree preservation order, the only tool
available to local planning authorities to curb the impact of
farming and forestry change on the landscape is the Article Four
Direction. This enables a planning authority to withdraw the
planning consent deemed to exist for all farm and forestry roads,

forestry buildings, and agricultural buildings less than 5,000 square feet in ground floor area (this is equivalent to the area of two and a half tennis courts). But only a handful of such Directions are made each year mainly because the law requires that farmers and foresters subjected to Orders have to be compensated for any extra profit foregone as a result (unlike the urban developer denied planning permission). So new farm buildings, like the 105,500 constructed on Britain's farms between 1978 and 1984, alone, have imposed great change on the countryside.[19]

Rural landowners also remain free to bulldoze new roads across 'their' land. More than three thousand miles of new vehicular track were laid across the countryside of Britain between 1978 and 1984.[20] In Grampian region many of the new roads bulldozed to ease access for deer stalkers leave conspicuous scars for miles around, often on formerly trackless wilderness areas. Seven hundred and fourteen miles of new road were constructed through this region alone between 1960 and 1981.[21] Since 1981, planning consent has been required for new estate roads rising about 980 feet in Scotland's highest tier of landscape designation, the 'national scenic areas'. These occupy a total of 4 per cent of the land of Grampian region.

South of the border, national parks are the only areas within which any sort of consent for new farm and forestry buildings and roads is required, and this only since 1986. After decades of calls for planning controls over such building throughout the countryside, the then Secretary of State for the Environment, Nicholas Ridley MP, finally made an order (the Town and Country Planning [Agriculture and Forestry Development in National Parks, etc.] Special Development Order, 1986) which requires landowners who propose to construct farm or forestry buildings or roads in the ten national parks and in the Norfolk Broads to notify their park authority or the Broads Authority before they go ahead. That authority then has the option of requiring the landowner to obtain formal approval for the design, siting and external appearance. The need for the road or building cannot be questioned; and Mr Ridley has told the park authorities that there will be a general presumption in favour of farmers and foresters carrying on their activities unimpeded.

Late in 1986, Mr Ridley announced another concession. He revealed that landowners would shortly have to seek planning permission for the construction of a new farm building if it was intended to house livestock or to dispose of waste products from the rearing of livestock and if the proposed building would lie within a quarter of a mile of an existing non-agricultural building. Welcome as this proposed move will be to those upset by smells from new intensive pig and chicken farms, it represents only a small concession to those who have campaigned for years to put farm buildings on a par with other industrial buildings under the town and country planning system.

One other recent advance is that woodland clearance and coniferization have become subject to what could prove effective controls by the government-appointed Forestry Commission. As we have seen (p. 433), anyone wishing to fell trees to clear space for agriculture or to convert deciduous woodland to conifers has always needed a felling licence from the Forestry Commission. In the past this was pretty much a formality: in the year ending 31 March 1979, for example, the Commission turned down only five of the 1,945 applications for felling licences it received, and of these only one was rejected on amenity grounds. However, in 1985, after a review of its policy on broadleafed trees, the Forestry Commission announced that when considering future applications for felling licences, it would operate a presumption against the clearance of broadleafed woods for agriculture and that it would not expect to see more than 25 per cent of a broadleafed ancient wood or 50 per cent of other broadleafed woods replaced with conifers.[22]

Through this single if belated step, the Forestry Commission may now make a real impact on landscape change. It remains to be seen however how the Commission will deal with one group of landowners who are not required to seek a felling licence. If a landowner has entered into a forestry agreement with the Commission whereby he agrees to plant or fell woodlands in accordance with a plan agreed between the two parties and in return receives a grant from the Commission, he does not need to apply for a felling licence each time he plans to clear fell. Nearly two million acres of privately-owned woodland in Britain are already subject to such agreements. If the Commission is serious about retaining the broadleafed character of Britain's lowland countryside then the coniferization of Britain's lowland woods must be reversed, since in many areas – like Dorset for instance – there is little pedigree broadleaf woodland left to conserve.

One form of broadleafed woodland completely out of reach of the Forestry Commission is coppice wood. The felling of coppices does not need a felling licence unless the poles are specially thick. The only means of protection available is the local planning authority tree preservation order. A landowner whose trees or woods are subject to a tree preservation order has to get consent from his local planning authority before he can fell or lop the trees in question. However, if the activities which would be inhibited by a refusal of consent under the order are farming or forestry, the law requires the planning authority to compensate the landowner financially for income foregone.

This can create great difficulties for planning authorities in areas where much of the woodland consists of coppice and where the main threats to it come from farming and forestry. Take Canterbury District Council. Much of the woodland it is anxious to conserve consists not of ancient woodland harbouring huge, old trees but of sweet chestnut coppice which, in this stretch of mid-Kent, typically supports a stunning display of wood anemones, primroses and bluebells in spring. Featherly and Quilters Wood in the Pett Valley south of Canterbury is just one coppiced wood on which the Council has imposed a tree preservation order. In 1986 this wood's owner won around £60,000 in compensation[23] for not being allowed to clear 39 acres of the wood for agriculture – more than twice the amount of money he had paid to buy the entire 88-acre wood five years earlier.

Despite this and other compensation claims, the Council is carrying on the fight. John Chater, the Council's conservation officer, explained his Council's philosophy to me in 1986: 'Woodland must be save for its average value. The ordinary man in the street isn't interested in the rare species, which are often less interesting in appearance than the common species. What's more, if we save our woods purely for the scientific community, access would have to be extremely restrictive because there would be so much pressure on the woods that were conserved.'

The Myth of the Parks

National park designation does, of course, provide some protection to some of Britain's countryside. The term 'national park',
however immediately misleads many people. In Africa, Australia,
North and South America and most of Europe, a national park
is a tract of wild, often spectacular scenery bought by the
government as a musuem piece; commercial activities like farming and forestry are usually completely banned. But the national
parks of England and Wales are different. They remain largely
in private hands; they cover a relatively high proportion of our
land surface (5.5 per cent of the United Kingdom, compared to
2.3 per cent of France); and they embrace not only activities
such as commercial agriculture, forestry, mining and Army
training but also many villages and even small towns.

The special character of the English and Welsh national
parks stems mainly from the conclusions of a committee under
the chairmanship of Sir Arthur Hobhouse which deliberated in
1947.[24] This committee rejected the idea of state ownership and
opted instead for planning as the means by which national parks
would be conserved. The proposals Hobhouse put forward bore
fruit in the National Parks and Access to the Countryside Act of
1949 which in turn allowed a string of national parks to be
established during the 1950s.

The problem of relying on planning rather than land ownership as the means of safeguarding the prime landscape areas has
turned out to be that the main forces for change in our countryside – farming and forestry – are little affected by planning.
When it comes to major developments like new quarries and
major roads, as well as the details of building design, our national
park system has been rather effective. But the requirements for
compensation introduced by the Wildlife and Countryside Act
ensure that such controls as national parks authorities possess
over farming and forestry change are of limited use.

Nonetheless, national park status does bring some protection.
Higher rates of grant from the Countryside Commission, together
with a special national park supplementary grant, provide the
park authorities with extra resources to provide facilities for
visitors as well as to take some action to curb damaging landscape

change. The remainder of Britain's countryside lacks even this flimsy protection.

Parliament charged the National Parks Commission and later the Countryside Commission to designate 'extensive tracts of country' as national parks and to base the selection of areas on two criteria: the 'natural beauty' of the areas concerned, and 'the opportunities they afford for open-air recreation, having regard both to their character and to their position in relation to centres of population'.[25] It might have been assumed that these requirements would have swept up such fine and accessible landscapes as the chalk downland scenery from Dorset and Sussex to the Chilterns; lowland vales like the Weald; landscapes centred on river valleys like those of the Wye, Test or Thames; coastal tracts like those of Cornwall and north Devon, or Dorset; or distinctive landscapes like the Norfolk Broads; the north Norfolk coast; the Malvern Hills; the Somerset Levels; the New Forest; or the Cotswolds. None of these areas came to be designated, however – although some, particularly in their closeness to centres of population, appear to fit the criteria laid down better than some of the areas that have been chosen. The nearest national park to London, for instance, is not the Chiltern Hills or the Kent and Surrey hills but the Brecon Beacons, 150 miles away.[26]

In fact, both the Norfolk Broads and the Cornish Coast were seriously considered by the National Parks Commission, members of which visited these areas. 'We ourselves have no doubt that the selected Cornish scenery eminently qualifies for designation as a National Park,' declared the Commission in its 1952–3 annual report. But both the Broads and the Cornish Coast national park proposals were dropped because of strong opposition to designation from the local councils concerned. The South Downs National Park was abandoned because so much of the open downland turf had been ploughed up during the early 1950s that the area was no longer considered worth designating. And while the Countryside Commission did get as far as selecting the Cambrian Mountains of mid-Wales for designation as Britain's eleventh national park in 1972, the Secretary of State for Wales refused not only to confirm the designation but even to hold a public inquiry into it.

In 1978, after decades of environmental neglect in which out of fifty-two broads only four still supported anything like their traditional wealth of wild birds, fish and flowers, the local authorities in Broadland finally set up a 'Broads Authority' of twenty-six members, including three appointed by the Countryside Commission, to try to stem the area's environmental decline. The Government plans to replace this body in 1987 with its own 'Broads Authority' which would be empowered to control navigation on the waterways. But like its predecessor, the powers of the new Authority will still fall short of those which would have been available to the national park authority urged by the Hobhouse Committee. For one thing, the geographical area covered will be less than two-thirds that covered by the Hobhouse Committee's proposed Norfolk Broads National Park. For another, only 6 per cent of the members of the new Authority will automatically be drawn from those with a conservation or recreation background: the Countryside Commission and Nature Conservancy Council together are to be entitled to nominate only three of the new Authority's forty-five members.

There are no national parks at all in either Northern Ireland or Scotland. It was not until 1985 that enabling legislation for national parks finally came to the Province. The Nature Conservation and Amenity Lands (Northern Ireland) Order of that year empowers the Department of the Environment to designate national parks in Northern Ireland. Yet it was nearly forty years before, in 1947, that a committee appointed by the government's Planning Advisory Board and which included representatives of local government, civil service departments, business and professional organizations and voluntary conservation groups called in its report for the designation of five national parks centred on the Mourne Mountains, the Sperrins, the Antrim Coast and Glens, Upper and Lower Lough Erne and Slieve Gullion. The purpose of the parks was 'to safeguard scenery of great beauty which is a national asset and not merely of local interest and concern; to protect the natural flora and fauna of the areas; and to ensure that the public generally – particularly the rapidly growing numbers of young people who spend their holidays camping, walking and cycling – should have free access to them.'[27]

Although the Department of the Environment may, if it sees fit, designate national parks in Ulster, the 1985 Order gives no indication of what the designation should mean in practice and certainly no hint of special national park planning authorities (direct rule would pose difficulties here). The Order simply empowers the Department to 'formulate proposals' for the conservation of the natural beauty, wildlife and historic objects of any national park and for the provision of public access and the promotion of public enjoyment within it. In the meantime only designations like 'area of outstanding natural beauty' have been applied to the Province. Professor Ronald Buchanan of The Queen's University, Belfast commented in 1981:

Instead of the positive management of scenic landscapes through National Park designation, Northern Ireland has been forced to rely on negative sanctions operated within the AONBs. Inevitably this had led the public to conclude that scenic beauty is to be equated with economic sterility, and in the absence of any significant leadership from local politicians, amenity planning has become expendable in the light of sustained public criticism of planning in general.[28]

Northern Ireland does at least enjoy enabling legislation for national parks. Scotland lacks even that.

In 1947 a parallel committee to the Hobhouse Committee, chaired by Sir Douglas Ramsay, recommended the creation of national parks in Scotland.[29] These parks would have been on the state ownership model employed overseas (an idea invented by a Scot called John Muir).[30] They were to cover 2,000 square miles of Scotland's finest scenery and the land would have cost £1.3 million to acquire. But while the Hobhouse Committee's report led swiftly to legislation, the Ramsay Committee's more radical ideas were made the subject of further inquiries and momentum was gradually lost.[31]

In 1974 the Countryside Commission for Scotland asked government to give it powers to designate what it called 'special parks' which would have been essentially the equivalent to the national parks of England and Wales with one-third of their members appointed by the Secretary of State for Scotland to represent the national conservation and recreation interest.[32] The Labour Governments of the 1970s made some positive

noises about these special parks but did not put them into
legislative form. The Thatcher Government's Countryside (Scotland) Act 1981 made provision for a lesser form of designation –
the regional park – but it did not proceed with special parks for
Scotland.

Had any serious effort ever been made to create the equivalent
of national parks in Scotland it might well have been beaten off
by Scotland's peculiarly powerful landowning lobby. Regional
parks are no more than areas within which extra central government finance will be provided for outdoor recreation provision:
they involve no extra curbs on landowners' freedom to alter the
landscape. Yet the Pentland Hills Regional Park, proposed in
1984 by Lothian Regional Council, was vigorously opposed by
the farming and landowning lobbies.

But the idea of national parks for Scotland is by no means
dead. In 1985, Highland Regional Council launched a campaign
to get the Cairngorms designated as a national park. The
Council sees the national park accolade as bringing three main
advantages to the Cairngorms. First, it would bring money from
central government to help finance a range of measures for
visitors such as better picnic sites, new footpaths and higher
standards of caravan parks. At present, Highland Region has to
finance provision for visitors largely out of local rates, and the
Council believes national park designation would provide a
means for the channelling of central government funds into the
provision of facilities for visitors in the way that areas like
Cumbria already benefit through the Lake District National
Park. It would also alter the emphasis on who recreation should
be provided for: Councillor John Robertson, the region's vice-
convener, explained that the national park designation would
bring 'the positive aspect of catering for the many, providing
access and leisure for the vast majority, in contrast to the mean
and petty sort of restrictions seen in many of our conservation
areas which appear to be set up by the few to keep out the
many'.[33] Secondly, the park designation could bring extra curbs
on the freedom of farmers and foresters to alter the landscape.
It is not clear precisely what extra controls over farming or
consultations with foresters for instance would be involved, since
south of the border national park designation provides only a

slim sanction against damaging landscape change, but Highland Region planning committee chairman Councillor Francis Keith believes it 'could mean that farming and forestry interests would need approvals to put up silos, etc., in rural areas and that would be a step forward'.[34] Finally, the better conservation of the area's scenery coupled with the extra finance for visitor provision would give the tourist industry a boost – the third main advantage of the park designation.

The Countryside Commission for Scotland – the organization that would designate any national park – has, however, advised the Regional Council that the national park idea is a non-starter. Since the legislation to establish national parks has never been extended to Scotland, the Regional Council must think in terms of the vehicles that already exist. These are the national scenic area and the regional park. But Highland Council considers both these tools grossly inferior to the national park. Senior deputy director of planning Howard Brindley told me in 1985:

The national scenic area is just an administrative arrangement whereby certain planning applications within the national scenic area are referred to the Countryside Commission for Scotland. They are nothing more. You don't have special bodies set up; there's no special funding that comes to them as extra assistance by way of central government: they are just an administrative thing whereby certain planning applications get referred to the Countryside Commission. They are not really relevant, not what our members are looking for. The regional park possibility? The view of our members was that's fine, a regional park is something that every region can have. But we want something that identifies the very special nature of the scenery of the Scottish Highlands, and it's not good enough simply to call it a regional park.

The people of the Highlands are not alone in believing their region merits special recognition. The International Union for the Conservation of Nature singled out the Highlands in its *World Conservation Strategy* as one of the globe's 'priority biogeographical provinces for the establishment of protected areas'. If Britain does not respond positively to international calls to conserve its most significant areas for conservation, on what basis can it suggest to other, often poorer nations that they take steps to conserve the tigers and tropical rain forests on their doorsteps?

Conclusion: The Broken Shield

On the planning front, Attlee's social contract had two essential elements. First, the whole community, through elected local planning authorities, would be enabled to shape the destiny of the environment, since all potentially damaging changes to the environment would come within the scope of planning control. Today, this part of the contract is in ruins. The general public have no means of curbing the impact of modern agriculture and forestry on their countryside because no government has been prepared to extend the planning system to these industries even though they have come to pose the greatest environmental threat.

The second basic element of the Attlee arrangements for the protection of the environment was that while local people through their county councils would have the decisive say over the destiny of most of Britain's land, the nation as a whole would be entitled to a real voice in those areas deemed of greatest beauty and recreation value. This promise too has turned sour. Though national parks have appeared in the uplands of England and Wales, there are none in Scotland, Northern Ireland or the English lowlands. And even where parks do exist they provide no real protection against the unforeseen threats of agriculture and forestry.

PART FIVE
At Issue

11. The Heart of the Matter

The failure of the post-war order to resolve the differences between landowners and the landless leaves a deep gulf between the two sides. When we look carefully we find that the issue is not merely the allocation of a resource which both groups acknowledge must be shared. Instead, two sets of fundamentally opposed value systems confront each other.

The View of the Landowner

On one side stand Britain's landowners. However they have come by their holdings, they tend to regard them as theirs to do with what they will. They consider their ownership of land as absolute as their ownership of their household goods.

Samuel Whitbread, the owner of 10,800 acres of rural land in north Bedfordshire embracing several villages, an 800-acre park, a lake and a great house, told me in 1982 how he viewed his domain:

Possession is nine-tenths of the law. I am in possession here. I control what I have got here. In fact, in my case it happens to be 11,000 acres of farmland and forestry and in your case, if I may say so, it may be a flat in South London. The actual ethics of possession are the same. I think one should be at liberty to do what one likes with one's own.

Many people will recognize and sympathize with this naturally human desire to possess. It is part of what makes a child delight in a new toy and helps turn some of us into collectors. But this desire to own absolutely poses problems when it is exercised in respect of things whose fate affects the community generally in some way and not just their owner. Into this category come our children, animals, weapons and chemical plants. The owners of all these things find their ownership rights circumscribed by society seeking to protect its own interest in these 'possessions'. Land, making up the space in which the community lives, cannot escape inclusion in this category. And of course even in the case of rural land, society imposes its will on owners in certain ways. It insists that certain crops be grown in time of war; it demands that land be yielded up for roads or railways. A state that had no powers over its own territory but only over its citizens is conceivable in theory but nowhere exists.

Herein lies an enduring contradiction. Though ownership of land can never be complete, it is also the thing which Man most covets. As individuals, we all want to claim territory of our own, be it a suburban house and garden or a vast ranch in Oklahoma; but as members of a community, we must seek to claw back the meaning of title from those of our fellow-citizens who happen to be fortunate enough to secure it.

For British landowners, however, there is no contradiction. They do not wish to perceive the claim of society to rights over their land. If landscape quality, wildlife habitats or recreation opportunities are incompatible with a landowner's pursuit of financial gain, he usually feels these things can go by the board. The feeling is strong and genuine and is often unaccompanied by any perception that an alternative attitude is possible. As a Sussex farmer told me when I asked him whether he had cleared away a sixty-nine-acre wood he had intended to convert to more profitable use: 'It's none of your business.'

Some landowners do, of course, have a genuine interest in conservation. Others may conserve features for the sake of game. Others who sense a challenge to their own way of thinking may temper the pursuit of commercial advantage with concessions made in the interests of self-preservation. But they expect any concessions to the rest of the community to be made on their own terms.

The present struggle over the consequences of the commercial exploitation of land does not mean that contemporary land-owners have lost all of their predecessors' concern with land as a status symbol and as a place for their own recreation. The idea of land as capital has been comfortably added to these older considerations. Together they all give rise to an awesomely comprehensive sense of possession. Our landowners tend to see all access to their land as at their behest, to be granted as a privilege if they wish it and more often to be withheld. Where existing law recognizes the rights of others in their land, it may be flagrantly violated. Public rights of way along footpaths and bridleways are now obstructed by ploughing, barbed wire or bulls to an extent that would have shocked the people of medieval, nineteenth-century or even pre-war Britain.

The View of the Landless

Pitted against the attitudes of Britain's landowners are those of the landless. Within this very much larger group there is of course plenty of apathy, but growing numbers are coming to care about the countryside. Among those who care can be found feelings at least as intense as those of the landowners. But the ideas behind them are often fundamentally at odds with those of the landowners.

Not only is the landowner's claim to control his property contested, the right of any man or men to absolute sway over the natural environment is now widely questioned. The old Christian notion that God created the earth for Man to have dominion over it is no longer universally accepted. As traditional Christianity has withered, many people have come to see the environment as something in which all creatures have rights – not just human beings without title deeds but even animals. As animal rights campaigner Margaret Manzoni explained in 1983: 'We don't distinguish between animal life and human life. All life is equal.'[1] Or, in the words of Roger Smith, then chairman of the Scottish Wild Land Group and commenting on the chopping down of a 9,000-year-old pine wood: 'Trees like these have rights too, and we should treat them as such, not merely as a "crop" to be exploited when the time is seen to be right.'[2]

Even those who still see the natural environment as there to benefit mankind increasingly see it as something to provide recreation or spiritual refreshment for everyone and not just owners. And people who 'own' no particular stretch of land have come to consider themselves more and more entitled to influence what happens to the countryside and to be provided with access to it.

The 1949 legislation was designed to cater for these feelings, which swelled further after it had been passed. In the late 1960s and early 1970s a series of environmental disasters which included the wrecking of the Torrey Canyon in 1967, the poisoning of the fish in the Rhine, and the widespread death of wildlife caused by DDT, dieldrin and other chemical pestkiller abuse spread interest in the natural world deeper and wider. In 1965, a timely bestseller, Rachel Carson's *Silent Spring*, brought awareness of the threat to the environment to a far larger number of people than had ever cared about the countryside before. More people became aware of the Earth as an ecological system upon whose fragile health depended the survival of human beings as a species. It came to be generally appreciated that Man's ability to exploit his environment had been enhanced by technological development to the point where further unrestrained exploitation could kill the goose that had been laying the golden eggs. Soon everyone seemed to know all about the vulnerability of many different parts of the global environment – the seas and rivers which were being polluted by oil, oil dispersants, radioactive waste, industrial waste, sewage and chemical fertilizers; the ozone layer which was threatened by super-sonic transport and aerosol sprays; the air by sulphur dioxide; and the soil which was being contaminated by heavy metals and pesticides – or simply being ground to dust and blown away.

This new concern spawned a host of voluntary pressure groups, such as the Ecology Party and Friends of the Earth. The number of newspaper column inches devoted to environmental issues tripled between the period 1965 to 1973, according to one study.[3] By 1983, one in every ten of the British adult population was a member of an environmental group – 2.5 to 3 million people, or more than the membership of any political party or trade union.[4]

At first, the response to environmental problems from the urban population was largely fired by guilt. The cause of the problems was usually seen as greed – for cars and other consumer durables, for transport, for holidays, for food, and above all for babies. It was the sheer pressure of growing numbers of people that was identified as the prime concern. 'No Standing Room: Population Control for Britain?' an article about the threat to

Man's survival from over-population, was, significantly, the first article in the first issue of *The Ecologist* magazine in 1970. It was feared that the population explosion would spawn houses and roads which might simply bury the countryside in concrete. 'As far as Europe is concerned, it is prophesied that it will become a continuous conurbation from Manchester to Milan,' wrote Robert Arvill in 1967 in *Man and Environment*, a book that encapsulates as well as any other the mood of the time. Arvill went on: 'In the USA in particular, the problem is causing great concern. The pressures arising from the arrival of a new baby every twelve seconds and a new car every five seconds are estimated to lead to the loss of two acres of countryside every minute.'[5]

Not only would huge swathes of the earth be engulfed in concrete, but the cultivatable lands that remained would be degraded if not completely sterilized by the over-application of pesticides and fertilizers. Man's demand for more and more recreation opportunities would also have catastrophic results. 'On public holidays, huge populations surge to and from the coast and the countryside is bestrewn with cars,' wrote Robert Arvill. 'These mass movements are like a floodtide in their impact on the environment. They are creating a wear and tear never known before.'

During this period, the talk was of population control and even of banning people from the countryside lest they destroy the very thing they had come to enjoy. But as the 1970s wore on, urban Man's attitude to the issue of the environment changed.

First, the assumption that the blame for environmental problems lay with the sheer numbers of townspeople and their demands came to be undermined. Particular cases like Rio Tinto-Zinc's application to mine for copper in the Snowdonia National Park made people realize that it was the drive for profit on the part of particular groups or individuals that really mattered. Rio Tinto-Zinc argued that copper from the Coed-y-Brenin Forest was required to meet global demands for the metal that could not be met any other way; but groups like Friends of the Earth, which opposed the application – successfully – challenged this claim and pointed out that it was the company's drive to increase its profits which actually inspired the proposal[6]. Gradually the threat to the environment came to be attributed less to population pressure than to the untrammelled workings of capitalism. And during the early 1980s, as the extent of over-production of food became apparent, agriculture came to be seen as more and more akin to other forms of profit-motivated environmental despoilation.

A second change was a broadening of the philosophy of conservation. People whose concern had been aroused by self-interested anxiety for the survival of mankind came to take a rather different attitude, echoing that of Wordsworth and the nineteenth-century conservationists. More and more people came to see the environment as something to be respected for its own sake, rather than merely as a support system for their own species. The whale and the panda came to be symbols of conservation, defending the earth and its creatures from commercial exploitation – a rather different matter from defending mankind's habitat from over-population. Among the creatures with a right to enjoy their environment urban Britons included themselves. If their countryside was being damaged this was their concern. And if they were being denied access to it, this was a breach of their rights.

It was quickly appreciated that some of the phenomena identified as deplorable in the world as a whole had manifestations extremely close to home. Proposals to build a third London airport at Foulness, for instance, created controversy which quickly spread beyond the issue of aircraft noise to questioning the ethic of growth on which demand for the new airport was based and to the assertion of the rights of the Brent Geese that inhabited Maplin Sands. More alarming for landowners was the emergence of fox hunting and factory farming as important and extremely emotive political issues, while opposition was also mobilized against practices as central to agricultural practice as stubble burning and hedge removal.

The ideas emerging in the cities quickly developed in directions even more subversive of the rural status quo. Enthusiasm developed for forms of agricultural exploitation that were contained by natural limitations such as the size of a man's family or the amount of work a man could do with his hands in one day. The methods of 'primitive' tribes acquired more respect as the destructive effects of the introduction of Western technology into Third World agriculture came to be appreciated and a general revulsion against automation and the alienation it induced gathered pace. Some groups of city-dwellers went back to the land, living in communes and trying to develop a life-style rooted in subsistence farming. Many people who would never have dreamed of entering a rural commune shared the reaction against the ruthless exploitation of the Earth. By 1980, a new set of attitudes could be found not only among the middle classes but throughout the urban population. The natural environment and all its living creatures were generally regarded as the precious and threatened property of all people, rather than merely being available for exploitation by the 'owners' of the land. And although the environmental movement sprang in the 1960s from a sense of self-preservation, it soon took on an almost religious dimension as it became a creed to which people attached themselves altruistically.

On Course for Collision

In response to the new challenge to their values, few landowners today have resorted (as their medieval predecessors might have done) to the argument that God made the earth for men to exploit. Instead they have tended to rely on the more contemporary but hardly less theological argument that the creation of wealth is an absolute good which benefits everybody and must on no account be obstructed. One Norfolk farmer put this argument in typical fashion in 1977 when he said: 'I believe that while the rich are rich, the poor have a good standard of living. But when the rich are poor, God help the poor. If it wasn't for people like me who take risks, and thereby feed people, employ people, service industry, provide fodder for the workforce everything would come to a grinding halt.'[7]

Unfortunately for the landowners, this argument has not been sufficient to dispel criticism of them from the rest of the community. One reason is that the argument seems rather less valid in the case of agriculture in Britain today than it might be in other areas. It is by no means clear that the present model of land ownership optimizes the dispersal of the economic benefits

to the community at large. Farmers pay a far smaller proportion
of their income in taxes than other groups; and very few
people are employed in present-day British agriculture. Much
agricultural activity is now directed towards the consumption of
subsidies to produce surpluses which then have to be disposed of
at further cost to the taxpayer.

In any case, despite the efforts of the Thatcher Government, a
large proportion of the population remains obstinately unper-
suaded of the need to see wealth creation as an absolute good.
The twentieth-century reaction against untrammelled capitalism
persists, and there is instead general acceptance of the need to
regulate the pursuit of profit in the interests of society as a
whole. If urban capitalists have to put up with health and safety
standards, equal pay, pollution control and so on, their rural
counterparts cannot expect to be left alone purely on the grounds
that they are creating wealth.

In view of this some landowners have tried a very different
tack. This is to present themselves not as the target of conservationists but as the best possible instrument for implementing
the conservationists' objectives. These landowners do not emphasize the wealth they are creating. Instead they suggest that
absolute owners though they may be, their primary motive is not
to make money but to care for the land. That is, they are to be
seen as custodians, not exploiters. The land agent responsible for
managing the Duke of Northumberland's 105,000-acre estate in
Northumberland, W. F. P. Hugonin, told me in an interview in
1982 what he considered to be the typical attitude of large
landowners:

The actual fact of ownership is less important than the fact that they
feel that they are stewards, that they have been handed down to look
after something for a very short number of years which they would
hope to leave in a better state than when they took over. They are the
arch conservers, and the stewardship involved is management and
control and what that word management involves is something that is
very little understood.

In fact, this kind of stewardship often turns out to be very
different from what a conservationist might imagine it to be.
Many landowners who talk of themselves as 'stewards' see no

contradiction between such a role and the destruction of many of the attractions of their property in the pursuit of profit. Nor do they feel that as stewards they are required to allow their fellow-citizens to share with them in enjoying the benefits that their land can bestow. For the kind of 'stewardship' that landowners usually have in mind is not exercised on behalf of the community, but on behalf of their sons and their sons' sons. They want to pass on property as extensive and lucrative as that which they inherited or acquired. Indeed primogeniture provides an extension of ownership into the future which makes it even more 'absolute' than it appears at first sight.

In view of this, it is perhaps not surprising that landowners have failed to win the unqualified endorsement of society for their 'stewardship' of the countryside, just as they have failed to convince their fellows that activities which appear environmentally destructive are economically beneficial. The gulf between the two sides yawns deeper than ever. So where do we go from here?

The answer seems to be that we must now review the character of land ownership in rural Britain. We must seek out new arrangements which enable the feelings of those citizens who do not happen to be rural landowners to find adequate expression. 'Ownership' already takes many different forms in our society. If somebody who owns a transistor radio chooses to take a hammer to it and dash it to pieces, no one is likely to complain, so long as the pieces are tidily disposed of. Somebody treating his child or pet dog in a similar way would quickly discover that society considered his ownership less than absolute. Clear limits are placed on the extent to which we may exploit our children for financial gain. This is for the benefit of the children. But if we contemplate the condition of the owner of a building protected from demolition on account of its historic importance or architectural merit, we see that limitations may be imposed on ownership in the wider interests of society as a whole. The fact that historic buildings are subject to planning permission, repairs notices and listed building consents means that nobody owns them quite as absolutely as our landowners like to believe that they own the land. In other times, in other places, very different arrangements have related the land to those who have exploited it. If we wish, we can revise the concept of land 'ownership' in Britain to accommodate the rights of others than the land 'owner'.

So what can be done to take some of the benefits which our countryside can bestow out of the hands of a privileged élite and into the bosom of the nation as a whole? Support is growing for some attempt to modify the rights of our rural landowners. More and more ideas for protecting the rights of the rest of the community are now being put forward. It is to examine these ideas that we now turn.

PART SIX
Repossession

12. Other Owners

If the ills of rural Britain spring ultimately from the land ownership régime, should that régime be changed? Why grapple with the symptoms, when the disease could be tackled at source? If conservation and recreation are not being adequately catered for it obviously makes sense to consider placing the countryside in hands more likely to provide these things. The advantage of this approach is that it eliminates the practical problems of management and enforcement that bedevil other approaches. But is this approach really consistent with the social and political realities of Britain's countryside today?

Nationalization

The nationalization of agriculture would provide a tidy means of resolving many conflicts over land-use. A number of individual private landowners have done much to enhance conservation and some have provided for public recreation. But as a group, landowners have tended to exploit their holdings in ways which conflict with the public interest. Ownership by the State would short-circuit the search for controls over landowners' actions. If the State owned the agriculture industry then the people, through the machinery of democracy, would decide precisely what form farming should take and how it should interact with other rural activities. The Government would necessarily have to address itself to the role of agriculture in the environment in the widest possible way. It would also, however, have to run the agriculture industry, and even the fiercest critics of our private landowners could hardly argue that State control is good for farming.

Before 1917, when Russia was owned by private landlords and farmed by tenants, the country regularly exported large amounts of grain to the West. Now, its endemic food supply problems would be even worse were it not for the high productivity of the small amount of farmland under private control. In 1979, private plots made up only 1.4 per cent of all Soviet farmland, yet they produced 30 per cent of the country's meat, milk and eggs, 60 per cent of the potatoes and over 50 per cent of the fruits and berries. In China, the total private plot area is to be increased from 6 to 15 per cent of the total cultivated land as the country's rulers have begun to appreciate the enormous difficulties in the path of state agriculture. The problem with state farming is that in an industry manned by a highly dispersed workforce which is often required to work unsocial hours, individual incentive is crucial.

The efficiency of British agriculture could not be expected to survive nationalization. What is more, a nationalized agriculture industry would be extremely vulnerable to industrial action. Under our present system, farmworkers never strike because they are scattered all over the country and work for a large number of different bosses. But if farmers and farmworkers alike were paid out of a central fund, central bargaining for wages with the State as boss would have to take place. A short strike at harvest-time would destroy much of the entire year's output. The consequence of this situation would doubtless be that a fall in output would be accompanied by a huge rise in costs. This might lead to a withering of the agriculture industry and would hardly be in the national interest. Nor might the nationalization of agriculture be as appealing a prospect for conservationists as it might appear. Because the profitability of agriculture would be bound to decline, the main headache of a national agriculture board would be its financial position. As it struggled to improve its figures it might prove even more desperate to destroy the landscape, whatever environmental objectives the Government to which it reported might profess.

A less radical alternative to the nationalization of agriculture would be the nationalization of agricultural land alone. As part of its leases, the State could impose whatever terms it saw fit on its tenants, insisting on any conservation or recreation requirements it chose. If farmers were otherwise left free to make what they could from land they leased from the State, there is no reason why their efficiency should decline. At present about

60 per cent of all British farmland is owner-occupied. Land nationalization would put these freehold owners in a position similar to that now held by the tenant farmers responsible for the remaining 40 per cent of Britain's farmland. Two studies, one conducted by the National Economic Development Office in 1973[1] and the second by researchers at Wye College, London University in 1984[2], could find no clear relationship between farm productivity and form of tenure: there was no evidence to suggest that people farmed better on land they owned than on land they rented.

However, the restrictive covenants in the leases designed to protect conservation and recreation interests would introduce considerable difficulties. A farmer taking on land as a tenant of the State would have to covenant either to leave certain features like woods and hedges specified in the covenant intact, or to undertake to seek permission from his landlord before he altered them. Such a system would need an army of officials to decide whether or not tenants should be able to remove features, and to check that they were keeping to the terms of their covenants. These officials would have to grapple with the immense task of evaluating the agricultural needs of the nation, compile lists of important landscape features and decide what proportion of them, if any, should be sacrificed to agricultural production. Their decisions might mean that the conservation interest was inadequately protected even in the unlikely event that any government was tempted to institute the system of which they would form a part.

Experience of other public institutions does not suggest that an individual citizen or a voluntary group, say a village society, would find it that much easier to influence land-use decisions if the State were landlord than they do at present. As we have seen, the Forestry Commission has enveloped its land-use decision-making in a cloak of secrecy. Nor is it clear how the pressure for relentless agricultural expansion would be more readily challenged if the State owned all the land. In theory, State ownership would be totally democratic; in practice, the people might find it extremely hard to influence those who were managing the land in their name.

A further problem with the nationalization of farmland is that it would require the taxpayer to find large sums of money to buy out existing owners. The Centre for Agricultural Strategy at Reading University estimated in 1978 that the cost of the transfer of all farmland in the UK to the State would be between £15,000 million and £20,000 million. If this were to be financed by means of government bonds at interest levels of 8 per cent over a fifty-year period, the annual financial burden would be £1,635 million.[3]

One consequence of this is that if the taxpayer were to get a reasonable return on his investment, farm rents would have to rise steeply. At present farm rents in Britain are relatively low: landowners are content to receive a return on capital through farm rent of only about 3 per cent (compared with a return on capital in the company sector of between 4 and 8 per cent). The reason is probably that they derive considerable capital gains through the appreciation of land prices from holding the land itself and because they derive satisfaction from other aspects of land ownership. High rents would put a squeeze on profits and might make it hard for the State to succeed in imposing strict covenants on tenants and still find takers.

Even if nationalization appeared more likely to advance the public interest, it would in any case be a political non-starter. In spite of the wrongs our landowners have done and are doing to the rest of the community, private landowning remains part of the British tradition as it has done for a thousand years. The right to own land is still seen as an important freedom and there is no will to get rid of it. What is required of our landowners is that they share their land with their fellow-citizens, not that they give it up completely.

Restricting Ownership

If wholesale land nationalization is not the answer to the problems of the countryside, is there scope for some lesser form of restriction on access to ownership rights?

In Britain, unlike some other Western countries, anybody can inherit or buy any piece of land; and anybody can hold as much land as he likes – so long as he can find the money or a donor. A buyer has to satisfy nobody that he should become a landowner save an existing owner seeking to sell. He rarely has to prove more than that he possesses the cash required. He certainly does not need to demonstrate that he is fit to own land.

In France, however, an Act of Parliament of 1960 requires that all sales of farmland be monitored by locally-based statutory agencies (*Sociétiés d'Aménagement Foncier et D'Etablissement Rural:* SAFERs). These agencies have powers of pre-emption over all land sales, buying land themselves if they consider a potential purchaser is unlikely to use the land concerned in the best interests of French farming. They also ensure that no new purchaser will exceed the personal farm holdings limit, set in many départments at 222 acres; an individual can buy more land than the threshold and let it, but he may not farm the extra himself. The SAFERs also control farm rents.

In Denmark and Norway, to take two more examples of countries in which the acquisition of land is treated differently from the acquisition of other chattels, nobody may buy agricultural land without first obtaining a permit from the Government indicating that he or she has the necessary technical qualifications to farm the land involved. No individual may own a farm in Denmark larger than 180 acres (the size of the average UK farm is 170 acres) without special permission; while financial and industrial institutions are prohibited from owning any rural land at all without government sanction.[4]

In Saudi Arabia, land can even be taken away from an owner who is considered not to be using it in the public interest. Indeed, in that country the way land is used is the very basis of a claim to ownership. A family comes to own land by reclaiming it and making it useable; conversely, an owner who leaves land idle for three years can lose it: the Government will take it back and give it to somebody else it considers a fit person to own it by virtue of the use to which he will put it.[5]

These examples from abroad serve to underline just how absolute land ownership in our own country has become. However, it is not obvious that they provide a useful model for extending the community's involvement in land ownership in Britain.

Any attempt to restrict ownership to one type of owner rather than another would achieve little while pressures towards anti-social activity act equally on all kinds of owner. As we have seen, financial institutions and foreign buyers often behave in remarkably similar ways to the landed gentry and family farmers, who in turn often display a great deal of commercial ruthlessness. When Countryside Commission consultant Tom Worthington examined approaches to land management on forty sample farms in England belonging to a wide range of owners he could find no hard and fast distinctions.[6] Among the financial institutions, for example, some were concerned with agricultural profits to the exclusion of all else, while others, more anxious about their public image than some traditional owners, were perfectly prepared to forego extra profit in the interests of the local community or wildlife conservation.

Funding Other Owners

If there is little scope for trying to exclude the kinds of owners most likely to abuse the powers of ownership, there is perhaps slightly more scope for encouraging ownership by owners who might be expected to behave well, like the National Trust, the Woodland Trust, the Scottish Wildlife Trust or the Royal Society for the Protection of Birds. But not much more. These bodies already buy as much land as they can afford to. If we all contribute more of our spare cash to them they will be able to buy more. At the same time, we could urge Parliament to vote more money in particular to the Nature Conservancy Council so that acquisitions like that of Creag Meagaidh in 1985 become more frequent.

More land for official and voluntary conservation agencies would be a splendid thing. However, these purchases are never going to make a real impact on the problem confronting the countryside. Rural land is an extremely expensive commodity and voluntary organizations are never going to be able to pluck more than a tiny amount of it out of the paths of the advancing combines and conifers. The National Trust and the Trust for Scotland together own far more land than any other voluntary conservation body. Yet, in 1986 their holdings made up no more than 1 per cent of the land of the United Kingdom. In the whole

of Northern Ireland, the National Trust owned in 1986 only
6,500 acres – equivalent to three Richmond Parks. Unlike the
National Trust, the Woodland Trust is not limited by Act of
Parliament to acquiring only outstanding land, and it has
bought a wide range of woodlands, from those of special wildlife
importance to unspectacular woods of local recreation value.
Active though it has been since its formation in 1972, by the end
of 1986 the Woodland Trust owned only 7,000 acres of woodland
in total. 'From the soulless conifer, good Lord and the Woodland
Trust deliver us!' declared the actor Sir Michael Hordern in one
of the Trust's newsletters in 1985. It is sad but true however that
on its own the Trust can have little impact on, say, the
coniferization of Scotland's woods and moors: in 1986 it owned
only five woods in the whole of Scotland. And, like all voluntary
organizations, the Woodland Trust can buy land only when an
owner is willing to sell. Opportunity buying confines it to land
that happens to come on to the market – which is not necessarily
the land most threatened with landscape damage.

In any case, the provision of pockets of land protected by
ownership would never really meet emerging public need in full,
however extensive they became. A collection of conservation
sites would not, for example, secure the future of our wildlife.

The marbled white, the high brown and the dingy skipper,
the brown hairstreak and the green hairstreak, the pearl-
bordered, silver-washed, dark-green and Duke of Burgundy
fritillaries – between 1950 and 1970 all nine of these beautiful
and increasingly rare butterfly species disappeared not from
meadows and woods converted to housing estates but from one
of the best conserved stretches of rural land in Britain – the
Monks Wood National Nature Reserve near Huntingdon. Excellent though it may be to fence and control the land on which
particular species happen to breed, this may not be enough to
guarantee their survival. Many birds, butterflies and other beasts
have needs that can be satisfied only in the wider environment.
Isolated sanctuaries cannot ensure the survival of species vulnerable to natural catastrophes if the reservoir populations outside
the reserves are sacrificed. The Nature Conservancy Council put
it like this in 1977:

For the present and for the foreseeable future, many plants and animals in nature reserves will need to be supported by outside populations to remain viable. Since about 80 per cent of the land surface of Britain is in some kind of agricultural use, conservation of wildlife on the farm is crucial for wildlife conservation in the country as a whole.[7]

However, it is not only the needs of our wildlife which require that it survives not just in isolated pockets in zoo-like conditions but throughout our countryside. Our own needs require the same thing. We need to feel that we are not alone in our environment – that we share it with other creatures. Conservation is not just about keeping species on the British list: it is about securing our relationship with them. The achievement of this objective does not mean all of Britain must be turned over to impenetrable swamp or jungle. What it does mean is that even in areas primarily devoted to agriculture or forestry, other considerations must also come into play. We are entitled to demand that whatever our landowners seek to achieve on their land must be consistent with the survival of those of our non-human fellows who have shared our island story with us for tens of thousands of years – birds like the nightingale, the kingfisher, the whitethroat and the barn owl; animals like the badger, the otter, the great crested newt and the common frog. Their survival is not too much to ask. It is our right as well as theirs.

13. Sensible Subsidies

The agricultural revolution now destroying our landscape is being fuelled partly by public money. Accordingly, it occurs to many people that the course that would make most sense would be the redirection of the subsidies away from destruction and towards conservation. Thus subsidies to agriculture would be designed to stimulate forms of farming that would help conserve the landscape beauty and wildlife interest of the countryside — rather than those forms that require the destruction of attractive and important features of the countryside. Such a redirection of subsidy is obviously desirable. It has the advantage that it might not necessitate a head-on confrontation with the farming community as readily as might other approaches. The question is, however, whether such an indirect approach would be sufficient to resolve the overall problem, landowners' attitudes remaining what they are.

Changing the Price Structure of the Common Agricultural Policy

The centrepiece of the farm subsidy arrangements is the price support system of the Common Agricultural Policy (CAP). It is the guaranteed market at guaranteed high prices for extra produce which the CAP offers which provides the single most important incentive for farmers to clear away features like spinneys, wetlands, moors and downs and use the land released to grow more crops that nobody needs.

A reduction in either guaranteed price levels or the introduction of limited quotas for production for which the guarantee is available would need to apply to all the main foodstuffs covered by the CAP or farmers would simply switch out of the affected product into some other foodstuff still covered by a guaranteed high price for unlimited quantities. It would also need to be a substantial price cut. Guaranteed prices for cereals, for example, would need to be slashed by at least one-fifth and possibly half if output were to be noticeably reduced.[1] Even more effective in stopping farmers intensifying and expanding production would be the abolition of the guarantee that all surplus produce will be bought up at a good price. If farmers, like other industrialists, faced the prospect of being unable to sell the extra produce they might hope to secure from the cultivation of marginal land, they would be far less likely to embark on it.

Dr Brynmor Green, author of *Countryside Conservation*, lecturer at the University of London's Wye College, former Nature Conservancy Council official and, since 1984, member of the Countryside Commission, is one of a number of conservationists who hope and expect the CAP to change to meet conservation needs. He wrote in 1981: 'The Common Agricultural Policy is vulnerable because of its huge cost, surpluses and inequitability within the farming community . . . A change to a system with differential income support and more product quotas seems inevitable. A concerted effort by a united conservation movement is needed to help bring this change about.'[2] Reminders of the absurdities of the Common Agricultural Policy together with farmers' talk of imminent ruin led in early 1986 to speculation that cereal prices were about to be slashed by 50 per cent and that, as a result of a major overhaul of the CAP, Britain's countryside would be returned to its former glories. The Labour Party's Environment Spokesman Dr David Clark MP, for example, said he envisaged as much as 10 million acres of Britain's farmland going out of production, thereby providing opportunities for a land revolution comparable with the agrarian revolution of the eighteenth century.[3]

But just what chance is there that the CAP will be radically reformed? Despite the talk of cereal land becoming jungle because it would not pay anybody to farm it, this has not happened. Cereal prices were not slashed in the 1986 Farm Price Settlement after all. The final agreement reached in April 1986 by the Council of Ministers for nothing more than a price 'freeze' in most products has in fact resulted in a price increase for British farmers of 2.7 per cent for animal products and 1.35 per cent for crop products because of a realignment of monetary compensation amounts, according to calculations by the Consumers in the European Community Group.[4] The Common Agricultural Policy has shown itself successful in resisting concerted attacks on it from quarters pulling vastly more weight than the UK conservation movement is ever likely to do at Brussels. Consumer groups within the Community in particular have long been urging radical reform of the CAP on the more immediately pressing grounds that Europe's consumers are having to pay too much for food. Since it is Western Europe's poorer citizens, including the 15 million unemployed people, who spend the highest proportion of their total income on food, the argument might be expected to have some force. Many Commonwealth countries, including Australia, Canada, New Zealand, Jamaica, Fiji, Guyana, Barbados and Swaziland have used their full diplomatic weight to push the case against the CAP, as has the United States, which in the crop-year 1983–4 (the most recent for which figures are available) was paying its own farmers $18,000 million to keep out of production 82,000 acres of good farmland (equivalent to one and a half times the total area of the United Kingdom) because the world market had been flooded with EEC surplus products. On top of the criticism from within and outside Europe there has even been a major attack on the CAP from within the Common Market's own institutional apparatus, as the European Commission has got down to preparing blueprint after blueprint for reform.

The failings of the CAP were appreciated as long ago as 1970. Dr Sicco Mansholt, the then vice-president of the European Commission with responsibility for agricultural policy, had this to say when introducing proposals for reform:

The current policy condemns three-quarters of Europe's farmers to stagnate on unprofitable holdings while producing utterly unmarketable surpluses. It costs as much each year as the Americans were spending on reaching the moon, and if the money we are wasting on the present system keeps increasing at the current rate, it should soon be enough to put a man on Mars. Under our plan the costs would be halved by 1980. ... Those with whom the decisions rest – the governments of the six countries – can no longer shirk their responsibilities.[5]

The essential weakness of the CAP, highlighted in many further critiques after Dr Mansholt's but never corrected, is that its uses the instrument of price to pursue two quite different objectives: maintaining farm incomes, and balancing supply and demand. So long as price support remains the central pivot, neither objective can be adequately achieved. Only a third of EEC farm holders are full-time, a situation that leads to low agricultural incomes, but not necessarily low total incomes of those who count themselves farmers at least some of the time. Many of the part-timers have small farms, and since small-scale production generally precludes economies of scale and is less suited to new technology, it usually entails high costs. The price levels needed to support the small, inefficient farmers are more than enough to galvanize the more efficient, lower-cost producers into the generation of surpluses – leaving the taxpayer to foot the bill for buying up and disposing of the unwanted produce. When the CAP simply subsidized inefficiency, as it was originally intended to, it fulfilled the social purpose of maintaining rural communities. It is the subsidy of efficient producers which is causing so much mayhem. Large-scale producers, among whom the British have played a prominent part, have exploited the CAP's failure to distinguish between large- and small-scale operations and taken the CAP to its logical conclusion. Not surprisingly, in the decade up to 1986, Community spending on agriculture increased in real terms by 7 per cent per year. In 1986, the Community was planning to spend £1,800 million over three years on the disposal of its food mountains (while still allowing more to accumulate). Dealing with the surpluses was costing the Community one-quarter of its entire budget.

'A decade and a half of empirical evidence has confirmed that as an economic policy for the Community as a whole, the CAP was irrational,' observed Joan Pearce, Research Fellow at the Royal Institute of International Affairs and the author in 1981 of 'The Common Agricultural Policy: Prospects for Change'. [6] Despite its deficiencies, the CAP has survived virtually unscathed since the Community was formed in 1962, entirely through the support of certain political forces. These forces work in the following way. Some countries, particularly net food exporting countries like France, Denmark, the Netherlands and Ireland, consider the CAP benefits them by ensuring a strong home market for a successful export industry. Net importers like Germany, the UK and Italy obtain through the CAP a means of maintaining the incomes of their farmers, a politically important group in all three countries. Throughout the Common Market, farming organizations are dominated by large farmers who benefit from general price support more than they would be likely to from more direct means of support for farmers, like income supplements payable only to those farmers who could show they needed them. In France, Germany and Italy in particular the vast majority of farmers own only small amounts of land (in Italy for instance 65 per cent of them own less than thirteen acres each). Yet in each case the farmers' representative organizations are just as effectively dominated by large efficient producers as they are in Britain. These organizations are in some ways even more politically significant in Europe than the National Farmers' Union is in Britain, as farmers in some continental countries switch their votes en bloc to an opposition party if they think they are not getting a good enough deal from the Government of the day. So although it may seem blindingly obvious that the guaranteed prices of the CAP should be lowered to reduce surpluses and the financial burden the CAP imposes on consumers and taxpayers, EEC Governments continue to support the existing system.

As long as these powerful political forces obtain, there seems little prospect of an across-the-board reduction in the guaranteed prices. Each year in the United Kingdom the House of Lords Select Committee on the European Communities hears evidence from consumers, farmers and food manufacturers. It then publishes its views on the CAP and on the European Commission's proposals for price changes in the coming year. This Committee has consistently advocated radical reform of the CAP and price reductions.[7] The British Minister of Agriculture receives this report before going to Brussels to attend the annual price-fixing session in the spring. But once he is in the meeting with the other agriculture Ministers, their lordships' recommendations seem to count for little. In the Brussels decision-making arena Joan Pearce believes that 'agriculture ministers tend to feel that their first obligation is to their country's farm sector regardless of whether this is consistent with the national interest'.[8] Once all twelve agriculture Ministers are together, the farmers' view seems to take on even greater weight. A series of trade-offs usually leaves the British Minister agreeing to considerably higher price levels than he originally said he would accept when he set out for Brussels.

Against this background it is clearly unrealistic to suppose that the CAP is going to be reformed in response to environmental considerations in Britain. Some member states, like Greece, have as their primary interest in the EEC the extraction of the maximum possible subsidy for their farmers. Environmental considerations, least of all those applying in other countries, are not likely to appear significant to their governments in comparison. As it happens, in no other country within the Common Market is the impact of agricultural change on the landscape so severe as it is in Britain – except for the Netherlands, where a new farm landscape is now so complete that there is almost no trace of the former landscape left to conserve. So the guaranteed minimum prices of the CAP are predominantly set by governments which do not face the same environmental problems as Britain and which have pressing reasons for keeping the prices high.

MILK QUOTAS: TWO DROPS IN THE OCEAN

Nonetheless, 1984 did see a change in the CAP. For the first time in its history production quotas were imposed in one important sector – dairy produce. Hitherto, quotas had existed only for sugar. But the story of how this apparently positive step came to be taken is salutary.

The move came after over-production of milk had bedevilled the Common Market for twenty years. Technology had provided Europe's farmers with a growing array of aids to step up milk output. The most dramatic results came from the use of commercial nitrate fertilizer (which increased fivefold in the Community countries between 1950 and 1979) and selective breeding facilitated by computers, frozen sperm and artificial insemination.[9] By 1968, Dr Mansholt was already recommending

price reductions for dairy produce to cope with growing surpluses. But no production curbs were introduced and pleas to
farmers to hold back milk production went unheeded. By 1980,
surplus milk had reached nearly a fifth of annual production, or
15 to 20,000 million litres, and the Community was spending
£2,900 million every year disposing of it.[10]

Britain was one of the prime offenders. As British farmers are
more efficient than those in most of the rest of Europe, it is not
surprising that excess milk production was a serious problem in
Britain at least twenty years before Britain joined the EEC.
Back in the 1950s, subsidies to farmers coupled with new dairy
farming methods like the enrichment of grassland with fertilizers
were already leading to increases in herd sizes and yields per
cow with the resulting production of far more milk than the
country needed. As early as 1954, the Minister of Agriculture
was warning the nation in his *Annual Review of Agriculture* that
there was a need to reduce the national dairy herd to offset
dramatic increases in milk yields per cow.

Warnings continued throughout the decade, but by 1960
surplus milk production had gone up to between 10 and 15 per
cent of total output.

The Common Market had made some attempts to curb milk
production before 1984. One method was a financial inducement
to give up dairying: UK farmers, for instance, received £115
million between 1977 and 1980 through a scheme whereby they
could claim £450 per cow for agreeing to stop milk production
for a minimum of five years. A producer tax on milk, the co-
responsibility levy, was also introduced in 1977. But it has
always been set at a very low level: 0.5 per cent of the Community
target price for milk in 1979, for instance, and only 2 per cent by
June 1982, with a reduced rate of 1.5 per cent for farmers in less
favoured areas. These two measures made no noticeable dents in
the mountains of surplus skimmed milk and butter.

Eventually a financial crisis in the Community forced member
states to go further. The quotas introduced in 1984 meant that
farmers (except the Irish) could expect the guaranteed price to
cover only the amount of milk they had produced in 1981. Any
extra output would be taxed at a punitive level. Even this
scheme still assumed that the EEC would over-produce each
year by 10 million tonnes of milk.

The second drop in the CAP milk ocean came in December 1986. EEC farm ministers agreed to reduce milk over-production still further over the following two years by a cut in milk quotas of 5.5 per cent and to reduce beef production by a cut of 13 per cent in the price at which beef is bought into intervention. Though the media were persuaded to treat this as a breakthrough, the cut in quotas was accompanied by other measures which reduced its effect. Guaranteed prices for beef were actually increased in the UK through a devaluation of the green pound; those for milk had already been raised in April 1986. At the same time the premiums paid on all beef cattle (including heifers) were increased with no limit to the number of stock on any one farm for which this £45 per head payment could be claimed. Another premium payable on every suckler cow was also increased. The December 1986 deal also provided for EEC governments to continue arrangements introduced in 1985 which allowed them to operate the milk quota system at regional and at dairy level rather than farm by farm. This meant that large producers could continue to over-produce so long as some other farmers in their regions or their dairy areas changed to other products or continued under-producing milk.

There is one other reason why the introduction of dairy quotas, whatever their limitations, does not seem to mark the beginning of the end of the CAP. In 1984, the budget ceiling which used to prevent member governments from giving more than 1 per cent of the revenue raised from VAT to the Common Market was lifted. At a meeting at Fontainebleau in 1984, heads of government of the Community countries agreed that the budget limit be raised to 1.4 per cent in 1986 with provision to raise it to 1.6 per cent in 1988. Hitherto, this budget limit had provided the main spur to CAP reform: its relaxation makes it possible for the cost of agricultural support to rise higher than ever. Certainly this move is vastly more important as far as the farm lobby is concerned than the dairy quotas. Long-time observer of the CAP Stefan Tangermann, Professor of Agricultural Economics at Gottingen University in West Germany, considered that 'The budget expansion dashes hopes that the 1984 CAP reform decisions could one day develop into a real reform.'[11]

The plain fact is that the incentives to agricultural intensification provided by the price support system of the CAP will be around for a long time to come.

Suppose, however, that the grip of the CAP were to be weakened. How far would this in itself go to securing the British landscape?

The leading political group in Europe advocating radical reform of the CAP is the British Labour Party. In 1981, Barbara Castle, then chairman of the European Labour Group's Working Party on Agriculture, spelt out the way in which her group would like to see the CAP recast.[12] In an overall reform of the CAP to be brought about mainly for social and financial reasons, all intervention prices would be brought down to the level at which supply and demand would come into balance. If this happened, the surpluses should disappear naturally. To ensure that such an approach did not cause hardship for some farmers, the socialist MEPs propose that national governments, working under Community rules, should support poor farmers directly with income subsidies.

In other words, Mrs Castle and her colleagues would still guarantee the Common Market's farmers an income but not such a high income as at present. The abolition of high guaranteed prices would mean that the large-scale producers of Western Europe would no longer have the spare cash to plough back into schemes to intensify production still further; nor would they have such a large financial incentive to do so.

In Britain such an approach would reduce the general profitability of agriculture and therefore the availability of funds for land reclamation schemes as well as the financial incentive to pursue them. This would obviously enhance landscape conservation greatly. It would not, however, eliminate the environmental problems posed by agriculture completely. Poor farmers might use their direct income aids to clear away landscape features in order to produce more income than the basic levels, and some of the richer farmers might still consider it worthwhile to increase production if they estimated that they could secure a good price for what they intended to produce on the open market. In other words, even a fundamental reform of the CAP would not provide a complete answer to the threat posed to the

British landscape by agriculture since its effect would be hit and miss. Some fields might stay unploughed that would otherwise have come under cultivation, but it is hard to predict where these fields might be, let alone whether they would have any conservation significance anyway. Particularly valued landscape features might still find themselves in the path of an agricultural improvement scheme that remained profitable even without CAP subsidy.

Changing the National Subsidies

The price guarantees of the Common Agricultural Policy are the single most important subsidy for destruction of the British countryside. But on top of the Euro-subsidies, there exists a host of ways in which British taxpayers' money is poured into British agriculture and forestry. All of these subsidies are of course subject to democratic control. So even if the CAP proves resistant to British pressure for radical change, there are still ways in which subsidies could be re-routed which are open to us as a nation.

It can certainly be argued that subsidies to agriculture from our own government should have been eliminated when we entered the Common Market, for they conflict with its purposes. While the Common Agricultural Policy is designed to stimulate output artificially it is supposed to do this by means which apply uniformly throughout the Common Market. Its tariff walls protect all the farmers of member countries equally from foreign competition, and its guaranteed prices offer the same level of security to all. The idea of a uniform agricultural régime was that it would ensure that the land surface would be used to the best advantage. Because prices for individual products would be much the same everywhere, crops would be produced in those parts of the Community best suited to them. If this meant that dairying died completely in one member country, that would be no bad thing if the country involved were better suited to citrus growing.

Specialization of this kind might have given Europe a healthier agriculture industry. One of the main reasons why it has not occurred is that national governments have insisted on retaining powers of their own over farming within their borders. They have used these powers in ways which have obstructed progress towards specialization. The main instrument of agricultural policy available to individual governments is the provision of cash aid. Partly to ensure that they do not become dependent on food from other EEC countries and partly in response to pressure from threatened sectors of their farming industries, Common Market governments are injecting very substantial subsidies through this route – on top of those coming into farming via the EEC. National subsidies to agriculture now add up to more than the whole cost of the CAP. If tax relief and social security spending on farmers are included, nationally financed spending on agriculture was twice as high as EEC spending in 1978, the most recent year for which figures are available at the time of writing.[13]

Given the scale of the spending involved, it is easy to see why these national subsidies can make nonsense of the idea of free competition within the EEC. But national governments have further room for manoeuvre in deciding how some EEC subsidies should be allocated. Take the allocation of hill livestock compensatory allowances to farmers within the EEC's designated less favoured areas. These payments are made on a livestock headage basis in respect of the difficulty faced by farmers rearing sheep, goats and cattle within these areas (which range from the Mezzogiorno and the mountains of Greece to the Scottish Highlands and half of the agricultural area of Eire). In 1982, French farmers, for instance, grazing livestock in high mountainous areas were receiving ninety European Currency Units or ECUs per livestock unit, to an upper limit of forty livestock units or 3,600 ECUs, while their counterparts on lower slopes but still within less favoured areas were getting 20.6 ECUs per animal with an upper limit of thirty animals.[14] The subsidy works as an instrument of income support, enabling French hill-farmers to stay in business when their activities would be uneconomic even by the standards of the CAP. This system may be good for the French hill-farmer. But not as good as the system operating in Britain in 1982. For in allocating the livestock compensatory allowances within British less favoured areas, the UK Government imposed no upper limit whatsoever on the amount of money any one person could receive or on the number of animals for which he could claim an allowance. Bigger British hill-farmers, benefiting from various economies of scale as well as their government grants, had an advantage over their French counterparts who nonetheless in turn had an advantage over their counterparts in countries like Greece in which in 1982 the upper limit per beneficiary was 1,765 ECUs, or Italy where it was 1,837 ECUs. In 1982, each person in receipt of compensatory allowances in the UK received on average 2,860 ECUs – far higher than that of any other EEC member country (the comparable figure for Greece was 923 ECUs, Germany 521 ECUs and France 898 ECUs).

National subsidy to agriculture and differences in the ways in which EEC cash is channelled heap further absurdity on the absurdity of the CAP. Britain, however, exacerbates still further the landscape damage being wrought by subsidies. Blanket subsidies – like generous tax reliefs and exemption from rates – have the effect of putting more money into farmers' pockets. This provides more funds which rich farmers can reinvest in schemes to produce yet more profits, many of which involve landscape destruction. Taxpayers' money can be seen funding landscape destruction even more obviously in the case of capital grants given specifically for the draining of meadows and the ploughing of cliff-top roughland. But other effective subsidies such as exemption from rates produce similar results by generating more funds for investment.

Withdrawal of these handouts would undoubtedly improve the prospects of the British countryside as well as the workings of the CAP. If the money saved could be redirected towards conservation purposes so much the better. And this is a step that need not wait upon the agreement of our Common Market partners; it would incidentally be welcomed by them. Some changes to national subsidies could be made through executive action. The Thatcher Government, for instance, cut grants to farmers for field drainage from 30 per cent to 15 per cent in 1984 simply by announcing the fact in its autumn financial statement. More substantial changes, such as the re-rating of agriculture or forestry, would require simply an Act of Parliament.

Some proposals for change in the UK subsidies to agriculture

have been advanced by conservationists. Most of them are
perfectly desirable, but would operate on a scale that could not
be expected to have a major impact on the landscape given the
forces for intensification that would still be at work. Nonetheless,
these proposals, many of them worked out in considerable detail,
do offer some pointers towards ways in which national subsidies
could be re-routed in the interests of conservation.

It is the most obviously damaging of the UK subsidies which
has attracted most attention, the capital grant. Clive Potter, an
environmental scientist at the University of East Anglia, has put
forward detailed proposals for change.[15] Under his scheme, no
farmer would be able to claim more than £10,000 in any one
grant application. At the same time, the Ministry of Agriculture
would be empowered to offer a farmer a 'supplementary grant'
that could help finance steps to soften the impact of the scheme
for which capital grant was being given – say tree planting
around a new farm building. The system whereby farmers
outside sites of special scientific interest and national parks may
carry out work and apply for capital grant retrospectively would
be replaced by one based on prior approval. Grant applications
would be submitted to local authority planning committees for
comments and suggestions before the Ministry of Agriculture
took a decision. Mr Potter hopes that the result would be a large
number of small schemes bringing about improvements both to
conservation and to farmers' incomes rather than a smaller
number of large capital projects wreaking havoc on important
landscape features.

Mr Potter's plan could be developed: landowners who wished
say to replace underground drains in fields already intensively
farmed could be allowed grant, while proposals to drain completely new areas could be excluded. Further grants could be
introduced on top of the small measures already taken to help
fund the maintenance of features like hay meadow and ancient
woodland, rather than their destruction. All of this would be
beneficial. But however Mr Potter's proposals were modified,
they could not provide a complete answer to the problems of the
countryside alone for several reasons.

Some activities which are causing serious landscape damage
are not eligible for capital grant. Grant has not been available

for hedgerow removal per se since the 1970s, and since the
introduction of new grant arrangements in 1985, the awarding of
grant for hedgerow removal where this is part of a drainage or
fencing scheme is at the Minister of Agriculture's discretion. Yet
hedgerow removal continues apace. No capital grant has ever
been available for the felling of woodlands – until 1985 grant
could be claimed only on the removal of tree stumps in order to
put the land down to farming use. Nonetheless, a third of
Britain's small woods were cleared away between 1947 and
1972.[16] The withdrawal in 1962 of a grant for ploughing downland turf, following a sustained campaign by Dorset conservationist Ruth Colyer, illustrates neatly how marginal the impact
of capital grants can be. The Ministry of Agriculture's cancel-
lation of the grant seems to have had no noticeable impact at all
on the rate of ploughing of chalk downland turf in Dorset or
anywhere else. There are no figures relating exactly to the
periods before and after 1962, but in the eleven years between
1956 and 1967, 4,000 acres of Dorset downland turf went under
the plough, while in the five years between 1967 and 1972, a
further 2,500 acres – more than 30 per cent of the 1967 acreage –
were lost.[17] The withdrawal of the downland ploughing grant
did not cause reclamation to drop off: the rate of ploughing
actually accelerated during the late 1960s and early 1970s.

Many farmers will go ahead with investment schemes like
land reclamation or the erection of new farm buildings or roads
without grants, even where these are available for the activity in
question. For grant aid is only one of the components of
investment finance. Other forms of support have helped make
agriculture so profitable that many schemes still make economic
sense even without Whitehall grants. Big farmers in particular
can usually lay hands on the capital for schemes with good
prospects, and often the bigger the scheme (and therefore the
higher the potential profit) the easier this is. What other investment opportunity can compete in the eyes of a banker with one
in which the market is guaranteed at the end of the day by the
taxpayers of twelve of the world's richest countries? If capital
grants were abolished tomorrow, many schemes would still go
ahead. Already, according to a recent study,[18] between 80 and
90 per cent of the cost of farm investment is generated on the

farm – in profits, gifts, sales of assets or from non-agricultural earnings. The remaining 10 to 20 per cent covers not only government capital grants but borrowing too. This can only mean that the greater part of farm investment is unaffected by government grant. In the great agricultural depression, farmers did not have the money for investment. Some of today's huge profits are literally being ploughed back, and more would be if the Government withdrew its contribution. Rather than a modification of the capital grants system, some new tool more precisely attuned to the needs of the landscape is now required.

A similar picture emerges when we examine the possibility of reforming the grant arrangements for forestry. It is possible to imagine a more attractive alternative to the great blocks of soulless conifers sprawling over Britain's wild country. There might be a variety of broad-leafed woods, here small, there large, of varying shapes containing loosely spaced trees of a variety of species but perhaps on Dartmoor predominantly oak, in the Yorkshire Dales predominantly ash, in East Anglia small-leafed lime, in Northern Ireland hazel and in the Highlands Scots pine. So long as plenty of wild moor were allowed to remain alongside new forests, tourists, sightseers, holidaymakers, hill-walkers and students of wildlife would welcome the new trees. In fact, if grant alone were the determining factor, broad-leafed trees are what landowners would already be planting. Since 1947 the Forestry Commission has awarded the planting of broad-leafed trees a higher rate of grant than conifer planting. This has not stopped conifers continuing to dominate large-scale afforestation schemes, for they grow more quickly than ashes, oaks, maples and beeches and therefore yield a quicker profit.

The difficulties of existing subsidy arrangements are tackled by Charlie Pye-Smith and Richard North, the authors of *Working the Land: a New Plan for a Healthy Agriculture*, published in 1984.[19] Though they concentrate on agriculture, the principles they lay out could be applied to forestry as well. They offer a plan to reshape British agriculture through the capital grants and some other national subsidies not only in order to conserve and enhance rather than destroy the wildlife and natural beauty of the countryside but also to bring about other changes they consider desirable: a switch from battery to free-range rearing of pigs and chickens, the production of more nutritious food, support for the small farmer, the encouragement of mixed and organic farming and the reduction of public spending on agriculture. Instead of the Ministry of Agriculture to hand out their re-jigged national subsidies, Pye-Smith and North propose new county committees. They have drawn the idea of these committees from the county war agricultural committees set up during World War II to ensure that even recalcitrant farmers attained the targets for home food production set by the Government. Two-thirds of the members of the Pye-Smith and North county committees would be farmers, landowners and agricultural experts; the remaining one-third would include representatives from the local planning authority, the Nature Conservancy Council, Countryside Commission and the regional water authority. Local farming and wildlife advisory groups would draw up maps of features like hedges and heaths deemed to be important, and the county committees would try to ensure they were conserved by withholding grants for projects which threatened them. If a farmer denied grant proposed to proceed without it, the committees would be empowered to impose 'freeze orders' which would make the destruction of the feature concerned a criminal offence and also jeopardize all that farmer's future applications for farm subsidies. Once-and-for-all compensation payments (as opposed to the annual, index-linked compensation payments made under the Wildlife and Countryside Act) would be available, at the committees' discretion, to farmers asked not to develop a particular habitat.

These proposals, though going further than Mr Potter's, suffer from similar limitations. No amount of control over the national farm grants will in itself secure the countryside from the threat posed by modern agriculture, since these represent only about 4 per cent of the total subsidies to British agriculture. At the same time, it is hard to see Pye-Smith and North's county committees acting with authority. The situation of war-time emergency created a very different atmosphere from that of peace-time Britain today. In war-time, the nation has committees to get things done and the urgency of war impels people to act together. Without this unifying force, the county committees would probably be beset by conflict. Farmers on the committees would not find it easy to cut off grants to their fellow-farmers. Rows and boycotts could be expected. At the same time, if the county committees were to be really effective in the conservation sphere, they would need expert technical staff in order to take such steps as imposing freeze orders. Established institutions whose authority is accepted, like local authorities, many of which already employ qualified professional staff, would seem better suited to such a purpose. Pye-Smith and North's acceptance of the principle of compensation could also lead to grave difficulties in practice. If a farmer receives a 'once-and-for-all' compensation payment one year, why should not the same man receive another once-and-for-all payment in respect of another land-use change on the same field in the following year? And if these payments are, as the authors suggest, to be related to a farmer's financial position, will this not leave the way open for unscrupulus farmers to shift their bank balances in order to be able to display 'need'? In any case, the idea of criminalizing the removal of features identified by committees of worthies is too momentous a step to be readily imaginable. The thought of farmer heroes going to gaol after refusing to pay their fines on principle would be enough to daunt even the most radical of legislators.

Another proposal for recasting national subsidies – this time the subsidies for upland farming – has been put forward by conservationists Malcolm MacEwen and Geoffrey Sinclair. In *New Life for the Hills*[20] they suggest ways in which both capital grants and headage payments in the uplands could be made to sustain rural communities without threatening environmental destruction. MacEwen and Sinclair want to see public money used not for the ploughing of moors, the planting of conifers, the draining of wetlands and so on, but on the conservation of wildlife and the development of facilities for tourism and for forms of agricultural improvement that enhance the environment. MacEwen and Sinclair propose the imposition of lower ceilings both on the amount of money any one person can get through a capital grant and the amount of headage payment available per acre of grazing land. This latter proposal would eliminate the existing incentive to farmers to re-seed their pastures with ryegrass so they can overstock them in order to claim the maximum possible number of headage payments. MacEwen and

Sinclair would like to see farmers drawing up 'farm management plans' showing how they proposed to improve their economic performance without damaging the environment. Local Ministry of Agriculture officials would advise on the drawing up of these plans and then use them to work out what level of subsidy each farm would receive. Subsidy levels could then be tied more closely to actual needs than is possible under the headage payments system.

The idea of the farm management plan has much to commend it. Such plans would provide a means of ensuring that the landscape was given the rehabilitation so much of it now needs more than mere preservation. However, there must be doubt about whether the Ministry of Agriculture is best placed to preside over the preparation and evaluation of the plans if these are really supposed to be a tool of landscape enhancement as well as agricultural management. MacEwen and Sinclair recommend the Ministry of Agriculture, Fisheries and Food should take on this role because they say it 'enjoys the confidence of many farmers'. But the reason why farmers like working with Ministry men is that the latter have always seen their function as serving the interests of the agricultural industry. The Ministry has so far shown reluctance to blur this objective. The House of Lords Select Committee on the European Communities, for instance, in a report in 1984 on *Agriculture and the Environment*, criticized the Ministry for its narrow interpretation of the economic possibilities of the uplands and its 'backward-looking tendency' in administering grant aid and offering advice in this field.

Yet another proposal for curbing the impact of modern agriculture and forestry on the landscape comes from Professor Timothy O'Riordan of the University of East Anglia. In 1983 Professor O'Riordan proposed that the existing exemption from capital transfer (now inheritance) tax granted to owners of outstandingly attractive stretches of land who have agreed to conserve it should be substantially widened to embrace about 30 per cent of the countryside of the United Kingdom.[21] To the landowners, this extra subsidy from the taxpayer would then have been worth many hundreds of millions of pounds annually. In return landowners would be expected to tell the Countryside Commission or the Nature Conservancy Council of any plans for changes in the use of land covered by the tax exemption. If the Commission or the Council considered a proposed change undesirable, it could seek to resist or modify the proposal through a management agreement; in the event of disagreement the Minister would be empowered to impose a 'countryside conservation order', with payment of compensation to the landowner. At the same time, capital grants would be withheld for environmentally damaging activities; a new package of grants would be available to encourage conservation.

Under Professor O'Riordan's plan, these arrangements would apply in two categories of land whose boundaries would be carefully designated by the Countryside Commission and the Nature Conservancy Council. One category would be known as 'heritage sites' and would cover 10 per cent of the countryside; the other category known as 'conservation zones' and enjoying lower conservation priority would cover 20 per cent of the countryside. In the remaining 70 per cent of the countryside, which Professor O'Riordan would designate as 'agricultural and forestry landscapes', there would be no automatic CTT exemption and none of the obligations for landowners which would accompany this in the other two zones. However, new grants and tax reliefs would be available for conservation work for those landowners who cared to avail themselves of them. And within the agricultural and forestry landscapes, local planning authorities would be empowered to designate small areas, even single important hedgerows, as 'areas of local conservation importance', a fourth new landscape category. Local authorities would designate these spots in their structure plans and safeguard them through management agreements or, in the last resort, through conservation orders which they would become empowered to make.

While some of Professor O'Riordan's ideas are interesting, the plan as a whole would be unlikely to prove either effective or easily practicable. This has become even more true since the replacement of capital transfer tax with inheritance tax provides landowners with the opportunity to evade the tax completely by making transfers within their lifetime. In any case, the idea that 70 per cent of the countryside can be more or less written off from the point of view of conservation, save for small spots within it, will not satisfy those for whom the countryside matters as a whole. However, the measures that Professor O'Riordan proposes for the 30 per cent of the land which is to be generally protected could not be guaranteed to safeguard even this. Landowners could still destroy landscape features without notifying anyone if they calculated that they would gain more by so doing than they might lose if their exemption from inheritance tax was withdrawn. Providing the exemption could, however, cost a substantial sum, and it is hard to see any government agreeing openly to improve the position of such a privileged group as landowners when the rest of the community seems certain to be subjected to continuing financial stress. To be politically feasible, any new subsidy to conservation-minded landowners will surely have to come at the expense of less responsible landowners rather than from society generally.

14. Pleas and Urgings

In 1977, the Countryside Commission for England and Wales launched an ambitious new publicity campaign. Its aim was to persuade everybody involved in the farming industry that the charms of the countryside should be conserved rather than destroyed. The Commission believed that farmers as a whole were ignorant of the environmental significance of their land. So a battalion of advisers set out to educate them.

Spokesmen and women appeared at a host of conferences up and down the countryside preaching conservation. A Commission-sponsored consultant drew up plans for reconciling conservation and modern agriculture on ten existing farms as object lessons; by 1983, 3,000 farmers and landowners had visited these 'demonstration farms'.[1] In five other areas, the Commission posted 'project officers' to spread the message. Each officer was charged with the task of trying to persuade landowners and farmers individually to plant amenity trees, manage or allow others to manage features of conservation interest like ponds, and to refrain from clearing away important landscape features.[2]

The Commission worked closely with the Farming and Wildlife Advisory Groups (FWAGs), which grew up in the 1970s to put the idea of voluntary conservation into practice on a county-by-county basis. Each Group contains representatives of local conservation and farming bodies: it has been the custom for the secretary of the county FWAG to be a Ministry of Agriculture employee and for the chairman to be a local farmer. FWAGs provide advice to farmers on conservation matters when invited to do so: by 1985, they had been asked to give advice to about 12 per cent of the farmers of England and Wales, according to national FWAG adviser Eric Carter, himself a former Ministry of Agriculture man.[3]

By 1986, sixty-three FWAG groups had been formed in Great

Britain. Describing the FWAG situation in Scotland, Dr Alan Mowle, Adviser on Rural Land Use to the Nature Conservancy Council, said:

The essence of a successful FWAG is that it is a group of interested farmers who can turn to conservation bodies and other experts for assistance. Conservationists are not trying to impose their will on the countryside in some trial of strength, but establishing a dialogue with the farming community which is intended to be a two-way process.[4]

In 1984 the then Countryside Commission chairman, Sir Derek Barber, launched the Farming and Wildlife Trust, a body whose main task is to raise funds for the county FWAGs. Prince Charles made a substantial donation to the new Trust when it was launched, and the Countryside Commission is providing it with grants.

As well as giving grants for conservation work to voluntary bodies like the county FWAGs and to local authorities and other public bodies, the Countryside Commission also offers landowners themselves a variety of grants to support conservation activities. Grants covering up to 50 per cent of the costs involved are available for the planting of trees and shrubs (but only broad-leafed species suitable to the locality), for conserving existing trees (perhaps through fencing, thinning or pollarding), and for conserving other landscape features (for example through hedge-laying, repairing dry stone walls, fencing and planting). Between 1974 and 1984, the Commission spent £8.5 million on steps to reconstitute the agricultural landscape of England and Wales and to advise others how to do so.

In 1982, a survey was conducted to try to discover how effective all this activity had been. Countryside Commission consultants Richard Westmacott and Tom Worthington were asked to revisit study areas they had examined ten years earlier. This original study, published in 1974, had provided some of the basic evidence about the impact of farming on the landscape. It had examined landscape change between 1947 and 1972 in seven widely dispersed study areas in England, each about 3,000 acres in size. In each of these areas the consultants uncovered extensive landscape change either already having occurred or in prospect. In the re-survey of 1982, Westmacott and Worthington returned to each study area, asking farmers what changes they had made and then going out and observing changes on the ground.[5]

What they found, though doubtless unwelcome to the Country-side Commission's optimists, came as no surprise to more realistic students of the rural scene. Essentially, Westmacott and Worthington's second survey showed the degradation of the English countryside they had identified in 1974 continuing uninterrupted in spite of all the efforts that had been made to 'educate' farmers into changing their ways.

Trees and hedgerows had continued to be cleared away and winding streams to be turned into straight drainage channels to meet the needs of agricultural technology and to produce more food-producing land. The rate of loss of landscape features was slower in the later period, but that was usually because there were far fewer features left to remove.

It was not just the deliberate removal of landscape features that concerned Westmacott and Worthington. They also found that landscape features like hedges, which had survived up till 1972 even if trimmed very close to the ground, had since then simply been allowed to deteriorate to nothing. Farmers in the Huntingdonshire study area, for instance, said they had removed very few hedgerows during the preceding decade. But when Westmacott and Worthington themselves plotted the situation on the ground, they uncovered extensive losses. In fact, over 85 per cent of the hedges lost during these nine years had been of poor quality at the start of the study period. Continual hard trimming, intensive cultivation all around them, plus possible occasional spraying with herbicide and burning, seems to have been enough to finish most of them off without deliberate uprooting.

So far the most obvious achievement of the education cam-paign is the planting of young broad-leafed trees. Millions of saplings have been planted since the early 1970s on roadsides, in field corners and on otherwise unused patches of ground. If these trees are properly nurtured, they should prove a delight to our descendants fifty years from now when they come to maturity.

Unfortunately, many of these saplings seem unlikely to survive that long. For while Westmacott and Worthington noted a considerable amount of tree planting in odd corners and on patches of unproductive land, they also found that the saplings were frequently dying through lack of proper after-care. In any case, they point out: 'While it is excellent that new planting is being carried out, it cannot fully offset the loss of ancient features. Once a 500-year-old hedge has been removed, planting half a dozen horse chestnut and sycamore in some awkward corner of an arable field is not much better than nothing.'

In the light of their study Westmacott and Worthington predicted the continuing loss of natural features throughout the countryside. They suggested that the result would be the drawing of a blanket of uniformity over the countryside smothering the regional diversity imparted by landscape features such as particular species of woodland tree, hedgerow styles or the pattern of water-courses.

There is no doubt that the enormous effort that has gone into persuading farmers to change their ways has had some good effects. But the Countryside Commission's own study does demonstrate that there is no point in expecting this approach alone to protect the British countryside against agricultural change. It does seem that farmers now appreciate the environmental implications of their activities more thoroughly than they did in the past. But that is by no means the same thing as agreeing to change their practices in consequence. For 'education' cannot force somebody to sacrifice his personal economic interest for the greater good if he does not want to. And in fact, economic self-interest has its own evangelists who are at least as energetic as the Countryside Commission's. One Lake District farmer told me: 'I get reps pushing spray chemicals every week in my yard, telling me that I am not doing the job right unless I use their spray to kill some weed I did not even know existed.'

The Commission said at the start of its campaign that it could take between twenty-five and thirty years to bring about the reversal of trends that was needed. If such a reversal was on the way, however, we could have expected to see more sign of it by 1982. Given the character of our landowners as it has developed over the ages, it would be strange indeed if they were to turn overnight into environmentalists because others sought to persuade them to. They have their own purposes and these are nowadays fundamentally at odds with those of many of their fellow-citizens who have an interest in the countryside but are not fortunate enough to own land.

There have been plenty of occasions on which farmers have destroyed landscape features in full knowledge of their importance. No one can imagine that the farmers anxious during the early 1980s to drain the Somerset Levels or the Halvergate Marshes had heard nothing of the case for conserving them. Unfortunately, many of the farmers who visit demonstration farms and read conservation booklets are the very ones who would not have removed a landscape feature anyway without first consulting their local conservation group. We can and should plead with our landowners to show restraint. But we should not treat this activity as a substitute for a more thorough-going review of the rural régime that is now required.

15. Planning

> We must introduce into the countryside the same wise planning development control as that which helps to preserve many of the finest features of our built environment. Sooner or later the House will require the same restrictions on material development of the countryside as are an obligation in our towns and cities. If someone needs planning permission to build a car-port next to his house, the same permission should be required to uproot a hedge or to drain a pond.
>
> Gerald Kauffman, MP, the then Shadow Spokesman on the Environment, during the second-reading debate on the Wildlife and Countryside Bill, 1981[1]

If the re-organization of the Common Agricultural Policy is beyond our power as a people; if re-arrangement of Whitehall subsidies to agriculture and forestry would be insufficient to save the countryside; if land nationalization might be ineffective and would certainly not be politically feasible; if pleading for concessions can have only limited impact; how might we rescue our rural heritage?

The answer lies, I believe, in a revision of our idea of what land ownership should mean. In the late Middle Ages, landowners accepted that they must share their rights over their land with the rest of the community. That principle was forgotten in the eighteenth century. Now we need to return to it. And our own age has provided one model of how it might be applied.

Town planning is an existing mechanism for providing the community as a whole with a say in the fate of land. Though operating at present only in the built environment, the system could be extended to the countryside.

What happened in 1947 when the Town and Country Planning Act was passed was that a share of the available rights over land was appropriated by the State. From that point on, anybody who wished to develop his land for industry, housing, mineral extraction and certain other activities required the approval of his democratically-elected local planning authority, though he could appeal against its decision to central government. The State had effectively nationalized development rights in land and the landowner had to apply to get these back through the process of planning consent.

Without this system of development control, the face of Britain would have been ravaged by building operations. The built-up area of London, for example, quadrupled in area during the first forty years of the twentieth century. Since 1947, however, it has hardly increased at all. This is largely because of a green belt policy enforced by planning authorities who may annually turn down as many as twenty planning applications to build on a single site. Development has been forced into specially selected satellite towns, where building densities are far higher than they would have been if developers had been allowed free rein. In the Surrey Green Belt alone, thousands of planning applications have been rejected since 1947, relating to anything from heliports, hotels and housing estates to golf courses, airfields, hypermarkets, mineral workings and garden centres. Elsewhere, in locations where the community deems it fit, developments like these are allowed.

Now this same instrument of development control, extended to embrace landscape features, could be applied to the task of rescuing our landscape. It could do this without toppling the landowners from the position they have held in the countryside for so long. All they would be required to do would be to recognize the rights of the rest of society in the land they hold in trusteeship for us all.

Trusteeship is not an idea alien to landowners today. As we have seen (page 480) many landowners like to present themselves as the mere stewards or custodians of their land, but some who talk in this way feel free to destroy the attractions of their property in the pursuit of profit, and feel no obligation to allow their fellow-citizens to share with them the benefits that their land can bestow. Landowners usually want to pass on property at least as extensive as that which they inherited or acquired. To do this they need profits, and the pursuit of profit may mean landscape damage. So this kind of trusteeship can bring about opposite effects to those that might spring from trusteeship on behalf of the community.

The extension of planning to the rural environment could provide the community with a means of ensuring that landowners did indeed operate as trustees on behalf of society rather than themselves and their heirs. Such a step would be an entirely natural extension of a system which has been universally accepted for four decades. The aim of the Attlee Government in passing the Town and Country Planning Act was to give to the community control over all the activities then thought to threaten the environment, rural as well as urban. Farming and forestry were given special exemption mainly because they were not at that time considered damaging. Now that it is clear they are doing far more harm than any building activity, the spirit of the original proposal, it could be argued, requires them to be brought under planning control.

An extension of the planning system to embrace the landscape could take many different forms. One way things might work would be as follows.

A new Act of Parliament would require any landowner or land occupier to seek planning permission from his local planning authority before he carried out any operation that could have a significant impact on the rural environment, such as removing a hedge or wood, tunnelling a stream underground, filling in a pond, draining a marsh, planting an area with coniferous trees, ploughing up a stretch of rough heath, down, moor or meadow, putting up a farm or forest building of any size, or bulldozing a new estate road. Once a planning application had been received, a local authority could grant it, refuse it or grant it subject to certain conditions. Local planning authorities would, as now, be required to issue a decision on any planning application within two months of receiving it, and any applicant aggrieved by a planning decision would have the usual right to appeal against it to the Secretary of State for the Environment. He would also have the right, as now in the built environment, to serve a purchase notice on his planning authority requiring it to buy the land if this became incapable of beneficial use as a result of the withholding of planning consent or the imposition of conditions.[2]

The framework within which councils would decide the fate of planning applications would be the existing county structure plans and local district plans. During the preparation of these plans, county and district councils are required to involve the public in an extensive public participation exercise. So the public would not only gain a say over the fate of particular landscapes and landscape features; they would also have a unique opportunity to challenge the orthodoxy on which agricultural and forestry expansion is presently based. The future of the countryside would be discussed and decided in public, not in private. Major decisions would be taken by people chosen by the whole community to take decisions on its behalf: locally elected councillors working through an extended planning system, not individual farmers and landowners alone concerned only with their own convenience or profit.

Of course, one problem would be that farmers and landowners dominate many local planning authorities in the countryside. But in 1981, the then Opposition Spokesman on the Environment, Gerald Kauffman MP, proposed a mechanism for dealing with planning authorities which favoured farmers at the expense of the public interest. Just as the applicant for planning permission may appeal to the Secretary of State for the Environment against the refusal of planning consent, so Mr Kaufman suggested that members of the public aggrieved by the granting of a permission could appeal against the decision.[3] Clearly, if such a change were made it would need to cover the whole of the planning system, but there have been plenty of cases which suggest that such a provision might play a useful role in the built environment as well as the countryside.

Unlike some other proposals for protecting the landscape, a system of planning control would provide a universal safeguard operating throughout the countryside. 'Conservation should not simply be a matter of protecting a small number of key sites, whether they are nature conservation sites or sites which are important from an amenity point of view. It should be an ethic which affects the whole of the British countryside,' were the words by which Lord Melchett, the Chief Opposition Spokesman on the Wildlife and Countryside Bill, introduced an amendment seeking to extend planning controls to the countryside in 1981 –

an amendment he said he considered the most important of any
of the large number which the Opposition tabled in the House of
Lords.[4] Of course, any form of effective rural planning would
inevitably involve the zoning of some areas as more important
for conservation – or, at the other end of the spectrum, for
industrial development. But, as the Vale of Belvoir and Til-
lingham Hall controversies for instance have shown, it is often
the less spectacular stretches of country, which are frequently
devoid of any special conservation designation, that turn out to
matter most to most people.

Failure to confront problems throughout the countryside is
the chief weakness of the existing approach embodied in the
Wildlife and Countryside Act. The Act specifically confines the
requirement for advance notification to sites of special scientific
interest, to areas of moor and heath in national parks covered by
special orders none of which had been made by the beginning of
1986, and to activities taking place in national parks for which
farm capital grant is sought. A further limitation is implicit in
that the Act specifies that compensation must be paid where
changes of use are blocked, and there is only a small amount of
money available to be paid out.

But if planning control would provide a reasonably straightforward means of conserving existing landscape features throughout
the countryside, it would not provide a complete solution to the
problems confronting Britain's landscape. One weakness would
be that it would not provide for the maintenance that might be
required by a stretch of downland turf, woodland or a wetland
saved from the plough.

In a letter to *The Times* published on 28 February 1984,
Professor Kenneth Mellanby picked up this theme. He wrote:

To retain its value, [the countryside of lowland Britain] needs to be
managed, often in an uneconomic way. Thus we deplore the loss of
hedges ... and the suggestion that they should be protected by
planning legislation is attractive. However, I believe this might well be
counterproductive. We could prevent a farmer from grubbing up a
hedge, but he could get rid of it simply by leaving it alone. In a few
years it would be a gappy thicket. A hedge needs to be cut or laid, a
meadow to be grazed or mown, to retain the features which we value.

The gradual deterioration of the upland woods of Britain provides a good example of this problem. In areas in which woodlands are surrounded by grazing lands, stock are frequently allowed to wander into the woods, where they eat tree seedlings and saplings. As a result, many woodlands in the Yorkshire Dales and Dartmoor, the Highlands of Scotland and the Welsh hills are failing to regenerate themselves and in seventy years or less could consist only of old and dying trees. Take Snowdonia for instance. Many of the oak and birch woods that clothe valley- and mountain-sides in this national park have been in existence from around 3,000 B.C. They are remnants of the ancient Wildwood and have been managed for timber production for much of the last thousand years. But in our own century, grazing animals have been allowed to get into the woods in an unregulated manner and this is preventing their natural regeneration. Nature Conservancy Council local official Dr Malcolm Smith estimates that: 'If present trends continue, and there is no indication that they will not, Snowdonia stands to lose between 80 and 90 per cent of its native broad-leafed woodland within the next 100 years.'[5] All that is required is the fencing of these woods so that any grazing that does take place is the result only of the woodlands' natural populations of herbivores, like voles and mice. At present, however, landowners have no ongoing financial incentive to fence the woods or financial disincentive to prevent their insidious destruction.

The Countryside Commission's 1984 report *Agricultural Landscapes: A Second Look*, which examined the impact of agricultural change on seven study areas of English countryside between 1972 and 1982, highlighted other kinds of erosion that can befall landscape features redundant to modern agriculture apart from out-and-out removal: 'As well as the conscious acts of removal and replacement, there is the constant unmeasured change of "natural" wear and tear. Events which "happen" are almost always deleterious – fire, spraying, over-zealous trimming, damage by vehicles, stock breaking out, lightning strike. All of these exact their toll.'[6]

If planning controls cannot provide for the maintenance of the features they save from destruction, they can do still less to

provide for the reconstitution of landscape features in areas
where these have already been eliminated.

Yet some provision for reconstitution would be an essential
part of any scheme designed to rescue our countryside, and not
only because reconstitution would be a desirable thing in itself.
For the announcement that controls on landscape change were
on the way would precipitate an orgy of destruction as farmers
sought to get rid of unwanted features while they still could. The
knowledge that reconstitution might be required would serve to
make farmers who were so minded think twice.

Overall, the reality seems to be, however, that while planning
controls would provide a great step forward, they would be
unlikely to provide a complete solution. So is there an alternative
approach consistent with Britain's long-standing land ownership
régime which could provide a more comprehensive defence
system for the countryside?

PART SEVEN
The Way Forward

16. A Tax on Land

I am a twenty-eight-year-old dairy farmer from the Lorton Valley in Cumberland. I do not *like* just keeping milk cows. I would rather keep twenty cows, thirty-five sheep, a few beef animals, free-range hens and some ducks and pigs. That would be farming and enjoying my way of life the way I always wanted to ... This is not possible for me now. I would like to keep all my dykes (hedges) in order (I am laying one at the moment), but on ninety-three acres with forty-five milk cows and rent, interest and loan repayments on the scale I have it is impossible to make a good job of the farm ... I cannot refuse to use high levels of nitrogen because I could not keep enough cows to pay the rent or the interest rates on all the money I had to borrow to get a start ... Capital grants are no use to me if I do not want to put up a building or drain a field. But the NFU men who matter tell us that the farming 'industry' is better off with capital grants ... I want to be able to farm this farm as a mixed farm. I want to stop making myself old quickly by chasing my tail producing food surpluses. I would like to have the pride in the appearance of my farm that there was forty-five years ago ... This is what is called rural life.

Letter to the author, 1980

What is objectionable is that subsidy should destroy important sites irretrievably in order to add to surpluses ... Anyone who farms in a highly populated country should embrace the concept of stewardship. He has a responsibility to hold the land in trust for the future ... Where farming is inherently unprofitable, and needs to be sustained for social reasons, some support system sympathetic to the environment must be accepted.

Kenneth Carlisle MP, *Conserving the Countryside: A Tory View*, Conservative Political Centre, 1984

If there are limits to what could be achieved through planning controls, there is a completely different approach to the problem of protecting our countryside which is being discussed increasingly widely.

Since it is an economic process which is damaging our
countryside, it has come to be argued by some people that
economic counter-measures are the appropriate response. An
early idea was that subsidies for conservation activities should
be made available alongside the existing agricultural subsidies
which turn out in practice to amount to subsidies for the
destruction of the rural environment. However, it quickly became
apparent that pressure on public funds would not permit the
creation of a whole new set of subsidies in the countryside,
especially in view of the fact that the existing subsidies to
agriculture are now widely considered to be a waste of public
money. Attention therefore turned to the idea of redirecting
certain of the present subsidies in ways that made them support-
ive rather than destructive of the environment. UK capital
grants to agriculture, for example, might no longer be given for
the reseeding of chalk downland turf but made available instead
for its reinstatement. Unfortunately, however, the modifications
that could be made without calling into question the whole price
support structure of the EEC (an impracticable objective) would
not be anything like large enough to outweigh the remaining
incentives for destruction.

A more radical form of economic attack on the problems
confronting the countryside is however conceivable. This would
involve applying taxation – not in order to raise revenue for the
Exchequer but as a means of regulating economic activity in the
public interest. Because agriculture and forestry, supported as
they are by almost unlimited bounty from Brussels or Whitehall,
seem set to remain profitable industries, they ought to be able to
bear the imposition of a new form of taxation. A new tax
with relief for those who meet conservation requirements could
conserve the countryside at no cost to the Exchequer.

Such a tax could take the form of a new rural land tax,
payable annually on every acre of rural land in the United
Kingdom. This would immediately serve to counteract the
financial incentives for landscape destruction provided at present
by national farming and forestry subsidies and by the Common
Agricultural Policy.

To achieve its full effect the tax would need to be levied
negatively as well as positively so that a taxpayer whose reliefs

amounted to more than what he was obliged to pay could be given the difference. In this way, some of the proceeds of the take from the great wealth of the landowning community could be redistributed towards its more public-spirited members. Where an owner was managing his land in ways deemed conducive to the national interest he might be rewarded by payments from the tax fund. Such payments would overcome the real problem faced by well-meaning landowners today that they cannot afford to maintain landscape features.

This would need to be a tax earmarked for specific activities – like the television licence fee but unlike vehicle excise duty – if it was to work purely as a regulator of the rural scene. Clearly, the cost of collection would have to be deducted from receipts. But what was left could be used solely to fund activities which had been rated negatively for land tax purposes. A landowner, say, who owned commons in Dorset with Dartford warblers on them and who proposed to keep them as commons rather than ploughing them up would get a subsidy through the land tax.

Of course the land tax would make intensive agriculture and forestry less profitable. But if the profitability of agriculture and forestry were reduced, there would be less incentive for owners to plough up the marginal land on which the quality of our landscape and the future of our wildlife depends. Some low-grade agricultural land could therefore be expected to revert to the roughland, woodland or marshland from which it had doubtless been reclaimed. Obviously the owners of such land would lose out financially. But landowners are a group capable of incurring some such losses without suffering unduly. So who would suffer? Not the workers, as agriculture and forestry have become so highly capitalized on the back of subsidy that employment in the industries is now minimal. Certainly not the citizen, who would have to fund less stockpiling of surplus food and provision of tax relief to conifer foresters.

Existing Fiscal Sticks and Carrots

It might appear that a rural land tax would involve a quite new and daunting level of state intervention in the economics of land-use. Already, however, there is a vast amount of state intervention in rural economics. Some of this is destructive. Some of it is beneficial. But all of it is haphazard and because of this it cannot serve as an effective tool of coherent policy-making.

Inheritance tax exemption is one of the obvious existing forms of intervention which would be superseded by a rural land tax. As we have seen (Chapter 10), the inheritance tax exemptions fail to achieve their supposed purpose of safeguarding the countryside and instead serve to enhance the position of landowning families. These exemptions would be swept away if a land tax was introduced and replaced by tax credits which would apply whether or not land changed hands, in line with clear policy objectives. But the story of these exemptions highlights one important point about a rural land tax. It would have to operate in public. Inheritance tax exemption is enveloped in a cloak of secrecy on the grounds that it concerns an individual's private affairs. It is this characteristic which has helped landowners turn the system to their own advantage and prevented citizens from assessing what benefit, if any, they are receiving from these subsidies. A rural land tax would firmly establish the principle that land is different from other capital assets. Because the community as well as its 'owners' has a stake in it, the terms on which it is held must be made known to all. In so far as this would involve a further sacrifice from landowners it is one they ought to be required to make. Arrangements under the Wildlife and Countryside Act for conservation in return for compensation are already made public. Details of the deals struck between landowners and the rest of society over the national landscape heritage through the land tax should be equally fully within the public domain.

Another existing form of state intervention in the rural economy which would be superseded by a rural land tax is the direct subsidies paid to farmers and foresters by central government, such as farm capital grants. These would disappear to re-emerge as positive or negative payments under the land tax in so far as national policy dictated. Where such payments remained – as might those from EEC sources – the land tax could simply be adjusted to take them into account. In place of the counter-productive mish-mash that exists at present, there would be a means of implementing a genuine national policy on the country-side which would be not only effective but also capable of responding quickly to change in society's demands from rural land. If at some future date field drainage became nationally desirable again, there should be no need to reinstate the capital grants system to encourage it. Drainage could simply become tax deductible while undrained but drainable land could be made to attract a high rate of land tax. Indeed, if agriculture as a whole were to become unprofitable and Britain seemed in danger of losing an effective agriculture industry, it would be possible to provide immediate support through adjustments in the land tax rates.

Imagine the impact of such a scheme on the farmer in the Lake District, who is quoted at the beginning of this chapter. He would lose his capital grants (which he does not want) and his headage payments (which encourage him to intensify production in environmentally harmful ways). Instead, so long as hill-farming was accepted as an activity to be encouraged, he would get a single subsidy designed to encourage the environmentally desirable activities in which he wishes to engage now but cannot afford to. The new subsidy would be continuous, rather than a one-off payment, so fencing to allow the natural regeneration of woodlands, for example, could be erected in the knowledge that funds would exist for its maintenance. The enhancement of his holding would not be brought about at the expense of the general taxpayer as are the constraints on changes in land-use wrought by management agreements under the Wildlife and Countryside Act. The money would be generated from the profits of other landowners whose activities were more economically successful than his but less socially desirable.

Introducing Democracy

If a land tax of this kind were to be created, there would still be the question of just what activities it should encourage and discourage. This is clearly something in which the community at large should have a say, and decision-making could and ought to take place at both national and local levels.

At national level, priorities would have to be set, based on a

clear view of the public policy priorities of the day. One government department would have to be responsible for setting rates,
positive or negative, for each major form of land-use in each
region of the United Kingdom. This would be the Department
of Environment, the Welsh Office, the Scottish Office or the
Northern Ireland Office. In setting rates, these departments
would consider representations from other affected departments,
such as the Ministry of Agriculture and the Ministry of Defence,
the feelings at local level as represented through county structure
plans and the views of pressure groups. But eventually, from
Whitehall would come rates per acre of tax for, say, cereals
(doubtless positive in most regions), broad-leafed woodland
(doubtless negative in most regions). Superimposed on these
basic rates, however, could be a subtle fine-tuning of the system
at local level that could allow for the achievement of almost any
kind of objective.

All this would provide a means of determining the different
policies which the tax would bring about at different places
within the United Kingdom. But what mechanism would ensure
that the tax levied accurately reflected a landowner's actions?
For this an instrument would be needed which would allow
scrutiny and influence by the general public but which would
also exploit a landowner's own instinct for change on his land.
The instrument would be a land plan.

Essentially, landowners would be entitled to certain levels of
relief from the land tax if they were in possession of a land plan
for their holdings approved by their local planning authority.
Local authorities, instead of devoting time to rural development
control, would negotiate the contents of these plans with landowners in the light of local feeling, the county structure plan and
guidelines from the Department of the Environment. Clearly,
the maintenance of landscape features of value might be an
ingredient of an approved plan. But a landowner might qualify
for relief at a higher level if his plan showed that conserved
features were to be adequately maintained or that new features
were to be created through reconstitution.

Local opinion would make itself felt through the consultation
process that goes with structure planning. Agreed land plans
would be open to public inspection. Citizens who felt their

council was being too easy on landowners as well as landowners who felt the council was being too hard could appeal to the Department of the Environment.

Suppose, for instance, that in west Bedfordshire, songbird populations were at a dangerously low ebb. Birdwatchers might bring this to the attention of their county council. The structure plan would set targets for the reinstatement of features that songbirds particularly favour like hedgerows and copses, while observing that such features should, where they already exist, be retained wherever possible. Landowners would note these objectives in preparing their land plans for approval.

Such a system might seem extremely radical but many of its principles would be familiar enough. Already the Department of the Environment determines the character of the built environment through the development control appeals system. It has to arbitrate the potential conflict between fulfilment of the national objective of job-creation and hence factory building and the safeguarding of the residential environment. What would actually happen if this process were extended to the countryside not through the extension of development control, but through the workings of a land tax?

A dialogue between the structure planning process and the Department of the Environment would yield regional policies for the countryside. This would doubtless mean that certain parts of the United Kingdom, because of the inherent fertility of their soils and their special climatic conditions would be designated prime farming regions. But in such areas, like East Anglia, where very little uncultivated land survives, landscape reconstitution could be encouraged. The structure planning process would identify particular types of landscape feature it would be desirable to reintroduce, whether for wildlife or landscape reasons. Negative rates of land tax would not only protect desirable forms of landscape, say, rough heathland; they would also encourage their reconstitution.

In some areas, like perhaps the Highlands and Islands of Scotland, the Scottish Office might well conclude that agriculture and forestry should be supported for reasons of employment. Here, particular rates of land tax might encourage labour-intensive agriculture like crofting. But in areas of grade 4 or 5 agricultural land where agriculture employs few people at present, such as parts of Surrey and Dorset, the land tax rates and management plan requirements might encourage the retention of many of those landscape features that remain and the reinstatement of many more. In areas such as this landowners might find that it paid them to turn substantial areas back to nature.

More than anything else, however, the emergence of the land plans would make every landowner (or at least every landowner interested in tax relief) think hard and continuously about conservation, harnessing and rewarding his own creative instincts. Each plan would be the owner's statement of the steps by which he proposed to meet the objectives set down in his county structure plan. It would differentiate between land now and in the future committed to supporting natural features like marsh, meadow, moor, heath, hedge, stream, salting, wood or copse and land under crop, ryegrass or conifer. In the case of a conifer plantation (which might be attracting a high rate of tax), a landowner could pledge that he would make provision for wildlife conservation within the plantation and arrange felling in stages and other ways that would benefit wildlife.

When the plan was submitted to the local planning authority it could be approved as meriting a certain level of tax relief, or made the basis for the negotiation of something very different. Some landowners might of course refuse to submit a plan, preferring to pay the full level of tax. If too many did this the system would fail, but the evidence is that Britain's landowners respond well to financial incentives if they are big enough.

The procedure for submitting a land plan for approval to a planning authority could follow the well-tried model of the planning application. This would mean that an authority would have to advertise the plan and receive any objections to it from members of the public. The authority could be required to issue a decision on any plan within a certain time of receiving it, as in the case of planning applications. Approved land plans would be available for perusal at council offices, and concerned citizens, seeing for example a wood being cleared away, would be able to go and check its status on the approved plan. If they considered the activity in question was in breach of an approved plan they could inform the planning authority which could then order the owner to take whatever action it deemed necessary to bring things into line with the plan. Its sanction would be immediate withdrawal of all tax reliefs.

Each land plan might last for five years. But within that time, the advent of a new owner or changes in financial circumstances or methods of cropping might mean that a landowner wished to alter his land plan. In that case, he could get a form from his local planning authority and send it in, completed, to his planning officer, indicating what departure he wished to make from his approved land plan. Such forms would go in a batch before the planning committee, after opportunity for public comment, following again on the model of the planning application.

Decisions on changes to an approved land plan could be taken, as for the plan itself, not by reference only to the feature in question, but within the context of the overall land plan. Thus, if a planning authority considered a landowner was making good provision for conservation perhaps by making ponds or creating tracts of roughland, they might allow him, say, to remove a hedgerow so long as it was not itself of outstanding historical or other significance. In other words, decisions could be taken within the overall context of conservation requirements, not on a site exclusive basis, as occurs in the planning system as it exists at present.

Some may detect in all this the ghostly voice of Henry George. But the proposal differs in one important respect from the nineteenth-century calls for a land tax. George advocated an across-the-board tax on site values, all of the revenue from which was to have gone direct to the Exchequer, reducing the need for other forms of national taxation, in particular taxes levied on income. The land tax, on the other hand, would involve the redistribution of wealth not within society as a whole, but within the landowning community. Nonetheless the two proposals share common features. In particular, the underlying objective of both is to enable the land to be put to the optimal use for the whole of society. George deplored the existence of idle land badly needed for housing or factory building but which its owners were holding back, often in the hope of higher profits in future. The new rural land tax would encourage the optimal use of land, though in some cases this might mean turning land over to the needs of recreation and conservation.

Of course, a land tax could be put to other uses other than safeguarding the rural environment. It could be used to encourage organic farming, or free-range hen rearing while discouraging the use of certain kinds of chemicals and battery cages. It could also stimulate the growing of certain crops or uses of farmland compared with others – say fruit and vegetables as against dairying, if that were considered a desirable component of agricultural policy. The tax could regulate the use of environmentally undesirable fertilizers and pesticides. And it could be used to stimulate employment on the land. The massive reduction in the numbers of people employed on the land has damaged the countryside by undermining rural communities. One day it might be considered sensible to support forms of labour-intensive farming which might provide work for the urban unemployed.

All of these things are examples of the rural policy-making for which a rural land tax would be such an effective tool. Any such policy-making would of course undermine the power of the landowner to do as he wishes with his land. But it would do so in a way which ought to allow for the maximum possible interplay between the landowner's ancient desire for control and the legitimate but long-ignored interests of the rest of the community.

17. A Right to Roam

> Every man, without distinction of race or colour, is entitled to
> nourishment, housing, covering, medical care and attention ...
> employment and ... the right to roam over any kind of country,
> moorland, mountain, farm, great garden or what not, where his
> presence will not be destructive of its special use, nor dangerous to
> himself nor seriously inconvenient to his fellow citizens.
>
> H. G. Wells, 'War Aims: The Rights of Man', in a letter to *The Times*,
> 1939

During the post-war era, opportunities for the people of Britain
to roam their countryside have steadily been reduced. Publicity
has attended the opening of the official long-distance footpaths
and country parks to which those who want to walk out of doors
are increasingly directed. But those who prefer to wander at
will through ordinary woods, commons and by-ways within
reasonable distance of their homes are finding this simple pleasure harder and harder to come by. As those who own land have
devoted ever more of it to the ever-more intensive pursuit of
wealth, they have eliminated much of the hitherto marginal
areas – the hedges, woods, streams and roughlands – that made
walking both possible and enjoyable. At the same time, our
landowners' long-standing preference for private pleasure
coupled with the power to indulge it has ensured that the
sanctuaries they have kept from the plough have remained
firmly closed to their fellow-citizens. Even the network of public
footpaths and bridleways which by tradition provided the landless with at least the opportunity to glimpse the glories of the
countryside, has been successfully eroded in recent years. And
measures provided by Parliament to improve access have lain
largely unused by local authorities anxious to avoid antagonizing
their local landowners.

In the face of these trends, action would be required merely to restore access opportunities to the levels existing in the past. But growing interest in rural recreation requires rather more.

One particularly comprehensive set of proposals for improvements in existing procedures and powers was put forward in 1983 by Andrew Bennett, the MP for Stockport North. In an (unsuccessful) Private Member's Access to the Countryside Bill Mr Bennett proposed several new measures to strengthen the rights of the walking public. Had this Bill become law, in cases where a highway authority failed to take action to secure the removal of an obstruction on a right of way, it would be open to anybody to apply to the magistrates' court for a new type of order that would require the highway authority to remove the obstruction. If the authority still declined to act, the court could authorize the complainant to remove the obstruction himself. A similar procedure would apply for the reinstatement of a public highway after ploughing; while any land-occupier who allowed any bull over the age of ten months to be at large in a field or enclosure crossed by a public footpath would be liable to prosecution.

To extend public access to so-called 'open country' (mountain, moor, cliff, heath, foreshore, woodland and waterside), Mr Bennett proposed to lay a new duty on every county council or access authority (such as a national park authority) to prepare and publish a draft access map defining land which is 'open country', common land subject to a right of access and land over which access agreements might be made. The Secretary of State for the Environment would hold a public inquiry into any objections or representations made about the map, and would, if necessary, direct the access authority to modify it. Thereafter, the map would be published. If an access authority declined, after a request from any person, to make an access order, the applicant could appeal to the Secretary of State for the Environment who could direct the authority to make the order.

Welcome though such proposals may be, they would not be as effective as a simpler but more far-reaching measure. What is really needed is an attack on the blanket presumption against access afforded by the law in Britain, reflecting as it does the dominant position which landowning interests have enjoyed for centuries. If there is to be a real attempt to provide for general enjoyment of the countryside alongside the requirements of the landowners, then this presumption has to be challenged. The character of land ownership in Britain needs to be redefined to exclude the landowner's right to bar his fellow-citizens from the face of the earth. We need a change from a system that treats presence on rural land as trespass except in special circumstances, to one that presumes a public right to walk on the land except in circumstances where there are good reasons why it should be withheld. In this way, we could break with our feudal inheritance and recover from the landowners a right which was taken for granted a thousand years ago.

Such a step may seem radical, even Utopian. But it would not seem so in many of the neighbouring countries of Northern Europe in which feudalism either never developed or was less persistent than it has been in Britain, and which have an arrangement of this kind.

In Sweden, the Right of Common Access, or *Allemansrätten*, gives everyone the right to cross another person's land on foot provided no damage or disturbance is caused. The landowner or tenant does not have to give permission. Carefully defined exceptions ensure that walkers are not allowed to enter the private land surrounding a house, or cross newly-planted woodland, growing crops or other land likely to suffer damage.

Swedish local authorities may prosecute landowners who obstruct access or erect signs to deter people from using their right of common access. On the other hand, people who leave litter in the countryside may be fined or sent to prison for up to six months.

Some areas used by the armed forces continue to be barred to the general public; in addition some nature conservation areas are also excepted from the right of common access. However, hunting and shooting in the countryside (and shooting pheasants is common in southern Sweden in late summer) take place without any suspension of *Allemansrätten*.

Of course, Sweden differs from Britain in many ways. It has a small population and much of it is remote forest. However, Sweden does have its densely populated areas. The highly industrialized southern parts of the country contain 90 per cent

of the population and most of the important farmland. Yet
Allemansrätten seems to work as well here as on the Arctic borders.

In Britain, movement in the direction of a right of access has at
least been contemplated in the last half-century. The Hobhouse
Committee on Footpaths and Access to the Countryside set up
during the war to consider what form access to the countryside
should take when the war was over did not recommend the
approach based on access agreements and access orders
embodied in the legislation that materialized in 1949: it proposed
that there should be a legal right to wander over all uncultivated
land, including lakeside, shore and cliff-top, mountain, moor,
heath and down.[1] From this 'access land' certain kinds of land
would have been exempted, including crop land, buildings,
golf courses and race courses. A decade after the Hobhouse
Committee's unproductive deliberations, the Royal Commission
on Common Land came out in favour of a public right of access
to all the common lands of England and Wales, which now
cover over 1.5 million acres.[2]

However, we now need a measure applying to a much wider
area than either Britain's common land or even to the moors,
mountains and coasts singled out by the Hobhouse Committee.
The woods and lanes of lowland Britain must also be opened up.
So what might be the shape of a new system that gave the public
the right to enjoy Britain's countryside to the full?

A new Act of Parliament could provide a right of pedestrian
access in principle to all woodland, parkland and rough grassland, lakeside, riverbank, streamside and coastline, field edge,
farm track and forest path throughout the United Kingdom.
The new right would apply whether the land was owned by
private individuals or public authorities. The effect would be
that legitimate access would no longer be confined as it is at the
moment to areas or routes over which specific provision has
been made, through the public footpath and access agreement
arrangements, with entry anywhere else constituting trespass.
Instead, people would enjoy a legal right that could be upheld in
the courts to walk along all the private tracks and open areas at
present reserved for the owners of land. At the moment a
landowner may use such force as is necessary to evict people
from any part of his land which is not subject to a public

footpath or other specific access arrangement. Under the new legislation he would be liable to prosecution if he attempted to prevent people from walking on land covered by the new right. Examples of such illegal obstruction might be the erection of fences not demonstrably required for some other purpose such as stock control, padlocking gates, or stationing fierce animals on likely routes for no other purpose than obstruction. Local authorities would be expected to conduct prosecutions in response to complaints, but private individuals or organizations like the Ramblers' Association could do so as well. For their part, landowners would not be required to take any particular action but would merely be required to refrain from stopping others walking on their land. They would retain the right to sue in respect of damage caused by members of the public, even if the damage was caused in the exercise of the new rights.

The only circumstances in which a landowner or occupier would be entitled to obstruct access would be when the land involved was excluded from the application of the new right of access because it was in a category defined in the Act as excluded or was the subject of a special exclusion order authorized by the Secretary of State for the Environment. Categories of land excluded in the Act would doubtless include land covered by buildings or the curtilage of such land, land used for growing crops or supporting trees less than fifteen years old, aerodromes, racecourses, railways, gardens, mineral workings and land on which development was being carried out. The special exclusion orders could be made by the Secretary of State for the Environment at any time in response to an application from a landowner who wished to restrict access for some good reason not covered by the categories for exclusion in the Act. The Ministry of Defence could be expected to apply for orders covering its lands on grounds of public safety or national security, but the orders need only be given where and when the Secretary of State was satisfied that exclusion was really necessary – in certain places, perhaps on days when firing was taking place but not on other days. The Nature Conservancy Council is another public owner whose lands need not all receive automatic exemption: the Council could be required to demonstrate that exclusion really

was necessary. It is far from clear that this is the case in all NCC
land from which the public are presently barred.

The procedure for applying for exclusion orders might perhaps
follow the model provided by the present system for development
control. Applications for orders would need to be publicized in
at least one local newspaper and on site; there would be a period
for objections to be made in writing to the Secretary of State for
the Environment, perhaps two months; if objections could not
be resolved by agreement the Secretary of State could be obliged
to hold a public inquiry. It would then be up to him to approve
or reject the order or approve it with modifications. The effect of
an exclusion order (which would relate to sites indicated on
maps and could be temporary or permanent) would be that
landowners or land occupiers in possession of an order would be
able to restrict access to the land covered by the order.

At present two of the forms of land use most often presented
as incompatible with public access are shooting and fishing. Yet
if the new legislation was to achieve its intended effect it would
be important to ensure that use of land for bloodsports should
not be one of the activities automatically securing exclusion from
the application of the new right of access. As we have seen,
there is plenty of evidence that pheasant, partridge and grouse
shooting, deer stalking and fishing can co-exist with public
access, except perhaps in small areas on particular days of the
year. Landowners could apply to the Secretary of State for a
temporary exclusion order, for instance along particular rides
where shooting was to take place for the period of the shoot or
the environs of coops at key breeding periods. People whose land
was subject to temporary exclusion orders would be required to
post notices indicating the circumstances when the public were
forbidden entry, just as advance warning is presently given in
respect of land covered by agreements permitting public access
to grouse-shooting moors except on certain days.

A law such as this would sweep huge tracts of Britain's
countryside from the exclusive grip of a small number of men. It
would also ease the position of some landowners who might be
prepared to open up their land if they knew they would not be
the only ones doing so. Some landowners have put it to me that
they would be prepared to let people in but they fear they would

be overwhelmed since so little land around them is accessible. But if a general right of access existed, the fear of being swamped by visitors could be allayed. Another similar fear that apparently inhibits otherwise liberal landowners at present is that disturbance will lead all their game to flee to their neighbours' lands. If disturbance of game were uniform, a landowner could expect that any pheasants he lost would be balanced by the arrival of someone else's.

Perhaps the greatest problems would arise over deer stalking since by its nature this activity involves the pursuit of the prey over considerable distances with the possibility of the deer being shot at any spot in a huge area. Compounding the problem of public safety is the stalkers' claim that the scent of one human being can drive deer miles away. At present the effect of this attitude is the exclusion of the non-deer-stalking public from vast tracts of Scotland at the very time when most people are on holiday. Landowners who wished to exclude the public from their land to facilitate the breeding and shooting of deer would have to convince the Secretary of State for the Environment that the restrictions they sought were necessary, not merely convenient.

As in Sweden, the new Act should provide not only for the right of access and make the obstruction of access an offence; it should also prohibit the erection of signs which appeared to prohibit access to land to which the right of access existed. Local authorities and private individuals would need the right to remove obstructions or offending signs as well as launch prosecutions. Also as in Sweden, the Act could provide stiff penalties for dropping litter and for vandalism.

Apart from eliminating some of their privacy, what harm would the new arrangements cause landowners? It would not stop stately home owners charging the public admission, since most of the areas to which they admit the public at present – houses and gardens – would enjoy automatic exclusion. Some landowners seem to fear that the introduction of public access would require them to provide picnic tables and the like. There need be no such requirement: all that is needed is for landowners to stop persecuting people who walk on their land.

For landowners who chose to provide way-marking, picnic

areas and so on, support could be provided through the workings of the new land tax. Specified activities for facilitating visitor use could be made tax deductible. But this would be quite separate from the workings of the new right of access.

The new right of access need not affect the existing network of public rights of way and the machinery for maintaining them: these could remain alongside the general right of access. Indeed, the existing network of footpaths and bridleways should benefit in one respect from the introduction of a general right of access. Landowners would have far less incentive to block them than at present. At the moment, the obstruction of one public path can keep people out of a landowner's territory extremely effectively. But after the Act is passed, blocking public footpaths would just push more walkers on to field edges and private tracks where landowners would like to see them even less than on public footpaths.

One of the basic principles of the new right of access would need to be that no particular owner of land would be exempt, only particular uses. So apart from land specifically exempted under the legislation, land owned by the Royal Family would be as open as anyone else's. This includes land owned by members of the Royal Family in their capacity as private individuals, as well as in that of holder of the Crown Estates. The applications the Royal Family could be expected to make for exclusion orders over parts of Sandringham or Balmoral for reasons of security, for bloodsports or whatever, would be subject to objection by members of the public with the Secretary of State for the Environment having the final say, as would be the case with any other landowner. And, as in other cases, such exclusion orders that were made, would be temporary or permanent as the need arose: for instance, the exclusion of the public from part of Windsor Inner Park on grounds of security might well be granted only for periods when the Royal Family was in residence.

Clearly, putting a new right of access on the statute book would not be an easy task. The landowning lobby could be expected to deploy its very considerable muscle against the measure. But if such a measure finally reached the statute book, what might be the greatest problems in putting the new system into effect on the ground?

In practice, such is the tradition of deference to the landowning classes in Britain, it might be some time before many people ventured off footpaths and out of country parks. In countries where widespread access to the countryside is already enjoyed by ordinary people, they do so because they understand the philosophical basis of their rights of access. In Sweden for example the absence of a feudal history has left the Swedes today without the feeling of mystical deference to the landowning classes that is common in Britain. *Allemansrätten*, or the Swedish right of access to the countryside for everybody, is accepted as a basic human right which it would be as unthinkable to abolish as it would be to abolish democracy in Britain.

PART EIGHT
Conclusion

18. This Land is Our Land

To wrest a share of control over the countryside from its firmly entrenched rulers may seem an almost impossibly difficult task. After centuries spent consolidating their power, can we really get our landowners to start yielding access rights, paying over part of their financial gains and allowing the public a say in the destiny of the landscape?

In fact, the chance of change is real enough. Circumstances are combining to create pressure for reform in our rural land ownership régime.

Before 1980, rural landowners – unlike, say, property speculators – were respected as the legitimate guardians of the nation's landscape heritage. Now, all that has changed. The landowners' carefully nurtured base of public acceptance has been kicked from under them as the media have woken up to the damage being done to the countryside.

The sudden public revulsion against modern agricultural methods that took place in the early 1980s has changed the atmosphere in which rural affairs are discussed. Between early 1981 and late 1982, it came to be accepted that the traditional English landscape was under threat from a group who had hitherto been seen as its protectors – our farmers.

Now the emphasis is shifting to another threat which is poised to ravage our countryside. Conifer afforestation, which is already destroying the attractions and wildlife of upland Britain, is now moving into the lowlands. Like agriculture, forestry is subsidised by the citizenry whose birthright it is laying waste. But resistance, primed by the earlier struggle with the farmers, is rising. Widespread concern is already being voiced and the bizarre economics that make the destruction of the environment a tax-efficient investment are already being laid bare.[1]

Looking back, the only surprising thing about the arousal of public concern about the impact of agriculture on the countryside is that it was so slow in coming. The crisis which finally woke up the nation had been building up for a generation.

By the 1970s the impact of agricultural change on archaeological sites, wildlife habitats and recreation areas was causing intense concern in specialist circles. It was in 1980 that this discussion spilled over into the public domain. The publication of *The Common Ground*[2] by the naturalist Richard Mabey focused attention on the ordinary humdrum countryside which is both most highly valued by most people and most threatened by agricultural change. My own book, *The Theft of The Countryside*,[3] published a few months later, catalogued the destruction being wrought and the scale of the public subsidy which made it possible. Media response was immediate. A review of *The Theft of The Countryside* in *The Times* generated a correspondence running to thirty letters. At first the idea of the destruction of the countryside by modern agriculture was seen in the light of pre-existing issues, in particular the debate about whether Britain should be in the Common Market. But gradually the subject came to be recognized in its own right. The question of whether or not the countryside really was being transformed dominated the debate for a matter of months. Once it had been accepted that change was occurring, the argument moved on to whether or not it mattered. Once the leader writers had found against those who praised the grand sweep of the hedge-free landscape, the way was open for the general airing of what seemed to be a clear-cut wrong. Television programme after television programme moved in upon a subject well suited to this medium.[4]

Perhaps concern about the subject would have died away had not chance moved things on. Against the background of mounting public concern about what was being called 'the battle for the countryside', the Government stumbled accidentally into what had become the minefield of countryside policy-making. In the process, it focused attention on the idea of solutions to a problem now universally recognized.

The immediate precursor of the Wildlife and Countryside Bill 1981, the Callaghan Government's 1978 Countryside Bill, had attracted virtually no public attention, completing its second-reading debate in the House of Commons in a mere six hours.

The similar 1981 Bill was therefore expected to pass unremarked even by elements in politics and the media most starved of subject matter. But things turned out very differently. In a climate of rising concern about the landscape, a Bill called the Wildlife and Countryside Bill was taken as being the Government's solution to what had come to be seen as a new but important national problem. Since the Bill had not been intended as any such thing, it was inevitably found to be hopelessly deficient. Uproar resulted.

By the time the Bill had completed its passage through Parliament, it had consumed hundreds of hours of Parliamentary time, been the subject of three leaders in *The Times* and had attracted 2,300 amendments.

Knocked sideways by the unexpected commotion, the Government sought to make some concession to the interests of conservation. Originally, the Bill had proposed that landowners responsible for between forty and fifty particularly important Sites of Special Scientific Interest should be required to notify the Nature Conservancy Council of any intention to change land-use on their sites. The final Act required advance notification of landscape change in respect of all 3,900 (but by 1986 4,842) SSSIs. This modest step was received with exaggerated enthusiasm by the media, now anxious to announce a solution to the problem they had made so much of. But though the Act itself may be relatively unimportant the furore it provoked may prove to have a lasting effect. The Act's very deficiencies have encouraged organizations to think up more convincing solutions. Several conservation groups, including the Friends of the Earth and the Ramblers' Association, have opted for a policy of planning controls over agriculture and forestry as the solution to the problem of damage to the landscape, as has one political party, the Labour Party. In spite of the implications of a head-on confrontation with the landowning community which this policy implies, it has come to be seen as a reasonable step in response to intense public concern. One particularly telling verdict came in the *You the Jury* radio programme in 1984, in which a large majority of ordinary people (81 per cent) found for the extension of planning controls to cover major farming and forestry change. They were not convinced by the well-rehearsed arguments to the contrary of National Farmers' Union President Sir Richard Butler.

One thing that did not emerge in the early 1980s was any link between the landscape damage caused by new agricultural practices and some of landowners' other anti-social behaviour such as blocking public rights of way and enclosing common land. One of the farmers' main propaganda achievements was to persuade some people that all that was required was a little bit more concern from them for the requirements of conservation when going about their business – concern which would henceforth be forthcoming. Attention did not get round to the heart of the issue – the ownership of land. I hope this book will help to direct attention to the ownership arrangements which now need to be rethought.

A second factor in the sharpening debate about agriculture, forestry and the countryside has been growing appreciation of the extent to which farmers and foresters depend on the generosity of the taxpayer and the consumer. A growing number of observers from Enoch Powell to Gerald Kauffman have contrasted the massive subsidies received by agriculture to the far smaller but hitherto more widely publicized subsidies received by other British industries. The landless of modern Britain know they have it in their power to de-subsidize most of Britain's farmers and foresters out of existence.

Six hundred years ago, without this particular lever to help them, our forebears in late medieval England succeeded in wringing from the landowners a social contract for the countryside that included substantial common rights, a general right of access and the right to take game. They did it by exploiting the economic lever they did have – the scarcity and therefore the value of agricultural labour following the ravages of the Black Death. Today the landless are in an even stronger position: their labour may no longer be necessary to the landowners but their taxes and the votes which sustain them are essential. If the landless want a say in the fate of the land they are in a position to get it.

The time is ripe for other reasons. Concern for the environment is moving from the fringes of British politics to the centre ground. The political parties are now vying with each other to secure what is seen as the 'Green' vote. The issue of control of the countryside is tailor-made to capitalize on this new concern. It coincides too with another topic that is coming to concern our political leaders more and more. Increasingly it is being accepted that however successful our economy becomes, it will never again provide full employment for all those available to work. Work-sharing and training for leisure are themes whose time has come. And they endow the countryside as a huge recreation resource with new-found importance for policy-makers.

In late medieval England, without the benefit of national newspapers and television to inform them of the actions of their counterparts outside their own villages, and, even more important, without the benefit of democracy, the landless managed to extract from Britain's seemingly all-powerful landowning class substantial concessions. Successive generations including our own have allowed these rights to be eroded. Now it falls to us to recover our countryside for ourselves and for our children. If we sometimes falter, we need look no further for inspiration than to the commons and public paths won for us in a far more difficult struggle by our medieval ancestors.

REFERENCES

Part One: Points of Reference

1: THE WORLD

1. For a fuller discussion of the impact of the British system of land organization on Maori land tenure, see I. H. Kawharu, *Maori Land Tenure* (Oxford: Clarendon Press, 1967); P. G. McHugh, 'The Economic Development of Native Land: New Zealand and Canadian Law Compared', *Saskatchewan Law Review*, Vol. 47, No. 1, 1983; and P. G. McHugh, *Maori Land Laws of New Zealand*, Studies in Aboriginal Rights No. 7 (University of Saskatchewan Native Law Centre, 1983).

2. T. McCarthy (Chairman), *Report of the Royal Commission of Inquiry into the Maori Land Courts* (Wellington, New Zealand, 1980).

3. The account of land rights among the Ojibwa is based on R. Landes, 'The Ojibwa of Canada', in M. Mead (ed.), *Cooperation and Competition Among Primitive People* (Boston: Beacon Press, 1961).

4. This account is based on I. Goldman, 'The Zuni of New Mexico', in M. Mead (ed.), op. cit., note 3. For a discussion of land allocation among 'primitive' tribes see also J. Bugajski, *An Assessment of the Significance of Cooperation and Reciprocity in Selected Hunting and Gathering Societies*, unpublished M Phil. thesis (London School of Economics and Political Science, University of London, 1981).

5. This account is based on M. Gluckman, *Politics, Law and Ritual in Tribal Society* (Oxford: Basil Blackwell, 1965), pp. 36–43.

6. For details of the changes to land organization in the Pacific Islands wrought by the introduction of the gun and technological change see R. Crocombe (ed.), *Land Tenure in the Pacific* (Oxford: OUP, 1971).

7. For a fuller discussion of the emergence and nature of European feudalism see D. Herlihy (ed.), *The History of Feudalism* (Brighton: Harvester Press, 1970); B. H. Slicker Van Bath, *The Agrarian History of Western Europe A.D. 500–1850* (London: Edward Arnold, 1963); M. Bloch, *Feudal Society*, vols 1 and 2 (London: Routledge and Kegan Paul, 1965); R. Allen Brown, *Origins of English Feudalism* (London: Allen and Unwin, 1973).

8. For a fuller description of the nature of Japanese feudalism, see C. P. Fitzgerald, *A Concise History of East Asia* (Harmondsworth: Penguin Books, 1974).

9. The account of feudalism in South America is based on S. Lindqvist, *Land and Power in South America*, (Harmondsworth: Penguin Books, 1979). See also K. Duncan and I. Rutledge, *Land and Labour in Latin America* (Cambridge: CUP, 1977).

10. For a discussion of the philosophical basis of peasant proprietorship in France and the United States, see R. Schlatter, *Private Property: The History of an Idea* (London: Allen and Unwin, 1951).

11. The descriptions of land reform in Egypt, Mexico and India are based on R. King, *Land Reform: A World Survey* (London: Bell and Sons, 1977).

12. For a discussion of the role of land reform in solving problems of world hunger, see G. Hunter (ed.), *Agricultural Development and the Rural Poor* (London: Overseas Development Institute, 1978) and C. Whittemore, *Land for People: Land Tenure and the Very Poor* (Oxford: Oxfam, 1981).

2. THE PAST

1. Lord Derby, 'Ireland and the Land Act', *Nineteenth Century*, October 1881, p. 474.

2. The section on land organization in prehistoric Britain is based on information from the following sources: P. J. Fowler, *The Farming of Prehistoric Britain* (Cambridge: CUP, 1981); R. Mercer (ed.), *Farming Practice in Prehistory* (Edinburgh: University Press, 1981); R. Muir, *History from the Air* (London: Michael Joseph, 1983); J. V. S. Megaw and D. D. A. Simpson, *Introduction to British Prehistory* (Leicester: University Press, 1979); H. C. Bowen, 'The Celtic Background'; in A. L. F. Rivet (ed.), *The Roman Villa in Britain* (London: Routledge and Kegan Paul, 1969).

3. For further details about land organization during the Roman occupation see Rivet, op. cit., note 2; M. I. Finley (ed.), *Slavery in Classical Antiquity* (Cambridge: Heffer and Sons, 1960); M. Todd (ed.), *Studies in the Romano-British Villa* (Leicester: University Press, 1978).

4. For further details about land organization in Saxon Britain, see H. R. Loyn, *Anglo-Saxon England and the Norman Conquest* (London: Longman, 1962); H. C. Darby, *Domesday England* (Cambridge: CUP, 1977); F. M. Stenton, *Anglo-Saxon England* (Oxford: Clarendon Press, 1971); H. P. R. Finberg (ed.), *The Agrarian History of England and Wales, Vol. I, 43–1042 A.D.* (Cambridge: CUP, 1972); M. L. Faull and S. A. Moorhouse (ed.), *West Yorkshire: An Archaeological Survey to 1500 A.D.*, Vol. 1 (Wakefield: West Yorkshire County Council, 1981).

5. For further details of the nature and development of common rights from prehistoric times to the present day, see W. G. Hoskins and L. Dudley Stamp, *The Common Lands of England and Wales* (London: Collins, 1963).

6. For further details of land organization in medieval England, see

R. H. Hilton, *A Medieval Society: The West Midlands at the End of the Thirteenth Century* (London: Weidenfeld and Nicholson, 1966); M. M. Postan, *The Medieval Economy and Society* (Harmondsworth: Penguin Books, 1975); A.G. Ruston and D. Witney, *Hooton Pagnell: The Agricultural Evolution of a Yorkshire Village* (London: Edward Arnold, 1934); M. L. Faull and S. A. Moorhouse (ed.), *West Yorkshire: An Archaeological Survey to 1500 A.D.*, Vol. 3, (Wakefield: West Yorkshire County Council, 1981); H. C. Darby, *Domesday England* (Cambridge: CUP, 1977); E. Lipson, *The Economic History of England, Volume 1: The Middle Ages* (London: Black, 1959); R. A. Dodgshon and R. A. Butlin, *An Historical Geography of England and Wales* (London: Academic Press, 1978). For further details of land organization in medieval Wales, see G. R. J. Jones, 'Field Systems of North Wales' and M. Davies, 'Field Systems of South Wales' in A. R. H. Baker and R. A. Butlin (ed.), *Studies of Field Systems in the British Isles* (Cambridge: CUP, 1973); for Scotland, see G. Whittington, 'Field Systems of Scotland', in Baker and Butlin (ed.) op. cit.; and for Ireland, R. H. Buchanan, 'Field Systems of Ireland', in A. R. H. Baker and R. A. Butlin (ed.), op. cit.

7. 'The Dialogue of the Exchequer', quoted by J. T. Bagley and P. B. Rowley, *A Documentary History of England*, Vol. 1 (Harmondsworth: Penguin Books, 1966), pp. 67–8. For further details of royal forests, chases and deer parks, see L. M. Cantor (ed.), *The English Medieval Landscape* (London: Croom Helm, 1982); L. M. Cantor and J. Hatherly, 'The Medieval Parks of England', *Geography*, Vol. 64, Part 2, April 1979; L. M. Cantor and J. D. Wilson, 'The Medieval Deer-parks of Dorset', *Proc. Dorset Nat. Hist. and Arch. Soc.*, Vol. 83, 1961; J. C. Cox, *The Royal Forests of England*, (London: Methuen, 1905); R. Cunliffe Shaw, *The Royal Forest of Lancaster* (Preston: The Guardian Press, 1956); C. R. Young, *The Royal Forests of Medieval England* (Leicester: University Press, 1979); C. R. Tubbs, *The New Forest* (London: Collins: The New Naturalist, 1986); P. A. J. Pettit, 'The Royal Forests of Northamptonshire', *Northamptonshire Record Society*, Vol. 23, 1968.

8. Quoted by W. G. Hoskins *The Age of Plunder: The England of Henry VIII, 1500–1547* (London: Longmans, 1976), p. 11.

9. See for instance, J. M. Neeson, *Common Right and Enclosure in Eighteenth Century Northamptonshire*, unpublished PhD thesis, University of Warwick, 1977.

10. Ibid.

11. For details of the early history of roads and footpaths see S. and B. Webb, *The Story of the King's Highway* (London, 1913); B. P. H. Hindle, 'Roads and Tracks' in Cantor, op. cit., note 7; B. P. H. Hindle, 'The Road Network of Medieval England and Wales', *Journal of Historical Geography*, Vol. 2, No. 3, 1976; C. W. Scott-Giles, *The Road Goes On*, (London: Epworth, 1946).

12. See for instance R. W. Malcolmson, 'A Set of Ungovernable People: the Kingswood Colliers in the Eighteenth Century', in J. Brewer and J. Styles (ed.), *An Ungovernable People* (London: Hutchinson, 1980).

13. For further details of changes in land tenure during Tudor and Stuart times, see ed. J. Thirsk (ed.), *The Agrarian History of England and Wales, Volume IV, 1500–1640* (Cambridge: CUP, 1967); Hoskins, op. cit., note 8; R. A. Butlin, *The Transformation of Rural England c. 1580–1800* (Oxford: OUP, 1983; W. E. Tate, *The English Village Community and the Enclosure Movements* (London: Gollancz, 1967).

14. Quoted by Hoskins, op. cit., note 8, p. 30.

15. Thomas Lever, 1521–77, quoted by Lipson, op. cit., note 6, p. 160.

16. For details see ed. A. Charlesworth, *An Atlas of Rural Protest in Britain 1548–1900* (London: Croom Helm, 1983).

17. For further details of these changes, see C. Hill, *Reformation to Industrial Revolution* (Harmondsworth: Penguin Books, 1969).

18. For details of the decline of the English yeoman farmer class, see ed. P. D. A. Harvey, *The Peasant Land Market in Medieval England* (Oxford: OUP, 1985); D. R. Mills, 'The Peasant Tradition', *Local Historian*, Vol. 11, 1976; M. Spufford, *Contrasting Communities* (Cambridge: CUP, 1974); J. L. and B. Hammond, *The Village Labourer* (London: Longman edition, 1978).

19. For further details see, C. Hill, *The World Turned Upside Down* (London: Temple Smith, 1972); H. N. Brailsford, *The Levellers and the English Revolution* (London: Spokesman Books, 1976); G. E. Aylmer, *The Levellers in the English Revolution* (London: Thames and Hudson, 1975). See also Caryl Churchill's play about the treatment of the Diggers and Levellers under Oliver Cromwell: *Light Shining in Buckinghamshire* (London: Pluto Press, 1976).

20. Ed. C. Hill, *Winstanley: The Law of Freedom and Other Writings* (Harmondsworth: Penguin Books, 1973).

21. Further details in M. A. Kishlansky, 'The Army and the Levellers: The Roads to Putney', *The Historical Journal*, vol. 22. No. 4, 1979.

22. For details of the way in which large landowners controlled parliamentary representation in the eighteenth century, see the Victoria County Histories of Cheshire, Leicestershire and Yorkshire, for example.

23. Further details of the situation in Cornwall in S. Baring-Gould, *A Book of the West of Cornwall* (London: Methuen, 1899).

24. E. P. Thompson, *Whigs and Hunters: The Origin of the Black Act* (London: Allen Lane, 1975).

25. Adam Smith, *The Wealth of Nations* (London: Everyman edition, 1910).

26. D. Hay, P. Linebaugh and E. P. Thompson, *Albion's Fatal Tree: Crime and Society in 18th Century England* (London: Allen Lane, 1975), p. 249.

27. The scope of the eighteenth century game laws and their operation is explained in detail by P. B. Munsche in *Gentlemen and Poachers: The English Game Laws 1671–1831* (Cambridge: CUP, 1981).

28. Bacon, quoted in Hay, op. cit., note 26, p. 191.

29. L. Radzinowicz, *Cambridge Law Journal*, Vol. IX, 1945, quoted by Thompson, op. cit., note 24.

30. Hay, op. cit., note 26, p. 249.

31. C. Hill, *Reformation to Industrial Revolution*, (Harmondsworth: Penguin Books, 1967), p. 270.

32. For further details, see R. W. Malcolmson, *Life and Labour in England, 1700–1780* (London: Hutchinson, 1981).

33. M. Briggs and P. Jordan, *Economic History of England* (London: University Tutorial Press, 1967), p. 298. For further details of the eighteenth and nineteenth century enclosures, see T. S. Ashton, *An Economic History of England: The Eighteenth Century* (London: Methuen edition, 1972); J. D. Chambers and G. E. Mingay, *The Agricultural Revolution, 1750–1880* (London: Batsford, 1966); Tate, op. cit., note 13; J. L. and B. Hammond, op. cit., note 18.

34. Notice at Hampshire Record Office, 8M/62/72, quoted by P. Horn, *Labouring Life in the Victorian Countryside* (Dublin: Gill and MacMillan, 1976), p. 229.

35. M. K. Ashby, *Joseph Ashby of Tysoe, 1859–1919* (London: The Merlin Press, 1974), p. 38.

36. In fact, as J. M. Neeson points out in *Common Right and Enclosure in Eighteenth Century Northamptonshire*, op. cit., note 9, who refers to Lord Spencer's threat (p. 13), transportation was not a legal punishment for trespass, although he hoped to convince the nutters that it was.

37. R. Jefferies, *The Gamekeeper at Home, 1878*; referred to by Neeson, op. cit., note 9.

38. Details in R. Carr, *English Fox Hunting: A History* (London: Weidenfeld and Nicolson, 1976).

39. R. A. Slaney, *Essay on the Direction of Rural Expenditure* (London, 1824), as quoted by R. W. Malcolmson, *Popular Recreations in English Society, 1700–1850* (Cambridge: CUP, 1973), p. 108.

40. Quoted by E. Richards, *A History of the Highland Clearances: Agrarian Transformation and the Evictions, 1746–1886* (London: Croom Helm, 1982), p. 9.

41. For more details of the operation of the infield-outfield system, see G. Whittington, 'Field systems of Scotland', in Baker and Butlin, op. cit., note 6; and R. A. Dodgshon 'The Origins of Traditional Field Systems' in M. L. Parry and T. R. Slater (ed.), *The Making of the Scottish Countryside* (London: Croom Helm, 1980).

42. For further details of the Clearances, see Richards, op. cit, note 40; J. Hunter, *The Making of the Crofting Community* (Edinburgh: John Donald, 1976); G. Whittington, 'Was there a Scottish Agricultural Revolution?' *Area* Vol. 7, No. 3, 1975; J. B. Caird, 'The Making of the Scottish Rural Landscape', *Scottish Geographical Magazine*, Vol. 80, No. 2, 1964; James Hunter's columns in the *West Highland Free Press*, 1983 and 1984.

43. J. Prebble, *The Highland Clearances* (London: Secker and Warburg, 1976).

44. For details, see (ed.) Charlesworth, op. cit., note 16, Chapter 3.

45. For details see E. P. Lawrence, *Henry George in the British Isles* (East Lansing, Michigan: Michigan State University Press, 1957).

46. H. George, *Progress and Poverty* (London: The Hogarth Press edition, 1966).

47. *Irish World*, 3rd December 1881, referred to by R. Douglas, *Land, People and Politics: A History of the Land Question in the United Kingdom, 1878–1952* (London: Allison and Busby, 1976), p. 44.

48. The account of the Irish land war is based largely on Douglas, op. cit., note 47.

49. *Oban Times*, 24 May 1884, quoted by J. Hunter, op. cit., note 42, p. 159.

50. For further details of the Highland Land War, see Douglas, op. cit., note 47, and Hunter, op. cit., note 42.

51. *Agricultural Returns, 1887*, quoted by J. Davis 'The End of the Estates and the Rise of Freehold Farming', *Welsh History Review*, Volume 6, No. 3, 1973.

52. For further details of the Rebecca Riots, see D. Williams, *The Rebecca Riots: A Study in Agrarian Discontent* (Cardiff: University of Wales Press, 1955); D. Jones, *Before Rebecca: Popular Protests in Wales 1793–1835* (London: Allen Lane, 1973).

53. For further details of the Welsh land movement, see Douglas, op. cit., note 47, and D. Howell, *Land and People in Nineteenth Century Wales* (London: Routledge and Kegan Paul, 1977).

54. For further details of the conditions of the English tenants in the nineteenth century, see C. S. Orwin and E. H. Whetham, *History of British Agriculture, 1846–1914* (London: Longman, 1964).

55. Quoted by P. Horn, *Labouring Life in the Victorian Countryside* (London: MacMillan, 1976), p. 245.

56. D. J. V. Jones, 'The Poacher: A Study in Victorian Crime and Protest', *The Historical Journal*, Vol. 22, No. 4, 1979.

57. A. J. Peacock, 'Village Radicalism in East Anglia, 1800–1850' in J. P. D. Dunbabin (ed.) *Rural Discontent in Nineteenth-Century Britain*, (London: Faber and Faber, 1974).

58. For further details of nineteenth-century riots by farm labourers, see (ed.) Charlesworth, op. cit., note 16, pp. 131–163.

59. For further details of the early development of the farmworkers' union, see R. Groves, *Sharpen the Sickle! The History of the Farm Workers' Union* (London, 1949); J. P. D. Dunbabin, *Rural Discontent in Nineteenth-Century Britain*, op. cit., note 57; B. and S. Webb, *History of Trade Unionism* (London, 1894).

60. For further details of the history of allotment provision, see *Departmental Committee of Inquiry into Allotments*, Cmnd. 4166 (London: HMSO, 1969).

61. D. Lloyd George, speaking in Newcastle, 9 October 1909, in (ed.) P. Guedella, *Slings and Arrows: Sayings Chosen from the Speeches of the Rt. Hon. David Lloyd George* (London: Cassell, 1929).

62. For further details of the campaign for land taxation in the late nineteenth and early twentieth centuries, see Douglas, op. cit., note 47, *Land and Liberty* magazine of the early 1900s, and Land Nationalization Society Tracts published in the 1920s.

63. The Land Song is reproduced in full in A. G. Huie, *Natural Rights*, (London: Land and Liberty Series No. 6, United Committee for the Taxation of Land Values, about 1913).

64. For further details of the New Domesday Survey see David Spring in J. Bateman, *The Great Landowners of Great Britain and Ireland, with an Introduction by David Spring* (Leicester: University Press, 1971).

65. Bateman, op. cit., note 64.

66. For more details of ownership of the Highlands in the 1870s, see A. M. Armstrong, *Geographical Aspects of the Ownership, Management and Use of Rural Land on Landed Estates in the Northern Highlands*, unpublished PhD thesis, University of Aberdeen, 1980.

67. For further details of these land sales see F. M. L. Thompson, *English Landed Society in the Nineteenth Century* (London: Routledge and Kegan Paul, 1963).

68. According to a survey by Lawrence and Jeanne C. Fawtier Stone, reported in their book *An Open Elite? England 1540–1880* (Oxford: OUP, 1984).

69. For details of the development of grouse shooting and deer stalking during the late nineteenth century, see R. Eden, *Going to the Moors* (London: John Murray, 1979); G. K. Whitehead, *Hunting and Stalking Deer in Britain Throughout the Ages* (London: Batsford, 1980); D. Hart-Davis, *Monarchs of the Glen* (London: Cape, 1978); W. Orr, *Deer Forests, Landlords and Crofters* (Edinburgh: J. Donald, 1982); R. Longrigg, *The English Squire and his Sport* (London: Michael Joseph, 1977).

70. Figure from Hart-Davis, op. cit., note 69, p. 208.

71. Richards, op. cit., note 40, p. 485.

72. T. Stephenson, 'The Battle of Glen Tilt', *Rucksack*, Vol. 10, No. 1, Winter 1980.

73. E. A. Baker, *The Forbidden Land* (London: Witherby, 1924), p. 9; see also E. A. Baker, *The Highlands with Rope and Rucksack* (London: Witherby, 1923).

74. G. M. Trevelyan, *The Call and Claims of Natural Beauty*, The Rickman Godlee Lecture, University College, London, 1931.

75. Quoted by K. Thomas, *Man and the Natural World: Changing Attitudes in England 1500–1800* (London: Allen Lane, 1983), p. 249.

76. T. De Quincey, *Recollections of the Lakes and the Lake Poets* (Harmondsworth: Penguin Books Edition, 1970), quoted by J. P. Rossiter, *An Analytical Study of the Public Use of Private Land for Outdoor Recreation in England 1949–1968*, unpublished PhD thesis, University of Cambridge, 1972, p. 3.

77. For a description of the nineteenth-century campaigns to save England's commons, see Lord Eversley, *Commons, Forests and Footpaths*

(London: Cassell, 1910); W. H. Williams, *The Commons, Footpaths and Open Spaces Preservation Society: A Short History of the Society and its Work* (Henley: The Commons Society [now The Open Spaces Society], 1965); and W. G. Hoskins and L. Dudley Stamp, *The Common Lands of England and Wales* (London: Collins, 1963).

78. P. Abercrombie, *The Preservation of Rural England* (Liverpool: University Press and Hodder and Stoughton, 1926).

79. For a flavour of the ideals of the founders of the CPRE, see G. M. Trevelyan et al., *Britain and the Beast* (London: Dent, 1937); and C. Williams-Ellis, *England and the Octopus* (London, 1928). John Sheail gives an account of CPRE's early campaigns in *Rural Conservation in Inter-War Britain* (Oxford: Clarendon Press, 1981).

80. For further details of the early history of the access movement in Scotland, see R. Aitken, *Wilderness Areas in Scotland,* unpublished PhD. thesis, University of Aberdeen, 1977; P. Bassett, *A List of the Historical Records of the Scottish Rights of Way Society,* Centre for Urban and Regional Research, University of Birmingham, 1980.

81. Rossiter, op. cit., note 76, p. 28.

82. C. E. M. Joad, 'The People's Claim', in G. M. Trevelyan et al., op. cit., note 79, p. 78.

83. P. A. Barnes, *Trespassers will be Prosecuted* (Sheffield, 1934), quoted by H. Hill, *Freedom to Roam* (Ashbourne, Derbyshire: Moorland Publishing), 1980, p. 35.

84. B. Rothman, *The 1932 Kinder Trespass* (Altrincham, Cheshire: Willow Publishing, 1982).

85. Lord Justice Scott, *Report of the Committee on Land Utilisation in Rural Areas,* Cmnd. 6378, (London: HMSO, 1942).

86. Ministry of Town and Country Planning, *National Parks in England and Wales: Report by John Dower,* Cmnd. 6628 (London: HMSO, 1945).

87. Ministry of Town and Country Planning, *Report of the National Parks Committee (England and Wales),* Cmnd. 7121 (London: HMSO, 1947).

88. Ministry of Town and Country Planning, *Footpaths and Access to the Countryside: Report of the Special Committee (England and Wales),* Cmnd. 7207 (London: HMSO, 1947).

89. J. S. Huxley, *Conservation of Nature in England and Wales,* Cmnd. 7122 (London: HMSO, 1947).

90. J. D. Ramsay, *National Parks,* Cmnd. 7235, (London: HMSO, 1947).

Part Two: Who are Britain's Landowners?

3. IN SEARCH OF OWNERSHIP

1. In 1977, local authorities in the UK owned 993,652 acres, mainly of tenanted farmland and woodland; water authorities 318,630 acres,

mainly reservoirs and water catchment grounds; and the Ministry of Transport 148,200 acres under motorways and trunk roads. These figures are taken from A. Harrison, R. B. Tranter and R. S. Gibbs, *Landownership by Public and Semi-public Institutions in the UK*, Centre for Agricultural Strategy Paper 3, University of Reading, 1977.

2. This figure is derived from adding together the holdings of public bodies listed in A. Harrison et al, op. cit., note 1.

3. W. B. Mercer, *A Survey of the Agriculture of Cheshire*, Royal Agricultural Society of England, 1963.

4. House of Commons, *Hansard*, Written Answers, 16 January 1985, col. 164.

5. A. and M. MacEwen, *National Parks: Conservation or Cosmetics?* (London: Allen and Unwin, 1982), p. 157.

6. Ibid.

7. Department of the Environment, *Common Land: Preparations for Comprehensive Legislation: Report of an Interdepartmental Working Party, 1975/ 77*, (London: DOE, 1978), p. 1.

8. Further details in 'Pension Fund's Farming Venture Shows Big Profit', *Farmers' Weekly*, 12 October 1979.

9. *Report of the Committee of Inquiry into the Acquisition and Occupancy of Agricultural Land, Chairman: The Rt. Hon. Lord Northfield*, Cmnd. 7599 (London: HMSO, 1979). For further details of the ownership of land by financial institutions, see J. Shutt, *The New Leviathans: A Study of Pension Funds in the UK and their Investment in the Land and Property Sector*, unpublished PhD. thesis, University of Birmingham, 1980; A. Steel and P. Byrne, *Financial Institutions: Their Investments and Agricultural Landownership*, Department of Land Management and Development, University of Reading, 1983.

10. For further details of the extent of land acquisition by financial institutions in 1984, see *The Savills-RTP Agricultural Performance Analysis* (London: Savills and Roger Tym and Partners, 1985) and J. Rhind, 'Sale and Leaseback', *Landowning in Scotland*, Summer 1984.

11. D. Massey and A. Catalano, *Capital and Land: Landownership by Capital in Great Britain* (London: Edward Arnold, 1978), p. 74.

12. R. Perrott, *The Aristocrats* (London: Weidenfeld and Nicolson, 1968), p. 160.

13. This figure was calculated from maps by John McEwen and published in *Who Owns Scotland?* (Edinburgh: EUSPB, 1978). Anxious to get an up-to-date figure for the total amount of land owned by the Duke of Buccleuch and Queensbury, I wrote to the Duke in 1985 asking him if John McEwen's figure of 277,000 acres as the amount of land he owns in Scotland was still accurate. The Duke replied that he would give me an accurate figure only on certain conditions – conditions which I found unacceptable.

14. B. Masters, *The Dukes: The Origins, Ennoblement and History of 26 Families* (London: Blond and Briggs, 1975).

15. Details of the Buccleuch subsidiary companies come from records at Companies House.

16. W. D. Rubinstein, *Men of Property* (London: Croom Helm, 1981), pp. 196–7.

17. R. Perrott, op. cit., note 12.

18. K. Pugh, *Estate Villages: Who Cares?* (London: SAVE Britain's Heritage, 1982), pp. 8–9.

19. J. McEwen, op. cit., note 13.

20. This estimate was made in Perrott, op. cit., note 12. p. 140.

21. R. Callander, 'Landownership in Birse 1800–1980', 'The Nicols of Ballogie' and 'Owner Occupation 1880–1980' in *History in Birse*, Vol. 1, No. 2 (Finzean, Aberdeenshire: R. Callander, 1980).

22. Country Landowners' Association, *The Future of Landownership* (London: CLA, 1976).

23. House of Commons Select Committee on Wealth Tax Session 1974–1975, Vol. III, *Minutes of Evidence (Sub-Committees A and B)* (London: HMSO, 1975), pp. 765–6.

24. The figures on the size of farm holdings in Common Market countries are taken from *The Agricultural Situation in the Community, 1984 Report* (Brussels: Commission of the European Communities, 1985).

25. Ministry of Agriculture, Fisheries and Food, *Agricultural Statistics* (London: HMSO, 1984).

26. H. Newby, C. Bell, D. Rose, P. Saunders, *Property, Paternalism and Power: Class and Control in Rural England* (London: Hutchinson, 1978).

27. For further details of the ways in which the various rights over land were allocated during the Irish land reforms, see W. F. Bailey, *The Irish Land Acts: A Short Sketch of their History and Development* (Dublin: HMSO, 1917).

28. David Musson, Director of the National Trust's Southern Region, personal communication, 1984.

29. G. Turner, 'Noblemen in the Age of the Common Man', *Sunday Telegraph*, 2 October 1983.

30. Quoted in Massey and Catalano, op. cit., note 11, p. 82.

31. Church Commissioners, *Report and Accounts 1985*, (London: Church Commissioners, 1986).

32. R. Norton-Taylor, *Whose Land is it Anyway?* (Wellingborough, Northants: Turnstone Press, 1982), p. 40.

33. Ibid., p. 40.

34. R. P. Pugh, *The Crown Estate: An Historical Essay* (London: HMSO, 1960).

35. The most recently published information on the properties owned by the Crown Estate is in *The Crown Estate: Report of the Commissioners for the Year Ended 31st March 1986* (London: HMSO, 1986). Other published information on the Crown Estate included in this section is taken from the Commissioners' 1985 report.

36. McEwen, op. cit., note 12, p. 54.

37. P. Chorlton, 'Lone Marcher Tracks Down M.P.', *The Guardian*, 29 May 1981, p. 2.

4. WEALTH

1. World in Action, *Harvest Gold*, Granada TV, 11 April 1983.

2. Royal Commission on the Distribution of Income and Wealth, *Report Number 7*, Cmnd. 7595 (London: HMSO, 1979), p. 151.

3. W. D. Rubinstein, *Men of Property* (London: Croom Helm, 1981), p. 229. See also W. D. Rubinstein, *Wealth and the Wealthy in the Modern World* (London: Croom Helm, 1980).

4. I calculated this figure in September 1985 as follows. The average price of the first houses on the site was then about £90,000 (and rising fast). At this rate, the total receipts from house sales here would be £34.2 million. A local estate agent told me that the value of such land without houses but with planning consent for residential development is about one third of the total selling price of the houses. This would make the land value £144 million or £268,235 per acre. Agricultural land in this area in September 1985 without planning permission for housing was worth about £5,000 an acre.

5. 'Royal Isle up for Sale at £150,000', *The Times*, 3 July 1984.

6. J. Tweedie, *The Guardian*, 31 January 1984, p. 8.

7. Benwell Community Project, *The Making of a Ruling Class* (Newcastle: Benwell Project, 1978), pp. 72–3.

8. J. Kerr, 'Oil Exploration and The Landowner', *Country Landowner*, Vol. 36, No. 2, February 1984.

9. 'Landowners Harvest Big Bonus from Oil Explorers', *The Guardian*, 27 December 1985.

10. For further details of the fortunes made by landowners through mineral extraction in the nineteenth century, see J. T. Ward, 'Landowners and Mining', in J. T. Ward and R. G. Wilson (ed.), *Land and Industry: The Landed Estate and the Industrial Revolution* (Newton Abbot: David and Charles, 1971).

11. Ibid.

12. G. Rogers, *Social and Economic Change on Lancashire Landed Estates During the Nineteenth Century with Special Reference to the Clifton Estate 1832–1916*, unpublished PhD thesis, University of Lancaster, 1981, p. 10.

13. Duchy of Cornwall, *Revenue and Capital Accounts of the Duchy of Cornwall for the Year Ended 31 December 1985*, (London: HMSO, 1986); *The Crown Estate: Report of the Commissioners to the Year Ended 31st March 1986* (London: HMSO, 1986).

14. British Geological Survey, *UK Mineral Statistics, 1985*, (Keyworth: British Geological Survey, 1986).

15. Memorandum supplied by Dr R. J. C. Munton, University College, London published in *First Report from the Environment Committee*

Session 1983–84: Green Belt and Land for Housing, Vol. III Appendices (London: HMSO, 1984), p. 564.

16. See D. Spring, 'English Landowners and Nineteenth Century Industrialism' in ed. J. T. Ward and R. G. Wilson (eds), op. cit., note 10; and D. Cannadine, *Lords and Landlords: the Aristocracy and the Towns 1774–1967* (Leicester: University Press, 1980).

17. For further details of the ways in which long-established landowning families in Lancashire made large sums of money from building in the nineteenth century, see Rogers, op. cit., note 12.

18. Ibid.

19. See for instance M. J. Hazelton-Swales, *Urban Aristocrats: the Grosvenors and the Development of Belgravia and Pimlico in the Nineteenth Century,* unpublished PhD. thesis, University of London, 1981.

20. O. Marriott, *The Property Boom* (London: Hamish Hamilton, 1967).

21. The size and extent of these central London estates is taken from O. Marriott, *The Property Boom,* op. cit., note 20. See also 'Who Owns London?', *Investors' Chronicle,* 27 August 1982; 'London Estates', *The Valuer,* March 1984; R. McKay, 'Landlording it over London', *City Limits,* 18–24 March, 1983.

22. F. Harrison, *The Power in The Land: Unemployment, The Profits Crisis and the Land Speculator* (London: Shepheard-Walwyn, 1983), p. 19.

23. K. J. Thomson, 'Evaluation of the EEC 1986/87 Price Proposals', *Proceedings of the Fifth European Agricultural Outlook Conference, 5–6 February 1986,* (London: Agri-Europe Ltd, 1986). See also A. W. Dilnot and C. N. Morris, 'The Distributional Effects of the Common Agricultural Policy', *Fiscal Studies,* Vol. 3, No. 2, July 1982.

24. Intervention Board for Agricultural Produce, *Report for the Calendar Year 1985,* Cmnd. 9540 (London: HMSO, 1986).

25. In fact, the agreement includes a small price increase for sheepmeat in the UK through a devaluation of the green pound.

26. House of Lords Select Committee on the European Communities, Session 1985–86, *1986–87 Farm Price Policy* (London: HMSO, 1985), p. 22.

27. Reported in *Farmers' Weekly,* 12 April 1984.

28. House of Commons Hansard, 12 February 1984.

29. R. Body, *Agriculture: The Triumph and The Shame* (London: Temple Smith, 1982), p. 24.

30. Ibid., p. 25.

31. Ibid., p. 23.

32. M. Shoard, *The Theft of The Countryside* (London: Temple Smith, 1980), pp. 29–31.

33. S. Milligan, 'Slim the Farmer', *The Sunday Times,* 8 April 1984.

34. V. Keegan, 'Should Industry be Left to Sink or Swim While the Farmers Reap Subsidies?', *The Guardian,* 6 February 1984.

35. Thames TV, *Against the Grain,* 26 July 1983.

36. Ministry of Agriculture, Fisheries and Food, *Farm Rents in England and Wales*, 1985 (London: MAFF, 1986).

37. *Annual Review of Agriculture 1986: Presented to Parliament by the Secretary of State for Northern Ireland, the Secretary of State for Scotland, the Secretary of State for Wales and the Minister of Agriculture, Fisheries and Food by Command of Her Majesty January 1986*. Cmnd. 9708 (London: HMSO, 1986).

38. A. Harrison, *Farmers and Farm Businesses in England*, University of Reading, Department of Agricultural Economics and Management, Miscellaneous Study No. 62, 1975, quoted by B. Hill 'Concepts and Measurement of the Incomes, Wealth and Economic Well-being of Farmers', *Journal of Agricultural Economics*, September 1982.

39. I. Jack and G. Rose, 'Warm Comfort Farm', *The Sunday Times*, 27 February 1983.

40. World in Action, op. cit., note 1.

41. For more details of post-war changes in farm rents and land values, see Jones Lang Wootton, *The Agricultural Land Market in Britain: An In-depth Study of its Mechanisms, for Owners, Investors and Advisers* (London: Jones Lang Wootton, 1984).

42. Ministry of Agriculture, Fisheries and Food, *Agricultural Statistics, 1983* (London: HMSO, 1984).

43. K. Mellanby, *Can Britain Feed Herself?* (London: Merlin Press, 1975).

44. C. Tudge, *The Famine Business* (Harmondsworth: Penguin Books, 1977).

45. See for instance J. Morrell, *Employment in Tourism* (London: British Tourist Authority, 1985).

46. Thames TV, *Against The Grain*, op. cit., note 35.

47. R. Body, *Farming in The Clouds* (London: Temple Smith, 1984).

48. J. Wiggin, MP, 'Agriculture and Conservation', *Ecos*, 2(2), 1981.

49. House of Commons First Report from the Agriculture Committee Session 1979–80, *Economic, Social and Health Implications for the UK of the Common Agricultural Policy on Milk and Dairy Products*, Vol. II, Minutes of Evidence (London: HMSO, 1980), pp. 246–52.

50. C. P. Righton, letter to *The Times*, 17 November 1980.

51. S. George, *How the Other Half Dies: The Real Reasons for World Hunger* (Harmondsworth: Penguin Books, 1976).

52. This report is summarized in W. Schwarz, 'Empty Stomachs that Fill Rich Men's Stomachs', *The Guardian*, 27 January 1984, p. 12.

53. Shoard, op. cit., note 32.

54. C. Barr et al, *Landscape Changes in Britain* (Huntingdon: Institute of Terrestrial Ecology, 1986).

55. Sussex Archaeological Field Unit, *An Extensive Survey of Plough Damage to Known Archaeological Sites in West and East Sussex*, Institute of Archaeology, University of London, 1976.

56. Ed. F. H. Perring and S. M. Walters (eds), *Atlas of the British Flora*, Botanical Society of the British Isles, 1982, p. 201.

57. Nature Conservancy Council, *Nature Conservation in Great Britain* (Peterborough: NCC, 1984), p. 56.

58. F. W. Simpson, *Simpson's Flora of Suffolk* (Ipswich: Suffolk Naturalists' Trust, 1982), p. 53.

59. Nature Conservancy Council, op. cit., note 57, p. 64.

60. T. J. C. Beebee, 'Changes in Status of the Great Crested Newt *Triturus Cristatus* in the British Isles', *British Journal of Herpetology*, Vol. 5, 1975.

61. T. J. C. Beebee, 'The Natterjack Toad (*Bufo Calamita*) in the British Isles: A Study of Past and Present Status', *British Journal of Herpetology*. See also A. S. Cooke and H. R. A. Scorgie, *The Status of the Commoner Amphibians and Reptiles in Britain*, (Peterborough: Nature Conservancy Council, 1983).

62. G. White, *The Natural History of Selborne* (London: Ducimus Books, 1974 edition), p. 92.

63. F. C. Gribble, 'Nightjars in Britain and Ireland in 1981', *Bird Study*, Vol. 30, Part 3, 1983.

64. Ibid.

65. Nature Conservancy Council, op. cit., note 57, p. 104.

66. The East Sussex Downs were proposed as a national park by the Hobhouse Committee in its report Ministry of Town and Country Planning, *Report of the National Parks Committee (Chairman: Sir Arthur Hobhouse)*, Cmnd. 7121 (London: HMSO, 1947), and the Berkshire and Marlborough Downs by John Dower in Ministry of Town and Country Planning, *National Parks in England and Wales: Report by John Dower*, Cmnd. 6628 (London: HMSO, 1945).

67. R. A. Canham, J. Richards and R. T. Schadla-Hall, 'Archaeology and Agriculture in Wessex', in J. Hinchcliffe and T. Schadla-Hall (eds.), *The Past Under The Plough: Papers Presented at the Seminar on Plough Damage and Archaeology held at Salisbury February 1977* (London: Department of the Environment, 1980), p. 58.

68. P. J. Fowler, 'Archaeology, the Public and the Sense of the Past' in D. Lowenthal and M. Binney (eds), *Our Past Before Us: Why Do We Save It?* (London: Temple Smith, 1981).

69. Ministry of Agriculture, Fisheries and Food, *Forestry May Offer the most Promising Alternative Use of Land no Longer Needed for Agricultural Production*, (London: MAFF, Press Notice No. 73, 20 March 1986).

70. National Farmers' Union, *Farming Trees: The Case for Government Support*, (London: NFU, 1986).

71. Figures on past rates of forest planting and the type of species involved are taken from the Forestry Commission's annual reports and Centre for Agricultural Strategy, *Strategy for the UK Forest Industry*, CAS Report 6, University of Reading, 1980.

72. A Forestry Commission survey in 1924 showed that there were then 2.924 million acres of woodland in Britain. The Forestry Commission return up to 31 January 1985 gave a figure of 5.451 million

acres. But in the meantime at least 205,000 acres of existing forest was converted to other uses, mainly agriculture. The increase in forest since 1924 is therefore around 2.719 million acres.

73. House of Commons, *Hansard*, 10 December 1980, col. 927.

74. Sir David Montgomery, 'Forestry and the Environment', speech to the Royal Forestry Society, 20 March 1980, as reported in A. Gilg, *Countryside Planning Yearbook 2* (Norwich: Geo Books, 1981).

75. For further details of the activities of Fountain Forestry in north-east Scotland, see 'Forestry Group Set Up in a Massive Empire', *The Scotsman*, 5 October 1984.

76. House of Commons, *Hansard*, 10 December 1980, col. 927.

77. Letter from B. P. Moor in *Farmers' Weekly*, 20 June 1986, p. 45.

78. House of Commons, *Ninth Report from the Committee of Public Accounts, Session 1977–78* (London: HMSO, 1978), p. 111.

79. 'Evidence Submitted by O. Rackham for the Botanical Society of The British Isles' in House of Lords Select Committee on Science and Technology, *Scientific Aspects of Forestry, Vol. II: Minutes of Evidence* (London: HMSO, 1980).

80. Nature Conservancy Council, op. cit., note 57, p. 56.

81. M. S. Warren, *The Dorset Woodlands – Their History and Conservation*, unpublished MSc thesis, University of London, 1976.

82. Loughinosholin was the name given in the seventeenth century to an Irish barony situated in the Lagan and Upper Bann valleys. It no longer exists as a place name.

83. For details see A. Jackson, *Forestry and Archaeology: A Study in Survival of Field Monuments in South West Scotland* (Hertford: Rescue – The British Archaeological Trust, 1978).

84. R. D. Ratcliffe, *The Peregrine Falcon* (London: Poyser, 1980).

85. *Effect of Afforestation on Birds in Galloway and Carrick*, unpublished paper supplied to me by Dr D. A. Ratcliffe, Chief Scientist, Nature Conservancy Council, Peterborough.

86. House of Lords Select Committee on Science and Technology, *Fourth Report of the Select Committee on the Scientific Aspects of Forestry* (London: HMSO, 1983).

87. Royal Society for the Protection of Birds, *Hill Farming and Birds: A Survival Plan* (Sandy, Bedfordshire: RSPB, 1984). For further details of the extent of moorland loss, see D. Goode, 'The Threat to Wildlife Habitats', *New Scientist*, 22 January 1981; M. Parry, A. Bruce and C. Harkness, 'The Plight of British Moorlands', *New Scientist*, 28 May 1981.

88. For further details of the impact of coniferization on moorland birds, see Royal Society for the Protection of Birds, op. cit., note 83; Memorandum Submitted by the Nature Conservancy Council: Submission by D. R. Ratcliffe, Chief Scientist, to House of Lords Select Committee on Science and Technology, *Scientific Aspects of Forestry, Vol.*

II: Minutes of Evidence (London: HMSO, 1980) and Nature Conservancy Council, *Nature Conservation and Afforestation in Britain* (Peterborough: Nature Conservancy Council, 1986).

89. S. Tompkins, 'Birds, Conifers and Money', *Birds* Autumn 1986, p. 22.

90. Royal Society for the Protection of Birds, *Forestry in the Flow Country – The Threat to Birds: A Critique of Afforestation in East Sutherland and Caithness* (Sandy, Beds. RSPB, 1986), p. 6.

91. Highland Regional Council Planning Department, *Structure Plan Review: Issues Paper* (Inverness: Highland Regional Council, 1985), p. 17.

92. For a further discussion of the attractions of moorland as a wilderness environment, see my chapter 'The Lure of The Moors', in J. Burgess and J. Gold (ed), *Valued Environments* (London: Allen and Unwin, 1981).

93 National Audit Office, *Review of Forestry Commission Objectives and Achievements* (London: HMSO, 1986).

94. B. Masters, *The Dukes* (London: Blond Briggs, 1977), p. 106.

95. See A. Sutherland, 'Capital Transfer Tax: An Obituary', *Fiscal Studies*, November, 1981.

96. *Savills Agricultural Land Market Report* (London: Savills, June, 1984).

5. POWER

1. M. Constable, *Shelter Report on Tied Accommodation* (London: Shelter, 1974).

2. T. Gould, 'The Decline of Community', *Landworker*, January 1985.

3. L. Paul, *The Deployment and Payment of the Clergy* (London: Church Information Office, 1964).

4. Figures from *The Clerical Guide and Ecclesiastical Directory* (London: Rivington, 1836).

5. R. Perrott, *The Aristocrats* (London: Weidenfeld and Nicolson, 1968), p. 191.

6. L. Paul, op. cit. note 3.

7. Benwell Community Development Project, *The Making of a Ruling Class: Two Centuries of Capital Development on Tyneside* (Newcastle: Benwell CDP, 1978).

8. 20: 20 Vision, *Divided Britain: A Club in the North*, Channel 4 TV, 27 April 1985.

9. I. Brotherton, *Ministerial Appointments to National Parks: A Report to the Council for National Parks*, (Department of Landscape Architecture, Sheffield University, 1983).

10. R. W. Howarth, *Farming for Farmers?* (London: Institute of Economic Affairs, 1985).

11. Country Landowners' Association, *CLA Game Fair*, CLA, 1984.

12. Ibid.

13. World in Action, *Harvest Gold*, Granada TV, 11 April 1983.

14. Ibid.

15. P. Self and H. J. Storing, *The State and the Farmer* (London: Allen and Unwin, 1982).

16. World in Action, op. cit., note 13.

17. Ibid.

18. HM Treasury, *Forestry in Great Britain: An Inter-departmental Cost-benefit Study* (London: HMSO, 1972).

19. *Forestry Policy*, (London: HMSO, 1972).

20. Countryside Commission, *A Better Future for the Uplands* (Cheltenham: Countryside Commission, 1984).

21. C. Hall, *The Countryman*, Summer 1984, pp. 20–21.

22. The Law Commission, *Property Law: Second Report on Land Registration: Inspection of the Register* (London: HMSO, 1985).

23. S. Glover, 'The old rich: a survey of the landed classes', *The Spectator*, 1 January 1977.

24. House of Commons Committee of Public Accounts, *Session 1983–84: Quinquennial Revaluation of Assets and Review of Performance* (London: HMSO, 1984).

25. *Report of the Committee of Inquiry into the Acquisition and Occupancy of Agricultural Land, Chairman: The Rt. Hon. Lord Northfield*, Cmnd. 7599 (London: HMSO, 1979).

26. Royal Commission on the Distribution of Income and Wealth, *Report No. 7*, Cmnd. 7595 (London: HMSO, 1979), p. 152.

6. PRIVATE PLEASURE

1. E. M. Forster, 'My Wood', 1926, in *Abinger Harvest* (London: Edward Arnold, 1936).

2. R. Lacey, *The Aristocrats*, BBC TV, 1983.

3. Figure quoted by A. Watson in 'The Grouse Moor Problem', Edinburgh: *Question*, May 1976.

4. Figure quoted by Cobham Resource Consultants in *Countryside Sports: Their Economic Significance: Main Report Prepared for the Standing Conference on Countryside Sports* (Oxford: The Consultants, 1983), p. 107.

5. J. A. Jolowicz with T. E. Lewis and D. M. Harris, *Winfield and Jolowicz on Tort* (London: Sweet and Maxwell, 1971), p. 306.

6. J. M. S. Thompson, 'Recreation and Access to the Countryside – The Estate Involvement', paper given at a conference at the National Agricultural Centre, Stoneleigh, 17 February 1982.

7. C. Watkins, *Woodlands in Nottinghamshire since 1945: A Study of Changing Distribution and Use*, unpublished PhD thesis, University of Nottingham, 1983.

8. Countryside Commission, *Study of Informal Recreation in South East England* (Cheltenham: Countryside Commission, 1978).

9. T. H. Blank and J. Meads, 'Hunting and Shooting', *Shooting Times and Country Magazine*, 4 December 1971, p. 22.

10. T. H. Blank, 'Co-operation in the Thurlow Country', *Shooting Times and Country Magazine*, 30 December 1972, p. 18.

11. T. H. Blank, 'Foxes and Pheasants: Cubs in Coverts', *Shooting Times and Country Magazine*, 17 November 1973, p. 20.

12. C. E. M. Joad, 'The People's Claim' in (ed.) C. Williams-Ellis, *Beauty and the Beast* (London: Dent and Sons, 1937), p. 78.

13. Brathay Exploration Group, North-West Highlands Expedition July–August 1973, *Interim Report on the Ecological Effects of Public Recreation in the Gairloch Conservation Unit: the Disturbance of Hill Red Deer by Walkers and Climbers* (Cumbria: Brathay Hall Trust, 1974).

14. For further details of the operation of the Peak Board's access agreements, see H. Gunton, 'Walking on the Wild Side', *Chartered Surveyor Weekly*, 8 December 1983 and H. Gunton, 'Landowners, Grouse and Thousands of Walkers', *Country Landowner*, August 1984.

15. N. Picozzi, 'Breeding Performance and Shooting Bags of Red Grouse in Relation to Public Access in the Peak District National Park, England', *Biological Conservation*, Vol. 3, No. 3, April 1971. For further details of the impact of public access on grouse rearing and shooting, see R. S. Gibbs, *The Impact of Recreation on Upland Access Land*, Agricultural Adjustment Unit, University of Newcastle-Upon-Tyne, 1976.

16. C. Tubbs, 'The New Forest: Conflict and Symbiosis', *New Scientist*, 1 July 1982.

17. See for instance, J. E. Satchell, *The Effects of Recreation on the Ecology of Natural Landscapes* (Brussels: Council of Europe, 1976) and M. C. D. Speight, *Outdoor Recreation and its Ecological Effects*, Discussion Papers in Conservation No. 4, (University College, London, 1973).

18. Royal Society for the Protection of Birds, *Silent Death* (Sandy, Beds: RSPB, 1980).

19. H. Newby, C. Bell, P. Saunders and D. Rose, 'Farmers' Attitudes to Conservation', *Countryside Recreation Review*, Vol. 2, 1977, p. 25.

20. Countryside Commission, *National Household Survey*, (Cheltenham: Countryside Commission, 1978). For details of a similar survey on the relative popularity of visiting the countryside see note 1 to Chapter 7.

21. R. M. Sidaway et al, *Access to the Countryside for Recreation and Sport*, (Cheltenham: Countryside Commission, 1986).

Part Four: The Broken Contract

7. RIGHTS OF WAY

1. Adrian Phillips (Director, Countryside Commission) and Jeremy Worth (Head, Recreation and Access Branch, Countryside Commission), 'Developing a Strategy for Leisure in the Countryside', *Institute*

of Leisure and Amenity Management Conference Proceedings, 11 June 1985, available from the Countryside Commission, Cheltenham.

2. Nobody knows the precise current mileage of public footpaths and bridleways. The 120,000 miles comes from figures supplied to the Ministry of Transport and the Welsh Office by the old county councils of England and Wales in 1973.

3. Phillips and Worth, op. cit., note 1.

4. For further details of conflicts over footpaths during the nineteenth century, see H. Hill, *Freedom to Roam*, (Ashbourne, Derbyshire: Moorland Publishing, 1980) and Tom Stephenson's regular column in *Rucksack* in the early 1980s.

5. Ministry of Town and Country Planning, *Footpaths and Access to the Countryside: Report of the Special Committee*, Cmnd. 7207 (London: HMSO, 1947).

6. See P. Clayden and J. Trevelyan, *Rights of Way: A Guide to Law and Practice* (Henley: The Open Spaces Society, 1983), for a clear exposition of the law relating to public footpaths and bridleways in England and Wales.

7. For further details, see *Rights of Way Legislation: 1st Monitoring Report: A Report Prepared for the Countryside Commission by the Ramblers' Association*, (Cheltenham: Countryside Commission, 1985).

8. M. Holroyd, 'Where are the Footpaths?', *Rucksack*, Vol. 6, No. 1, Winter 1970.

9. 'Melbury House, Dorsetshire: The Seat of the Earl of Ilchester', *Country Life Illustrated*, 19 August 1899.

10. D. Rubinstein, *The Wolds Way* (Clapham, North Yorkshire: Dalesman, 1979), p. 5.

11. The figures on the proportions of the South-West Coast Peninsula Path, North Downs Way, South Downs Way and Wolds Way that follow established rights of way were supplied to me by the Countryside Commission.

12. Quoted by E. Grice in 'Long-distance footpaths face a lonely future', *The Sunday Times*, 7 February 1982.

13. Foreword by D. Barber to *The Wolds Way* by R. Ratcliffe (London: HMSO, 1982).

14. H. Newby, C. Bell, P. Saunders and D. Rose, 'Farmers' Attitudes to Conservation', *Countryside Recreation Review*, Vol. 2, 1977, p. 25.

15. Lord Justice Scott in *Jones v. Bates* (1938), 2 AER 237.

16. J. Bugler, 'Public: Farmers will be Prosecuted', *The Observer*, 24 October 1971.

17. J. Jefcoate, 'Footpath Scene', Ramblers' Association: *South-Eastern Rambler*, Vol. 3, No. 27, Summer 1983.

18. Ramblers' Association Sussex Area, *Public Rights of Way in East Sussex*, February, 1983, unpublished paper available from Ramblers' Association, London.

19. R. and J. Moreton, 'Surveying the Paths of South Cambridgeshire', *Rucksack*, Vol. 11, No. 7, Ramblers' Association, April, 1984.

20. Countryside Commission, *Ploughing Footpaths and Bridleways: A Study of the Law and Practice, Undertaken for the Countryside Commission by the Rights of Way Review Committee* (Cheltenham: Countryside Commission, 1985) and Ramblers' Association, 'Ploughing Research', *Footpath Worker*, Vol. 6, No. 4, Ramblers' Association, April, 1985.

21. F. Thompson, *Still Glides the Stream* (Oxford: OUP, 1948).

22. *The Sunday Times*, 8 March 1981, p. 3.

23. Further details in J. Saville, *Rural Depopulation in England and Wales, 1851–1951*, (London: Routledge and Kegan Paul, 1957).

24. I describe the impact of agricultural change on the landscape of Graffham Down in detail in *The Theft of The Countryside*, (London: Temple Smith, 1980), pp. 129–135.

25. Further details in B. and B. Webb, *The Story of the King's Highway* (London, 1913).

26. Quoted by C. Hall, 'One Countryman to Another', *The Countryman*, Spring 1984, p. 181.

27. G. E. Jenkins, 'A Policy for Footpaths', *District Councils' Review*, November 1978. See also Preseli District Council Public Services Committee, *Report of Chief Executive Officer: Review of Footpath Legislation*, 13 September 1978.

28. *Pembrokeshire Coast Path: A Report to the Countryside Commission on the 180-mile Long Distance Route*, (Cheltenham: Countryside Commission, 1982).

29. *Report of the Inquiry held on 20 October 1982 into the Proposed Reorganization of Footpaths and Bridleways in Brinkhill, Somersby, South Ormsby and Tetford in Lincolnshire*, London: Department of the Environment.

30. Ramblers' Association Gloucestershire Area, *Survey of the Public Paths of Gloucestershire, July 1981*, unpublished paper available from Ramblers' Association, London.

31. Ramblers' Association Sussex Area, op. cit., note 18.

32. Parliamentary Debates House of Commons Official Report, *Standing Committee D: Wildlife and Countryside Bill (Lords)*, 23 June 1981, col. 1034.

33. T. Huxley, in an interview with the author in September 1983.

34. *Tak' Tent: Newsletter of North East Mountain Trust*, (Aberdeen: NEMT, May 1982).

8. FREEDOM TO WANDER

1. House of Commons, *Hansard*, 31 March 1949, col. 1485.

2. *Footpaths and Access to the Countryside: Report of the Special Committee, Chairman: Sir Arthur Hobhouse*, Cmnd. 7207, HMSO, 1947.

3. Foreword by Tom Stephenson to *Keep Out: The Hundred Year Struggle for Public Access to the Hills and Mountains of Britain, 1884–1984*, (London: Ramblers' Association, 1984).

4. R. S. Gibbs and M. C. Whitby, *Local Authority Expenditure on Access*

Land, Agricultural Adjustment Unit, University of Newcastle Upon Tyne, 1975.

5. R. S. Gibbs and M. C. Whitby, op. cit.

6. J. P. Rossiter, *An Analytical Study of the Public Use of Private Land for Outdoor Recreation in England 1949–1968*, unpublished PhD thesis, University of Cambridge, 1972, p. 316.

7. J. P. Rossiter, op. cit., p. 150.

8. J. P. Rossiter, op. cit., p. 150.

9. N. W. Moore, 'The Heaths of Dorset and their Conservation', *Journal of Ecology*, Vol. 50, 1969; B. Rippey, *The Conservation of the Dorset Heaths*, unpublished MSc thesis, University of London, 1973.

10. Devon County Council and the Nature Conservancy Council South West Region, *The Changing Face of Devon*, (Exeter: Devon County Council, 1979).

11. Gloucestershire Trust for Nature Conservation, *Wildlife in Gloucestershire: a Habitat Survey*, (Stonehouse, Glos: The Trust, 1981).

12. For details of some of the first access agreements secured in Stirling District, see M. Dobson, 'Access Agreements in the Countryside', *Scottish Planning Law and Practice*, Vol. 1, September 1980, pp. 12–13.

13. M. Dower, *Fourth Wave*, (London: Civic Trust, 1966).

14. Ministry of Housing and Local Government, *Leisure in the Countryside*, Cmnd. 2928, (London: HMSO, 1966).

15. S. Waterhouse, *Country Parks and the West Midlands*, (University of Birmingham Centre for Urban and Regional Studies, 1972), p. 20.

16. Quoted in *The Countryman*, Winter, 1983, p. 133.

17. *Northampton Chronicle and Echo*, 5 March 1975.

18. A. Kemp, 'Access to the Forest of Wychwood', *Rucksack*, Vol. 9, No. 4, Summer, 1978.

19. Ibid.

20. *The Secret Forest: The Case for Access to the Ancient Forest of Wychwood*, (Charlbury: CPRE Oxfordshire Branch, 1982).

9. COMMON LAND

1. D. Wells, 'The Nature Conservancy Interest' in *Conference on the Future of Common Land and its Management* (Henley: The Open Spaces Society, 1983).

2. For further details of the history of Wimbledon Common, see *Extracts from the Court Rolls of the Manor of Wimbledon* (London: Wyman and Sons, 1866); T. B. Bishop, *Remarks on the Wimbledon Court Rolls* (London: Cawston and Sons, 1867); and Lord Eversley, *Commons, Forests and Footpaths* (London, 1910).

3. For a summary of the law on commons see P. Clayden, *Our Common Land: The Law and History of Commons and Village Greens* (Henley: The Open Spaces Society, 1985).

4. P. F. Brandon, *The Common Lands and Wastes of Sussex*, unpublished PhD thesis, University of London, 1963.

5. The figures on the extent of common land are taken from J. W. Aitchison, E. J. Hughes and S. D. Masters, *The Common Lands of England and Wales: Commons Registers and Designated Conservation Areas in Selected Counties*, (Department of Geography, University College of Wales, Aberystwyth, 1984); W. G. Hoskins and L. Dudley Stamp, *The Common Lands of England and Wales* (London: Collins: The New Naturalist, 1963); and J. W. Aitchison, *The Common Lands of Wales*, (Department of Geography, University College of Wales, Aberystwyth, 1983).

6. Department of the Environment, *Common Land: Preparations for Comprehensive Legislation: Report of an Interdepartmental Working Party, 1975/77* (London: DOE, 1978), p. 1.

7. *Royal Commission on Common Land 1955–1958 Report* (London: HMSO, 1958).

8. It used to be thought that the Secretary of State could give permission only if a proposal would be for the 'benefit of the neighbourhood'. However, when in 1980 the Secretary of State took counsel's opinion on this point he was advised that he need do no more than take into account the benefit of the neighbourhood when reaching a decision. For further details see P. Clayden, op. cit., note 3, p. 54.

9. The Commons, Open Spaces and Footpaths Preservation Society, founded in 1865, changed its name to The Open Spaces Society in 1982.

10. Welsh Office, Cardiff, decision reference P22/549, 18 August 1983, para. 19.

11. Those commons covered by access deeds of covenant are listed in the *Annual Report of the Commons, Footpaths and Open Spaces Preservation Society, 1930*.

12. J. Perrin, 'Speed the Plough – and Pass the Ammunition', *The Guardian*, 5 November 1983, p. 9.

13. Department of the Environment, Bristol, decision reference CRD2/MB/720, 4 December 1978, paras. 9, 10.

14. *The Common Land Forum Report* (Cheltenham: Countryside Commission, 1986).

15. For further details of the history and present extent of common grazing land in the Scottish Isles see A. Fenton, *The Northern Isles: Orkney and Shetland* (Edinburgh: John Donald, 1975); and S. A. Knox, *The Making of the Shetland Landscape* (Edinburgh: John Donald, 1985).

10. ENVIRONMENTAL PROTECTION

1. A. G. Tansley, *Our Heritage of Wild Nature: A Plea for Organized Nature Conservation* (Cambridge: CUP, 1945).

2. R. Vaughan Cornish, *National Parks and the Heritage of Scenery* (London: Sifton Praed, 1930).

References

3. Ministry of Town and Country Planning, *National Parks in England and Wales: Report by John Dower*, Cmnd. 6628, (London: HMSO, 1945), p. 48.

4. Ibid., p. 48.

5. Forestry Commission, *Consultation Procedures for Forestry Grants and Felling Permissions, Revised June 1986*, (Edinburgh: Forestry Commission, 1986), p. 5.

6. Eighteen thousand, seven hundred and seventy-two acres of Great Britain's farmland were converted to urban uses in 1981, the most recent year for which calculations have been made, according to expert on the conversion of rural to urban land Dr Margaret Anderson of Wye College, University of London (personal communication). Answering a question in the House of Commons on 19 December 1985 Mrs Peggy Fenner, the then Parliamentary Secretary at the Ministry of Agriculture, stated that around 10,000 acres of farmland in England had been converted to urban and industrial uses each year during the preceding five years.

7. The proceedings of this conference, organized by the Council for the Protection of Rural England and entitled 'The Forestry Industry: A Case for Scepticism', are reported in the *CPRE Bulletin*, Winter 1980/81.

8. Letter from Sir David Montgomery on 'Forestry planting' to *The Scotsman*, 17 September 1985.

9. Forestry Commission, *The Composition and Procedures of the Forestry Commission's Regional Advisory Committees*, (Edinburgh: Forestry Commission, 1986). See also House of Commons, *Hansard*, 24 March 1986, cols. 353–355.

10. These were the EEC Bird Directive, the Convention on International Trade in Endangered Species, the Ramsar Convention on Wetlands, the Convention on the Conservation of Migratory Species and the Berne Convention on the Conservation of European Wildlife and Natural Habitats.

11. J. Tubbs, *The Concept of Sites of Special Scientific Interest: A Review*, unpublished thesis, University of Southampton, 1977.

12. Nature Conservancy Council, *Loss and Damage in SSSIs in 1980* (Peterborough: NCC, 1981).

13. J. Wiggin, MP, speaking at the Game Conservancy's Three Counties Conference in Cheltenham in 1981, as reported by A. Gilg in *Countryside Planning Yearbook 3*, (Norwich: Geo Books, 1982), p. 26.

14. The Countryside in 1970, Third Conference, London, 26–28 October, 1970: *Reports of Advisory Committees and Groups*, (London: Nature Conservancy, 1970), pp. 1.36, 1.37.

15. Department of the Environment, Ministry of Agriculture, Fisheries and Food, Welsh Office, *Wildlife and Countryside Act 1981: Financial Guidelines for Management Agreements*, Circular 4/83 (DOE and MAFF), 6/83 (Welsh Office) (London: HMSO, 1983), para. 29.

16. *Statement by the North York Moors National Park Committee to the House of Commons Environment Committee on the Operation and Effectiveness of the Wildlife and Countryside Act, 1981*, (Helmsley, North Yorkshire: North York Moors National Park Authority, October 1984).

17. For details of the capital transfer tax exemption system, see HM Treasury, *Capital Taxation and the National Heritage* (London: The Treasury, 1983).

18. Trustees of Nawton Tower Estate and D. C. Statham (National Park Officer), *The Bransdale Moor Management Plan* (Helmsley, North Yorkshire: North York Moors National Park Authority, 1982).

19. C. Barr, C. Benefield, B. Bunce, H. Ridsdale and M. Whittaker, *Landscape Changes in Britain*, (Huntingdon: Institute of Terrestrial Ecology, 1986).

20. Ibid.

21. A. Watson, 'A Survey of Vehicular Hill Tracks in North-east Scotland for Land Use Planning', *Journal of Environmental Management*, Vol. 18, 1984, pp. 345–353.

22. Forestry Commission, *Guidelines for the Management of Broadleaved Woodland*, (Edinburgh: Forestry Commission, 1985), pp. 13, 14.

23. The Lands Tribunal awarded Mr Bell £46,547 plus the cost of taking the case to the Lands Tribunal which was expected at the time of writing to run to about £20,000.

24. Ministry of Town and Country Planning, *Report of the National Parks Committee (Chairman: Sir Arthur Hobhouse)*, Cmnd. 7121 (London: HMSO, 1947).

25. Section 5(2), National Parks and Access to the Countryside Act, 1949.

26. I discuss the reasons why no tract of lowland England has ever been designated a national park on pages 141–143 of *The Theft of The Countryside*, (London: Temple Smith, 1980), and go on to propose six new lowland national parks on pages 239–254.

27. Northern Ireland Planning Advisory Board Committee on Amenities, *The Ulster Countryside*, (Belfast: HMSO, 1947).

28. R. H. Buchanan, 'Landscape', in J. G. Cruickshank and D. N. Wilcock (ed), *Northern Ireland: Environment and Natural Resources* (Belfast: The Queen's University and the New University of Ulster, 1982), p. 282.

29. Department of Health for Scotland, *National Parks and the Conservation of Nature in Scotland: Report by the Scottish National Parks Committee and the Scottish Wild Life Conservation Committee*, Cmnd. 7235, (Edinburgh: HMSO, 1947).

30. For details of the influence of John Muir on America's national park system, see R. Nash, *Wilderness and the American Mind* (Yale: University Press, 1973).

31. The events of this period are described in detail in G. E. Cherry, *Peacetime History: Environmental Planning, Volume II: National Parks and Recreation in the Countryside* (London: HMSO, 1975), pp. 141–145.

32. Countryside Commission for Scotland, *A Park System for Scotland*, (Perth: CCS, 1974).

33. Quoted in 'Moves for Highland National Park', *The Scotsman*, 3 July 1985.

34. Ibid.

Part Five: At Issue

11. THE HEART OF THE MATTER

1. M. Manzoni of the British Union for the Abolition of Vivisection, speaking on BBC Radio Four's 'Today' programme, 16 February 1983.

2. R. Smith, 'The Tragedy of the Pines', *Scottish Wild Land News*, Spring 1984.

3. P. Lowe and J. Goyder, *Environmental Groups in Politics* (London: Allen and Unwin, 1983), p. 9.

4. Lowe and Goyder, op. cit., note 3, p. 1.

5. R. Arvill, *Man and Environment* (Harmondsworth: Penguin Books, 1967).

6. 'Mining in Snowdonia', *The Ecologist*, June 1971.

7. Quoted by H. Newby, C. Bell, D. Rose and P. Saunders in *Property, Paternalism and Power: Class and Control in Rural England* (London: Hutchinson, 1978), p. 331. For an interesting account of the defence of landownership see R. Schlatter, *Private Property – The History of An Idea* (London: Allen and Unwin, 1951).

Part Six: Repossession

12. OTHER OWNERS

1. Agriculture EDC, *Farm Productivity: a Report on Factors Affecting Productivity at the Farm Level* (London: National Economic Development Council, 1973).

2. R. Gasson and B. Hill, *Farm Tenure and Performance* (Wye College, University of London, 1984).

3. Centre for Agricultural Strategy, *Capital for Agriculture* (CAS, University of Reading, 1978), p. 48.

4. For further details of the controls on the acquisition of farmland in Denmark, see *A Report by W. K. Turner of a Visit to France, Romania, Denmark and West Germany in 1980 to Study the Impact of Modern Farming Systems on the Social and Physical Environment*, (Olney, Bucks: The Nuffield Farming Scholarships Trust, 1980).

5. For further details of land ownership in Saudi Arabia, see H. H. Hajrah, *Public Land Distribution in Saudi Arabia* (London: Longman, 1982).

6. T. R. Worthington *The Landscapes of Institutional Landowners* (Cheltenham: Countryside Commission, 1979).

7. Nature Conservancy Council, *Nature Conservation and Agriculture*, (Peterborough: NCC, 1977).

13. SENSIBLE SUBSIDIES

1. House of Commons, *Hansard*, 10 March 1986, col. 690.

2. B. Green, 'What's Wrong with Conservation?' *Ecos*, 2(4), 1981, p. 29.

3. P. Johnston, 'Back-to-nature Farmland Plan: A Green Revolution is Ploughing Ahead', *Today*, 30 March 1986.

4. Consumers in the European Community Group, *Outcome of the 1986–7 Farm Price Review*, (London: CECG, 1986).

5. S. Mansholt, 'European Community', *The Guardian*, 14 December 1970, quoted by J. G. S. and F. Donaldson in association with D. Barber, *Farming in Britain Today*, (Harmondsworth: Penguin Books, 1972).

6. J. Pearce, *The Common Agricultural Policy: Prospects for Change*, Chatham House Papers 13, (London: Routledge and Kegan Paul, 1981).

7. See for instance House of Lords Select Committee on the European Communities Session 1980–81, 19th Report, *The Common Agricultural Policy – Directions of Future Development and Proposals for Prices and Related Measures*, (London: HMSO, 1981).

8. Pearce, op. cit., note 6, p. 15.

9. For further details of the post-war agricultural revolution in Europe, see G. Thiède, 'L'Agriculture Européene et La Révolution Technique', in M. Tracy and I. Hodac (eds), *Prospects for Agriculture in the European Economic Community*, (Brussels: De Tempel, 1979).

10. House of Commons First Report from the Agriculture Committee, Session 1979–80, *Economic, Social and Health Implications for the United Kingdom of the Common Agricultural Policy on Milk and Dairy Products*, Vol. I, (London: HMSO, 1980), p. 5.

11. S. Tangermann, 'EEC farm policy: the "reforms" that change nothing', *Financial Times*, 5 September 1984.

12. Socialist Group European Parliament Press Notice, *Mrs Barbara Castle's Amendment to the Plumb Report*, Strasbourg, 16 June 1981. See also The Labour Party, *Withdrawal from the EEC: Statement by the National Executive Committee to the 1981 Conference*, (London: The Labour Party, 1981).

13. Commission of the European Communities, *The Agricultural Situation in the Community: 1978 Report*, (Brussels: EEC, 1979).

14. Further details in The Arkleton Trust, *Schemes of Assistance to Farmers in Less Favoured Areas of the EEC* (Langholm, Dumfries-shire: The Arkleton Trust, 1982).

15. C. Potter, *Investing in Rural Harmony: An Alternative Package of Agricultural Subsidies and Incentives for England and Wales* (Godalming, Surrey: World Wildlife Fund, 1983).

16. Department of the Environment: Countryside Review Committee, *Report of Working Party on Trees in the Countryside*, unpublished, 1975, referred to in M. J. Feist, *A Study of Management Agreements*, (Cheltenham: Countryside Conmmission, 1975).

17. C. A. Jones, *The Conservation of Chalk Downland in Dorset* (Dorchester: Dorset County Council, 1973), pp. 7–8.

18. Centre for Agricultural Strategy, *Capital for Agriculture*, (CAS, University of Reading, 1978), p. 28.

19. C. Pye-Smith and R. North, *Working the Land: a New Plan for a Healthy Agriculture*, (London: Temple Smith, 1984).

20. M. MacEwen and G. Sinclair, *New Life for the Hills* (London: Council for National Parks, 1983). Michael Dower puts forward a similar proposal for farm management plans in 'Farmers and the Landscape', *Town and Country Planning*, January, 1981, pp. 30–31.

21. T. O'Riordan 'Putting Trust in the Countryside' in World Wildlife Fund, *The Conservation and Development Programme for the UK: A Response to the World Conservation Strategy* (London: Kogan Page, 1983).

14. PLEAS AND URGINGS

1. R. Cobham et al., *Demonstration Farms* (Cheltenham: Countryside Commission, 1984).

2. P. Hamilton and J. Woolcock, *Agricultural Landscapes: An Approach to their Improvement* (Cheltenham: Countryside Commission, 1984).

3. Quoted in D. Lovibond, 'FWAGs of Convenience', *The Countryman*, Spring 1985, p. 54.

4. A. Mowle, 'Experience of Agriculture and Conservation in Scotland', unpublished paper delivered at Regional Studies Association Edinburgh Conference, 30 March 1984 (available from Dr Mowle, Nature Conservancy Council, Edinburgh).

5. R. Westmacott and T. Worthington, *Agricultural Landscapes: A Second Look* (Cheltenham: Countryside Commission, 1984).

15. PLANNING

1. House of Commons, *Hansard*, 1980–81, Vol. 3, 27 April 1981, Cols. 541–2.

2. I examine in detail how the extension of planning controls to major changes to the rural environment could operate in practice in *The Theft of the Countryside* (London: Temple Smith, 1980), pp. 204–25.

3. The Socialist Countryside Group advocate this step in *The Countryside: A Rescue Plan: The Case for Controls Over Farming and Forestry* (London: Socialist Environment and Resources Association, 1982).

4. House of Lords, *Hansard*, 13 February 1981, col. 410.

5. M. Smith, 'How to Save the Forests of Snowdonia', *New Scientist*, 1 July 1982.

6. R. Westmacott and T. Worthington, *Agricultural Landscapes: A Second Look* (Cheltenham: Countryside Commission, 1984).

Part Seven: The Way Forward

17. A RIGHT TO ROAM

1. *Footpaths and Access to the Countryside: Report of the Special Committee, Chairman: Sir Arthur Hobhouse*, Cmnd. 7207 (London: HMSO, 1947).

2. *Royal Commission on Common Land 1955–1958 Report* (London: HMSO, 1958).

Part Eight: Conclusion

18. THIS LAND IS OUR LAND

1. See S. C. Tompkins, *The Theft of The Hills* (London: Ramblers' Association and World Wildlife Fund, 1986).

2. R. Mabey, *The Common Ground* (London: Hutchinson, 1980).

3. M. Shoard, *The Theft of The Countryside* (London: Temple Smith, 1980).

4. I trace the development during the early 1980s of the debate about the conflict between modern farming and conservation in 'Viewpoint', *Footloose*, August 1982.

Index

Abercrombie, Professor Patrick 110
Aberdeenshire 138–40
access agreements 303, 373–84
access and bloodsports, conflict between
    270, 282–304, 542–3
access and farming, conflict between 310–13
access, deeds of 415
access, proposals for right of general
    of Hobhouse Committee 371–2, 540
    of Marion Shoard 538–45
    see also Allemansrätten
access to the countryside
    history of 46–7, 67–9, 112–14
    loss of open access lands 203–4, 347,
        382–3, 385
    see also access agreements; country parks;
        paths, permissive; Public Order Act,
        1986; rights of way, public; trespass
Access to the Countryside (Northern
    Ireland) Order, 1983 369–70, 385
Access to Mountains Bills 112, 114
Acquisition of Land (Authorisation
    Procedure) Act, 1946 412
Adopt-A-Path 350
Africa 19–20, 195–6, 463
agricultural revolution, post-war 197–8
Aitken, Dr Robert 294, 362–3
Agricultural Act, 1947 180, 249
Agricultural Act, 1986 453
agricultural and conservation, conflict
        between *see* conservation and
        agriculture, conflict between
Agriculture and Fisheries of Scotland,
    Department of 121
Agriculture, Fisheries and Food, Ministry
    of 180, 248–50
agriculture, history of 32, 44, 72, 179–80,
    197–99, 428–9
Alker, G. A. 358
Allemansrätten 271, 311, 539–40, 543, 545
allotments 91–2
Althorp estate *see* Spencer, Earls

America, South 21–3, 463
America, United States of 23, 59, 79, 463,
    495
Anglesey 281–2, 326, 408
Angus District 126, 296, 362, 365, 367
Animals Act, 1971 313
animals, wild 210–13
    see also birds; butterflies; deer stalking;
        dogs; fox hunting; grouse shooting;
        natural world; nature conservation;
        newts; pheasant shooting; salmon and
        trout fishing
Arran Mountains 397–9
Arbuthnott, Viscount 258–60
archaeology 30–31, 199–200, 204, 220, 224,
    445
Archers, The 143
area plans 425
aristocracy, landed 127–37, 150
    see also under names of individual titled
        landowners
Arundel Park 287–8, 313–14
Arvill, Robert 477
Ashdown, C. J. 234
Association for the Preservation of Rural
    Scotland 110
Atholl, Dukes of 111, 132–3, 290–91, 299,
    301, 323, 362
Attlee Government 114–15, 322, 331
Attwell, Les, 317
Avebury 460
Ayrshire 221

Baddesley Common 448–50
Baker, E. A. 103
Baker, Ralph 252
Baldry, MP, Tony 359
Balfour, Dr Jean 259
Barber, Sir Derek 261, 391–2, 340
Barden Moor and Barden Fell 373–7
Batchelor, Hughie 166–7, 188
Bateman, John 98

Batty, Mike 161
Baxter, Donald 365
Beba, Douglas 193
Beckett, Clive 335
Bedford, Dukes of 99, 131, 277
Bedfordshire 140–41, 217, 273, 276, 326, 533
Bedfordshire County Council 335
Beebee, Dr Trevor 202
beef cattle 500
Bell, Robert 458
Belvoir Castle 37, 229
    see also Rutland, Dukes of
Benefices Measures 236–7
Bennett, MP, Andrew 538
Benwell Community Development Project 239–41
Berkhamsted Common 108–9
Berkshire 203–4
Berthon, Sir Stephen 357
Berwick-on-Tweed 460
Berwick District 362
birds 200–3, 221–3, 409, 438, 492
Birse 138–40
Black Act, 1723 64–5, 90
Black Death 41
Blackstone, Sir William 59–60
Blakiston-Houston, Dick 151
Blaxell, Peter 148–9
Blenheim Park 378
bloodsports *see* deer stalking; fox hunting; grouse shooting; pheasant shooting; salmon and trout fishing
bloodsports and access, conflict between *see* access and bloodsports, conflict between
bloodsports and conservation, relationship between *see* conservation and bloodsports, relationship between
Bolton, Lord 67
Boote, Robert 445
Boughton Estate 131, 395
Boulsbury Wood 452
Bradley, J. H. 437
Braes, Battle of The 84–5
Brecon Beacons 166
Brecon Beacons National Park 242, 437
bridleways, *see* rights of way, public
Brindley, Howard 469
British Field Sports Society 142, 285
Broadlands 278–80
    see also Romsey, Lord
Broads Authority 149, 465–6
Brocket, Lord, 231
Brotherton, Dr Ian 242

Bryce, MP, James 112
Buccleuch, Dukes of 98, 130–31, 134, 143, 170–71, 226–7, 261
Buchanan, Professor Sir Colin 197
Buchanan, Professor Ronald 466–7
Buckinghamshire 155, 351–2, 326
Buckinghamshire County Council 238, 260
Bugler, Jeremy 341–2
building 110–11, 166, 173–9, 424, 428
    see also farm buildings; roads, estate
Burns, Mr and Mrs John 449–50
Burritt, Elihu 324
Burton of Dochfour, Lord 383
butterflies 491

Cadogan Estate 176
Caernarvon, Earl of 234, 284
Caernarvonshire 86, 152
Cairngorm Mountains 293–5, 467–9
Caithness 222–3
Callaghan Government 227, 438, 550
Callander, Robin 138
Cambrian Mountains National Park (proposed) 465
Cambrian Way (proposed) 339
Cambridgeshire 99, 342, 410
Cannock Chase 65
Canterbury District Council 462–3
capital gains tax, 166, 190, 227
capital transfer tax 226–7, 454–60, 510–12
    see also death duties, inheritance tax
Capper, Wilfrid 337
Carlisle, MP, Kenneth 527
Carrington, Lord 245
Carter, Eric 513
Castle, MEP, Mrs Barbara 501
Castle Ashby 131, 395
    see also Northampton, Marquesses of
Catalano, Alejandrina 127
ceorls 32–3
cereal farming 77, 180–83, 187, 191, 193, 195, 197–9, 494
    see also quotas, cereal
Chamberlain, MP, Joseph 88, 93
Charles, Prince 130, 413, 514
    see also Cornwall, Duchy of
Charnwood District Council 324–5
chases, hunting 39
Chater, John 463
Chatsworth Settlement, Trustees of the 174, 459
Chelsea, Viscount 176–7
Cheshire 120, 136, 330, 352, 393
Cheshire County Council 393
Cheshire, Paul 185

China 21, 27, 486
Cholmondeley Castle Estate 393
Christianity 205, 475
Church Estate 156–7
Church Estate Commissioners 153, 156–7
Church of England 156–7, 177, 233, 237
Churchill, Winston 93–4, 381
Clandon Park 153
clan system 71, 74–5
Clark, Dr David 419, 494
Clearances, Highland 69–75
Clowes, Mrs Hazel 256
Clywd 217, 408
coal 166, 169–71, 239–40
Cochran, Hugh 139
Coke, Sir Thomas 67
Collier, Major Brett 353, 358–9
Collins, Lady Clarissa 456
Colyer, Mrs Ruth 506
Combermere Estate 393
Common Agricultural Policy 181–3,
     493–504
  Farm Price Settlement, April 1986 182,
     494–5, 500
  Farm Minister's Agreement, December
     1986 182, 500
common land
  definition 122, 407
  history of 33–4, 43–6, 107–9
  see also enclosure
  existing situation 408–19
  in Northern Ireland 420–21
  in Scotland 420–21
Common Land Forum 419
Common land, Royal Commission on
     411–12, 416, 419
Commons Act, 1965
Commons, Footpaths and Open Spaces
     Preservation Society 109, 412–3, 417
Commons, House of 61–2, 75–6, 94–5,
     244–5
commonties 72
Commonwealth countries 495
compensation to landowners 312, 424–5,
     443–6, 450–53, 461
compensatory allowances, livestock 184,
     503–4
conifer afforestation *see* forestry
conservation and access, conflict between
     305–7
conservation and agriculture, conflict
     between 196–205, 347, 438–53, 478,
     549–52
conservation and bloodsports, relationship
     between 268–70, 288–9, 309–10

conservation and forestry, conflict between
     215–25, 429–38, 452–3, 461–2, 549
conservation and grazing, conflict between
     288–9, 306
Conservative Party 527
Consumers in the European Community
     Group 495
copyhold tenure 54
co-responsibility levies 182, 499
Corn Laws 77–8, 88, 100
Cornwall 61, 141, 217, 331, 335–6, 356, 392,
     465
Cornwall County Council 141, 238
Cornwall, Duchy of 130, 141, 158, 161, 168,
     171, 408
Cotswolds 383, 464
Council for the Protection (formerly
     Preservation) of Rural England
     (CPRE) 110–11, 430–31
  of Rural Wales 110
Country Landowners' Association 141,
     143–4, 245–7, 315–16, 445
country parks, 301, 377, 385–94
Countryside Act, 1968 382, 385–6
Countryside Commission 256–8, 315, 321,
     339–40, 380, 391–2, 454, 456, 465,
     513–16
Countryside Commission for Scotland 256,
     259, 361, 366, 454, 456, 467–8
Countryside in 1970 conferences 444–6
Countryside (Scotland) Acts 360, 363, 467
county councils, membership of 237–8, 240,
     328–9, 332, 352, 380
Court of Wards 54
Cowdray, Viscount 139
Cowley, Geoffrey 243
Cranborne, Viscount 452
Craston, Canon C. R. 235–7
Creag Meagaidh 452
crofts 85, 420
Crown Estate 157–61, 171, 176–7, 413–14,
     544
Crown Estate Commissioners 159–60,
     413–14
Cumbria 217
  see also Lake District

dairy farming 182, 197–8, 498–500
  see also co-responsibility levies; quotas,
     milk
dairy herd conversion scheme 499
Dartmoor 41, 219, 223, 383, 410, 430, 523
Dashwood, Sir Francis 155
Dawson, Michael 458
death duties 140, 176, 226–7, 277, 454

see also capital transfer tax, inheritance tax
Dee River (in Scotland) 269, 299, 368
deer parks 40
deer stalking 37–40, 100–1, 269, 288–98, 542–3
see also royal forest
Defence, Ministry of 119
deficiency payments 180
definitive maps *see* rights of way, public
Denmark 489, 496
demonstration farms 513
Derby, Earls of 29, 97, 175, 234, 261
Derbyshire 152, 172, 229
'development', definition of 424, 460–61, 518
development land tax 227
development plans 425
Devon 326, 382
see also Dartmoor, Exmoor
Devon County Council 382
Devonshire, Dukes of 152, 171–2, 174–5, 229, 373
Diggers 56–9
Dissolution of the Monasteries 50, 53, 131
district councils, membership of 148–9, 238
Dobson, Maurice 384
dogs 313
Domesday surveys 97–8
Dorset 89, 152, 162, 203, 218, 326–7, 341, 383, 408, 452, 534
Douglas, Dr Roy 86–7
Doune 460
Dower, John 115, 429–30
Dower, Michael 386, 580n
Down County 151
Downe, Viscount 135–6
downland, chalk 203–4, 408, 464, 506
drainage, land 197, 202, 214, 447, 449, 505, 517, 520, 531
see also internal drainage boards, water authorities
Drake, Tony 339
Drewett, Dr Peter 199
Ducker, Brian 282
Dulverton, Lord 294
Dumfries-shire 131, 222
Dundee District 366–7
Dundee District Council 366–7
Dunning, John 260–61
Dyfed 122, 217, 242, 326, 338, 356

East Anglia 147–8, 232, 507
see also Essex, Norfolk, Suffolk
East Midlands 276

Ecology Party 476
Edinburgh 112, 183
Edwards, MP, Nicholas 416
Egremont, Lord 154–5
Egypt 24
employment in
agriculture 193, 223
forestry 214–15, 225, 255
manufacturing industry 193
tourism 193, 223
enclosure 51–3, 65–7, 76, 210, 416–19
Enclosure Acts 107
enclosure, riots against 52–3, 67, 74, 86, 90
environmentalism, development of 475–9, 552–3
environmentally sensitive areas 453
Epping Forest 108, 409
Esher Common 412
Essex 169, 203
see also Epping Forest
estate workers 231–2
European Communities, House of Lords Select Committee on 510
European Parliament, membership of 244–5
Evans-Freke, John 396
Evelyn, J. P. M. H. 434
Exeter, Marquess of 235
see also Stamford Estates
Exmoor 223, 383, 442

Fagan, Michael 316
Falmouth, Viscount 335–6
farm buildings 199, 461
farmers
owner-occupier 99, 145–9
small 145, 193, 253
farm buildings, size of 144–5, 193–4
farm income 186–8
farming and wildlife advisory groups 513–14
farmland prices 123–4, 146–7, 167, 188–90
farm workers 76, 88–92, 161, 231–3
Farquharson, Captain A. A. C. 137
Farquharson, Angus 139
Featherly and Quilters Wood 463
felling licences 433, 461–2
de Ferrers family 35
feudalism 20–22, 34–6, 53–4, 83
Feversham, Countess of 456
Finance Acts 94–5, 97, 226–7, 454
financial institutions 123–7, 490
Finland 23–4
fishing, salmon and trout 101–2, 269, 298–302, 366, 368, 542

Fitzwilliam family 43, 166, 276, 283
  see also Milton Estate
flowers, wild 200–1, 451–2, 458, 463
food aid 195–6
food prices 76–8, 181–2
food riots 77, 86
food surpluses 182–3, 496
footpaths, public *see* rights of way, public
footpaths, origins of 46–7
forestry 205–225, 416, 446
forestry and conservation, conflict between
  see conservation and forestry, conflict
  between
Forestry Commission 119–21, 207–8, 211,
  214–15, 221, 225, 254–60, 263–4, 280,
  378, 393, 430–38, 445, 461–2
  regional advisory committees of 254,
  432–4, 437
Forster, E. M. 266–7
Fowler, Professor Peter 204
Fountain Forestry 165, 209, 452
fox hunting 99, 154, 268, 285–6, 308,
  311–12, 478
Framlingham 460
France 23, 145, 271–2, 463, 489, 496–7,
  503–4
Friends of the Earth 476–7, 551
Fritton Lake Country Park 387

Galloway 220–21
gamekeepers 232
game laws 63–5, 86, 88, 90, 100–1
George, Henry 78–81, 92–3, 178–9, 535
Geikie, Sir Archibald 70
Germany, West 21, 144, 497
Giffard family 141
Glen Ample (Stirling District) 206–7, 209,
  434–6
Gloucestershire 285–6, 357
  see also Cotswolds
Glover, Stephen 263
Goldstone, David 152
Goodwood Estate 391
Graffham Down (Sussex) 346–7
Grampian Mountains 296–8, 461
grants
  for agriculture 180, 184–5, 442, 505–11,
  527
  for forestry 210
Grant, Lt. Col. J. P. 383
grazing, impact on wildlife of *see*
  conservation and grazing, conflict
  between
Greece 498, 503–4
Green, Dr Brynmor 494

green pound 500
Greenwood, Mr and Mrs John 141, 174,
  286–7
Gribble, F. C. 203
Grosvenor family *see* Westminster, Dukes of
grouse shooting 113, 266, 268–9, 302–4,
  374, 457, 542
Gwent 217
Gwynedd 217, 408

Hall, Christopher 257–8
Hampshire 131, 155, 203, 234–5, 349, 408,
  417–18, 448–50, 452
Hampshire County Council 351
Hampstead Heath 108, 409
Hanna, Robert 149
Harris, Sir Ronald 157
Harrison, Fred 178–9
Hay, Dr Douglas 63, 65
Hazeley Heath 417–18
headage payments 184, 500, 503–4
Heathcote Ball, J. E. 324–5
Heath Government 255, 259–60, 431
heaths, lowland 383
hedgerows 199, 515, 520, 522–3, 533–4
Hebrides 420
Herefordshire 125
Hertfordshire 77, 100, 168, 217
Hertfordshire County Council 351
Highclere Estate 284
Highland Land League 85
Highland Regional Council 223, 364
Hill, Professor Christopher 66
Hill, J. W. 331
Hill, Octavia 110, 422
Hobhouse Committee on Footpaths and
  Access to the Countryside 323, 347,
  371–2, 403, 540
Hobhouse Committee on National Parks
  464–5
Holbeche, Barney 248–50
Holmes, George 214
Holroyd, Michael 326
Hordern, Sir Michael 491
horticulture 252
Hose, John 255
Howard, Lord 322
Howarth, Richard 244
Hudson, W. H. 204, 302
Hugonin, W. F. P. 274, 480
Hulme, Tim 451
Humberside County Council 351
huntservants 231–2, 304
Huntingdonshire 515
Huxley, Tom 366

Income and Wealth, Royal Commission on the Distribution of 165, 265
India 21, 25–6
inheritance tax 152, 226, 453–60, 510–12, 530
Institute of Terrestrial Ecology 199
internal drainage boards 149
International Union for the Conservation of Nature 469
Intervention Board 182
Inverness County Council 383
Inverness-shire 383, 452
investment income surcharge 246
Ireland 81–3, 494
 see also Northern Ireland
Italy 145, 497

Jack, Ian 187–8
Japan 21, 23–4
Jefferies, Richard 68
Jenkins, Eric 356
Joad, Professor Cyril 112–13, 288
Jolowicz, J. A. 271
Jopling, Michael 205

Kauffman, MP, Gerald 518, 521, 552
Keegan, Victor 185
Keith, Councillor Francis 468
Kemp, Mrs Alison 257, 400
Kent 167–8, 327, 342, 410, 450–51
Kent County Council 334
Kimball, Sir Marcus 142, 289–90, 316, 358–60
Kincardineshire 138–9, 259
Kinder Scout 114, 303
Knights, Frank 300–1
Knoydart 230–31

Labour Party 96, 551
Lacey, Robert 267
Lake District 110, 272, 322, 371, 380, 430, 468, 516, 527
Lanark 131
Lancashire 171, 175
Lancashire County Council 350–51, 358
Lancaster, Duchy of 120, 158–9
land agents 136–7
land nationalization *see* nationalization, of agricultural land
Land Nationalisation Society 93
land ownership, ideas about 17–20, 26, 40–41, 59–60, 71, 79–81, 84, 91, 93, 198, 473–5, 480–82, 489, 519
land reform 23–8
Land Registry 262

Land's End 152, 331
Land Song 95
land tax proposals
 of Henry George 79–80, 178–9, 535
 of Lloyd George 95–6
 of Marion Shoard 528–36
land value 166–7
 see also farmland prices
Lane, Walter 445
Last Labourers Revolt 90
Law Commission 263
Law, Graham 435
Leconfield, Lord 154–5
Leicestershire 229, 217, 324, 346
Leicestershire County Council 237, 351
less favoured areas 184, 499, 503–4
Levellers 56, 59
Levellers' Rising 74
Lever, Revd. Thomas 51–2
Liberal Party 94, 96
limestone 170, 172
Lincolnshire 193, 217, 229, 235, 238, 326, 358
Lincolnshire County Council 353
listed buildings 441, 481
Lloyd George, David 87, 92, 94–7
Locke, John 60
London 129–30, 133, 159, 162, 175–8, 274–5, 427, 465
Londonderry 149
long-distance paths 336–40, 356
lord lieutenants 52, 240, 243–4, 259–60, 335
Lords, House of 60, 76, 94–5, 129, 244–5
Lothian Regional Council 467
Lowrey, Joseph 351–2
Lozi tribe 19–20
Luton Hoo 140, 171, 273

Mabey, Richard 550
McCulloch, Norman 291
MacDonald, Lord 84
MacDougall, Archie 231
McEwen, John 137, 562–3n
Malcolm MacEwen 509–10, 562n
McGuire, Gerald 224, 257
machair 420
Mackworth-Praed, H. W. 434
MacMillan, MP, Harold 381
management agreements 441–8, 452–3
Man, Isle of 133
Mansfield, Earl of 160, 366
Mansholt, Dr Sicco 495-6, 498-9
Manswell, B. W. 336, 356
Manzoni, Margaret 475

Maoris 17–18
March and Kinrara, Earl of 390–91
Marlborough Downs 204
Marlborough, Duke of 134, 378
Marriott, Oliver 176
Marten, Commander George 226
Massey, Dr Doreen 127
meadows 200, 410
Meakin, Tom 281
Melchett, Lord 396–7, 521–2
Mellanby, Professor Kenneth 191, 522–3
Merton, Statue of 46, 52
Mexico 25
Middleton, Lords 233–4, 340
milk *see* dairy farming; quotas, milk
Milligan, Stephen 185
Milton Estate 276, 283–4
mineral extraction 166, 169–73, 405, 423, 426–7
Montgomery, Sir David 121, 209, 254
Moor, B. P. 212–13
moorlands 220–25
  see also Dartmoor, Exmoor, North York Moors
More, Sir Thomas 51, 204
Morrison, Simon George Strangways 161–2
Mountbatten of Burma, Earl 278
Mountgarrett, Viscount 135
Mourne Mountains 385, 420, 466
Mowle, Dr Alan 514
Muir, John 467
Munro, Sir Hector 258
Munros 103, 206
Murray, Anthony 187

National Audit Office 225
National Farmers' Union 180, 184, 194, 205, 215, 247, 253, 261, 441, 445, 497
national park authorities, membership of 241–3, 260
national parks 115, 121–2, 241, 424, 432, 463–70
  in Northern Ireland 122, 466–7
  in Scotland 122, 466–9
National Parks and Access to the Countryside Act, 1949 241, 323–4, 336
National Parks Commission 464
national scenic areas 432, 468–9
National Trust 110, 151–6, 280, 310, 393, 490–91
National Trust for Scotland 151, 290–91, 389, 490
nationalization
  of agricultural land 486–8
  of agriculture 485–6

of minerals 169–70
Nature Conservancy Council 123, 217, 256, 258–60, 281–2, 304, 401, 439–43, 445–6, 449–55, 465, 491–2, 541
nature conservation 491–2
  see also wildlife
Nature Conservation and Amenity Lands (Northern Ireland) Order, 1985 466
nature reserves 123, 289, 401
Nawton Tower Estate 456–8
Neagh, Lough 151
Netherlands 496
New Domesday Survey 97–8
New Forest 41, 305–6, 409, 464
New Zealand 17–18, 194, 325
Newby, Professor Howard 147–8, 310, 341
Newcastle 239, 409
newts 201–2, 492
Nicol, James Dyce 139
Nightingale, Dennis 329–30, 354
nightjars 202–3
Norman Conquest 33–37
North Downs Way 339
North East England 239–41
North East Mountain Trust 257, 361, 367
North, Richard 507–8
North Norfolk District Council 148–9
North York Moors National Park Authority 447–8, 456–7
North Yorkshire County Council 238
Norfolk 67, 90, 148–9, 326, 397
  see also East Anglia
Norfolk Broads 148–9, 371, 465–6
  see also Broads Authority
Norfolk, Dukes of 177, 287
Northampton, Marquesses of 131–2, 332
Northamptonshire 44, 52, 68, 100, 131, 136, 142, 217, 331, 393–6
Northamptonshire County Council 394–6
Northern Ireland 122, 149–51, 218–9, 262, 369–70, 384–5, 389, 419–20, 507
Northfield Committee on the Acquisition and Occupancy of Agricultural Land 124, 264–5
Northumberland 100, 128–9, 223, 273–4, 430
Northumberland, Dukes of 40, 128–30, 134, 273–5, 396, 480
Norton-Taylor, Richard 157
Norway 489
Nott, Sir John 245
Nottinghamshire 162, 229
Nottinghamshire County Council 280, 351, 353–4
nutting 67–8

Offa's Dyke Path 338
oil 170
Ojibwa Indians 18
Onslow, Earl of 153
Open Spaces Society *see* Commons,
    Footpaths and Open Spaces
    Preservation Society
O'Riordan, Professor Timothy 510–12
Oxfordshire 280–81, 376–8
Oxfordshire County Council 238, 246,
    399–402
oxlips 198, 200

Paine, Gordon 364–5
Paine, Thomas 59
parish councils 330–32, 349, 353
Parliament, membership of *see* Commons,
    House of; Lords, House of
Parnell, Charles Stewart 82
Paths, permissive 399, 402
paths, public *see* rights of way, public
patronage in Church of England 233–7
Peak District 112–14, 302–4, 322, 371, 430
Peal Park Special Planning Board 303, 353,
    379
Pearce, Joan 496–8
Pearson, Charles 139
Peasants' Revolt 42–3, 270
Pembroke, Earl of 131
Pembrokeshire 217, 326
Pembrokeshire Coast National Park 122,
    242, 356
Pembrokeshire Coast Path 338, 356
Pennine Way 338
Pentland Hills 103, 467
Percy, Ralph 287, 313–14
Perrott, Roy 127–8, 134–5
Perth and Kinross District Council 363, 365
Perthshire 290–91
pesticides 197, 516
Peterborough 276, 283–4, 314
Petworth Estate 154–5
pheasant shooting 99–100, 268–70, 281,
    283–8, 309–10, 542
Phelps, H. V. 332
Phillips, Adrian 321
Phillips, Nicholas 140, 142, 273
picnic sites 377, 385, 387
Picozzi, Nicholas 304
plants, wild *see* flowers, wild
planning, town and country 111, 115, 179,
    422–8, 460–63, 518–22
Planning Acts, Town and Country 422–6,
    439, 518–9
Planning Appeals Commission 149

planning controls on agricultural and
    forestry change, proposals for 518,
    520–22
Plumb, Sir Henry 244–5, 248
Plynlimon Common 409, 413–14
poaching 63–5, 90
political reform 75–6, 95
pollution 476
population change in countryside 344–5
Portman, Viscount 176
Post Office Pension Fund 124
Potter, Clive 505
Powell, Enoch 552
Powys 408
    see also Cambrian Mountains National
    Park
Prebble, John 75
prehistoric times 29–31
Preseli District Council 356
primogeniture 132
Prior, MP, James 245
privatization 120–21
Property Act, 1925, Law of 109, 412–15,
    417–18
Prudential Insurance Company 125–6
Public Accounts Committee of House of
    Commons 214
Public Order Act, 1986 317
public owners of Britain's land 119–21
Pye-Smith, Charlie 507–8
Pym, MP, Francis 245

Quakers 56, 135
Queen Elizabeth II 157–61, 544
    see also Crown Estate, Lancaster,
    Duchy of
Queen Victoria 18, 101
quotas 493
    cereals 199
    milk 182, 205, 500

Rackham, Dr Oliver 217
Radzinowicz, Professor Leon 64
Ramblers' Association 113–14, 253, 264,
    324–6, 340, 353, 359, 371, 431, 551
Ramsay Committee on National Parks in
    Scotland 115, 467
Ratcliffe, Dr Derek 221
Rebecca riots 86
recreation, countryside
    history of 69, 104, 106–7
    popularity of 315, 321, 406
    see also access to the countryside
Red Deer Commission 259, 291
regional parks 467–9

Register of Sasines 262, 362
rent 80, 82–3
    farm rents 157, 185–6
Rhodes, Philip 233
    see also Knoydart
Rhum, island of 103
Richards, Professor Eric 102
Richmond, Duke of 390
Richmond Park 64, 288
Ridgeway, The 339
Ridley family 240, 461
Righton, Christopher 194–5
Rights of Way Bills and Act, 1932 323
rights of way, public
    creation of 332–40, 458–9
    definitive maps of 329–32, 398, 400, 459
    in Northern Ireland 369–70
    in Scotland 360–69
    legislation concerning 322–4
    obstruction of 331, 341–3, 346, 348,
        350–56, 538
    signposting of 356–9
Rio Tinto-Zinc 477
rivers, access along 269, 299, 336, 365–6,
        368, 464
roads, estate 461
Robertson, Councillor John 468
Rogers, Dr G. 175
Rockingham Estate 142, 395
roll-over relief 189–90
Romans 20, 31, 34
Romsey, Lord 168, 278–80, 305
Rose, Chris 257
Rose, Graham 187–8
Rose, Howard 395–6
Rossiter, Dr Judith 380–82
Rotherwick, Lord 410–12
Rothman, Benny 114
Roxburgh, Duke of 266
Roxburghshire 131
royal forest 37–9, 47–8
Royal Society for the Protection of Birds
        222–3, 310
Rubinstein, Dr W. D. 132, 166
rundale agriculture 72
runrig agriculture 72
Rural Voice 260
Rutland 49
Rutland, Dukes of 37, 143, 171, 229–30,
        233–4, 237, 244, 306
Rutland Water 300
Russia 21, 26, 485–6
Rye 460

salmon fishing *see* fishing, salmon and trout
Sampher, The 450–51

sand and gravel extraction 172–3
Sandwich Bay 168, 450
Saudi Arabia 489
Saunders-Watson family 142, 332
Savills 227
Saxons 32–4
Sayer, Lady Sylvia 219–20, 257
scattald 420
Scotland 69–75, 83–5, 98, 100–3, 115, 122,
        128, 137–40, 206–9, 220–23, 230–31,
        243, 262, 360–69, 383–4, 388–9,
        419–21, 523, 533
    see also Atholl, Dukes of: Birse; Balfour,
        Dr Jean; Buccleuch, Dukes of;
        Cairngorms; Clearances; Countryside
        Commission for Scotland; Creag
        Meagaidh; Dee, River; Glen Ample;
        Grampians; Knoydart; Mansfield, Earl
        of; Montgomery, Sir David; National
        Trust for Scotland; Register of Sasines;
        Roxburgh, Duke of; Southern Upland
        Way; Speyside Way; West Highland
        Way; and under the names of
        individual counties and local
        authorities
Scott, Lord Justice 115, 341
Scottish Landowners' Federation 245, 259
Scottish Rights of Way Society 361, 363–5
Scottish Wildlife Trust 289
Scottish Woodland Owners' Association
        209, 215
secrecy over ownership of land 261–5
Self, Professor Peter 249
Selkirk 131
serfs 35–6
Shaftesbury, Earl of 151
Shakespeare, William 198
Sharp, Thomas 332–3
Shaw-Lefèvre, MP, George 108
sheep farming 50–52, 66, 70, 73, 75, 84,
        181–2, 503–4, 509
Shelter 231
Shetland 420
Shropshire 217, 411
Silkin, MP, John 115, 248, 250
Silkin, MP, Lewis 115, 371–3
Simpson, Francis 200–1
Sinclair, Geoffrey 509–10
Sinodun Hills 376–7
sites of special scientific interest 439–42,
        448–52, 551
Skye, Isle of 83–5
small farmers *see* farmers, small
smallholdings 99, 121
Smith, Adam 62

Smith, Dr Malcolm 523
Smith, Roger 475
Snowdonia 371, 377–9
Snowdonia National Park Authority 242, 397–9
social contract for the countryside
late medieval 43–8, 62–9, 552–3
twentieth century 115, 318–470
Somerleyton, Lord 387
Somerset 217, 326, 464, 517
Somerset County Council 351
South Downs 109, 172, 204, 371, 391, 424, 429, 465
South Downs Way 338–9
south Esk, Earl of 126
South West Peninsula Coast Path 338
South Pembrokeshire District Council 356
South Yorkshire Metropolitan County Council 349–50, 353, 358
Southern Upland Way 338
Southill Estate *see* Whitbread family
Spence, Thomas 59
Spencer, Earl 107–9, 168, 332, 394–5, 405
Sperrin Mountains 369, 385, 420, 466
Speyside Way 338
Staffordshire 65
Stamford Estates 174, 235
Stirling District 362, 460
Stirling District Council 206, 384, 435–6
Stocker, Anthony 146–7
Storing, Dr Herbert 249
Straker, Sir Michael 240
strict settlement 54
structure plans 425–6, 521, 532
subsidies to agriculture 181–5, 493-510
justification for 190–96
see also Common Agricultural Policy, grants for agriculture, concessions for agriculture
subsidies to forestry 210–15, 225, 255, 507, 528, 530
justification for 211–5, 225
see also grants for forestry, tax concessions for forestry
Suffolk 90, 146–8, 200–1, 285, 326
see also East Anglia
Suffolk County Council 238
Surrey 129, 153, 166, 217, 274, 396, 410, 519, 534
Sussex 141, 154–5, 199, 203, 235, 248, 342, 346–7, 357, 408
Sutherland 142, 222–3
Sutherland, Dukes of 98
Sweden 539–40, 543, 545
Syon Park (London) 129–30, 274–5

Tangemann, Professor Stefan 500
Tanley, A. G. 428
Tawney, R. H. 48
tax concessions
for agriculture 183–4
for forestry 210–11, 219
see also inheritance tax
tenant farmers 81–8, 98, 246, 251–2
Test, River 153, 333, 464
Teulon, Alan 395
Thatcher Government 120, 165, 183, 227, 245, 257, 265, 317, 428, 438, 453, 467, 504, 551
Theft of The Countryside, The 198, 550
thegns 33
Third World countries 195–6
Thompson, Andrew 307, 313
Thompson, E. P. 62
Thompson, Flora 344
Thompson, Michael 283–4, 308, 314
tied housing 231–2
Tilhill Forestry Company 208, 436
timber, demand for
demand for 211–13
price of 225
trade in 212–13
Timber Growers United Kingdom 253
Tolpuddle martyrs 91
Tong, J. R. 332
tourism 103, 223
Treasury report on forestry 225, 255, 570n
tree planting (amenity) 199, 513, 515–16
tree preservation orders 460, 462
Tregothnan Estate (Cornwall) 335–6
trespass 114, 271–2, 316–7, 325, 372, 539
Trevelyan, Professor G. M. 104
Tubbs, Dr Colin 305–6, 449
Tubbs, Mrs Jennifer 440
Tudge, Dr Colin 191
Tweedie, Jill 169, 226
Tyrone, County 151

Ulster Countryside Committee 149
Ulster Farmers' Union 149
Ulster Way 337–9
Unna, Percy 290–91
usufruct 17

vandalism 308
Vaughan Cornish, Ralph 429
Velcourt 125, 165
Verney, Sir Ralph 260
Vestey, E. H. 137
villages, estate 136

Wake, Sir Hereward 332
Walden, Lord Howard de 176
Wales 85–7, 223, 242, 339, 345, 408–9, 413–14, 416, 430, 465, 523
  see also Arran Mountains; Brecon Beacons National Park; Cambrian Mountains National Park (proposed); Cambrian Way (proposed); Pembrokeshire Coast National Park; Pembrokeshire Coast Path; Plynlimon Common; Rebecca riots; Welsh Land League; and under the names of individual counties and local authorities.
Warwickshire 77, 131, 410
water authorities, regional, membership of 238–40, 252
Watkins, Dr Charles 280
Watney family 400–1
Watson, Dr Adam 577n
Watson, Drennan 237
Watson, Graham 437
Wealth Tax, Commons Select Committee on 144, 264
Wells, Dr Derek 404
Wells, H. G. 537
Welsh Land League 86
Wernher, Sir Julius 140
West Highland Way 338, 340, 368
West Midlands 388
West Oxfordshire District Council 402
West Riding County Council 374, 376
Westmacott, Richard 514–16, 523
Westminster, Dukes of 35, 111, 133–4, 142, 150, 176–8, 160, 235, 267
Whitbread family 140–41, 276, 314–15, 473
White, Gilbert 105, 202
Wickstead, Rollo 349
Wiggins, MP, Jerry 194, 441
wildlife
  attitudes towards 104–6, 475–9, 492
  see also animals, wild; butterflies; flowers, wild; nature conservation; newts; nightjars; oxlips

Wildlife and Countryside Act, 1981 438–43, 446–53, 551
Wildlife and Countryside (Amendment) Act, 1985 443–4
Wildlife and Countryside Bill, 1981 438–9, 441, 550–51
Williams, Julian 141
Williamson, Dr Bill 240–41
Wills family 137, 294
Wiltshire 203, 418, 440
Wimbledon Common 107–8, 404–6
Winans, W. L. 102
Winchester, Statute of 47
Windsor Forest 64, 159
Winstanley, Gerrard 56–9, 78, 84
Woburn Estate *see* Bedford, Dukes of
Wolds Way 339–40
Woodland Trust 491
woods 523
  access to 280–81
  ancient 200–1, 216–17
  deciduous 199, 218
  coppice 462–3
  see also conservation and forestry, conflict between; forestry
Woolley, Nicholas 126
Worcestershire 326, 410
Wordsworth, William 106–7, 272
Worsley, Sir Marcus 153
Worthington, Tom 490, 514–16, 523
Wychwood Forest 40, 400–402

Yorkshire 124, 135, 187, 203, 223–4, 276, 329–30, 349–50, 408, 430, 447–8
  see also North York Moors; Wolds Way; Yorkshire Dales
Yorkshire Dales 373, 458, 507, 523
Yorkshire Dales National Park Authority 374, 458
Younger, MP, George 208, 212

Zuni Indians 19